AMERICAN BUSINESS & PUBLIC POLICY

THE POLITICS OF FOREIGN TRADE

SECOND EDITION WITH A NEW PROLOGUE

RAYMOND A. BAUER·ITHIEL DE SOLA POOL·LEWIS ANTHONY DEXTER

ALDINE PUBLISHING COMPANY/ *New York*

First Edition published 1963
First Paperbound Edition, 1972
Second Edition published 1972
Third printing, 1981

Aldine Publishing Company
200 Saw Mill River Road
Hawthorne, New York 10532

ISBN Cloth 0-202-24128-9
ISBN Paper 0-202-24129-7
Library of Congress Catalog Number 63-8171

Printed in the United States of America

AMERICAN
BUSINESS
&
PUBLIC
POLICY

PROLOGUE

Introduction to the Paperback Edition

Among the reactions to this book, several have particularly gratified its authors. One of these was the American Political Science Association's Woodrow Wilson Award for the best book published in the United States in 1963 on government, politics, or international affairs. Others were by Robert Peabody in Huitt and Peabody, *Congress: Two Decades of Analysis,* by Charles Lindblom in *The Policy Making Process,* by Theodore Lowi in a review in *World Politics* (1964), and by Lewis A. Froman in a review in *The American Political Science Review* (1963).

    Most of these evaluations tried to place this book in relation to the mainstream of writing in contemporary political science. While generous in their praise, most reviewers saw the book as a case study needing to be linked more closely to empirical or normative political theory. The publication of a new edition permits us, in this introduction, to attempt one such linkage and to suggest others.

    The most active theoretical debate in American political science in the past 25 years has perhaps been that on pluralist democracy. The classic theory of democracy, expressed in extreme form by Rousseau, postulates an ideal in which each individual citizen involves himself as much as possible, and roughly equally, in deliberations on the general interest. Each citizen then votes for the general interest rather than for his own special interest. In that classic view, the public authorities too should represent as best they can the common good and should resist special interests. Apathy in portions of the citizen body, nonvoting, ignorance about public affairs, political action motivated by self-interest, and actions by public officials on behalf of special interests are all, in that view, deformations of the democratic process.

Candid observation, however, finds such deformations widespread. The discovery of what really happens in democracies, in contrast to what doctrine proposes, has been one of the main activities of muckraking journalists and empirical social scientists for almost a century. Among them is a group of writers who may be called the "realist" critics of democratic theory. Our concluding chapter relates what we found in this study to their work. Writers like Ostrogorski (1902), Michels (1915), Weber (1919), Lippmann (1922), Steffens (1931), Pareto (1935), Mosca (1939), Berelson (1954), and Key (1961) have demonstrated that in one respect or another democracy does not actually work in the way the classic theory postulates. Among these writers, some may be called "elistist" critics of democracy, for they argue the inevitability of inequality. Not all citizens are or can be equally involved, effective, wise, or powerful. Michels observed that the "iron law of oligarchy" compelled the emergence of a self-interested elite even in radical democratic social movements. Lippmann argued for the desirability of having an educated, informed elite provide leadership to what he saw as an inevitably uninformed mass.

Against this background of empirically grounded scepticism about democratic theory, there emerged, especially since 1950, a set of treatises that accepted and developed the empirical evidence of imperfections in the functioning of democracy, but which argued nonetheless, that even such democracy is valuable. These treatises formulated a "pluralist" theory of democracy. Its defense of democracy accepts the fact that a democratic system operates by bargaining and the resulting coalitions among interest groups; on any given issue only minorities are active. However, it also maintains that this process produces a reasonable representation of the desires of the public. Note that this pluralist theory emerged, on the one hand, as an attack on radical Rousseauian democratic theory, and, on the other hand, as a defense of democratic practice in the United States against elitist criticisms —but not as an *elitist* theory, as is sometimes asserted.

This "pluralist" position was best formulated in a number of studies of the processes of "group representation" in politics, some of the earlier of which are discussed in this book under such labels as "the group approach to politics" or "pressure group theory" rather than under the currently more fashionable term, "pluralist democracy." Truman's *Governmental Process* (1951) was one such study. At about the time our own book appeared, debate was mounting on the issue of whether the American political system

was best described as elitist or pluralistically democratic. Hunter's (1953) community study of Atlanta, portraying a town run by a unified power elite, had appeared 10 years earlier. Mills (1956) popularized once more the characterization of the American national scene as dominated by a power elite. These authors, squarely in the tradition of the realist critique of democracy (even if their value stance was quite different from that of Mosca or Pareto), were answered most effectively by Dahl in *Who Governs* (1961). Dahl described the leadership of New Haven as consisting of a whole series of only partially overlapping elites, each of which might assume leadership on some special issue in their domain, but none of which had broad power over the city as a whole. His description of a process of fluid, dispersed power allocations contradicted the notion that there was a single local power elite. With Dahl's reply to Hunter, the lines of debate were drawn. For most of a decade, political science reverberated with discussions of community power.

In some ways the debate on community power has been unsatisfying, because the issue of whether the elite is a concentrated class or a floating and rotating populace is quantitative. To some degree it is each; but no writer has provided a metric of the degree of concentration of power to make his statements rigorous. That there are such things as upper classes is no discovery, nor is it a surprise that different individuals exercise authority in different fields of activity. Yet community study after study was devoted to stressing one or the other aspect of this dual reality (see Dye, 1970). Such documentation was useful for readers interested in learning about prevailing practice in particular kinds of American communities in the mid-twentieth century, but did not contribute to theory. Sooner or later the sense of discovery had to wane. Until someone invents a measure that will compare degrees of concentration of influence over various fields and at different times and places, the empirical discussion has probably reached a dead end. Whatever one's epistemological views of the role of theory in social science, theory clearly means something more than the choice of emphasis on one aspect or another of a mixed reality. A theory of democratic politics must be more than that.

Many of the criticisms leveled at the pluralist theory of democracy, however, have not been empirical; they have been normative. The pluralists were characterized, and in our opinion not unfairly, as providing justification for democracy as practiced. They were therefore criticized as justifiers of the status quo, and, at the same time, unfairly labeled "neoelitists." (The pluralists were defending a *dispersion* of power that they perceived as prevailing in the status quo, not its *concentration*.) The writers who took this critical line did not necessarily challenge the empirical findings of the pluralists about the dispersion of power among special interest groups. What they were saying was that, from their value stance, pluralism of power is not democracy enough (Bottomore, 1964; Bay, 1965; Walker, 1966; by far the best statement is Davis, 1964).

Thus the antipluralists argued two theses. They argued that among the many struggling groups there is one dominant establishment that wins most of the battles and exploits deprived classes and groups such as the poor, the nonwhites, and the young. They further argued that this undesirable outcome of group conflict can and should be reversed by the government, acting on behalf of all to redistribute rewards and to prevent undemocratic dominance by certain privileged groups.

The distribution of benefits in society is clearly and grossly unequal. The pluralists did not disagree with this observation. They did not question John F. Kennedy's aphorism that "life is unfair," nor did they refain from commitment to doing something about it by protest, by reform, and by redress of grievances. What they did deny was that the cost/benefit ratio of unfairnesses always accrues to the advantage of the same, small class. They argued that interest conflicts produce a many-sided, if not always just, mix of both deprivations and rewards to various elements of the population, that these conflicts do not result in a simple, one-sided outcome. Their contention, certainly heavily documented by many empirical studies of recent American politics, has been that any two-class summary of the outcome of group conflict is a distortion; that group conflict, in fact, distributes its payoffs widely.

The debate on pluralist democracy really concerned not just one but three different issues. First, a normative issue: whether pluralist democracy is participatory or equalitarian enough to satisfy a true democrat. Second, an empirical issue: how pluralistic the distribution of power was in the United States in the middle of the twentieth century.[1] The third issue, which is the one raised in this book, is the extent to which groups in the political arena actually do act as simple political maximizers, each struggling to serve its own well-defined interests.

On this third issue we, in this book, take our departure from pluralists and antipluralists alike. It is also on this issue that we see the discussion of pluralist democracy raising some genuine problems of social theory, going well beyond mere differences in value preferences and beyond factual observations about the character of contemporary American political practice. The issue in a nutshell is this: how adequate is a theory of political behavior and political outcomes that postulates that people act on behalf of their group interests? What are the limitations of such a theory, and how can such a theory be used in ways that take account of its limitations? Our book may be considered a critique of an assumption that has been widely shared by pluralists and antipluralists alike: that interest groups act rationally to serve their own interests.

For the most part, the existing literature describes (and describes well) how special interests struggle effectively, each on its own behalf. Both pluralists and antipluralists, however, make unrealistic assumptions

---

[1] Pluralist theory is largely derived from the American experience. As Wilson (1964) has pointed out, the description of American federalism by Grodzins (1966), for example, in terms of multiple access points, does not apply to Great Britain.

about the clarity of human motivations, and an even more unrealistic assumption that group motivations get readily translated into policy. The point that is missed in both assumptions is that individual and group interests get grossly redefined by the operation of the social institutions through which they must work. The political outcome is something very different from the simple product of a parallelogram of forces input by the conflicting groups. Summing up the conflicting interests at work is only the beginning of political analysis. The heart of political analysis is the discovery of the transformation processes that make the political outputs something very different from what any of the interested parties wanted or sought.

The identification of such transformation processes is, indeed, the central thesis of this book, as was recognized by Theodore Lowi (1964) in his perceptive and frequently cited review. He saw that our approach fell outside either the pluralist or the opposed school of thought, which he called the "elitist" school. He says of our work: "What they have found severely tests the assumptions of both schools of thought. Without significant adjustment, the pluralist framework will be able to encompass a great many of their propositions and findings only with extreme difficulty. But for every single problem that the tariff decisions of a decade pose for the pluralist model, they pose several for the elitist or stratification approaches" (p. 682).

Lowi's review recognized that, in important respects, the structure both of an issue and of the arena in which it is discussed shapes the way in which group conflict—which clearly does occur all the time—gets translated into a policy outcome. In particular, Lowi drew attention in his review to one very important structural parameter, the significance of which we had not noted in our book. That parameter is whether the resources on which the government is operating in a policy action are sufficiently abundant so that giving some of them to citizen or group A does not significantly reduce the possibility of giving some to group B; or whether the resources are, on the contrary, scarce or indivisible, so that the decision to favor A implies a denial to B. The first situation Lowi called "distributive" politics. Examples are nineteenth century land policy, grants and contracts, "pork barrel" legislation, and traditional tariff policy as it was described by Schattschneider in the 1920s (when the basic rule that Congress applied in tariff-making was to give each applicant some protection, though a little less than he asked). "Regulatory" politics differs in that the decisions involve "a direct choice as to who will be indulged and who deprived" (pp. 690–91). As Lowi correctly notes, tariff legislation in the era about which we write was increasingly of a regulatory nature. Clearly also, the nature of group interactions and their effects upon the outcome are different in these two types of situations.

There is room for difference of opinion about the consequences of a given structure on particular policy outcomes. That is what much of political science theory and research is about. Lowi later concluded (1969), for example, that the growth of regulatory and redistributive relative to distributive politics requires central political action on behalf of the public interest, very much in the tradition of Rousseau and Lippmann. From our review of the history of the trade controversy in a period when it had already become a regulatory issue, it is far from clear to us that there is any realistic basis for expecting central political action to serve a broad national interest (as interpreted by top-level political leadership) rather than the narrow self-interests of subordinate groups. There were indeed complex divisions of labor in the trade debate, with some persons playing an overview role and some a narrower interest role. But the balancing of many kinds of interest, short and long range, national and group, personal and corporate, took place at every level, not excepting the White House. Whatever conclusion one draws about the prospect of government transcending special interest, we welcome Lowi's clear perception of our thesis that the role and structure in which a political person finds himself will greatly affect the interest of which he becomes conscious and which he expresses in action.

Social scientists have long been fascinated by how individual preferences in a competitive arena end up being translated into social choices to which they may have but remote resemblance (cf. Arrow, 1963). If that awareness has not been discussed adequately in the literature on pluralist democracy, it is nonetheless central in a growing body of literature that has tried to apply the approaches of economic analysis to political decisions. Many outstanding authors have illustrated the usefulness of carrying into the political realm the kind of rational, normative analysis that is used in economics. One who, regrettably, is little known these days is Philip Henry Wicksteed, whose general theory of choice (1933) is, as one would expect, a marginal utility theory of action. Among more recent authors we might mention Dahl and Lindblom (1953), Downs (1957), March and Simon (1958), Homans (1961), Riker (1962), and Olson (1965). These authors offer analyses that are normative in a sense very different from that of the criticisms of pluralist democracy mentioned above. They are not tracts on behalf of a particular value position. They are analyses that start with the postulate that men rationally strive to achieve norms.

There is much to be said for this approach to political and social theory-building. It seems more realistic to look at the political marketplace (as economists look at the economic marketplace) as a complex system with outcomes determined by interactions, rather than to try to identify power-holders whose wills somehow determine outcomes independent of the total context.

The assumption of rational behavior on behalf of self-interest is where pluralists and antipluralists alike tended to end their analysis. But if it is taken rather as only the beginning of analysis, it becomes a powerful simplification that makes it possible to treat in an elegant theoretical way the otherwise baffling complexity of reality. Significant analysis has come more often from understanding the process of goal-seeking than from accumulating data about decisions in a substantive area such as foreign trade or housing or schools or whatever. The latter kind of effort has produced no significant theory on any major topic of public policy. There is, however, a significant general theory of bargaining behavior, for the dynamics of rational choice gives structure to an otherwise inchoate picture of the political process.

While economics has provided political science with a powerful tool in the form of rational normative theory, there are also contributions to be made by political science in return. The theory of choice behavior is essentially tautological. People maximize whatever it is that they maximize, and whatever they maximize is defined operationally as what they want. Logically, that tautology presents a problem for economics, but practically it is more of a problem in politics. When economists assume that money crudely approximates the utility that people maximize, that is not a catastrophic oversimplification, when they assume that the unit which behaves as an economic self-seeker is the firm, that is something of a falsification, for firms are complex organisms with all sorts of fuzzy boundaries, but still it is not a bad simplification. When we move into politics, the relationship of abstract theoretical terms to well-defined entities in the real world is far more complicated. In politics there is no natural empirical surrogate for utility, like money, and the organized entities in the political marketplace are a seamless web of overlapping institutions. Political science has to look closely at the empirical complexities.

For the most part, this book consists of a critique of an oversimplified application of the notions of self-interested behavior to the foreign trade issue. Most writers on this issue (without working out the complexities of a rationalized normative analysis) simply take it as axiomatic that each interest group seeks its own advantage. For us, that turned out not to be a useful assumption, not because it was wrong but becasue it failed to pose the important theoretical questions. It failed to provide critical information about the structural parameters that in fact determined how people saw their interests, to what they attended, and therefore how they behaved.

In this book we try to specify some of these crucial parameters— those that determine how people define their interests and thus how they frame the issues in terms of which they may then act rationally. Among these are time perspective: Is he maximizing for the short or the long run, and what is his time discount? Who is the "I" or "we" for whom a person acts? Does he seek benefit for a firm, a community, a party, a constituency, a nation, or some combination of these, to all of which he belongs and which he values in some complex differential way? What is the good that he is maximizing? Is it earnings or security or political influence, and again in what combination? How are costs to be measured in a mix of scarce resources of which money is but one, and time and friendship are others? Also, in calculating what is rational action, the political activist weighs what is feasible, which introduces a vast circularity: what is in the interest of each are policies that he perceives as likely to be perceived as sufficiently in the interest of many others so that these others will act to make them realities, provided they too see them in the same way.

In short, a rational theory of public policy can borrow much from the formalizations of welfare economics and game theory, but it also requires much analysis of the paramenters that these theories take for granted. Psychology, sociology, and political science may contribute a more systematic analysis of the conditions that define choice situations than they have provided in the past. That is what we try to do in part through this case study and also in its concluding analytic chapters. One answer, then, that we offer to those who have asked about the theoretical relevance of this study is that it questions both pluralist and antipluralist analyses of interest group behavior by showing how circumstances determined the perceptions that groups formed of their interests and of their options. Self-interest is not an objective fact.

It is evident that the foregoing analysis of pluralism, and for that matter of rational behavior, is simply one way of relating this book to a theoretical framework[2]. If space permitted, several other ways could be developed. For instance, it is entirely possible (and in Dexter's view likely) that a focus of attention upon the democracy issue, however posed, obscures significant contributions that the study may have made to the understanding of the nature of action in *any* complex political situation. Our theoretical analysis from one standpoint would seem to be close to that developed by Braybrooke and Lindblom (1963) on "incrementalism." From another standpoint, our analysis is close to that of Burke (1837) on wise statesmanship. One might also argue the extent to which this book contributes to organization theory in politics, on the one hand, or to communication theory in politics on the other. This introduction may perhaps, by its focus on the former, blur the book's focus on the latter. While at least one of us (Pool) sees in this a corrective to an omission in what we originally wrote, another (Dexter) who developed some aspects of the communications analysis further in a subsequent book (1969), is concerned that the emphasis here may obscure for the reader the fact that the theoretical approach of the book is, above all, that of communications theory.

Political analysis in the 1970s can perhaps find more powerful and less ambiguous concepts for describing interpersonal linkages than that of the "group." An increasing number of British-trained political anthropologists have been making this point recently. Boissevain, in his essay on "The Place of Non-Groups" (1968), has presented the thesis that social scientists have overstressed the group and neglected "forms of social organization

---

[2] A book is like the elephant in the fable: three coauthors looking back at it do not necessarily see their joint product alike. Pool (writing first) has chosen to place this book in relation to recent political theory on the functioning of democracy, while Dexter has chosen to stress the significance of the communications approach, and to suggest the outdated character of "group" concepts and of some of the normative political theory based upon it. Bauer (writing last) has focused on foreign trade and how it has evolved in a changing world economy.

that lie somewhere between interacting individuals on the one hand, and formal corporate groups, on the other." "Networks," "links,"and "quasi-groups" are terms found with increasing frequency in studies such as Barnes on Norwegian committees and Ngoni politics (1954), Mayer on Indian elections (1966), and Bott on British social relations (1957). One of us (Dexter) has begun an effort to show the relevance of these conceptions to our study and related work. We certainly believe that the interactions we found as we studied the foreign trade debate fit a communications approach better than one predicated on the existence of well-defined groups in conflict.

There are many other points on which the authors have had second thoughts. We have been interpreted, for example, as saying that congressmen are vastly overworked. What we tried to say is that as for any other free professional with heavy decision-making responsibilities, time is a scarce resource for congressmen, and their allocation of time over its many alternative uses can substantially affect the character of the decisions made. Congressmen are like many high officials in the executive branch, businessmen, judges, or lawyers—some are fiercely overburdened, many less so. But for all such people the constraints of time are critical in the performance of their work.

Had we been writing today, we certainly would have written differently about some aspects of our specific subject matter of foreign trade. As this new edition goes to press we are in the aftermath of the great dollar crisis of 1971. For a quarter of a century after World War II the world economy was fueled by a flow of American dollars. At the time we started our research in the mid-1950s, after the end of the Marshall Plan, the public policy question seemed to be how to keep that flow going. The slogan "trade not aid" expressed a program for doing so by encouraging a rebuilt Europe to sell products to us. By the early 1960s, when we finished our research, the dollar flow was beginning to be seen as a problem, and keeping foreign doors open to American goods became an increasing concern in the "Kennedy Round" of international trade negotiations. By 1971 the bottom of the well was reached; the era when the American government would allow a continuing dollar flow came to a drastic end. Bargaining with a toughness which makes clear that trade wars are still very much with us, the Nixon administration compelled Europe and Japan to accept a devaluation of the dollar without retaliating by counterdevaluations or trade barriers. In the coming decades trade policy will continue to be a major issue for the United States as it faces an enlarged Europe, a modernized Japan, the Communist powers and the Third World, and particularly as the easy days of dollar dominance lie behind us.

The main matters with which this book deals are renewals in the Congress of the Reciprocal Trade Program. We completed the writing of this book as the Trade Expansion Act of 1962 was passed. The book was first published as the Kennedy Round of negotiations in 1963 began to implement that act. These negotiations continued into 1967, producing, in a mix of successes and failures, a pattern of results that can be considered a landmark in implementing freer international trade. But the agreements were scarcely signed (and, in fact, had not yet been implemented) before a countercurrent set in. Since then, a number of authors have tried to put the Kennedy Round and other developments into perspective.[3] Let us briefly discuss some of what has happened.

As the historical portions of this book indicate, American trade policy has been marked by fairly long periods of a trend toward protectionism, and by other periods toward freer trade. Within these secular trends, however, there have been shorter cycles of policy. Ever since the Reciprocal Trade Act of 1934, the trend has been toward a more liberal trade policy, but with distinct periods of regression. For all of these four decades of liberal trend, as we note in the text, the arguments for protectionism have been arguments of exception. Seldom in that era did a protectionist spokesman argue his case in principle. More often he accepted the premise that increased trade is in general desirable, but pointed to the special needs of a particular industry or region or section of the economy, or to a foreign power's actual or seeming violation of generally agreed-upon principles.

Regardless of the relative legitimacy and political appeal of protectionist and liberal arguments in the abstract, the day-to-day staying power of particularized protectionist arguments has permitted them to have an erosive effect on liberal trade advances, which have come in relatively discrete surges. The first Reciprocal Trade Act during the Great Depression came as a response to a dramatic decline of foreign trade. The post-World War II movement, including the General Agreement on Trades and Tariffs (GATT), was bolstered by the argument that America had the moral obligation to help the less fortunate inhabitants of this small world. Finally, there was the Kennedy Round.

We can now see with perhaps a little more clarity the significance of the events that led up to the Kennedy Round. During the fifties the liberal advances made with GATT at the end of the forties were eroded by pleas of special circumstances. As the European and Japanese economies recovered, two things happened simultaneously: sympathy for their needs declined as the needs themselves declined, and as the strength of their industries grew, their imports into the United States also grew. Perception of the impact of these imports was probably sharpened by the rather slower rate of growth of our own economy.

In past decades it has traditionally been the executive branch that for a variety of reasons—including the fact that it saw commercial policy as an integral part of foreign policy—has carried the banner of liberal trade. The executive has succeeded to the extent that it could muster support from a Congress which during this same period has been the target of protectionist influence, and throughout the middle and late fifties, the Eisenhower ad-

---

[3] The interested reader who wants to get into this literature can begin with Allen and Walter (1971), Evans (1971), Malmgren (1970-'71, and Preeg (1970). The recency of these several sources makes them, in turn, an adequate point of entry to the more extensive bibliography of the past five years.

ministration fought such a battle. Though Eisenhower himself undoubtedly saw trade liberalization as a cause to which he had a primary commitment, most present writers see his administration as one in which protectionism was whittling away at past gains. His was a relatively liberalizing trade policy compared to the balance of forces building up within Congress. However, the events of the time (or the administration's perception of them) did not seem to offer his administration an issue around which it could rally sentiment for a dramatic or substantial new effort to reduce trade barriers. Each successive renewal of the Reciprocal Trade Act involved compromises of such an extent that it was not clear who won.

The advent of the Kennedy administration was marked by new personnel and by new circumstances, chief among them the development of the European Economic Community. As we point out in the text, it was not possible for us at the time to judge the extent to which the new administration used the evolution of the EEC as a pretext for doing that which came naturally versus the extent to which the evolving EEC presented a significant new circumstance that "demanded" a new response. From today's vantage point it is clear that, regardless of what truly moved the Kennedy administration, the EEC has emerged as such a significant factor in world trade that it was fortunate the response came when it did. While the full significance of the EEC may not have been seen by all, its potential significance was sufficiently widely perceived to make it a rallying point for the Trade Expansion Act, which offered the President negotiating powers well beyond those granted by any legislation of the past decade or more.

The intricacies and complexities of the negotiation of the Kenndy Round defy a short treatment; the interested reader is referred to Evans' account. (1971) The negotiations, which lasted well into 1967, were characterized by seemingly insurmountable impasses and missed deadlines. Though generally considered successful, their successes were mixed, and were most marked in the cutting of tariffs on industrial goods. The complexities of judging the significance of a tariff level or tariff cut, of what weights and criteria to employ, are well known to professionals and are discussed at some length in the body of this book. Suffice it to say that most recent commentators on the Kennedy Round take as a working figure that industrial tariffs were sliced by about one-third. Since after a couple of decades of systematic whittling down the existing tariff levels were already relatively low, it is generally conceded that, on the whole, tariffs on industrial goods ceased to be a substantial barrier to international trade.

Little or no progress was made in the Kenndy Round on other barriers to trade. Negotiations on nontariff barriers such as import quotas, regulations actually or ostensibly designed to protect health, and the like, proved virtually a dead end. And, since tariff barriers have receded in importance while nontariff barriers have remained unreduced or have increased, the relative importance of the two types of barriers has shifted to a point where, at present, nontariff barriers are of primary importance.

Just as nontariff barriers in general proved intractable, so did both tariff and nontariff barriers to agricultural trade. This was due mainly to the EEC policy of leveling barriers to agricultural trade within the Community while maintaining a price-support level, a policy that has stimulated, if anything, an overproduction of agricultural products. The device that the EEC employed is the so-called "variable levy," whereby the tariffs on imports of food are adjusted to bring the price of imports in line with domestic costs regardless of world market prices. Some writers estimate that the barriers to export of agricultural commodities to the EEC have doubled or tripled in importance. The significance of these failures of the Kenndy Round lies not so much in evaluating the effort itself as in the fact that the very success of tariff cutting on industrial goods has left nontariff barriers and barriers on agricultural trade as the key agenda items for future trade policy, along with the increasingly important problem of monetary flows and rates of exchange.

It is impossible briefly to give an adequate analysis of the trade arrangements and issues that characterize the post-Kennedy Round world.[4] No sooner were the agreements signed than each side charged that the other was evading their word, their intent, or both. Currency difficulties caused one country or another to take unilateral action. The devaluation of the British pound, for example, reduced the value of Britain's tariff concessions.

With the Kennedy Round agreements barely in force, the 1968 session of Congress was deluged with a variety of protectionist bills. Of a hundred witnesses before the House committee, only eight testified in favor of freer trade (Evans, 1971, p. 302). Delaying tactics in the committee seem to have frustrated the neoprotectionist drive. While this sentiment has as yet produced little in the way of concrete results, it persists with the oddity of the Chairman of the House Ways and Means Committee in 1971 "negotiating" a voluntary quota on textile imports with the Japanese as a device for avoiding more widespread protectionist steps. The actions of the Nixon administration in temporarily imposing a 10 per cent tariff surcharge on imports and then devaluing the dollar, so heightened a consciousness of the competitive difficulties of America in the world market that, at the moment of writing, it seems likely that after 1972 there will be a surge of proposals in Congress for quotas and other measures of protection.

Allen and Walter cite the following combination of reasons for the increase in American protectionism: "the increased competitiveness of Europe and more particularly Japan, relatively higher recent rates of inflation in the United States than abroad, technological and product improvement by American competitors, and the internationalization of business activity. The result has been damage or foreseeable damage to important import-competing sectors. These include textiles, steel, shoes, dairy products, electronic, and others" (1971, p. 53).

While it is difficult to give proper weight to all factors, we must comment on the extent to which the whole pattern of international business has

---

[4] A quick introduction can be found in Malmgren (1970-'71) and Evans (1971, chapters 16 and 17).

changed from the period of the fifties to the beginning of the seventies. As Allen and Walter observe, business has become internationalized. Increased worldwide intelligence of business opportunities and conditions has facilitated the international flow of money and other productive factors. The extent of U.S. investment in Europe during this period is well known; many see direct U.S. participation in the EEC economy as more important than exports to the Community.

Indeed, among the points to which hindsight tells us we should have paid more attention in the book, the internationalization of business is one of the foremost. The whole national perspective of many corporations has changed as both their capital and their executive staffs have become multinational and as their communication systems have become more cosmopolitan. The opening of world markets has significantly broadened competition and trade among multinational corporations, weakening cartel arrangements and oligopoly, and increasing support for freer trade arrangements.

On the other hand, the defection of the labor movement from the cause of freer trade is especially noteworthy. Such practices as the exporting of American-made parts for assembly abroad and the reimportation of finished products have caused anxiety over the "exporting of jobs."

The Vietnam war not only contributed to inflation and thereby facilitated an increase in imports, but also hastened a shift of America's attention away from international concerns toward domestic concerns, which were already rising in saliency during the sixties. Additionally, the Nixon administration in its first two years appeared to underplay the role of commercal policy as an integral part of its foreign policy.

Finally, the EEC has grown into a formidable economic entity, exceeding the U.S. in trading power. If Britain enters the EEC, as seems probable, the relative power of the U.S. will be affected even more. In sum, the United States has lost both the disposition and the capability to exercise the role in world economic affairs that was its lot in the fifties and to some extent in the sixties. If we consider that the remaining barriers to trade will be more difficult to reduce than were industrial tariffs, and that the EEC has entered various complicated trading relationships with a number of non-EEC Eastern Hemisphere countries, it becomes clear that some entirely new formulas of trade policy are likely to come into discussion soon.

BIBLIOGRAPHY

Allen, R. L. and I. Walter. The Formation of United States Trade Policy: Retrospect and Prospect. *The Bulletin.* February, 1971, Nos. 70–71, N.Y.U. Graduate School of Business Administration, Institute of Finance.

Arrow, K. *Social Choice and Individual Values.* New York: Wiley, 1963.

Baldwin, R. E. *Non-tariff Distortions of International Trade.* Washington, D. C.: The Brookings Institution, 1970.

Barnes, J. A. Class and Committees in a Norwegian Island Parish. *Human Relations,* 1954, 7, 39–58.

Bay, C. Politics and Pseudopolitics. *American Political Science Review,* 1965, 59, 39–51.

Berelson, B., P. F. Lazarsfeld, and W. McPhee. *Voting.* Chicago: University of Chicago Press, 1954.

Boissevain, J. The Place of Non-Groups in the Social Sciences.*Man,* 1968, New Series 3, 542–56.

Bott, E. *Family and Social Network.* London: Tavistock, 1957.

Bottomore, T. B. *Elites and Society.* London: C. A. Watts, 1964.

Braybrooke, D. and C. E. Lindblom. *A Strategy of Decision.* New York: Free Press, 1963.

Burke, E. Speech at the Guildhall in Bristol (1780). In *Works,* Vol. 1, 256–72. London: Samuel Holdsworth, 1837.

Dahl, R. A. *Who Governs?* New Haven: Yale University Press, 1961.

Dahl, R. A. and C. E. Lindblom. *Politics, Economics, and Welfare.* New York: Harper, 1953.

Davis, L. The Cost of the New Realism. *World Political Quarterly,* 1964, 17, 37–46.

Dexter, L. A. *The Sociology and Politics of Congress.* Chicago: Rand McNally, 1969.

Downs, A. *An Economic Theory of Democracy.* New York: Harper, 1957.

Dye, T. R. Community Power Studies. In Robinson, J. A., *Political Science Annual,* Vol. 2, 1969. Indianapolis: Bobbs-Merrill, 1970.

Evans, J. W. *The Kennedy Round in American Trade Policy.* Cambridge, Mass.: Harvard University Press, 1971.

Froman, L. A., Jr. Review, American Business and Public Policy. *American Political Science Review,* 1963, 57, 671–72.

Grodzins, M. *The American System.* Chicago: Rand McNally, 1966.

Homans, G. *Human Behavior, Its Elementary Forms.* New York: Harcourt, Brace, 1961.

————. *The Human Group,* New York: Harcourt, Brace, 1950.

Huitt, R. K. and R. L. Peabody. *Congress: Two Decades of Analysis.* New York: Harper, 1969.

Hunter, F. *Community Power Structure.* Chapel Hill: University of North Carolina Press, 1953.

Key, V. O., Jr. *Public Opinion and American Democracy.* N.Y.: Knopf, 1961.

Lindblom, C. *The Policy Making Process.* Englewood Cliffs, N.J.: Prentice-

Hall, 1968.

Lippmann, W. *Public Opinion.* New York: Harcourt, Brace, 1922.

Lowi, T. American Business, Public Policy, Case Studies and Political Theory. *World Politics,* 1964, *16,* 676–715.

————. *The End of Liberalism: Ideology Policy and the Crisis of Public Authority.* New York: Norton, 1969.

Malmgren, H. B. Coming Trade Wars? (Neo-mercantilism and Foreign Policy). *Foreign Policy,* Winter 1970–71.

March, J. G. and H. A. Simon. *Organizations.* New York: Wiley, 1958.

Mayer, A. C. The Significance of Quasi-Groups in the Study of Complex Societies. In Banton, M., *The Social Anthropology of Complex Societies.* New York: Praeger, 1966.

Michels, R. *Political Parties.* First published 1915. N.Y. : Free Press, 1966.

Mills, C. W. *The Power Elite.* New York: Oxford Press, 1956.

Mosca, G. *The Ruling Class.* New York: McGraw-Hill, 1939.

Olson, M. *The Logic of Collective Action: Public Goods and the Theory of Groups.* Cambridge, Mass.: Harvard University Press, 1965.

Ostrogorski, M. *Democracy and the Organization of Political Parties.* New York: Macmillan, 1902.

Pareto, V. *The Mind and Society.* New York: Harcourt, Brace, 1935.

Preeg, E. H. *Traders and Diplomats.* Washington, D. C.: The Brookings Institution, 1970.

Riker, W. *The Theory of Political Coalitions,* New Haven: Yale University Press, 1962.

Rousseau, J. J. *The Social Contract.* Translated by Gerald Hopkins. New York: Oxford University Press, 1948.

Steffens, J.L. *The Autobiography of Lincoln Steffens,* N.Y.Harcourt, Brace,1931.

Truman, D. *The Governmental Process.* New York: Knopf, 1951.

Walker, J. L. A Critique of the Elitist Theory of Democracy. *American Political Science Review,* 1966, *60,* 258–95.

Weber, M. *Politics as a Vocation.* Reprinted in Gerth, H. H. and Mills, C. W,. From *Max Weber: Essays in Sociology.* New York: Oxford University Press, 1958.

Wicksteed, P. H. L. Robbins (ed.), *Common Sense of Political Economy,* Vol. 1, London: Routledge, 1933.

Wilson, J. Q. An Overview of Theories of Planned Change. In R. Morris (ed.), *Centrally Planned Change.* New York: National Association of Social Workers, 1964.

Preface

Some ten years ago, the authors, interested in the workings of public opinion in foreign policy, began a research project to test accepted theories of pressure groups and decision-making. We chose as our data the politics of foreign trade from Eisenhower's inauguration to the Kennedy Trade Expansion Act of 1962. The research included a 900-interview poll of heads of corporations and some five hundred interviews with congressmen, lobbyists, journalists, and others. We present here the results of that research in the hope that they transcend the limits of a case study and contribute to the understanding of decision-making, communication, and democratic processes.

In the course of these ten years of work, we have contracted many obligations, which it is a pleasure to acknowledge here. The study itself—part of a program of comparative studies of international communication by the Center for International Studies, Massachusetts Institute of Technology—was financed primarily by The Ford Foundation. To a number of other institutions, too, we owe gratitude for support: to the Harvard Graduate School of Business Administration, which Mr. Bauer joined after M.I.T.; to the Center for Advanced Study in the Behavioral Sciences, where two of the authors worked on this study while fellows; to the Bureau of Social Science Research of Washington, D.C., where we had Washington headquarters; and to the National Opinion Research Center, which conducted a survey of American businessmen for us. That survey was organized at NORC by Eli Marks and Herbert Hyman, and we are especially grateful to them and to Clyde Hart, then director of NORC, for their active role and continued interest in our work.

The qualitative interviews were done by the authors themselves and by a number of colleagues and associates, among whom we particularly wish to note Harold Isaacs, who observed Textiletown, and Kenneth Fry, of the *Milwaukee Journal,* who did the same in Midwest.

Suzanne Keller and Doris Held did much of the survey analysis which forms the backbone of the various chapters on public and business opinion. William Miller prepared a valuable historical survey of American foreign-trade policy which served as the basis for the chapter on that topic. Frank Bonilla helped with analysis, editing, and many other things.

In the course of the study, many others worked on pieces of the analysis, among them: Stanley Wellisz, William R. Leitch, Rosanne Mandler, Robert Melson, and Samuel Popkin. Elmo Roper, the Standard Oil Company of New Jersey, and the New York City League of Women Voters each made cards from public-opinion surveys available to us. Richard Hatch gave the manuscript an over-all editing.

Among the authors themselves, responsibility varies. Messrs. Bauer and Pool both worked on the entire manuscript in its several drafts and bear the full responsibility for its various defects. Mr. Dexter, who was our representative in Washington, did the basic study of Congress, the results of which may be found at greater length in his "Congressmen and the People They Listen To." [1] He also prepared the original reports on Delaware, Appalachian City, the Fifty-third Congressional District, and portions of other chapters. He wishes to record his dissent to some of the historical interpretations in chapters 2-4. The treatment of the partisan division within legislative bodies and the omission of certain important legislative and administrative details which would belong in a book about foreign trade, if not in one about political communication, remain at issue between us.

Secretarial assistance, as on all such projects, was a crucial factor in making this work possible at all. We owe a debt to Elizabeth Hopkins Colt, Martha Tucker Harris, Rosemary Parkins, and Dorothy Gilligan. Very special thanks are due Elly Terlingen, who arrived on the scene after most of the fun was over and has worked so diligently at the tedious job of handling successive revisions of the manuscript, checking facts, preparing the index, and correcting our errors.

---

[1] Copyright M.I.T.; submitted in partial fulfillment of the requirements for the Ph.D. to Columbia University, 1959.

The administration of the Center for International Studies made a contribution to the complex operation of this group research which usually goes unacknowledged. We would like to mention the encouragement received from Max F. Millikan, the director of the center, and the constant and cheerful support of the center's administrative staff, especially James Baldwin, Donald Blackmer, Arthur Singer, Roger Bull, and Mary Burns.

The list of credits could be extended at great length, and the question would still arise as to where to draw the line. Various journalists, economists, and social scientists served us as consultants in varying capacities. We are particularly indebted to our many informants, a few of whom are mentioned by name in the text, but most of whom are either given pseudonyms or not mentioned at all, in order to preserve their anonymity. Many persons in business, Congressional, and other organizational offices were helpful in arranging appointments, taking messages, making facilities available, and so on. We hope that each of them will individually forgive us for not mentioning him by name. We considered at length how to thank our 1,400 interview respondents—congressmen, busy businessmen, and important public figures—who gave their precious time. A few, especially, went to great length to help us. Although we would like to mention them for the help they gave, some would prefer to remain unnamed, and it would be impossible for us to attempt to discriminate. We therefore content ourselves with thanking these people collectively and thanking the major organized groups on both sides of the trade debate for their tolerance and friendliness to our academic curiosity. The Committee for a National Trade Policy; The Nation-wide Committee of Industry, Agriculture, and Labor on Import-Export Policy; and the American Tariff League all offered cooperation and candor in support of our endeavors.

Contents

PART IV · THE PRESSURE GROUPS   321

INTRODUCTION

The Study and Its Methods

This is a study of American politics and of international communication. Its subject is the ethos and actions of business executives when confronted by a political issue—foreign-trade legislation—with repercussions throughout the world as well as at home.

The issue of foreign trade links the smallest domestic business to the broadest questions of foreign policy. The jobs of coal-miners in West Virginia are affected, but so is the power of NATO and the modernization of developing countries. In the foreign-trade issue, foreign policy becomes domestic politics.

The politics of trade legislation is our subject. We start with the renewal of the Reciprocal Trade Act in 1953 and end with the passage of Kennedy's Trade Expansion Act in 1962. The latter act set this nation on a path toward what may some day be a boundaryless Atlantic economy. The Common Market is already becoming an economic unity. The Trade Expansion Act allows the United States to press for a still-greater West straddling the Atlantic. Before such a bill could be enacted into law, American attitudes had to change. That attitude change and its translation into action is our story.

1

In 1952, for the first time in twenty years, the party in control of the government changed. Within its first months, the new Republican administration had to decide what to do with the Reciprocal Trade Act. This act, framed under the New Deal to lower the barriers to international trade, automatically expired within six months of the inauguration of the new president.

"The Tariff" had once been a central issue of American politics. Many new men in Congress still remembered it as the touchstone which separated Democrats from Republicans—Democrats for low tariff, Republicans for high.

It has been the political issue par excellence for the first century of the Republic. No other had wrung such fervent rhetoric from Congress or created such controversy in the hustings. But by 1953, when Eisenhower took office, the questions which faced the nation in relation to foreign trade had changed their character. Tariffs were no longer the only barrier and probably not even the most important barrier to trade or regulator of it. Nor was the tariff the important source of revenue it once had been. Few if any "infant" industries stood in need of protection. Furthermore, tariffs, which over the years had been debated as a matter of domestic politics, came after World War II to be regarded as integrally related to the country's foreign policy. Eisenhower and most of his close supporters favored extension of the Reciprocal Trade Act, for they saw the stimulation of international trade as a necessary step toward a stable and peaceful international order.

However, other considerations and interests stood in the way of renewal of the act. A number of American industries were feeling the impact of foreign competition, in part a result of the postwar revival of European and Japanese industry. Influential members of Congress, principally representatives of the anti-Eisenhower wing of the Republican Party, who had long opposed the very fundaments of the Reciprocal Trade Act as contrary to American interests and sound American policy, both political and economic, remained protectionists in principle. The Eisenhower Republicans had to find some formula to protect themselves from the charge of having gone "me too" and now voting for a New Deal bill they had once opposed. On the other hand, some Democrats in Congress found that, as a result of shifts in the location of American industry and other changes in the economy, they were representing for the first time in their memory constituents who desired protection from foreign competition.

Not only were conflicting interests at stake, but political processes produced something more than a direct translation of public opinion into public policy. Congress, the administration, and the American people at large were concerned with events and issues other than foreign trade.

Limitations on the time and energies of all parties concerned coupled with the relative priority and urgency of other matters affected the fate of the Reciprocal Trade Act.

In 1953-1955 the decision whether the act should be renewed and in what form was deferred by two moratoria: a one-year extension in 1953 and another such extension in 1954. In 1955, as Bill HR 1 of the Eighty-fourth Congress, the act was finally extended for three years in such ambiguous form that the outcome was variously interpreted as victory for the proponents of protection, victory for a liberal trade policy, or a compromise, the final import of which was unpredictable.

The events of those two years provide the main materials for this book. But there have been two further rounds of legislation since. In 1958, the act was renewed once more with but little change and little controversy. By making some concessions in advance and not asking for further power toward liberalization, the Eisenhower administration avoided in 1958 the bruising Congressional battle it had had three years earlier. In 1962, a new bill was enacted in place of the Reciprocal Trade Act, the Kennedy Trade Expansion Act. It was designed to pick up once more the movement toward lower tariffs where it had been dropped. Labeled as a new law, justified by new arguments—namely the threat of the Common Market— it nevertheless kept the broad principles of reciprocal-trade legislation as it has existed since 1934, though significantly extending the powers of the president.

There are many ways in which one might approach the struggle which took place in the years after 1953 over American foreign trade policy. The main emphasis might be placed on the problems which faced American business and the world economy. It might equally be put on the strictly political factors involved in the passage of legislation. But there are questions which fall outside the framework of these usual schemes of explanation. How closely do the policies adopted reflect the wishes and interests of the business community and/or the general public? How far are businessmen motivated by rational computations of self-interest? How do they determine what their self-interest is? To the extent that factors other than "rational self-interest" enter the picture, what are these factors? How do they get expressed? If there is one single, central question to which this book is addressed, it is this: How did processes of information and communication, both international and domestic, change decisions from what they would have been had simple economic determinism been operating alone?

When we inaugurated this study, one prominent economist told us we were wasting our time. "Tell me what a businessman manufactures," he said, "and I will tell you where he stands on foreign trade." If this economist's genie could have so performed, then indeed a study of com-

munication, persuasion, and influence about reciprocal trade would have
but little interest. It would be a study of mediating variables incapable of
affecting the outcome.

But if processes of communication do in part determine how men
behave and if self-interest alone does not predict the decision reached,
then there may be much to learn from studying how the decisions are
reached. Who exercises influence on Congress? How, why, and to what
effect? How far do congressmen know what their constituents want or
even what the pressures on Congress are? When policy is made, what
information is available to the policy-maker? When policy affects both
domestic and foreign interests, what are the images of the relevant foreign
events and what are the sources of information about them? Consideration
of these questions is not absent from previous studies of foreign-trade
policy. But in many instances the processes of communication by which attitudes and decisions are reached occupy a status analogous to unexplored
territories on ancient maps marked with such a legend as, "Hereabouts
theyre be wilde beastes." The existence of wilde beastes is recorded, their
importance for potential travelers is noted, but they are seldom described in
any detail. For us, this terra incognita is our primary interest. It is the
process of policy-making to which we shall pay attention, rather than to
the substantive questions which preoccupied the executives, the lobbyists,
and the politicians concerned with the passing of trade legislation.

There has been a tendency for students of politics and economics to
regard the processes with which we are concerned as imperfections or
perversions of a proper political process. Writers reviewing the foreign-
policy debates in the United States Congress often complain that the
arguments used fail to reflect adequate comprehension of basic economic
theory! But such lapses from perfect wisdom happen regularly and are
inevitably part of the political process. They are neither curiosa nor subjects for moral condemnation. They are as legitimately and necessarily the
object of systematic study as are theoretical economic considerations and the
formal political process from which they are deviations.

□ Objectives

This volume is one in a series which reports studies in several areas
—initially the United States, France, the Middle East, and India—on communications and foreign policy.[1] We have referred to the project as a study

---

[1] Volumes resulting from the International Communication Program of the Center
for International Studies, Massachusetts Institute of Technology, have been:

George V. Coelho, *Changing Images of America*, "A Study of Indian Students' Perceptions" (Glencoe, Ill.: The Free Press, 1958);

of international communications and also as a study of elite decision-making. Neither of these labels conveys adequately what we did, why, or how we did it. What distinguishes the research is an emphasis on the flow of communications to and within the groups involved in the foreign-policy decision-making process. In the present study, we examined the communications behavior of the American business community, that influential stratum with most interest and most voice in the shaping of foreign-trade policy. Second, we examined the communications behavior of Congress, the group that finally had to arrive at a decision. And, third, but to a very small degree, we have looked into the behavior of the general public as it bore on the behavior of the Congress and the business community. We were interested in the sources of information for each of these populations, the bases of its attitudes on the trade issue, and the circumstances which lead some individuals to take active roles in the making of policy.

In the summer of 1953, at the time we were designing the present project, the first one-year interim extension of the Reciprocal Trade Act had just been passed. It seemed clear that, one year hence, when our field work would be in full swing, a major issue of foreign policy would be another renewal of that act. Furthermore, the issue promised to be one of highest interest to the business community, the particular American elite which we most wished to study and which we felt had been least perceptively and adequately studied before.

The American businessman as a social force has often been excoriated. He has as often been extolled. He has seldom been analyzed. That he is an important mover in American life both his friends and enemies would admit—even if he is not the all-powerful member of a cabal or ruling class that is often portrayed. Nor is he a barefoot boy being pushed around by powerful politicians and labor leaders, as he sometimes sees

Harold R. Isaacs, *Scratches on Our Minds,* "American Images of China and India" (New York: John Day, 1961) ;

Idem., Emergent Americans, "A Report on 'Crossroads Africa' " (New York: John Day, 1961) ;

Idem.. The New World of Negro Americans (New York: John Day, 1963) ;

Hidetoshi Kato, ed. and trans., *Japanese Popular Culture,* "Studies in Mass Communication and Cultural Change" (Rutland, Vt.: Charles E. Tuttle, 1959) ;

Felix and Marie Keesing, *Elite Communication in Samoa,* "A Study of Leadership" (Stanford: Stanford University Press, 1956) ;

Eric H. Lenneberg and John M. Roberts, *The Language of Experience,* "A Study in Methodology," Memoir 13, supplement to *International Journal of American Linguistics,* 22 (April 1956), No. 2;

Daniel Lerner with Lucille W. Pevsner, *The Passing of Traditional Society,* "Modernizing the Middle East" (Glencoe, Ill.: The Free Press, 1958) ;

Daniel Lerner and Raymond Aron, eds., *France Defeats EDC* (New York: Frederick A. Praeger, 1959) ;

Edward A. Shils, *The Intellectual between Tradition and Modernity,* "The Indian Situation" (The Hague: Mouton & Co., 1961).

himself. He is part of a stratum whose efforts and energy have been a source of many of the distinctive features of American society. That stratum is worthy of study even if it does not constitute, as some believe, the "bosses" of that society.

□ Methods

The methods we employed were diverse. They included sample surveys of the heads of American business firms, analysis of historical and contemporary documents, and relatively informal interviews, such as are employed by newspaper reporters.

A survey of 903 business leaders was designed by us in close collaboration with the National Opinion Research Center and carried out by that organization. These business leaders constituted a carefully selected sample of the heads of United States firms with more than 100 employees. The interviews inquired into the sources from which these business leaders learned news in general and that of foreign-trade problems in particular, their attitudes toward foreign-trade policy and toward international relations, the stake of their businesses in foreign trade and in other issues of national policy, and the extent of their activities on such issues in communicating with their trade associations, Congress, or the administrative agencies of government. (The reader interested only in the main lines of foreign-trade policy-making and not in the details of our survey of businessmen's attitudes may wish to pass over most of Part II except Chapter 13.)

A sample survey of the heads of American businesses could not, of course, give a complete picture of the making of American foreign-trade policy, nor even of the communications behavior of businessmen. Accordingly, the systematic sample survey was complemented by more than 500 interviews with members of Congress and their staffs, persons in the national administration, businessmen particularly active in the foreign-trade controversy, lobbyists and trade association representatives, leaders of labor unions, and journalists. These interviews, less formal and less rigidly structured, served a variety of purposes, one of which was to study the inflow of communications to Congress and the reaction of the national legislature to such communications. These findings are discussed in Chapter 12 and parts IV and V.

Our earliest interviews with businessmen and with persons actively involved in the making of foreign-trade policy were to a great extent intended to aid us in the design of the sample survey, but they gave us much additional information on the activities of men in various industries and various communities. Historically, it had been argued that foreign-trade policy is largely a local issue in the sense that Congress is more likely to respond to the demands of local constituencies than to act in terms of the national interest. Furthermore, the characteristics of different communities might affect markedly the concern and behavior of businessmen in those localities. Where a single large business is dominant, it might mobilize the citizens behind its interests. Small, locally owned businesses might find in their Congressional representatives a more receptive ear than would branches of large firms, nationally owned. Many such propositions (some of them mutually contradictory) are upheld by students of the problem. It therefore seemed more worthwhile to turn a certain amount of attention to ascertaining just what was happening in a half-dozen American communities. Part III is a series of such local case studies based on our informal interviews.

A book on attitudes of American businessmen toward foreign-trade policy would be incomplete were some attention not paid to their similarities to and differences from the attitudes of the general public. Several polling organizations—Gallup, the National Opinion Research Center, Elmo Roper, and the Survey Research Center of the University of Michigan—were generous in making available to us their findings conducted under various sponsorships. The League of Women Voters submitted to us for analysis the results of a special survey in New York City.

Many queries and objections to our procedures may be anticipated and, we hope, answered at some point; but only one seems sufficiently important to dwell on before proceeding to the substance of the book. We touched on it briefly at the beginning of this chapter. The issues of foreign-trade policy facing the United States in the period following World War II were exceedingly complex, both politically and economically. For over a century tariff problems seem to have been central in American politics, and "the tariff" came to symbolize the whole range of questions associated with the regulation of trade, despite the fact that dumping practices, subsidization of American shipping, and a variety of related issues made their appearance at an early date. It is quite probable, however, that, by the second half of the twentieth century, tariffs were actually a relatively minor factor in the control of trade between countries. Certainly the tariff was only one among a number of important problems—export-import licenses, bans on shipment of "essential goods" to Iron Curtain countries, customs procedures, currency convertibility, dumping, "Buy-American" Act, shipping in American bottoms, long-term credits extended with governmental support by nationals of some countries, and so on. Nevertheless, most, although not all, of our analysis is focused on the question of the tariff and on attitudes toward it.

Many friendly critics have already protested that focusing on tariffs vastly oversimplifies the problems of foreign-trade policy. This is true, but without such simplification the study would have been impossible. More-

over, although a selective focus on attitudes toward tariffs oversimplifies
the economics of the issue, it is unlikely that it oversimplifies the politics
of the issue to the same degree. To this day, "the tariff" still serves as a
symbol of where a man stands on a wide range of problems concerned
with foreign-trade policy. There is no more eloquent testimony to this
than the fact that many who wrote in protest against the provisions of HR 1
for tariff revision had themselves no interest in tariffs per se, but rather
in related issues. Yet these people reacted to the possibility of lowered
tariffs as a symptom of a broad policy which would affect all foreign-trade
policy. (This is discussed in more detail in Chapter 8.) For us, too, attitudes
toward tariffs were the most convenient index of attitudes toward the broad
range of problems involved.

PART I

The Setting

PART I

Chapter 1

Foreign-Trade Policy
Prior to 1934 [1]

The passage of the Reciprocal Trade Act in 1934 marked a turning point in American foreign-trade policy. For the first time, the leading role in tariff-setting passed from Congress to the Executive. Also, the act reversed a long-range trend of increasing American tariffs. This trend, which ran from the first Congress in 1789 to the passage of the Smoot-Hawley tariff in 1930, was interrupted by only two periods of lowered tariffs: from 1832 to the beginning of the Civil War and from 1913 to 1922.

In this chapter we shall review the trend of tariffs in the era when Congress dominated tariff-making. We shall find that the upward trend, at least until after the Civil War, was a result of the government's need for revenue, particularly in wars, and of the working of politics, rather than of a settled national policy of protection. The latter appeared only

[1] This chapter is based mainly on a historical review of American foreign-trade policy prepared for us by William Miller. We have taken considerable liberties with Mr. Miller's manuscript, and he should be given all credit for the merits and none for the demerits of this chapter.

later, as the arguments used to justify protection changed from pleas for exceptional measures on behalf of infant industries to doctrines that made of protection a right and a principle. That was to a considerable degree the accepted view by the time of the passage of the Smoot-Hawley Act, with which we close this chapter.

The first tariff bill, introduced by Madison in the House in 1789, was intended to raise urgently needed revenue by taxing the heavy spring imports which were already on the high seas. Madison did not intend that his bill should act as a regulator of imports. He proposed that the duty should fall on "such articles . . . only as are likely to occasion the least difficulty." [2] But other members of Congress saw that the economic interests of their constituents were involved. Clymer of Pennsylvania asked that steel be added to Madison's list on the grounds that, "the manufacture of steel in America was rather in its infancy; but as all the materials necessary to make it were the produce of every state in the Union, and as the manufacture was already established, and attended with considerable success, he deemed it prudent to emancipate our country from the manacles in which she was held by foreign manufacturers. . . ." [3] A duty was put on steel, and a tariff which had been intended solely for revenue became an instrument for regulating both the flow of trade and domestic economic policy.

The debate of 1789 also foreshadowed other characteristics of succeeding tariff debates. Any tariff tends by its very nature to be discriminatory. One person gains at the immediate expense of another. In 1789, land speculators were wooed into supporting the bill by the imposition of a duty on hemp, with the prospect that this would increase land values. This incensed shipbuilders. Both the tariff on hemp and that on iron worked to their disadvantage. To placate the shipbuilders, discriminatory rates were voted in favor of goods arriving in American bottoms. As legislators were to discover over the next century, it was simpler to compensate those injured by tariffs by protecting them in turn rather than by reducing the protection originally granted to the first party. This tendency was enhanced by the fact that any one business, once granted protection, tended to regard that level of protection as its natural prerogative, even though in many instances the circumstances that warranted the original protection had since disappeared. Pressure was thus built into the tariff-making process for all revisions to be upward.

---

[2] D. R. Dewey, *Financial History of the United States* (8th ed.; New York: Longmans-Green and Co., 1922), p. 80.

[3] C. A. Beard, *Economic Origins of Jeffersonian Democracy* (New York: The Macmillan Company, 1915), pp. 163 f.

□ The War of 1812 and Its Aftermath

One of the events which has ordinarily brought about an upward revision of trade barriers in American history has been a war. The War of 1812 was the first to have such an effect. Tariffs were approximately doubled in the hope of increasing revenues, a hope that was not realized because the war itself blocked the sea lanes, and foreign trade almost ceased. Under the physical protection thus accorded domestic manufactures, a host of new industries were born, while old ones expanded. Manufacture of cotton goods, woolens, iron, glass, pottery, and other articles increased rapidly. When the war ended, Congress felt that these war-born industries were entitled to some measure of additional temporary protection from the normal revival of foreign trade, so the general duty was raised again in 1816. At that time, though, little sentiment in favor of protection as a permanent policy was expressed either by the public or by Congress.[4] It was genuinely believed that these increases were temporary.

The period after the War of 1812 proved to be one of economic difficulty for the United States. British manufacturers, with plant capacity swelled by the demands of the Napoleonic Wars, began to ship excess commodities to American shores in ever-increasing quantities. The influx threatened war-born American firms. Many industries suffered, despite unprecedented tariff protection. The action of the British manufacturers was viewed by many Americans as a deliberate attempt to ". . . stifle in the cradle those rising manufactures . . . which the war has forced into existence." [5] Thus it was for the first time possible for American protectionists to make the tariff issue a popular one by linking it to anti-British feeling and the spirit of American nationalism.

Budding Eastern industrialists found advocates of protection in the agricultural Midwest and Western states. There, corn-, wheat-, and hemp-growers gradually became supporters of Clay's "American System." [6] Faith grew in the argument that the future of agriculture in the United States lay in the development of a domestic urban market for agricultural produce.

The core of the protectionist doctrine was the "infant-industry" argument. With sufficient protection, American manufacture could develop. The consumer and farmer were assured that American manufacturing,

---

[4] F. W. Taussig, *The Tariff History of the United States* (7th ed., New York: G. P. Putnam's Sons, 1923), p. 18.

[5] T. C. Cochran and W. Miller, *The Age of Enterprise*, "A Social History of Industrial America" (New York: The Macmillan Company, 1949), p. 11.

[6] H. J. Carman and H. C. Syrett, *A History of the American People to 1865* (New York: A. Knopf, 1952), pp. 358 f.

if encouraged by temporary protection, would develop to the point where its products would become cheaper than European ones. The tone of that protectionist argument was optimistic, aggressive, expansionist. It contrasts with the conservative, static, defensive themes in protectionist arguments today. Then, unlike now, protectionism had strong popular support behind it. But one element of early protectionism which has persisted is nationalism. These were the political factors which helped produce a rising tariff level after the War of 1812.

From the panic of 1819, precipitated by the postwar events referred to above, came tariff increases, until in 1828 the level of duties was 44 per cent ad valorem. The basic tariff rate before the War of 1812, with the exception of certain luxury items, had been 5 per cent.

□ The Civil War and the Tariff

The South strongly opposed protectionism, both because it increased the price on goods which it purchased from abroad and because it feared the British would impose retaliatory duties on cotton. However, not until 1833 could the South make its voice effective. In that year, Calhoun, leader of the free traders, and Clay, who had been the strongest of protectionists, agreed on a compromise tariff with rates to be lowered progressively over the next decade. Although there was a slight reversal of trend in the act of 1842, tariffs continued in general to decline until the Civil War.

But, with the Civil War, circumstances again brought about a sharp increase in rates, and others prevented their postwar reduction. Wartime need for revenue caused some of the increase. In order to finance the war, other taxes were also introduced, one of which was a set of excise taxes on domestic manufactures. Imports of the same goods were assessed an additional tariff to compensate for the internal taxes.

Such fiscal considerations were reinforced by the protectionist disposition of the men remaining in Congress, which naturally included no Southerners, and by anti-British sentiment, which, though endemic in this period of American history, was heightened by Britain's support of the South, both in the war and in prewar efforts to keep tariffs low. Taussig reports that the average rate of dutiable commodities under the act of 1864 rose to 47 per cent.[7]

At the end of the Civil War, the internal revenue taxes were abolished, but it was quietly forgotten that a good portion of the existing tariffs had been intended as compensations for these internal taxes. The

---

[7] *Op. cit.,* p. 167.

so-called war tariff became permanent, both on the statute books and in the minds of the public and of the protected industries.

Efforts were made to reduce tariffs after the war, but they failed. In fact, more often than not what started out as a movement for reduction produced an increase. The act of 1870 was one such example. Some items were put on the free list, a few significant duties were lowered, but the increases overshadowed the reductions.

Low tariffs, identified as a Rebel policy, were labeled by protectionists as treachery. Greeley's influential *Tribune* referred to the Union's own advocates of reduced tariffs as "the traitorous section of Northern politics," among whom it was "consistent for Americans to advocate and plot with foreigners British Free Trade." Continued the *Tribune*:

> The cotton planters were educated by Calhoun to the policy of keeping the Yankees from manufacturing and confining them to raising cheap food for their slaves. The failure of their Rebellion has not softened the temper of this education. The reconstructed South would vote solid to destroy the wealth-producing industry of the Loyal States. And their unprincipled [Northern] slaves . . . would lick their shoes while they voted for them.[8]

Protectionism and nationalism were once again partners.

□ A Tariff for Protection, Not Revenue

The same period marked the beginning of the shift in the function of the tariff from a source of revenue to a device for the frank regulation of trade. Even though both the internal excise taxes and income tax introduced during the war were repealed as soon as hostilities ended, wartime experience taught that there were means of raising money other than by tariff.

Although the tariff continued for many years to be the chief source of national revenue, it was by the time of the Civil War being challenged by other sources. It was, however, assuming increasing importance as a regulator of trade. A subtle move by the protectionists was to lower revenue by cutting the duty on items in which they were not interested. Then, under the pretext of the necessity of maintaining the level of income, duties on competitive items were raised. Thus, the tariff revisions in the decades after the Civil War were marked by reductions on noncompetitive goods or their transfer to the free list.

A little later, pressure for lowering rates came from the fact that the Treasury began enjoying a surplus. The tariff was raising more money

---

[8] Quoted in H. Beale, *The Critical Year,* "A Study of Andrew Jackson and Reconstruction" (New York: Harcourt, Brace & Co., 1930), p. 275.

than the government spent. But this fact was not sufficient to stem the protectionist surge. Congress acted to limit revenues, as just indicated, by lowering or removing duties on noncompetitive imports, shifting them to cover products manufactured in the United States. The general principle of tariffs for protection was strengthened even as some rates were being lowered.

Maneuvering on individual items perhaps reached its peak in 1894, when the Senate, in revising the tariff act of that year, produced over 600 amendments to the House bill. During the late years of the nineteenth century, the influence of the trusts on behalf of particular items began to be felt. The president of the sugar trust frankly avowed that profits depended on maintaining the sugar duty. To this end, the trust contributed liberally to political campaigns.

During the 1880's, the tariff became the prime political issue of the time. Under the personal leadership of Grover Cleveland, the Democrats made tariff reduction a central plank. The Republicans took up the challenge, and their party platform in both 1884 and 1888 also set forth the tariff issue as the party's major stand. By 1888, the Republican platform stated:

> We are uncompromisingly in favor of the American system of protection. The President [Cleveland] and his party . . . serve the interests of Europe; we will support the interests of America. . . .[9]

The Cleveland victory of 1884 was too much a product of the bitterly personal campaign with Blaine to be interpreted as a mandate for tariff reform. Indeed, a sizable minority within the Democratic ranks joined with the Republicans to prevent any legislation to reduce tariffs during Cleveland's first term. However, Cleveland's annual message of 1887 was devoted entirely to the tariff and drew the battle-lines tighter. The 1888 campaign was fought on the tariff issue and was won by the Republicans. The victory may not have stemmed from public support of protectionism, but, having won with this as their platform, the Republicans could interpret their victory as a mandate to push through an upward revision.

Although the protectionist 1890 McKinley tariff had been followed by a Democratic landslide in that autumn's Congressional elections, the slower turnover which characterizes the Senate delayed complete Democratic control in Washington until Cleveland's personal triumph of 1892. With friends of tariff reduction in power, it appeared that a reversal of the protectionist trend would follow. However, the emergence of fiscal troubles in 1893 and the concomitant development of the currency question as a major national issue, combined with somewhat inept party leader-

---

[9] Kirk Porter, ed., *National Party Platforms (1840-1924)* (New York: Macmillan, 1924), p. 147.

ship in Congress, led to an act that the President allowed to become law
without his signature, evincing his displeasure with what had materialized
from such a promising start.

It is interesting to note that, throughout this period, the protectionists seem to have been more effective than their opposition in mobilizing
their sources of support and exploiting their resources, a pattern which
holds to the present. A number of the protectionist tariffs were passed
through Congresses in which protectionists were actually in the minority.
Vote-bartering over particular provisions of tariff acts obscured broad
principles, and the regulations grew ever more lengthy and complex as
varying interests were served. Moreover, the tariff was not the only
political issue of the time. Since Western farm areas were joined to the
Republican Party on a variety of other issues, they did not become an active
source of opposition to protection, although the farmers were hardly tariff
enthusiasts.

It is a familiar political tale that organized special interests find
little opposition aimed directly at them on an individual basis. The proponents of a particular industry united and worked effectively on behalf of
measures favorable to them. Rate increases were obtained or cuts prevented
via campaign contributions, especially to the Republican Party.[10] Opponents of something as big as "the tariff" seldom joined together to fight
piecemeal tariff increases. Thus, in this era of vigorous tariff lobbying, the
proponents of special interests were better able to maintain or increase
protection than were free-trade advocates to gain general decreases.

From the mid-1890's, free silver, war, extracontinental expansion,
and trusts replaced the tariff as dominant national issues. The Democratic
Party, until revitalized by Wilson's New Freedom, was so politically weak-
ened as to give protection relatively free reign. The high rates of the 1897
Dingley bill were undisturbed for over a decade, and, save for moderate
reductions during the Wilson administration—when war itself served as
a protective buffer for American industry—the protective tradition continued. In 1922, the high rates of the prewar era were restored, as agricultural decline and a general wave of nationalistic fervor swept the country.
The climax of the trend toward ever-higher walls was the passage in 1930,
during the Hoover administration, of the Smoot-Hawley tariff.

That act is still the basic tariff law of the land. For the past two
or three decades, under the Reciprocal Trade Act of 1934, the Executive
has had the power to raise or lower rates in the basic Smoot-Hawley
schedule by negotiating reciprocal concessions in trade treaties with other
countries. By this act, on the surface a purely administrative modification,

---

[10] See Ida M. Tarbell, *The Tariff in Our Times* (New York: Macmillan, 1915), and
The Nationalizing of Business (New York: Macmillan, 1936), pp. 288 f.

Congress passed on to the president much of its tariff-making power. In so doing, it not only changed the entire politics of the tariff but also reversed a 150-year trend toward protection.

□ The Changing Role of the Tariff

In the course of a century and a half there were many profound changes in issues and conditions and many remarkable constancies in American tariff-making.

Trends during and after World War I were in some ways a reflection of those of the War of 1812 and the Civil War. With the imposition of the federal personal income tax in 1913, the already-much-reduced role of the tariff as a source of revenue was reduced still further. The coming of war, its attendant mushrooming of federal expenditures, and the transformation of the United States during the conflict from a debtor to a creditor nation all served to intensify the decline in the role that the tariff could play in the over-all revenue picture. Hence, by 1920, the tariff was almost solely an instrument for the protection of American industry and labor against foreign competition in the American market.

But it was not long before the tariff began to lose its significance as a booster of American industry, too. The economy of the United States had altered basically. Starting as an agricultural country in the eighteenth century, it was not until the end of the nineteenth century that the country became genuinely interested in the export of industrial products. Until then, the United States was concerned with exporting agricultural produce mainly and with obtaining finished goods and some raw materials from abroad. Then it developed into the mightiest industrial power of the twentieth century. But, even though the United States had become a great exporting nation, many Americans of the first few decades of this century showed little appreciation of the relation of exports to imports. They were willing to do anything to stimulate export trade except to provide other nations with a market within which to earn dollars to pay for United States exports. Consciousness that such one-way trade could not go on forever began to dawn in the Great Depression and reached its full tide in the years we are studying. A contemporary student of American foreign-trade policy, Samuel Lubell, dates Great Britain's departure from the gold standard in 1931 as the beginning of the decline of the tariff as the United States' main instrument of trade regulation.[11]

A multitude of factors have been operative in the period since Britain abandoned the gold standard and, with it, the automatic control

---

[11] *The Revolution in World Trade and American Economic Policy* (New York: Harper & Bros., 1955), p. 12.

of trade by the market place to reduce the importance of the tariff. The managed-trade practices of Nazi Germany, embargoes and quotas on vital materials during and after World War II, currency and import controls, and the coordination of U.S. trade policy with foreign political policy were all factors at work to diminish the tariff's role in foreign trade. Other devices for regulation, such as shipping subsidies and legislation for preferential buying from certain nations, came into existence. It might well be argued that today the tariff is no longer a major element in the conduct of U.S. foreign trade. Nonetheless, it clearly remains the symbol of protection to both its friends and enemies.

In stressing the relative decline in the importance of the tariff in recent decades, we do not mean to imply that all the alternative devices for regulating foreign commerce are new. In the very first tariff act there was a provision for preferential duties on goods arriving in American bottoms. At a fairly early period, the secretary of the treasury was empowered to raise tariffs automatically on any products which were being dumped on the American market as a result of subsidization by foreign governments. During the 1920's, the British attempted to control world rubber prices by cornering the market. Many countries used a quota system for regulating imports. Governments subsidized the export efforts of their citizens. All such devices had been used previously. After the 1930's, however, they increased in relative importance. The chairman of one of the important Congressional committees dealing with foreign economic policy in the Eighty-fourth Congress is quoted as saying impatiently that he hoped the committee's staff members would review the "tariff stuff" quickly and then "forget it . . . it's no longer of any importance."

□ The Arguments for Protection and Free Trade

We have already touched on most of the arguments introduced for and against protection. However, it may be well to review them and their development in a summary fashion.

In a sense there are today almost no truly new arguments, though the weight and salience of them have shifted. One, at least, has dropped from the discussion. No one advocates a high tariff as a device for increasing revenue even though this was the first and main argument employed for the imposition of duties on imports.

George Clymer's early pleas for a tariff on iron introduced the "infant-industry" argument which was to become the mainstay of early protectionist theory. It was contended that the national interest lay in the development of manufactures; that, after a period of infancy, these industries would be able to stand on their own feet; and that they would in fact be able to produce goods more cheaply than they could be imported. National pride reinforced economic arguments for encouraging the development of manufactures in the United States. This national pride was stimulated at several points in the nineteenth century by anti-British feelings. During the tariff debate of 1864, Zach Chandler epitomized prevailing attitudes:

> If I had my way, I would raise a wall of fire between this nation and Great Britain. I would not only not allow her iron to come here, but I would not let a single pound of any article she manufactured come here during this war. . . . Let the railroad interest suffer and any other interest suffer. It is nothing to me. I am for the tax, the highest tax.[12]

"Pig Iron" Kelly argued for protection even for the nonexistent tin-plate industry, an industry which might more properly have been called preconceived than infant: "In God's name do not . . . lead us to declare that the people of this country shall never manufacture tin plate." [13]

The infant-industry argument decreased in pertinency and plausibility with the course of time and the development of the American economy. The baton was passed to the "vested-interest" argument, namely, that established manufacturers should not be disturbed. Thus, what was once a subsidy for a struggling infant gradually became an old-age pension. Whether it be the interest of the businessman in his investment or of the worker in his job, vested interest is the mainstay of many present-day pleas for protection.

Although one could not fail to notice the individual benefits that would accrue to those who were working energetically to gain them, the phraseology of early protectionist pleading was nevertheless in terms of the country's welfare. When William Lowndes of South Carolina asked in 1828 for the information on which he could judge whether certain manufacturers were in need of a higher tariff, the newly established Committee on Manufactures replied that there was no relevance to his inquiry, since upward revision of duties was being proposed from consideration of national policy, not that of company or industry.[14]

An additional argument of national import was that we could not afford in the event of war to be dependent on supplies from abroad. This argument, heard as early as the War of 1812, has grown in its appeal since that time.

Protectionists made numerous attempts, sometimes successful, to persuade groups who imagined their self-interest to be opposed to protection that this was not so. Farmers were told that their future lay with the

---

[12] Quoted in Tarbell, *The Tariff in Our Times, op. cit.,* p. 22.
[13] *Ibid.,* p. 191.
[14] J. Dorfman, *The Economic Mind in American Civilization, 1606-1865* (New York: The Viking Press, 1946), I, 386 f.

development of the home market, that protected industries would draw workers into the towns and thereby prevent excessive farm production, which might lower farm prices. Consumers were told that the infant industries, on reaching maturity, would provide them with cheaper goods. The "home-market" appeal to the farmer has ceased to be a central protectionist argument, even though it may occasionally be used in local situations. Gone also is the assurance that consumers may look forward to lower prices from protected industries. This argument may still be found in vestigial form in warnings to the American public that foreign manufacturers intend to keep prices down only until their American competitors are driven out of business, at which point, having a monopoly, they will charge "all the traffic will bear."

The arguments for a low-tariff policy have been fewer. Shippers, traders, and merchants have feared that high tariffs would injure their businesses. Farmers, particularly those in the Southern agricultural states, have wanted to buy imported goods cheaply. For a brief period, Southern cotton planters feared that a high tariff might provoke retaliation from Great Britain in the form of high tariffs on cotton. They do not seem to have been concerned over the possibility that Britain and/or other European countries might need to earn American dollars via exports to the United States. In truth, this may not have been the case, since Britain was exporting capital to this country.

At the beginning, the proponents of lower tariffs spoke in personal or sectional terms. The South, for example, in the person of Dr. Thomas Cooper, president of the College of South Carolina, complained in the late 1820's:

> This is a combined attack to the whole manufacturing interest. The avowed object is to tax us for their own emolument; . . . to force on us a system which will sacrifice the South to the North, which will convert us into colonies and tributaries.[15]

By midcentury, however, the teachings of the classical economists and the example of Britain stimulated an interest in free trade as an economic doctrine, and a low-tariff policy could be supported on the basis that it was in the national welfare. To these considerations must be added one that today makes one feel nostalgic: the United States Treasury had a surplus, and either some way had to be found to spend it or tariffs had to be reduced so as to lessen the federal revenue. The latter of these arguments, as stated before, was the more effective.

The two low-tariff points that dominated discussions of foreign-trade policy after World War II had previously been heard only feebly, if at all. The one which came closest to having real roots in the history of

---

[15] Quoted in Cochran and Miller, *op. cit.*, p. 17.

the tariff debates was that it was necessary to import in order to export. This argument, though presented in classical form by Adam Smith, had not been heard before in American discussions with the vigor with which it was voiced in those years. The other point was a transitory political one, applicable only to the present unique bipolar world situation: to defeat Communism, we must strengthen the economies of the non-Communist countries, and the stimulation of trade in the Free World is one of the most potent weapons in this struggle. All in all, the issues as debated in the 1950's sounded quite different from those voiced in the early years of the growth of the country.

Chapter 2

The New Republicanism and
Renewal 1953

"I further recommend that the Congress take the Reciprocal Trade Agreements Act under immediate study and extend it by appropriate legislation." So said Dwight D. Eisenhower, the newly elected president, in his State of the Union Message on February 2, 1953.

There is more to these few words than meets the eye. In them is a commitment by the first Republican administration in twenty years to a large measure of the New Deal.[1] In them is also a commitment to internationalism.

The last previous Republican tariff legislation had been the Smoot-Hawley Tariff Act of 1930. It wrote into the law on the eve of the Depression levels of customs duties unprecedented in American history.

It was the triumph of rampant protectionism. Industrial lobbyists in effect took over the writing of the bill. The Connecticut Manufacturers Association, a leading high-tariff group, placed the assistant to its president on the staff of Sen. Hiram Bingham, chairman of the Finance Committee,

---

[1] Note in the Preface the remarks on the division of responsibility and on some differences in interpretation among the authors.

which prepared the bill. He attended its executive sessions and handled the senator's tariff correspondence. The hearings became a record of private interests rampant. Each industry filed claims for the public subsidy it wanted, its right to protection being no longer in question.[2] Even those few witnesses who advocated tariff cuts for particular raw materials they imported said, in effect, "we concede the principle of protection, but . . . ," and then proceeded to detail the special circumstances which made high tariffs in this one instance an affront to their pocketbooks.

The principle nominally applied throughout the hearings was that tariff rates should equalize costs of production at home and abroad. That criterion is, however, economically indeterminate. There is no one cost of a commodity's production; there are many. Costs at what volume of production? For which manufacturer? At what capitalization of his investment? These and even more complex questions must be answered before a cost of production can be ascertained.

The principle of equalizing costs of production had been written into the Fordney-McCumber Tariff Act of 1922, which included an elastic clause providing that, on recommendation of the Tariff Commission, the president might raise or lower any duty by half to equalize production costs. The commission was to conduct scientific investigations of such costs as a basis for recommendation. In two and a half years, between 1930 and 1932, with its staff of 300, the commission explored costs of seventy-four of the 25,000 dutiable products. At that rate, to do the job on only the 3,221 enumerated items in the tariff schedules would have taken a staff of 13,000 and cost $100,000,000. Yet the Ways and Means Committee of the House, in forty-three days of hearing witnesses, mostly for five minutes apiece, was supposed to produce a bill which when done filled 195 pages of legislative print with reasoned rates based on costs of production!

In practice, the criterion of production costs was ignored in 1929. The operating goals of Congress were to shorten the boring hearings, to get onto the record as efficiently as possible what each industry wanted, and to give it enough to satisfy it. As Schattschneider points out in his dramatic account of the events of 1929-1930,[3] there were several rules of thumb to guide decisions in practice.

> 1. Get a consensus from an industry as to what it needs. Don't listen to any one manufacturer, but make the industry's witnesses tell you what

---

[2] The momentary triumph of protectionist ideology may be documented by the fact that the 1928 *Democratic* platform advocated the protectionist principle of a tariff to equalize "the actual difference between the cost of production at home and abroad, with adequate safeguard for the wage of the American laborer."

[3] E. E. Schattschneider, *Politics, Pressures and the Tariff* (Englewood Cliffs, N.J.: Prentice-Hall, Inc., 1935), pp. 84 f.

80 per cent of them would agree to. They know their own business, and if they agree they are probably right.

2. Everyone asks for more than he expects to get, so take the figure asked and discount it some.

3. Where tariff increases raise someone's cost, raise their protective tariffs accordingly. The solution to injury by tariffs is more tariffs; for example, if you have raised tariffs on wool, raise tariffs on woolen textiles compensatingly.

4. People in similar situations should be treated equally; if you have given a 30 per-cent increase to one textile, give a 30 per-cent increase to another.

With these simple rules of thumb, the bill was written, but still not without turmoil and pressure. Seldom in American history have so many lobbyists beleaguered so many congressmen with so many missives, so many pleas, and so much pressure.

Schattschneider's book set the tone for a whole generation of political writing on pressure groups. The present volume is in some ways a dissent from Schattschneider's position. We find that what happened in 1929 is not a general model of the legislative process. We do not deny the facts of the case as Schattschneider presents them. He has reported an episode in the legislative drama during which selfish interests treated the halls of Congress as their own.

Out of that maelstrom came a bill with record rates and, on top of them, many such hidden gimmicks for protection as minimum valuations. Though 1,028 economists petitioned the president to veto the Smoot-Hawley bill and the American Bankers' Association denounced it, effective political opposition to the act was negligible. In 1930, the philosophy of autarky seemed firmly in the saddle.

It was not only in America that neomercantilism was riding the crest of the wave. The second quarter of the twentieth century saw a rapid and world-wide return to restrictions on goods, ships, currencies, and persons, of which higher tariffs were but one manifestation. Some of this movement started well before the Smoot-Hawley Act, and much of it continued in response to the Great Depression. That act, however, precipitated widespread foreign protest and retaliation and was itself undoubtedly a cause of the prolongation and intensification of the world-wide collapse of trade. It was one of the ways in which America contributed to the export of depression. If 1930 was the moment of pride for protectionism, the nemesis was not far behind. Depression set the stage for a reversal of policy.

In June, 1934, a year and a half after the Roosevelt administration took office, the Trade Agreements Act, which usually goes by the name of the Reciprocal Trade Act, was passed by Congress.[4] The new act did not repeal the Smoot-Hawley tariff, which even now remains the law of the land. Instead, it authorized the president for a three-year period to negotiate agreements with other countries for mutual reductions in tariff rates. The president could agree to make cuts down to 50 per cent of the basic Smoot-Hawley rates. The power was renewed in 1937, 1940, 1943, and again in 1945 with further power to reduce rates to one-half of those prevailing on January 1, 1945. It was substantially renewed in 1948, 1949, and 1951. Up to the outbreak of World War II, twenty-one reciprocal-trade agreements had been made, reducing about 1,000 tariff rates. Since each reduction under the "most-favored-nation" clause had to be applied not only to that nation to which it had been conceded but to other nations as well, these reductions constituted in effect executive rewriting of the tariff.

What bill could be better calculated to be an issue between Republican conservatives in Congress and the New Deal, Fair Deal presidents than one like the Reciprocal Trade Act?

It revived the great historic issue of American party politics—the tariff. Congressmen in the 1930's, 1940's, and 1950's belonged to a generation that had grown up being told that the Republican Party was the party of protection and the Democratic Party that of tariffs for revenue only.

It also exemplified the great new issue of American party politics—the power of the executive branch. Like most New Deal measures, it transferred decision from Congress to the president and did it in one of the areas most jealously guarded as a legislative prerogative—the power to tax.

Each renewal of the Reciprocal Trade Bill up to 1953 was a partisan battle on standard lines. Internationalism *vs.* isolationism, creeping socialism *vs.* vested interests, executive bureaucracy *vs.* Congressional log-rolling were among the specters raised. Each time the renewal passed, but in most cases a substantial majority of Republican congressmen voted to kill the program.[5]

---

[4] Although we call the Trade Agreements Act a New Deal measure, it is perhaps fair to note that it was indeed an anomaly in the early NRA phase of the New Deal. The spirit of national economic planning of the earliest New Dealers was better expressed by their torpedoing of the London Economic Conference. The introduction of a program to lower barriers to world trade into that package of odds and ends which ultimately became the New Deal owes more to the accident that a gentleman of traditional Southern Democratic views was secretary of state than it does to the economic policies of reformers. What justifies our calling the Reciprocal Trade Act a New Deal measure was its enhancement of the power of the president, not its low-tariff tendency.

[5] "Following is the Republican voting record on the original act in 1934 and on subsequent extensions:

It should be understood that these Republican votes were not mere acts of demonstrative irresponsibility under cover of assurance that the bill would pass anyway. If renewal had failed, tariff rates would not have precipitously and automatically reverted to Smoot-Hawley levels. Existing trade agreements would have remained in effect. All that would have been terminated would have been the president's power to make new agreements. Congress would then have had to turn to the business of devising a new and—from the protectionist and anti-New Deal point of view—a better program.

Even before the adoption of the Reciprocal Trade Act in 1934, the Republicans had indicated support for a new type of tariff legislation, different from the Reciprocal Trade Act but not entirely so. Their 1932 platform said:

> The Republican Party has always been the staunch supporter of the American system of a protective tariff. . . .
> To fix duties on some thousands of commodities subject to highly complex conditions, is necessarily a difficult task. It is unavoidable that some of the rates established by legislation should, even at the time of their enactment, be too low or too high. Moreover, a subsequent change in costs or other conditions may render obsolete a rate that was before appropriate. The Republican Party has, therefore, long supported the policy of a flexible tariff, giving power to the President, after investigation by an impartial commission . . . to modify the rates named by the Congress.

But the difference between being in and out of power is evident in the way the Republican 1936 platform reacted to the New Deal's im-

	Senate			*House*	
	For	*Against*		*For*	*Against*
1934	5	28		2	99
1937	0	14		3	81
1940	0	20		5	146
1943	18	14		145	52
1945	15	16		33	140
1948	47	1		218	5
1949	15	18		84	63
1951	34	2		(passed by voice vote)	
1953	(passed by voice vote)			363	34

The heavy support in 1948 by the Republican-controlled Congress was explained by the insertion of a restrictive 'peril points' clause. This was deleted by the Democrats in 1949, but put back in again in 1951 when most Republicans again supported extension." *The New York Times,* March 3, 1954.

plementation of these policies:

> We will repeal the present Reciprocal Trade Agreement Law. It is futile and dangerous. . . .
>
> We will restore the principle of the flexible tariff in order to meet changing economic conditions.

Basically, the Republican objections were two. First, "flexibility" as interpreted under the New Deal was in practice (though not by law) flexibility downward; as earlier advocated by the Republicans, it was mostly flexibility upward. Second, there was objection to the bypassing of Congress. As the 1940 platform said:

> We condemn the manner in which the so-called reciprocal trade agreements of the New Deal have been put into effect without adequate hearings, with undue haste, without proper consideration of our domestic producers, and without Congressional approval.[6]

Party lines in the United States are never clear-cut, but the Republican heritage until after World War II was protectionism and support for Congressional supremacy in the tariff-making field. It was that heritage which Eisenhower contravened by making extension of the reciprocal-trade program a major plank in his platform. Doing so was neither a one-man nor an unexpected act. Republican support for protection had long since suffered erosion. Until 1943, no more than five Republican votes had ever been cast for a reciprocal-trade bill in either house. From 1943 through 1951, a majority of Republicans supported it in six of nine roll calls on renewal (five in the Senate, four in the House).

The platforms show the same trend. The 1940 platform began the shift from an emphasis on protection to one on expansion of trade.

> We believe in tariff protection for Agriculture, Labor, and Industry as essential to our American standard of living. The measure of protection shall be determined by scientific methods. . . .
>
> We shall explore every possibility of reopening the channels of international trade through negotiations so conducted as to produce genuine reciprocity.

By 1948, statements of opposition to reciprocal trade had been reversed.

> At all times safeguarding our own industry and agriculture, and under efficient administrative procedures for the legitimate consideration of domestic needs, we shall support the system of reciprocal trade.

Eisenhower was the spokesman of that internationalist wing of the Republican Party which had made this shift in views. There was no

---

[6] It must be noted, however, that the Republican attitude toward executive as against Congressional authority in this field was highly affected by who was in office. The 1932 platform said: "We commend the President's veto of the measure, sponsored by Democratic Congressmen, which would have transferred from the President to Congress the authority to put into effect the findings of the Tariff Commission."

doubt where he would stand. Indeed, a common remark in Washington in the years of the first Eisenhower administration and even before he took office was that freeing of international trade was one issue on which the President had a deep and strong personal conviction. In an administration not marked by firmly held presidential views, this was an exception. As *Business Week* said on Dec. 13, 1952, "President-elect Eisenhower is pretty solidly committed to trying to strengthen the free world through a policy of 'trade, not aid.'"

The phrase, "trade, not aid," had been coined in a speech by British Chancellor of the Exchequer R.A. Butler. It was an enormous propaganda success, for it put in a nutshell what many people were trying to say. The European reconstruction effort had by 1952 made great strides. The Marshall Plan had succeeded. The tide of American opinion was turning against continuing gifts to countries which seemed no longer to need them. The American public had not yet habituated itself to the use of money as a continuing diplomatic instrumentality. Lend-lease had been viewed as an exceptional wartime measure, and even *it* had had to be camouflaged as lending. The minute the war was over, lend-lease was abruptly terminated. The Marshall Plan, put through by strong presidential leadership, was still political dynamite in 1952. With European recovery, the case for further aid was increasingly hard to make.

However, the dollar gap had not yet ended. It did indeed pass into history soon after. By the last year of the Eisenhower administration, the problem in Treasury circles was the reverse one, that of declining dollar balances and loss of gold. But in 1952 the dollar gap—the excess of foreign payments to the United States over American payments abroad— still seemed a monumental problem. How could the flow of American goods to other nations be maintained as the country cut off aid funds with which much of the flow had been financed? How could one avoid interrupting the process of recovery and growth while putting it back on a self-sustaining and free-enterprise basis?

That was a problem very much in the minds of American internationalists in 1952. It was in the minds of those businessmen whom Paul Hoffman and William Foster had recruited into Marshall Plan missions and in the minds of the leading New York bankers, who had, after all, been antiprotectionists even in the 1920's. It was a problem in the minds of the internationalist wing of the Republican and Democratic parties.

"Trade, not aid" seemed to be the answer captured in a snappy slogan. It caught the imagination of men like Eisenhower, but recently returned from his NATO assignment of trying to rebuild the strength of Europe. Eisenhower's call for renewal of the Trade Agreements Act was a symptom, not a cause, of a historical reversal which was already well under way. The New Republicanism had incorporated much of the New

Deal. The first Republican president in twenty years could ask for a lowering of tariffs on the ground of foreign alliances and by way of transferring taxing and treaty-making powers to the executive branch.

□ Renewal 1953

If Eisenhower had been converted to a new image of Republicanism, not all of his Congressional followers had been. The chairman of the Senate Finance Committee in the newly elected Republican Congress was Eugene Millikin, of Colorado, an able conservative and long-time protectionist. The chairman of the Committee on Ways and Means of the House was Dan Reed (N.Y.), stubborn and old guard. The third-ranking Republican on Ways and Means was Richard Simpson (Pa.), whom we shall meet again, one of the ablest men in the House and Chairman of the Republican House Campaign Committee.[7] Both Reed and Simpson told us that, as boys, learning to be Republicans, their fathers had told them that the crucial difference between the parties was that the Republicans believe in protection. Simpson was more than a supporter of protection; he was a crusader. Such were the men on whom Eisenhower had to lean to enact his legislative program.

When the new Republican president in 1953 asked the new Republican Congress to extend the Reciprocal Trade Act, the measure incorporating his request went automatically and by long-established precedent to the committees on which those men sat. Since tariff bills are tax bills, they start in the Committee on Ways and Means.

But that was not the only problem. The same committees had been asked to do a great deal of work on a number of other pressing issues and to swallow their principles on several of them to please the new administration. The efforts of Ways and Means to do anything about extending reciprocal trade were at best lackadaisical.

Indeed, more attention of the committee and of Congressman Simpson was given to a related bill, but one expressing an opposite policy, the so-called Simpson bill, to impose import quotas on petroleum products.

To understand the Simpson bill, it is necessary to digress for a moment. Crude oil as it comes from the ground is a complex mixture of hydrocarbons. In the cracking process, gasoline comes off as the most highly refined and valuable product, while fuel oil, kerosene, and other less-refined products are obtained simultaneously. At the lowest level of refinement, a residue remains which is still combustible, though of no other

---

[7] This committee assists House Republicans financially and in other ways in their election campaigns. Its chairman wields great power.

value. This is called residual fuel oil and should be distinguished from either crude or regular fuel oil.

The petroleum business is an international business par excellence. In most countries, petroleum is either a large-scale import or export. In the United States, it is both. Although the United States is one of the world's major oil producers, it is nevertheless economical to ship petroleum products by tanker from Venezuela to the U.S. East Coast. As a result, the industry is divided. There are five great firms with assets of over $250,000,000 apiece: Standard Oil of New Jersey, Shell, Texaco, Gulf, and Standard Oil of New York, each of which has vast investments abroad as well as at home. They import as well as drill at home, and they also buy from the so-called independents. The independents, the rest of the producers, are characteristically wholly domestic in their operations, located primarily in Texas, Oklahoma, or California. These "small" businesses, the source of most of the current crop of oil millionaires, have suffered in recent years from the glut of new oil finds. The Texas Railroad Commission, which sets the conservation standards, has at times held the producers to as few as eight days of pumping a month.

The independents, of course, want protection, but a tariff is no answer to their problem. The present 5 per-cent rate on crude oil could be doubled, trebled, or quadrupled without making it uneconomic to import from Venezuela to the East Coast. The independents wanted a more drastic measure than a tariff increase, and the answer seemed to be quotas. That is what the Simpson bill proposed.

Richard Simpson was a congressman from Pennsylvania. One may wonder why he should have been the sponsor of a bill to help the Texas and Oklahoma oilmen. The answer is coal. Let us see how the various interests stood.

The Southwestern oilmen wanted crude-oil imports cut. They did not care about stopping residual-oil imports, because the quality of the crude they pumped, when refined by modern catalytic methods, left but little residual fuel oil. The only way they could have produced more of the cheap residue was to cut into the production of the more valuable highly refined products, clearly an uneconomic thing for them to do. But they did want to stop some of the flow of crude oil which was being shipped here by tanker for refining. What they wanted was restriction on crude-oil imports, but, since their best customers were the Big Four, the main oil importers, they found themselves in a political bind. They did not campaign as aggressively as they might have for fear of antagonizing their customers.

The coal miners were particularly aggrieved by residual oil imports. They had long since given up on the struggle against regular fuel oil for home heating. Convenience, not price, was decisive in destroying the market for coal as a furnace fuel. But residual fuel oil was something they felt they could still fight. Residual fuel is burned by big industrial consumers, mostly along the Atlantic Coast. They are usually equipped to use residual fuel oil or coal alternatively, as price fluctuations dictate. For the miners, then, residual fuel oil was a menace, crude-oil imports a secondary matter.

The railroads are oil-burners and coal-carriers. In fact, as we shall see in a later chapter, they lined up with the miners, but their optimum strategy would clearly have been quotas on residual oil but no restriction on crude.

Those who carried the ball for petroleum quotas were the coal-mining interests, and it was a Pennsylvania congressman, Simpson, who introduced the bill for them. With support from both oil and coal states and from coal dealers all over the country, with a Republican, traditionally protectionist, majority in Congress, the drive for the Simpson bill was indeed powerful, and its chances of passing seemed good.

It was the fight over the Simpson bill, favorably reported by the Ways and Means Committee, and not the administration's proposal for Reciprocal Trade renewal, which absorbed the attention of Congress and the nation in 1953, as far as foreign trade was concerned.

In the end, the Simpson bill was defeated. Administration opposition contributed slightly to its defeat, though the main tactic of the Eisenhower administration in its first year in office was conciliation of the right wing of the Republican Party. Official silence at first surrounded the Simpson bill, despite its obvious conflict with the administration's desires (just as, even more dramatically, an official silence surrounded Senator McCarthy and his victims even when they were members of the administration). However, the lobby against the Simpson bill primed a friendly reporter at a news conference to ask the President his views on the bill just before the crucial vote. The President, inadvertently trapped, expressed his opposition to it.

More important than the President in beating the Simpson bill were certain private efforts. The Venezuelan business community, including some big oil companies, with vigor not often shown by foreign investors, responded to the danger to themselves and undertook an energetic and astute public-relations program in this country. The program was so effective that the entire New England delegation in Congress, for instance, was made conscious of the loss New England manufacturers and utilities would suffer from the fuel oil proposal. The story of the campaign that beat the Simpson bill is told below in the chapter on lobbies. The point to note here is that the main victory won by the administration in 1953 was the defeat of a bill wanted by the Ways and Means leadership, the very men who would have had to have been the pilots for a Reciprocal Trade renewal.[8]

The administration also bludgeoned the Ways and Means Committee into reporting out a bill to extend the excess-profits tax for six months. Chairman Reed had himself introduced an income-tax reduction bill (which the Rules Committee bottled up), and he obtained from his Republican colleagues on Ways and Means both a favorable report on his bill and a unanimous pledge to let the excess-profits tax die on June 30. But President Eisenhower was resolved to balance the budget. To achieve that, the Republican leadership threatened, through Speaker Joseph Martin, to use the unprecedented parliamentary device of having the Rules Committee report out a bill on which the standing committee (Ways and Means) had failed to hold hearings or report. Reed delayed and opposed to the bitter end, but when, on June 25, the Rules Committee voted this unique blow at his power, he yielded and permitted Ways and Means to outvote him and on July 8 to report out a retroactive extension of the excess-profits tax.

Under the circumstances, an administration following tactics of conciliation could hardly make a strong demand for Reciprocal Trade renewal. The President took office on January 20. The Reciprocal Trade Act expired on June 12, less than six months later. After a few months of shuffling, it became obvious that a reversal of the historical Republican protectionist position could not be engineered by the deadline date. The time had come for a deal, and the deal was made.

The act was extended for just one year, at the request of the President. The official reason given was that there was no time in the first year of the new administration to work out a whole new program on so complex a matter as foreign trade. To secure a one-year extension, the administration apparently stipulated that no use would be made during that year of the powers conferred upon it. Administration members argued that this was an academic matter, since there would be no time to work out any new trade agreement within the course of one year anyway. The President also gave the protectionists a further concession by naming Joseph E. Talbot, a strong protectionist, as his first appointee to the U.S. Tariff Commission. (There is one vacancy in the six-man body each year.) This addition to protectionist strength on the body which acted on escape-clause petitions could have been a more important action on foreign-trade matters than any 1953 legislative action.

---

[8] The administration made some other gains. Congress passed a Customs Simplification Bill, which facilitated correction of evaluations by importers and eliminated some excessive labeling requirements. Congress refused, however, to include the provision the President wanted most, one standardizing methods for determining values.

Finally, as a concession to the protectionists, the renewal bill provided for the establishment of a Commission on Foreign Economic Policy. The commission was to make recommendations to the next session of Congress for long-range action on the reciprocal-trade program and other foreign economic policies. It was heavily weighted with congressmen—ten, versus the seven public members appointed by the President. The ten Congressional members, three Republicans and two Democrats from each House, included Millikin, Reed, and Simpson. To balance this protectionist strength, the President appointed a convinced free-trader, Clarence Randall, as chairman.[9] But even among the public members of the Randall Commission the President appointed one known protectionist, Cola Parker.

With a guarantee against precipitous executive action to lower tariffs, with a commission dominated by congressmen and due to report to the Congress and not to the executive branch, and thus with Congress guaranteed the last word, the protectionist Republican leaders of both Ways and Means and Finance were satisfied to avoid for the moment any open breach between the two wings of the Republican Party and, in the closing days of the session, to quietly pass a one-year renewal.[10]

What was it that the protectionists wanted? The actual outcome was a compromise in which neither side got its way. What the President wanted, we know. It is less clear what the Congressional leadership was really after.

The answer does not appear on the record. An opposition can enjoy the luxury of irresponsibility. Critics can oppose without affirming what should be. The positive program of the protectionists, if it existed, could be pieced together only from scraps of evidence.

We know that the Republican Congressional leadership had voted

---

[9] Other members of the commission were:

Lamar Fleming, Jr., vice-chairman		
David J. McDonald		
Cola G. Parker		
Jess W. Tapp		
John Hay Whitney		
John H. Williams		
Sen. Bourke B. Hickenlooper	(R.)	Iowa
Sen. Prescott Bush	(R.)	Connecticut
Sen. Harry F. Byrd	(D.)	Virginia
Sen. Walter F. George	(D.)	Georgia
Rep. John M. Vorys	(R.)	Ohio
Rep. Jere Cooper	(D.)	Tennessee
Rep. Laurie C. Battle	(D.)	Alabama

[10] There was one other major controversy, which we skip over lightly here. A rider was added to the renewal bill by the Republican leadership adding one member to the bipartisan Tariff Commission. That would have given the new administration an extra appointment and, by making the commission membership seven, would have given the party in office a majority. Democrats, whose votes were essential to passing the renewal bill, were able to kill this change as a price for their support.

each triennium against the Reciprocal Trade Bill; but that fact alone does not tell us much. They could vote against the bill, confident in the knowledge that it was going to be passed despite their gesture of protest and knowing further that, if they ever had enough votes to defeat the bill, the result would not be a total and irrevocable defeat of it but a whittling-away of the bill by its sponsors to the point at which enough marginal votes could be captured to pass some bill. A vote against the bill was, indeed, a vote for something different from the bill, but just how different we cannot precisely determine.

We can discern some outlines of protectionist policy in the Simpson bill. Though its 1953 version dealt only with petroleum, in 1954 it was developed into a more general program. Quotas, not tariffs, were the new protectionist panacea. Since tariffs were not protective enough, the purposes of reciprocal trade were to be undermined by the quota system. But in some respects the Simpson bill followed the pattern of the Reciprocal Trade Act. It did not return regulative authority to Congress. It made the imposition of quotas an administrative act to be taken when certain findings of fact showed injury to American industry. It was not Congress that was to specify by legislation what commodities were to have quotas imposed at any particular time.

The fact of the matter is that no one was seeking to restore to Congress the powers it had lost under Reciprocal Trade. Neither in the matter of quotas nor in the matter of tariff rates did Congress wish to see a return to the legislative procedures which produced the Smoot-Hawley Act. The protectionist votes against Reciprocal Trade were not really what they seemed. They were not votes to kill the system permanently, but essentially votes used as bargaining devices to affect the spirit in which the law was administered. The entire controversy took place within a broad consensus that a law should be passed turning over to the executive branch the function of regulating the import of particular commodities within certain broad guide-lines set by Congress.

That is the usual situation in legislation. Before a bill can be passed, there must ordinarily be strong consensus that *some* bill should be passed. Under those circumstances, it may be possible to construct a majority coalition for a particular bill. But, in the absence of agreement that some action is better than none, there will seldom be enough steam behind a coalition to force the necessary compromises. Note, for example, Stephen Bailey's *Congress Makes a Law*.[11] In the case which Bailey describes, there were in Congress two diametrically opposed primary purposes. One was to foster deficit spending to maintain employment, the other to check federal deficit-spending programs. There was agreement only on the importance

---

[11] (New York: Columbia University Press, 1950).

of having a bill passed to prepare or to appear to prepare for the demobilization crisis, whether in one of these opposed ways or the other. Within that consensus, it was possible to draft a compromise bill which left unresolved the main issue—whether it would work out to favor or restrict deficit spending. That is a usual pattern. Majorities are not usually so one-sided nor minorities so compliant that a final solution is legislatable. Generally, a legislative solution is a provisional action which permits the debate to continue while life is going forward. The bill adopted must not settle the controversial issue. It must not foreclose possible future victory to either side, while it fulfills the shared desire that some action be taken at once. It was much the same with reciprocal trade.

The seemingly vital question whether the spirit of executive action was to be protectionist or liberal was in fact a second-order one. It evoked controversy and therefore attracted everyone's attention. But underlying this controversy was a common view in which the controversy was embedded, a consensus on the need for tariff legislation which would have the general character of administrative regulation.

That was a new consensus in American politics. The drafting of tariff rates had been a jealously guarded prerogative of Congress, though a dozen acts prior to 1890 gave the president power to make specified adjustments of rates. Reciprocity, albeit without flexibility, first appeared in American tariff legislation in the McKinley Tariff Act of 1890. In that act the presidential power was limited to enforcing a specific schedule of tariffs on certain items on the free list as a penalty against countries which did not deal favorably in their duties with American goods. The Payne-Aldrich tariff of 1909 gave the president more flexible powers, allowing him to add duties up to 25 per cent ad valorem in case of discrimination by a foreign country. The Underwood Tariff Act of 1913 extended this type of penalty provision. But none of these provisions was viewed as more than an exceptional measure designed to provide a bargaining weapon for fair treatment of American commodities.

It was only in the Fordney-McCumber Act of 1922 that a broader conception of flexibility was introduced. The elastic clause was amended to allow the president on recommendation by the Tariff Commission (which had been created in 1916) to raise or lower rates by 50 per cent with the objective of equalizing costs of production. The percentage elasticity in this act was no less than that in the Reciprocal Trade Act of 1934, though the criterion, production cost, was much more restrictive. The biggest difference, however, was in the presidents who executed the acts and in their purposes. Actions under the elastic clause were few. The pre-eminence of Congress in tariff-making was still beyond question in the minds of the presidents. Executive branch action was still by mutual consent a matter of secondary adjustments to meet changing circumstances. When Congress passed the Reciprocal Trade Act, the words might have suggested only a mild broadening of the legislative intent, but the agreements negotiated by a vigorous president soon represented in effect a total rewriting of the law. Median tariff rates today are about 13 per cent, less than a quarter of what they were under the Smoot-Hawley Act, before Reciprocal Trade. Hardly an important rate still stands where Congress fixed it.

Why has this assumption of executive power, so controversial when it first occurred, come to be part of the consensus between Republicans and Democrats, protectionists and free traders alike? Why is it that today most legislative proposals fixing a specific tariff rate for any commodity, no matter how just or meritorious, are drowned in a majority of negative votes from congressmen who above all do not wish rate-fixing to be part of their responsibility? Responsibility brings with it intolerable pressure. The power to dole out favors to industry is not worth the price of having to beat off and placate the insistent pleas of petitioners.

This is a dilemma for a congressman. The commodity in which he deals is favors, whether personal or ideological. His ability to do something which his clientele wants done is his political capital. The constituent clamoring for a favor is a potential supporter at the polls or campaign contributor. He is not a nuisance to the congressman; without him, the congressman would be nothing. Thus, the congressman is reluctant to give up any power which brings petitioners to his door, be they for patronage or West Point appointments or post offices. But every favor which can be conferred is also a danger, because it must sometimes be refused. Responsibility involves blame. And, if the demands exceed what the congressman can effectively handle, then he may happily yield up a significant portion of his power.

That is what happened with the tariff. The demands became such that even ordinary honesty and a modicum of independence became hard to maintain. Well-financed industrial interests were all too willing to pour substantial funds into the coffers of those who supported them. Congressmen need and want this sort of support, but they want it within limits—not to the point where the congressman is no longer in the driver's seat. It may be argued that the difference between a campaign contribution and a bribe, between integrity and corruption, is whether the receiver retains his freedom of action after the money is passed. To protect their own freedom, congressmen needed to reduce their power to be immediately helpful to their constituents.

The Congressional work load which the tariff generated also had become onerous. The conference committee on the Smoot-Hawley Tariff Act made 1,253 adjustments of differences between the House and Senate

bills. This is but one index of the unmanageable mass of detailed problems from all directions thrown at every congressman under the old system.
Tariff mail and tariff visitors led all the rest.

And so it came about that tariff-making became a scandal and
farce. The congressman was no longer free to do his job in the national
interest as he saw it. The tariff became a burden to him. That is the situation which led to a consensus in Congress—cutting across theoretical views
about the role of the executive and legislative branches—that Congress
should fight the battle of the tariff at one step removed from the final
decision. A congressman, no matter how keen his desire to help the toy
marble-makers, does not want to be given the right of voting them an
increase in tariff rates. He prefers to be in the position of being allowed
merely to place a speech in their favor in *The Congressional Record* as an
extension of his remarks or to appear as a witness before the Tariff Commission, free to indulge the irresponsibility afforded those who do not
participate in the final decision. Rather than rule on the plea himself, he
prefers to debate and vote on legislation that sets general principles gov-
erning how the marble-makers' plea should be considered. If he is a protectionist, he wants those principles lax; if a free trader, rigid—but both
agree that Congressional decision on particulars should be avoided.

This agreement makes the events of 1953 understandable. Not
even the most extremely protectionist congressmen wanted a collapse of
the existing system of tariff-making, although they wanted it changed very
much indeed. They, no less than the administration, regarded passage of
some legislation as essential.[12] To have let the Reciprocal Trade Act die on
June 12, at least if a protracted vacuum had followed, would have been
regarded as irresponsible by almost the entire Congress. Thus, Reed and
Millikin were almost as dependent on getting a bill passed which the
liberals would accept as the liberals were dependent on them.[13] Given
the consensus on the desirability of legislation and the narrower consensus
on the need to maintain apparent unity in the Republican Party, a formula
had to be found on which a majority coalition, including both protectionists and liberal traders, could be formed to pass a bill.

The formula required that Reed and Millikin, now the leadership
instead of the opposition, propose (after years of ostensibly opposing) a
renewal of Reciprocal Trade, albeit a short one and with some attached

---

[12] The best indication of what the protectionists wanted is the contents of the Reed-
Simpson dissenting report to the Randall Commission. They recommended a new tariff
structure for the country based on an industry-by-industry and product-by-product study
to be undertaken by the Federal Tariff Commission, not Congress. And they recommended
this as part of a two-year renewal, not rejection, of the Reciprocal Trade Bill.

[13] A hiatus, as we noted above, would not have been a catastrophe, at least in protectionist eyes, and would even have been a tactical victory for them, but it would have
brought public blame on those seeming to be responsible for it.

gimmicks which they hoped would strengthen their bargaining power on the next round. No entirely new system that might be proposed could win support of a majority on short notice. The most acceptable changes in the existing system would be ones which each side believed likely to help it in the next round of the battle. Establishing a study commission and delaying action are both ideal measures for this purpose. With any optimism at all, each side can see opportunities for using time and facts to its own advantage. Under such a legislative formula, both sides can agree to go on with the battle without introducing the incalculable consequences of sudden abandonment of the existing system.

The protectionists faced a dilemma, however. They shared in the consensus that somebody outside Congress should set tariff rates or impose and remove quotas. But the executive branch, the logical place to which to pass such responsibility, was committed to a liberal trade policy. These facts determined the character of their proposals. Their goal became to constrain the executive branch from taking liberalizing moves while imposing on it requirements of procedures as favorable as possible to interests claiming protection. This meant giving power to the Tariff Commission, rather than to the president. It meant categorical rather than discretionary requirements that tariff increases or quotas be imposed when injury was demonstrated.

In short, the goal of the protectionists, just as much as of the liberals, was to change the system at its margins, though for historic reasons the liberals did so in the name of favoring and the protectionists in the name of opposing the slogan name, "Reciprocal Trade." Even on this one issue, there were no "revolutionists" in the leadership of Congress. The sound and fury, the intrigue and backbiting that marked the struggle over protection served to hide a fundamental agreement about how the system should work. The consensus that all interested parties should be allowed to go on fighting for marginal changes led to a one-year extension of the Reciprocal Trade Act in 1953.

Chapter 3

The Randall Report

When, in the spring of 1953, the White House announced its acceptance of a one-year trade act extension and the establishment of what came to be called the Randall Commission, it did not require much foresight to recognize that reciprocal trade was bound to be a major political issue of 1954. The partisans on each side girded for the battle.

Expressing the liberal view, a group called the Committee for a National Trade Policy was formed. In the summer of 1953, Harry Bullis, chairman of the board of General Mills, at the behest of White House aides, called a gathering of industrialists. Among those present were Joseph Spang, Jr., of the Gillette Safety Razor Company, Gen. John McCloy of the Chase National Bank, and George Ball, who had spearheaded the successful campaign against the Simpson bill. For chairman of the new organization they obtained John Coleman, president of the Burroughs Manufacturing Company, who accepted at White House urging. The CNTP came to be known as the Coleman committee. As president and full-time executive officer it chose Charles Taft, brother of the late senator, who, though himself a liberal Republican, might be hoped to have some familial acceptability to conservative Republicans.

As its first act in the fall of 1953, the committee sent lengthy telegrams to hundreds of business leaders asking for contributions. The goal, never realized, was $300,000. It opened a Washington headquarters and became a major source of releases, speeches, facts, and statements. In its first half-year of operations, the committee issued eleven mailings.

Working the other side of the political street was another organization formed in 1953, the Nation-wide Committee of Industry, Agriculture, and Labor on Import-Export Policy, headed by O. R. Strackbein. This organization was much more the vehicle of a single man, its president. Strackbein had originally been an American Federation of Labor organizer. Then, from 1924 to 1940, he was a trade commissioner with the Department of Commerce overseas. In the years that followed, he developed his interest in protection and his activities in tariff matters. In 1950, he organized a group which he called the National Labor-Management Council on Foreign Trade Policy. Both this and the later organization drew their membership primarily, though not exclusively, from relatively minor labor unions and from trade associations of industries affected by foreign competition. The Nation-wide Committee, usually called the Strackbein committee, also included the United Mine Workers, which was indeed its backbone and to some extent called the turns, the National Coal Association, and the Manufacturing Chemists Association among its sixty-five members. But more typical of its membership were such groups as the Wine Institute, the Tuna Research Foundation, the Window Glass Cutters League of America (AFL), and the United Wall Paper Craftsmen and Workers of North America (AFL). The Strackbein committee lacked the big names which graced the Coleman committee. Strackbein brought together a group of professional association executives, and the strong voice among them was Strackbein's own.

Strackbein was a prolific and quite gifted pamphleteer. He testified frequently at hearings, but probably made more dent with such flamboyant and ingeniously argued pieces as his tract, "Free Trade, a Form of Economic Pacifism," which, though conceding that both pacifism and free trade represented ultimate ideals, argued in effect that you could not accept one in practice until you were ready to accept both.

The first substantial target for action by both these groups was the Randall Commission. The Coleman committee's first job was mobilizing support for Clarence Randall and for publicizing his expectedly liberal report. The Strackbein committee had as its first tasks the discrediting of Randall and the commission, publicizing conflicts within it, and in general making the whole operation testify to the impracticability of tariff liberalization.

The Randall Commission, though set up in the summer, held its organizational meeting, with the President appearing, only on September 22. By mid-October, a staff was in operation [1] and hearings began behind closed doors on October 21. They were held in public for two days, October 28 and 29, and continued in Paris, November 9-12. The report was issued January 23, 1954.

Clarence Randall, formerly president of Inland Steel, a lawyer with a classical education and a gift for words, an industrialist devoted to free enterprise, came to the task with a naïveté about politics that would have soon brought to catastrophe any man less able to generate respect by his moral stature. Peremptory in manner, he neglected the flowery deference to which congressmen are accustomed. He ran hearings, one congressman commented, "like he was running a board meeting." He began them at 9:30, a little early by Capitol Hill standards. Public witnesses were given twenty minutes to present their cases. Witnesses and commissioners alike were gaveled down. At the commission's brief public hearing, Senator Millikin was questioning a witness when Randall snapped, "May I suggest we ask one more question?" "There is no use asking an isolated question," Millikin retorted, and asked no questions thereafter.

Randall's clock-watching drive, aside from habit, arose from his awareness of the magnitude of the task and the shortness of the time. The report was due March 6, but, if it had arrived at that point in an election year, the prospect of Congressional action before the end of the session would be negligible. To have effect, a report should be submitted shortly after Congress convened in January, and that was the goal Randall set and achieved over the practiced procrastination of hostile congressmen, for whom the whole idea of a commission was only a time-killer. As the Simpson-Reed dissent complained:

> The report is now submitted six weeks before the deadline set by Congress with the complaint that adequate time was not permitted. However, of the seven months available, less than four months had been fully used when the report was frozen and submitted to the members of the commission with only one week allowed for development of their dissents.

To limit the number of witnesses, Randall sent out 1,500 letters asking for written statements and suggestions. No spokesmen for particular industries were allowed to testify. Even foreign states were denied inclusion in the carefully chosen list of witnesses at the Paris hearing. The

---

[1] The director of research was Alfred C. Neal, first vice-president of the Federal Reserve Bank of Boston. Other staff members included Joseph C. Davis, Food Research Institute, Stanford University; Howard S. Piquet, Legislative Reference Service, Library of Congress; Raymond Vernon, Department of State; William L. Batt, Jr.; Emilio G. Collado, Standard Oil of New Jersey; and Lewis C. Mattison, the one public-relations man along with fourteen economists.

staff digested written testimony and prepared 800 pages of staff papers. Drafting was divided section-by-section among the public members. Members were asked to write sections which would commit them to stands that were particularly hard for them to swallow. David McDonald of the United Steelworkers (CIO) did the section on labor standards and foreign competition. Protectionist paper manufacturer Cola Parker did the section on tariffs. The Commission went through the sections one-by-one. Randall started with one he thought least controversial—the section on foreign investment—to get his members "in the habit of agreement."

The section held for the last was McDonald's on adjustment to increase imports. That one, read a few days before Christmas, proposed subsidies and similar aids to firms, communities, and workers injured by increased foreign imports due to reciprocal-trade agreements. A direct subsidy from the Treasury was to replace the indirect subsidy of the tariff, a proposal which, if adopted, could destroy the political basis of protectionism by giving the injured an alternative way out. The McDonald proposals were foreshadowed in the testimony of Meyer Kestnbaum for the Committee for Economic Development, Stanley Ruttenberg for the then-CIO, and John Coleman of the CNTP. The proposals were worked out by William Batt, Jr., of the commission staff, and Elmer Roper, of the Steelworkers. Batt, son of the prominent manufacturer who had headed the pressure group for the Marshall Plan and who had been active in the moves leading up to the CNTP, was himself an assistant to the secretary of labor and had specialized in community efforts to cope with dislocation. Later, in the Kennedy administration, he headed the depressed-area redevelopment program.

No votes were taken as the commission discussed section-by-section, and few objections were registered. The protectionist congressmen did not waste their energies quibbling at that stage. Only McDonald's proposal produced a protest, by Sen. Prescott Bush backed by his colleagues, against the theories of the paper. The commission rejected McDonald's ideas 16-to-1. Randall, though voting against subsidies, ordered the paper published and personally wrote an explanation of why he thought the "admirably prepared" proposal merited attention. That action produced one of the sharpest dissents to the Randall report, Congressmen Reed and Simpson saying: "The mere insertion of the proposal in the report indicates a dangerous sentiment in its favor."

The McDonald proposal, though excluded from the Randall report, had great delayed impact. It was the origin of the Kennedy-Williams-Humphrey-Eberharter proposals at the next session of Congress. Though their bill was not successful at the time, its existence gave a significant number of congressmen from areas suffering import injury a way of demonstrating their solicitude for their constituents while still supporting the liberal-trade policies they felt to be in the national interests. How many votes were thus saved for reciprocal trade no one can say, but there were some. More important, the sponsor of the bill eventually became president, and what had originally been the rejected McDonald proposals became in 1962 the readjustment provisions of the Trade Expansion Act. Their inclusion then did serve to undercut protectionism by giving injured labor and other interests an alternative mode of self-defense.

Throughout the months of the Randall Commission deliberations, the main drama was the quiet struggle between Randall on the one side, striving to draft a near-unanimous report that would be a strong plea for liberalization and would bear the signatures of many congressmen, and on the other side the protectionists Reed, Simpson, and Millikin, attempting to discredit him.

It soon became clear that Simpson and probably Reed were hopeless cases, from Randall's point of view. At the start Randall laid down a rule for himself, hoping the others would follow it, that nothing of what went on in the commission's deliberations would be divulged to the press. He believed that in truly private discussion men would be honest and that, in being honest, they could not help but reach liberal conclusions on the nation's interest. He saw his problem not as one of political bargaining but one of group dynamics. The European trip taken by twelve of the commissioners, for example, he valued because on it they "developed a fine spirit of companionship."

Randall adhered to his own rule of external silence, even promising his fellow-commissioners, especially the Democrats, that he would not consult Eisenhower during their deliberations. Indeed, the President was not informed of what was going on until the report came to his desk. The price Randall paid for enveloping his commission in privacy was loss of press support. He refused all press conferences, except one in Europe which for reason of international good will he felt compelled to endure. In that one, he consciously dodged reporters' questions and "said nothing."

But, though silenced by his own rule, Randall had to tolerate the free-wheeling of Congressman Simpson, who disregarded Randall's unilaterally imposed edict. Simpson reported to the press daily. Every few nights a blast to the press would emanate from Strackbein about the day's secret proceedings, the information having been fed to Strackbein by Simpson. Strackbein in effect served as Simpson's public-relations man in his battle with Randall. One day Simpson stepped out of the commission meeting without a word, heading, Randall assumed, for a few minutes' respite, but in fact to address a meeting which the Strackbein committee had arranged for the purpose of giving Simpson a sounding board. When Simpson finished his speech, the committee passed a resolution calling for the resignation of Randall on the grounds that he was biased. Simpson did not make the accusation, except in a quiet instruction to Strackbein. The assemblage made it, and Simpson returned the next day to the session that Randall was trying to make into a detached, apolitical examination of national interest.

Although Randall had to give up on Simpson and Reed, he saw that their dissent would not have serious effect if he could separate Millikin from them. A report bearing the signature of the studious and respected protectionist Millikin, perhaps the most powerful man in the Senate, would lose little of its bite from the snapping dissent of two men known to all as unreconstructed conservatives and committed lifelong spokesmen of protection. The strategy of Randall was "to land the big fish," Millikin.

The process was one of successive surrender, point-by-point, in the seriatim discussions, on the assumption that, if Millikin and others got virtually all that they asked, they would go along with the report. Protectionist Cola Parker, loyal to the administration which appointed him, turned in a draft calling for further tariff-cutting powers for the president, but he wrote in what for protectionists were key points: the peril-point and escape clauses.

In the 1948 one-year extension of the Reciprocal Trade Bill, the protectionist forces in the Republican Eightieth Congress bestowed on the Tariff Commission a new power designed to inhibit (for it did not bind) the State Department negotiators of trade agreements. It was embodied in a provision that, before the negotiation of an agreement on any product, the Tariff Commission must be asked to indicate a limit below which a cut in rate would imperil the domestic industry—that is, the peril point.

In 1943, the State Department had persuaded the Swiss to accept in a new trade agreement an escape clause which would permit either party to the agreement to restore any of the rates being lowered if, wholly or partly as a result of the agreement, imports increased enough to threaten serious injury to a domestic industry. In 1951, Congress followed suit and wrote such a provision into the law. Under that escape clause, an injured manufacturer might appeal to the Tariff Commission. If the latter found that imports were causing serious injury, it ordered an increase in tariff rates. This order would go to the president, who might accept or reject it on grounds of national interest.

These provisions and others like them, giving threatened interests administrative tools with which to struggle against imports, were the great objectives of the protectionists and conversely the *bêtes noires* of the free traders. It was on precisely such issues that the Congressional struggle centered.

Cola Parker put into the draft report an endorsement of the peril-point provision, the escape clause, and countervailing duties. Randall and the other liberals accepted those deviations from their liberal doctrines to keep Parker and Millikin in camp. The commission also agreed to limit the presidential bargaining authority more sharply than it had been limited in the existing law. Thus, the ringing call for a new economic policy was progressively muted. As Randall said, "I'm slicing pieces out of my back."

All the while the courteous and even-tempered Millikin baited the trap. Not until the last session before Christmas, when the McDonald proposals were discussed, were there signs of open conflict. Even in the last two weeks, as final revisions were made on the report, the friendly protectionists got modification after modification to make the report more acceptable. Randall assumed that their silence meant consent. Not until after the report was finished, on January 9, did the dissents come in, expectable blasts from Simpson and Reed and the unexpected mild but deadly blow from Millikin. His was a subtle but devastating letter, in effect relegating the whole report to the status of a provisional document by a working team preparatory to serious consideration of the issues by responsible people:

> The programs for Congressional and Executive action suggested by the report will be subject to further study and hearings by the appropriate committees in Congress and those who work in these fields in other departments of the government.
>
> Additional facts and debate will develop and may change conclusions which now seem to be firmly seated.

Thus, Randall failed to win his near-unanimous report.

We may ask ourselves who won by the 1953 compromise which made a study commission a condition of a one-year renewal. There were points scored by both sides.

1. Thanks to Randall's driving energy, the protectionists failed to get the opportunity for procrastination that they thought lay in the commission. Even at the last moment, Randall scored in this respect. On January 6, he issued a confidential memorandum (published in *The New York Times,* January 9) calling for final action on January 11. It said in part:

> At the meeting, Tuesday, January 5, . . . we went through all of the tentative drafts in the order in which they will appear in the report, making revisions as those were suggested, and limiting as best we could the few areas of differences of opinion.
>
> On [next] Wednesday I shall start putting the whole report together. This involves a good deal of mechanical processing and will probably take three days.
>
> The Commission will please, therefore, meet at 10 A.M. on Saturday, January 9, at which time I intend to read the whole report straight through and receive final suggestions.
>
> I shall have to assume that the drafts are acceptable to all the

members, except as they notify me to the contrary. . . . I ask that these written dissents be placed in my hands not later than Friday noon, January 8. . . .

I hope that changes may be held within moderate limits at the Saturday meeting. On Saturday night, January 9, and Sunday, January 10, we hope to produce the final copies. I ask the commission, therefore, to meet at 4 P.M. on Monday, January 11, at which time I shall expect to submit the proposed report for final action.

I then intend to file the report as soon as the printing can be accomplished, which is estimated at perhaps five days thereafter.

I suggest that this schedule be held in strict confidence.

The reaction was sharp. Senators Walter George and Harry Byrd, influential Democrats and not protectionists, conferred and decided to make clear their refusal to accept the assumption that the draft would be acceptable to members unless notified to the contrary; one called it "perfectly ridiculous." Reed and Simpson protested, said *The New York Times*, "that there was insufficient time even to digest the draft, much less prepare dissents, and they ignored the deadline of noon," January 8. There was also protest over Randall's plan to permit dissents in the form of footnotes, rather than as a second report. Randall's system would give the impression that the report was acceptable to all members except for scattered reservations.

Randall stood firm on his schedule. He offered Reed and Simpson a compromise. He would go ahead and publish the report, allowing them to have their dissents published by the commission at a later date. The representatives, themselves trapped this time by their procrastination, chose to rush through their dissents as a letter plus scattered footnotes, to appear at the same time as the report was published, though in their letter they also accepted Randall's offer to publish a fuller dissent later, for whatever added value such a later publication might have had. Thus, despite protectionist protests. Randall succeeded in getting a report out in time for impact on the 1954 session of Congress. That was a score for the liberals.

2. On the other hand, the process of compromise to get an agreed report left the administration committed to a far weaker program than that with which it started. That is what generally happens in the process of legislation. A bill is introduced by its more extreme partisans. But they are not a majority, and to win a majority their bill is gradually whittled away (sometimes thus losing a few disgruntled extreme supporters who feel the cause has been betrayed) to pick up needed votes from those in the middle. That was bound to happen when the bill came into Congress, but in this case, thanks to the Randall Commission, it happened before the bill ever reached the floor. The administration, without the Randall Commission, would have submitted a far more daring set of proposals, but

after the Randall report the administration policy could be only that to which the compromise Randall report was committed. The liberals had started out asking for a permanent or ten-year extension to stop the process of triennial whittling-away at America's liberal-trade policy. The report ended up calling just for the standard three years.

The liberals started out opposing the escape-clause and peril-point provisions, but gave up on these. When they accepted the escape clause, they surrendered on perhaps the most important question of all, for the greatest burden on import development in recent years has not been the rates in American tariffs but the unpredictability of the consequences of import development. The late Adriano Olivetti, for example, resisted the pressure of his American typewriter distributors to expand his market here, as he could easily have done by aggressive promotion, because he believed that, if he expanded his share of the market, escape-clause proceedings would be instituted by his competitors to impose tariff increases on him. For similar reasons, both the Japanese textile industry and the big oil companies have followed policies of voluntary market restriction. By accepting the escape clause, the liberals gave up in advance on the hope of radically improving this situation.

By rejecting the McDonald proposal, the liberals excluded the possibility of getting administration support for a program of readjustment aid for injured industries.

The report, by another compromise, dashed hopes of foreign nations for direct financial aid from the U.S. Treasury to help achieve currency convertibility. The British had asked for a monetary stabilization loan and had been told that the reply would depend on the Randall report. The report threw the main burden of achieving convertibility on foreign countries. It took seriously the slogan of "trade, not aid" and talked about foreign aid as something that was about to decline drastically.

Finally, the report asked only very moderate tariff-cutting powers for the president. Under the previous law, the president had power to cut any tariff to as low as 50 per cent of its 1945 level. Under the Randall Commission proposals, he would lose that power. Rates in 1954 would become the new base, and he would be authorized to cut a rate 5 per cent per year during the three years of the act, or 15 per cent in total. For rates which had already been cut the full 50 per cent previously authorized, this new authority would constitute some increase of the president's tariff-cutting power. For rates which had not yet been cut and which he could still cut 50 per cent under the previous authorization, the new law would represent a decrease in his powers.

Along with these equivocal provisions, the report did contain support for some standard liberal-trade measures, including relaxation of the Buy-American Act, insurance for foreign investments, custom simplification, and repeal of the requirement for use of 50 per cent American bottoms in government-financed shipments. The report also recommended that the president have the right to make large nonreciprocal cuts in token tariffs—tariffs on goods that are not imported in any event.

But, all in all, the Randall report left the liberals campaigning to put through the Congress a tepid compromise which generated little enthusiasm among their potential supporters, either in Congress or in the nation. It left them to start the legislative bargaining and concession process from a point already far from what they wanted. This was a score in the protectionists' favor.

3. The report disappointed U.S. allies. This was another failure from the liberal point of view. From the beginning, the Randall Commission majority had its eye cocked to foreign reactions. As Reed and Simpson said in their dissent, "Witnesses in the United States were allowed two days for appearances; [2] those appearing at private hearings in Europe, whose primary interest was to obtain help for foreign countries, were allowed four days." Among those heard were Pierre Calvet, Lord Ismay, Jean Monnet, Robert Marjolin, and R. A. Butler. The gap between what they proposed and what the commission recommended was obviously large. But the tepid European reaction to the text of the report itself was cooled still further by awareness that the report was only the first step in a Congressional process that would trim it more. The report was not a success in creating an image of American economic cooperativeness with the country's allies.

4. There was one final point, however, in which the report clearly scored for the liberal traders. It provided them with an agreed platform and a leader. Clarence Randall, after finishing his job on the report, became special assistant to the President for foreign-trade matters. The report made him not merely a citizen with some views on free enterprise and foreign trade but also a recognized spokesman for the American majority point of view on the subject of world trade. In thus crystallizing leadership for the liberal side, the commission clearly hurt the protectionists who had originally insisted on having it. The report, although weak, was clearly a liberal and not a protectionist platform. No one asked the question which side it was on—only the question of whether it made a good case for its side. Thus the report cast the liberal-trade side as the majority and the protectionists as the opposition in all subsequent debate.

We shall not cast up a balance sheet of the points scored by each side. Suffice it to note that the commission had served its purpose of postponing decision, allowing the system to function and allowing the discourse to go on while each side jockeyed for position. The lines were now formed for the next round, which was to take place in the halls of the Congress.

---

[2] Not quite accurate; this excludes the closed hearings.

Chapter 4

Renewal 1954

Well before the Randall Commission submitted its report, it had become the view of Washington insiders, though not of most others, that few major reforms in American trade policy would be passed by the 1954 session of Congress. It was an election year, no time to ask congressmen to vote for legislation opposed by powerful interest groups. It was a recession year. Protectionist sentiment was strong in Congress, and public expression of it was increasing. European competition had revived, thanks partly to the Marshall Plan. American industries between 1945 and 1950 had expanded their exports to fill the vacuum caused by the destruction of European industry in such markets as Latin America, to which Europe had once exported heavily. They now found the traditional European suppliers coming back into their own. By going back to a 1938 base, one might show that American sellers were not doing badly, but figures using, say, a 1947 base showed a trend of rising European competition.

When the Randall report appeared dotted with dissents, even less astute observers recognized that major reforms faced a long, hard fight.

It became apparent that the only chance for quick action lay in exceptionally vigorous presidential leadership.

Prospects looked even dimmer when, two months after the hectically prepared Randall report was published, the White House finally, on March 30, got around to issuing a special message to Congress on foreign-trade policy. Foreign trade was by no means the center of everyone's attention. As Walter Lippmann put it:

> Last week was certainly not an ideal moment for a message from the President on foreign economic policy. Even if it were a more fascinating subject than it is, it had to compete for attention with the hydrogen bomb, the heart-rending defense of Dienbienphu, another major doctrinal speech by Secretary Dulles, another big move by Moscow on the peace front, and always and of course McCarthyism. The competing news would in itself be enough to explain why not every citizen spent all of last Wednesday evening reading the President's message.[3]

Inside White House circles there was already talk of settling for the *status quo* for another year and trying for more fundamental reforms after the Congressional elections. The President's message on foreign trade asked for five pieces of legislation, two of them controversial. Of the three noncontroversial ones, customs simplification and tax incentives for foreign investment were both already under consideration by Congress.[4] Increases in tourist exemptions were the subject of the third noncontroversial bill. Changes in the Buy-American Act[5] and Reciprocal Trade renewal were the difficult bills. On these, at the end of March the President urged the Randall Commission recommendations, but there was still no bill.

The bills were being drafted in the White House by an interdepartmental committee under the chairmanship of Randall with representatives from the departments of Commerce, Labor, State, Treasury, and Agriculture and other agencies. A bill was finally delivered to Capitol Hill a few days before the Easter recess began on April 15. According to a widely circulated story, when the measure went to the House Committee on Ways and Means, Chairman Reed tossed it on the table and said, "Who wants to take this?" After a long pause, Robert W. Kean of New Jersey, *fourth*-ranking Republican on the committee, finally said, "I will." Kean was the highest ranking Republican willing to touch it. The story, or indeed even its circulation, attests to the chilly atmosphere into which the bill was introduced.

Representative Kean got little help. Since he was not a committee

---

[3] *New York Herald Tribune,* April 5, 1954.

[4] "Noncontroversial" does not mean that they passed. Customs simplification died in the Senate.

[5] That act requires the government to purchase from domestic suppliers unless a foreign bidder quotes a substantially lower price.

chairman, he had only a small personal staff at his disposal, and this staff had to work on constituency problems, too. Since the committee clerks were overworked with other legislation, clerks on the majority side knew that the chairman was opposed, and those on the minority side would not extend themselves for a Republican, he could not call on staff for help with the same freedom as is normally the case with an administration bill. He also got no cooperation from Reed in scheduling hearings. When Kean introduced the bill, HR 8860, on April 15, Representative Simpson asked ironically, "When is Congressman Kean going to hold hearings on this measure?"

The Easter recess passed. April moved into May, but Congress did not move. Nor did the administration. We quote a May 8 editorial from *The Washington Post*.

> What is the Administration doing. . . . Are speeches being made in support of the program? Are key members of Congress being called to the White House to hear the President's arguments? Is the Republican National Committee using its resources to try to persuade GOP dissenters? Are the Republican leaders in Congress holding caucuses to discuss the program and ways to keep it on the tracks?
>
> The President's work was not completed when he submitted his program to Congress.

It was not just the trade bill which was tied up. So were foreign aid, labor legislation, taxes, and social-security extension. The latter was of particular significance, for it, too, needed hearings before the Ways and Means Committee, scheduled to begin the first week in May. The middle of May came, and still no progress. The Reciprocal Trade Bill was due to die in less than a month. Typically, it would take a month to schedule and hold hearings in the House, some time for floor action, another month for hearings in the Senate, then time for floor action, and at least a few weeks for a conference committee. In short, three months would have been a reasonable schedule for a bill as important and controversial as this one.

The third week in May was "Foreign Trade Week." Kean read a speech into *The Congressional Record*. The same day, Rep. Oakley Hunter (R., Calif.) introduced a protectionist tariff bill transferring from the president to Congress the right to reverse Tariff Commission findings on rate increases. Still there were no hearings scheduled.

Increasingly, commentators began to say that the best the President could get was another one-year extension. *Newsweek* as early as February 1 had labeled the outlook as "a one-year extension, possibly two."

The Washington Post on May 17 said:

> The President will be fortunate if he gets a one-year extension . . . without severe new restrictions. . . .
>
> There is talk again that "next year" it will be possible for the Ad-

ministration to make progress on the program Mr. Eisenhower has described as "urgent." That was the prediction all last year, too.[6]

Drew Pearson on May 20 said:

Uncle Dan Reed (R., N.Y.), chairman of the Ways and Means Committee, is trying to make a deal with the White House to kill reciprocal trade.

The Congressman has secretly offered to help put the President's social-security program through Congress if the President, in turn, will abandon his campaign to liberalize the reciprocal trade agreement. . . . So far—no answer.[7]

The same day, the President faced reality. We quote *The New York Times:*

President Eisenhower disclosed today that he would accept a one year extension of the Reciprocal Trade Agreement Act. . . .

The President let it be known, however, that he believed Congress should get on with the task of holding hearings on his original proposal so that it could act on the three-year extension early in the 1955 Congressional session.[8]

What the President neglected to note was that there would certainly be objections to one Congress holding hearings for a new one.

Thus, once again, in 1954 as in 1953, the Congressional leadership and the White House—or fate or events—made a decision not to push for a three-year extension. We have heard different accounts as to who made the decision, and probably different people became aware of the political and procedural problems more or less simultaneously. The social-security hearings were still on in Ways and Means and were expected to last until May 30, and other legislation was scheduled for discussion there until June 15. The only period in which hearings could have been held on the Kean bill was about four days in between. The committee had more than enough pending legislation which had been requested by the White House and had been waiting for some time.

The decisive consideration, however, was the grass-roots political question. Several political leaders felt that, if the Republicans were only to get by the 1954 elections, the reciprocal-trade extension would have a lot of votes from men who would have to oppose it in 1954. In other words, what held off a showdown on the three-year reciprocal-trade extension in the House was political caution, a surfeit of legislation—in particular the tax and social-security bills—the fatigue produced by months spent on them, and the calendar. Neither side wanted to plunge into

[6] *The Washington Post,* May 17, 1954.
[7] Drew Pearson, *The Washington Post,* May 20, 1954.
[8] *The New York Times,* May 21, 1954.

hearings or into a floor debate which might take several days out of an overcrowded calendar at the end of a session.[9]

After Memorial Day, most congressmen, particularly in an election year, begin to look forward hopefully to adjournment. If Congress stays in session much after the Fourth of July in an election year, there is no real chance of vacation before the campaign. Consequently, the desire to wind things up quickly was an important factor in leading the protectionists to accept a one-year extension gracefully. Then, too, Representative Simpson, the most influential Republican protectionist, was also chairman of the House Republican Campaign Committee and presumably felt some reluctance to force Republican members in close districts to record themselves against Eisenhower on this issue.

In the end, it was Reed himself who introduced in the House and piloted to success the bill requested by the administration for a one-year reciprocal-trade extension. That did not happen without some bargaining. "Key Congressional figures" (presumably Reed) asked the administration for a commitment such as had been given in 1953 against any actual negotiations of trade agreements during the year. The reward for that would be a year's renewal of the act "as is," without amendment, and the giving of top priority at the 1955 session to hearings and action on a three-year extension. The White House refused. The reason for both the demand and the refusal lay in negotiations with Japan. The administration considered the Japanese economic situation critical and planned to enter into trade-agreement negotiations to help Japan increase its exports. Nothing could have been more alarming to protectionists; cheap Japanese competition was their *bête noire*.

But an event helped silence the protectionists temporarily. The Communist armies made great advances in Indo-China; the whole American position in Asia became more evidently precarious. So Reed was probably wholly sincere when, despite the administration's refusal to make a deal, he introduced a one-year extension "as is" on the administration's terms. In asking the House to support it he said:

> We know the conditions in the world today. Let us lay the cards on the table. We know the situation in Japan. We know that . . . there is a great reservoir of people out of work and the Communists are working to the best of their ability among these people. We need

---

[9] As Representative Reed said when it finally came to floor action on a compromise, "The sole purpose of [this bill] is to preserve the status quo until a sound tariff policy can be developed." He explained the tremendous work load the Ways and Means Committee had had during the 1954 session and said, "There is a limit to physical and mental endurance. . . . The choice . . . is . . . to enact [the extension] or to allow the Trade Agreements Act to expire. The expiration . . . would not have any effect upon the trade agreements which are presently outstanding. . . . It would not grant any additional tariff protection to any of our industries, workers, and farmers."

Japan on our side in this troubled world, and we are not going to gain their support by starving them to death. We have to do at least this much for them, at least give them a chance to be heard through trade negotiations. I am not willing . . . to take the responsibility under present conditions of the world of killing this bill and shutting the door to such negotiations.[10]

Simpson took the same view:

Because of the plea made today by the Administration, which I will not contradict, namely that we can, by making an agreement between now and next year effectively prevent the spread of war in Asia, possibly making permanent the peace which we now enjoy, I am unwilling for this 12-months period to stand in the way of those who affirm that trade agreements possibly will prevent war in the foreseeable future.[11]

The bill was introduced by Reed on June 8, unanimously approved by the Ways and Means Committee on June 10, and passed by the House the next day, 281 to 53.

It took two more weeks for the Senate to act, although the Finance Committee, under Senator Millikin, held no hearings and sent the bill to the floor, 13 to 2. These were two dramatic weeks, indeed.

The balance of power in the Senate was quite different from that in the House. It was partly accidental that in the House two men, Reed and Simpson, were simultaneously fanatical protectionists and in the most strategic possible position for control of tariff legislation. In the Senate, Millikin resembled Reed, but he was a far less dogmatic and committed man. More important, he had less control. That was assured by the nature of the Senate. A small club of powerful men with flexible rules of procedure, compared to the House it is unbossed. The House, a large and cumbersome body, is dominated by the leadership. If Kean had been a senator, he would have been far less effectively boxed-in.

Of all the differences between House and Senate, the most crucial for our purposes is the rule on amendments. In the Senate, any senator may introduce any amendment. It need not even be germane to the subject of the bill on the floor. On the other hand, in the House, each bill, before coming onto the floor, goes to the Rules Committee for the adoption of a rule under which it will be discussed. Occasionally it may be an "open rule," allowing unlimited amendment. At the other extreme, is a "closed rule," specifying that no amendment is permitted; the bill must then be accepted or rejected as it stands. Other rules lie in-between, for example, a closed rule which allows only one specified amendment for which there is substantial support.

The one-year renewal was taken up by the House under a closed

---

[10] *Congressional Record*, June 11, 1954.
[11] *Loc. cit.*

rule. It was renewal of the bill "as is" or nothing at all. The action of the Senate could not be as fully fixed. It was bound to reflect more nearly the basic division of strength existing in the body. And that was good for the liberal traders.

The balance of votes of the Congressional members on the Randall Commission, who generally supported the report, 7 to 3, was one indication of the true balance of sentiment in Congress. So was the bald fact that reciprocal trade has been the policy of the United States since 1934, eleven times renewed by Congress. In short, the liberal traders were bound to be stronger in any situation where Congressional sentiment was better reflected than it was in the House, under the fortuitous circumstances of Reed's and Simpson's dominance.

So it was that, in the Senate, initiative fell into the hands of the liberal traders, whereas in the House it had been in the hands of the protectionists. The man who took the initiative was Sen. Albert Gore (D., Tenn.). Gore's strategy was to offer an amendment substituting the original three-year extension, for which the President had asked, for the House-approved bill.

Senator Gore, as one of his associates said,

> . . . has always been interested in Cordell Hull's work. . . . They lived in the same little community [Carthage, Tenn.], and when Mr. Hull was home for the Congressional recess he'd sit on the courthouse lawn and chew the fat with the [future] Senator [then a boy and young man]. Personal factors and relationships and his 14 years of strong support [of reciprocal trade] while in the House explain why Mr. Gore took the lead.

Gore's scheme was to give the President exactly what he wanted, not what he had settled for, putting him in the position of either supporting the move and thereby going back on his latest word to the House right-wing leadership or of opposing his own program and appearing weak.

When Gore first acted, the protectionists did not take him seriously. The Democratic leadership also regarded his move as frivolous and opposed it. They may have genuinely feared a "knock-down, drag-out" fight which would push the Senate, with its tradition of unlimited debate, into August before adjourning. But more important was the fact that Lyndon Johnson did not believe that Gore's tactics had any chance of working. But Gore's move, a sly device to embarrass the Republican administration, caught fire among the Senate Democrats. When it did so, Johnson reversed his ground. He put the Senate whip to rounding up votes.

One key man who might have enabled the Gore amendment to pass the Senate was Walter George (Ga.), senior Democrat on the Senate Finance Committee. His unwillingness to go along with the amendment largely shaped Senator Johnson's early attitude. George's reluctance was attributable to several factors. He was friendly with Senator Millikin, and they maintained an amiable working relationship similar to the more widely publicized Martin-Rayburn relationship. He was in his late seventies and under physician's orders against excessive work. Several other tough conference-committee fights on fiscal matters, in which George, as senior Democrat on Finance, would have to serve, were unavoidable. He hoped to avoid another one. Also, George was aware of the unhappiness or potential unhappiness of Georgia textile interests about reciprocal trade. Lastly, even if Gore could get a three-year extension through the Senate, the House would never accept it.

Despite George's defection, the Gore amendment lost only six Democratic votes altogether and fell seven votes short of passing.

The amendment was indeed a coup for the Democrats. Dramatic enough to win national attention, it enabled Gore to make a four-hour speech notable for something other than its length. He introduced into the reciprocal-trade debate a theme which had hardly been present until then but which has since come into the focus of much attention. "The Reds," he said, "are driving hard to take over our foreign markets and we must forestall them." And with this theme went the dominant one that the President had "surrendered" on his own program. As Senator Fulbright added, a one-year extension would mean "another year of indecision and delay." The Republicans, he said, had killed "trade, not aid" through "procrastination, hesitation, and doubt."

If the Democrats rallied to the marvelous opportunity for attack which Gore's tactics had given them, the Republicans rallied to the President's defense.

Thirty-nine Republicans opposed Gore's amendment and not one supported him. Among the Republicans were many men who favored the Eisenhower-Randall program. Senator Bush (R., Conn.), himself a member of the Randall Commission, probably spoke for them when he said:

> I have a good deal of sympathy with the substance of the amendment. . . . I am compelled to vote against [it] because it can serve no useful purpose at the present time. . . . Our friends on the other side of the aisle have claimed that they are supporting the President of the United States in offering this amendment. The claim is without foundation. . . . The actual choice before us is a one-year extension or nothing.
> I say that because of the knowledge which I have . . . as to the attitude of the House Ways and Means Committee, which simply will not accept the amendment.

Senator Bush was speaking for the White House. One Eisenhower senator, who supported the reciprocal-trade program, called the White House and was told not to support the Gore proposal. If one looks at the

Republicans who probably would have followed White House leadership in favor of the amendment, it is clear that the White House could have pushed a three-year extension through the Senate had it desired. But the White House considered the Gore amendment "political gunplay" designed to highlight the schism within the Republican Party and to force it and its supporters in the Senate into a profitless hassle with the senior Republicans in the House.

On final passage, on June 24, with seventy-one votes in favor, only three votes were cast against the one-year extension—the two senators from Nevada, Malone (R.) and McCarran (D.), and Butler of Nebraska (R.). And so reciprocal trade survived for another year.

Chapter 5

Renewal 1955 and Since

When the returns came in from the 1954 elections, a Democratic Congress had been chosen.

The new chairman of the Committee on Ways and Means was Jere Cooper (D., Tenn.) an old-school Southerner, traditionally and personally committed to lower tariffs. His right-hand man was Wilbur Mills (Ark.), third-ranking Democratic member of Ways and Means, a convinced liberal trader and one of the ablest men in the House. The chairman of the Senate Finance Committee was Byrd of Virginia, hardly a liberal, but a traditional Southern Democrat and therefore not a protectionist. The speaker of the House, Rayburn, and the Senate majority leader, Johnson, were convinced long-time supporters of Reciprocal Trade.

On the first day of the Eighty-fourth Congress, some 1,000 bills were dropped into the hopper of the House. Exercising his traditional prerogative, Speaker Rayburn took one of them and labeled it House Resolution 1. It was Cooper's Reciprocal Trade Renewal Bill, essentially the same as the Kean bill, and also drafted by Clarence Randall. Thus Rayburn signaled that this bill was of top importance and that this time

59

there was to be no delay. The bill was ready on the first day of the session, January 5. Five days later, the President sent a special message to Congress on foreign economic policy, supporting renewal legislation. One week after that, January 17, over the protests of Strackbein against "an unwarranted and perhaps unprecedented brevity of time allowed to prepare," Chairman Cooper started sixteen days of hearings on HR 1.

The hearings, when published, filled 2,601 pages. The witnesses were a star cast, led off by Secretary of State John Foster Dulles, followed by the secretaries of Agriculture, Commerce, Defense, Treasury, and Labor. A week was devoted to supporters of the bill and a week to its foes, and then there were the executive sessions.

There, Chairman Cooper and Wilbur Mills had trouble holding the line against all amendments. The four-man protectionist team in the twenty-five-man committee—Reed, Simpson, Noah Mason (R., Ill.), and Thomas Jenkins (R., Ohio)—managed to get some close votes on strengthening the power of the Tariff Commission and weakening the power of the president in escape-clause proceedings. In the end, the committee made no substantive changes and reported out the bill 20 to 5. Rising protectionist sentiment was kept in check. But, when the House started to consider the measure, it ran into trouble.

The general expectation was that a Democratic House and Senate would be more sympathetic to liberal trade than the previous Republican ones. However, it happened that areas of great current unemployment— the Appalachian mountain areas, Oklahoma, and Rhode Island—were chiefly Democratic and that a case could be made to attribute that unemployment to foreign imports. Congressman Burnside of West Virginia (D.), who may be described in general as a New Deal progressive and by training a specialist in international affairs, testified or spoke on behalf of no less than seven industries in his district, urging protection for each of them. West Virginia congressmen stated that over 225,000 persons in West Virginia were being aided by the surplus food program; Rhode Island congressmen maintained that there were as many as 30 per cent unemployed in a city like Bristol.

But the most important political development of 1955 in regard to reciprocal trade was the way in which textiles entered the protectionist picture. Over the years, textile manufacturers and unions have grumbled about foreign imports, but, with a few local exceptions, they have not been notably vociferous on the matter. In 1955, all this was changed; textiles entered the battle in full force. Letters poured in on the congressmen from the textile districts. The Georgia and Alabama delegations, longtime mainstays of Southern free-trade sentiment, went over to the protectionist side.

One influential Southern congressman, Lanham of Georgia, told the story thus:

> I started to get a lot of letters from employees in the textile mills about the tariff. Now, of course, these letters were inspired by the mill people, the owners, and I didn't feel very kindly about their way of going about it. I had fought their battles on a lot of things . . . so I pushed them aside by pointing out that peril point and escape clause protected them. . . . After a while (since this kept up) I got sort of irritated and wrote to a friend of mine who's in the textile business in the district saying in effect to him "why don't you get these guys to shut up?" only I didn't want to put it so crudely. . . .
> "Well," my friend replied, "no, peril point and escape clause do not protect us." So I started digging into it, consulting Congressman Cleveland Bailey [(D., W.Va.), the most dedicated protectionist in the House] and others, and I found out that . . . peril point and escape clause are being administered by visionaries without practical experience. . . . I consulted all the Congressmen from my area and they took up the matter and we agreed to testify on behalf of the textile people . . . and most of us went along with Dan Reed on the vote.

Many of the Southern congressmen receive very light mail; Northern congressmen's secretaries used to make a joke of the 10-to-3:30 schedule of Southern congressmen's secretaries, since there was so little mail to handle. But, on this matter, the mail flooded in; one Alabama congressman reported receiving 5,000 pieces of mail on the issue in six weeks or less. In addition, a number of Southern congressmen were phoned by local businessmen or by local managers, sometimes acting out of intense conviction, but at least as often as a result of requests from a trade association or as a favor to somebody else.

The textile unions, and in particular the former CIO unions, have sometimes tried to act as a brake on the protectionist tendencies of some of the manufacturers. This year they had to go along, although they maintained that "the really hysterical letters and campaigns come from the unorganized mills," of which there are a good many, especially in the South. "These manufacturers are just crazy; we have to go along with them," a liberal union leader rationalized, "to see they don't go completely wild."

In fact, the interests of the textile industry are by no means unified with regard to imports. Congressman Harrison (D., Va.) forced Seabury Stanton, chairman of the board of the National Cotton Manufacturers, to admit that "our [total national] exports in cotton goods are twelve times our [total national] imports [6 per cent as against one-half of 1 per cent]" and that "if we returned to a protectionist policy . . . we would [be likely to] lose 6 per cent in exports and be protecting one-half of 1 per cent in imports." [1] It was not at all clear why such a company as Berkshire-Hathaway, which Stanton heads, should fear foreign trade. On the other hand, "coarse linen towelling and hemmed linen handkerchiefs from the United Kingdom, cotton hosiery from France and the United Kingdom, woolens and worsteds from the United Kingdom, and apparel wool from Australia . . ." did constitute a real threat to domestic firms.[2]

So the textile industry is rather bitterly divided between unions and management and, to some degree, between North and South. Controversies over wages, differential wage rates, and the like are acute. The trade association leaders and others whose devotion is to the industry rather than to a firm admit that they regard the tariff issue as a godsend because it is one of the few issues which comes near uniting the industry.

Tactically, the textile industry in 1955 seems to have borrowed its procedures from those successfully followed by Pittsburgh Plate Glass and to a lesser degree by Westinghouse Electric in 1954 in their campaigns against reciprocal trade. Pittsburgh Plate Glass got almost every worker to write demanding protection for his job. Then it got surgeons, automobile dealers, grocery-store owners, high school teachers—anybody in a town where it had a plant—to send in obviously individually written letters to the congressmen. Although they did not equal the technical brilliance of this campaign, textiles and other protectionist industries adopted this grassroot approach in 1955.

The force of the opposition to the bill began to make itself clear when the members of the Ways and Means Committee went before the Rules Committee to ask a closed rule for the bill. One after another, members of the Rules Committee raised problems of local industries in their constituencies and questioned the closed rule. An open rule would allow commodity amendments in favor of special interests. Even if none passed, and some amendments would, congressmen could make a record for the folks back home.

The ironic event of the day came when Chairman Smith of Rules called on Reed, who supported the closed rule. Because Jere Cooper had backed him on the closed rule the previous year when he was chairman, Reed was now backing Cooper.[3] Having thus paid his debt by giving the Democrats what they wanted, he launched without further ado into a tirade against the bill itself.

---

[1] Ways and Means Committee, *Hearing on HR 1*, 1955, p. 1669.

[2] Commission on Foreign Economic Policy (Randall Commission), *Staff Papers*, 1954, p. 299.

[3] Note, however, that, while in private and in reality he was paying off his debt to Cooper by backing the closed rule, in press statements he was attacking it and lining up with his ideological colleagues. See *New York Times*, Feb. 16, 1955.

> I've been listening to these internationalist arguments for twenty years. The whole business is not constitutional, and the courts will prove it so one of these days.
>
> I formed my opinion about low tariffs as an infant during the administration of Grover Cleveland. Yes, I formed my opinions when, gentlemen, I walked miles and miles to sell a dozen eggs for ten cents!

His fist crashed down with a bang.

The speeches after Reed were sixteen to two against the bill. The six hours of debate behind closed doors before the Rules Committee were far more of a clue to the sentiment that existed than was the eight-to-three vote by which the Rules Committee finally decided to allot two days of floor debate according to the normal and traditional closed rule under which tax and tariff matters are nearly always discussed.

Two days later, on February 17, when the House met to consider HR 1, the first business was to adopt the proposed rule. Rarely does the House fail to do so. During the decade 1939-1948, it rejected the Rules Committee's request for a closed rule only six times.[4] But that was just the strategy which the protectionists proposed. A series of speakers rose nobly to protest against "gagging" the House. Again, the one maverick was Reed.

> Last year when I had a desperate fight on tax revision and other legislation, the distinguished gentleman from Tennessee [Cooper] was in the minority. I asked him to cooperate with me for a tight rule to get the legislation through. He did it. I told him I would reciprocate. I am doing that on this legislation.

Then came the first of two complicated votes. The motion on the floor was for the closed rule. The first vote was on the previous question. Only if that were defeated would the floor be open for an amendment instituting an open rule. A vote for was a free-trade vote—it was a vote to shut off any amendment to the closed rule. A vote against was a protectionist vote—against shutting off debate and amendments to the closed rule. The pundits had been saying that the liberals had a fifty- to one-hundred-vote margin (perhaps 220 to 160). The results were 178 for, 207 against. Protection had won by about thirty votes.

The joyful victors moved promptly to the second step: an amendment changing the rule so that it would permit unlimited amendment to the bill.

Then Rayburn did something a speaker does only once or twice a session. He left his rostrum, went down as a member, and took the floor.

---

[4] Louis J. Lapham, "Party Leadership and Rules Committee" (unpublished Ph.D. dissertation; Harvard, 1953), p. 346.

> The House on this last vote has done a most unusual thing and under the circumstances a very dangerous thing. . . . Only once in the history of the House, in forty-two years in my memory, has a bill of this kind and character been considered except under a closed rule. . . . So as an old friend to all of you, as a lover of the House of Representatives and its procedures, I ask you to vote down this amendment.

The House went from silent listening to feverish activity. The whips worked on the votes. Rep. Cleveland M. Bailey (D., W.Va.) for the protectionists promised that not more than four or five amendments would be offered. He was trying to quiet the fear that the protectionists would use the open rule to create pandemonium, loading the proceedings and perhaps the bill with so many incompatible amendments as to get the whole thing sent back to committee.

Then came the crucial second vote. It was much closer. Among the Republicans, the protectionists actually picked up three votes (from 106 to 109). But among the Democrats the influence of Rayburn paid off. The end was a photo finish. As the roll call proceeded, the protectionists seemed to win by seven votes. Then the "corrections" began. One man after another rose to ask how he was recorded and then corrected his vote from "for" to "against" the amendment. The amendment lost 193 to 191.

Every vote now counted, and there was another to come, the vote on the closed rule itself. The roll was called for the third time: 193 to 192.[5] The closed rule had carried by the narrowest House vote in fourteen years. The House was in turmoil, and there was still one crucial vote to go. Under the closed rule, one, but only one, amendment was permitted: a motion to recommit the bill to committee, that is, to kill it.

But there was no time for the vote that day. The anticlimactic debate on the bill itself was now going on to an audience of two dozen members. President Eisenhower's legislative representatives, Gen. Wilton B. Persons, I. ("Jack") Martin, and Gerald Morgan, met with Minority Leader Joseph Martin and arranged a special plea by the President, two-thirds of whose party had deserted him. The next morning, February 8, Rayburn met with all the freshman representatives for breakfast. He advised them earnestly: "If you want to get along [in the House] go along [with the leadership]." No one could miss the point.

The one amendment permitted under the rule was offered by Reed. Carefully, he made it a very modest one which some middle-of-the-roaders might be able to accept. There were no special safeguards for any industry. It was a motion to recommit with instructions to the Ways and Means Committee to write in a provision changing the escape clause only slightly, by providing that Tariff Commission rulings under the escape clause

---

[5] Note that Reed continued to be loyal to his obligation to Cooper. He voted for the closed rule despite the one-vote margin.

should be final except where the president found that national security would be adversely affected. There was a good deal of wrangling about the phrase "national security." Some stalwart protectionists felt that Reed was too mild and should have limited the president's discretion to findings of adverse effects on "national defense." The liberal-trade leadership declared that they would accept the term "national interests," but not "national security." This was no quibble. It makes a vast difference whether the president can overrule the Tariff Commission only on military defense grounds or on any basis which seems to him to be in the national interest. The word "security" fudges that issue. The administration offered to accept "national interest." Reed refused. "We'll vote it up or down." The real issue—which makes it hard to understand why the administration panicked into making such an offer—was that, if the bill were recommitted for any change at all, it would probably not come out again that year in recognizable form. Recommitted bills do not.

The debate went on all day Friday. Among the many speeches, one deserves to be noted. Henderson Lanham of Georgia, one of the most respected members of the House, who had previously been a lifelong low-tariff supporter, spoke in favor of the Reed motion. He was a weather vane and also an influence on a substantial group of votes.

At the end of the afternoon, Minority Leader Martin rose as the debate drew to a close. "A little while ago," he said, "the President handed me a letter." The letter was conciliatory. In effect it said: "This program . . . will be administered to the benefit of the nation's economic strength and not to its detriment. No American industry will be placed in jeopardy."

Once again there was a roll-call vote. Once again the protectionists really won until the "corrections" came in. Martin, Rayburn, and the whips called on their credits. The Reed motion to recommit was rejected, 206 to 199. Actually, these close votes are misleading. The leadership may lose in a landslide, but the leadership need never lose in a close vote. The Martins and the Rayburns have enough long-standing credits outstanding to round up a dozen votes as needed. The number who switch is a function of the gap to be closed. There are others who would switch if someone else had not done it already. The protectionists simply did not have the substantial margin needed to deny the leadership its way, but they had enough to impose a real check on the liberal traders.

The Reed proposal was beaten, and the Eisenhower administration saved for one major reason—Sam Rayburn. As Rayburn himself said in conversation, the bill was a "Rayburn Bill," not an "Eisenhower Bill." Had there been a new speaker, a weaker leader, or one less devoted to reciprocal trade, the Reed motion would have won.

The last step in the House drama was an anticlimax. Once the

Reed motion was beaten, the bill itself was adopted, 295 to 110, showing that quite a number of protectionists did not wish to record themselves as opposed to reciprocal trade. One of our interviewees put it that nowadays there are two kinds of reciprocal traders, "protectionist reciprocal traders" and "lower reciprocal traders." Also, having been beaten, many of those who strayed off the reservation wanted to work their way back into the good graces of Rayburn and Eisenhower.

Thus the House, with a liberal-trade leadership, completed action on the three-year renewal on February 18, six weeks after the session began. The narrow escape made it clear that the bill was still in danger, but at least it went to the Senate with time enough to ensure action. The Senate Committee on Finance scheduled hearings beginning March 2, which were in many respects a replay of the House hearings.

Because he was overseas, Secretary Dulles, who was supposed to be the lead-off witness, could not be present; and Secretary George M. Humphrey, who was to be second, according to the account we heard, had not organized his testimony for the lead-off spot and did not wish to take Dulles' place. Assistant Secretary of Agriculture Earl L. Butz was therefore thrown into the breach. Listening to the reading of his testimony, one received the impression of a scholar conning a lesson not thoroughly grasped, an impression which Senator Millikin, senior Republican on the Finance Committee, was quick to confirm by asking him to explain various points about the rates, which the witness was unable to do. State Department representatives in the room were presumably prepared, since Millikin had on previous occasions asked similar questions of them, but there was not enough interdepartmental liaison for Butz to escape his embarrassment. Then Millikin forced Butz to admit: "As long as we have our domestic price support program, we must have some way of protecting it." Millikin commented, "I am glad to see you are very firm and clear on that," making the point that in fact the Agriculture Department does not support reciprocal trade in farm crops, but quite the contrary.[6]

The hearings became what it would be fair to call tedious. A contributor to tedium was Senator Malone (R., Nevada); nearly three-fifths of the record—that is, 1,200 pages of testimony—resulted from his questions and statements. The following is a sample:

> Isn't that right . . . that if a man knows his business and he sits down on one of these committees in Geneva, 3,000 miles away from Washington and 3,000 miles away from the mines, and if he knows what he is doing he can murder you and still it will look all right on paper. . . . I have worried with this thing now—it is my ninth year in the Senate—and I worried about it ten years prior to that time. . . . How it happened, of course, you are entirely unfamiliar with that. . . .

---

[6] "Hearings Before the Committee on Finance," U.S. Senate, on HR 1, 1955, pp. 6-53.

Of course, you are. You are just trying to pay the wages and pay the help and get this stuff on the market. And when Congress can allow something to be done that even they don't understand through an agreement clear beyond any agency of theirs, then if we don't understand it, is it a cinch nobody else is going to? Isn't that about right?

The witness in this case, as in many other instances, was confined to saying in answer to these statements, "That is right," and Malone through his own remarks made the bulk of the record. Frequently the chairman urged Malone to speed up, but to no avail. Evening sessions were conducted, at which it appears that frequently Senator Malone alone was present to interrogate witnesses and hear testimony; the record does not clearly indicate when senators leave the hearings. This procedure did little to publicize the viewpoint that Malone was trying to get across. He received little newspaper or radio coverage. Even his colleagues became irritated with him; his most acrimonious run-ins were with two of those most likely to oppose HR 1, Kerr (D., Okla.) and Millikin (R., Colo.).

The Congressional balance of power in 1955 was a mirror image of what it had been in 1954. House and Senate differed for identical reasons in the two sessions, but the direction was reversed. It was the Senate which was more protectionist in 1955. Senator Byrd, though not a protectionist, was no Cooper, and, even if he were, he had no such power to check amendments. Sen. Walter F. George was in his last desperate fight for political survival, and Herman Talmadge, the challenger, was using George's internationalism and lack of interest in local industries as a weapon. George was being forced to retreat.

In the Senate, the battle centered on a series of amendments. First there was the Neely amendment, which was in effect the old Simpson bill broadened. Introduced by Sen. Matthew Neely (D., W.Va.) and sixteen other senators, it would limit petroleum imports, including residual fuel oil, for any quarter of the calendar year to 10 per cent of the domestic demand in the corresponding quarter of the previous year. This provision was in the Simpson bill. But to expand the coalition beyond coal and oil states the Neely amendment applied the same technique also to other commodities. A provision required the president to restrict imports whenever they "threaten to retard the domestic development and expansion or maintenance of domestic production of natural resource commodities or any commodities which he determines to be essential to the national security."

This extreme program of the protectionists was but one of a number of amendments debated in the executive sessions of the Senate Finance Committee.[7]

On March 17, Sen. Leverett Saltonstall (R., Mass.), the Senate

---

[7] Neely used open hearings on unemployment before his own subcommittee of the Labor Committee to publicize his bill.

Republican whip, proposed two amendments, one to cut the renewal from three years to two (an amendment also sponsored by Senator Millikin), the other to limit possible concessions on textile imports by changing the base date. The power to be granted the president to negotiate tariff cuts had been stated as 15 per cent of the June, 1955, level. By changing that to the January, 1955, level, lowered rates already conceded in then-current Japanese negotiations would fall within the permitted cuts and not form the basis for new reductions.

Senators Styles Bridges (R., N.H.), chairman of the Republican Policy Committee, and John Pastore (D., R.I.) proposed what had been the barely defeated Reed amendment in the House, that is, to limit the grounds on which the president might overrule the Tariff Commission in escape-clause proceedings to "national security."

There was also a series of special commodity amendments—one for an import tax on lead and zinc, one for a quota on fluorspar, sponsored by Alben Barkley (D., Ky.), and one for higher tariffs on hardboard. Senator Millikin moved to make it clear that the Senate was not approving GATT.

An amendment was introduced to make Tariff Commission recommendations public when sent to the president, not after sixty days, as hitherto. The point was to bring the president under the pressure of public opinion while he was reaching a decision. Another amendment removed from the president the power to reduce token tariffs on things not currently imported.

The Finance Committee which pondered these amendments was closely divided. The canniest insider could not be sure what the outcome would be. The first test, on Tuesday, April 19, was on Millikin's amendment cutting the three-year renewal to two. When the votes were cast, there was a seven-seven tie, defeating the amendment. Voting for the amendment were five Republicans and two Democrats. Voting against were five Democrats and two Republicans, the latter being the liberal trader Ralph Flanders (Vt.) and the protectionist fanatic Malone.

Protection was the victim of Malone's own intransigence. He was against reciprocal trade for "three years, two years, one year, or three minutes." The ethos of a parliamentary body was lost on him. Like most laymen outside the Capitol, he saw the issue as a bipolar one—for reciprocal trade or against it, and against it meant voting down the whole bill. Malone was the sort of man—laudable in the public arena but indigestible in a negotiatory, decision-making body—whose decision rule on voting was simple. He voted for what he believed in and against what he opposed.

We have already noted how alien this was to the responsible parliamentary approach of protectionists and liberal traders alike. In acting on this bill, as on most, a Congressional consensus recognized that an existing system must continue to function. The goal of everyone was to modify it to his taste if possible, but, if not, at least to keep the issues open, all the while assuring the continuing functioning of the system and maintaining his own position to participate on good terms in the future decision process. If the reader finds this compromising attitude too sophisticated for his taste, let him conceive what would happen to a national defense system, for example, if decision-makers did not agree to keep it going as is while arguing about its character. Or let him conceive what would happen to foreign policy if Congress refused to appropriate money for presidential policies of which it disapproved.

In their actions, the majority of congressmen recognized that a parliament can be stable when the members seek as much as they can without risking larger dangers. It becomes unstable when strategies are selected by some absolute criterion of rightness. Malone shows this. He was opposed to reciprocal trade, so he opposed a two-year extension—and opened the way for the three-year extension.

Not secure in their rescue by Malone, for he could switch his vote, the liberals got on the telephone to New Orleans and added the vote of Russell Long, making it eight to seven against the two-year amendment.

But, while the liberals were repulsing that attack, the same afternoon the balance of power shifted sufficiently to pass an amendment—the one for publicizing Tariff Commission reports at once as a pressure on the president.

Within the next days, by votes of ten to one, the committee also adopted the amendment on GATT and the George amendment on the base date for computing cuts and eliminating the power to cut token tariffs. George and the committee had thrown their sop to the textile industry, which feared the outcome of the Japanese negotiations.

But the ten-to-one votes were more than met the eye. The administration was yielding. The senators who were backing the President's line would not have gone along without a green light from the White House. Indeed, Senator Barkley asserted that the State Department and the administration had agreed to the amendments.

The crucial break came on Sunday, April 24. Senator Byrd, chairman of the Finance Committee, has an estate at Berryville, Va., where he sometimes assembles key people to discuss important matters in an unpublicized way. The house guests that Sunday included, besides several senators (among others Millikin and Flanders), the then-strong man of the Eisenhower administration, George M. Humphrey, a few presidential aides, and some Randall Commission staff members.

The bill as it came out of that day's gathering at Senator Byrd's was a far cry from what the Randall Commission had produced or what the President had called for. The escape clause was rewritten. An amendment like the Neely one, providing for quotas on oil and other imports affecting national security, was accepted by Secretary Humphrey in principle, but agreement on mechanics failed. The secretary wished quotas to depend on elaborate Congressional action, their advocates wished easy presidential action. Although a final deal was therefore not reached, the administration's power to take a position of principle against changes was gone. The bill the administration agreed to was far more protectionist than that which had prevailed when it entered office.

On Monday, amid blasts of distress to the press by Senator Gore and other determined liberal traders, the committee sat down for the crucial votes. The liberals denounced the President for lack of leadership, for failure to bring pressure, for leaving them holding the bag. As *The New York Times* headline said, "Democrats call Eisenhower Lax in Tariff. Bill Struggle." Indeed, the administration could not deliver many Republican votes. In the previous week, White House staff members had approached the Democratic leadership agreeing to turn over both leadership and credit for success to the Democrats if they would put the bill through. The Democratic answer gave two alternatives: either give them the services of one leading Republican behind whom they could fall in, or give them a guaranteed twenty-five Republican votes. The executive branch could promise neither.

The President ended seeking to hold the line against extreme protectionist amendments by agreeing to some moderate ones. Ironically, that same day on which the Finance Committee sat down to accept at least part of the old Simpson bill and the former Reed amendment with administration blessings President Eisenhower was in New York delivering a speech to the annual meeting of the Associated Press in which he called on Congress in general terms not to cripple the trade bill.

At the Finance Committee meeting itself, discussion focused on the details of oil quotas. Votes were balanced so closely that a single vote could tip the issue for or against the Neely amendment. But at this point Senator Millikin turned his authority to the service of the administration. As the final twist in this complex story, he did in the Senate what Reed had once done in the House. As a Republican, as a man schooled in that moderation needed to make a parliament govern, he piloted through a bill which gave him as a protectionist only a few concessions and which would at the same time meet the demands of the administration. Loyal to the tradition of *do ut das,* he became the broker of an agreement for which the administration would have to be grateful to him. Having pushed the President to accept what could only be considered defeat, he did not demand his pound of flesh, but with the instinct of a skilled parliamentarian he sought just that fine line of compromise that would make it unclear who won.

It took another day, but on Tuesday, April 26, the Finance Committee adopted a substitute for the Neely amendment which did not mention oil but gave the president authority to fix quotas on imports if in his opinion they injured domestic industries vital to national security. (Under this provision, oil quotas have since been imposed.) This action, because it omitted all mention of specific commodities, was construed as an administration victory.

The negotiations on the escape clause paralleled the footwork on quotas. Millikin himself had introduced an amendment giving the president the right to overrule Tariff Commission recommendations on grounds either of national security or of national interest; if national interest were his grounds for overruling a recommendation, the whole thing would go to Congress for final action.

In the final revision, Millikin dropped all reference to the national security-national interest controversy. The escape clause was amended in entirely different ways. Under the old clause, one had to show that a whole industry was being injured. Under the new provision, relief could be considered for any one product which was suffering competition, even if the industry as a whole was thriving. The amendment also ordered the commission to find injury if imports were to any degree at all responsible for the damage.

The whole bill as thus amended was favorably voted, thirteen to two, by the Finance Committee the same day.

The three-day Senate floor debate which began on May 2 was an anticlimax. Millikin had forged an uncomfortable truce. Many senators —liberal traders, reluctant protectionists, and Republican protectionists— wanted to avoid a break in it which would result in a free-for-all of amendments on the floor. Only an extreme protectionist and one indifferent to the administration's political standing could welcome that with equanimity. Yet every roll call could threaten the truce, for senators have to think about how their constituents will interpret a roll-call vote, not only what their colleagues think.

By various devices, including numerous quorum calls, the leadership kept debate, votes, and changes to a minimum. All amendments were defeated except one by Senator Morse for the benefit of cherry-growers.

At a crucial point in the debate Sen. Carlson (R., Kan.), supposedly a close friend of the President but also a sponsor of the Neely amendment, rose to assure the protectionists that the administration would in fact use the new quota-fixing powers that had been incorporated into the bill: "I was assured by those in the Administration responsible for the administration of the trade-agreements program that, if such amendment were adopted by the Committee and by Congress, action would immediately follow, and that imports of petroleum and its products would be definitely restricted." In short, the administration was committed to a deal. On final vote, the bill was passed, seventy-five to thirteen.

The conference committee proceedings were languorous. Cooper and the others in the liberal House leadership had no stomach for the Senate bill, but, with no administration backing, they had no prospect of defeating it. The administration had destroyed its bargaining base by agreeing to the Senate amendments. Once thus committed, it could not appeal to the conference committee to scrap them. Indeed, no sooner had the Senate bill been passed than James Hagerty, presidential press secretary, described the bill as "satisfactory to the administration" because it "preserves the principle of Reciprocal Trade which the President has so ardently advocated for the past two years." The same line was followed in a letter from presidential aide Gerald Morgan to the chairmen of Ways and Means and Finance. He endorsed all the amendments except that by Sen. Wayne Morse (D., Ore.) in behalf of cherry-growers. The administration had become enmeshed in its net of compromises.

It was the Senate bill (minus the Morse amendment) which was finally passed on May 15 and sent to the White House.

Our narrative of what happened on Reciprocal Trade in 1953-1955 has been unduly focused on Congress. From many points of view much more important things were going on elsewhere. Before the Tariff Commission, for example, toy marbles, bicycles, tuna fish, wallpaper, machine tools, and watches all had their day in court.

The watch controversy is perhaps the most familiar. The only three American manufacturers of jewelled watches—Hamilton, Elgin, and Waltham—were being swamped by imports of Swiss movements, usually loaded into watch cases here. Thanks partly to a public-relations-minded union leader, these companies had been trying their case in full-page ads in the papers for many years. They had also been trying it before the Tariff Commission. The commission had recommended relief to President Truman, who had overruled the recommendation. But Eisenhower, on July 27, 1954, accepted the proposal for rate increases. This hardly ended the watch controversy, since Switzerland felt the impact immediately, while imports remained massive. In fact, the next controversies involved an antitrust suit against the Swiss manufacturers and a dispute about what rate should be charged when jewels are inserted into otherwise-assembled imported works in the United States.

Such details simply indicate how much the story has been simplified here. The issue of reciprocal trade was not a single one, but a nexus in which a myriad of special interests came together. Often, reciprocal trade meant nothing to the interests who fought over it except to provide a platform for their coalition.

In a broader sense, the bill was such a platform for an even broader alliance, including both protectionists and liberal traders. For all of them, it was an instrument for getting on with the business of government while working on the particular problems each had in mind.

Whose victory was the 1955 renewal act? Later events alone could determine whether the administration was justified in regarding the bill as "acceptable" to it, as White House Press Secretary Hagerty said, or whether Senator Douglas was correct in regarding the amended measures as one to be "spewed forth" by all "honest" believers in reciprocal trade. What the bill really meant would depend on administrative practices and court decision over the years.

□ Developments since 1955

Two extremely important events followed rather quickly after Congress adjourned. First, as a result of an escape-clause recommendation by the Tariff Commission, the President approved a considerable tariff hike (50 per cent over the previously prevailing duties) on bicycles imported into the United States.

At almost the same time, the Defense Department, on rather tenuous grounds, threw out a British bid which was considerably lower than any American bid for heavy generating equipment, and, to add apprehension to injury, stories were released that the Defense Department was considering ruling out all foreign bids on all its contracts.

Three years later, in 1958, reciprocal trade was renewed with few changes, little controversy, and slight further concessions to protection, most notably a provision whereby Congress by a two-thirds vote could force the president to accept an escape-clause recommendation of the Tariff Commission.

In 1962, when the bill came up for renewal again, the new Kennedy administration asked for substantially expanded power to cut tariffs and also decided to call it a new bill, not a renewal.

Shortly after the presidential elections of 1960, before the new administration took office, a series of task forces consisting of scholars and opinion leaders was organized. They drafted reports with policy ideas for the new administration. The task forces reporting to the President-elect were initiated and organized by a Washington lawyer, George Ball, assisted by a younger partner, John Sharon. One of the task-force reports dealt with foreign-trade policy. That report more than any other reflected the special interests of the organizers of the task-force program themselves. Ball had for years been a convinced and devoted advocate of trade liberalization. He and his colleagues, as we shall have occasion to note later, played a key role in the defeat of the Simpson bill in 1953 and in the formation of the Committee for a National Trade Policy. Ball had also represented the European Common Market in Washington as its attorney. Trade and Western integration were the subjects closest to his heart. A few months later, when the new administration had to draft a trade program to offer to the 1962 session of Congress, Ball was no longer a Washington lawyer; he was undersecretary of state and the man who was personally responsible for the conduct of the nation's foreign economic policy.

In the summer of 1961, a year before the act was to expire, Ball posed to the President a series of questions. Should there be a dramatic new bill? If so, who should take the lead? The State Department could not. The Commerce Department should not. As when Randall was appointed, it had to be a White House task if any significant bill was to be passed.

Howard Peterson was appointed presidential aide for the task. The bill he and his staff drafted by October was a modest one, with liberalized escape-clause and trade-adjustment provisions. A controversy immediately developed, with Ball contending that an ill-defined anxiety about the growing Common Market, the gold flow, and the world in general made the public ready for something new. The same old bill stood little chance.

Early in December, the President received two alternative memorandums. One from Ball proposed a big new bill, but said that it would take until 1963 (with a stop-gap 1962 extension) to get it. One from Peterson proposed a more conservative bill immediately. The President accepted Ball's bill with Peterson's timing.

The counsel's office in the State Department then went to work to draft the bill to be ready for Congress in January. In it could be seen the task-force report.

The heart of the new bill was a revived authority for the president to negotiate tariff reductions of 50 per cent of existing rates. That was the power the president was given in the Reciprocal Trade Act in 1934 and cumulatively once again in 1945. The 1955 extension had permitted a further 15 per-cent cut, and the 1958 extension a further 20 per-cent cut. The provision allowing a new large cut is limited, however, in that it must be made in stages over at least five years.

A most significant change in the new proposals was that reciprocal tariff reductions could be negotiated multilaterally by broad categories of goods. Past negotiations have been item-by-item. This change is important to enable the United States to bargain with the European Economic Community, whose common market arrangements are stated in broad categories indeed. Broadened categories would also free the State Department of some of the pressures from particular interests when negotiations concern their particular item. Maraschino cherry packers, for example, are less likely to have crucial weight in a negotiation about packaged foods than they are in a negotiation about cherries.

The new proposals also permitted negotiations for total elimination of tariffs in some circumstances. The Reciprocal Trade Act had explicitly prohibited the transfer of items to the free list. The Trade Expansion Act permits it for tropical products not produced in the United States, agricultural products which are exported rather than imported, products whose duty rate is under 5 per cent, and, most important of all, products largely produced in Western Europe and the United States.

More precisely, this provision authorizes the president to negotiate the reduction of tariffs to zero on groups of products where the United States and the Common Market countries jointly supply 80 per cent or more of the world's trade, not including trade within the Soviet bloc. That provision could turn out to be the first of a series of steps toward the integration into a single vast free-trade area of the economies of the Western world.

At the time the bill was passed, it was impossible to know how the 80 per-cent provision would function, for it was not known whether Great Britain and perhaps other members of the Outer Seven would end up in the EEC. Without Great Britain's inclusion, there would be few commodities which met the criterion; with England in, there would be many. The Senate tried to eliminate that uncertainty by adding the free-trade area of the Seven to the Common Market of the Six for calculating the base 80 per-cent figure, but the conference committee refused. Thus, the bill as passed left it as a possibility, but only a possibility, that a major part of the trade between the United States and Europe would be altogether freed from the burden of tariffs.

The Kennedy plan would do this through the complicated 80 per-cent formula, rather than by an overt regional arrangement, to avoid having to amend the most-favored-nation clause, which has been part of the Reciprocal Trade acts from the beginning and excludes the granting of special tariff rates to particular nations. A reduced rate granted by the United States to one country is automatically extended to all, with certain qualifications for Soviet bloc countries. The 80 per-cent provision was designed to permit a different tariff policy to prevail on trade that is largely within the West and that where a major producer is another country, such as Japan.

The 1962 plan also dropped the peril-point provision, but kept the escape clause substantially as before.

Finally, the 1962 proposals adopted the scheme of the rejected McDonald proposals to the Randall Commission and of the Kennedy-Eberharter bill to help industries and workers injured by foreign competition by subsidies other than tariffs. Injured industries could receive government loans or government guarantees of private loans to facilitate their conversion to new fields of enterprise. Workers could receive allowances while being retrained or relocated.

These significant changes in American trade policy certainly justified the decision of the administration to drop the name Reciprocal Trade Act and to give the bill a new name, the Trade Expansion Act. Yet the change in label was clearly not required by the changes in the law. It could equally well have been described as a renewal of the basic act, had that description been strategically expedient. The compelling reasons for change were political, not legislative. They concerned the image the administration wished to project, the tactics of getting the bill passed—avoiding entrapment in outworn identifications and shibboleths—and the consequences of passage for further steps in American foreign policy.

The change of name could help promote the imagery of the New Frontier. A bill which President Kennedy agreed to make the top-priority item on his legislative agenda could hardly be a retread of an old scheme that the previous Republican administration had also labeled as its pet project. And the bill was not a retread. Hidden in its moderate changes in presidential authority was actually a start in a process the terminus of which may well be the uniting of the economies of America and Europe. The great decision that the United States faced in 1962 was not whether to have higher or lower tariffs. It was whether to react to the competition of the Common Market by isolation and protection of the American market or on the contrary by insisting on full U.S. participation in the unified economy of Europe. If the latter, the country would have to pay for it with acceptance of European competition at home.

Europe, in 1962, was a new entity whose shape was still unformed. The Common Market of the Six was already an outstanding success. Its industry was increasingly competing with America's. The disappearance of tariffs within it while retaining a tariff wall around it could turn it into another major internal market, excellent for the economy of those who belonged but disconcerting to those on the outside. The outsiders included Great Britain, Russia, and the United States. They reacted in three different ways. Great Britain decided that its prosperity required that it be inside the new trading area, and it applied to join. Russia issued blasts against discriminatory regional trading blocs and proposed a vague world-wide nondiscriminatory trade arrangement. The United States, under other circumstances, might well have taken the same position as did Russia. Seeing in the Common Market a threat to itself, it might have attacked it in principle. But the United States had been a prime supporter of European integration and the Common Market. For fifteen years the cornerstone of American policy had been to build a strong, united Europe. Political interests which could only be served by a thriving European economy overrode parochial considerations of competition. The Common Market had to be sustained, while somehow America's interests were protected from its effectiveness.

The British option was not yet open to America. An Atlantic Common Market was not yet economically feasible and certainly not politically acceptable on either side of the ocean. The Kennedy program was a brilliant compromise, offering bargaining concessions to keep the external wall of the Common Market as low as possible and to provide the market with additional incentive to broaden itself by admitting Great Britain and other powers. That strategy looked to the increasing mingling of the American and European economies to prevent the hardening of the Common Market into an opposed force. If this is to be the line of American policy, then the bargaining powers of the president will be only the first of a series of economic measures, each of which will raise the issues of isolationism versus internationalism, protection versus world trade. If there is more to come, then setting the ideological direction of the nation toward trade expansion by getting Congressional approval of a brave new course is a better strategy than palming it off as just another renewal. In spirit and purpose, the act President Kennedy presented did, indeed, represent the most significant turn in American trade policy in thirty years.

Though the goals were bold, the tactics adopted were cautious. They might also be described as brilliant. In later chapters, we will have occasion to note the differences between the political tactics adopted by the Kennedy and Eisenhower administrations in getting their bills through. The Kennedy lieutenants had the experience of the 1950's to learn from, and they made few of the same mistakes.

For example, they brought their bill in on time. On January 25, the President sent Congress his special message proposing the new legislation. The administration could not avoid the fact that once again the Trade Act expired in an election year, but, in the tempo of the New Frontier, even in an election year Congress was kept in session through the summer. But, even under the New Frontier, Congress moves in its deliberate way. The House Ways and Means Committee, under the chairmanship of Wilbur Mills (D., Ark.), the bill's sponsor, began hearings on March 12 and did not report the bill out until the middle of June. It passed the House at the end of June under a closed rule by 298 to 125. The key vote rejected recommittal, 253 to 171.

It then went to the Senate, which took until September 19 to pass it, 78 to 8. As in earlier years, it had to await the completion of tax legislation. The test vote in the Senate was on restoring the peril point, an amendment which failed, 40 to 38, with no Republicans on the administration side.

The administration strategists understood this time what the protectionists have always understood, that defense against an imminent danger gets more public and Congressional reaction than do broad principles of good policy. The trade bill in 1962 was often presented as a defense maneuver against the threat of the European Common Market. A man from Mars reading some of the statements supporting the bill would have found it hard to believe that their authors favored the EEC, rather than viewing it as a threat. A repeated theme was that, if we fail to associate ourselves with the European union, "we will be on the outside looking in." The outflow of gold was another fear cited as a reason for the bill, as was the tendency of American firms to establish plants in Europe so as to be inside the Common Market, thereby reducing their use of American labor.

The administration's strategy consisted of satisfying in advance the demands of enough injured industries to neutralize them or even give them a stake in the passage of the bill. The outstanding instance was textiles. From the start, the administration argued, as the textile industry had for years, that textiles were a special case. First, the government brought pressure to bear on Japanese and Hong Kong manufacturers to restrict their textile exports to the United States. Then, in February, 1962, a nineteen-nation international textile agreement was concluded in Geneva under GATT, permitting the United States to impose special limits on imports of cotton goods. In April, a special bill was put to Congress to empower the president to bar cotton-textile imports from any country not party to the agreement. In May, the woolen industry was promised similar solicitude by the administration. In March, President Kennedy also approved tariff increases on Belgian carpets and sheet glass under an escape-clause action. The bill itself prohibits the president from negotiating tariff cuts on any product on which escape-clause or national-security action has been taken in recent years, indeed on any product on which the Tariff Commission has made a finding of injury. A few textile products, lead, zinc, and oil are the important products thus specially protected.

The administration's bargains with special interests were handled by White House political aides, especially Meyer Feldman. His strategy of special concessions alarmed devoted liberal traders, not only in the CNTP and Congress, but also in the Department of State and White House foreign-trade staff. A couple of times a week, letters and calls from the men who framed the bill pleaded with Feldman not to sell out their principles. But his strategy was subtle. It was to preserve the bill intact by concessions outside it. The bill as passed was virtually intact. The concessions that were made and the obligations that were incurred concerned administrative action or special bills. The theory seems to have been that history will not ask what price was paid in current concessions if the charter itself is grand. And, in the end, that may prove true.

In the short run, however, as in the cases when Eisenhower had yielded on particular commodities, such as watches, to save the chances for his big bill, one result was anger in Europe and doubts about the real direction of American policy. Clearly, a proliferation of exceptions can make a farce of the principle.

There are those, furthermore, who argue that the strategy of concessions did not work. They can point to the fact that on key votes, such as that on the Bush amendment, which but for a two-vote margin would have restored the peril point, those congressmen who can be labeled, for example, as textile congressmen, gave little support to the administration. But that may be misleading. It takes only a few pivotal people to make the difference between success and failure. At least a few textile senators did switch their votes to beat that amendment. Sen. Robert S. Kerr (D.) from the oil state of Oklahoma guided the bill through the Senate.

A combination of a general decline in protectionist ideology, a widespread malaise about the prospects of American export trade in the face of the Common Market and the administration's calculated and massive individualized approach to such industries as chemicals and textiles did cut the protectionist coalition to shreds. It would have been a rash man in the fall of 1961 who, after the experiences of the 1950's, would have predicted that a drastic liberalization of trade could get through the House of Representatives. Yet, in the end, the opposition there never got organized, and what opposition there was focused on the readjustment provisions. Those interests from which congressmen expect to hear asking for protection were simply not being heard. The crowning event was the textile industry's reversal. On March 31, the American Cotton Manufacturers Institute, representing 80 per cent of the country's textile-manufacturing industry, adopted a resolution. "We believe," it said, "that the authority to deal with foreign nations proposed by the President will be wisely exercised and should be granted."

It remains to be seen how far the mortgages the administration incurred to get its bill passed will burden its movement toward freer trade in the future. In 1962, as in 1955, no one could know from the text of the bill what the nation's trade policy is or will be. A trade bill is a set of rules of the game. Each interest wants the rules so defined as to ensure that its desires will not be slighted. The administration has its goals and interests, too. It is the job of Congress to adopt rules under which each party seeks its goals. Sometimes the rules lean one way, sometimes another. But the one thing that in a democracy the parliament must not do is to settle controversial issues. While the reader is reading these lines, the reformulation of American trade policy is undoubtedly continuing.

Chapter 6

Public Attitudes on Foreign Trade

The detailed and technical aspects of the legislation the passage of which through Congress we have just followed never entered the consciousness of the general public. In the public mind, there was at most awareness only of a general issue of "high" versus "low" tariffs. Yet public opinion had to be considered by both Congress and the business community. Moreover, public opinion offers a base line against which to assess the attitudes of business leaders. There is now a considerable collection of opinion-poll data which gives a basis for understanding the man-in-the-street attitudes toward the issue.

□ What Was Public Opinion?

Trend of Opinion

In American history, the tariff was for many decades one of the most important of national political issues. At times it was *the* issue. Unfortunately, however, we cannot know much about the opinions of the general public or even whether the public was much interested in or aware of this hottest of political issues.

It has become a cliché to lament the absence of public opinion polls (their limitations notwithstanding) over the centuries of history. This lamentation is based on the assumption that there may be only a loose fit between official policy and public opinion. Poll data, available since approximately 1937, give substance to this assumption. There is evidence of a general shift of opinion in the direction of a more liberal trade policy, a trend that parallels national policy on this issue. But the trend lagged behind policy. There is every evidence that opinions on this subject have not been well crystallized or firmly held and that a large proportion of the public has been neither informed on nor interested in the topic. The shift toward liberalism was accompanied by a slight increase in interest and involvement, but the opinions of the general public on this issue are still far from being a vital force imposing itself on policy-makers.

Assessment of changes in public attitudes on foreign-trade policy is complicated by the fact that, in the considerable body of polling data available, the questions put to the public have varied sufficiently from time to time to make the comparability of many findings subject to considerable reservation. The problem is especially difficult because, on a topic on which opinions are so poorly crystallized, a slight change in question wording can produce a considerable shift in the proportion of persons supporting one or another position. Despite the obvious caution with which one must proceed, certain broad trends seem nonetheless firmly established. It is only since 1945 that a question on general attitudes toward tariff policy has been asked of the public over a period of years in approximately the same form. In September, 1945, the American Institute of Public Opinion asked a cross-section of American adults: "Are you in favor of high tariffs or low tariffs for this country?" Of the people asked, 37 per cent favored high tariffs, 33 per cent low tariffs, and 30 per cent had no opinion. These data may be interpreted as reflecting a predominantly protectionist sentiment. In 1953 and 1954, this question was asked in the spring and fall of each year.[1] In this period in every instance, the proportion of persons who would favor lowering tariffs was about twice that which would favor raising them. A poll taken in the late summer of 1954 is typical for this period. Of "informed voters" (that 46 per cent of the adult population which had heard about the tariff controversy) 27 per cent would favor higher tariffs, 49 per cent would favor lower tariffs, 16 per cent would keep them the same, and 8 per cent had no opinion. One taken at the very end of 1954 gave the following results: 25 per cent favored higher tariffs, 42 per cent

---

[1] The wording was slightly changed: "By and large, do you favor higher or lower tariffs than we have at present?" Respondents were offered the additional choice of saying "The same."

favored lowering them, 22 per cent would keep them the same, and 10 per cent had no opinion. This might be interpreted as a very slight regression toward protectionism, but such an interpretation would be risky in view of the allowances one must make for sampling errors. By January, 1962, the picture was still much the same. According to the Gallup poll, 40 per cent favored lower tariffs, 31 per cent higher, 14 per cent no change, and 15 per cent had no opinion. By April, a sharp increase in indecision cut into the protectionist sentiment, with 38 per cent saying "lower," 15 per cent saying "higher," 18 per cent "no change," and 29 per cent had no opinion. Such a rapid shift from a committed position to indecision is often the first clue that a major change is taking place, but, as of the 1962 debate, public opinion had remained fairly stable over a decade or more. There was a clue in the shift of the balance of mail in the final weeks of action by the Senate that, as a result of the whole debate, a change in sentiment in a liberal direction may have then been in the making. Granting all the reservations which will be introduced below, there seems little doubt on the basis of these figures that, over the decade 1945-1955, there had been a shift in popular opinion away from protectionism. The generally nonprotectionist position prevailed into 1962. Evidence for a similar shift in businessmen's attitudes is discussed in a subsequent chapter.

Level of Interest

In addition to knowing the general direction of public sentiment on foreign-trade policy, we are concerned with whether this topic was one in which the public was much interested. The level of public interest and information remained generally low throughout the period for which we have poll data. Over a period of a decade, from 25 to 50 per cent of national cross-sectional samples polled by various agencies were unable to give an accurate definition of a tariff. The proportion of "uninformed" persons varies mainly according to the strictness of the criteria invoked as to what was an "acceptable" or "correct" definition of a tariff.

In 1946, the National Opinion Research Center polled a national cross-sample on several questions relating to foreign trade. The NORC comments: "The majority of the public report little or no interest in the subject of foreign trade":

> Q. Do you yourself take a good deal of interest, only a little, or no interest at all in the subject of our trade with other countries?

	Per cent of total sample
Good deal of interest	39
Only a little	34
None at all	21
Don't know	6
	100

The report continued with the following data:

Compared with other issues presented to the public at the same time, foreign trade ranks a poor last in terms of interest:

	Per cent of total sample reporting good deal of interest
Shortages of food	73
Our relations with Russia	64
Control of inflation	51
Atomic bomb	55
Trade with other countries	39

In a survey conducted in 1947 by the Survey Research Center, the tariff question was second in percentage of "don't-know" responses, out of a series of nine foreign-policy issues, being exceeded only by international control of atomic weapons.

With regard to the salience of this issue, an additional point to be made is that, on a series of polls from 1946 to 1954, the public gave a very low rating to all problems in foreign affairs when asked to rate their importance relative to other issues. The New York League of Women Voters surveyed the New York metropolitan area in 1954 and asked a cross-sectional sample which of eight subjects noted on a card they had talked about in the preceding few weeks. The three they rated as most discussed were high prices, crime and juvenile delinquency, and high taxes. The possibility of another depression was in fourth place, and danger of World War III in fifth. The atomic bomb, economic aid to other countries, and the United Nations tied for the last three places.

There is fairly good evidence of a perceptible increase in public information about and interest in trade policy in the years 1953-1955. In the fall of 1953, only 32 per cent of a national sample had heard of the tariff controversy. By the spring of 1954, this proportion had reached 45 per cent, and, by the end of 1954, a majority of adults, 52 per cent, had heard of the issue. At best, however, this is not a high degree of public involvement in an issue which was receiving constant and thorough coverage in the press and on radio and television. Attention to the issue of trade fell off after the 1955 peak of 52 per cent informed, not to reach the same level again until 1962. The same figure appears in a January, 1962, Gallup poll, but by April only 46 per cent claimed to have heard of the Kennedy plan. We have already noted that the strategy of administration supporters in 1955 was one of propaganda and public education in behalf of the general interest, whereas in 1962 it was one of quiet approaches to special interests, deals offered to split the opposition, and work with businessmen rather than the general public. Thus, in 1962 a rather more drastic reform got, if anything, rather less public attention.

So, having said that there was a trend away from protectionism in the post-World War II period, we hasten to qualify the practical importance of this trend by pointing to the relative lack of interest in foreign policy and in foreign trade in particular.

Stability of Opinion

An additional dimension of public opinion—other than direction of sentiment and degree of interest—is the degree of stability of those opinions. One of the surest signs of instability is the degree to which apparent expressions of opinion vary according to the way the issue is posed. Judged by this criterion, attitudes toward foreign trade are very unstable.

It is possible, by posing the issue in various ways, to get from the same type of sample and occasionally from the very same sample answers that might seem to point in opposite directions.

From 1937 until the 1962 change of name made it a dead issue, national cross-sectional polls (with a single questionable exception in 1940) have consistently indicated support for continuation of the Reciprocal Trade Act when this act was mentioned by name and when the questioning was restricted to voters who knew what it was. The proportion of persons who supported the act was ordinarily two, three, or more times the proportion which opposed it. In May, 1945, the American Institute of Public Opinion reported that it had asked a cross-sectional sample of Americans: "Should the trade agreements program be continued or not?" Only 7 per cent said "no," 18 per cent were undecided, and 75 per cent said "yes." Yet, throughout this period, several national polls indicated a predominance of protectionist sentiment when the public was asked the rather general question of "raising" or "lowering" tariffs. On the same AIPO poll mentioned above, the same sample which had indicated such strong support for the trade-agreements program was asked: "Is it a good or bad thing to reduce tariffs further in the United States and other countries under the trade agreements program?" Only 57 per cent thought it was "a good thing," 20 per cent thought it was "bad," and 23 per cent had no opinion. This would seem to indicate less support for the trade-agreements program than was exhibited in response to the previous question, but still a majority support for lower tariffs. This was the same year in which another national sample polled by the American Institute of Public Opinion found slightly more people favoring high tariffs than favored low tariffs.

Replies in polls on an issue with as low a saliency as foreign trade represent, not considered judgments of the problems actually at hand, but rather projections of highly general underlying attitudes which the poller taps by his superficially precise question.

One underlying attitude that seems to affect responses to questions on foreign-trade policy is "conservatism," a disposition to accept any existing state of affairs. Thus, continuance of trade-agreements programs designed to lower tariffs would be approved, but lowering of tariffs might be opposed as a change in whatever is. A 1939 *Fortune* poll of businessmen produced the same tendency to favor or oppose a liberal trade policy depending on whether it was presented as current practice or something new.

Another underlying attitude that has been shown to have considerable influence on the public's response to questions on foreign-trade policy is approval of the notion of reciprocity. On a number of polls, including our own poll of business leaders, many proponents of lower tariffs indicated that they would not advocate this policy if tariffs were not lowered reciprocally by other countries. The notion of reciprocity also has the power to shift people away from a protectionist stand. When the National Opinion Research Center asked in 1946 whether reducing tariffs was a good or bad thing, only 35 per cent said initially that it was good, 35 per cent said bad, and 30 per cent had no opinion. But when those who said that it was a bad idea or had no opinion were asked if the United States should reduce tariffs "providing other countries reduce their tariffs on goods we want to sell them," an additional 38 per cent thought that tariff reductions would be good under such circumstances.

Since 1953, the Gallup poll has never failed to find more people favoring lower tariffs. But in that same year, 1953, a Roper poll asked: "Would you rather see this country import *more* goods from foreign countries than we do now, or put *more restrictions* on goods imported into this country from abroad?" More people favored increasing restrictions than favored an increase in imports (37 and 26 per cent, respectively; the others were undecided or favored leaving things as they were).

In 1946, a year in which Gallup and Roper polls tended to find the public quite evenly divided, the Survey Research Center asked:

> Some people think we should keep our tariffs high in order to keep out foreign goods, *even if this means we will sell less to other countries.*[2] How do you feel about that?

The inclusion of the italicized contingency apparently swung the sample to the support of a low tariff policy. Two and one-half times as many persons favored low tariffs as favored high tariffs.

What Was Opinion?—Summary

In summary, such divergences in poll data should not be regarded as a criticism of the polls themselves but only as a warning to exercise

---

[2] Italics supplied.

extreme caution in interpreting the poll results. Foreign trade is a complicated issue on which the public's attitudes are unstable by reason of
its complexity and of their lack of information and interest in it. The
economically sophisticated reader will inject the further caveat that foreign-
trade policy can no longer be posed realistically as exclusively a tariff issue.
The question of raising or lowering tariffs or any other such simplistic
posing of the issue could do no more than tap on a symbolic level very
generalized attitudes toward foreign-trade policy. But the simplistic formulation of the issue is correct for a poll. Because of the complexity of the
issue and the lack of information on the part of even generally well-
informed persons, it does not seem possible that, with the general public,
the issue could be fruitfully explored in any more detailed fashion.

□ Who Holds Which Opinions?

Educational Level

The most important pattern to be noted in the distribution of
public attitudes toward foreign-trade policy is that they are closely related
to level of education. The more education a person has had, the less likely
he is to be protectionist and the more likely is he to be informed about
and interested in the tariff question. Fig. 6-1, from an AIPO poll of June,
1953, shows a typical relationship between level of education and opinion
on raising or lowering tariffs. In addition to large differences in the proportions of persons having no opinion, the college-educated group favored
low tariffs over high tariffs by a ratio of 4 to 1, whereas the grade school
group favored it by a ratio of only 2 to 1.

The Roper poll of 1953 [3] referred to above permits us to look
further into the relationships of attitudes toward foreign-trade policy with
level of education and other personal characteristics. From this poll it was
possible to develop a typology which identified persons of varying consistency and firmness of attitudes in five groups: (1) ultraliberal traders—
persons who gave antiprotectionist answers to two different questions, one
on imports in general, the other on oil imports,[4] and who held their posi-

---

[3] This poll was conducted for the Standard Oil Company of New Jersey by Elmo Roper.
We wish to acknowledge our gratitude to them for making the full data available to
us for additional analysis. Although we were able to borrow freely from the original
analysis, neither Standard Oil of New Jersey nor the Elmo Roper organization should be
regarded as responsible for any of the interpretations we make.

[4] The general question read: "Taking everything into consideration, would you rather
see this country import more *goods* from foreign countries than we do now, or put *more
restrictions* on goods imported into this country from abroad?" The question relating to
oil imports read: "Taking everything into consideration, would you be for or against
putting more restrictions on the oil being brought into this country from abroad (restrictions like limiting the amount of oil coming in or putting a high tariff on it)?" Four
thousand adults were interviewed.

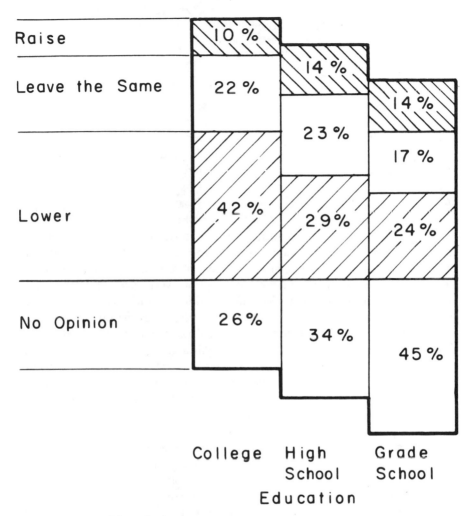

Fig. 6-1 TARIFF ATTITUDE BY EDUCATION

tion without change when presented with a series of contingencies; (2) consistent liberal traders—persons who gave consistent antiprotectionist answers but were swayed by arguments against their position; (3) switchers —persons who gave inconsistent responses; (4) consistent protectionists; and (5) ultraprotectionists.

The general question on attitudes toward imports elicited somewhat more protectionist responses, as noted above, than did most polls conducted in that year. The question pertaining to oil imports produced the following answers, generally nonprotectionist on this specific issue:

	Per cent
For restrictions	29
Against restrictions	35
Depends (various)	6
Other	3
Don't know	27

If we confine our attention to those who had opinions on these questions and who took a definite stand for or against import restrictions, we find that 70 per cent of them gave consistent answers, that is, they were either protectionist or antiprotectionist on both questions. Lack of consistency does not indicate lack of logic. There may be good reasons for favoring imports under some conditions and opposing them under others. We are enabled by this device, however, to locate persons whose opinions lie rather consistently in one direction or another.

In addition to these two questions, a series of contingencies were introduced which gave additional tests to the stability of the attitudes of these respondents. Those persons who gave a committed liberal-trade or protectionist answer on the oil import question were asked if they would retain their position under a series of conditions which would challenge their views. For example, a person who opposed restrictions on oil imports would be asked: "Suppose having no more restrictions on this imported oil means some companies in the United States might be forced out of business. Would you still be against the restrictions or in favor of them?" There were three such contingencies presented as a challenge to whichever position the respondent took on the question of oil imports.

We used these data to develop the category of "ultraliberal" traders and "ultraprotectionists," namely, persons who not only gave consistent answers on the two major questions but also held their positions despite the consequences which might result from their positions.[5]

On the general question as to whether one favored an increase in imports, those persons having grade school education and offering an opinion on the issue favored restrictions on imports twice as often as they favored increasing imports (44 to 23 per cent). Among persons with a college education, the relationship is reversed, and almost twice as many would increase imports as would restrict them (47 to 28 per cent).

The relationship of level of education to foreign-trade attitudes is increasingly striking with those persons who showed stable attitudes on the issue. Among the grade school group, consistent protectionists out-

---

[5] One contingency (whether one would continue to favor restrictions on oil imports even though through this policy our armed forces might be short of oil in case of war) proved so powerful that virtually every protectionist (83 per cent) reversed his position when confronted with this possibility. For this reason, it was not employed in setting up the typology.

number consistent liberal traders by more than 2 to 1, whereas in the college-educated group, consistent free traders dominate by a margin of over 3 to 1. If we turn to the ultraprotectionists and the ultrafree traders, those persons who not only give consistent answers on the two trade questions but also held to their positions despite contingencies which were introduced, we find the relationship to be even stronger. (See Fig. 6-2.) The more stable the protectionist opinion, the more likely it is to be held by a person of grade school education. The more stable the antiprotectionist opinion, the more likely its holder is to have a college education.

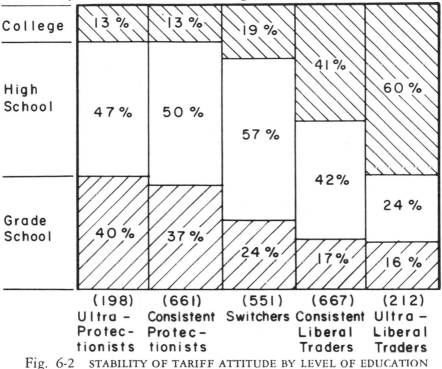

Fig. 6-2   STABILITY OF TARIFF ATTITUDE BY LEVEL OF EDUCATION

Economic Level

Attitudes toward import policy show a relationship to the economic level of respondents similar to that which they show to the level of education. This is not surprising, since these two factors are so closely related to each other. However, it is important to note that the relationship between education and attitudes toward import policy is considerably stronger than that between economic level and attitudes. Fig. 6-3 presents the proportion of protectionists (of those who had an opinion) among persons of various economic and educational levels. It is obvious that education is by

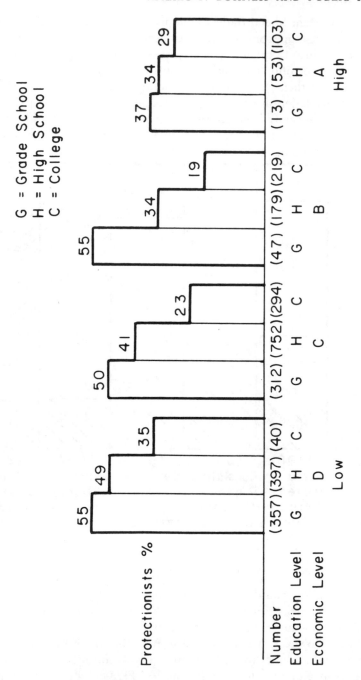

Fig. 6-3 PROPORTION OF PROTECTIONISTS AMONG PERSONS
OF VARIOUS ECONOMIC AND EDUCATIONAL LEVELS

far the more important determinant. Except for a very small group of grade school individuals in the highest economic bracket, half of all persons of that educational level, regardless of economic class, favored protectionism when they had an opinion. Among the college-educated group, however, the proportion was less than 1 in 3, except for the small group in the lowest economic category.

Party Affiliation

Historically, the tariff was one of the major issues separating the Republican and Democratic parties. Early poll data showed that adherents of the two parties were in fact quite different in their attitudes toward the tariff, the Republicans being substantially more protectionist. This was revealed as early as 1932 in a questionnaire survey conducted by the League of Women Voters and presented by S.P. Hayes, Jr.[6]

In recent years, poll data have shown that this difference has been dwindling, at least insofar as the rank-and-file voters attached to the two parties were concerned. Gallup polls in the years before 1955 showed consistently that differences between the adherents of the two major parties on foreign trade had virtually disappeared. On the Roper poll, there were no major differences between people who acknowledged a party affiliation (or for that matter between them and the self-styled independents) on the general import policy question. On the question of oil imports, Republicans turned out to be appreciably less protectionist than were Democrats.

The really striking differences between Democrats and Republicans emerge in the distributions of "stable," or "ultra," answers. Quite contrary to what we would expect on the basis of the historical stand of the two parties, we find in Fig. 6-4 that the ultrafree traders are strongly Republican. The ultraprotectionists are most often Democrats.[7]

This amazing historical reversal of party stands is attributable to the educational and income differences between the people affiliated with the two parties. The hard core of protectionism has come to be among the poor, the less educated, and the industrial workers who see a threat to their jobs. They are generally Democrats. The hard core of a liberal policy has come to be among the college-educated business and professional people, who are mostly Republicans. On the same educational level, however, Democrats and Republicans are about equally likely to fall into either of the "ultra" categories. On tariffs, there is no genuine party difference left

---

[6] "The Inter-relations of Political Attitudes: 1, Attitudes Toward Candidates and Specific Policies," *Journal of Social Psychology*, 8 (1937), 459-482.

[7] On other polls, Democrats may still sometimes show up as somewhat less protectionist than Republicans, depending on question-wording. But one must keep in mind the difference between amorphous opinions and the hard cores.

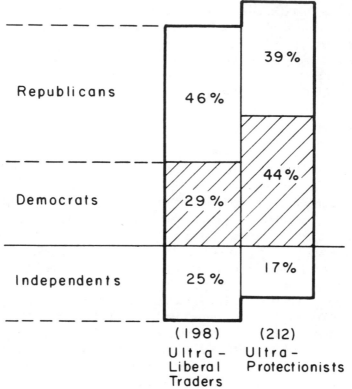

Fig. 6-4   TARIFF ATTITUDE BY PARTY

among the voters, only a difference derivative from social differences. The fact remains, however, that Republicans are better educated. As a result, the hard core of supporters of each side of the foreign-trade issue is to be found in the party opposite to that with which the particular policy has historically been associated.

Political Activity

Some people are more likely than others to do something about their beliefs. They vote more often, take part in public discussions, write their congressman, contribute money to political campaigns, and so on. The Roper organization often includes in its polls a series of questions which enables one to identify those persons who are most or least politically active.[8] The data from the 1953 Roper poll showed a strong rela-

---

[8] The Roper political-activity index is built from responses to seven questions which are concerned with: (1) membership in public-interest organizations, such as school,

tionship between political activity and attitudes toward oil imports and imports in general; the more politically active a person, the less was his concern with protection. Of those who were most active politically, 63 per cent were opposed to additional restrictions on trade, whereas this was true of only 24 per cent of those who were least active. Again, the strength of these relationships was more marked among the groups which held extreme positions on foreign-trade policy. Among the persons who were most active politically, the proportion of ultraliberal traders to ultraprotectionists was 17 to 1.

We have dealt with four personal characteristics of citizens which were strongly correlated with attitudes toward foreign-trade policy—level of education, economic level, party affiliation, and political activity. There are other relationships of potential importance. On the whole, women are less interested and informed than men, but those women who are interested and informed hold about the same opinions as men of comparable status. Younger people are generally less protectionist than comparable older people. If the latter relationship represents a genuine generational change, then there may be a long-run trend away from protectionism. It remains to be seen, however, how far the age difference is a life-cycle phenomenon rather than a trend. It could represent a contrast of "idealism," associated with both youth and a liberal-trade stand, as opposed to "realism," associated with both greater maturity and protectionism.

Naturally, support for or opposition to protectionism is especially strong among persons associated with industries threatened by foreign competition on one hand and those directly dependent on imports on the other. Such relationships would, of course, cut across the ones which we have outlined above. In general, poll data do not permit us to identify such groups with appreciable precision. On the Roper poll, the strongest protectionist sentiment was found among factory workers, where it would be expected on the basis of the traditional problem of competition with low-paid foreign labor. The fact that factory workers were more protectionist than farmers suggests that something more than mere differences of education were at work. However, only a detailed analysis of the particular industries—impossible on the ordinary national poll—would enable us to

---

housing, etc.; (2) frequency and extent of participation in conversations on political or economic issues, such as labor unions, taxes, etc.; (3) whether respondent has written to his senator or congressman, and how often; (4) whether respondent has contributed money to political parties or candidates; and (5) how often respondent has voted in the past four years. The responses to these questions are then assigned a weight; e.g., "voted five or more times" is given four points, whereas "voted once or twice" is given one point; "belong to two or more organizations" is given three points, and "belong to one" is given only one point. It is then possible for a respondent to get an activity index score of from zero to twelve points.

identify the special effect of foreign competition on the attitudes of these working men and women.

Speaking of the population as a whole, we can say that the strongest support for protectionism comes from those people who are older than average, have less than a high school education, are factory workers, vote Democratic, and are relatively low in political activity. The strongest opponents of protectionism are young, college trained, wealthy, Republican, and politically active. All these statements apply most correctly to the "ultras," those persons who have the firmest commitment to one or the other polar position on this issue. They are generally, although less strongly, true of persons with less firm convictions.

It follows from such facts that there should have been more effective support in the general public for the liberal-trade position than for the protectionist one. The supporters of a liberal-trade position were politically active, well off, and well educated. They were therefore persons whose opinions as individuals might be presumed to carry weight. Insofar as public opinion was a factor, the cards seemed stacked in favor of reciprocal trade. Protectionism had become a minority view held mostly by poorly educated, uninfluential, and politically inactive adherents of the opposition party. Backed by such a public opinion, the Eisenhower administration should have had an easy time with its proposals in Congress. We know already that that was not so. The answer must lie outside public opinion.

Whose Opinion?—Summary

When the over-all level of public interest and involvement is low, an increase in public interest may change essential aspects of the over-all public-opinion picture without there being any switching between sides. The mere fact of a spread in the base of informed citizens can change the results of national cross-sectional polls. The more people in the population who are aware of and interested in a question, the greater will be the proportion of informed persons found in the lower-level educational groups. By virtue of their values, perspectives, and possibly their personal interest, they are disposed toward protectionism. Thus, continued discussion of the foreign-trade issue may result in an apparent popular swing toward protectionism, whereas it would be more accurate to say that a higher proportion of persons predisposed toward protectionism had become interested and involved in foreign-trade policy.

Indeed, that is what probably happened between 1954 and 1955. In general, protectionism seemed stronger in 1955 than in 1954. Despite the liberal and Democratic swing at the polls and despite the resulting transfer of Congressional leadership from rock-ribbed protectionists to convinced liberal traders, reciprocal trade legislation, according to all observers, faced stronger opposition both in the country and in Congress in 1955 than in 1954. The explanation seems in part at least to be in the rising prominence of the issue.

The public may be thought of as an iceberg. Visible at the top are the active, the alert, the influential few who are always in the open air of political activity. Invisible below water are the generally apathetic many who appear only on rare occasions, such as in election campaigns, when strong tides of politics expose them. On some issues, and trade is one, distributions of attitudes at the top and bottom of the iceberg differ. The appearance of public opinion changes when something raises the iceberg higher out of the water.

The Congressional battle of 1954 and the resulting one-year renewal did at least one thing: they alerted the public. We noted earlier that the proportion of the public which had heard of the reciprocal-trade issue rose from 32 per cent in late 1953 to 45 per cent by spring 1954 and to 52 per cent by the end of 1954. It took a two-year battle to activate opinion that was already there. Probably few persons were converted; it takes longer than that to convert. But the seeds for later conversion may have been sown then, to be reaped in 1958 and 1962. The campaigns launched by both sides made trade less of an "elite" issue. It became an item of concern for more of the public in 1955 than in 1954.

That fact suggests a dilemma. Did groups like the League of Women Voters and the Committee for a National Trade Policy which campaigned to arouse the public in support of liberal trade actually harm their own side in the short run? In part, undoubtedly so. Their own propaganda was largely responsible for bringing discussions of foreign trade into the press and mass media. They certainly exposed more of the iceberg as their efforts progressed. Their net effect in the short run was probably to increase the proportion of protectionists in that part of the public which was making itself heard.

True, the liberal-trade pressure groups probably had little choice. They might have got Eisenhower's and Randall's proposals through more easily if they could have confined the discussion to the alumni of the Ivy League, to the leading civic clubs in the major cities, and to the "experts." But American politics does not work that way. To achieve long-run results they had to do an educational job. Even to achieve short-run results in overcoming vigorously mobilized opposition on the other side they had to rally their own forces. But, once they did so, to their astonishment and dismay they faced a mounting opposition, an opposition unconsciously generated by themselves.

We doubt that the liberal-trade propagandists ever realized the problem they were making for themselves. We doubt that in 1953-1955 they considered the alternative strategy of quiet and subdued action. We also doubt that, even if they had considered it, they would on balance have adopted it then. Perhaps they would have acted exactly as they did, although in 1962 they did act differently. The Kennedy strategy went as far in the direction of avoiding broad public agitation as was possible. The strategy was to negotiate with particular industrial groups to meet their objections and pull the sting of their opposition in advance. Given the administration's late decision to have a major new trade bill, no preparatory propaganda was possible. In December, 1961, there was one short burst of statements of support by such prestigious figures as William Clayton and Christian Herter coincident with the revelation of the Kennedy proposals. Public discussion was then sustained at a low key until, in May, a month before hoped-for House action, there was again a burst of presidential speeches, Washington conferences, and World Trade Week activities. Public House hearings through late winter and early spring served their function, however, of forcing the discussion of the issue into the press and the public arena. A strategy of quiet elite persuasion could be maintained only up to a point. The hope was to keep public agitation to a sufficiently short period to avoid the boomerang effect of activization of latent opposition which occurred from 1953 to 1955. In summary, we see that, in the instance of trade legislation, as in many instances in the study of public opinion, it is more important to look at which part of the public is activated than at which is converted.[9]

□ Why Do They Think That Way?

Isolationism vs. Internationalism

Socioeconomic facts may tell us who are protectionists and who are free traders. But why do they think that way? A simplistic assertion is: "Protectionists are isolationists, and free traders are internationalists." The evidence introduced ordinarily rests on the characteristics of the political spokesmen for each point of view. Typically, one might contrast Rep. Noah Mason (R., Ill.), as an isolationist-protectionist, with a member of the Eisenhower internationalist wing of the Republican Party. There is a large element of truth in the conclusion, and in this and subsequent chapters we plan to introduce evidence to indicate that attitudes toward foreign-

---

[9] Cf. Paul F. Lazarsfeld, Bernard Berelson, and Hazel Gaudet, *The People's Choice* (New York: Duell, Sloan and Pearce, 1944), and Bernard Berelson, Paul F. Lazarsfeld, and William McPhee, *Voting* (Chicago: University of Chicago Press, 1954), for a similar finding in the study of an election campaign.

trade policy are in a good measure influenced by broader attitudes toward America's role in the world and perhaps by some rather different general values and ways of thinking, too. However, we must disavow any simple explanation in this direction.

Considering the generally amorphous nature of public attitudes toward foreign-trade policy and the relatively low degree of interest and involvement in the issue, it may well be anticipated that the stand many persons will take with respect to this policy will in some way derive from more general attitudes. Direct evidence of the truth of this among the general populace is spare, but such evidence as there is, is clear.[10]

Respondents on the Roper survey were asked: "How do you feel about American companies going into foreign countries to develop and produce natural resources like rubber, minerals, etc.? Do you think this is generally a good thing or generally a bad thing?" This question has no necessary, logical relationship to the question of whether we should import more or whether we should take a given stand on oil imports. It deals only with American activities abroad. For our purposes, it may be regarded as a crude index of the involvement people would like to see America have in the external world. A strong relationship between answers to this question and answers to the two questions on import policy would indicate that attitudes toward import policy are related to a broader complex. It turns out that 66 per cent of those persons who think American development of foreign resources is a "good thing" oppose restrictions on oil imports, whereas this is true of only 26 per cent who think it a "bad thing."

In Fig. 6-5 we have gone further and isolated the stable liberal traders and stable protectionists, and we show the proportions of each favoring or opposing American development of foreign resources.

Since three-fourths of the sample thought that American development of foreign resources was a good thing, it is almost inevitable that a majority of each trade-attitude group would also favor it. But for the stable liberal traders there is virtual unanimity in favor of American development of foreign resources, whereas only about half the stable protectionists are in favor.

This is further evidence that public attitudes toward development of foreign resources are a reflection of internationalist and isolationist attitudes in general. However, it may be objected that foreign investment involves economic activities, too, and may overlap with the issue of foreign-trade policy itself. To forestall this objection, we would like to present other data gathered in connection with some local surveys, one made in

---

[10] Cf. William A. Scott, "Rationality and Non-rationality of International Attitudes," *Journal of Conflict Resolution*, 2 (1958), 8-16; "International Ideology and Interpersonal Ideology," *Public Opinion Quarterly*, 24 (1960), 419-435.

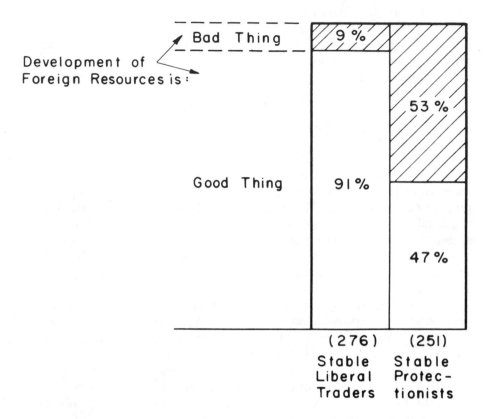

Fig. 6-5   RELATIONSHIP OF ATTITUDES TOWARD FOREIGN TRADE AND
FOREIGN INVESTMENT

Minnesota in 1955 [11] and the other in the New York metropolitan area in
1954.[12]

The poll of a cross-section of adult Minnesotans contained a number of questions which constituted a scale of internationalism-isolationism.
From these items, we selected seven unrelated in content to the problem

---

[11] This survey was part of a study conducted by Herbert McClosky at the Laboratory
for Research in Social Relations, University of Minnesota, with the assistance of the Minnesota Poll. The findings were made available to us through the kindness of Professor
McClosky.

[12] The poll of the New York metropolitan area was made by the New York League
of Women Voters in collaboration with the Bureau of Applied Social Research and the
Elmo Roper organization.

of foreign-trade policy.[13] The respondents were also asked if they thought American tariffs were "too high," "too low," or "about right." In Fig. 6-6 we see once more that protectionists are more likely to be isolationists than are the supporters of a liberal-trade policy.

The survey of the New York metropolitan area conducted by the League of Women Voters in 1954 revealed a similar relationship between attitudes toward United States participation in the United Nations and attitudes toward tariffs. Of those persons who thought we were doing less than our share in the United Nations, the number who favored lowering tariffs was greater than that favoring raising them by a proportion of 3 to 1. On the other hand, there was a small percentage of the sample (7 per cent) which felt that we should drop out of the United Nations. In this group, the proportion favoring lower versus higher tariffs was much smaller, being 1 to 2. Those who took intermediate stands on the United Nations fell between these two extreme groups.

There can be little doubt that attitudes toward foreign-trade policy are related to more general attitudes toward internationalism and isolationism. It is equally obvious, however, that isolationism and protectionism are far from synonymous. In each instance of data we have cited, there has been a considerable proportion of protectionists who were internationalists and a reasonable proportion of liberal-trade supporters who were isolationists. More refined techniques of measurement and analysis might reveal a higher association between internationalism-isolationism and attitudes toward foreign-trade policy than was exhibited in the preceding data. But there is every reason to conclude that attitudes toward foreign-trade policy are determined by many factors, among which internationalism-isolationism is only one, albeit an important one.

---

[13] The seven propositions—unrelated to foreign-trade policy—with which respondents were asked to agree or disagree, were:

(1) George Washington's advice to stay out of agreements with foreign powers is just as wise now as it was when he was alive.

(2) The federal government should be prevented from giving away any more of our wealth to foreign governments.

(3) In spite of all the claims to the contrary, America can defend itself as it has always done without the aid of our so-called allies.

(4) Any time American boys are found fighting on foreign shores, it is doubtful that the war is one that the United States should really be in.

(5) By belonging to the United Nations we are running the danger of losing our constitutional right to control our own affairs.

(6) Most of the countries which have got economic help from America end up resenting what we have done for them.

(7) These foreign wars America has been in are just part of the old quarrels Europeans have been having among themselves for centuries.

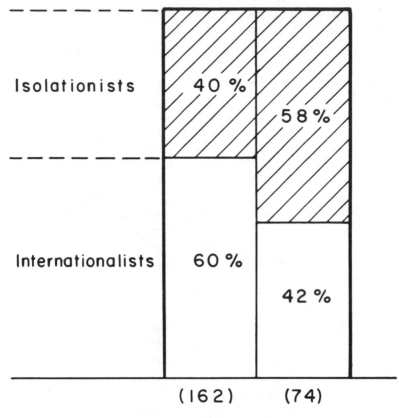

Fig. 6-6   RELATIONSHIP OF TARIFF ATTITUDE TO ISOLATIONISM/
INTERNATIONALISM IN MINNESOTA *

---

* Respondents were given a "plus" score for every isolationist answer they gave on the seven questions. Then the total group of approximately 800 respondents was divided as nearly as possible in half, and those who gave the fewer numbers of isolationist answers put in the "internationalist" category, and vice versa. This figure includes only that minority of the total sample which gave committed answers on the tariff question, i.e., who did not say "don't know" or "tariffs about right."

Arguments

On a number of polls, people have been asked the reasons for which they held their stand on foreign-trade policy.

An American Institute of Public Opinion release on March 1, 1954, gives a typical summary of the reasons which people offer:

The principal reasons given for favoring lower tariffs were that they would promote freer trade, mean lower prices, eliminate the need for dollar aid to foreign countries, and help to establish better international relations.

Those in favor of higher tariffs said they were necessary to protect American products, to protect U.S. wages and employment, and to keep certain products from coming into this country.

Other polls show the same picture. The respondents to the League of Women Voters survey in metropolitan New York were asked, after they had stated their attitudes toward raising or lowering tariffs, "Why do you think so?" Their answers, reported in Table 6-1, are consistent with the AIPO poll.

Respondents on the Roper poll previously referred to were asked the reasons for their attitudes.

TABLE 6-1

REASONS GIVEN FOR ATTITUDE TOWARD TARIFFS

Per cent	*Protectionist reasons*
82	Concerned with threat to the domestic economy; to avert unemployment, depression, dumping by foreign countries, etc.
17	Isolationist, xenophobic, suspicious, resentful, retaliatory, etc. E.g., "Because they have taken enough from us in the past. Let them pay." "We must help ourselves first." "Everything we send over there, they tax us double." "Since they are giving us a dirty deal we should raise tariffs."
1	Benefit to United States of tariff revenues.

	Liberal-trade reasons
33	Advantages for "international trade," "mutual advantages," "trade, not aid." E.g., "We have to encourage world trade." "High tariffs are a barrier to free world trade." "Lower prices mean more trade."
28	Advantages for consumers in the United States; lower prices. E.g., "Being that my husband is a working man, we would be able to buy more."
15	Homely morality; direct, outgoing sympathy for other nations. E.g., "To help other countries." "The common citizen of all countries benefits." "Other countries have it hard."
12	Benefits to business in the United States; exports only possible reciprocally with imports. E.g., "More trade would increase our business." "We would buy more and they would buy more."
8	Support of United States foreign policy. E.g., "It would keep other countries from becoming a prey to Communism."
4	Considerations bound up with comparative advantage. The country that can produce each commodity cheapest should produce that commodity for the rest of the world. E.g., "If things can be produced cheaper in other countries, we should buy them." "Foreign competition would force domestic producers to produce economically or not sell."

Once again, protectionists were concerned with the interests of such special groups as labor or particular businesses which might be harmed by foreign imports, whereas the proponents of freer importation of oil saw their preferred policy as promoting international relations and international trade and aiding the American consumer.

Although there are difficulties in the use of the material from any one of these polls, each supports the generalization that protectionists defend their position either in nationalist terms or in terms of the interests of special groups in the population. The advocates of a liberal-trade policy couch their arguments in a broader framework of interests. They sometimes speak from a nationalist point of view, being concerned with the special interests of domestic consumers. However, they are distinguished from the protectionists in the extent to which they invoke the argument that their policy improves international relations and by the tendency for their nationalist arguments to be phrased in terms of America as a world power which cannot isolate itself from what goes on in other countries.

The strong correlation between educational levels and attitudes toward foreign-trade policy described above becomes more understandable if we assume that these attitudes are at least partially determined by one's underlying feelings toward the world at large. On almost all political issues, the better-educated persons have proven not only more interested and informed but also to have a broader perspective and, more particularly, to be more internationalist and less nationalistic than persons of lesser education.

On the Roper poll, where it was possible to make detailed analysis of the data, we found not only that the better-educated respondents were less likely to be protectionists, but also that persons of different educational levels were likely to give different reasons for their support of their chosen position. For example, among the opponents of restriction on oil imports, 25 per cent of the persons of high school education or less gave as their argument the fact that consumers would benefit from increased oil imports, whereas the college-educated group cited this reason only half as frequently (12 per cent). Of all the reasons cited, this one was closest to the type of argument advanced by protectionists, namely, benefits to a specific group. In other words, even among opponents of protection, persons of lower educational status tended to cite arguments against protection which were similar to the arguments offered in favor of protection. On the other hand, the college-educated proponents of a liberal oil-import policy were more likely to favor free trade in principle (22 per cent) than were the high school (14 per cent) and grade school (11 per cent) groups.

Since almost all the reasons for supporting a protectionist policy with respect to oil were couched in terms of the interests of particular groups, we find no such difference among the protectionists. However, there were variations among protectionists of varying educational back-grounds as to which group's interests concerned them. Persons of less than college education were more likely to be concerned about protecting labor (20 per cent) as compared to those with college training (6 per cent), whereas the latter group was proportionately more involved with the interests of the domestic oil industry (53 per cent) than were the respondents of lower education (32 per cent). Clearly, the role of per-ceived self-interest must not be forgotten as we note also the influence of generalized ways of viewing the world. Among protectionists, people are most concerned with protecting those groups with which their own interests are more closely identified.

The greater protectionist sympathy among lower-educated groups may be largely the traditional anxiety of the workingman over losing his job because of foreign competition. But, since education shows a strong relationship to attitudes on this issue even within each occupational and economic group, we suspect that this greater support for protection among the less educated also stems from a rather distinctive set of values which are a function of being less educated per se. Since such persons usually ap-proach political, social, and economic problems from a relatively narrow frame of reference, they are less likely to see their own interests as in-tegrally linked with those of the nation as a whole or with the entire inter-national community. This leads to a limited definition of their self-interest and, quite naturally, to protectionism.

☐ Public Attitudes—A Summary

American foreign-trade policy has not been a burning issue in the minds of the American people for the past two decades. Even at the height of the controversy over the Reciprocal Trade Act in 1955, a bare half of the adult voters were aware of what was going on. On the whole, those Americans who are interested, aware, and have an opinion of the subject, have switched from a protectionist doctrine to what appears to be a predominant support for a liberal position. Although a plethora of qualifications and caveats is warranted when we make this statement,[14] it seems that the available evidence says that the public wants a liberal-trade policy.

Opposition to protectionism in the general public is concentrated selectively in those segments of the population that are better educated,

---

[14] For example, large groups of persons reply that we should leave tariffs about as they are. A protectionist might contend that this is a stand against tariff reductions. A proponent of a liberal trade policy might argue that this is a stand against raising tariffs. In practice, however, the answer appears to be the equivalent of having no opinion, at least among the general population.

wealthier, more politically active, and younger. We may well anticipate a broadening popular base of support for liberalization of trade barriers as the American educational level rises.

Although such an extrapolation seems justifiable, it cannot be made without appropriate sensitivity to other factors which may offset its effect. There is always the possibility that, under changing world conditions, the very values that led people away from protectionism might conceivably lead them back to favor some form of control over trade. The growing public consciousness of the dependence of America on its world relations can lead to quite opposite conclusions. Under certain conditions of competition with Communism, the internationalist point of view might dictate the adoption of a form of state-trading that would make it possible to wage more effective economic war. Ironically, the growth of the European Common Market could also stimulate American protectionism; as Europe emerges as the third great trading superpower, it competes in world markets with a more slowly growing United States. The 1962 Kennedy proposals are an attempt to avoid that eventuality. They are an attempt to deal with the problem by plunging into a close and increasingly free-trading relation with the incipient competitor. That is a daring strategy and clearly not the only one that could follow from a consciousness of how deeply the world market can affect us.

Unless the issue as a whole becomes a matter of increased popular concern, however, the popular approval of trade liberalization may not affect the national policy decision. As in the past, the potential support resting in the citizen body may be entirely offset by the political activity of relatively small groups with particular and immediate stakes in the issue.

PART II

Businessmen's Attitudes and
Communication on
Foreign-Trade Policy

PART II

Chapter 7

Introduction to Part II

In the following chapters, we shall look at the attitudes and communications of businessmen on foreign economic policy. Our main source of information is a sample survey conducted for us in the spring of 1954 by the National Opinion Research Center after consultation between the NORC and the Center for International Studies of M.I.T. Herbert Hyman and Eli S. Marks directed the survey for the NORC. It was supplemented by a self-administered questionnaire mailed out by the Center for International Studies in the spring of 1955. (As remarked above, the reader interested only in the main lines of foreign-trade policy-making and not in the details of our survey of businessmen's attitudes may wish to pass over most of this part except Chapter 13.)

The goal of the NORC survey was to interview 1,000 "heads of firms," a term to be defined and explained later, of whom 903 were actually interviewed. A large portion of our concern was with the manner in which the economic interests of a firm, however defined, were converted into political and economic policy on the national level. This meant that we had to interview men whose attitudes and opinions could be accepted as representing the position of their firms. This is not always indicated by a man's position. In some firms, the chief policy-maker is the chairman of the board of directors, in others, the president. Since every business has a president and not every one has a board of directors and since in most firms the president is identified more directly with the interests of the particular firm (the chairman of the board may be on the board of additional companies), we tried in the first instance to interview the president of each company we had selected. In descending order, we accepted as substitutes the chairman of the board, executive vice-president, some other vice-president with generalized responsibilities, or the general manager. Even though vice-presidents and general managers seldom are the setters of company policy, we felt that they would be sufficiently identified with company policy in the majority of cases for us to accept their views as those of the company. Of the 903 men interviewed, more than 90 per cent and perhaps as many as 95 per cent were acceptable as men who by virtue of their position presumably reflected company policy. The positions of the men interviewed are listed in Table 1.

There was a natural tendency for busy executives to shunt interviewers off toward the "man concerned with foreign trade." Since the heads of export divisions are frequently at odds with company policy, the interviewers were especially instructed not to interview such men. Public-relations directors were also natural substitutes whom our interviewers were instructed not to accept. The total of these and other such unacceptable respondents was less than 5 per cent; therefore we did not bother to separate them out from the analysis. Their evidence was valuable for its own sake on matters that did not necessarily involve the firm's official stand.

Our sample, a modified clustered probability sample, was selected from firms with at least 100 employees on the Old Age and Survivors' Insurance list.[1] Sample design was complicated by our anticipated analysis objectives. For example, we expected that size of firm might become a crucial variable in our analysis. (It did.) Since there are many more very small firms than there are very large firms, a random sample of all firms with more than 100 employees would include very few very large firms. Accordingly, we divided the universe of business firms into three strata: "small," having 100 to 999 employees; "medium," having 1,000 to 9,999 employees; and "large," having 10,000 or more employees. We sampled proportionately more heavily among the medium and large firms so as to have adequate representation for analysis. Among firms with more than

---

[1] Certain industries, such as newspaper publishing, motion pictures, restaurants, hotels, etc., were excluded on the grounds of irrelevance of our questionnaire to their situation.

10,000 employees (there were slightly more than 200 in 1954) we attempted to get every firm, except for about twenty-five which were located at particularly inconvenient distances from the NORC sample points. This left a universe of 176, all of which we tried to interview. We succeeded in interviewing a chief executive officer from 94 per cent of these firms. The refusal rate for the sample as a whole was 17 per cent.

TABLE 7-1

POSITION OF RESPONDENTS IN COMPANY

	Size of firm		
Position	*Large Per cent*	*Medium Per cent*	*Small Per cent*
President	41	62	55
Chairman of board of directors	4	2	3
Executive vice-president	14	8	9
Vice-president	19	13	16
General manager	1	2	3
Other acceptable respondent	8	6	9
Foreign-trade expert	3	1	1
Economist or financial-policy expert	2	1	1
Public-relations representative	1	–	0
Legal counsel	0	–	0
Other "dubiously acceptable" respondents	2	3	3
Other unacceptable respondents	0	1	1

Similarly, we anticipated that the objective economic interest of firms would have an important bearing on our analysis. But, despite the importance of protectionist sentiment from a political point of view, there are actually only a small proportion of United States firms that have a clear and unequivocal interest in protection. A simple random sample would therefore leave us with few such cases to feed into our analysis. We therefore had a panel of four economists rate the industries in the *Standard Industrial Classification Manual* [2] as to what their economic self-interest ought to be. The economists were instructed to ignore any generalized

---

[2] Technical Committee on Industrial Classification, Office of Statistical Standards, *Standard Industrial Classification Manual* (Washington, D.C., Government Printing Office, 1957). The manual used a decimal outline form to classify and subclassify industries. For our purpose, the four-digit classification seemed to represent the necessary degree of fineness and was used.

benefits which might diffuse to all sections of the economy as a result of increased foreign trade and concentrate only on the immediate, direct interest of the industry in question. The categories into which they were asked to sort these industries were: high-tariff interest, low-tariff interest, mixed interest, and no perceivable direct interest. (When at least three of the four did not agree on the objective interest of a given industry, that industry was classified as "mixed.") This initial classification was then used as a basis for oversampling in what appeared to be the more scarce categories.

Similar oversampling was done on other variables presumed to be of relevance for our analysis: region, industrial grouping, and the like. Once the interviews were collected, each was weighted so that it would occupy its proper proportionate place in the universe of business firms. Thus, if data on firms from the various size groups are combined, figures on the largest firms are weighted at unity, figures on the medium group are divided by two, and figures on the smallest firms multiplied by six before adding the figures together. These factors compensate for over- and undersampling. In this manner, the information gathered from each size of firm contributes its proper weight to the total. Similarly, in any given size of firm an interview from a "no-interest" business had to be weighted to represent several firms, since this group was undersampled with respect to its true proportions in the population. By this device of reweighting, it was possible to regard our sample as representative.

Our sampling procedure increased the efficiency of our 903 cases by giving us more adequate representation in scarce categories. However, it complicated the analysis and presentation of the data. The reweighting of underrepresented categories to their proper proportions resulted in a marked inflation of the apparent number of cases with which we were dealing in analysis. Without rerunning each analysis on an unweighted deck of IBM cards, it was not possible to know exactly how many cases we were dealing with in any given result. Accordingly, the standard convention of presenting the number of cases involved at each stage of analysis had to be abandoned.[3] In the more elaborate analyses presented in the next several chapters, the number of cases is often so small that individual figures should be regarded as no more than suggestive.

Because the variable of size of firm proved to be so crucial, we have as a standard practice kept the several sizes of firms separate in all presentations of data. (There are several instances in which this practice is violated for practical reasons which are explained in each case.) The reader may use the following numbers as guide-lines in looking at the

---

[3] For estimating significance, we here present some of the most often used unweighted N's, where the breaks are sufficiently fine or lopsided as to be troublesome.

data from the several sizes of firms. From firms of more than 10,000 employees, 166 interviews were collected, representing about three-fourths of all existing firms of that size. From firms with between 1,000 and 9,999 employees, there were 404 interviews. From the smallest firms, with between 100 and 999 employees, there were 333 interviews. These numbers, however, should be used only as rough guide-lines for estimating the number of cases in any subcategory within a given size of firm. For example, 3 per cent of the medium-sized firms were rated as having a high-tariff interest, but the actual number of cases in this subcategory is considerably more than fourteen, because this, being one of the scarce categories, was oversampled. Because they were scarce categories which were oversampled, the actual number of cases in minority subcategories will usually be larger than one would estimate from our total number of cases. For persons who are interested in further aspects of our survey data, we have published the code book and marginals of both the NORC 1954 survey and our 1955 mail questionnaire follow-up.[4]

Attitudes toward tariffs: 1954

Size of firm	Raise	Lower	Leave	Other	Total
Large	4	72	52	38	166
Medium	22	161	140	81	404
Small	28	109	107	89	333
Total	54	342	299	208	903

Communicating with Congress: 1954

Size of firm	Had done so within two years	Had not	Total
Large	37	129	166
Medium	68	336	404
Small	47	286	333
Total	152	751	903

[4] Raymond A. Bauer and Ithiel de Sola Pool, *American Businessmen and International Trade,* "Code Book and Data from a Study on Attitudes and Communications" (Glencoe, Ill.: The Free Press, 1960).

Chapter 8

Attitudes of
American Business Leaders
1954-1955

By the postwar period, the issues involved in American foreign-trade policy had become exceedingly complex. We have noted that the tariff question no longer was the only issue, and many persons argued quite cogently that it was one of the least important ones. There was the problem of currency convertibility, the Buy-American Act, shipping in American bottoms, quotas, dumping, simplification of customs regulations, American investment abroad, political and economic stability of foreign countries, American economic aid to foreign countries, restrictions on trade with Communist countries, cartelization of world markets, and so on. Any one of the issues, it might be contended, had as much effect on the pattern of American trade as did the structure of either American or foreign tariffs or of both. However, if it is true that the Reciprocal Trade Act and tariffs in general had more symbolic than practical importance, attitudes toward tariffs nevertheless remained the best single summary index to attitudes toward foreign-trade policy.

112

☐ Trends in Opinion to 1954

The general impression of persons in contact with the American business community in the postwar period was that it had shifted away from protectionism during or after World War II. Little in the way of sample survey data was available for the prewar period, but such as they were they indicated that the business community had been predominantly inclined toward protectionism. The Elmo Roper organization, in a poll which was published in *Fortune* in September, 1939, found a sample of American businessmen favoring higher tariffs over lower tariffs in a ratio of 2 to 1, with the usual accompanying high proportion of undecided persons.

In the spring of 1954, on our NORC poll, one of the questions asked was: "Taking everything into consideration, would you favor raising most tariffs, reducing most tariffs, or leaving most tariffs at their present level?" [1] The proportion favoring reduction of tariffs was more than seven times as great as that favoring a raising of tariffs: 38 as compared to 5 per cent. However, it is equally important to note that fewer than half were willing to commit themselves to either a general reduction or a general raising of tariffs. Thirty-one per cent wanted to leave tariffs as they were, 22 per cent said they did not know which general policy they favored, and 4 per cent simply refused to generalize, stating that a general position was untenable. We shall return to a consideration of this uncommitted group shortly, but for the moment we concern ourselves with the question of the trend of opinion in the business community.

Certainly the data from the NORC survey supported the notion that American businessmen had shifted away from protectionism in the period since 1939. The magnitude of the differences between our poll and the Roper poll of 1939 is so marked that this conclusion must be held even though the samples interviewed on the two surveys were not entirely comparable. (We interviewed heads of firms and sampled no firms as small as the smallest ones in the Roper survey.)

There is additional internal evidence in our survey data to indicate a trend away from protectionism. The younger men in the sample were more likely to favor reducing tariffs. Among men over fifty, 33 per cent thought we should reduce tariffs, whereas the proportion among men under fifty was 44 per cent.

Additionally, our respondents were asked if they recalled having shifted their "ideas toward tariffs and trade policies over the years." Over 40 per cent reported that their attitudes had shifted, and of those who had

---

[1] This question was practically identical with the one on the Roper survey.

shifted more than 3 to 1 had shifted toward support of lower tariffs. (See Fig. 8-1.)

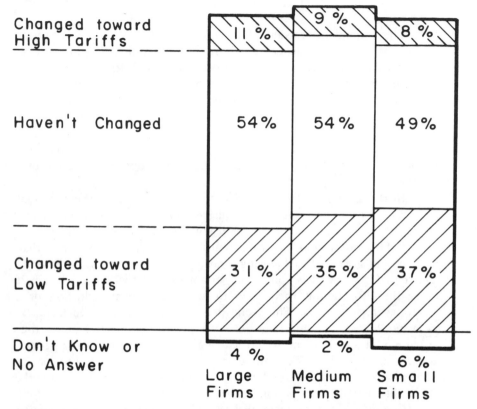

Fig. 8-1   RECALLED SHIFT IN TARIFF ATTITUDE OF BUSINESSMEN

It will be noted in Fig. 8-1 that the change toward support of lower tariffs was somewhat stronger among the heads of small firms. This reflects another trend in the business community and one which was not entirely anticipated. There was a general belief that liberalism on trade was strongest among the largest business firms. It was thought that, except for importers, they were the representatives of the giant mass-production industries, able to compete effectively with "cheap foreign labor," who were for lower tariffs. As one protectionist spokesman said to us: "The big companies are safe, but the small ones are vulnerable. They cannot produce by their methods efficiently enough to meet foreign competition." This we found to be incorrect in 1954, or at least not reflected in the attitudes of the men we interviewed.

The 1939 *Fortune* poll had shown a clear relationship between the size of a man's firm and the stand he took on tariffs. Among the smallest manufacturers, 42 per cent favored raising tariffs, whereas this was true of only 7 per cent of the largest manufacturers. Among the retailers, the differences were almost as marked: 47 per cent of the smallest retailers wanting higher tariffs, in contrast to 18 per cent among the largest retailers.

But, contrary to expectation, this was no longer true in 1954. The responses of men from the several sizes of firm show that, notwithstanding size, they held substantially the same attitudes. One might argue for some slight trace of the old pattern, but obviously there is nothing to warrant the conclusion that small businessmen are protectionists and big businessmen are free traders.

The change in attitude from 1939 to 1954 is thus above all a change among smaller businessmen. By 1939, the heads of the biggest firms had already adopted an orientation toward world trade. If 1928 poll data existed, we would perhaps find an earlier shift in their views from a traditional protectionism. But by the 1940's big business had already become trade-minded, and small business was gradually adopting the new norm with something of a lag. By 1954, size differences in attitudes had disappeared.

TABLE 8-1

TARIFF ATTITUDES OF BUSINESSMEN BY SIZE OF FIRM: 1954

	Size of firm		
Attitude	*Large* *Per cent*	*Medium* *Per cent*	*Small* *Per cent*
Favor:			
Raising most tariffs	2	7	5
Reducing most tariffs	41	41	37
Leave at present level	32	34	31
Don't know	17	11	24
Refused to generalize	8	7	3
	100	100	100
Total number	166	404	333

Nor did any large sector of the economy dissent en masse from the current business view of trade barriers. Obviously, there were specific industries and businesses which were strongly protectionist or radically for freer trade, but the differences between such broad sectors as banking, retailing, manufacturing, and the like were not striking. Manufacturers as a whole, while not quite as solidly agreed as transportation executives, gave predominant support to lowering rather than raising tariffs. In only one major industry grouping did as many as 10 per cent of the businessmen interviewed favor higher tariffs, namely the extractive industries, 18 per cent.

Minimally, these data indicate a swing away from protectionism. On closer inspection, however, we shall see that they are nothing like the solid, strong support for a liberal-trade policy that the proponents of such a policy might hope for.

□ Trends in Opinion, 1954-1955

In the spring of 1955, a year after our initial survey, we sent out a mail questionnaire to those businessmen whom we had interviewed the previous year. Since the year 1954-1955 had been an active one with respect to the debate over foreign-trade policy, we wanted to see if any perceptible shift of opinion had occurred.

The questionnaires were returned by 632 persons, over two-thirds of our original sample. Because of the factors of self-selection that are ordinarily involved in the return of mail questionnaires, we made a detailed comparison between the sample which responded to the mail questionnaire and the original group of respondents. Contrary to our expectation, the second group was virtually identical with the original sample on all those dimensions which appeared to us to be crucial to the issue—subjective tariff attitude, information on foreign-trade policy, objective interest (as measured by economists' ratings), salience of foreign-trade policy as an issue, and contacting Congress on foreign-trade policy. The only factor which seems to have been related to whether people returned these questionnaires—apart from the obvious interest and cooperativeness of the men concerned—was that of size of firm. Men from smaller firms were less likely to respond, reflecting their smaller public relations and secretarial staffs and a tendency, which we find at various points in our data, to devote a smaller proportion of their time and attention to things external to their firm. Apart from this, the 1955 sample appears to be as representative as was the 1954 one.

In Fig. 8-2, we compare the responses to the 1955 mail questionnaire with those to the original 1954 interview survey.

The major apparent shift is a larger proportion of protectionists among the largest and smallest firms. Because of differences between the oral interview and the self-administered questionnaire, we do not know from these data how much of this shift is apparent and how much is actual, though we shall present more substantial evidence that there was. a slight growth in protectionist strength from 1954 to 1955. The present data, however, have some holes. In the oral interview situation, the interviewer's probing might get a man who began with an uncommitted position to take a committed one. On the written questionnaire, a considerable group of men who took an uncommitted position, such as "leave tariffs as they are," included qualifying remarks indicating the direction in which they were leaning. These men were assigned to the appropriate "committed" category. Though similar in concept, the effects of the procedures in the oral and written situations might be different.

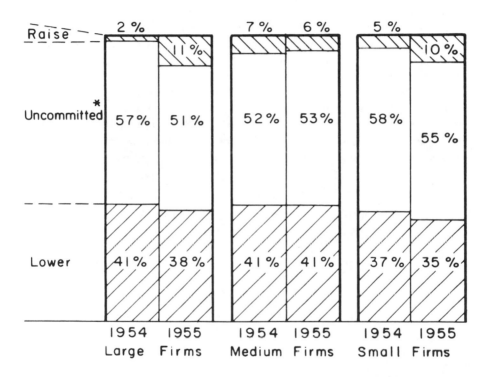

Fig. 8-2 ATTITUDES TOWARD RAISING AND LOWERING TARIFFS: 1954 VERSUS 1955

---

* Virtually no one said "don't know" or refused to answer on the mail questionnaire, and proportionately more said "leave tariffs as they are." The very nature of the mail questionnaire makes it improbable that a person would say "don't know" or refuse to answer the main question on a form which was being returned. From the fact that the combined proportion of "leave," "don't know," and other uncommitted responses were almost identical on both surveys, we inferred that persons who would have said "don't know" on oral interviews replied "leave" on the self-administered questionnaire. We lump all such answers under the general label, "uncommitted."

There is in any case no evidence of a major reversal of the long-term trend away from protectionism, though there might have been a slight one. The ratio of "reduce" to "raise" remains at least 3.5 to 1.

More instructive than the over-all distribution of answers are the changes which took place in the answers of individual respondents. Since the pattern was very nearly identical for each size of firm, we have presented the combined results of the entire sample in Table 8-2.

The table is organized so that 1954 attitudes can be used to "predict" 1955 attitudes. Thus, if we read down the first column, we find that, of those men who favored higher tariffs in 1954, 53 per cent continued to favor higher tariffs in 1955, 4 per cent favored lower tariffs, and 43 per cent had gone into one of the uncommitted categories. The majority pattern was for the men in each category to give the same answer in both 1954 and 1955 (53 per cent of raise, 55 per cent of reduce, and 67 per cent of uncommitted).

This table shows that, although there had been relatively little shift in the net distribution of attitudes throughout the business community in the year 1954-1955, many individuals shifted their position between committed and uncommitted categories. However, there was for practical purposes no shifting between committed positions.

TABLE 8-2

SHIFTS IN ATTITUDES TOWARD TARIFFS

(Spring, 1954, to spring, 1955)

	1954 attitudes		
1955 attitudes	Raise tariffs Per cent	Reduce tariffs Per cent	Uncommitted Per cent
Raise tariffs	53	(1)*	15
Reduce tariffs	(4)*	54	18
Uncommitted	43	45	67
	100	100	100

* A total of seven men in these categories.

The most interesting group is the large uncommitted category, which comprised over half the men in the sample. This was the pool of potential switchers to which either polar position could look for recruits or for replacements for its own wavering adherents.

If the protectionists had gained members from the uncommitted group in proportion to their strength in the 1954 poll, they would have added to their numbers only about one-seventh as many persons as would have been added to proponents of lower tariffs. Yet we find that they made a relative gain. Of the 1954 uncommitted group, 18 per cent shifted to the side of lower tariffs, as compared to 15 per cent who shifted to the side of raising tariffs. These data indicate that heightened interest in the reciprocal-trade controversy in 1954-1955 served to activate latent support for higher tariffs somewhat more readily than for lower tariffs.

In summary, we may say that there was strong evidence of a shift away from protectionism in the business community between the beginning of World War II and 1954 and evidence of a halt in that trend, even a slight reversal, between 1954 and 1955. The reciprocal-trade controversy during the year 1954-1955 tended to crystallize opinions somewhat and to move men out of uncommitted positions, but for practical purposes there were no "conversions" from one committed position to another. There was no real decline in liberal-trade sentiment. A proportionate increase in protectionist sentiment which did appear did not in those circumstances constitute a significant reversal of the long-term trend of business opinion.

☐ The "True State" of Opinion

Up to this point we have been accepting the answers to our question on tariff policy in an uncritical fashion. But we may now ask legitimately to what extent our findings approximate the "true state" of business opinion, if we may be permitted to use that unmeasurable and hypothetical notion. In the pages which follow, we try to estimate the range within which the true state may lie.

As previously mentioned, more than one-half our respondents favored neither generally higher nor generally lower tariffs. It will be remembered that 31 per cent wanted to leave tariffs as they were, 22 per cent said they did not know what position they favored, and 4 per cent refused to generalize. Analysis of the sort of public-opinion-poll data presented in the previous chapter indicated that, for the general public, such uncommitted responses were essentially an expression of lack of interest in and/or lack of knowledge of the subject and in effect were no more than additional evidence of the low level of public involvement in the issue. "Leave tariffs as they are" is for the general public most likely a way of evading the issue.

This is not entirely true of the answers given by our sample of businessmen. True, foreign-trade policy was an issue of low salience and interest relative to other issues with which businessmen were concerned. Nevertheless, compared to the general public, the heads of business firms were interested and informed. For many businessmen, our question of whether they would favor high or low tariffs in general was an over-simplification of the problem, and many said so. It is interesting for example that the men who refused to generalize were on the whole better informed, more interested, and more involved in the issue of foreign-trade policy than was the rank-and-file member of our sample. Furthermore, many publicly known protectionists—men who were working actively against the Reciprocal Trade Act—were not so much concerned with raising tariffs as with preventing further reductions. Indeed, many businessmen are not so concerned with the general level of tariffs as with their structure; a man may want low tariffs on the raw materials he imports and high tariffs on the manufactured products he sells in the American market.

An over-all question about what the level of tariffs should be served to identify men whom we might label protectionists in principle, that is, those who said "raise tariffs generally," and it identified liberal traders in principle, that is, those who said "reduce tariffs generally." We shall use these groups in much of our further analysis. These data were adequate to the task of documenting the historical trend of a shift away from protectionism, particularly since the question we asked was equivalent to the Roper question of 1939. But the responses to these questions cannot be taken as a statistical description of the distribution of latent protectionist and antiprotectionist sentiment in the business community. A careful reading of the interviews showed that many men who refused to give a committed answer on the general question of raising or reducing tariffs were actually inclined in one or the other direction when judged by their answers to other questions and their volunteered comments and qualifications. In an effort to get another approximation of the distribution of sentiments for and against protectionism, we classified as many of our respondents as possible on the basis of such additional information as was available in the interviews.

One reason for making this revised estimate is that an argument might well be made that the answers to our general question may not reflect the extent of protectionist sentiment in the business community. "Raise tariffs" in general is a fairly drastic stand to take in an era of internationalism. Therefore, a man who said some tariffs should be raised and some should be lowered we reclassified as a protectionist, since this is a position taken by many active, publicly known protectionists.[2] This and other conventions employed in reclassifying our respondents were probably biased toward overestimating protectionist sentiment. However, it

---

[2] Some of these men would contend that they are not "protectionists." Obviously, there cannot be complete agreement as to just where this label should be applied; but our attempt is to plumb the full extent of the support of this general position, no matter what the exact terminology may prove to be.

seemed worth while to see what such a counterbiasing of the original question might produce.

The data derived from this reclassification are presented in Table 8-3.

TABLE 8-3

ATTITUDES TOWARD FOREIGN-TRADE POLICY

(Based on the tariff question plus additional evidence available in 1954 interviews)

	Size of firm		
	Large Per cent	Medium Per cent	Small Per cent
Protectionists	14	15	12
Liberal traders	49	50	44
Leave as is	19	24	22
Don't know	17	9	21
No answer	1	2	1
	100	100	100

One thing that seems clear is that this search for latent leanings increases the proportion of apparent protectionist sentiment. According to these criteria, there would appear to be almost one-third as many adherents to protectionism as there are to a liberal-trade policy. It will be remembered that the proportion elicited by the general question was less than 1 in 7.

There is yet another procedure which can be adopted. It will be remembered that many men shifted between committed and uncommitted categories between 1954 and 1955. Let us suppose that a man who took a committed position in either year was revealing the true direction in which his sentiments lay. Under these conditions, a man who said "raise tariffs" one year and who said "leave," "don't know," or "refuse to generalize" the other year would be classified as a latent protectionist. To make this classification as inclusive as possible, that is, to reduce to a minimum the number of uncommitted respondents, we have employed the 1954 recoded estimated attitudes rather than the more stringent criterion of the respondents' own self-assignment. For purpose of compactness of comparison we now have combined all three estimates in Fig. 8-3: (1) the direct answer given to our 1954 interview question; (2) our recoding of "leaners" on the 1954 survey; and (3) our classification on the basis of combined 1954 and 1955 answers.

Although the combined 1954-1955 rating reduces the proportion of uncommitted men still further, the picture derived from the three estimates is, all in all, not very different. It leads us to estimate sentiment in the business community as at least three to one in favor of the liberal-trade policy, a figure that also comes up in a *Dun's Review* survey of corporation presidents in 1962.[3]

But suppose we assume that in the final analysis nobody is uncommitted and that in some residual fashion everyone has a preference for either a protectionist or a liberal-trade policy. Suppose further that our reclassification of the 1954 leaners gives us an estimate of how the rest of the population would go. We found that our leaners who had not initially taken a committed position divided approximately equally between protectionist leaners and liberal-trade leaners. Using this finding as a guide, we may estimate that those persons for whom we did not have evidence for classifying might divide in about the same proportions. On the basis of this, we shall therefore assign all of those as yet uncommitted on the 1954 survey to either the protectionist leaners or the liberal-trade leaners. When this is done, we get just about exactly [4] 33 per cent protectionists and 67 per cent liberal traders among the men from each size of firm. This is about as far as we can go in doing justice to whatever latent protectionist sentiment there may have been in the business community in 1954. This device still leaves the protectionists outnumbered by 2 to 1, and it furthermore gives what is undoubtedly an overestimate of protectionist sentiment.

Which of these estimates is more valid? Which is more representative of the true state of opinion? These questions are, as we have suggested, not meaningful. Opinions and attitudes are abstractions, the true state of which can be approached only through procedures such as these, and each procedure measures something different. If one is interested in firm attitudes, in men who are willing to take a position, then our first procedure is probably preferable. It shows that a very large proportion of men are unwilling to take a categorical position and that protectionists are in a small minority both absolutely and relative to supporters of reduced tariffs. If, on the other hand, one is interested in estimating latent sentiments which might become activated, then probably one of our later procedures is preferable. However, the last of these procedures—assigning everyone to a committed category—is unwarranted. It is difficult to envisage a situation in which everyone would become actively involved in

---

[3] John Maughan, "Business and the Common Market; a President's Panel Report," *Dun's Review and Modern Industry*, 79 (March 1962), No. 3, 35, 130-136.

[4] There is a variation of 1 per cent with the various firm sizes.

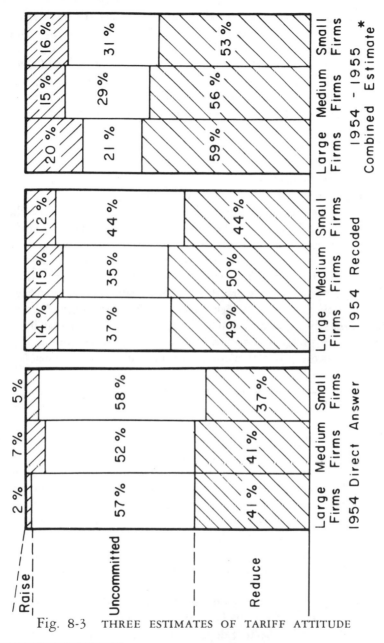

Fig. 8-3 THREE ESTIMATES OF TARIFF ATTITUDE

---

* Based on both the 1954 and 1955 surveys, but including only those persons who answered both. For the 1954 survey, we employed the recoded criterion. For the 1955 survey, we placed respondents according to their own self-assignment and in addition assigned to their proper category those who said "leave tariffs as they are" but gave evidence of the direction in which their sentiments lay.

the issue of foreign trade. We carried out this procedure merely to show that even the most extreme estimate available to us would have left the protectionists in a minority in 1954-1955.

Although we have contended that the extent of protectionist sentiment is not as great as our most extreme estimate would indicate, we must admit that, after spending several years analyzing these data, we felt it much stronger than had been our initial impression in looking at the straightforward answers to our main tariff question. When one studies attitudes of the general public, one is inclined to take the uncommitted answers—"leave," "don't know," and "refuse to generalize"—as indications of noninvolvement in the issue. But in the business community this was often the ambivalence that comes with knowledge, not the camouflage of ignorance. The men who knew most about the complexities of the real situation were the least willing to issue a categorical platitude about the level of tariffs. A refusal to generalize could come from two quite different kinds of businessmen—those who did not know enough to answer and those who knew too much. The latter might be on either side of the broad issue of protection. As we worked with these data, we came increasingly to appreciate the extent to which many of the uncommitted men were inclined in one direction or another and to the recognition that in general there was more protectionist sentiment in the business community than was reflected in the proportions of men who said "raise" versus "reduce" tariffs.

Though we have no cause to doubt the propositions put forth in this chapter concerning the swing away from protectionism in principle among the American business community, much of the remainder of this book will be devoted to showing how misleading these findings would be if they were to be interpreted as meaning that the American business community was in any over-all way united behind liberal-trade legislation. Although liberal-trade proponents appear more likely to give verbal support to their attitude, this does not mean that they are more likely to take action on the basis of this verbal position. Only a limited portion of the business community cared enough to act.

□ Salience of the Issue

In the previous chapter on the attitudes of the general public, we made much of its lack of involvement in foreign-trade policy. Opinion pollers have regularly rejected, depending on the criteria used, from one-quarter to one-half of the public as being so uninformed that it is not worthwhile even soliciting their opinions on tariffs and trade. This is obviously a different matter with businessmen, foreign-trade policy having a direct impact on so many businesses and businessmen themselves being more concerned with public policy than is the average citizen. Yet, interest in and salience of issues are relative matters. Relative to the rank-and-file citizen, the American businessman was interested in foreign-trade policy. But in the business community how salient was this issue relative to others?

Certainly the data already presented show that it was not a burning issue on which the business community was either militantly united or in a state of deep cleavage. Granted all the complications of foreign-trade policy to which we have already referred, the fact remains that almost all businessmen recognized the existence of two broad, contrasting points of view, two general orientations which would be recognized by the labels of "protectionism" and "liberal trade." Yet, only a minority felt itself clearly aligned with either camp.

How did foreign trade and foreign-trade policy fare in comparison with other issues with which American businessmen were concerned during the time of our 1954 NORC survey? Respondents were asked to rate the importance of various topics to their business. The proportions of men saying that a given topic was very important to their business is recorded in Table 8-4. The topics are listed in their approximate order of importance.

Taxes and tax rates were an issue of the highest saliency, being labeled "very important" for their firms by virtually all men interviewed. Three-fourths of all men regarded wages and union demands as very important. But, with respect to topics bearing on foreign trade and foreign-trade policy—tariffs, export markets, foreign competition—the picture is qualitatively different. Approximately one-fourth or less of the men from any size firm indicated that such topics were very important to their firms, while a third to one-half found them not important at all. They were of high saliency to a relatively few men, but of second-order saliency for the business community as a whole. Foreign-trade policy was indeed a matter of which most businessmen were aware, about which most were in some measure concerned, but on which only a relatively few would exert major effort and exhibit major interest.

The extent of their interest depended in part on the size of their firm. A substantially larger proportion of large firms are to some degree concerned with export markets or are somewhat affected by foreign competition. But, when a small firm is affected, it is affected in a very different way. A large firm is normally a multiproduct company with no one product decisively affecting its business. Typical large firms, for example, DuPont and General Electric, have some divisions which have severe competition from abroad but also other divisions with large export sales. A small company is often a single-product company which lives or dies by its one product. Thus, the chance of a small firm being affected at all

TABLE 8-4

IMPORTANCE OF VARIOUS TOPICS FOR A MAN'S BUSINESS

	Proportion saying "very important"			Proportion saying "not important"		
	Size of firm			Size of firm		
	Large	Medium	Small	Large	Medium	Small
	Per cent					
Taxes and tax rates	91	90	83	1	2	4
Wage rates and union demands	75	75	76	3	7	9
Political stability abroad	50	46	39	15	22	23
Tariffs	29	28	23	30	37	51
Export markets	26	19	18	30	45	53
Defense contracts	24	15	19	41	50	53
Foreign competition	24	22	15	49	52	66

by foreign competition may be considerably smaller than for a large firm, but if it is affected its stake is large and so is its incentive to protect itself.

Our statement that foreign-trade policy was an issue of secondary salience must be taken as a proposition descriptive of the business community as a whole and not as applicable equally to all its segments. It was obviously an issue of high salience for some industries, some men, and some businesses.

Chapter 9

The Roots of Conviction—
Self-Interest and Ideology

What determines the stand a businessman will take on foreign-trade policy? It was easy to find people who gave us simple, categorical answers. We were told on one hand that it was "self-interest," "it depends on whose ox is gored," and "businessmen just look at the balance-sheet." But we were also told: "Isolationists are protectionists, and internationalists are for lowering trade barriers." The picture turned out to be more complicated. Both economic self-interest, to the extent that this elusive concept can be identified, and attitudes toward internationalism turned out to be correlated with attitudes toward foreign-trade policy; but so did a number of other things, most notably a man's role in business and society.

□ The Notion of Self-Interest

The history of foreign-trade policy has been written largely from the point of view of competing interest groups. It has been assumed that attitudes toward foreign trade are predominantly determined by economic self-seeking. "People act according to their self-interest" is stated as though it were a self-evident truth and as though most people knew where their self-interest lay.

A large portion of the populace does, indeed, have an image of its stake in foreign trade. The image has psychological reality regardless of whether it corresponds to objective economic facts. In 1946, the National Opinion Research Center asked a representative sample of the American public if they thought that they personally would be better or worse off if the United States bought more things from foreign countries. Of those who thought they would be better off if we bought more, 65 per cent favored tariff reductions, in contrast to only 25 per cent of those who thought they would be worse off. Those who felt that it would make no difference to themselves took an intermediate position. The tariff policy a citizen favored usually corresponded to his perceived self-interest.

It is worth noting that a parallel question as to whether the respondent had a stake in United States selling abroad produced less striking results. Of those who felt they would personally be better off if the United States sold more abroad, 56 per cent favored tariff reductions. The proportion of those who thought they would be worse off if we sold more abroad and favored lowering tariffs was only moderately smaller—44 per cent.

Both sets of figures argue that a person's attitudes toward foreign-trade policy are related to what he conceives his self-interest to be. It is instructive, however, that there is so noticeable a difference in the strength of the relationship when the issue is posed differently. The gain or loss from buying imported goods is perceived as more directly and immediately affected by tariff policy than the gain or loss that may accrue from selling more goods abroad. Direct and immediate benefits readily perceivable had a much more powerful impact than potentially equally important factors whose effect was less directly perceived. This is one reason why economic determinism is habitually frustrated; people fail to see where their self-interest lies.

The way in which an individual defines his self-interest and the relation of this perceived self-interest to his attitudes are considerably more complicated than is ordinarily assumed. Self-interest permits some latitude of definition. Indeed, the presence of such ambiguity is a crucial assumption of this study, for, if everyone were motivated by self-interest and had a clear and unequivocal awareness of it, there would be little room for argument and persuasion between people and nothing for the social psychologist or political scientist to study. The pattern of controversy would be predetermined and would be a simple power struggle.

The reader may accept our assertion that few members of the general public have a clear image of their economic self-interest on foreign-trade policy, but he may still believe that with the business community the situation is different. The head of a business organization should know his self-interest. Yet even for him it is not as clear as it might seem. Although there are groups whose immediate interest on foreign trade is obvious and relatively unequivocal, even in sophisticated business circles the partisans of each side argue that men on the other side miscalculate what is to their advantage. For example, the DuPont Corporation was generally, though not officially, identified with the side of protectionism. Yet many supporters of the Reciprocal Trade Act contended that DuPont would gain as a firm if it concentrated on increasing foreign trade and were not overly concerned with protecting the production and sales of organic chemicals which comprised only a minor portion of DuPont products. The American watch manufacturers appeared to be a clear case of an industry that was suffering from foreign competition. Yet it was argued that Elgin and Hamilton had diversified under this competition, started importing works and assembling finished watches in this country, and, in the process, could increase their profitability. On the other side of the fence, users of fuel oil opposed quotas on the imports of this product, and protectionists argued that this would make them vulnerable in the long run to foreign control over the prices of these imports. The automobile industry favored lower tariffs, but men on the other side of the issue nodded their heads sagely and said that things would be different once foreign cars grabbed a larger share of the market. Among businessmen, certainly, everyone did not agree on where everyone else's interest lay.

Smaller firms, in particular, often do not have the information necessary to assess their interest in foreign-trade policy. They do not hire economists; they seldom have a foreign-trade specialist.[1] The head of the firm, especially if it has less than 400 employees,[2] is a production manager along with everything else. He is, as we shall have occasion to note, more of an inside man, whereas the head of a large firm is essentially an outside man. Day-to-day production responsibility leaves the head of a small firm few resources with which to explore the alternatives existing in the world market. Is there a market for his product somewhere in the world, or is there a potential market for a slightly different product which he could make? The small businessman with a limited staff cannot generally know. Most often he must calculate self-interest on the assumption that basically all he can do is what he is now doing, but do it a little better.[3] As seen

---

[1] The percentage of firms having no foreign-trade specialist was: large firms, 30 per cent; medium-sized firms, 44 per cent; small firms, 72 per cent.

[2] In our sampling, we arbitrarily took as cutting points 100, 1,000, and 10,000 employees. Our data, however, suggest that there is an important structural change at about the level of 400 employees. Firms with more than that number tend to be like our medium-sized firms. Firms with fewer employees tend to be quite different.

[3] What we are describing here is what Herbert Simon calls "satisficing," as contrasted with maximizing, behavior. Cf. *Models of Man* (New York: John Wiley, 1957), p. 261. We agree with Simon's view that satisficing is what people generally do.

from Olympus, foreign-trade opportunities which he will never know may exist for him. Not knowing his opportunities in wider markets, he may see himself as hurt by policies which theoretically open up other markets to him but also open up his own markets to others.

One reason why businesses, especially small ones, often find it hard to know where their foreign-trade interest lies is that they sell to wholesalers and frequently have no idea what proportion of their manufactured product ends up in foreign lands. Or they buy through jobbers and do not know the effect of import restrictions on the prices of the things they buy. In the Venezuelan campaign against petroleum import quotas, an effective device used by the Venezuelan interests was to go to a U.S. manufacturer who sold to middlemen or processors and show him figures on Venezuelan imports of his commodity or things made from it. Surprised in most cases to learn of the market Venezuela represented, the manufacturer often agreed to write his congressman about a measure which, he was told, would curtail that market. It was the propagandist who identified the businessman's self-interest.

Another common reason why U.S. companies are unaware of their own interest in foreign trade is that Canadian sales are handled by the sales manager, not the export manager. If you ask a business firm how much it sells abroad, you will most often be given the figure of sales handled by the export department. Canadian sales, which are often as great as all other foreign sales put together, are thought of as domestic and are not separately accounted. Since they involve none of the red tape, anxiety, or special problems associated with foreign business, there is no awareness of that large segment of what, economically if not administratively, is really foreign trade.

Even large organizations find it difficult to make an accurate assessment of their interest. We attended a meeting at which a representative of the steel industry told of a staff study which had been made to answer this particular question. When a careful study of the raw materials consumed by the steel industry was made, they discovered, entirely to their surprise, that the steel industry consumed more paper in dollar volume than it did alloys, which went directly into the making of steel. Although the interest of the steel industry in low tariffs on alloys had long been discussed, it now turned out that it had even more interest in a low tariff on the importation of wood pulp!

As difficult as self-interest is to assess, there is little doubt that there are variations in the immediate short-run interest of various American businesses in foreign-trade policy. Though their judgment may be askew and their information incomplete, most businessmen have a fairly fixed notion of what that interest is, and it is a notion which is not devoid of objective basis.

Perhaps the most independent criterion we have of business interest is the ratings which a group of economists made for us of the industries in the *Standard Industrial Classification Manual*. As described in Chapter 7, we instructed the economists to rate each four-digit industry classification according to its immediate self-interest. This was to be done independently of any mediated benefits which might come to an industry through general economic conditions as affected by foreign-trade policy. These industries were placed in one of four interest categories: high tariff, low tariff, mixed interest, or no interest. Where the economists were not in substantial agreement on a particular industry, it was placed in the mixed-interest category.

The ratings of the economists suggest that only a small proportion of American industries have a clear, uncomplicated interest in a high-tariff policy and that a majority are affected by foreign-trade policy only as they have a stake in the economy as a whole. The distribution of firms in our sample according to the ratings of the economists is presented in Table 9-1.

It is worth noting that, among the largest firms, the proportion of mixed- to high-tariff interest is 18 to 1, in comparison with 3 to 1 among the smallest firms. This reflects a state of affairs already noted in Chapter 8, namely, that the interests of larger and more complicated firms are seldom wholly in the direction of one or another over-all tariff policy.[4]

TABLE 9-1

OBJECTIVE TARIFF INTEREST BY SIZE OF FIRM

	Size of firm		
Interest	*Large* *Per cent*	*Medium* *Per cent*	*Small* *Per cent*
High	1	3	4
Low	30	32	26
Mixed	18	14	12
None	51	51	58
	100	100	100

[4] The distribution of these ratings also bears on our sampling procedure. Since so few industries were rated as having an over-all high-tariff interest, we oversampled among these industries in order to have an adequate number of cases for statistical analysis. However, among the largest firms we attempted to get the entire population. There were only two firms in this entire category which came from industries rated as having a simple high-tariff interest. Therefore, in the analysis which follows we have combined the largest with the medium-sized firms, for which we were able to get a more adequate numerical representation of the scarce high and mixed categories.

In Table 9-2 we present the relationship between self-interest as judged by the ratings of our panel of economists and the attitudes of our respondents toward tariffs. In Section A of the table we have used as a criterion of our respondents' attitudes their answers to the general question whether they preferred to raise, reduce, or leave tariffs at about the present level. Section B employs the more elaborate criterion of our own ratings assigned not only on the basis of the general question but also on the basis of information garnered from answers to other questions and incidental remarks which served as clues to the uncommitted respondents' leanings.

These data confirm a relationship between the objective self-interest of the industries which the firms represent and the attitudes of the chief officers of these firms. The proportion of men who favor lowering tariffs is greatest among firms with a low interest or with no interest, and protectionism is highest among the heads of those firms with a high-tariff interest.

We owe it to the reader to point out that even this banal finding, that businessmen were affected by their objective self-interest, may be a little suspect. How objective is our "objective" rating? Although our economists were supposed to use their independent judgment, they could not help but be aware of the historical stand of various industries. An economist would know that the entire history of the synthetic-organic chemical industry has been one of fighting German competition, and he would be influenced by his knowledge. So the economists' rating may be tainted, and the correlation as it appears in Table 9-2 between objective and subjective interest may be too high.

Yet, even as it stands, the correlation between our respondents' attitudes toward tariffs and our criterion of self-interest is far from perfect. Only in one instance do a majority of respondents in any interest category commit themselves to the tariff attitude that is clearly and unequivocally in line with their own "objective self-interest."

To some extent, this failure of our respondents' expressed attitudes to correspond to their own economic advantage may be attributed to the criterion of self-interest employed here. The judgments made by the panel of economists were made for the industries into which the firms fell and not for the firms themselves. Industries are not so homogeneous that a rating given to the industry as a whole will apply equally well to all firms within the industry. Therefore, it should not be assumed that the 5 to 7 per cent of persons with a low-tariff interest who favored high tariffs or the 21 to 26 per cent of persons with a high-tariff interest who favored low tariffs were opposing their business interests out of civic altruism. Each of those respondents could conceivably be precisely representing the needs of his single firm. The United States exports pharmaceuticals, but the manufac-

TABLE 9-2

RELATIONSHIP OF ECONOMISTS' RATING OF INDUSTRIES' TARIFF
INTEREST TO RESPONDENTS' OWN TARIFF ATTITUDES

Attitude	Economists' ratings *			
	High	*Low*	*Mixed*	*None*
		Per cent		

A. *Own directly expressed attitude*

Large firms:

	High	Low	Mixed	None
Raise tariffs	⑫	⑦	7	6
Reduce tariffs	㉑	❹❼	26	42
Leave	39	22	52	35
Don't know	4	20	8	10
Refused to generalize	24	4	7	7
	100	100	100	100

Small firms:

	High	Low	Mixed	None
Raise tariffs	⑱	⑤	6	4
Reduce tariffs	㉖	❸❻	27	41
Leave	31	32	38	29
Don't know	16	21	23	25
Refused to generalize	9	6	6	1
	100	100	100	100

B. *Own attitude reclassified*

Large firms:

	High	Low	Mixed	None
Raise tariffs	㉜	⑬	20	11
Reduce tariffs	㉕	❻❶	36	52
Leave	31	13	34	24
Don't know	6	13	7	12
Refused to generalize	6	1	3	1
	100	100	100	100

Small firms:

	High	Low	Mixed	None
Raise tariffs	㉟	⑩	16	10
Reduce tariffs	㉟	❹❷	38	47
Leave	17	24	23	23
Don't know	10	24	23	20
Refused to generalize	3	—	—	—
	100	100	100	100

* Circled white numbers are cases where there is complete correspondence of respondents' own expressed view and economists' rating of interest. Circled black numbers are cases of direct contradiction of own expressed views and economists' rating of interest.

turer of a single drug may find he needs protection. The camera industry would be rated as having an objective interest in protection, but Polaroid, with a monopoly on its product, might well see its advantage in exports. Such a consideration suggests that the correlation of objective and subjective interest as reported in Table 9-2 may be too low.

Despite the inevitable imperfections, the table supports the thesis that self-interest and attitudes toward tariff policy are correlated, though not perfectly; precisely how strongly we cannot be sure.

We may add a further observation about the behavior of those businessmen with a mixed interest. The low-tariff element in this mixed interest has a relatively weak impact on their thinking. In either section of the table and for both size groups, the men from the mixed-interest industries are less likely to favor a lower tariff policy than those from low- or no-interest industries. On the other hand, they are only moderately inclined toward raising tariffs. The tendency of mixed interest seems to be to drive men toward the semiprotectionist position of leaving tariffs as they are. If the reader wonders why we call "leave as is" a semiprotectionist answer, we would point out that protectionism in the 1950's was on the defensive. Proposed legislation would lead to tariff cuts. The *status quo* meant no further reductions. Men and organizations committed to the protectionist side seldom argued for high or higher tariffs as such. They formulated their demands in terms of leaving over-all levels of tariffs as they were, while giving added protection in special instances where needed. By comparing parts A and B of Table 9-2, it will be clear that protectionism more often than the reverse lurked behind the noncommittal answer that current tariffs were "about right." As noted in Chapter 8, respondents whose overt answer to our query on tariffs was "leave" or "refused to generalize" when reclassified by their remarks on other questions added more cases to the protectionist than to the liberal-trade categories. Protectionism shows up substantially stronger in Table 9-2 B than in Table 9-2 A. Among men whose firms had mixed interests, especially, the tendency was for the *initial* reaction to be an indecisive "leave things as they are."

It is frequently asserted in discussions of attitudes toward foreign-trade policy that such attitudes are not merely a function of a businessman's interest in foreign trade per se but also of the general state of his business. More specifically, it is contended that a man is not very likely to worry about foreign competition in the domestic market if his business is generally going well.

Now, there is no simple rationality in predicating a tariff policy on the general state of one's business. If higher tariffs are good for a man's business, they may be good for it whatever his absolute rate of profit. So, too, if lower tariffs are good for him, they may be good for him whether he is already making a fortune or currently losing money. The effect of the tariff is at the margin, and the difference between a high- and a low-tariff interest is a difference in the direction of movement at the margin. Simple self-interest regarding tariffs has no relation to the level of current business.

But, empirically, the tariff stand which businessmen take does have a strong relation to the level of their current business. The data which illustrate this relationship are presented in Fig. 9-1. Protectionists were more likely than liberal traders to say business was "worse last year." And in both instances the leaners who were identified on reclassification were less extreme than the overtly committed proponents of the position. Let us imagine two men of fundamentally protectionist orientation, one of whom has had a bad business year and the other a good year. We might suppose that the man who had had a bad year would be more likely to say "raise tariffs" and that the other might be content to leave tariffs as they are. The interest in protection being given, it might be reasonable for the man in greater need to press for relief the harder. But now imagine two men of fundamentally liberal-trade orientation, one of whom had had a good and one of whom had had a bad year. A simple self-interest theory would tell us that the man who had had the bad year should be at least as firmly in favor of tariff reductions for expanded trade as the other, but it does not turn out that way. The man who had had the good year is more likely to say "reduce tariffs," and the other to say "leave them as they are." A liberal-

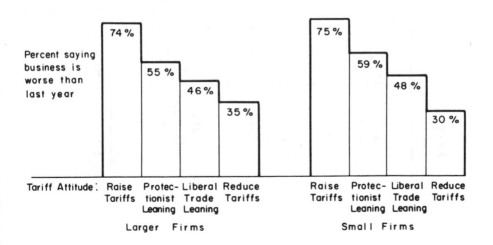

Fig. 9-1   STATE OF BUSINESS RELATED TO TARIFF ATTITUDE

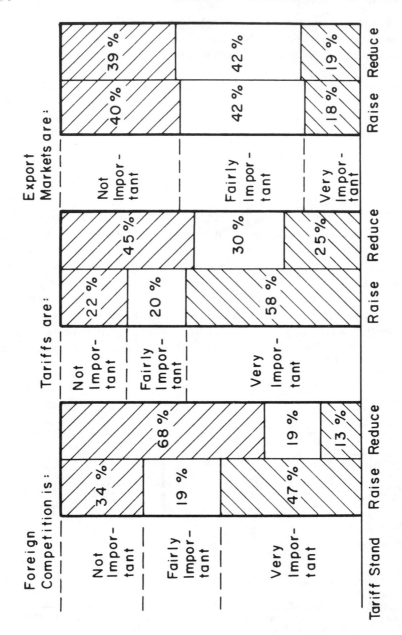

Fig. 9-2(a)   LARGE FIRMS: IMPORTANCE OF VARIOUS TOPICS AS
RELATED BY THOSE WHO FAVOR RAISING AND REDUCING TARIFFS

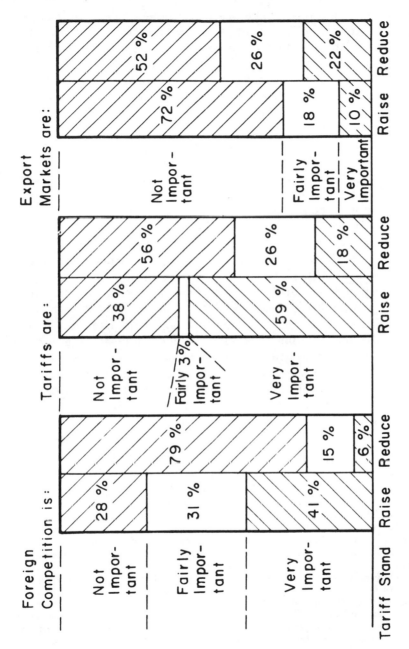

Fig. 9-2(b) SMALL FIRMS: IMPORTANCE OF VARIOUS TOPICS AS
RELATED BY THOSE WHO FAVOR RAISING AND REDUCING TARIFFS

trade policy seemed to appeal to businessmen who were doing well, regardless of any specific contribution of it to their business. And protection seemed to appeal to businessmen who were hurt, again independently of any specific help that tariff increases would provide.[5]

In addition to the relatively objective criterion provided by the economists' assessment of interest in foreign-trade policy, we have a number of more subjective indexes of how our respondents themselves saw their own situation. First of all, there is the respondent's own rating of how important tariffs, foreign competition, and export markets are to his own firm. In the left-hand bars of Fig. 9-2 we explore this matter. It is clear that men who favor raising tariffs tend to think that foreign competition is important to their firms and that men who favor lowering tariffs think it is not important.

A similar relationship is found in Fig. 9-2, middle, between attitudes toward raising and lowering tariffs and the perceived importance of tariffs to their firms. It is conceivable that a man might say tariffs are important to his firm meaning that high tariffs are a handicap. But that is not generally the way in which tariffs are viewed, as is evidenced by the strong relationship between being a protectionist and saying tariffs are important. The liberal trader is not the man who sees high tariff rates as a serious problem and harmful to him. The liberal trader is generally the man for whom tariffs are not personally an important issue.

On the other hand, a man who felt that export markets were important to his firm ought to favor lowering tariffs. The data to test this proposition are to be found in the right-hand bars of Fig. 9-2.

It turns out not to be equally so that an export interest corresponds to a man's views on tariffs; the relationship is by no means clear. Men from large and medium firms favor either raising or lowering tariffs independently of their firms' interest in export markets. The tariff stand of

---

[5] Note, however, that a closely related hypothesis failed of confirmation. We thought that protectionists might be temperamental pessimists and liberal traders optimists. As one index of that, we asked not only about this year's business but also about next year's.

Presumably we may take at face value a man's statement of how business is, compared to the previous year. He would have sufficient objective evidence to incline us to regard this as a statement of fact. There is, of course, a certain amount of factual evidence on the basis of which to estimate the future trend of one's business, but such an estimate must of its nature contain an element of guessing. When we asked our respondents how they expected business to be in the following year, we found that those men who favored raising tariffs were more optimistic than were the men who favored lowering tariffs. In every size of firm the proportion saying business would be better was higher: in the largest firms, the proportions were 75 to 46 per cent; in the medium, 55 to 44 per cent; and in the smallest firms, 61 to 55 per cent.

Perhaps businesses which were down in a year when most business was not down had realistic reasons to expect the next year to be better. In any case, the psychological factors which entered the choice of a tariff stand were not as simple as generalized optimism or pessimism.

men from the smaller firms, on the other hand, is somewhat related to the self-interest of their firms in export markets. But an inspection of these data in comparison with the previous two sets of data shows quite clearly that, in general, the association between attitudes toward tariffs and a liberal-trade self-interest is far less strong than the association of foreign-trade attitudes with a protectionist self-interest.

In addition to affirming—with complications to be mentioned below—that there is an association between a businessman's attitudes toward foreign-trade policy and his perceived self-interest, these data call our attention to two less obvious and therefore more interesting propositions.

The first is that in general any criterion of self-interest is likely to show more impact among the small firms than among the larger ones. We saw, for example, that interest in export markets appeared to have no relationship to attitudes toward tariffs among the heads of the larger firms, but that it did have a perceptible relationship among the small firms. An inspection of the two other sets of data will show that, in general, the strength of association of attitude and interest was somewhat higher among the small firms. This is a phenomenon that we shall encounter at various points. It does not mean that the heads of larger firms are less motivated by self-interest, but rather that their self-interest is more complicated and therefore seen as less dependent on a single factor. This point can be illustrated here with two fairly simple statistics.

Respondents were asked a series of questions about the impact of decreases or increases of tariffs on their own business. At the end of this series of questions, those who had indicated that their business would benefit from an increase in tariffs were asked: "Would high tariffs be good for your business in some ways and bad in other ways?" Among the men from the largest firms to whom this was applicable, two-thirds said that some parts of their business would be affected differently than others, whereas among the smallest firms a full three-fourths said just the opposite, namely, that all parts of their business would be affected the same way. Hence, in assessing their self-interest, the men from the larger firms were faced with a more complicated decision.

Furthermore, apropos of the criteria we have just been discussing, the heads of larger firms are more likely to find themselves in a situation of cross-pressure—the condition of a firm simultaneously having tariffs important (a protectionist force) and having export markets important (an antiprotectionist force). Among the largest firms, 55 per cent were under such cross-pressure; among the medium-sized firms, 44 per cent; and, among the smallest firms, only 34 per cent.

The second point to be made is that the prospect of gain apparently has less impact than the prospect of loss. Concern with export markets involves the prospect of increasing profits, whereas the threat of foreign competition involves the prospect of losing a share of the existing market. We saw that, both among businessmen and among the general public, self-interest in increasing exports was less strongly associated with attitudes toward tariff policy than was self-interest in restricting imports. It seems that one reason for this is that increases in exports are associated with a gain above the present level, and protection from imports is associated in people's minds with maintaining that which they have—and, by implication, that to which they are entitled—and also that which they can assess more directly.

It seems clear that, at the time of our survey in 1954, trade liberalization was perceived as a way of opening up business opportunities, not of protecting vested positions. In 1962, the perception of the situation was somewhat different, and that is one of the reasons for the augmented strength of the liberal position. In 1962, the liberal-trade argument was that, if the president did not receive fresh bargaining powers, American firms would find themselves shut out of the Common Market. This identification of liberal-trade policies with the protection of existing markets was almost wholly lacking in 1954-1955.

One small but interesting piece of evidence on this point comes out of our data. Those men who felt that their firms were suffering substantially from foreign competition or who feared the threat of such competition were asked what they anticipated would be the effects on their business of raising or lowering tariffs. Specifically, they were asked:

> Would a 15 per cent cut in U.S. tariffs hurt your business materially?
>
> Would a 15 per cent increase in U.S. tariffs help your business materially?

The answers to these questions in relation to the men's attitudes toward tariffs in general are tabulated in Fig. 9-3.

We note, first, that there were some men, actually a majority, who felt that, although they were indeed threatened by foreign competition, a 15 per-cent change in tariffs one way or another would not affect their businesses. Such men were conspicuously less protectionist than those who thought a tariff change would affect them (columns 2 and 4 in comparison with columns 1 and 3). This may be considered a reaffirmation of the linkage between attitudes and perceived self-interest.

A comparison of columns 1 and 3, that is, a comparison of those who fear loss with those who anticipate gain from a change in policy, is even more interesting. One might expect that those men who expected to benefit from an increase in tariffs would be more anxious to see them raised than would those who anticipated a loss from a cut in tariffs. The latter should be content to leave them as they are. Yet, to some extent, the

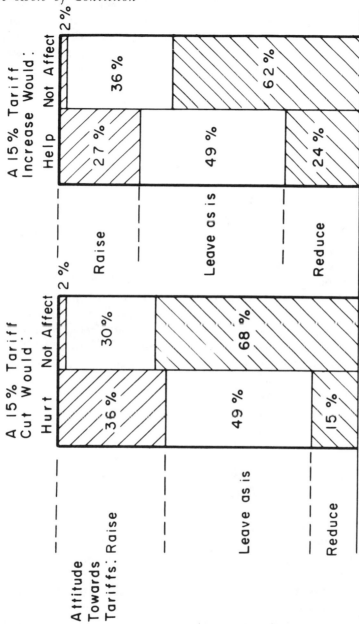

Fig. 9-3 PROSPECT OF GAIN OR LOSS FROM TARIFF CHANGES RELATED
TO OWN ATTITUDES TOWARD TARIFFS *

* Since this figure includes only men who felt substantial injury or substantial threat
from foreign competition, there were so few cases that we have grouped all businessmen
together.

opposite is true. The men who feared loss from a tariff cut were more in favor of raising tariffs than were those who explicitly asserted that they would gain by the increase. We see that fear of loss is a more powerful stimulus than prospect of gain. This finding is in accordance with the contention of some recent commentators on business decision-making that firms are not operated so much to maximize profit as to minimize loss.

We may summarize our discussion of self-interest to this point as follows: the concept of self-interest is sufficiently complicated that there may be genuine arguments as to what the self-interest of any man, firm, or industry is. Nevertheless, one way or another, most men arrive at an image of what this self-interest is, and this image, according to our data as well as according to common sense and casual observation, is correlated with the stand taken on foreign-trade policy.

Because the range of involvements of firms varies with their size, no single criterion of self-interest will have as much impact on the head of a large firm as on the head of a small firm.

Protectionist attitudes were more closely linked to perceived self-interest than were liberal-trade attitudes. We have explained this in part with the intervening proposition that prospect of loss is a stronger motivating force than is prospect of gain. The expansion of foreign trade raises a prospect of gain. Protectionism is primarily a matter of defense against loss of domestic markets. Hence, self-interest acted more powerfully on behalf of protectionism. In 1962, the liberal-trade advocates tried to change that situation by trading on fear of the Common Market.

We are not finished with the problem of self-interest and its relation to attitudes and actions, but we take leave of it for the moment. The impact of self-interest and of persuasion will run as a thread throughout this study. There are more questions still to be asked about self-interest.

Whose self-interest—that of the individual executive, or of management as a group, or of the firm (whatever that may be), or of its major stockholders, or of any combination of the many claimants? Over what period of time? In what values? Is it only the maximum amount of money that counts or also the security of the enterprise, power, and the like? And what about uncertainty? What of a small return at low risks versus unexplored horizons?

For the moment, it is sufficient to note that self-interest does indeed operate on the behavior we are studying; yet, when that has been said, nothing has been determined. Self-interest is but a name for what a man wants. It does not tell us what it is that he wants. Unlike our friends who told us, "Tell me a man's interest and I will tell you his stand," we would say, "Tell us where a man stands and we will tell you what perceptions of his interests will serve to make that stand a self-consistent and stable one." There are perceptions of self-interest available to bolster any stand by any individual. To say that a man arrived at any position via consideration of his self-interest is no more determinative than to say he arrived at it by cognitive processes, or by logical steps, or by discussion. It is true, it is important, it is worthy of attention and study, it shapes and limits the process in part, it excludes certain outcomes; yet it does not tell us what the outcome will be. The theory of self-interest is an "empty-box" model—a valid one, a useful one; but it remains for us now to fill some of the boxes by seeing what further determinants entered into businessmen's decisions.

☐ Tariff Attitudes and Internationalism

It was asserted by many observers that, as with the general public, the attitudes of businessmen toward foreign-trade policy were associated with their attitudes toward internationalism and isolationism. This we found to be in some measure true.

Most businessmen in the postwar era are internationalists in principle. In the survey which the NORC conducted for us, 87 per cent either agreed that we should take an active part in world affairs or said that we had no choice but to do so and indicated that they did not mind this enforced internationalism. Furthermore, economic autarky was rejected. Eighty-five per cent thought that American prosperity and security would best be served by an increase, rather than a decrease, in foreign trade.

But, even with this overwhelming majority ready to put itself on record verbally for internationalism, there remained some room for variation. In Fig. 9-4, we show attitudes on America's taking an active role in world affairs of men who favored raising and reducing tariffs. One conclusion is clear: the overwhelming majority of businessmen favored an

IMPORTANCE FOR ONE'S FIRM OF POLITICAL STABILITY ABROAD

RELATED TO ATTITUDES TOWARD TARIFFS

Political stability abroad	Large and medium firms		Small firms	
	Respondent favors:			
	Raising	Reducing	Raising	Reducing
	Per cent			
Very important	52	49	51	40
Fairly important	8	32	12	36
Not important	40	19	37	24
	100	100	100	100

internationalist foreign policy.

Even among proponents of raising tariffs, a substantial majority favored an active U.S. role in world affairs. However, there is a definite tendency for this group to be less internationalist than the proponents of reducing tariffs.[6] Among the men from the smallest-size firms, the isolationism of the protectionists becomes quite strong.

The question might well be raised whether attitudes toward foreign-trade policy and attitudes toward internationalism were accidentally correlated, both being a result of a man's objective self-interest. This does not appear to be so. The ratings made by our panel of economists on the self-interest of the various industries do not correlate with responses wishing the United States to take an active part in world affairs. Self-interest correlates with tariff attitudes, as noted before. Internationalism correlates with tariff attitudes, as we note now. But tariff interest does not correlate with internationalism. They are independent forces operating on tariff attitudes.

Further evidence for the association of protectionism with nationalism and of a liberal-trade policy with internationalism is derived from two questions asked on the poll conducted for us by the National Opinion Research Center. Respondents, regardless of their own feelings, were asked what they thought the best single argument for high tariffs, and, following this, what was the best single argument for low tariffs. Their responses are reported in Table 9-3.

Even the most casual scrutiny of these answers shows that our sample of businessmen saw a high-tariff policy as associated with a national interest—particularly that of American business, industry, and labor—and a low-tariff policy as benefiting international interests of foreign countries or the world in general. Some of the categories of argument are to a surprising extent restricted to one side. For example, only 1 per cent of the sample thought of a low-tariff policy as being for the benefit of American labor. Virtually nobody thought of a high-tariff policy as benefiting either foreign countries or the world in general. Little issue was seen by our respondents about the uncertain matter of what effects high

---

[6] A similar relationship exists between attitudes toward tariff and favoring U.S. investment abroad.

One anomaly must be reported, however. We expected that concern with political stability abroad would be another measure of internationalism, correlated with a liberal view on the tariff. It did not turn out that way. Rather, it seems that a concern that foreign political affairs remain stable may be a reflection of positive involvement with these affairs, an internationalist attitude, or a desire that they remain stable so that one need not be bothered with them—an isolationist attitude. We find that protectionists are more likely to say both that political stability abroad is very important and that it is not important. Unlike those who would lower tariffs, they avoid the middle category

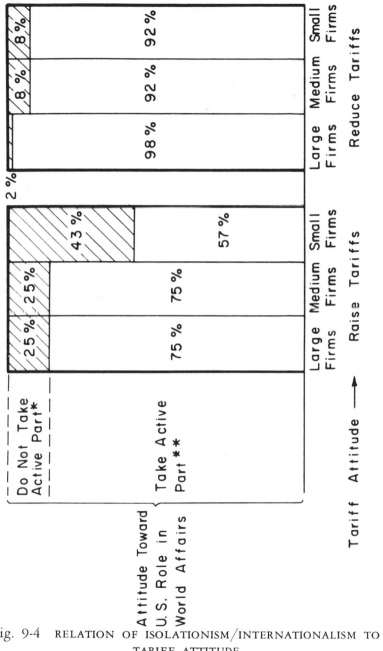

Fig. 9-4 RELATION OF ISOLATIONISM/INTERNATIONALISM TO
TARIFF ATTITUDE

* Includes those who felt that we have no choice but did object.
** Includes those who felt that we have no choice but did not object.

TABLE 9-3

BEST ARGUMENTS FOR TARIFF POLICY

A. Best argument for high tariff, classified by "who will benefit?"

	Size of firm		
	Large	Medium	Small
		Per cent	
1. American business and industry	34	34	42
2. American labor	23	25	24
3. American consumers, general public, or economy in general	29	26	20
4. Foreign countries	—	1	—
5. World in general	—	—	1
6. No "good argument," or only rebuttal offered	10	6	7
7. No answer	6	8	6
	102*	100	100

B. Best argument for low tariff, classified by "who will benefit?"

	Size of firm		
	Large	Medium	Small
		Per cent	
1. American business and industry	11	9	13
2. American labor	1	1	1
3. American consumers, general public, or economy in general	18	19	19
4. Foreign countries	20	21	14
5. World in general	28	30	26
6. No "good argument," or only rebuttal offered	7	7	11
7. No answer or benefit unclear or unspecified	23	22	22
	108*	109*	106*

* Some respondents named more than one beneficiary.

or low tariffs would have. The issue was joined over how much one cared about those effects. Were the important consequences the ones close to home or those overseas? That was seen as the issue.

The Ideological Initiative

With the decline of isolationism and the rise among businessmen of a concern for world events, protectionism has been losing its ideological base. Our younger respondents who favored higher tariffs gave business-linked reasons without adopting a generally isolationist attitude. Among the older generation of protectionists, a full 48 per cent said that we should stay out of an active part in world affairs if we can, whereas this is true of only 21 per cent of the respondents under fifty.

There is ample evidence beyond our survey data for the contention that protectionism is becoming less ideological. It has become relatively rare for a protectionist spokesman to argue for protection in principle. When they speak for protection of a particular industry, it seems that they often tacitly accept the arguments of their opponents and contend that their own industry is an exception.

When Schattschneider studied the passage of the Smoot-Hawley tariff in the Hoover administration, he commented on the extent to which protectionism then had the ideological initiative. Even men who argued for the reduction of specific tariffs professed their beliefs in protectionism in principle. "Many of the most passionate avowals of faith in the dogma of protective tariff to be found anywhere in the record," he says, "were made in the course of arguments against particular interests in the rate structure." [7] The prototype of the argument for lowering a particular tariff began in effect thus: "Of course I favor protectionism, but. . . ."

Today, as we have already noted, the tables are turned. More often than not one hears the advocate of protection begin his statement about as follows: "Of course I am for increasing trade and believe in lowering trade barriers, but. . . ." Typical of this point of view was that of a small Midwestern businessman whose business was fast dwindling, largely as a result of competition from foreign imports. He said: "In the broad view I understand that these countries have to get trade from us to exist, and I know that they need the trade to get funds to pay back their debts. But they can start erasing trade barriers somewhere else, not in the wallpaper business."

The deterioration in the ideological underpinnings of protectionism is evident in the following statement from Oscar Strackbein, whose efforts in postwar years won him the label of "Mr. Protection":

> No retreat into isolationism is entailed in the regulation of imports to assure fair competition. No ill will toward the foreign producer can be deduced. . . . There is nothing nationalistic in the principle of equal treatment of imports and domestic trade. There is no chauvinism involved. . . . There is no decline in our love of our neighbors and allies. [8]

---

[7] E. E. Schattschneider, *Politics, Pressures, and the Tariff* (Englewood Cliffs, N.J.: Prentice-Hall, Inc., 1935), p. 141.

[8] O. R. Strackbein, "The Tariff Issue Reviewed and Restated" (Washington, D.C.: The National Labor-Management Council on Foreign Trade Policy, 1951), p. 20.

While Strackbein argues that protectionism is not in fact linked with isolationism, nationalism, and chauvinism, he recognizes that a large portion of his listeners think it is.

Protectionists generally assume that intellectuals—and college professors and economists in particular—are opposed to their position. Although spokesmen for protectionist organizations treated us with the utmost politeness and helpfulness in our study, we were always painfully aware of the fact that they assumed that we were on the other side of the argument, no matter how much we reassured them of our neutrality on the substance of the issue. On the other hand, spokesmen of liberal-trade organizations took it for granted that we were on their side, and it sometimes took a fair amount of firmness to keep them from involving us in their activities.

We asked our respondents what sorts of people they thought favored lower tariffs and what sorts favored higher tariffs. Almost one in ten spontaneously mentioned professors, intellectuals, or economists as favoring lower tariffs. Not a single respondent mentioned this group among the proponents of a higher tariff policy.

One cannot come away from a study of the trade controversy without a feeling that, despite the very real effectiveness of the protectionist position in many quarters, the ideological initiative has shifted to the other side, and this had happened mainly because, in a period of expanding internationalism, protectionism was linked with isolationism in the thinking of so many people.

Chinks in the Liberal Traders' Ideological Wall

There were vulnerabilities to the liberal-trade position, too, the principal one of which was the notion of injury to domestic industries and workers. The power of this consideration was suggested in a poll reported by the Research Institute of America in the *Saturday Review* in 1954. Five hundred business and labor leaders were asked: "Do you favor further lowering of our tariffs?" "Yes" was the reply of 60 per cent, 21 per cent said "no," and 19 per cent were not sure which policy they favored.[9] However, when they were asked if they would continue to favor lower tariffs "despite the possibility of injury to the particular American industries involved," the proportion favoring lower tariffs dropped to 44 per cent, and opposition to this policy rose to 35 per cent. Certainly, this unwilling-

---

[9] The Research Institute of America, "Free Trade . . . A Survey," *Saturday Review*, Jan. 23, 1954, pp. 33-34 and 54-56. The differences between the Research Institute of America's sample, method, and question and ours are such that we should expect little correspondence in the distribution of answers. What we are interested in is the impact of the contingency question which the institute posed.

ness to hurt one's neighbor is in some sense an ideological support for protectionism.

There is a deep-seated feeling in the American business ethic that one must not injure another businessman gratuitously. This means, on the one hand, that it is ethical to compete with him if one has some direct stake in the matter, but one may not espouse a policy in the general interest which will hurt some particular person or business. For example, one businessman told us that he was reluctant to support a liberal-trade policy publicly for fear some one of his associates would say to him in effect: "Look, Joe, you have nothing to gain from this. Why do you want to hurt me?" This is substantially what was told to many public spokesmen for a liberal-trade policy.

Couple this general feeling with the fact that specific injury to specific businesses is much easier to communicate and comprehend than are diffuse benefits to the economy as a whole, and one can understand why the plea of injury had the capacity to immobilize a good deal of potential support for a liberal-trade policy.

It should be further emphasized that the substantial majority with which American businessmen supported a liberal-trade policy amounted to something less than evidence of crusading zeal. We have often used such phrases as "symbolic support" and "verbal support" for a liberal-trade policy and for internationalism. This has been because we are acutely aware of the fact that what a man favors in principle and what he does in practice are far from identical. True, the overwhelming majority of our sample of businessmen gave verbal support to some internationalist sentiments. But this does not argue that the business community was saturated with undiluted, militant altruism toward foreign countries. Many respondents expressed concern over "give-away" programs. The "trade, not aid" slogan was calculated to garner support for a more liberal trade policy from men whose general internationalism was complicated by the anxiety that we were playing the role of "Uncle Santa Claus." In light of this, it is pertinent that the present trade acts are based on reciprocity. The notion of reciprocity played an important part even in the thinking of advocates of generally lower tariffs.

We asked the respondents: "Some people think we should cut tariffs even when other countries do not make any reciprocal concessions. How do you feel about this in general?"

Most respondents who had favored reducing tariffs opposed reductions without reciprocity. Only 36, 39, and 49 per cent of low-tariff advocates in large, medium, and small firms, respectively, favored nonreciprocal tariff cuts. These data illustrate the importance of the notion of reciprocity. Protectionist spokesmen, sensing the vulnerability of reduction of trade barriers on a nonreciprocal basis, took pains to introduce into their arguments evidence that we had given more than we had received. For example, they repeatedly introduced statistics to show that our own tariff structure was one of the lowest in the world. On the other hand, the Kennedy administration in 1962 published a "box score" on its trade negotiations with foreign countries, claiming a 4-to-3 advantage in concessions.

□ Strengths and Vulnerabilities

The facts that the protectionist position was more firmly grounded in direct business considerations and that the liberal-trade position fitted better with the ideology of the times naturally controlled what the proponents of each position thought were the best arguments for their own and the opposing position. In Table 9-4 we have summarized the views of the committed proponents of raising and reducing tariffs as to the best argument for both their own and the opposing position.

With respect to the main arguments in favor of protectionism, both sides agree on two points: the main arguments for high tariff are the benefits they convey to American, as opposed to foreign, interests and that it is American business which mainly benefits. However, from this point on, there is some divergence of opinion. Men who favor raising tariffs are considerably more likely to claim for their side that high tariffs benefit American workers as well as business. Also, the advocates of higher tariffs are more likely to see them as serving the general American interest by promoting American peace and prosperity. Both sides agreed on the validity of a business interest in tariff protection, but the protectionists sought to bolster their position against the charge of being narrowly selfish by claiming benefits to other Americans, too.

In the lower portion of the table, the four arguments for low tariffs are listed in order from the most narrowly domestic to the most internationalist. The somewhat more isolationist protectionists tended to see the most domestic consideration as strongest; the liberal traders, the most international.

Grouping the arguments differently, the protectionists see the benefit of low tariffs as being to domestic consumption (#1), not to domestic business (#2); and to world politics (#3), not to world business (#4). The low-tariff advocates claim that their best arguments are neither the consumption argument nor the political argument, but the good of business (#2 and #4).

The reasons for this difference are complex. For one thing, the liberal-trade position suffers from a vulnerability opposite to that of selfishness. In an era of internationalism, the advocates of lowering tariffs run the risk of being called impractical, of sacrificing the interests of American

TABLE 9-4

BEST ARGUMENTS FOR RAISING AND LOWERING TARIFFS AS
PRESENTED BY PROPONENTS OF OPPOSING SIDES *

A. *Best arguments for high tariffs*

	Own attitude toward tariffs	
	Raise	Reduce
	Per cent	
Benefits American business	55	52
Protects American workers	50	28
Protects American security and prosperity	45	30
	150	110

B. *Best arguments for low tariffs*

	Own attitude toward tariffs	
	Raise	Reduce
	Per cent	
Lowers prices and increases demand	52	15
Makes business more efficient and develops export markets	8	36
Improves military strength and aids allies	28	18
Benefits world economy	25	46
	113	115

* Because of the relatively small number of cases giving relevant answers for any size of firm, all sizes of firms have been combined. Arguments are here classified by nature of argument, not by beneficiary mentioned. Respondents could give more than one argument.

business to the cause of internationalism. Their answer is that they, too, are interested in business and the economy, not just in doing good.

It should be remembered that we did not ask people the reasons for which they might personally favor one policy or another, but for their estimation of the best arguments regardless of their own position. In such a situation, we would expect to find what we did in fact find. The opponents of a position would grant as arguments for it those which were least debatable and which from their own perspective would be least convincing. Thus, protectionists are willing to grant that low tariffs benefit consumers and strengthen military and diplomatic alliances.

The strategy of the proponents appears to be to seek out arguments which counter the vulnerabilities of their own position. Protectionists indicate benefits of their position to the general interest and to groups other than business. Liberal traders stress the economic benefits of their position. Each cites those benefits of his own position that other people are, in his mind, likely to overlook or underestimate.

In these answers, we see the strengths and vulnerabilities of the protectionist and liberal-trade positions. In the chapters which follow, we shall see how these strengths and weaknesses on each side affected the communications activities of our respondents.

□ Summary

In Chapter 8, we saw that there was a shift away from protectionism in the American business community in the period before 1954. In the present chapter, we looked further into the origins and nature of our respondents' attitudes toward foreign-trade policy. We found clear linkages between tariff attitudes and self-interest and between tariff attitudes and internationalism. Prospects of loss had more impact than prospects of gain on our respondents' estimates of the interests of their firms, and, as a corollary, a protectionist interest had more power than a liberal-trade interest. We further observed that any single criterion of self-interest seemed to have more effect on smaller than on larger firms. The interest structure of larger firms is more complex, and they are therefore less dependent on any single factor.

There was a modest relationship between protectionism and isolationism, even though the respondents as a whole gave strong support, in words at least, to internationalism. The relationship between protectionism and isolationism was stronger among older than among younger men. This finding and others suggested a loss of ideological initiative on the part of the protectionists. Protectionism in 1954-1955 was in an ideologically vulnerable position; there seemed to be general agreement that a protectionist policy did not serve international objectives. This (as we shall soon see) did not mean that the protectionists were lacking in other real sources of strength.

It is worth pausing for a moment to take another look at the factors which produced a predominantly antiprotectionist sentiment in the American business community in 1954 and 1955. The bases of this sentiment were two: the postwar international situation and the general prosperity of American business. The predominantly protectionist sentiment of American businessmen as reflected in the 1939 Roper poll cannot be interpreted solely in terms of isolationism. American business in 1939 was not in a particularly optimistic mood, at least in comparison with the outlook of the mid-1950's. We have seen in our own data that protectionism is correlated with the over-all state of a man's business. During the recession of 1954 the liberal-trade forces seemed to lose strength as general business conditions worsened.

Also, the postwar position of the United States was different from the prewar one. Rather than being one among several great nations, the United States was the leader of an alliance. Much of the appeal of a liberal-trade policy was that such a policy was seen as strengthening the Free World economically and politically in the fight against Communism.

In addition to self-interest and ideology, one other set of factors bore on a businessman's attitudes toward foreign-trade policy. That social-structural set of factors was the man's role in the flow of business communication and decision. Small businesses did not have foreign-trade specialists to advise them of their interests. Large businesses found their interests mixed, since the marketing demands for different products placed them under cross-pressure. Companies frequently did not know how much they sold abroad because they used intermediaries and because Canadian sales were not included in foreign-trade figures. The characteristic response to doubts and cross-pressures seemed to be to settle for the *status quo*.

So far, we have only touched on such structural factors. We have touched on them only insofar as they served to influence perceptions of self-interest or of national interest. These goals are unclear and subject to a variety of definitions. They are little more than formal categories, the contents of which differ from man to man and from situation to situation. We turn now, for most of the rest of the book, to the situational factors which affected what went into those empty boxes. We shall examine the communications behavior of the men in our sample, their sources of information, their own outgoing communications, and, finally, their efforts to influence Congress.

Chapter 10

Channels of Information

What channels of information did our respondents use to keep up with the world around them? How well did their sources inform them? How did men with different roles in business and national life differ in the sources they used and in what they learned?

American business leaders are a generally well-educated group of men in highly responsible posts.[1] Since they must, if only to do their jobs well, keep posted on what is happening in the world, they are avid information-seekers. But they are extraordinarily busy with the daily affairs of their firms. News of the political world must compete for their attention with that of the economy and technology and problems of their own company.

What an executive can learn about public or international affairs depends on the way channels are set up to brief him. What he needs to learn depends on whether his firm is small or a nation-wide, diversified giant; the structure of the staff which feeds him information varies with the

---

[1] Even among the small firms, 50 per cent were college graduates, and, among the large firms, 61 per cent.

firm's size. His job thus makes a difference in what a man learns about world affairs, a greater difference even than does his education. By the time he has become the head of a company, a man has become a certain type of individual. His chances of getting there are better if he has had a college education, but, if he is the exceptional man who has got there without such an education, he has long since made up the deficiency. He has become indistinguishable from his more formally educated colleagues. It was role more than background which controlled what our respondents learned about the world.

On matters not closely bearing on their own businesses, executives rely heavily on conventional printed media. Despite the other demands on their time, they do much reading of newspapers and magazines. As a matter of fact, a study made by Bursk in 1957 (described below) indicates that in the business world they are the men with most responsibility and hence with the greatest pressure on their time who do the most reading.

On matters that touch their business more closely than the news in a magazine or daily paper, our respondents learned a great deal from conversation. To a surprising degree, the American business communication system is oral or by memorandum. In many instances, requirements for information are so technical that the businessman must rely on specialists to brief him. Specialized reading can be made almost impossible by the pressures of other demands. On the other hand, highly informed advisers are readily available. American businessmen thus get a considerable amount of their information face-to-face, on the telephone, or in the form of letters or condensed memorandums.

International information comes to our respondents via one more major channel, foreign travel. Travel supplements the standard American news media and the oral advice of experienced colleagues. Our respondents traveled abroad often, and, when they did, their travels had a profound effect on their views.

In this chapter, we shall try to document these conclusions. The data on which they are based come from a series of questions on the NORC survey concerning the reading and travel experience of our respondents as well as from our informal interviews. We shall also include certain comparable data from studies by Bursk and by Erdos and Morgan, the latter being referred to as "E. and M." [2]

---

[2] Edward C. Bursk, "New Dimensions in Top Executive Reading," *Harvard Business Review*, 35 (September-October 1957), 93-112, and Erdos and Morgan Research Service, "The Reading Preferences of Corporate Officers and Executive Personnel" (1957; private circulation). Both studies were done on a sample of executives drawn from *Poor's Register of Directors and Executives*. The samples which were drawn in both studies consisted of "top executives," but were not as much confined to heads of firms as was our sample.

The Bursk study was done in 1957, three years after ours. The E. and M. report gives

□ Reading Habits

Regular reading of one or more newspapers is virtually unanimous,[3] and a majority of our respondents say they read two or three regularly. Among the newspapers cited, the most important numerically are local papers.[4] Second is *The Wall Street Journal,* which was mentioned by almost one-half of the group (Bursk, 75 per cent; E. and M., 49.8 per cent). In third and fourth places were *The New York Times* (about one in three; Bursk, 33 per cent; E. and M., 26 per cent) and the *Herald Tribune* (about

---

results of surveys done in 1952, 1954, and 1957. Both studies were done by mail questionnaire. The Bursk study was supplemented by 100 telephone follow-ups on non-respondents. Bursk used aided recall, giving respondents a list of publications from which to check those which they read for business purposes. The Erdos and Morgan study, done for *The Wall Street Journal,* asked respondents to indicate spontaneously, without the aid of a list, the newspapers and the magazines they read "regularly for general or business news."

There are certain obvious differences between these two studies and ours. (1) The samples were somewhat different. (2) Ours was a personal, oral interview, and the others were mail questionnaires. (3) Each of the three studies put the question somewhat differently. (4) The other studies report findings for years other than 1954. Yet, when all this is taken into account, the picture drawn from each of the three studies is remarkably similar. Only if one had an interest in selling space in one of the media concerned would he be inclined to quarrel over the differences in the findings. The precise findings on reading habits are so inevitably a function of the details in design of study and question-wording that it has been our policy not to emphasize the precise figures, but only the over-all patterns. However, where the Bursk and the E. and M. studies report on the same newspapers or magazines as we do, the comparable figures are inserted for the reader's guidance. The Bursk figures refer to 1957, the E. and M. figures to the 1954 portion of their findings.

It will be seen that Bursk, using aided recall, generally reports higher readership for specific media. This should be expected from the difference in method. However, it should be remembered that aided recall has a tendency to produce overreporting, though data introduced by Bursk indicate that his own study may not have produced such over-reporting. On the other hand, E. and M., using spontaneous recall, tend to report lower readership than we do. This would be expected on a self-administered questionnaire in comparison to an oral interview, in which the interviewer can keep probing. It is probably also a function of the limited number of spaces provided in the questionnaire. This discourages the really active reader from listing all his sources. (Cf. the discussion of the *Harvard Business Review,* below.) Finally, the E. and M. question is more restrictive, specifying reading for news. Bursk has shown that much of the disparity between his and the E. and M. figures disappears when one corrects for this difference in question-wording—a correction he was fortunately able to make by virtue of further questions which he asked.

[3] Respondents were asked about the newspapers and magazines they read. Apparently some, in concentrating on magazines, overlooked mentioning newspapers. The total proportion of men who did not mention reading some newspaper was slightly over 5 per cent. A look at their interviews indicates that most and probably all of the limited number of men who reported no newspaper actually were newspaper-readers. We are assuming that newspaper-reading was for practical purposes universal.

[4] Outside New York, 83, 68, and 76 per cent of large, medium, and small businessmen, respectively, mentioned local newspapers.

one in six; E. and M., 16.6 per cent). General business newspapers (not trade papers) other than *The Wall Street Journal* were read by about one person in ten.

The Times, Herald Tribune, and to some extent *Wall Street Journal* may be viewed as substitutes for each other. They are means for keeping currently informed at a level of detail above that possible with an ordinary local daily alone. It is significant that relatively few of our respondents used none of these superior daily sources. Only 37 per cent of our sample did not read either *The Times* or the *Herald Tribune* on the one hand or *The Wall Street Journal* plus a local paper on the other.

There are, of course, great regional differences in newspaper-reading. In each locality, local newspapers predominated. In New York, where one-fifth of our sample of American corporate heads was located, *The New York Times* and the *Herald Tribune* served as both national and local papers, and one or both were read by 90 per cent of the executives. Those two papers also enjoyed a considerable national readership; 33 per cent of non-New Yorkers read them (and that was before the West Coast edition of *The New York Times* existed). *The Wall Street Journal* was read explicitly as a national newspaper. As one proceeds away from New York, readership of *The Wall Street Journal* in one of its three editions (New York, Chicago, San Francisco) increased in comparison to the New York papers. The regional distribution is presented below in Table 10-1.

TABLE 10-1

REGIONAL PATTERNS IN THE READING OF "NATIONAL" NEWSPAPERS

| | Percentage of respondents who read: | | | Regional distribution of the sample Per cent |
	New York Times	Herald Tribune Per cent	Wall Street Journal	
New York	71	40	43	21
Northeast	38	19	44	25
North Central	19	6	38	29
South	28	—	50	13
West	6	2	53	12
				100

Thus we find not only that business leaders are habitual newspaper-readers but also that the majority read a newspaper of relatively broad scope giving them adequate coverage of both national and general business news. If they lived in New York—or for that matter in the same-day-delivery area around New York, from Boston to Washington—they tended to rely on the two New York papers which gave them national, general business, and local news simultaneously. The farther they lived from New York, at least in 1954, the more they relied on *The Wall Street Journal* in combination with local papers. Improving air mail delivery and the publication of national editions of leading papers will undoubtedly change the details of the picture.

Magazine-reading was not as pervasive as newspaper-reading. It was nevertheless general. At least three out of four men checked one or more national news magazines which they read. Although half the heads of firms with more than 10,000 employees said they read two or more news magazines regularly, this proportion drops off for the smaller firms, and we find only 33 per cent of the men in this group saying that they read two or more. Among news magazines, *Time* was read most often (by slightly over half the men; Bursk, 53 per cent; E. and M., 44.7 per cent); *U.S. News and World Report* was second (approximately one in three; Bursk, 44 per cent; E. and M., 26.5 per cent); and *Newsweek* was third (about one in four; Bursk, 31 per cent, E. and M., 20.6 per cent). Only about one business leader in ten read any of the liberal magazines of commentary, such as *The Reporter, The Nation,* and *The New Republic.*

General business magazines were read about as often as news magazines, and about one-half of the men in our sample read two or more. Readership was concentrated mainly on two magazines: *Business Week* (45 per cent; Bursk, 46 per cent; E. and M., 29 per cent) and *Fortune* (25 per cent; Bursk, 38 per cent; E. and M., 16.8 per cent). The *Harvard Business Review* (Bursk, 24 per cent; E. and M., 3.2 per cent) and *Kiplinger Letter* (Bursk, 48 per cent; E. and M., negligible) were mentioned by about one in ten.[5] The residual reading of general business magazines was scattered.

Journals devoted to the problems of specific businesses and indus-

---

[5] Our own method did not limit the respondent to any specific number of titles or any specific subject matter, but it also did not provide a list. The respondent's own tendency to name four or five titles and then stop or his sense of fitness probably tended to reduce mention of less salient titles. For these reasons, there are marked disparities in these findings, with ours falling midway between the other two. The Bursk method of aided recall detected a much higher proportion of readers of the *Harvard Business Review* and *Kiplinger Letter.* (Bursk produces very convincing evidence that these men were actually readers of the *Harvard Business Review.*) The E. and M. study, on the other hand, may have discouraged the reporting of these relatively specialized sources by virtue of the limited number of lines it provided for the listing of magazines. Also, the specification "general or business news" may have affected the reporting of these two relatively special sources. We would be inclined to accept the Bursk findings over either our own or those of E. and M. for at least occasional readership.

tries were almost as widely read as newspapers. Nine out of ten respondents said that they read at least one, and two out of three cited two or more.

Whereas businessmen tended to read news and business magazines with considerable frequency, this was less true of their reading of less serious material. Among general magazines, *Life* was clearly first, with one-fourth of the men from the largest firms and more than one-third among those from the smallest firms citing it (E. and M., 29.7 per cent). The *Saturday Evening Post* came next, with about one fourth of all the men mentioning it (E. and M., 17.5 per cent). Finally, *Reader's Digest* was checked with some frequency by the heads of the smallest firms (23 per cent), but only infrequently by the men from the largest (6 per cent). Only about one-sixth of the men said that they read any of the "high-brow" magazines, such as *Atlantic Monthly, Partisan Review, National Geographic, New Yorker,* and others.

Some Similarities and Differences in Reading Habits

Viewed in the perspective of the over-all population, the business leaders whom we interviewed constituted a remarkably homogeneous group with respect to reading habits. Even the most diverse subgroups in our sample were more like each other in their choice of reading material than they were like the rest of the population. For example, in the population at large it can be taken for granted that the higher educated will read more of most categories of materials than will the less educated. For certain publications there will, of course, be a reversal; highly educated people will read relatively and sometimes absolutely fewer tabloid newspapers, confession magazines, and the like. Although our business-leader group was quite highly educated, a quarter had not attended college, and one in ten or twelve had not completed high school.[6] Surprisingly enough, the differences in reading habits that are associated with these educational differences were exceedingly small. For those who became leading officers of good-sized businesses, factors of selection, experience, and responsibility subtantially wiped out any disparity based on early education, at least insofar as reading of newspapers and business and news magazines is concerned.

The homogenizing effect of role on our sample was most clearly brought home to the authors by an episode which concerned the data on foreign travel, rather than that on reading. As with reading, we found no over-all difference between our better-educated and less-well-educated respondents in propensity to travel abroad. More accurately, we found, as Fig. 10-1 shows, that, among the heads of small firms, the better-educated

---

[6] For the statistics on education by size of firm, see Raymond A. Bauer and Ithiel de Sola Pool, *American Businessmen and International Trade* (Glencoe, Ill.: The Free Press, 1960), pp. 66f.

men, as expected, traveled more. But among the larger firms the difference disappeared, and, if statistically unreliable differences are to be treated as plausible, it may indeed be the other way around. We queried an intelligent big-business informant about these results, which did not surprise him at all. "In those [top finance] circles, one is expected to know that little street off the Champs Elysées, and, if a man comes from a background where he doesn't, he will seize the first free forty-eight hours to hop over there." At

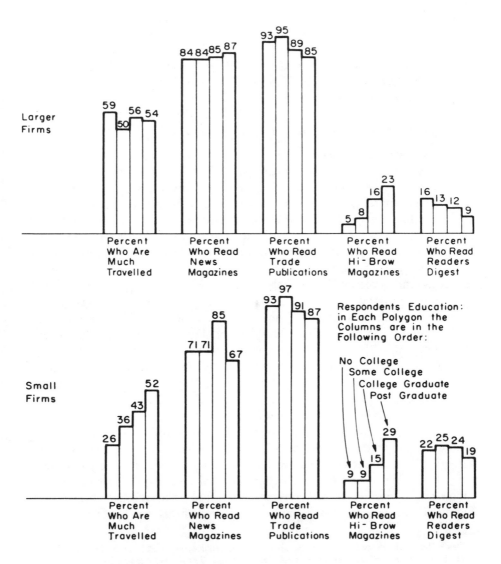

Fig. 10-1   EDUCATION AND COMMUNICATION BEHAVIOR

that level, the cost is no obstacle, but it still is for the man with 100 to, say, 400 employees. The latter may have a harder time leaving his plant for even a few days. His reference group consists of less-widely traveled persons. At the big-business level, travel was a means of demonstrating achieved status by those who needed to show it. The man who had risen to the top despite the fact that he had not gone to the right schools is a man of energy, prone to seize every opportunity to acquire the status symbols of his colleagues. Travel is one of the easiest of these symbols for him to acquire and one which a wife, married early, can also share as she rises with him. Thus, in our sample, which was defined by achieved status, educational background, which normally correlates well with symbols of status, was no longer predictive of them.

Reading for self-education, like travel, could be a way to establish one's identity with a social group into which one has risen. Indeed, as we have already noted, the successful though uneducated executive did behave exactly like his more privileged colleagues in regard to business- and news-reading. But changing one's reading habits is a more arduous way to establish one's status than is travel. Thus we find that, in sophisticated reading, education did make a difference. For businessmen of any given size of firm, there was a positive correlation between the amount of education a man had and his reading of such high-brow magazines as *The New Yorker, Harper's,* and the like. Among the heads of larger firms, there was a negative correlation between education and reading of the *Reader's Digest.*

Some variations in reading habits depend on the size of the firm which a man heads. The representatives of the larger firms, when contrasted with those from smaller firms, showed a concern for national as opposed to local affairs and for broad business matters as opposed to the problems of their own industry. In Fig. 10-2, we present some of the data on reading habits which reflect this trend. In general, the heads of the larger firms read more and, as we shall see further in the next chapter, were exposed to more of all sorts of communications. However, they were the heads of the smallest firms who read the most local newspapers [7] and the most trade journals.

The larger the firm he represents, the more must a man see things with what may be called "the broad view," the wider the variety of information he must have. The general level of the communications behavior of the smaller businessman was lower and concentrated relatively on

---

[7] This result is accounted for by the concentration of large firms in New York. Taking only firms outside New York, the citing of local papers occurred among 83 per cent of large, 68 per cent of medium, and 76 per cent of small businessmen. Whether the explanation is the geographical structure of small and large businesses or the psychology of each of them, the fact remains that the reading habits of small businessmen were more parochial.

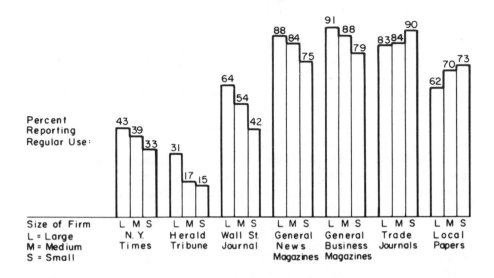

Fig. 10-2   READING HABITS OF HEADS OF FIRMS OF VARIOUS SIZES

matters concerning his local community and his own industry. In these areas, his reading actually exceeded that of his opposite number from larger companies. As we note repeatedly in this study, the concern of the head of a big business is largely with the external environment, whereas that of the head of a small business is with internal management.[8] Their reading corresponded with this difference.

Such differences in reading habits between large and small businessmen are not of extraordinary magnitude. When viewed in the perspective of the American population as a whole, these men are alike in their communications behavior. For example, it would be difficult to find another occupational group in the United States comparable in size to the business community—unless it be physicians—in which at least 40 per cent read any one paper (*The Wall Street Journal*) and 80 per cent read a small group of general occupational magazines.

[8] Cf. Carroll L. Shartle, *Executive Performance and Leadership* (Englewood Cliffs, N.J.: Prentice-Hall, Inc., 1956), which shows public relations to be the single most time-consuming activity in the big-business executive's day.

□ Foreign Sources of Information

American foreign trade policy is an issue which is in large part involved with information about events outside the United States. It is therefore relevant and interesting to note that the reading of our respondents was confined almost exclusively to domestic sources. We found that our respondents had two main sources of information about foreign affairs: the American media which report foreign news and their own foreign travel. They read scarcely any foreign printed material. Even though our questioning about news sources concluded an interview which had been largely focused on foreign affairs, only thirty-five of our 903 respondents listed foreign publications among the newspapers and periodicals which they read regularly. (Cf. Table 10-2.) These thirty-five men cited a total of forty-seven sources, most of which (thirty-six) were British. *The Economist,* London, was the source most often mentioned (fifteen times) and was the only one mentioned with any frequency.

This overwhelming reliance on domestic as opposed to foreign printed material for information does not stem from indifference to foreign affairs. A fair portion of our respondents' firms were involved in foreign operations. Among the largest firms, 60 per cent had foreign subsidiaries, as did 37 per cent of the medium and 13 per cent of the smallest firms. (And, as we shall see shortly, American businessmen as a group do a great deal of traveling abroad.)

More surprising than that the top men in American firms do not read foreign newspapers and magazines is that this was true also of their aides who are directly responsible for overseas business.

We interrogated a number of import-export managers in unstructured interviews. An interview with the export manager of a fair-sized American chemical company was typical. There was, he said, a tremendous amount of travel from headquarters to other countries, and vice versa. Much of the company's information about conditions abroad came from its own men overseas and from the observations of home-office men when they went on trips. He himself read American newspapers, magazines, trade journals, and bank letters. When pressed for foreign sources, he named a publication of the American Foreign Trade Council.

Another respondent, an importer who himself traveled often, stated that, when he was in this country, he relied mainly on the foreign division of the Big City Bank [9] for information on developments in foreign countries. This bank exemplifies those few organizations which act as transmission belts for foreign information to the American business com-

---

[9] Like most names of individuals and firms in this book, this is a pseudonym.

TABLE 10-2

READING OF FOREIGN PUBLICATIONS

Country of origin	Number of publications read	Number of respondents (out of 903)
Great Britain	36	26
Canada	4	3
Latin America	3	2
France	1	1
Australia	1	1
Unspecified	2	2
	47 publications	35 respondents

munity. When we interviewed the head of the bank's foreign division and asked him where it got information about what was going on abroad, he said, "First of all, from foreign banks." For example, a bank in Europe might write him, saying that it had a textile manufacturer who wanted to find a market for a certain kind of fabric. He in turn would approach an American organization that might be interested. A certain amount of economic and political information is picked up via such correspondence. He added that bank personnel keep in touch with foreign affairs, mainly through the "important dailies," of which he mentioned *The New York Times*. One man in the office, the only one of foreign birth, read the *Neue Zürcher Zeitung;* another read the London *Economist*.

Among the most international-minded of American business leaders, one had a staff member who read foreign sources and called his attention to items which might be of interest to him. But this practice was, to the best of our knowledge, exceptional. More often, specialized organizations, such as foreign-trade departments of banks; the Foreign Trade Council; export associations for particular industries; foreign investment, marketing, and public-relations consultant firms; or international editors of business publications were the direct consumers of foreign printed matter. They then relayed part of the contents to a wider segment of the business community. In most instances, however, materials did not exceed two or three titles.

Aside from such "gatekeepers," who have direct contact with foreign sources and who process them for the American consumer, American businessmen paid negligible attention to foreign printed matter.

Failure to use foreign printed media did not entirely deprive American businessmen of direct exposure to foreign attitudes. Whereas the average American is unusual if he has traveled outside the United States

once in his lifetime, one of our respondents was very unusual if he had
not done so. The travel experience of the interviewees is summarized in
Table 10-3. Even among the smallest firms, six out of seven had made at

TABLE 10-3

TRAVEL EXPERIENCE OF AMERICAN BUSINESSMEN

	Heads of		
	Large firms	Medium firms Per cent	Small firms
A. *Extent of travel*			
Number of trips abroad:			
None	7	11	14
1 trip	9	9	13
2-4 trips	18	20	28
5-9 trips	21	22	19
10-24 trips	20	21	18
25 trips or more	14	10	2
Many, unspecified	6	5	3
No answer	5	2	3
	100	100	100
B. *Recency of last trip abroad*			
Last trip was within:			
Last year	58	52	43
1-5 years	25	31	31
Over 5 years ago	17	17	26
	100	100	100
C. *Purpose of last trip abroad*			
Business only	55	41	22
Vacation only	28	39	55
Business and vacation	8	12	12
Other *	9	8	11
	100	100	100

* Includes military service and study abroad.

least one trip abroad. The men from the larger firms were even more active
travelers; most of the heads of the largest firms had made five or more
trips. About half of the sample had been out of the United States in the
preceding twelve months. Three-fourths had been in the preceding five
years.

The countries most often visited on the last trip were Great Britain and Canada (about equally), followed by Western Europe and other European countries, South America, and Mexico. Other areas of the world were visited by only small minorities.[10] Communist countries were virtually unvisited at the time of our 1954 survey, a situation which has now presumably changed.

Our respondents traveled abroad for both business and pleasure, often for both at once. Motives for travel are not easy to assess.[11] Often a traveler himself cannot tell you the exact proportion of these two motives. And, even if he does know, the Bureau of Internal Revenue discourages him from saying. In general, statistics on purposes of travel are highly artificial. Those based on visa applications are biased in favor of tourist travel, for it is simpler to get a tourist visa than any other type. Those based on U.S. passport or other application forms may be biased, for tax purposes, in favor of business travel. But, then, how does one classify a trip in which a man meets and talks socially to leading businessmen in other lands while he also visits cathedrals? Who can say what social contact may eventually provide a client or associate? At the business level, as in the free professions, private and business life merge into an indistinguishable whole in a way which it is hard for a salaried man or wage-earner to grasp. Everything the executive does may promote or injure the business in which he serves as guide and symbol, be it activity in the Community Chest; membership on the board of a college; participation in politics; establishing social friendships; or expanding his own areas of experience, information, and expertise.

But, whatever vagueness there is about the statistics on travel motives, they do measure something. Our respondents were able to cut the continuum of motives in some way, and the replies show important differences. Among the heads of the largest firms, 66 per cent of the most recent trips were stated to have been for business or for business in combination with vacation. This was true of only 34 per cent of the most recent trips made by men from the smallest firms. The men from the smaller firms not only traveled somewhat less frequently but also were proportionately less likely to travel for business. Note the parallel between the figures on traveling abroad for business and the proportions of firms with subsidiaries abroad (60 and 13 per cent for large and small firms, respectively). The heads of larger business organizations are more often directly involved in business abroad.

We must also note the small but important proportion of business-

---

[10] Bauer and Pool, *op. cit.*, p. 77.

[11] Cf. Ithiel de Sola Pool, Suzanne Keller, and Raymond A. Bauer, "The Influence of Foreign Travel on Political Attitudes of American Businessmen," *The Public Opinion Quarterly*, XX (Spring 1956), No. 1, 161-175.

men who traveled abroad for reasons other than business or pleasure and more particularly that very small minority whose reason was government service, especially in connection with the Marshall Plan. A great deal has been said in recent years about the sobering and broadening effect of government experience on business leaders. Many of these executives have served in foreign areas on technical-aid and other missions.

The theory of the business community being educated by such experiences is not without validity, but it is easy to overstate. Only a minority, though among big businessmen a very substantial minority, of our respondents had ever held policy-level government jobs. (See Table 10-4.) Except among the heads of small companies, these jobs were overwhelmingly federal.[12] Most of them were domestic, but close to half were concerned with foreign affairs, and some of those four per cent of top executives of both large and medium firms—had worked for the government abroad.

Although those businessmen who had once had to look at foreign affairs from a role of responsibility for national interest were few in numbers, the part they played in the leadership of the organized liberal-trade effort was enormous. We have reason to note such names as Clarence Randall, who had been involved in technical assistance to Turkey, and Ralph Straus, George Ball, Gen. William Draper, and William C. Foster, all of whom had played significant roles in the Marshall Plan and all of whom participated actively in the reciprocal-trade controversy and, with one exception, in the formation of the Committee for a National Trade Policy, the low-tariff organization. These men with deep foreign-affairs involvement were transmitters of information to the rest of the business community.

But foreign observation came not only through gatekeepers. A well-traveled group, our respondents had all in all a good deal of opportunity to observe events abroad with their own eyes.

We may ask ourselves what kinds of effect such travel experiences had upon them. Travel abroad is a quite different source of information from the mass media. Travel is for all except a small minority an intermittent matter, and it is selective in that each man visits only one or a few of the many possible sectors of the globe.

Yet, travel is a deeply personal experience which turned out to have a profound impact on the frame of reference in which our respondents viewed foreign affairs. Few of them went to gain political insight or to study foreign relations. But, whatever happened as they bathed on the Lido, bought souvenirs, or transacted business turned out to be politically important, too.

---

12 Cf. Bauer and Pool, *op. cit.,* pp 104 ff.

Table 10-4

PUBLIC-AFFAIRS AND FOREIGN-AFFAIRS EXPERIENCE

Per cent who had held a:	Among respondents from		
	Large firms	Medium firms	Small firms
		Per cent	
Policy-level government job	20	10	3
Foreign-affairs government job			
(e.g., FOA, ECA, UN, consul)	8	6	—
Overseas government job	4	4	—

Summarized in a sentence, the political effect of travel on tariff attitudes was to counteract the force of self-interest. It made a man see the trade issue in national terms, rather than in the parochial terms of his own industry.[13]

The highly traveled respondents—those who had made five or more trips abroad and at least one in the previous five years—were not in general more liberal on trade matters than their less-traveled colleagues, nor were they more protectionist. However, they differed in one important way. Their view on tariff policy was less predictable—from knowing the industry in which they were engaged—than was that of their more provincial colleagues.[14] (See Fig. 10-3.) For those businessmen who had not traveled much, if we knew what their firm made, we could make a reasonable prediction of where they as individuals would stand on tariff policy. For those who had traveled, a better prediction could be made, not by knowing what they manufactured, but by knowing the nation's foreign policy. From either atypical extreme, the travelers moved to support that norm.

Foreign travel introduced international political problems and America's relationship to them increasingly into the businessman's con-

---

[13] These results are more fully reported in Pool, Keller, and Bauer, *op. cit.*

[14] We might briefly note some qualifications at this point. Among the much-traveled, a small group had been abroad twenty-five or more times. These continuous travelers were mostly in businesses where foreign trade is life and death. They therefore tended to line up fairly well behind their firms' self-interest. Among the little-traveled, there was one particularly interesting group, those who had made their first trip abroad recently. There were only sixteen of them who also had an identifiable tariff interest. These few were the most extreme in defense of their self-interest: eight defended it in extreme form, only two opposed it. This is in line with our hypothesis about the contrary effects of much and little travel. One trip may provide ammunition for one's previous views. Time and more experience may shake them. However, the data are too sparse for reliance.

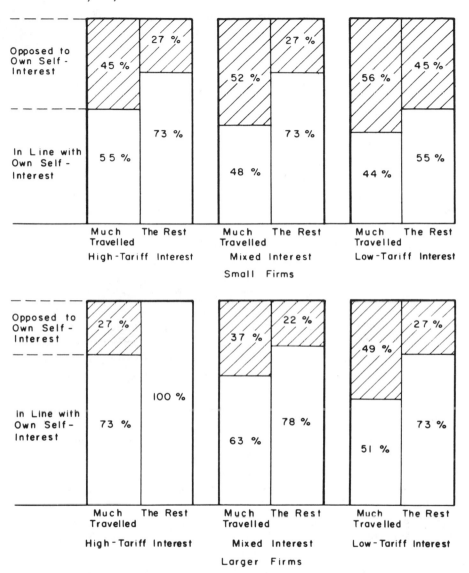

Fig. 10-3 TRAVEL AND SELF-INTEREST *

* Definitions:

Own self-interest is:	Reply in line with own self-interest is:	Reply opposed to own self-interest is:
High tariff	Raise or leave as is	Lower
Mixed	Raise or leave as is	Lower
Low tariff	Lower	Raise or leave as is

sciousness. As he traveled, he found himself being role-cast, not as the representative of a particular industry, but as an American. He found himself playing at being secretary of state and talking for his country, not for his firm.

The influence of travel was not primarily to bring European or other foreign ideas to the traveler, leading him to diverge from his national norm. On the contrary, it moved him toward that norm. There was a shift in center of gravity away from narrow parochial interests *toward* international interests, but with views quite close to the national standard. Thus, foreign travel broadened the frame of reference in which the businessman considered the foreign-trade issue to one which took account of world political and economic circumstances. But the responses he gave to the facts that he learned abroad were ones that his own domestic reference group would approve. The reference group perceived as relevant changed from a parochial to a national one, but it remained a domestic one.

Thus the very partial and often irrelevant experiences of foreign travel, either on the Lido or in an office, could affect a man's broad foreign-policy conclusions. Whether the traveler acquired his sense of responsibility to an American role in an argument with a perverse waiter or in a study of foreign production costs made little difference. The effect was to shake his established convictions and to make him see himself in a more statesman-like role, defined, it is true, as the American business community sees that role.

The way in which foreign travel related to public-affairs attitudes was illustrated in a most striking way by data on political party affiliation of our respondents. Our theory postulates that, if any shift of opinion on matters of substance occurs as a result of travel, its direction should be toward the standard business position—in this case, toward the Republican Party. Though this prediction follows from our theory, we cannot claim advance wisdom. Like most of our colleagues, we expected that travel would liberalize and that liberals would be less often Republicans. We were wrong. We find, as our theory should have led us to expect, that the most traveled businessmen are most uniformly Republican.

This finding deserves a little more elucidation. Virtually no businessmen switched from the Republican to the Democratic Party. Those who switched party were switching from an ancestral Democratic affiliation to a Republican affiliation more appropriate to their career role. Thus, the Republican homogeneity of the highly traveled business executives simply means that a larger proportion of the travelers who chanced to be born Democrats had abandoned their ancestral party than did so among the nontravelers. Those who were born Democrats, if they exposed themselves to new and unsettling experiences, moved away from that "devia-

tion" toward the central ideology of their group. Those who continued
to hold a more sectional (for example, Southern), familial, or otherwise
particularistic traditional stand, which is what being a Democrat means if
one is head of a company, are found among the nontravelers.

The same kind of shaking-up which appeared in party politics explains our findings about travel and foreign-trade attitudes. Although
travel shook men loose from their industry stands, its net result was to
permit them by changing to solidify, not weaken, their bonds to their
decisive domestic reference group. Attention to foreign attitudes, to foreign
reactions to American trade policy, and to varied foreign facts became

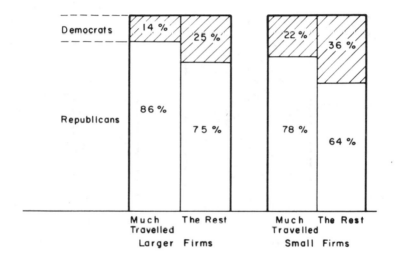

Fig. 10-4   TRAVELERS MORE SOLIDLY REPUBLICAN
THAN NONTRAVELERS *

* The findings hold up separately for both Democrats and independents, but the numbers are small. In the graph, they are combined.

greater among those respondents who had traveled much than it was among
those who had not. But we must not confuse this increased awareness of
foreign views with acceptance of them.

Although much-traveled men were not more likely to favor lower
tariffs, they differed from the less-well-traveled men in what they thought
were the best arguments for a low-tariff policy. We see in Fig. 10-5 that
men who had been frequently abroad were more likely to favor low-tariff
arguments with an international orientation than were those who had done
less traveling.

An interesting instance of broadened perception has to do with the ideas our respondents had for increasing foreign trade. When asked what actions might result in an increased volume of foreign trade, the much-traveled respondents more often than the less-traveled cited actions by foreign agencies (Table 10-5). They blamed foreigners more often than did the less-well-traveled respondents for existing difficulties in international trade.

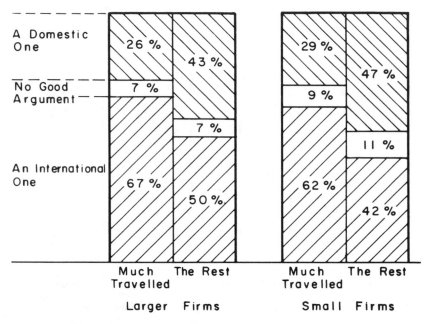

Fig. 10-5   BEST ARGUMENT FOR LOW TARIFFS

TABLE 10-5

WHICH ACTIONS WOULD INCREASE FOREIGN TRADE

	Per cent citing action by, or stability of, foreign country or people
Large and medium firms	
Much-traveled	25
All others	17
Small firms	
Much-traveled	19
All others	10

At first glance, that might suggest that our well-traveled respondents were more isolationist in the sense that they were more likely to lay blame abroad. However, there is independent evidence that they are neither more nor less isolationist than are those who have traveled less. The groups are identical in their attitudes toward United States participation in world affairs. These data represent, instead, a direct manifestation of the greater familiarity with foreign facts among the frequent travelers. They knew what obstructions there were to trade abroad as well as to that at home.

We have said that foreign travel—except for a very few men who spend a very high proportion of their time abroad—is not to be regarded as a regular news source for events abroad. True, men who travel abroad do return with a certain amount of specific information, both concerning their own particular businesses and also concerning general economic and political conditions. However, it seems clear that the major day-to-day impact of foreign travel is on the man's reaction to the news which he gets from domestic American sources. He is enabled to bring a broader background of experience to bear on the interpretation of what he reads in the American press.

□ Sources of Information on the Reciprocal-Trade Controversy

Considering the reading habits of our respondents and the media coverage given the reciprocal-trade controversy in the years 1953-1954, the men we interviewed had ample opportunity to become acquainted with the general features of the controversy. Although most newspapers and practically all national magazines favored the extension of the Reciprocal Trade Act, there was also adequate reportage of the statements of protectionist spokesmen. There was quite frequent reporting of the complaints of injury on the part of the watch, textile, coal, chemical, and other industries.

Granting that it is difficult to judge just what is "adequate reporting" and granting also that the general run of local papers paid only sporadic attention to the reciprocal-trade debate, it nevertheless seems safe to say that *The New York Times, Herald Tribune,* and *Wall Street Journal* (at least one of which 72 per cent of our respondents read), the national news magazines, and the general business magazines reported the controversy adequately, certainly to the point where everyone could know that it existed and what its general alignment was.[15]

Perhaps the coverage was inadequate on one point, the concern

---

[15] *The New York Times Index* had 12.5 column inches of entries under "Reciprocal Trade Act" in 1954 and 35 column inches in 1955. Stories appeared on about 60 days during 1954 and 110 days during 1955.

of foreign countries over whether American trade barriers were going to increase or decrease. News stories on reciprocal trade tended to originate in Washington. Foreign correspondents wrote about more salient subjects. Anyone who had access to foreign sources at that time perceived a greater sense of involvement and urgency on the part of foreigners than was conveyed by the American press on the whole, although Swiss reaction to United States tariffs on watches was effectively reported. However, about half of our respondents had been abroad in the preceding year and would in all probability have been exposed to foreign attitudes on this subject. So, even on this point, our respondents had access to substantial information.

But access to copious information does not guarantee its assimilation. Selective attention, perception, and recall among businessmen, as among any other human beings, assured that those who learned about a controversy were those with specific interest in it.

Before proceeding in the next chapter to consideration of communications specifically dealing with foreign-trade policy—a type of communication generally confined to businessmen with concrete foreign-trade concerns—we may pause to look at the impact of two events which were thoroughly covered in the public press, namely, the Randall Commission report and the President's message. The Randall Commission report, which had been delivered some months before our interviews, was well covered at that time in the local press, as well as in the prestige papers and news magazines and to some extent on radio and television. It was the subject of considerable later debate, too. The Randall report was also sent by the Committee for a National Trade Policy to its entire mailing list, which included businessmen from virtually all the larger firms in our sample. The President's message was delivered the day before we began interviewing, and, although there was therefore not time for it to become the topic of wide discussion, it should have been fresh in the minds of our respondents if they had been following the ordinary domestic news sources. In Fig. 10-6 are presented the proportions of men in each size of firm who had heard or read about either of these reports.

Since the President's message had been delivered so recently before our interviews began, there had been little time for it to be discussed or reported in trade journals or even in the general business or news magazines. Accordingly, most respondents who said that they had read or heard about the President's message had read about it in a newspaper. This was true of a minority of the people who said they had heard or read about the Randall Commission report. General news magazines, general business magazines, and trade journals—all having a longer time-lag in reporting than do newspapers—were somewhat more often mentioned as sources of information about the Randall report.

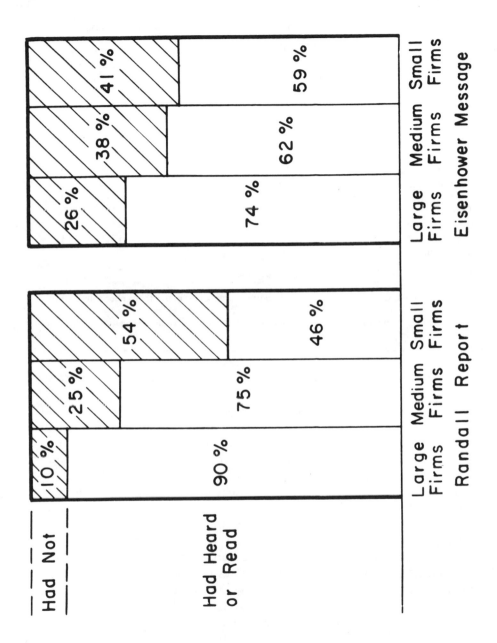

Fig. 10-6 PROPORTION OF MEN HAVING HEARD OR READ ABOUT
RANDALL REPORT AND EISENHOWER MESSAGE

TABLE 10-6

SOURCES OF INFORMATION ON RANDALL REPORT AND
EISENHOWER MESSAGE *

	Large firms		Medium firms		Small firms	
	Randall	President	Randall	President	Randall	President
			Per cent			
Newspapers	36	60	43	57	39	61
News magazines	16	7	29	13	17	15
General business magazines	9	3	6	3	7	5
Trade journals	10	1	8	2	11	3
Special communi- cations **	24	5	15	5	13	3
Saw report or mes- sage itself	29	7	22	5	11	3

* Adds to more than 100 per cent because some gave more than one source. Only those who had heard of report or message are included in this table.

** Includes communications from men in own business, trade associations, lobbyists, congressmen, etc.

One difference between the sources of information for the President's message and the Randall report is especially interesting. That difference is in the reading of quite specialized documents—either the report itself or other items that we have lumped under the heading of special communications. The latter are communications from one's trade associations, industry representatives, lobbyists, or even one's congressman in a few instances. What such materials have in common is that they do not come to the respondent as part of a regular media flow to which he subscribes, but come to his desk episodically and more often on the initiative of the communicator than that of the recipient. The special communications may be viewed as a second wave, activated by the first wave of reporting in the general media. Ironically, the Randall report itself or the President's message may most often be viewed as part of this second wave. For, though they actually start the media flow and though a few of our most influential and involved respondents may have had copies at the moment of release or earlier, for most of our respondents the act of looking at the full text which someone had mailed to them was a follow-up to being informed through the newspapers that this was an important document and worth pulling out of the pile of incoming printed material.

The second-wave material is specialized in its points of origin, its content, and its selection of audience. The second wave also takes time to get organized and heard, even though the major documents themselves are mailed out as quickly as possible after release. For that reason, if for no other, such special communications had come to constitute at the moment of interviewing but a small proportion of the sources of knowledge concerning the President's message. They accounted for a much larger proportion of the sources concerning the Randall report.

Such specialized communications are more likely to be directed at the men in the largest firms, apparently because the latter are publicly more visible and have better lines of communication. It will be seen in Fig. 10-6 that the spread between the largest and the smallest firms in knowledge of the President's message is but 15 percentage points, whereas in knowledge of the Randall report the spread is 44 percentage points. The President's message being still the news of the week, the difference in awareness of it among large and small firms was not great and reflected above all individual differences in competence, political interest, and cosmopolitanism, rather than in communication exposure. The Randall report, however, was far enough in the past to have fallen out of the news, to have been forgotten by those who did not care about it, and to have been maintained in the focus of attention above all for those businessmen who continued to receive specialized follow-up communications. Those were largely the heads of larger firms.

This analysis suggests that the media of general communication play a dual role in the transmission of information to the business community. They convey initial news of events, and they stimulate a secondary wave of specialized communications, which have a delayed and relatively selective effect.

The general communications media are also somewhat selective in effect. Such events as the Randall report and the President's message, though universally reported, were not universally read. Selective perception is a pattern found in every study of news-reading. We have seen, and shall continue to see in the next chapter, that men from larger firms, presumably having a wider range of interests, were consistently better informed and more active in communicating about foreign-trade policy.

Size of firm was but one of the factors which affected which news businessmen read and remembered. Self-interest, or, more particularly, fear of loss, was another. For example, among the heads of the smallest firms, only 25 per cent of those men who had said that foreign competition affected their firms had not heard of the Eisenhower message, but as many as 46 per cent of the men who had said that their businesses were not affected were ignorant of it. Again it turns out that those who saw a threat to themselves in foreign imports informed themselves about foreign-trade news.

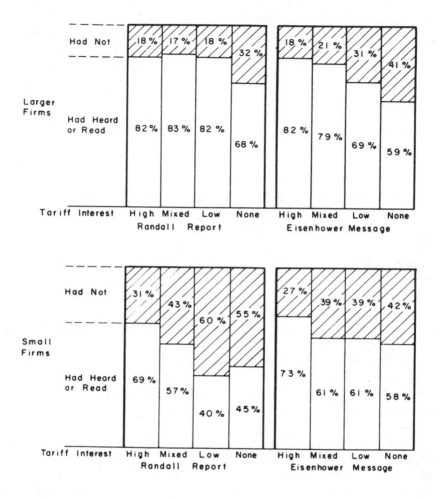

Fig. 10-7   PROPORTION OF MEN HAVING HEARD OR READ ABOUT
RANDALL REPORT AND EISENHOWER MESSAGE RELATED TO
OBJECTIVE TARIFF INTEREST

Thus we find that either fear of foreign competition or an externally oriented business role was a force which would lead a businessman to select foreign-trade news for attention from among the flood of items available to him in the general media.

Chapter 11

Communications about
Foreign-Trade Policy

The media read by businessmen contained copious information, at least about the main course of debate over major pieces of trade legislation. Yet we found that, among the heads of the smallest firms, only about half professed knowledge of the Randall report, the most widely publicized event concerning foreign-trade policy in the previous months. It is not stretching things to say that to have avoided learning about the Randall report may have taken a little effort. Such selectivity of attention, recall, and response will appear repeatedly as we look at specialized communications dealing with foreign-trade problems. The mass media reached everyone in our sample, forcing some information even on readers without an active interest. The specialized media came only to those individuals who felt some need for information on foreign-trade policy.

The notion of "information concerning foreign-trade policy" defies precise specification. For American businessmen it may include topics as broad as the political stability of foreign countries and as narrow as the decisions of customs authorities on the procedure for counting the jewels in watches. In our own research group, we found that each of us had a

179

slightly different perspective on what was relevant to the study. All, of course, would be interested in the Swiss reaction to watch tariffs and in the speeches of Oscar Strackbein. But one of us might clip an article on the health of a particular congressman because it bore on the potential membership of the Ways and Means Committee. Another might note a drought in Brazil which could affect coffee imports. A third would read a report that Japanese cameras had improved in quality.

The above is by no means far-fetched. Our informal interviews clearly established the fact that American businessmen in the years 1953-1955 viewed information concerning foreign-trade policy in many and varied ways, ranging from the broadest of policy considerations down to the most narrowly technical details. For businessmen, information on tariff and foreign-trade policy is far from being exclusively information on newsworthy matters.

We asked our respondents what they considered the best sources of information on tariff and foreign-trade policy, however they defined that subject matter for themselves. Their answers to this question are characterized in Table 11-1. The distribution of responses offers an interesting contrast to the sources from which they had learned about the Randall and Eisenhower messages. It will be remembered that the vast majority of men who knew of the Eisenhower message reported having heard about it in general news media. However, our respondents, when asked about their preferred sources of news on whatever they called matters of tariffs and foreign-trade policy, replied by naming highly specialized sources. They were presumably thinking of tariff policy as embracing a narrower and more technical domain than that of the public-policy statements embodied in the Randall report and Eisenhower message.

Men from large firms, in particular, voted confidence in specialized sources. In this preference, they reflected their greater need for, their better access to, and their superior knowledge of such detailed and thorough information media. Many more, for example, have foreign-trade specialists in their firms to whom they can turn. They have more communications directed at them from industry specialists, lobbyists, and the like. They have better contact with government agencies. They are more knowledgeable themselves and are aided by better and larger staffs.

There is an anomaly in the fact that men from the smaller firms are more likely to prefer general media. Use of general sources might be taken to imply less concern with the narrower and more technical features of foreign-trade policy and more concern with matters of broad policy. But breadth of interest does not characterize the men from small firms. They are, on the contrary, less concerned with issues of wide public policy. Another factor in this instance overrode the usual proclivity of small businessmen to read trade publications rather than those dealing with national

TABLE 11-1

SOURCES OF INFORMATION ON TARIFF AND FOREIGN-TRADE POLICY RESPONDENT CONSIDERED BEST

Source	Size of firm		
	Large	Medium	Small
	Per cent		
A. *General public printed sources*			
1. Newspapers	15	15	21
2. News magazines	15	15	15
3. General business magazines	13	11	19
4. Other general publications	4	6	6
Total public printed sources	47	47	61
B. *Special sources*			
1. Individual business associates, including foreign-trade specialists	13	17	8
2. Communications from business and trade associations and lobbying groups	43	31	27
3. Political figures	3	4	4
4. Government agencies, reports, and officials	30	25	22
Total special sources	89	77	61
Total all sources	136	124	122

affairs, and that factor was indifference. Being less involved with foreign-trade policy, they had less demand for detailed technical information. Those few small businessmen who were actively involved in the issue had a frame of reference generally narrower than that of the men from the larger firms. Those more-interested small businessmen, along with their colleagues from larger firms, thought of rather specific business consequences when they thought of foreign-trade policy, and, accordingly, they preferred specialized sources for information on the subject; but they were a minority.

□ Talking about Tariffs and Foreign-Trade Policy

The media, the use of which we reviewed in the previous chapter, are inputs into the business community. The Randall report, the President's message, and the vast majority of the articles read and speeches heard originated outside that community, in government or in the professions. Reviewing now more focused communications, we turn first to a type which occurs largely within the confines of the business community—conversations.

We asked our respondents three questions: whether in the preceding month they had talked to any persons in their organization specially designated to handle matters concerned with foreign trade, whether they had talked about trade to other persons within their company, and whether they had talked with persons outside their company. The proportions of men who had talked about foreign-trade matters under any of these three conditions is summarized in Fig. 11-1.

The amount of conversation reported was surprisingly large. In the large and medium firms, over 60 per cent of the men had talked about tariffs and foreign-trade policy in some circumstances. The men from the small firms were conspicuously less active. Note, also, that twice as many members of the business community had discussed the issue face-to-face in the previous month as had read or heard some particular article or speech on it (Fig. 11-2). The system of communication about trade matters was to a large degree an oral one. But participation in it was highly selective. Fig. 11-1 indicates that some men talked a great deal and some not at all. Except in the smallest firms, if a man talked at all, he was more likely than not to have talked both inside and outside the firm.

About 40 per cent of all discussion inside a man's firm took place with someone in charge of foreign-trade matters. To some extent, talking with such a man was a function of his availability, and we find that such foreign-trade specialists were much more likely to be found among the larger than among the smaller firms (74, 63, and 41 per cent, respectively). Discussion with other persons within one's firm almost always meant talking with other top officers. A few men talked with representatives of the sales department, and still fewer with a scattering of staff personnel.

Discussion outside the firm was also often with business contacts (about three-fifths of the time for large and medium businessmen and half the time for the smallest businessmen, who had a less elaborate structure around them with which to interact). In other words, the issue was more apt to appear to leading businessmen as a business topic appropriate for discussion within his industry and with suppliers and customers than it was to present itself as a political issue for citizen consideration, appropriate for civic groups, neighbors, and the breakfast table (Fig. 11-3). We shall note in Part III further evidence that the channels of discussion tended to fall within industry lines rather than within the community. A businessman or a congressman was less likely to have a sense of how a geographical constituency felt than of how an industry felt. Furthermore, those who attempted to promote expression of civic feelings about the issue had less

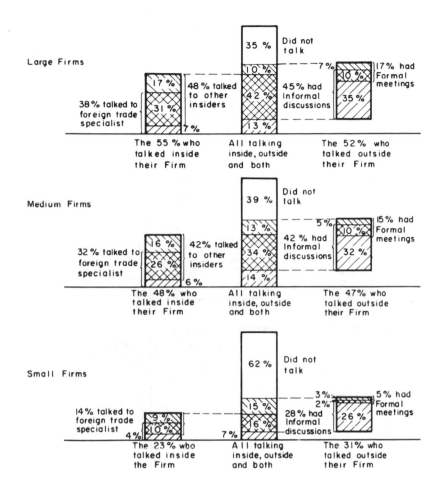

Fig. 11-1 TALK ABOUT FOREIGN TRADE IN PRECEDING MONTH

success than those who attempted to organize representation of direct business interests.

Most of the outside talking consisted of informal discussion. Yet one-sixth, except in the small firms, had discussed foreign trade at a formal meeting within the previous two weeks. Some men attended repeated meetings, and others attended none; yet, over a period of a year, many of our respondents would find themselves at a meeting where foreign-trade policy was discussed.[1]

---

[1] About half those meetings were called specially for the purpose. Cf. Bauer and Pool, *op. cit.,* p. 41.

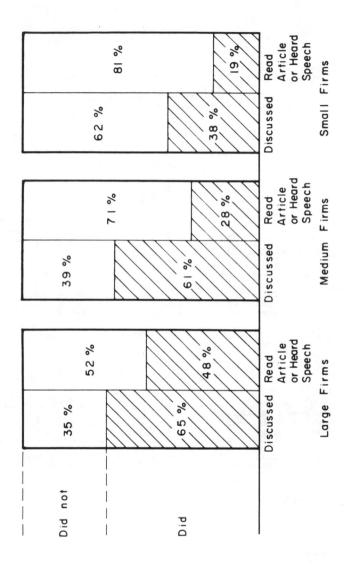

Fig. 11-2   DISCUSSION VERSUS READING *

* In the context of the question as asked, reading an article would not include reading a news story. Many more respondents had done that. Reading a special article represents a higher level of involvement. Note, also, that reading articles outweighed hearing speeches by more than three to one, but some such hearing is here recorded along with reading. To that extent, the dominance of oral communication is even more marked than indicated.

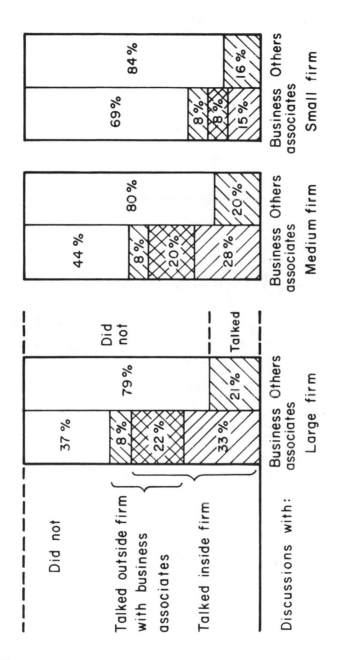

Fig. 11-3 DISCUSSION OF FOREIGN TRADE WITH BUSINESS ASSOCIATES OR WITH OTHERS

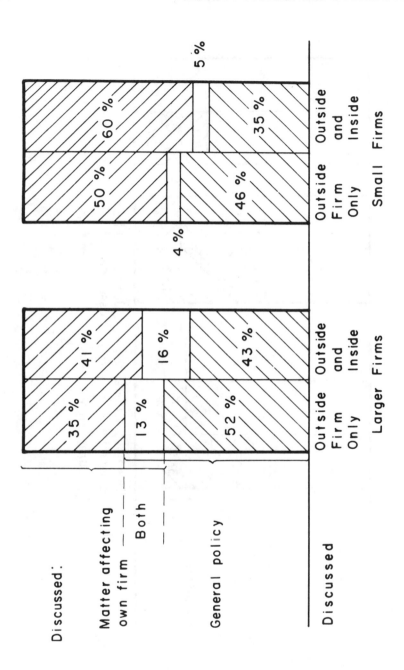

Fig. 11-4   TRADE DISCUSSIONS OUTSIDE FIRM·

We have already pointed out that foreign-trade policy extends over a wide range of issues from general policy to the narrowly technical problems of a specific business or industry. Discussions inside a firm are likely to be focused on the problems of that firm. Discussions outside may either continue such focus on the specific problems agitating the firm or industry or they may be couched in symbols of ideology or national interest. We asked which way the discussions outside the firm had gone. When we look at the men who talked only outside their firms and compare them with the men who had talked both inside and outside their firms, we discover that the men who had talked only outside their firms were likely to have entered into general discussions, whereas men who had talked also inside their firms were more likely to have talked about matters affecting their firms specifically, even in their outside conversations.

We have now established, at least in a sketchy way, who talked to whom and what they talked about. What significance did such conversations have? We take talking about foreign-trade policy to be an indication of involvement in the subject. Note as evidence on this point that talking about foreign-trade matters is correlated with reading about them, too.

Talking is also correlated with knowledge. Indeed, men who were active by any communications criterion showed consistently more knowledge concerning the men and organizations involved in foreign-trade policy. For example, those who had discussed foreign trade were more likely to know the views of their congressmen—among the larger firms by about two to one.

Communications activity with respect to foreign-trade policy may thus clearly be treated as an indication of interest. We can rule out the alternative hypothesis, that communicators on the trade issue were simply men who communicated on everything. There is no clear indication that having discussed foreign-trade policy (holding size of firm constant) is generally related to total newspaper-reading, magazine-reading, and so on. A high level of communication on foreign trade is in general specific to the issue.

This talk was more than idle chatter. Arising from a real interest in the issue, it often led to action. Fig. 11-6 presents the relationship between talking and reading about foreign-trade policy and the probability that a man will have communicated with his congressman on trade matters in the years immediately preceding our 1954 survey. The most dramatic contrast is between those who did no talking and those who talked both inside and outside their firms. Among the nontalkers, only a negligible number communicated with Congress. Among the most active talkers, the proportions approach a quarter or a third.

Reading or hearing mass-media material without further discussion of it produced little action. Conversations outside the firm were perhaps

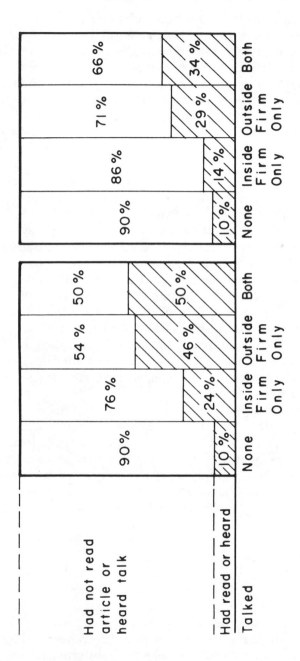

Fig. 11-5 PROPORTION OF RESPONDENTS HAVING READ ARTICLE OR
HEARD SPEECH SPECIFICALLY ABOUT FOREIGN-TRADE POLICY RELATED
TO THEIR PATTERNS OF DISCUSSION

slightly less related to action than were those inside. A small but highly revealing difference appears when we compare Figs. 11-5 and 11-6, a difference of a sort which will be confirmed again in other results. In Fig. 11-5, we see that persons who talked outside the firm were more likely to read articles or listen to speeches than those who talked only inside. But, in Fig. 11-6, we see that those who talk only inside are, if anything, the ones more likely to act. To be more precise, among bigger businessmen, those who talk inside the firm and those who talk outside are equally likely to act, even though those who talk outside are more likely to inform themselves by reading, too. Among smaller businessmen, those who talk inside the firm are even more likely to act, though less likely to read.

This result reveals two alternative patterns of communication. One of these, in which the foreign-trade issue figures as a broad political question, involves use of the published media and of conversations in the broad civil community of which the respondent is a part. The other pattern of communication, where foreign trade figures as an operating problem of the respondent's business, involves much oral communication with fellow executives and less use of published media. Such a pattern was the more conducive to action.[2]

Sociological studies in recent years have repeatedly established that oral communication with reference persons located in the immediate social environment of an individual is far more likely to lead to action by him than will mass-media material alone. This has been found to be so among farmers,[3] housewives,[4] physicians,[5] and others. We find it again among business executives, and that is not surprising.

Furthermore, the whole organization of business is geared to producing action easily and quickly on any current business problem. It takes much more initiative for the executive to act as a private citizen outside his office, where he has no secretary, staff, in-box, and out-box. Executives of the kind we were interviewing arrive at the office to face a neatly arranged pile of mail and memos. A first precept is that every letter must be answered and every proposal get some action decision. A staff is waiting

---

[2] Note that causality goes two ways. The usual interpretation in the literature is that word-of-mouth communication has a greater causal impact on action than do written media. It is probably also true, however, that, when a man is ready to act, he is prone to talk about the topic.

[3] Everett Rogers and G. M. Beal, "The Importance of Personal Influence in the Adoption of Technological Changes," *Social Forces*, 36 (1958), No. 4, 329-335; Bryce Ryan and Neal Gross, *Acceptance and Diffusion of Hybrid Seed Corn in Two Iowa Communities* (Ames, Iowa: Iowa State College of Agriculture and Mechanic Arts, Research Bulletin #372, 1950).

[4] Elihu Katz and Paul Lazarsfeld, *Personal Influence* (Glencoe, Ill.: The Free Press, 1955).

[5] Elihu Katz and Herbert Menzel, "Social Relations and Innovation in the Medical Profession," *Public Opinion Quarterly*, 19 (1955), 337-352.

to discuss and facilitate decisions. (Discussions with staff are some of the conversations which appear in our data.) If a letter to an executive is a plea from a business colleague to write Congress about a particular difficulty of the industry, he must either present reasons for declining—devise an "out," such as referring it for study—or send the requested letter, and that usually within a few days. Although a form request from a trade association may simply go unanswered, the option of letting the problem slide by sheer indecision is not approved for proposals more weighty than that.

Many of the letters sent by our respondents to their congressmen arose out of this compulsion for action. We review in Part IV a case in which the major Eastern railroads came to the support of fuel-oil quotas, though their self-interest was not at all clear. Nonetheless, they responded to a request in almost all cases by agreeing to sign a statement. Had their diesel-fuel suppliers approached them first, they might have been found on the other side.

The initiators of the low-tariff lobby were conscious of the advantages of using business channels and of relating themselves to operational problems of firms. But, as we shall have occasion to relate, that strategy was replaced in 1954-1955 by civic appeals through lectures, luncheon meetings, and public exhortation. Whatever educational value those activities may have had, and in the long run that may have been very great indeed, they did not produce much immediate action. In 1962, the strategy of making individualized appeals to businessmen with foreign markets was revived with good effect.

The fact that generalized views find expression less readily than special demands may be demonstrated by reference to the otherwise-puzzling

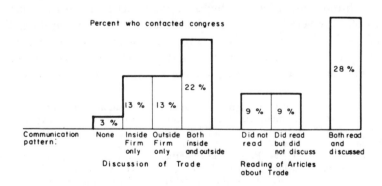

Fig. 11-6(a)   PROPORTION IN LARGE FIRMS WHO HAD RECENTLY
CONTACTED CONGRESS ON TRADE POLICY AMONG RESPONDENTS
WITH VARYING COMMUNICATIONS PATTERNS

figures on letter-writing to Congress. Although both business and public opinion strongly favored a liberal-trade policy, the weight of the mail was the contrary. We had no opportunity to systematically sample Congressional mail, but a few congressmen opened their files to us, and some mail clerks gave us estimates. That left us with the impression that the mail was perhaps ten-to-one for protection. Even if one subtracts the stimulated campaigns of a few organized industries, which accounted for perhaps two-thirds to four-fifths of all the mail, the majority of the mail still consisted of pleas for protection. Especially if one subtracts that portion of the residual mail from other than businessmen—for example, that from members of the League of Women Voters—the majority of business mail was clearly protectionist. It became apparent, as we spoke to congressmen about situations that we knew, that the discrepancy was to a large extent explained by letters from businessmen who in our interview would have been rated as liberal traders and, indeed, were that. But they wrote their congressman, not about their general feeling on foreign trade from home in their capacity as citizens, but from their offices, as executives, about some particular problem of customs classification or administrative procedure which was hurting their competitive position. In the environment of Congress, these letters were read as protectionist.

Thus, the structure of the communications system favored the propagation of particular demands. Internal consultation in a company generally preceded action. Outside discussion and reading often followed. Just as the man who has bought a new car reads the advertisements for it both to reassure himself and because of his newly found interest in that brand, so, too, a businessman who had written his congressman often talked

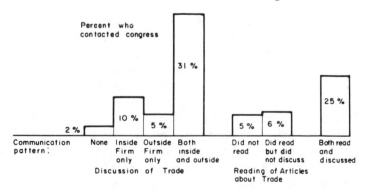

Fig. 11-6(b)   PROPORTION IN SMALL FIRMS WHO HAD RECENTLY CONTACTED CONGRESS ON TRADE POLICY AMONG RESPONDENTS WITH VARYING COMMUNICATIONS PATTERNS

about that act and read articles supporting what he had done. He also discussed and read in advance of his action, as he sought to inform himself better about the issues which faced him. But reading and general conversation alone, without the final stimulus of discussion within an institution geared to action, were unlikely to lead to an action in the short run.

□ The Genesis of Communications Activity—Interest and Attitude

What makes some heads of firms more likely to talk about foreign-trade policy than others? We often take issue with simple notions of economic self-interest, but never to deny that it is an effective motive to action. Our reservations have to do with the difficulty of arriving at an unequivocal criterion. Yet, having entered these reservations, we find that there is a positive correlation between communications activity on foreign-trade policy and virtually any criterion of economic self-interest which we may employ.

Men who said that tariffs were important for their firms were more likely than others to have talked about foreign-trade policy in the previous month. Similar relationships hold between talking (also reading or hearing a particular article or speech) and other subjective criteria of self-interest, such as the importance of foreign competition and export markets. But statements that tariffs, export markets, foreign competition, and the like are important to one's firm—that is, subjective criteria of self-interest—though to some extent unquestionably reflecting objective facts, may be contaminated by the respondent's personal involvement (or lack of it) in the issues.

Let us take the existence of a foreign-trade specialist in a firm as objective, prima facie evidence that the firm has an interest in foreign-trade policy. We find that, among firms which have a foreign-trade representative on their staff, the chief officer of the firm is twice as likely as otherwise to have talked about foreign-trade policy to members of his firm other than his foreign-trade specialist (Fig. 11-7).

It may well seem self-evident that men with an interest in a topic would be likely to talk about it. It is not equally obvious, however, that the amount of discussion should be related to the direction of a man's interest, but we see in Fig. 11-8 that it is so related. The self-interest of our respondents' industries are consistently related to whether they have talked and read about trade matters. Regardless of the criterion of activity or of size of firm, the men from high-tariff industries are most active, those from mixed industries come second, those from low-tariff industries are next, and in all instances those from no-interest industries are least active. High-tariff interest seems to be conspicuously more effective in stimulating communica-

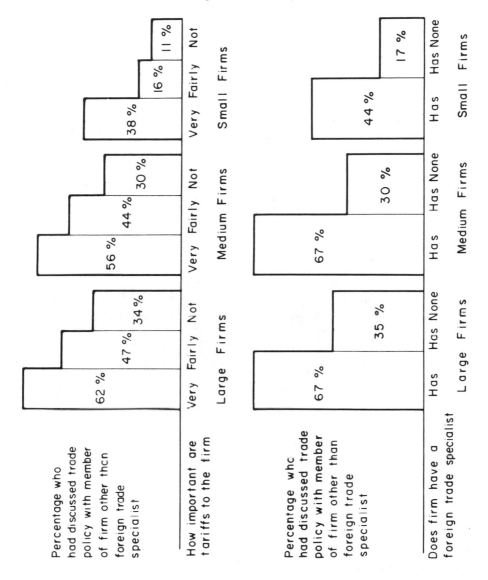

Fig. 11-7 DISCUSSION OF FOREIGN-TRADE POLICY AS A FUNCTION OF ITS IMPORTANCE TO THE FIRM

tions than is low-tariff interest. In almost all cases, the low-tariff group is closer in its reported activity to the no-interest group than it is to the high-tariff group. The protectionist component of a mixed interest apparently makes even that group more active than the low-tariff group.

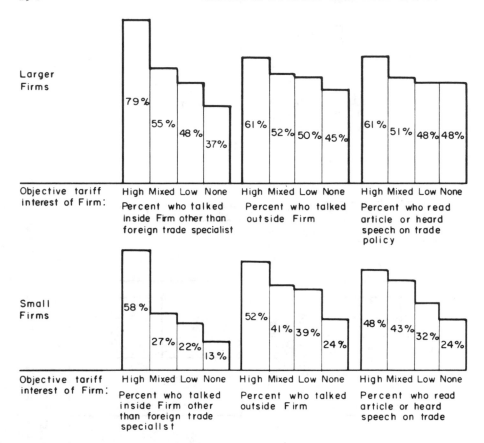

Fig. 11-8 PERCENTAGE TALKING AND READING ABOUT FOREIGN-TRADE
POLICY AS A FUNCTION OF THE OBJECTIVE TARIFF INTEREST
OF THE INDUSTRY

There is one difference between the smaller and the larger firms that should be noted. Company interest had more impact in producing communication about foreign trade in the smaller firms. More accurately, among the heads of smaller firms, attention to the foreign-trade issue depends heavily on their having some direct business interest in the matter. Among the heads of larger firms, the foreign-trade issue often attracted their attention even in the absence of special business involvement. It attracted their attention also in their general reading and sometimes involved their participation in civic affairs outside their firms. The heads of large businesses more often than those of small saw themselves as having a responsibility for the general condition of the national economy. The head of a giant insurance company could hardly say, as could a small-town manufacturer, that the state of dollar balances or of national economic policies was none of his affair. He could not see himself as a little man, having to accept whatever national trends the economy produced. He had, and recognized that he had, channels by which his voice could affect any national policy of significance to him, even if its significance arose through its impact on the position of the nation in the world. The heads of large firms therefore participated more than those of small firms in the public affairs of business through such organizations as the Committee for Economic Development, the International Chamber of Commerce, and the Committee for a National Trade Policy and through reading and discussing foreign trade as a national policy issue, independent of their own firms' special interests.

Despite this difference of degree between large and small firms, we may conclude that any interest is likely to increase communications activity, though a high-tariff interest is markedly more effective in evoking action than is low-tariff interest. A high-tariff interest is particularly effective in stimulating discussion inside the firm and by implication, therefore, of its own problems, in contrast to broad matters of policy. It is thus all the more conducive to action.

This conclusion is buttressed by Fig. 11-8, where talking about foreign-trade policy is compared to objective tariff interest. Those who advocated raising tariffs did the most talking, especially within their firms. Fewest did no talking. More talked both inside and outside their firms. But few talked only outside their firms. If they did not talk both outside and inside, then they talked inside only.

A high-tariff interest and/or attitude proved a more effective stimulus to action than did a low-tariff interest, because, in part, a high-tariff interest and/or attitude stimulated discussion within a firm along lines directly concerned with its specific interests, rather than discussion of general policy.

Chapter 12

Communicating with Congress

Ultimately, our concern is the influence of the business community on the federal government. The channels of influence examined in this book are those that were used in the course of a single legislative event. The resulting picture is a simplification. Nonlegislative foreign-trade problems and other kinds of legislative problems might each suggest use of somewhat different lines of influence.

The businessman may approach Congress directly, by writing, telephoning, or speaking to some representative or senator. He may give a public speech. He may stimulate his trade association or an organization like a Chamber of Commerce to take action. Those he has stimulated may in turn hold meetings or otherwise address larger publics, members of which may communicate with their congressmen. The businessman may write to a general or business newspaper. He may get in touch with one of the administrative agencies of the government, which, in turn, will be presenting a case before the Congress. He may contribute money and/or verbal support to some organized interest group working on the question. He may organize his employees to communicate with Congress, or he may organize representative groups in the community to act in his behalf. He may talk to his associates and thereby raise the general temperature of those around him to the point where more of his associates take some direct action on their own which they would not have taken if the topic had not been so much discussed.

These are examples of the complex of ways in which, by our own observation, businessmen actually have exerted or at least have attempted to exert influence on Congress. Not only is the list not exhaustive, but the elements on the list cannot be assumed always to stand in the same relation to each other. Sometimes the businessman stimulates his trade association to action, and sometimes the trade association stimulates him to action. The same is true of his relations with newspapers and magazines, lobbying groups, federal agencies, general interest groups, unions, and perhaps even Congress itself. There are innumerable cases in which interested members of Congress get businessmen to make statements which it is hoped will influence other members of Congress. The most common illustration of this is when a member of Congress arranges to have a businessman testify before a Congressional committee. In this chapter we isolate for study one element of this complex system, namely, the circumstances under which the businessman communicates directly with Congress.

In the American political tradition, the way to get things done is to "get in touch with your congressman." The matters on which a constituent may approach his representative or senator range from the advocacy of specific legislation through requests for advice on how to build a chicken coop. There are people other than congressmen who influence legislation, and all congressmen are by no means equally important. But, in the end, the passage or nonpassage of legislation depends on the votes of the 435 representatives and 100 senators. Accordingly, interested parties are prompted to write, telephone, or buttonhole their representatives and senators to make known their views and interests.

Since foreign-trade legislation bears on so many specific and local interests, it has historically produced much activity designed to influence the members of Congress. By the 1930's, the variety and complexity of interests turned the setting of tariff rates by Congress into such a legislative shambles that Congress passed tariff-making powers on to the administrative branch of government under the Reciprocal Trade Act. Nevertheless, Congress retained important legislative functions bearing on foreign-trade policy and is still looked to by many interested persons as the source for getting things done in this area.

Respondents were asked: "If you thought that some particular tariff or trade regulation should be changed, who would you be likely to turn to for help or advice on what to do?" Despite the fact that this question was posed sufficiently broadly to permit some respondents to interpret "tariff or trade regulation" as a nonlegislative matter, a representative or senator was the first choice of our respondents. (See Table 12-1.) Trade associations were the second most favored channel. Other replies were widely scattered and attest to the variety of available channels.

Under this direct probing, only a small minority indicated that they would not turn to Congress or to trade associations for support. (See Fig. 12-1.)

TABLE 12-1

PREFERRED SOURCE OF HELP OR ADVICE ON CHANGING SOME TARIFF OR TRADE REGULATION

Source	Per cent of respondents from each size of firm citing each source		
	Large	Medium Per cent	Small
Congressman or senator	27	32	39
Trade association	23	19	19
Direct approach to government body involved	15	8	3
National association other than trade association	5	4	5
Top U.S. government executives	5	3	1
Lobbyists, Washington representatives	5	3	1
Legal counsel	3	3	6
Local Chamber of Commerce or other local organization	2	2	5
Various other replies	11	7	6
No answer or don't know	21	27	27

What did our respondents in fact do during the period of 1953-1955 by way of getting in touch with the Congress?

In the course of the 1954 survey, we asked our businessmen if they or their company had "ever got in touch with a congressman or senator on any tariff or foreign-trade matter." The proportion who said that they or their company had done so in the previous two years was 19 per cent among the largest firms, 13 per cent among the medium-sized firms, and 8 per cent among the smallest firms. More than half of these had made their most recent contact in the preceding year.

Since Congress in 1954 deferred any definite action on the Reciprocal Trade Act for one year, 1954-1955 was a year of heightened inter-

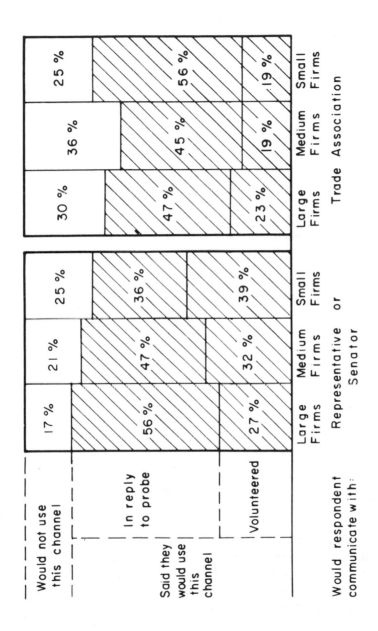

Fig. 12-1 USE OF CONGRESSMEN OR TRADE ASSOCIATIONS
FOR CHANGING TRADE REGULATIONS

est for the various trade associations and interest groups. In the follow-up survey in 1955, we asked our respondents if they had communicated with a congressman or senator in the period between the two surveys. Considerably more men now said that they had written to a representative or senator on foreign-trade or tariff matters. The proportions reporting communicating with Congress in 1954-1955 were 38 per cent of the heads of the largest firms, 30 per cent of the heads of the middle-sized firms, and 18 per cent of the heads of the smallest firms. Figures for the two surveys are summarized in Table 12-2.

It would be wise to be conservative in assessing the increase in political activity reflected in our 1955 survey. This increased activity may have been partially a function of our having aroused their interest in the issue by our previous survey. We certainly would not attribute the entire increase to our earlier wave of interviews. However, it would be safer to assume that the increase in activity in the business community as a whole may have been less than the increase in our sample.

TABLE 12-2

COMMUNICATING WITH CONGRESS

Size of firm	In two years prior to 1954 (a)	In one year prior to 1954 * (b)	In the year 1954-1955 (c)
		Per cent	
Large	19	18	38
Medium	13	9	30
Small	8	6	18

* These figures are also included in Column *a*, the proportion of men who communicated with Congress over the two-year period. Therefore, columns *a* and *b* should not be added.

A second bias which might have inflated the 1955 figures on letter-writing does not appear to have done so. It will be remembered that the 1955 survey was conducted by mail questionnaire. Those persons who were most interested in the subject matter might have been most likely to return their questionnaires, and therefore the 1955 survey could be selectively biased in favor of those who had communicated with Congress. This much can be said as empirical evidence against this plausible assumption: those who did and those who did not return the 1955 questionnaires were equally likely to have communicated with Congress in the two years preceding the 1954 survey. On the basis of this and a number of other findings, we are convinced that, as of the time of the 1954 survey, the respondents on the 1955 survey were no more interested or involved than were the 1955 nonrespondents. Selective response to the questionnaire can have inflated the 1955 figures only by a small amount, if at all.

If we look at the business community as a whole—that is, weigh the several size groups according to their representation in the American business world—and make some slight downward revision of the 1954-1955 figures, we find that, whereas less than one in ten business heads had communicated with Congress in 1953-1954, apparently at least twice as many, or about one in five, had done so in 1954-1955.

There is no convenient (in fact not even an inconvenient) yardstick by which to decide if this is little or much activity. We may look for an empirical standard and ask how this level of communication compares with that by other groups on other issues, but there are no really comparable data. On the bases of the testimony of Congressional informants and those partial mail counts that we were able to make it appears that the flow of mail was heavy by most standards but did not measure up to any of the really outstanding letter-writing campaigns. Since mail contains many repeats by people who have written more, perhaps many more, than one letter, letter counts do not tell us the proportion of the total electorate which has written on any one issue; but it is certain that the proportion has never on any issue reached anything like the one in five of our business sample.

On cross-sectional surveys of the American electorate, people have been asked if they have ever communicated with Congress or any other lawmaking body. The results from the Roper poll referred to in previous chapters are typical: only about 20 per cent (about the proportion of our sample that communicated with Congress on one issue in one year) of the electorate claim that they have ever written to a legislator on any issue. In response to a similar question, three-fourths of our sample said that at some time they had communicated with Congress on some issue other than foreign-trade policy. By size of firm, the percentages were 88, 79, and 71. By a large margin, the heads of business organizations are more inclined than the average citizen to act on the assumption that one writes his representative or senator on matters of public policy in which he is concerned.

But the heads of business firms are something other than rank-and-file citizens, and what would be great activity on the part of the over-all electorate could well be little activity on the part of men responsible for institutions deeply and immediately affected by government policies. It must be remembered that we are dealing not even with a cross-section of businessmen, but with businessmen who are the spokesmen for their firms on policy matters. They certainly should not be compared with the rank-and-file electorate.

Writing a letter to a congressman is for our respondents a minimal political act. Nothing is easier than to ask an aide to draft a note for signature. It involves no break in the routine of daily activity, no meetings, no trips, no inherent issue of precedent or procedure, no visible cost, and very little drawn from the writer's bank account of good will. Hard political acts which carry serious costs in money, time, or good will are those such as hiring a lobbyist, organizing a committee, traveling to Washington, or asking a political favor.

Some few businessmen found the trade issue important enough to do such things, too. The one in five who wrote letters can be considered as that broader group which had any sense of personal involvement in the issue at all. Accordingly, we take that statistic to indicate that the issue was not one of high salience for the business community as a whole.

☐ Who Wrote and Why?

What was it that made the issue salient for some individuals but not for others? Why did some men communicate with Congress while others did not? Our informal interviews suggested the existence of certain rather clear distinctions between the active and inactive men. The difference, in a nutshell, is that those who wrote were the ones who saw the act of writing as part of a recognized professional role, likely to contribute to a specific and short-run objective and contributing effectively to the special interest for which the writer spoke. Moral conviction was not enough. A sense of the importance of the issue was not enough. Writing was not self-expression. A man was more likely to write on a trivial point if it were part of his job and a practical thing to do than if he were burning with deep conviction about the nation's future and welfare. For all these reasons, protectionists were more likely to write than were reciprocal-trade supporters.

Let us label as activists those who indicated on either the first or second wave of questioning that they had communicated with Congress on foreign-trade policy at any time over the three-year period, 1952-1955. However, because the number of respondents is considerably smaller for the 1955 mail questionnaire, we confine the main burden of our analysis to the period before the 1954 interview survey.

The Role of Self-Interest

It is no surprise that almost any criterion of self-interest is correlated with a tendency to communicate with Congress.

Respondents were asked to indicate the importance to their business of a series of issues: taxes and tax rates, wage rates and union demands, tariffs, export markets, defense contracts, foreign competition, and political stability abroad. The salience of such issues as taxes, wage rates, defense contracts, and political stability abroad bore no relationship to whether the representative of the firms had communicated with Congress on foreign-trade policy, so letter-writing is not part of any general propensity to see politics as important. But Table 12-3 does show a strong connection between communicating with Congress on foreign trade and importance attributed to tariffs and foreign competition. Those men who reported one of these issues to be important to their firms were more likely to have communicated with Congress on foreign-trade policy. "Export markets," as we have come to expect, were something of an exception. They played a less important role than the protectionist-associated "tariffs" and "foreign competition." Among medium and small firms, "export markets" had virtually no influence.

A man's statements that tariffs, foreign competition, export markets, and the like are important to his firm are subjective interpretations of his interest. There is, therefore, circularity in the argument. What has been shown so far is that activists perceived their self-interest as being involved, not necessarily that it was. It remains to show that they were responding objectively to self-interest. Fig. 12-2 shows that. It reveals that those respondents from industries which economists rated as having no interest in foreign-trade issues wrote their congressmen less than the rest.

That economic interest is a stimulus to action is hardly a surprise. Less obvious is the fact that the kind of economic interest determines how effective a stimulus it is. Just as we found that protectionists were more likely to talk to their colleagues about trade matters, so here we find that they are more likely to write to their congressmen.

An industrialist suffering from foreign competition sees his problem as clear and tangible. He is apt to believe that it can be coped with by protective legislation. A single product is being undersold in the market. The situation can be changed by changing a single tariff rate or customs classification or regulation. A letter to a congressman may be favorably received as a proper expression by a spokesman of a valid interest. It may be expected to have a discernible effect.

However, an industrialist believing that he stands to gain from a high level of foreign trade seldom perceives any one factor, and certainly not American tariff legislation, as determining the level of his sales.[1] He

---

[1] In 1962, the Common Market was an exception. It was a single factor, about which something could be done, which was seen as likely to cut sales if not responded to.

TABLE 12-3

RELATIONSHIP BETWEEN IMPORTANCE OF VARIOUS ISSUES TO FIRMS AND
PROPORTION OF RESPONDENTS WHO COMMUNICATED WITH CONGRESS

	Per cent who communicated with Congress		
	Large firms	Medium firms	Small firms
		Per cent	
1952-1954			
Tariffs are:			
Very important	32	24	15
Fairly important	18	9	11
Not important	9	7	4
Foreign competition is:			
Very important	33	25	13
Fairly important	22	15	3
Not important	11	6	6
Export markets are:			
Very important	25	15	17
Fairly important	21	9	7
Not important	13	15	6
1954-1955			
Tariffs are:			
Very important	68	37	30
Fairly important	32	32	22
Not important	21	23	11
Foreign competition is:			
Very important	53	42	28
Fairly important	54	34	26
Not important	22	24	13
Export markets are:			
Very important	56	25	19
Fairly important	34	34	20
Not important	27	28	16

sees himself as less uniquely responsible for action and perceives the relation between any letter he might write and the state of the world he desires
as indirect. He is also, as we have already seen, less apt to feel strongly.
For all these reasons, a self-interest on the side of foreign trade works far
less effectively on behalf of action than does a self-interest in protection.

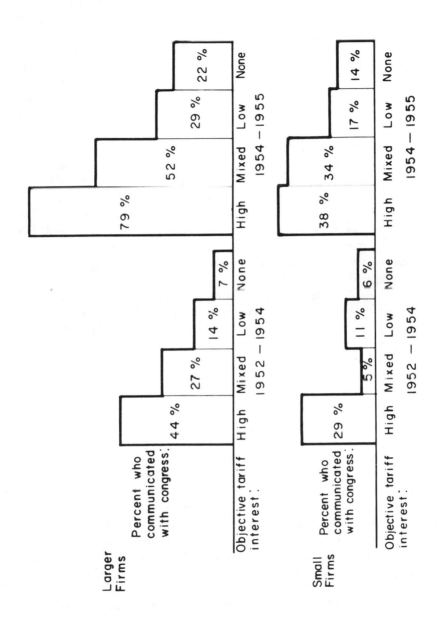

Fig. 12-2   OBJECTIVE ECONOMIC INTEREST AND ITS RELATION
TO COMMUNICATING WITH CONGRESS

These variations in the force with which self-interest acts stand out clearly both in Fig. 12-2, where self-interest is measured objectively, and in Table 12-3, where subjective criteria of interest are used. Those men who said export markets were very important were more likely (but not by a very wide margin) to communicate with Congress than those who said export markets were not important, whereas those who feared foreign competition were two or three times as likely to write as those who did not.

In Fig. 12-2, additional variations in the impact of self-interest on action become evident. In each category, men from the large firms were more active than those from the smaller firms.

In addition, it is important to note that, in three out of four instances, men from mixed-interest industries were more active than men from low-tariff industries. We had predicted the reverse. Psychological theories to the effect that cross-pressures generate apathy had led us to expect that men with mixed interests would withdraw, becoming less involved than men with either a clear high- or clear low-tariff interest. We expected that men faced with a conflict in their own desires would let the whole matter ride, rather than take action. Our error calls for examination, for a wrong prediction may be more interesting than a right one; the right ones are too easily dismissed as common sense. The source of our failure seems to lie in not anticipating that, when a man had mixed interests, the protectionist components would be psychologically much more compelling than the liberal components. A mixed interest worked in effect as a high-tariff interest.

Take the cases of two industrial giants, DuPont and General Electric. DuPont had ten divisions, G.E. dozens. In accordance with current administrative theory, each division had a large degree of autonomy. In each company, one such division had an intense and long-established concern over foreign competition. In DuPont, manufacture of synthetic organic chemicals had flowered during World War I, thanks to the cutting-off of German competition. Fear of the revival of that competition has haunted the division ever since. But other divisions, such as paints, have a significant export business. General Electric faces stiff competition in large turbines from Swiss, Swedish, and other foreign firms. The division that makes them has considerable interest in the Buy-American Act. But G.E. is also a large exporter and a foreign manufacturer of smaller appliances. Faced with such conflicting interests, neither firm took an official corporate stand on reciprocal trade. But, for practical purposes, the impact of the two firms was on the side of protection. G.E. permitted some of its divisions to sign a protectionist memorandum issued jointly by several electrical manufacturers. No division expressed itself on the other side, except perhaps within the company. DuPont permitted the chairman of its tariff committee, a vice-president, to act as an individual as the leading spokesman of the chemical industry on behalf of protection. Again, none of the division heads on the other side were publicly heard, although they were known to be opposed to, or at least not in favor of, protectionism.

Mixed interests did not produce the indecision that we anticipated they would because the merest breath of competition in any one established market was usually perceived as a threat to the self-interest of the firm and was acted on accordingly. It was acted upon to some extent regardless of ideology. For example, many liberal traders in principle wrote to complain about specific practices which injured them.

On the other hand, export opportunities had to be much more massive to be recognized. Even when recognized, they were less often perceived as constituting a valid interest, an interest requiring support by specific items of reciprocal-trade legislation, or one requiring such pinpointed action as writing a letter.

The Role of Attitudes

At least in outline, we have now made our point that, although self-interest stimulated action, just how much it did so depended on a number of attitudinal and political considerations. Let us look a little more closely at those conjunctions of attitudinal and objective variables which were conditions of action. We start by looking at the role of our respondents' attitudes taken by themselves. Later, we shall look at the combined effect of attitudes and self-interest.

In Table 12-4, we have summarized the attitudes expressed on both the 1954 and 1955 surveys in relation to the percentages of men who communicated with Congress at any time during the period 1952-1955.

There are a number of interesting features about these data. The most obvious, of course, is that respondents who said "raise tariffs" on either or both surveys are more likely to have reported communicating with Congress than are those respondents who said "lower tariffs" on either or both. Just as a high-tariff interest was a more effective stimulus to action than a low-tariff one, so is a high-tariff attitude a more effective stimulus than a low-tariff one.

The label "indeterminate" is a way of identifying those men who would not take a categorical stand on either side of this complex issue. In many respects, they were as involved in the issue as men who took a committed position. (Men who took a "raise" position on both surveys and those who took a "reduce" position on both were not generally any more active than those who took either of these committed positions on only one

TABLE 12-4

HOW TARIFF ATTITUDE AFFECTED COMMUNICATION WITH CONGRESS
1952-1955 *

Attitude	*Per cent communicating with Congress* (a)	*Size of group* (b) *Per cent*	*Proportion of letter-writers provided by that group* $\left(c = \dfrac{a \times b}{\Sigma[a \times b]} \right)$
Said raise in 1954 and/or 1955	43	13	24
Steadily indeterminate	23	36	32
Said reduce in 1954 and/or 1955	22	51	44
		100	100

* Excluded from the table are the seven men who shifted from one extreme position to another during the two surveys. On intensive analysis of these seven cases, no consistent pattern appears. They must be regarded either as "accidental" or idiosyncratic. Moreover, the classification of these cases on one or another of the surveys was in most instances dubious.

All responses other than "raise" or "lower" have been lumped together as "indeterminate." "Indeterminate" includes all such answers as "leave," "don't know," and "refuse to generalize." These are not necessarily the ill-informed, uninterested replies which don't-know responses are on cross-sectional surveys of the population. A refusal to generalize was sometimes an intelligent response by men too sophisticated to be glib.

Because of low frequencies, we have abandoned our usual practice of separating respondents by size of firm. Combining all size groups in one does not here affect the major conclusions drawn from the data.

survey.) As the table shows, the steadily indeterminate group is somewhat more active than the "reduce" groups.[2]

Thus, "indeterminate" does not mean inactive. The uncommitted respondents were heard in Congress, too. But they were not heard in defense of the Reciprocal Trade Act. They usually expressed themselves

[2] Of the 13 per cent who said "raise" in either year, only 3 per cent said it in both years. Of the 51 per cent who said "reduce" in either year, only 27 per cent said it in both years. The reader may raise questions as to whether those who shifted from committed to indeterminate positions and vice-versa between 1954 and 1955 were simply non-generalizers, as we have interpreted them, or people who actually experienced changes of attitude in the course of the year. We may apply a test by making the simple assumption that a shift to a genuinely uncommitted position ought to reduce the probability of a man's communicating with Congress, and a shift from a genuinely uncommitted position to a genuinely committed position ought to increase the probability of a man's communicating with Congress. Yet, among protectionists, we find the reverse, and, among liberal traders, no relationship. The individual shifts between committed and indeterminate answers were merely variability that occurred when sophisticated men tried to give simple answers to complicated questions.

on specific problems facing particular industries, and their letters were almost *ipso facto* read as pleas for protective measures. In the 1950's, liberal trade was a broad ideological position, whereas protection took the form of arguing the special case. Thus, those who wrote on the special case were construed to be protectionists. Adding the true protectionists to those who gave indeterminate replies, about half the letter-writers from management were in effect writing on behalf of protection.

In 1955, letter-writing increased substantially. Keeping in mind that proportionately more men communicated with Congress in 1954-1955 that in the years immediately preceding the 1954 survey, we may ask, "Who benefited from the increase in activity?" Tables 12-5 and 12-6 show that the increased activity occurred on both sides of the fence, but that protectionism benefited more. Of those who wanted tariffs raised, the proportion who wrote rose from 16 per cent in 1952-1954 to 40 per cent in 1954-1955. Of those who wanted tariffs lowered, the proportion who wrote rose from 10 per cent in 1952-1954 to 17 per cent in 1954-1955. Clearly, there was a larger proportionate gain for the protectionists. But we know that there are more persons on the low-tariff side, so even a smaller percentage gain could bring in a larger absolute gain in the number of low-tariff letters to Congress. Indeed, at first glance, it may look as though that happened.

In 1954, two protectionists wrote Congress from every 100 of our respondents, whereas five liberal traders wrote. In 1955, five protectionists wrote Congress from every 100 of our respondents, and nine liberal traders. But, if we add the letter-writers of indeterminate persuasion to the protectionist letter-writers, as, indeed, we probably should, the liberal traders appear as a diminishing minority. In 1954-1955, these liberal letter-writers were 5 per cent of the business elite, tied against 5 per cent writing on the other side. In 1955, the liberal letter-writers had risen to 9 per cent, but those on the other side had risen to 11 per cent.

We can add some further detail to these calculations. Let us try to compute how the correspondence would have looked from the Congressional end. It is not to be assumed that each letter-writer wrote one letter. On the contrary, a fairly common pattern is to write to one's representative and both senators at once. We have no quantitative data on that sort of multiplication of letters. It is also true that some men wrote repeatedly, and on that point we did collect data in 1954. Eight per cent of the heads of large companies said that they wrote continuously or a number of times; so did 4 per cent of the heads of medium-sized firms. Others indicated the date of the most recent letter. The distribution of these over time may be taken as a rough—though very rough—indication of the frequency of writing.

It turns out that protectionists write about twice as often as liberal

TABLE 12-5

ATTITUDES TOWARD TARIFFS (1954 AND 1955) AND COMMUNICATING WITH CONGRESS (1952-1954 AND 1954-1955)

Attitudes	1952-1954 Yes	1954-1955 Yes	1952-1954 Yes	1954-1955 No	1952-1954 No	1954-1955 Yes	1952-1954 No	1954-1955 No	Total
					Per cent				
Said "raise" in either year	13		3		27		57		100
Steadily inde- terminate	3		6		14		77		100
Said "reduce" in either year	5		5		12		78		100

Was Congress written to?

TABLE 12-6

LETTER-WRITERS ON THE TWO SIDES

	Per cent of sample (a)	Per cent communi- cating with Congress 1952-1954 (b)	Per cent of sample communi- cating with Congress 1952-1954 (c = axb) Per cent	Per cent communi- cating with Congress 1955 (d)	Per cent of sample communi- cating with Congress 1955 (axd)
All who said "raise" (either year)	13	16	2	40	5
Steadily indetermi- nate	36	9	3	17	6
All who said "re- duce" (either year)	51	10	5	17	9

traders, with indeterminate respondents midway between. Applying that estimate, we find that, from every 100 respondents in our total sample, Congress may have received about twenty-six letters asking for protection in 1952-1954 and sixteen letters from liberal traders.

We have also noted, furthermore, that a letter from a liberal trader is not necessarily a letter in favor of liberal trade. We noted that such a letter will often be a complaint about a trade problem, and, as such, whatever the unknown personal views of its writer on the larger issue, it will be read as support for protection. For that reason, the ratio of twenty-six to sixteen is still not the balance of letters which Congress received from our respondents on the two sides of the issue. The letters classified as they would be read on Capitol Hill would be yet a little further tipped to the side of protection.

Thus, we find that, with each selective factor in the flow of mail to Congress, the protectionists gained more. More protectionist businessmen wrote. Protectionist businessmen stimulated more letters from their colleagues. Those protectionists who wrote, wrote more often. Those liberal traders who wrote, wrote less clearly of their views.

So it happened that liberal-trade advocates among businessmen outnumbered protectionists three to one; letter-writers among these liberal businessmen in 1952-1954 outnumbered protectionist letter-writers by a substantially smaller margin. However, they still predominated. Nonetheless, letters received from business heads by Congress in 1952-1954, the purport of which was favorable to protection, outnumbered those calling for liberal trade.

As the debate became more intense in 1955, protectionist writing increased more than did liberal writing. Applying to our sixteen–to–twenty-six estimate of letters written in 1952-1954 the known percentage of increase in writing by liberal traders, indeterminates, and protectionists, we estimate that, in 1954-1955, every 100 of our respondents generated twenty-eight letters written by liberal traders and fifty-five written for protection. Thus it happened that a body of citizens represented by our sample could appear to Congress to be two-to-one protectionist when we know they were more nearly three-to-one liberal traders.

Interests and Attitudes Combined

We have seen that both self-interest and attitudes separately relate to the probability that a man will communicate with Congress. In each case, protectionism—whether protectionist interest or protectionist attitude—increases the chance that a man will write. In each case, also, mixed or moderate interests or attitudes operate in surprising ways. We are naturally led to the question of the interactive effects of interests and attitudes. The data on this matter are presented in Table 12-7. These data are for both the 1954 and 1955 surveys. We have combined the sizes of firms, for the pattern is about the same for all of them.

We note, first of all, that each factor retains some predictive power even when controlled by the other. Protectionist attitudes continue to exert a motivating force superior to liberal-trade attitudes. Regardless of the economic interest of the industry from which they come, the men who said "raise tariffs" were almost invariably more likely to have communicated with Congress than those who said "reduce tariffs."

TABLE 12-7

SELF-INTEREST AND TARIFF ATTITUDES IN RELATION TO
COMMUNICATING WITH CONGRESS

	Tariff attitudes in 1954				
Objective interest	Raise	Reduce	Leave	Don't know	Refused to generalize
				Per cent	
Per cent communicating with Congress 1952-1954					
High tariff	63	14	40	7	38
Mixed	14*	6	9	11	25*
Low tariff	24	15	8	6	19
None	—*	8*	20*	—	22*
Per cent communicating with Congress 1954-1955					
High tariff	56	18	30	—	40
Mixed	75*	40	28	—	85*
Low tariff	42	28	11	—	31
None	20	12	18	—	7

* The cells marked with the asterisk are the exceptions to the generalization that men who said "raise tariffs" were the most active men in any industry category. All but one of the exceptions come from men who refused to generalize, that is, men who gave an answer compatible with protectionism.

The numbers on which our conclusions are based are small, so let us look at a consolidated table (Table 12-8). We shall disregard the "don't-know" replies, treat "raise," "leave as is," and "refuse to generalize" as protectionist answers, and combine mixed-interest respondents with those with high-tariff interests.

The highest levels of activity, both in 1954 and in 1955, are found where some protectionist interest coincides with a personally protectionist view. Even such a coincidence of interests and views did not work, however, to activate the liberal-trade side so strongly. The coincidence of liberal interests and views produced more, but only moderately more,

TABLE 12-8

SELF-INTEREST AND TARIFF ATTITUDES IN RELATION TO
COMMUNICATING WITH CONGRESS: A SIMPLIFIED VIEW

	Tariff attitude	
Objective interest	*Raise or leave or refused to generalize*	*Reduce*
	Per cent	
Per cent communicating with Congress 1952-1954		
High or mixed	21	8
Low tariff	12	15
None	9	8
Per cent communicating with Congress 1954-1955		
High or mixed	50	29
Low tariff	15	28
None	17	12

action than that basal level of activity found among businessmen with no interest in the issue or with conflicts of attitude and interest. Low-tariff interests and low-tariff attitudes taken individually or even in interaction proved to be relatively weak stimuli to communicate with Congress.

The Role of Ideology

We have steadfastly tried not to take a position on the relative weight of ideological factors and self-interest, but to view them as part of a complex. We have also refused to identify protectionism with isolationism, since the majority of the men in our sample, including the protectionists, could not be considered classical isolationists. Nevertheless, the evidence we have introduced indicates that there is an association between protectionist attitudes and isolationism. High-tariff advocates are less willing to have America play its new role in the world than are low-tariff advocates. And, if that was true among our respondents as a whole, it is even more true among those of them who communicated with Congress.

High-tariff letter-writers were less likely to be wholeheartedly in favor of an active United States role in world affairs. About 90 per cent of the low-tariff letter-writers from each size of firm unqualifiedly favored an active role, but this was true of only 42 per cent of the high-tariff letter-writers from the larger firms and 50 per cent of the high-tariff letter-writers from the smaller firms. It will be recalled from Chapter 9 that 75 per cent of all high-tariff supporters from larger firms and 57 per cent from small ones advocated an active role for the United States in world affairs. Thus we see that the isolationist segment was substantially larger among those protectionists who wrote Congress than among those who failed to act.

To say the same thing the other way around, high-tariff advocates for whom isolationism reinforced their tariff stand, were more likely to take action in writing their congressmen than were those high-tariff advocates whose stand was being undercut by general support for American participation in world affairs. Among small businessmen no great difference appeared, but among larger businessmen one did. Of those who were both isolationists and protectionists, 26 per cent wrote their congressmen in 1953-1954. Among those who were protectionists but at the same time internationalists, only 17 per cent wrote. Internationalism acted as a brake on protectionist proclivities.

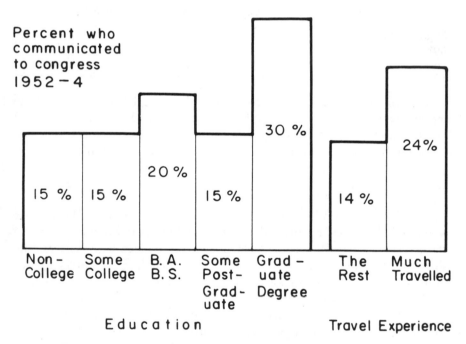

Fig. 12-3   RELATION OF EDUCATION AND TRAVEL TO COMMUNICATION WITH CONGRESS

All of this might suggest the hypothesis that the men who write their congressmen are the most troglodytic, unenlightened elements of the business community. They are those whose protectionist views unabashedly reflect a protectionist self-interest, and they are also the men most apt to be isolationists. Can we not take these facts as simply special cases of a general relationship between narrowness and recourse to Congress?

If education and foreign travel may be taken as indexes of breadth and perspective, this thesis must be rejected. Fig. 12-3 shows that the men of broader training and experience wrote their congressmen more often than their colleagues of less sophisticated experience.

That being so, the propensity of protectionists, and more particularly isolationist protectionists, to write their congressmen must be interpreted as a specific characteristic of the foreign-trade issue, not as a reflection of a general propensity of troglodytes to enjoy complaining by letter.

The letter to Congress has for years been the specific and characteristic mode of self-defense of an industry threatened by injury from foreign competition. That fact is the context in which all other factors operate. Anything which reinforces the impulse to write, such as an ideological belief in protection or having a better education, increases the probability of a letter being sent by a person who feels the need for protection. Anything that creates conflict, be it ideological belief in internationalism or in liberal trade, may interfere with the impulse to write a letter asking for protection.

But our respondents on the liberal side, even when all such reinforcing factors as education, ideology, and travel push them toward action, still do not write. Belief in the principles of liberal trade is not the sort of thing businessmen write Congress about.

□ The Channels of Communication

Congress, though our respondents' preferred place to turn for help, is preferred more by some than it is by others. Those who had communicated with Congress on foreign-trade policy were also more likely to have done so on other matters: 98 to 83 per cent, 86 to 70 per cent, and 89 to 68 per cent, for large, medium, and small firms, respectively.[3]

The men with an inclination to turn to Congress, as might be expected, knew better what to expect. Those individuals who communicated with Congress were more likely to know whether their congressmen and senators had taken a stand on foreign-trade policy and what that stand was.

---

[3] The proportion of men who expressed preference for Congress as a source of help is somewhat higher among those who actually communicated with Congress. Comparing those who did so prior to the 1954 survey with those who did not, we find the following proportions of spontaneous mentions of a congressman or senator as someone to whom to turn for help or advice: among the largest firms, 33 to 25 per cent; among medium-sized firms, 40 to 30 per cent; and, among the smallest firms, 57 to 36 per cent. Even under direct questioning, the people who had not communicated with Congress were less likely to say that doing so was a good idea.

Among writers and nonwriters from the various sizes of firms, the proportions knowing the stand of their congressmen were: 41 to 22 per cent, 40
to 25 per cent, and 42 to 19 per cent. For the senators, the proportions
were: 73 to 37 per cent, 62 to 38 per cent, and 65 to 36 per cent.

It is not surprising that the men who took action had more knowledge of the situation in which they were acting. It is worth noting, however, that fully half of the men who wrote their representative did so without knowing what his stand was and that this was also true of more than
one-third of those who wrote their senators. In other words, a surprisingly
high proportion acted in ignorance of the stand of the men whom they
were addressing. But this was not equally true of protectionists and liberal
traders. The protectionist letter-writers had more knowledge of the position
of the men they were writing.[4] In the ratio of about two to one, protectionist letter-writers were more likely to know the positions of both their
senators and their representatives than were their opposite numbers who
favored low tariffs.[5] The liberals, even when they wrote Congress, did
so without enough investment in what they were doing to ascertain the
views of the men to whom they were writing. To all intents and purposes,
their letters on behalf of foreign trade were manifestoes "to whom it may
concern." The thinness of their involvement in such manifestoes was wit-
nessed by their failure to know how the recipients might react to them.

Suppose a businessman does know how his congressman feels about
reciprocal trade. Does he tend to write a representative or senator with
whom he agrees or one with whom he disagrees? A priori, the case might
be argued either way. On one hand, there might be more point in writing
a man with whom one disagreed, since the aim of one's action is to shift the
balance of power in Congress in the direction of one's own position. Why,
therefore, write, telephone, or call on someone who already agrees with
you? However, when we look at those men who communicated with Congress and who knew the position of their representatives and/or senators,
it seems clear that these men wrote senators and representatives who agreed
with their own position. The reasons for this behavior will be considered
later.

In summary, to whom does one turn for help on tariff and foreign-

---

[4] This cannot be explained by a hypothesis of generally greater awareness by protectionists than by low-tariff advocates. It is true only of protectionists who wrote their
congressmen. They were better informed about what they were doing than were liberal
traders who wrote. In other words, protectionists who wrote were involving themselves
more deeply in that activity. Among those who did not write, liberal-trade advocates were
substantially better informed than protectionists.

[5] It is necessary to call attention to the fact that we are dealing with very small numbers of cases (only about one-quarter of our sample), and these comparisons can be
regarded only as suggestive. The fact that the same patterns are exhibited in both sizes
of firms is somewhat reassuring.

trade matters? The preferred person is a member of the national legislature, either one's representative or one or both of one's senators, and one who already supports one's point of view. The second choice is one's trade association, sometimes because the trade association will in turn write a member of the legislature. Only a small portion of all the men interviewed favored writing an administrative agency or any one of the organizations or institutions which are one way or another also involved in foreign-trade policy.

The men who actually did write a member of the national legislature were the ones who were better informed as to their senators' and representatives' positions. They were also more inclined to report that these men shared their position.

Everything said of the activists in general is even more true of the high-tariff advocates among the activists. Compared to low-tariff activists, the high-tariff ones were better informed of the views of their representatives and senators. They seemed to feel, according to data not reported here, that they had somewhat freer access to their legislators. They maintained more active, continuing contact with them. In the American system of government, there is greater legitimacy in speaking up for an injured industry than in arguing for the general good. The result is that the channels of communication between Congress and protectionist firms were both more open and more frequently used.

☐ The Supportive Environment

We have frequently had occasion to state that the businessman finds support from his environment. The people with whom he is associated tend to agree with him, and in most instances the forces bearing on him impel him in the direction of his interests and convictions. This is natural, since the circumstances of business life throw men of common interests and attitudes together. Furthermore, their own choices of associates and associations reinforce their attitudes and implement their interests. Yet, this is not a universal condition; there are many sources of conflict in the life-situation of the businessman.

Which environment stirs a man to communicate with Congress? Is it a hostile one, in which he is aware that he is in a fight and that, if he does not speak for himself, others will speak against him? Or is it, on the contrary, a sense that everyone around him feels the same way as he does and supports his political actions? The answer is complex. Both conditions are needed. We have already seen that a danger, such as the threat of foreign competition, generates letters. But such an external threat would not lead to strong political reactions by a man who felt that, as an isolated victim, he stood alone. Generally, before he will act he must feel support and strength in his immediate milieu. He must perceive those whose approval he desires as aligned with him. Either because it is a fact or through fantasy, he must believe that the danger comes from "them," but that "we" are united behind his views. That is when he will write.

Furthermore, our interviews revealed that, like other people, businessmen feel freer to act if they believe that their interests are not in conflict with those of the people about them. The motivations of this feeling are at least two.

It is part of the unwritten code of business to avoid actions which will gratuitously injure others. In Chapter 9, we noted that a businessman typically feels free to act in his own interest even though others may suffer incidentally, but he also feels that, where he lacks strong direct interest, he should not act, either from principle or for other reasons, in ways that hurt others. Under that code, businessmen without a vested interest in foreign trade are reluctant to advocate a policy in which they believe if others will thereby suffer injury.

Second, action against the interest of others may provoke counteraction. We have introduced numerous illustrations of men refraining from an active role in the foreign-trade controversy out of concern for possible retaliatory action by clients or competitors. Although actual instances of such retaliation proved difficult to find, the possibility loomed fairly large in business thinking.

Thus, the absence of contrary interests in the environment and the presence of like-minded men close at hand acted as stimuli to action. In like-minded groups, the content of discussions is one-sided. They therefore bolster action, rather than inhibit it.

The men who reported that they had communicated with Congress had such environmental supports. For example, they were apt to report that others in their industry agreed with their tariff stands. Comparing writers to Congress with nonwriters in the several sizes of firms, we find the following proportions saying that the men in their industry agreed with their own stand: large, 75 to 60 per cent; medium, 75 to 61 per cent; small, 70 to 60 per cent. Of course, we do not know whether in reality those who wrote their congressmen had more support in their industries than did the silent ones, but at least they perceived it that way.

The same pattern of protective perception appears on other questions, too. In Chapter 8, we have shown that the trend in business opinion seems to have been away from protectionism in recent decades. We have also shown that the members of our sample as a whole reported that their own attitudes had changed in the direction of a more liberal trade policy. On this item of information, the true, as distinct from perceived, direction of change for our sample as a whole seems clear. But the picture is somewhat different if we look at how the direction of change appeared to the men supporting one or the other position on foreign-trade policy. There was a quite marked trend for the advocates of either position to see the men in their own industries as shifting toward their own position (see Table 12-9) or in any event as not having shifted counter to their own position. This finding is of particular importance for understanding the behavior of the protectionists. When the tide was running against them, they found themselves and, even more, thought they found themselves, in eddies which ran counter to the tide. What they saw in their immediate environment protected them from the conflict between their own position and that of the business community at large.

Men who wrote their congressmen were much more likely to say that their industry had taken an official stand on tariffs and foreign-trade policy: 48 to 21 per cent, 57 to 29 per cent, and 48 to 14 per cent. This finding suggests that the industries of the activists had, or were thought to have, a direct stake in foreign-trade policy. This fact is also important

TABLE 12-9

PERCEIVED CHANGES IN TARIFF ATTITUDE AMONG BUSINESSMEN IN OWN INDUSTRY

Perceived direction of change of other men's attitudes	Own attitude			
	Low-tariff		High-tariff	
	Large firms	Small firms	Large firms	Small firms
	Per cent			
Those who had written Congress				
No change	25	12	41	66
Toward low	49 *	53 *	6	—
Toward high	3	19	53 *	9 *
Don't know	23	16	—	25
	100	100	100	100
Those who had not written Congress				
No change	18	20	24	37
Toward low	46 *	50 *	24	8
Toward high	4	2	20 *	30 *
Don't know	32	28	31	24
	100	100	100	100

* Asterisked numbers represent proportions in a supportive environment.

as an indication of the consensus which surrounded the activists. Finding the men in their industry agreeing with them and having in fact taken an official stand on the issue, they would have less inhibition on acting in their self-interest.

As usual, such relationships take on an even sharper focus when we compare protectionist activists with those who supported a policy of lowering tariffs. Protectionists said more frequently that the men in their own industries agreed with them. In the larger firms, 64 per cent of the high-tariff letter-writers said that the other men in their industries agreed with them, whereas this was true of a slightly smaller proportion (61 per cent) of the antiprotectionists. Among the smaller firms, the trend is more marked, the proportions being 97 and 52 per cent. On the question of an official industry stand, the differences are still more marked. Comparing protectionist activists with their antiprotectionist opponents, we get the following figures: larger firms, 71 to 32 per cent; smaller firms, 56 to 40 per cent. If we adjust the weights of these firms to their proper representation in the business community, 59 per cent of the protectionists and only 38 per cent of the active advocates of lower tariffs came from an industry which had taken an official stand.

Finally, we are interested in whether those who communicated with Congress did so under stimulation from a trade association or similar agency. Of those who reported communicating with Congress on the 1954 survey, 25 per cent of the men from the largest firms, 52 per cent from the medium-sized firms, and 46 per cent from the smallest firms said that they had been asked to get in touch with their congressman or senator.[6]

In the complex of data introduced above, causation may and probably does lie in several directions. However, whatever the origins of the relationships may be, once they exist, they tend to offer the businessman involved a protective and supportive environment. Activists, in addition to being more strongly motivated to act, were also subject to fewer cross-pressures of an environmental sort which might inhibit action and the mechanisms of support were more important for the protectionist than for his opponent. The former, although he lives in a business community which in principle is predominantly opposed to his position, is actually fairly well protected from cross-pressures by having immediately around him an environment that tends to support his own position, or at least he perceives it as such.

---

[6] Unfortunately, we did not ask the men who had *not* communicated with Congress whether they had been asked to do so. Therefore, we do not know how much pressure the latter group perceived. On this question, there were no consistent differences between the high-tariff activists and the low-tariff activists. Their writing was equally stimulated.

□ Summary

The data we have reviewed underscore the strength of the protectionist position for stimulating its advocates to take action to influence the
national legislature. Both the various criteria of self-interest which we
employed and the subjective attitudes of our respondents bore a relation to
whether they had communicated with Congress. But both low-tariff self-
interest and additional support for a low-tariff policy proved to be more
feeble stimuli than either a high-tariff interest or a high-tariff attitude.

More remarkable was the fact that a mixed interest, for example
on the part of a diversified company, stimulated action that could only
with difficulty be distinguished from protectionist action. The protectionist
component of the company's interest strongly dominated the export interest.

Other data show that an attitude which approached tariff matters
eclectically and empirically, rather than in terms of an ideological commitment, tended to result in more frequent letter-writing. The letters that our
businessmen respondents wrote were less the expression of their political
passion than a realistic or would-be realistic response to concrete situations.
They wrote in their roles of spokesmen for special interests, often, indeed,
writing on the side opposite to that which they themselves would have
generally espoused as national policy.

One result of this is that it was difficult to perceive, from the side
of Congress, the true meaning of all the correspondence. The mail grossly
overrepresented the viewpoint of the protectionists. They did, indeed, write
more often, and they stimulated their employees to write. But, in our own
sample, the largest part of the letters still came from men who in principle
believed in reciprocal trade. Yet, the majority of letters received on the
Hill were pleas for protection. Part of the explanation was that communication was incomplete. The letter that said, "I believe in the necessity for this
nation to follow a liberal-trade policy and expand its foreign trade, but
may I draw your attention to a special injustice which besets the widget
industry," was read on the Hill as a plea for protection with a bow to
prevailing ideology. It was often written quite sincerely by a man who
thought it his business to speak for his business. A large proportion of the
letters that liberal traders wrote were of this character.

Writing to Congress thus proved to be a function of self-interest,
but not, we must stress, of any self-interest whatsoever. It occurred when
a self-interest was reinforced or at least not counteracted by a series of
ideological and political considerations. Isolationist protectionists or protectionists in principle who felt a practical need for protection were more
likely to write than men who felt the same need but were restrained by

ideology. Men from large companies were much more likely to write. They had research and clerical staffs working for them, making the signature on a letter a routine operation. Better-educated and more-widely traveled men wrote more often.

Most important of all, the act of writing had to seem geared to producing a result. Whatever they may have said when citing political shibboleths, our businessmen in practice did not treat seriously the notion that mere citizen expression on matters of general interest was an effective way to spend their scarce time. They wrote, and wrote often, but primarily when they had a particular objective to serve and some reason to feel that, by writing, they, as individuals, had a chance to promote it. That fact served the side of protection in good stead. Foreign competition tends to be seen as specific. A narrowly defined commodity undersells an American commodity, and the intruder can be kept out by a tariff rate, a quota, or a classification change. Foreign markets, on the other hand, tend to be seen as a function of the general state of the world economy. Businessmen do not often take the same kind of political action to force a particular commodity into a particular foreign market as they do to keep out one that is injuring their established position. Rationally or irrationally, rightly or wrongly, foreign competition is seen as a specific problem, to which for years the letter to Congress has been the appropriate remedy, whereas the extension of export markets is seen as a matter of broad national policy in which every citizen's voice is as relevant as any other's.

It is difficult to assess the level of activity we observed on the Reciprocal Trade Bill, in view of the fact that even reasonably comparable data do not exist. Only 8 per cent of the men from the smallest firms had communicated with Congress on this subject in the two years preceding the 1954 survey. For them, it was clearly an issue of low salience at that time. On the other hand, 42 per cent of the men from the largest firms communicated with Congress in 1954-1955. That figure would indicate an issue of high salience, even though it is hardly an act of deep involvement for a big-businessman to write a letter. The sample as a whole fell between these two extremes. Men from larger firms were more active than men from smaller firms, men from each size of firm were more active in 1954-1955 than they had been previously, and protectionists in both years and for all sizes of firms were more active than their opponents. Furthermore, the increase in activity in 1954-1955 increased the protectionists' already-considerable advantage.

Some of the advantage of the protectionist position stems both from the immediacy of the loss perceived and the immediacy of the gain anticipated. But we found, additionally, that the protectionist acted in an environment that he perceived as facilitating his activity. More aware of the position which his senator and/or congressman held, he was more likely to feel that these legislators could or should be approached directly and more likely to believe that they already agreed with him. Furthermore, his immediate business environment was supportive in the sense that his industry was more likely to have taken a stand of which he was aware, and he did not perceive the men around him as having gone along with the general antiprotectionist swing. Although neither side was immune from cross-pressures exerted by the opposition, both were in a measure buffered from the full impact of the opposition. For the protectionist, we have argued, this condition was especially remarkable and fortuitous, in view of the facts that he was actually in the numerical minority and knew it.

Chapter 13

Businessmen's Attitudes and
Communication—
A Summary

We have asked how the members of the business community felt about foreign-trade policy and what they did about it. We have studied how they perceived their self-interest, how they gained information about foreign trade and world affairs, to whom they communicated their views, and who among them sought to influence Congress. We have examined them as an intermediate link in a communications process by which both world and local events came to impinge on Capitol Hill. We considered them as both receivers of news and transmitters of pressure.

Our main source of information was a sample survey of heads of corporations. Such data are more precise numerically and therefore perhaps more onerous for the reader than those to be discussed in subsequent chapters, in which we shall try to take the businessman whom we studied in the survey as an individual and set him within the institutional context of his community.

Thus far, our conclusions have dealt mainly with the interaction of self-interest and ideas in determining the conduct of businessmen. Self-interest was, of course, a powerful force in shaping men's views and impelling them to action, but we cannot accept the over-simple notion expressed by some of our advisors: "Tell me what a businessman makes, and I will tell you what foreign-trade policy he stands for."

What our respondents believed and how they acted were influenced by other factors, too. Some of these were ideological. Isolationists were more apt to act on behalf of protection than were internationalists. A man's ideas might serve as a brake on his economically determined impulses.

Some of the influences were social-structural. Heads of large firms were far more active than heads of small ones. They may have been abler men on the average, but, more important, they had staffs facilitating their operations, and their job was more that of the outside man than that of the inside man. On the other hand, some advantages in political action lay with the small firms; mergers tend to take the public-policy function away from local management and confine political expression to New York and Washington offices.

Some of the influences were communications variables. Our respondents were consumers of an extensive but quite uniform set of communications media. The overwhelming majority of them were reached by *The New York Times,* the *Herald Tribune,* or *The Wall Street Journal.* Virtually all were reached by both news weeklies and general business magazines. These, it is true, were a relatively larger part of the reading matter of heads of large firms, whereas publications of particular industries were a relatively larger part in the reading matter of heads of small firms. But, such small differences aside, reading was surprisingly uniform, with but few high-brow publications or foreign publications reaching even the elite stratum which we interviewed. Differences became larger when we looked at oral communication, which plays an enormous part in the information-gathering process of American businessmen. What they learn about world economic matters comes either from the few standard published media or through travel or conversation. Not reading of texts but talking to the expert is the top businessman's way of getting specialized information.

Specialized communications were the ones that induced action. Conversations with business colleagues, particularly effective in inducing action, played a relatively larger part in the discourse of protectionists, whereas conversations with others played that relatively larger part in the discourse of supporters of liberal foreign-trade policies.

Foreign travel served to blunt the power of narrowly defined self-interest to shape a man's views. Those men who had traveled extensively seemed to be formulating their views with an eye to the self-interest of the United States rather than to the self-interest of a single product. Their interaction with foreigners apparently made them assume the role of spokesmen of America vis-à-vis the world, rather than as spokesmen of a company vis-à-vis competitors and the government.

The theory of self-interest as a complete and all-embracing explanation of behavior breaks down when we realize that self-interest is itself a set of mental images and convictions. Whose self-interest does a man see it as his role to serve—his own as a physical individual, that of the corporation for which he works, or that of some other unit? If the corporation is the unit, who does he perceive as constituting the corporation? Over what period of time is he seeking a maximum—the short or the long term? What values does he pursue—solely money, or also respect and other values? The role businessmen played, the communications that impinged upon them, their ideology—all influenced their definitions and perceptions of their self-interest.

These considerations were introduced by a review of data on the foreign-trade attitudes of the general public, for it is in the context of the broader society that businessmen operate and arrive at their own views. Among the general public, too, attitudes toward foreign-trade policy were found to be related to people's perceived self-interest. But perceived self-interest did not pull equally on behalf of both sides. In looking at the relation between perceived self-interest and its political outcome among people at large, we received our first clue to the superior pulling power of protectionist interest. We found that attitudes toward tariff policy were more highly correlated with a perceived concern with the threat of imports than with the benefits of exports.

Among the general public as among businessmen, attitudes toward foreign-trade policy were also related to ideology. Isolationism correlated with protectionism, internationalism with a low-tariff stand. Support for a liberal-trade policy also proved to be highly related to the amount of education one had, perhaps more related to this than to any other factor with which we dealt. This relationship between education and support of liberal trade proved so strong that it offset traditional party alignments on this issue among the strong supporters of either side. In the general public, more strong protectionists were found among the Democrats, more strong low-tariff men among the Republicans!

Finally, supporters of a liberal-trade policy proved to be the people who were generally most active politically. On this score, however, we suspect that attitudes were in fact a poor predictor of specific activity on foreign-trade policy. Our observation of the national scene showed only one subgroup among the highly educated and the generally politically active to be actually active on the particular issue of foreign-trade policy during the years 1953-1955. This was the League of Women Voters. Similarly active on the other side were some few special groups of industrial workers who generally would not be heard in politics but who were moved in this instance by their perceived immediate self-interest.

There were both similarities and differences between the conduct of the general public and that of the business community. Self-interest and international ideology were important variables for both, but education was less so. It did have some relation to businessmen's activity, but not much. In general, the heads of business corporations were a homogeneous group who acted alike even when they differed in educational background. The less-educated among them had long since made up for any lacks en route to the status which made them part of our sample.

There has been a historical trend away from protectionism in the business community. But, even though there was by the middle of the century more support for lowering tariffs than for raising them, most businessmen were not inclined to take a categorical stand on either side of this symbolic issue. In the business community, this tendency stemmed less from ignorance and indifference than from a sense of the complexities of the problem. Certainly, our full reading of the interviews revealed that many men who would not take a simple, committed position in favor of either a high- or a low-tariff policy were thoroughly cognizant of the issues and had a clear, even if complexly qualified, position. The direction of leaning was generally toward low tariffs.

If a congressman were looking to opinion-poll data to tell him how the business community as a whole wanted him to vote, he would have concluded weakly that it favored his voting in favor of liberal-trade policies. However, though the situation may have been otherwise in specific Congressional districts, he could usually have voted as he pleased without arousing either the support or opposition of the business community as a whole.

If the congressman looked not at the polls but at the communications activity of the business community, the tables would be somewhat turned. In the 1950's, he would have found more messages suggesting he vote for protection than for freer trade.

All the men in our sample were exposed to a sufficiently wide range of general communications in their reading of newspapers, magazines, trade journals, and the like for them to have kept abreast of development in the foreign-trade controversy. Yet, we found that effective exposure was uneven. Men from larger firms were better informed, as were those who had an objective interest in the issue. These patterns in attention to the information available to them held also for their amount of oral communication either inside or outside the firm. However, a protectionist interest proved to be a considerably stronger stimulus to attention and action than did a liberal-trade interest. Furthermore, when we consider the final criterion of activity—communicating with one's congressman or senator—these differences become even more pronounced. Protectionists were considerably more likely to write.

One reason for the morale of the protectionists in the face of a swelling stream of opinion against them was that, to a perceptible degree, businessmen operated in a protective environment. They lived not in the business community as a whole but in industries which supported their own stand. They selected their incoming communications, at least to some degree, so as to support their existing position. They perceived the people around them as agreeing with them, and, if they communicated with Congress, they believed that the men to whom they wrote agreed with them.

These assertions are, of course, true in varying degrees. When we say that the protectionist businessman operated in a "protective environment," we mean that it was more protective of his own position than was that of the business community as a whole. In point of fact, that community in general disagreed with the protectionist position, and so did the majority of congressmen. Yet, protectionists more often saw their environment as in agreement with their own position than did their antagonists.

Our data confirmed the general assumption that a perceived protectionist interest or a protectionist attitude is a more powerful stimulus to action than is an interest in the liberal-trade position, or at least that it was until fear of exclusion from the European Common Market gave a new incentive to trade liberalization. The benefits of a protectionist position were seen in the 1950's as more direct and immediate than those of liberalization. The concept of the protective environment adds another dimension to our understanding of the greater activity of the protectionist. Not only is his initial stimulus to action more powerful, but his environment also supports this action and shuts off potentially inhibiting pressures.

Finally, we return to the ubiquitous factor of size of firm. Contrary to the belief prevalent at the time, we found no evidence that men from smaller firms were more protectionist than men from larger firms. In terms of attitudes and of objective interest as rated by our panel of economists, men from the various sizes of firm were virtually indistinguishable. We might put it this way: the size of the firm from which a man came was not related to either of the primary stimuli to action—attitude or interest. Yet, when it came to the activities which might have resulted from these stimuli, we found consistent and marked differences.

Judged by virtually every criterion of activity, men from the larger firms were more active than those from the smaller. This fact was so salient that, in the comparison of firms of various sizes, virtually every other consideration was wiped out. In most instances, the most-interested men from the smallest firms were less active than the least-interested men from the largest firms. This held true for exposure to incoming information, to participation in discussions, and to political activity.

The men from the smallest firms appeared to have a narrower frame of reference. They were relatively and sometimes absolutely more active with respect to narrow communications, for example, reading trade journals or local newspapers. Any single criterion of self-interest which we employed as predictor of activity produced proportionately more increase in activity among the men from the smaller firms. Furthermore, this induced activity appears to have been more narrowly focused; for example, they were more likely to talk inside the firm than outside it.

These differences arise in part from the range of involvements of businesses of various sizes. Larger businesses have a more complex and wider range of interests. They are more widely distributed geographically. Their sales are spread over more products. Therefore, any single criterion of interest is likely to have proportionately less importance in their total picture. Furthermore, the heads of larger firms are in touch with a wider range of external events. They travel more. They move in higher circles. They spend more time on public relations and public affairs. Finally, and perhaps most important, their jobs are set up differently. The greater division of labor within the firm makes it possible for the head of a large firm to be better informed and generally more active with respect to affairs external to his own firm; he is staffed to be so.

In summary, we would suggest that most significant of all to an understanding of what communication went out from business on foreign trade was neither self-interest nor ideology, but the institutional structures which facilitated or blocked the production of messages. Whether a letter to a congressman would get written depended on whether organization facilitated it, whether the writer's round of daily conversations would lead up to it, whether a staff was set up to produce it, and whether the writer conceived writing the letter to be part of his job. To look at the whole man and his views on the world, at the whole firm and its interests, is indeed useful, but communications are not generated by whole men or whole firms. They are generated by men in specific roles. It was the demands of their roles, the call of their jobs, and the round of their lives which largely shaped what our respondents actually communicated.

Appendix to Part II

Large and Small Firms—
The Varying Impact of Self-Interest

We have seen that men from the larger firms were more active in getting and exchanging information on foreign-trade policy. In most instances, even the least-interested men from the largest firms were more active than the most-interested men from the smallest firms. Those from the larger firms were conspicuously more active, whatever the criterion or condition.

Differences in discussion and reading on foreign-trade policy between large and small businessmen do not end with the over-all level of such activity. The heads of larger companies were not only better informed and had read and talked more about foreign-trade matters, but they also viewed the problems in a broader perspective. Narrow business interests determined to a larger extent in small firms than in big ones how much communication activity about foreign trade the head of the firm would engage in. That is only one fact which documents the narrower approach to the issue by the small businessmen.

Among respondents who had discussed trade matters with persons outside their firms, the heads of smaller firms were proportionately more likely to report that they had talked about things specific to their own business as opposed to matters of general policy, and that, by the way, despite the fact that they were somewhat less likely to have been talking to business associates.

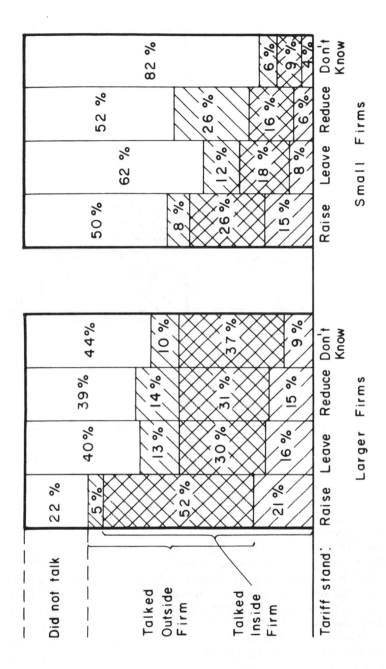

Fig. A-1 TALKING ABOUT FOREIGN TRADE BY TARIFF ATTITUDE

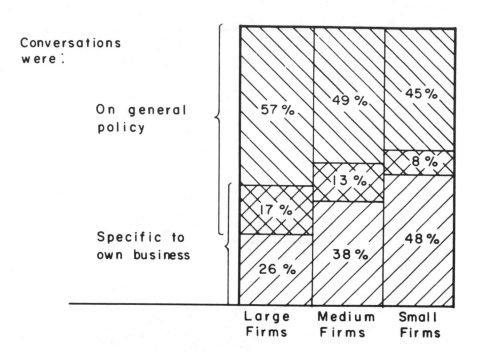

Fig. A-2   BREADTH OF ISSUES DISCUSSED IN CONVERSATIONS
OUTSIDE OWN FIRM

In seeking knowledge about foreign-trade policy, our respondents also use somewhat different information sources, depending on the size of their firms, as we see in Fig. A-3. There, we take as our criterion of desire for information about foreign trade an affirmative reply to the question as to whether the respondent had read an article or heard a speech on the subject within the past month. We want to compare the sources of information used by those large and small businessmen who thus showed an interest in being informed. We note, first, that, among the two larger groups of firms, those who had read about foreign-trade policy were more likely to read a general business magazine such as *Fortune,* but that this was not true among the men from the small firms. On the other hand, those from the smaller firms who had read something about foreign trade were more likely to read many (i.e., five or more) trade publications. The information-seekers from large and small firms turned in quite different directions to find the information in which they were interested.

Thus far, our data have repeatedly indicated that men from larger firms were more likely to communicate about matters of general policy, as opposed to matters specific to their own business. We may approach the same result from a different angle. ˙

It might be argued that the evocation of self-interest would stimulate

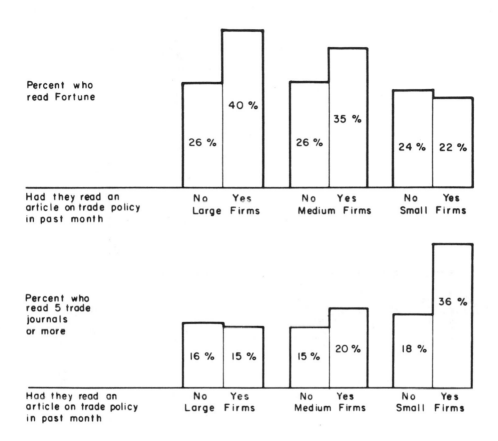

Fig. A-3   TYPES OF PERIODICALS USED BY THOSE WHO HAD
READ ON FOREIGN TRADE

different responses in men from different-sized firms. Some concrete data on this point are presented in Fig. A-4.

A quite small proportion of our respondents reported that their industries had taken a formal stand on tariff policy (27, 31, and 16 per cent). However, we see in this figure that men from industries which had taken a formal stand (again, this may be used as a reasonably objective criterion of self-interest) were more likely to have talked about foreign-trade policy in the previous month.

However, there was a differential impact on the men from the smaller and larger firms. When their industry was sufficiently involved in the tariff issue to take a stand, the men from the larger firms started talking to people both

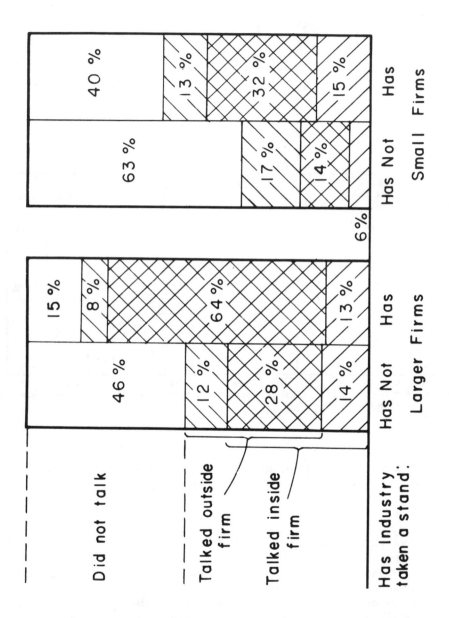

Fig. A-4   TALKING ABOUT FOREIGN TRADE BY WHETHER INDUSTRY
HAS OFFICIAL STAND ON TARIFF

inside and outside the firm. Among the small firms, a stand by their industry on tariffs, though somewhat increasing all discussion of foreign-trade policy, does not produce as much total talking, and the added discussion it stimulates is mostly internal to the firm. Internal communications increase by 27 percentage points, while external communications increase by but 14 points among the smaller firms.

That an active interest in foreign trade should lead small firms to increase their communications inside rather than outside is more remarkable than it might seem at first glance, since it works counter to the structure of their business organization. Heads of smaller firms, having fewer internal resources, are to some extent forced to turn outward, usually to their trade association, for information and guidance when confronted with an issue such as that of American foreign-trade policy. Furthermore, the heads of larger firms have in sheer numbers more people about them with whom it would be relevant and natural to discuss such matters, even in a casual context. Recall that men in large firms do talk more inside their firms than outside, whereas men in small firms talk more outside than inside. But smaller firms when they become involved in the issue exhibit a relatively greater increase in internal communications.

This fact matches with some precision our other findings on the relation of size of firm to breadth of approach to the issue.

Among the larger firms, we found that:

1. Those men from firms with an economic interest in the issue discussed it somewhat more—from about half again as much to twice as much, depending on the item of data chosen.

2. Those men from firms with an economic interest in the issue read about it only about a quarter more than did others.

3. If their interest in the issue made them read more, they turned to general business magazines as sources.

4. When they talked outside their firm, it was often about general policy on trade.

5. When their industry took a stand on the issue, it increased their conversations outside the firm as much as those inside.

Among small firms, we found that:

1. Those men from firms with an economic interest in the issue discussed it two or three times as much as their colleagues.

2. Those men from firms with an economic interest in the issue read about it twice as much as the others.

3. If their interest made them read more, they turned to trade journals.

4. When they talked outside their firm, it was less often about general trade policy.

5. When their industry took a stand on the issue, they increased their discussions inside the firm rather than outside.

These findings indicate differences in what it means to be the head of a large and of a small firm. The data might seem to reflect poorly on the heads of small firms. They are in general less informed, they are less active in discussing foreign-trade policy, and they employ a narrower frame of reference in their approach to issues. However, this judgment, if taken at face value, does them an injustice. To put the matter in better perspective, we have to look at the differences in the role of chief officer of such organizations, rather than at their personalities, though the role may find personalities to fit it. Our findings certainly cannot be interpreted as indicating that men from large firms are less motivated by self-interest. Rather, the heads of large firms see their self-interest differently, involving a longer time perspective and a wider range of considerations. They also represent a more varied set of interests, with the divisional manager speaking for the unified interest which a small-company president represents. Furthermore, the greater activity of the heads of larger firms on broad public-affairs issues is a function of having a job less concerned with production and sales and more with public relations.

□ The Protective Environment—Self-Selection in Communication

The notion that to a large extent people seek out and/or remember communications which reinforce their own positions and make it seem that the world agrees with them finds a good deal of support in the general literature on communications [1] and also in our own data.

The sources of concurrence between people's own views and those they believe they find around them are many.

People tend to associate with others in their own geographic locality. It is often true that a large majority of persons in one's own community agree with him, even when he is in the national minority. In the textile towns of New England and the piedmont, in the cherry districts of Michigan and Oregon, in the coal towns of the Appalachians, protectionists could conceivably have been a majority, though in fact we believe that this was only occasionally true.

People tend to associate with like-minded people. Old-line Republicans in their sixties mingle with old-line Republicans in their sixties. Young men with experience overseas have friends who are also young and cosmopolitan.

In the business community, discussion topics are chosen so that shared views are the ones that get expressed. This is not only because common problems bring people of common viewpoints together, but also because the accepted behavioral code calls for collaboration on points of common interest and avoidance of points of disagreement. The man with whom one differs on one point may be an ally whose friendship one needs on another. Trade associations are organized on this principle. Separate trade associations are formed to cover each range of agreement. So, too, in the market place competitors do not berate each other, and only racketeers damage their competitors' resources. In addressing third parties, too, the code is to praise oneself, not run down one's competitor. Each

---

[1] Cf. Joseph T. Klapper, *The Effects of Mass Communications* (Glencoe, Ill.: The Free Press, 1960).

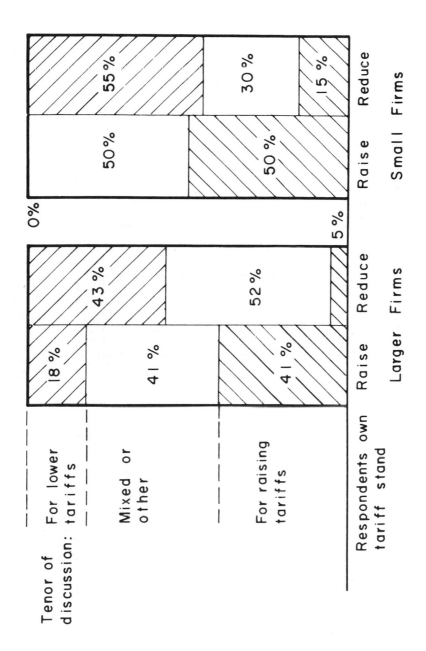

Fig. A-5   TENOR OF DISCUSSION AND READING IN WHICH
RESPONDENT PARTICIPATED COMPARED WITH
HIS OWN TARIFF STAND

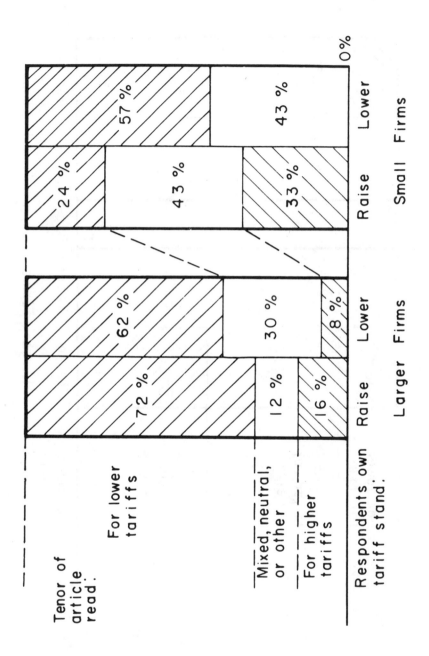

Fig. A-6   TENOR OF ARTICLE READ OR SPEECH HEARD IN PAST MONTH
COMPARED WITH RESPONDENT'S OWN TARIFF STAND

interest is treated as legitimate and entitled to its own expression. So, too, in community business discussion and, indeed, also in Congress, the practice, as we shall see, is not to engage in polemics addressed at a man who does not share one's interest. The rule is to organize one's own side and let the other side be.

People select news sources that fit their own views. In the sources that they read, they note those items which support their beliefs. They misperceive other items they encounter to bend them into congruence with their beliefs. And, finally, the items they remember they misinterpret if necessary to keep them in line.

All this we know already from the literature on communications behavior. It explains why, even though our respondents were all fully exposed to news sources, some in the minority could perceive themselves to be in the majority, not only among those they talked to but also among those whose articles they read. Most respondents, regardless of their own position, found the public opinion to which they were exposed to be supporting them.

Our respondents were asked about the point of view advocated in the articles they read and in the discussions in which they had taken part. Had the articles or discussions tended generally to support a high-tariff position, low-tariff position, to be neutral?

Both free traders and protectionists report that the discussions in which they took part strongly tended to favor their own position. Although many of the discussions were mixed, those which were partisan favored the respondent's own position in proportions mostly of 3 to 1 or better.

Our respondents were less selective in the articles they read. They had less control over the contents of the newspapers and magazines they saw than

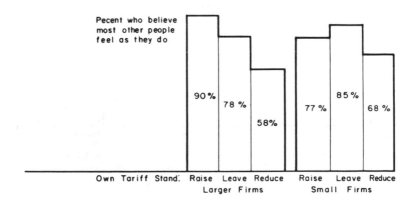

Fig. A-7   HOW OWN TARIFF STAND AFFECTS PERCEPTION
OF HOW OTHERS STAND

over their discussions. They were all reading the same mass media, and those were liberal on the trade issue. That fact could not entirely escape the attention of the protectionists. Among the larger firms, the protectionist respondents recognized that they were exposed to speeches and articles that ran counter to their own position. Indeed, they often complained bitterly that the press was against them, sometimes attributing that to the publishers' self-interest in cheap imports of newsprint.

Thus, the protective envelope was only relative. The reality of the balance of forces in the world intruded upon it. The advocates of higher tariffs were less protected in their reading than those of lower tariffs, but they compensated by their perception of "the people." Though they were really in the minority, they saw people more solidly on their side than did the liberal traders. (Cf. Fig. A-7.)

Reading, discussion, and physical mobility did, however, penetrate the protective enevelope. Those persons who were the most active communicators on this controversial issue became most aware of conflicts of opinion on it. Those who had read an article or heard a speech in the preceding month were less likely to report that they felt most people agreed with them. People who talked a good deal about foreign-trade policy were also more aware of people who disagreed with them, as were men who had traveled a good deal abroad.

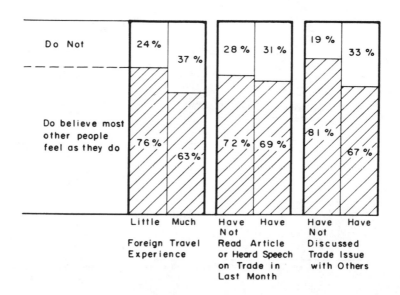

Fig. A-8(a)   HOW INFORMATION IN LARGE FIRMS AFFECTS
PERCEPTION OF WHERE OTHERS STAND ON TARIFF

But, granting the fact that men cannot isolate themselves entirely from their environment, the facts remain that exposure to rebutting evidence was much less than one might expect and that systematic forces worked to favor exposure to reinforcing information.

☐ Summary

We have found that communication on foreign-trade policy is in various ways selective. Men who by various criteria had an interest in foreign-trade policy were in all respects most likely to have read or talked about foreign-trade matters in the month preceding our survey.

However, interest does not have a uniform impact. A protectionist interest is more powerful than one in a liberal-trade policy. Not only is a protectionist interest more likely to make a man into an active communicator, but it is also proportionately more likely to make him active inside his firm, where he talks about foreign-trade matters more in the context of the specific interests of his firm than in terms of general policy. That is a significant fact because talking within the institutional structure of the firm leads to action more often than does general communication on the outside.

Two distinctive patterns of communication existed in the reciprocal-trade

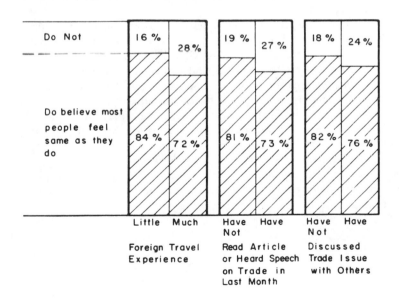

Fig. A-8(b) HOW INFORMATION IN SMALL FIRMS AFFECTS
PERCEPTION OF WHERE OTHERS STAND ON TARIFF

controversy. In one, foreign trade was treated as a broad political issue fit for discussion in the mass media and in the civic forums of community life. In the other, trade was treated as an operating problem of a business, and communication about it was oral within the firm and, when outside the firm, still within industry channels and in such specialized, nonmass media as letters, memoranda, and trade journals. Liberal-trade advocates tended to communicate in the first pattern (with exceptions in the Simpson bill controversy and in 1962) ; protectionists in the latter. This was important because the first pattern failed to produce much action in view of the amount of communication which took place. The second pattern was action-oriented.

In general, the structure of the action-oriented business communication system and of the communication system between business and the Congress favored the active propagation of particular demands and left general views about public policy unexpressed. What businessmen wrote to Congress was often unrepresentative of their own views, reflecting rather what happened to be in the in-box.

Larger firms have a greater variety of involvements with respect to foreign trade than do small firms Furthermore, their chief officers play more the role of the outside man. As a result of this combination of factors, the heads of larger firms are more likely to be active in the realm of general public policy than are those of smaller firms.

When stimulated to action, the head of a small firm is likely to act within a relatively narrow frame of reference, being concerned with the problems of his own firm. That self-interest is itself usually less complicated than that of a large firm.

Cutting across the above considerations of self-interest is a further factor of selectivity. Men tend to be exposed to, and to take part in, communications which agree with their own point of view. This is by no means an absolute matter. Neither protectionists nor liberal traders are by any means completely shielded from the opposing point of view. The man who travels is by virtue of his physical mobility more exposed to the fact that there are people who disagree with him. So, too, is the man who engages in much discussion. But strong selective forces do exist and inhibit the flow of information and influence between the two opposing camps.

The tendency to talk to one's own may lessen the possibility of conversion of people in the opposite or neutral camp; but it reduces cross-pressures on the committed individuals and therefore also lessens their inhibitions against action.

PART III

Eight Communities

PART III

Chapter 14

Introduction to Part III

In our survey of businessmen's communications and attitudes on foreign-trade policy, we treated our respondents as individuals and only minimally as parts of an organized community. We took note of what industry a man came from and with whom he talked, to whom he wrote, and whence he got his information. But we did not trace such networks of interrelations more than one step in either direction from the man whom we interviewed. We now concern ourselves with the more organized aspects of the business community. We shall deal with the extent and manner in which eight local business communities were or were not organized on the issue of foreign-trade policy in 1953-1955.

American politics as a whole is rooted in local politics. The set-up of Congress and particularly of the House of Representatives gives priority to the representation of local interests. The House is an extension of Main Street into Washington.

The point is sharpened by comparison with the situation in Britain. There a candidate for Parliament is adopted by the local constituency party, but he need not be a local man. A constituency is often honored to run a national figure, recommended to them by party headquarters, who may never have been to his new constituency before. Once in Parliament, he is under tight party discipline. Important bills are introduced, not by him, but by the cabinet, and, when the chips are down, he votes for or against the cabinet's program according to whether he is in the majority or opposition party. Public-policy-making in that system is highly concentrated in the members of the cabinet, whose high position and over-all view make them consider national interest rather than think of themselves as each a spokesman for his home town.

An American congressman, in contrast, is a local man sent to represent the interests of the folks back home. He must reside in the district he represents. A large part of his job is to run errands for his constituents. To be re-elected, he needs only to keep in their favor and that of the local party. The views of the administration or the national party have little to do with his chances. On a regional issue, he does better to buck the national party and vote as his constituents feel, and often he does just that. As the congressman from Textiletown said:

> After all, what am I down there for? I am supposed to look after my own people. I cannot come back here and say that I voted because of the interests of the country at large, and it was just too bad if it isn't good for the people at Textiletown. People just do not buy that sort of thing. They send you down to Washington to look out for them, and that is what you are rightly supposed to do. . . . I don't see what other position I can take. The party leadership in Washington . . . asked me several times to change my vote, but I never would agree to do so.

We shall see that other congressmen gave national interest more consideration. Yet, the viewpoint of the Textiletown member is so far encouraged by the organization of the House of Representatives that that attitude toward local service has become a wellspring of American political activity.

The tariff is no exception to the general rule. It is, of course, an issue of foreign policy, but it is also a domestic issue and even a local issue. In the days before the Reciprocal Trade Act, when rates on individual products were set in the halls of Congress, it was a leading local issue. Congressmen represented the products of their home districts. Mr. Dooley has "the sinitor fr'm Virginya" say:

> I loathe th' tariff. From me arliest days I was brought up to look on it with pizenous hathred. At many a convintion ye cud hear me whoopin' against it. But if there is such a lot of this monsthrous iniquity passin' around, don't Virginya get none? . . . I will talk here ontil July fourth, nineteen hundred and eighty-two, agin th' proposed hellish tax on feather beds unless something is done f'r the tamarack bark iv old Virginya. . . .[1]

---

[1] Finley Peter Dunne, *Mr. Dooley at His Best* (New York: Scribner's and Sons, 1938), pp. 91 f.

Today, Congress has freed itself from much local pressure by yielding up to the executive branch the power of setting specific rates. The individual representative can placate a local industry by writing to the Tariff Commission about an escape-clause proceeding or to the Committee on Reciprocity Information when a trade agreement is about to be negotiated. But letters are cheap. He can also make a speech on the floor of Congress or before a trade association. Having done his bit for local industry in this way, he is not necessarily called upon to try to translate local interests into the law of the land. Since he never gets a chance to vote on a specific rate for the local product, he represents his community only on the much broader legislative question of how the process of tariff-making should be organized. He may favor or oppose the entire trade program as his way of getting high or low rates for the products with which he is concerned. He may also work for or against escape clauses or new Tariff Commission procedures. Only a few and relatively dominant interests of a community can be served in such complex and indirect ways, however. The congressman may still listen to and represent his community, but, if he does so, it is by balancing total and often conflicting community interests as they impinge on the few key issues affecting world trade which may come before him at any one session. Yet, on those decisions, the tariff is still local politics as well as world politics.

If the tariff was local politics to 435 congressmen in 435 districts, then to understand what happened in Congress we ought to look at some communities and see how opinion was mobilized in them. If the congressman thinks of himself as a representative of local interests, then the most effective communications will be those from his district. We shall shortly examine how community opinion developed in eight American communities.

We must note, however, that, if communications to Congress came only from local communities, many important American interests would go unrepresented. American business has long since outgrown Main Street. A billion-dollar company speaks to Congress from its executive suite, its public-relations department, and its legal counsel, all possibly located on lower Manhattan Island. Its factories and its workers may be in scores of cities throughout the country, but a plant superintendent in a small town, unlike an independent entrepreneur in the same town, may not even know where his company stands on a piece of legislation; much less will he regard it as his job to approach his congressman about it.

The point may be clarified by describing two opposing models of the ways in which communication from business might reach Congress. There could be a situation in which tariff issues were discussed vertically within industries, but not at all horizontally between industries in the same communities. That would tend to happen if, for example, businessmen viewed the tariff as a purely business question on which they took their stand in terms of their own balance sheet with no reference to ideology, national interest, or the world's needs. Communications about trade and tariff matters, if viewed in that light, would be thought of as appropriate for referral to higher echelons and central offices within the company and from them to trade association executives, attorneys, and legislative agents. Those professional emissaries in Washington would express the industry's needs to government agencies, Congressional committees, and key congressmen. One result of such a communication pattern is that there would be no genuine public opinion of a community-wide character, since businessmen, viewing tariff questions as a pure workaday business matter of no broad interest to others, would seldom discuss them with friends and neighbors. Competitors and colleagues in the same town might be taking opposing views without realizing it or debating it. That is one extreme type of communications network, such as exists for some matters of purely internal business interest, where no communal or civic aspect is recognized.

The other, or horizontal, extreme type of communication network is that which is favored by the constitutional structure of the House of Representatives. It would exist in pure form if each congressman believed that his sole business were representing the interests of his district, irrespective of national interest. In that case, or if people who cared about tariffs thought that the only effective way to organize was by precinct work or local meetings, all communications would flow first from citizen to citizen within local communities for the purpose of mobilizing local opinion and then from the community to the congressman. The practice obviously lies somewhere between the two extremes.

It should already be clear that an interesting development has occurred in public representation on foreign-trade matters. The most powerful organizations in the economy have outgrown the districts on which political representation is based. They may have gained in wealth, prestige, expertise, organized representation in Washington, but they have lost in direct contact with their representatives. A firm with twenty plants in twenty cities may have far less influence politically than twenty different one-plant firms acting together, although it will usually have more influence than any one of them. Twenty independent firms mean twenty independent entrepreneurs, most of them community leaders in their home towns and known to their representatives. Great national interests, on the other hand, may fail because they lack grass roots in the constituencies.[2]

Let us now see what actually happened in a number of American

---

[2] A force contrary to this is that tendency of men from small, local firms not to take action discussed in various portions of Part II.

communities on the issue of foreign economic policy, and how far in each community communications were vertical within industries or horizontal across the community. We have noted that this depends on at least three factors:

1. Whether the constitutional structure of the policy-making body fosters representation of local interests or consideration of a central, over-all view.

2. Whether the structure of vested interests leads petitioners to express themselves district-by-district directly to the policy-makers or to express themselves through vertical channels to some top-level spokesman of the petitioners, who in turn approaches the policy-makers at the national level.

3. Whether the issue in question, here the trade issue, is viewed as something appropriate for internal discussion within specialized institutions only or whether it is a matter felt to be of general interest to the citizen body within a geographic district.

The eight communities we chose to study differed in a great many ways. Some had one dominant industry, others had mixed industries. Some had export industries, some industries with stiff competition from abroad. Some had traditions of protectionism, others traditions of favoring free trade. Some were large, others small. Some were prosperous, others depressed. Some sustained lively political and interest organizations, others were relatively dead. For reasons of budget, we examined only communities in the Eastern half of the country. Most were represented by Democrats, as are most industrial cities, but a few were Republican. Included in the eight was the financial district of New York, which is hardly a "town," but in some senses is a community and is important in its own right as a nerve center of American business. Wall Street, Detroit, and Wilmington we identify by name, because no camouflage would serve to disguise them. The other five have been disguised in name and other nonessential facts to enable us to describe what we found with somewhat more frankness than we otherwise could.

The communities in which we made case studies follow:

Detroit. A large metropolitan area dominated by the automobile industry. If any city could be said to have been organized in favor of a liberal-trade policy, it was Detroit.

Delaware. A small state containing a single dominant firm, DuPont, which has traditionally been identified as favoring protectionism.

Wall Street. The financial capital of the country, with a major interest in the financing of international trade and in the port of New York.

New Anglia. A fair-sized New England manufacturing city with varied industries, including textiles, metal products and machinery, accessories,

and plastics. It has a protectionist tradition, but is now strongly Democratic.

Midwest. A small city in "Chicago Tribuneland" with varied manufactures and a possible isolationist orientation.

Appalachian City. A community which had most of the characteristics
which would lead one to expect it to be in favor of protectionism.

Textiletown. A small city, previously dominated by the textile industry, with recent massive unemployment and a strong protectionist past.

The Fifty-third District. An Eastern Congressional district with diverse economic activities, chosen for study because, on the surface, there
should have been little or no direct interest in foreign-trade policy.

Into each of these cities we sent a senior member of our staff [3] who
interviewed leaders of opinion and of the business community. In the
larger communities, further interviews arose as businessmen within them
fell into the NORC sample. The interviews were supplemented by reading
the local press and by further interviews and background reports from
local representatives who were either knowledgeable journalists or professional persons resident in the community.

---

[3] L. Dexter, Delaware, Appalachian City, and the Fifty-third District; I. Pool, Wall
Street and New Anglia; R. Bauer, Detroit and Midwest; H. Isaacs, Textiletown.

Chapter 15

Detroit:
Hotbed of Free Traders

In the fall of 1952, the Detroit Board of Commerce issued a "Statement of Policy." It was a vigorous attack on barriers to trade and was distributed in the hundreds of thousands to American businessmen. In 1953, Henry Ford II made two widely publicized speeches in which he advocated liberalizing our foreign-trade policy. By the fall of 1953, largely on the basis of these two events, Henry Ford II, Detroit, and the automobile industry had become the symbolic heart of the support for a liberal foreign-trade policy, particularly in the eyes of protectionists. To give further substance to this image, a Detroit businessman, John Coleman, president of the Burroughs Corporation, became head of the newly organized Committee for a National Trade Policy. Although it is doubtful that the Detroit community was ever as solidly and energetically organized behind the liberal-trade movement as many protectionists thought, it nevertheless came as close to being a free-trade city as any large American metropolis.

In many of the cities and towns we visited, the protectionists were known, the liberal traders, relatively unknown. In Detroit, it was the reverse. When one of us arrived there in the fall of 1953, newspapermen, officials of the Board of Commerce, bankers, and the manufacturers whom we first contacted readily identified supporters of a liberal-trade policy— Henry Ford II, the automobile industry as a whole, John Coleman, officials of Reichold Chemicals, the UAW-CIO, and various staff members of business and community organizations—but they had difficulty identifying protectionists. Dow Chemical of Midland, Mich., 100 miles distant, came readily to mind in almost all interviews. But, beyond this, our informants were hesitant. The vice-president of a large bank suggested tentatively: "Find out what makes the machine-tool people tick on this. They might have a conflict of interests." The NORC interviews the following spring showed his hunch to be partially correct. A knowledgeable journalist, on being pressed for suggestions, thought erroneously that a certain pharmaceutical company might be protectionist. A ranking staff member of the Board of Commerce was able to identify two protectionists other than Dow because they had responded unfavorably to the Board of Commerce's policy statement. By and large, however, the picture was the reverse of that to which we were accustomed. Protectionists were less well known than their opponents.

There were and are businessmen and industries in the vicinity of Detroit that favor tariff protection, and, as we shall see, they made their voices heard in Washington. However, they had little effect locally, compared to that of injured industries in other towns and cities. Their reaction to their own position was expressed, possibly in an exaggerated form, by two members of a Detroit firm which opposed the Reciprocal Trade Act. One said: "The Detroit Board of Commerce likes unanimity: that's why they sort of overlook our views."

The second continued: "Here in Detroit, the export managers rule the roost."

Detroit, America's fifth largest city, was as much of a one-industry town as a metropolis of three million people can be. Almost half of the people employed in manufacturing were engaged in the production of automobiles and parts. Many others, too, derived their living directly or indirectly from that dominant industry. Not only is Detroit distinctive among giant American cities in its dependence on a single product, but the automobile industry is itself unique in its position in the American economy. The oft-quoted, though perhaps never-delivered, remark, "What's good for General Motors is good for the country," is not too far from the mark. No other business in the country is more clearly aware of the interdependence of America's economic health with its own fortunes. Nor is there any other business more representative of the system of mass production, high capitalization, and low unit labor costs—a condition providing a most favorable competitive position vis-à-vis cheap foreign labor. Auto officials whom we interviewed as late as the early summer of 1955 were unanimous and vigorous in stating their complete lack of concern over foreign imports.[1] The classical argument that trade benefits the economy as a whole has clear, immediate relevance to the automobile industry and to the city of Detroit. In addition, automobile manufacturers had a more immediate incentive for stimulating imports of foreign products, since their own export market was clearly affected by the difficulties foreigners had in getting dollars with which to buy American automobiles.

In addition we must note that to a surprising degree Detroit is a port city. Representatives of its Board of Commerce, speaking in support of HR 1 to both the Senate and the House committees, estimated that one of seven people engaged in manufacturing in Detroit owed his living to foreign trade.[2] Such estimates are, of course, always conjectural. However, the Port of Detroit Commission testified that the Michigan Customs District had ranked second in value of foreign trade in the preceding year and that approximately 15 per cent of total U.S. exports are produced in the Michigan area.[3] Consistent with this interest in foreign trade, the Detroit community, particularly as personified by its Board of Commerce, was a vigorous supporter of the St. Lawrence Seaway.

These are the economic facts behind the foreign-trade policy adopted by the Detroit business community. But there were certain relevant organizational facts, particularly about the Board of Commerce.

The Board of Commerce was both the voice and the organizer of Detroit's attitude toward foreign-trade policy. Various of its staff men were deeply committed to a liberal, perhaps even a free-trade, policy. Willis H. Hall, secretary-manager, Richard B. Frost, former secretary to the World Affairs Committee, and Gerald Heatter, who succeeded Frost, had not only worked hard to convey the doctrine of a liberal-trade policy to the national business community and to policy-makers in Washington, but had also taken unusual steps to convert their own members. The most effective of these steps was a series of guided foreign tours which the Board of Commerce organized. Each year for several years, approximately two dozen Detroit businessmen had been taken as a group to Europe, South America, or Asia. There was, of course, some self-selection of who went. Despite this, the staff as well as the men who had taken the trip were convinced that the trips had imbued those who went with an awareness of the need for increased world trade. One of us attended a luncheon at which board members who had taken the previous year's trip to the Far East met

---

[1] Perhaps their tone might have been different after 1958, but our continued contact with people in the automobile industry suggests that there has not been much change of attitude.

[2] "Hearings on HR 1," House Ways and Means Committee, p. 734; Senate Finance Committee, p. 2304.

[3] *Ibid.*, p. 761.

to greet an American whom they had met on their visit to Japan. There could be little doubt that these men had developed an interest in Japan's problems that could be described only as conversion.

Charles Helin, president of the Helin Tackle Co. of Detroit, testified in behalf of the Reciprocal Trade Act despite the fact that the design of his famous lure, the "Flatfish," had been pirated by several foreign manufacturers. He said that the trips he had taken to the Near and Far East sponsored by the Detroit Board of Commerce had convinced him of the need for more international trade.[4]

Two officials of motor car company *P.*, in discussing a top executive of motor car company *Q.* who had recently taken a leading role in civic affairs, had this to say: "It wasn't until he took over *Q.* and made one of these world trips that he saw the importance of trade, not only for *Q.*'s business, but for world peace."

It would, of course, be a mistake to attribute Detroit's support of the Reciprocal Trade Act entirely to the trips organized by the Board of Commerce.

The automobile industry has historically favored more liberal trade policies. As one junior executive of a major auto company said:

> You know, it's always been true that automobile people have been free trade. Old Black Republicans who elsewhere are protectionists, like . . . [a retired executive of his own company], who on everything else were reactionary as hell, they still weren't protectionist on trade.

Perhaps the top executives were not as acutely concerned with the issue as some of their subordinates might wish, but there was not much doubt about which side they were on. Such men as John Coleman of the Burroughs Corporation, officials of Reichold Chemicals, Parke Davis and Company, the Monroe Calculating Machine Company of Kalamazoo, and other businessmen from the Detroit area who had extensive exports and foreign operations had unquestionably been interested in lowering trade barriers for some time. But the Board of Commerce trips, beginning in 1950, and other promotional activities accomplished the activation of a sizable group of persons whose own direct participation in the issue would otherwise have been minimal or nonexistent.

It is difficult to separate the actions of the Board of Commerce staff from the leadership afforded to the community by John Coleman, president of the Burroughs Corporation. Coleman was president of the Board of Commerce in the years 1952-1953, when the famous policy statement was issued. But he was also active in stimulating interest in foreign trade in the Detroit area in previous years. Opinion was unanimous that Coleman was the one businessman of prominence who was a crusader on the issue.

---

[4] *Ibid.*, p. 868.

Not only had his influence been felt in the Board of Commerce and among his business associates, but Coleman was known as a man who "would give a speech at the drop of a hat" and was credited with bringing the liberal-trade message to civic groups outside the immediate business circle.

A final factor in the Detroit situation was the United Auto Workers (CIO) and the location in the city at that time of the national headquarters of the CIO. Industrial workers are probably the most numerous single group which can be readily mobilized on the side of protection. They are responsive by reason both of their general political and social orientation and of their anxiety about losing jobs from competition with foreign labor. Furthermore, the plight of the worker deprived of his means of livelihood has a strong appeal to the neutral public and to Congressional decision-makers. Several of the chemical companies succeeded in getting members of District 50 of the United Mine Workers to support their requests for protection. So far as we know, however, no CIO affiliate in the Detroit area joined the ranks of protection. The Reuthers and the top staff men of both the UAW and the CIO favored a liberal-trade policy, probably somewhat because of their association with the automobile industry, but more because of their over-all political and economic philosophy. The stand of the CIO on this issue was not, as has occasionally been alleged, a result of direct pressure by the automobile industry. The industry had not approached the union on this question. Although a few CIO unions, such as the Textile Workers, favored protection on the national scene, the international dampened the protectionist inclinations of its affiliates and attempted to "educate" its rank-and-file members. There seems little doubt that the policy of the CIO inhibited any potential labor support for protectionism in the Detroit area.

The extent to which the Detroit business community as a whole was oriented toward foreign trade and international relations was especially noticeable if one traveled, as did one of our authors, directly from there to Chicago. The standard, though not necessarily incorrect, image of the influence of the isolationist *Chicago Tribune* on the point of view of its readers seems scarcely an adequate explanation of the differences in orientation of the two communities. Part of the difference stems from the superior position of Detroit on the Great Lakes waterway, bringing it several days closer by steamer to Europe. (The Chicago Chamber of Commerce had favored the development of the Calumet-Sag Canal to the Mississippi in preference to the St. Lawrence Seaway, which was favored in Detroit.) Few Chicago industries of importance demanded protection, but the diversity of business in Chicagoland left the community without the strong unifying influence that the automobile industry was alleged to exert in Detroit. It may be objected that Clarence Randall, who spearheaded White House efforts in securing extension of the Reciprocal Trade Act, and his staff assistant, John Stambaugh, were both drawn from the Chicago business community. But, despite Randall's great prestige in Chicago, he was not able to muster any strong show of support from his colleagues comparable to the liberal-trade sentiment of a large segment of the Detroit businessmen.[5]

Thus far, we have enumerated the main elements that compounded the image of Detroit, Henry Ford II, and the automobile industry as united and militant in support of a liberal-trade policy. But, as we have hinted above, matters were more complex than that.

Though the automobile industry may have been united behind the Reciprocal Trade Act, it was far from militantly active. The World Affairs Committee of the Board of Commerce in 1952-1953, when the famous Detroit policy statement was issued, was composed of forty-four members, forty-two of whom were from business and industry. Of the latter, nine were officials of automobile companies, with every manufacturer except Packard Motor Car represented. Ford, Chrysler, and Nash each had two men on the committee, and General Motors, Kaiser-Frazer, and Hudson had one each. But almost every one of these men was from the export, overseas, international, or foreign division. They represented, rather than over-all company policy, the segment with a special interest in foreign trade. Two members of the purchasing staff of the Ford Motor Company were the major exceptions.

Foreign-trade policy had a relatively low priority on the agenda of most major auto executives. It was a matter left to subordinates whose specific responsibility was foreign markets. Of greater concern in the motor world in the years 1952-1955 were other topics: the fight for leadership in the domestic market, taxes, the struggle of the independents to remain alive (usually thought of in terms of the domestic market and mergers), a federal highway program, the guaranteed annual wage, and the like. Even insofar as foreign trade was concerned, the Reciprocal Trade Act attracted less interest than did the St. Lawrence Seaway. Officials of the UAW-CIO, for example, told us that they had not been approached by the automobile companies to support the Reciprocal Trade Act, although they had been approached several times in connection with the seaway, and of course on such issues as a federal highway program. In our NORC interviews, auto officials listed foreign trade and related issues relatively low in comparison with taxes and the like, as did businessmen in Detroit as a whole.

Foreign-trade policy, as we found at various other points in our

---

[5] We have no basis for revising this impression of the contrast between Detroit and Chicago for the period of our study, 1953-1955. But it must be reported that, in 1959, when the seaway was actually opened, Chicago appears to have been better prepared than Detroit. Cf. *Printers' Ink,* June 26, 1959, pp. 25-33.

study, had to compete for attention with many other problems in the minds of extremely busy men, and even in Detroit and in the automobile industry it was relegated to relatively low priority.

Probably the best illustration of this point is the case of Henry Ford II, who might ordinarily seem to be its chief exception. Ford came to prominence in the debate on foreign policy by virtue of a speech he made to the Inland Daily Press Association in February, 1953. Our several sources of information give us a cloudy picture of exactly what happened, but it seems certain that Ford accepted the invitation to speak with no particular topic in mind. Once the invitation was accepted, either Ford or a member of his staff thought of the subject of foreign-trade policy. Even if the idea originated with a staff member, it was one which Ford accepted readily and about which he was enthusiastic. Because of his prominence, not only as president of the Ford Motor Company but as a highly visible example of the young, progressive, public-spirited businessman, his speech received wide publicity.[6] When the Committee for a National Trade Policy was being launched, he made his second speech at a dinner of that organization in October, 1953. After this second speech, he became better known than perhaps any other individual in the forces behind the reciprocal-trade policy. Such personalities as Clarence Randall, John Coleman, and Charles Taft were clearly more actively involved in the debate, but Henry Ford II, at the age of thirty-seven, stood for "the mass-production industries," "the international point of view," "the younger generation of businessmen"— in short, the very principles that Randall, Coleman, and Taft were representing. However, it seems clear from conversations with associates of Ford that he had never sought the mantle of a crusader against protectionism. The two speeches he made constituted his contribution to the struggle. Requests came in for him and other Ford executives to make more speeches on this topic, and it became a minor but difficult task of the Ford organization to protect Ford from further demands on his time and to keep within manageable limits the notion that he was a crusading free trader or that the Ford organization was actively involved in the issue. This is not to imply that Ford was not interested in a liberal foreign-trade policy, but numerous other issues were pressing upon him more urgently. The readiness with which the public seized on him as a symbol of the liberal-trade view reflects not so much his own enthusiasm as the extent to which most other business supporters of the same policy gave it an even lower priority.

An element in muting the voice of liberal traders in Detroit is the

---

[6] The authors of this book were as aware as anyone of how effectively publicized Ford's stand on foreign trade was by the fall of 1953. Most of the men whom we interviewed wanted to know, "Who's behind your study?" Revelation of the fact that it was supported by a grant from the Ford Foundation was inevitably greeted by the assumption that we were supporters of the Reciprocal Trade Act.

sheer size of the automobile companies. Size is not an unmixed advantage; as a firm increases in size, its actions tend to become more visible and more subject to public scrutiny. Its associations and interests also tend to ramify further. Its representatives, when dealing with matters that are not of first priority, must carefully weigh side effects of their actions that might prejudice other relations with the business and political community.

The General Motors Corporation illustrates these facts. G.M. officials asserted in a number of interviews that their company was opposed to protectionism as strongly as any other motor-car manufacturer. But both they and other observers in Detroit bore out our impression that they had been less vocal in expressing this view. Ford, as we have mentioned, spoke on the topic, and so did Lester L. Colbert, president of Chrysler. In some quarters it was whispered that the reason for G.M.'s reluctance to speak out was to be found in the fact that DuPont, a protectionist organization, was the major stockholder in G.M. Such a pressure, if present, was exerted subtly, to such a degree that neither its presence nor absence could be ascertained. DuPont's influence over G.M. was at that time the subject of an antitrust suit, and it might well be argued that, though G.M. had a motive for appearing to act independently, in some subtle ways consciousness of the attitudes of DuPont executives could not help but be present. We could find no evidence that G.M. felt any need to conform to DuPont views.

G.M.'s reluctance to speak up for its views on foreign trade was at least in part a reflection of the marked sensitivity which certain giant corporations in America have developed over their public image. Large firms which have been the object of antitrust action or have been generally viewed as throwing their weight around may indeed sometimes use their economic strength to influence public policy or to take advantage of their business competitors. But, if they sometimes do so in fact, such industrial giants must take all the more pains to avoid the appearance of so doing. And, as many of them have learned by harsh experience, the best way to maintain the image of probity is to maintain its practice, too. One high official of G.M. who talked with two of our authors separately at intervals of fifteen months stated on both occasions that G.M.'s desire to avoid criticism was the reason for reticence. In the spring of 1955 he said:

> Because of G.M.'s peculiar position, we can't take a stand on issues of this sort. Now, Mr. X, after he retired but was still identified with G.M., gave a speech supporting reciprocal trade, and a West Virginia congressman said that that was all very well, but it didn't help West Virginia glass-workers. As your question implied, our taking a stand on this might sound selfish, and we were eager to stay away from that. . . . We feel if we have any position it is much better for an organization to support it than for us. . . . We're probably a little gun-shy

because of the way they twisted Mr. Wilson's remark; and we don't want to appear to do anything selfish like that suggested in its twisted form.

This official's reference to Charles E. Wilson's alleged "what's good for General Motors is good for the country" is a particular instance of such sensitivity to public reaction. It was referred to spontaneously by this man on both occasions, even though the event was almost two years old by the time of the second interview.

Though G.M. is the extreme case among the automobile companies, it is in no sense an exception. To some degree, the same concern over their public visibility and fear of being accused of throwing their weight around was expressed by representatives of all the large automobile companies. As one man said: "People are very much afraid to expose themselves to Congressional committees. Somebody gets up and testifies, and then Saltonstall from Massachusetts gets up and asks him about fish or somebody from Ohio about pottery, and he doesn't like it. It's embarrassing." Thus, the large firms hesitate to cast themselves in the role of seeming selfish or of acting against the public interest or, even worse, against particular interests.

Such sensitivity to external reaction stems from a mixture of motives: fear of public and particularly government action, fear of retaliation from business associates, moral conflict over violating a fundamental concept of business ethics. One does not offend the interest of another except while in clear pursuit of one's own self-interest. Among the largest firms, fear of economic retaliation is minimal, but concern over government retaliation or public reaction is very high, and a certain amount of ethical conflict is visible, although its importance is difficult to assess.

During the period of our study, there were repeated stories of boycott threats against liberal-trade spokesmen. Clarence Randall is reputed on good authority to have lost an important customer for Inland Steel as a result of his support of the Eisenhower administration's foreign-trade policy. After Henry Ford II's initial speech, it was rumored that he had been subject to similar pressure from business associates, to the effect of "Henry, what do you want to ruin my business for?" Ford himself announced in the text of his second speech that 98 per cent of the response to his earlier stand had been favorable. Nevertheless, more than a year after his second speech the slim minority of protesting letters had left a firm impression on certain of his associates. A prominent senator is reported to have informed Ford that the senator's protectionist constituents "buy Fords too, you know." A small group of suppliers threatened to boycott Ford products. A number of dealers were afraid that they would lose customers.

There is little evidence that these protests by themselves had any strong influence, but in many instances they added to a complex of factors.

When their own prospective benefit is less clear and immediate to advocates of a liberal-trade policy than the injury done to others, practical considerations become enmeshed with ethical ones. This was illustrated in an interview with several second- and third-echelon executives of one of the major auto companies as they were seeking to explain their company's relative inaction on this question. After introducing a number of the reasons we have listed above, they continued: "One reason you don't take a position is that you don't like to kick your casual business acquaintances in the teeth. Dow or Monsanto will be hurt, or think they'll be hurt. There's always that." A further comment: "The problem is, we never really have had any good reason to fight Dow and Monsanto. It's a matter, as we said, of not being able to place our fingers on the specific benefits to us to make it worth fighting them." The ethical dimension latent in this statement is, as we know from other interviews, widely shared in the American business community. Our respondents saw their own moral conflict diminished and the liability of incurring enmity minimized when they acted against their own colleagues out of the sort of clear, definite, urgent self-interest that these men found themselves lacking. The automobile industry recognized its involvement in the over-all economy and the dependence of the economy on trade, but its interest was not sufficiently immediate to warrant vigorous, all-out action.

The foregoing list of forces inhibiting the auto companies from action must be considered in conjunction with the low priority which they gave this issue. They were, as a result, unready to expend precious time, energy, and good will on it.

Factors we enumerated in the opening portion of this chapter explain the image which many people had of Detroit. These factors were sufficient to give the Detroit business community a façade of homogeneous support for the Reciprocal Trade Act; but, partially for the reasons just listed, they were not enough to convert the city into the free-trade hotbed which some people took it to be.

The chinks in Detroit's free-trade armor become clearer if we look at communications on the national, as opposed to the local, level. Nationally, the Detroit community continued to exercise a considerable influence. The Board of Commerce testified before both the House and Senate committees, as did businessmen and other representatives of the Detroit area. Mr. John Coleman, in part through his representative Edward Littlejohn, played a leading role in the Committee for a National Trade Policy, of which he was the national chairman. One of the automobile companies on occasion lent personnel to the committee. A considerable number of Detroit organizations contributed money to the committee and to other associations working for HR 1. Detroiters working with such national bodies reported that they were able to sway a number of influential votes in Congress. Furthermore, we must not discount the importance of Detroit, its businesses, and its businessmen as symbolic rallying points for other segments of American business. Compared with other cities, Detroit played an important role in the passage of HR 1.

However, viewed from Capitol Hill, the Detroit area seemed less like a solid free-trade phalanx than it did when one talked to civic leaders in that city or sat in the office of a protectionist spokesman who was expressing horror at the massed power and wealth of the automobile magnates. On the basis of our contact with the Michigan Congressional delegation, we have the impression that the bulk of Congressional mail from the vicinity of Detroit opposed HR 1. The following excerpt from one of our reports shows what was found in the mailbag of a leading member of the Michigan delegation:

> There was a folder of probably 200 letters since January 1. The two dominant groups were the League of Women Voters (I'd guess 50-75), favorable of course, and Dow Chemical employees and associates (50-60), and a few other chemical letters (15), opposed of course. A great deal of the mail originates around Midland (Dow Chemical). One letter was from a Chamber of Commerce, saying that their two major industries (gloves and some kind of machine) were dying or threatened by foreign competition. Among other industries protesting foreign competition (usually the president of a small company), were glass; iron ore; food products (several); X Electrochemical; Y Camera; Local 12075, UMW; Dow. The president of Z company wrote in a three-page letter supporting Randall's position. A sport-fishing guy wrote in a letter complaining about losses but saying foreign trade is good. Japanese crabmeat was protested against. A wholesale butter-and-egg firm sent in a ringing endorsement of a free-trade editorial from a Detroit paper saying they wanted to disassociate themselves from their industry. An industrial-furnace manufacturer urged an increase in the quota on Mexican sugar because he sells his furnaces to Mexico if Mexico has exchange.

Several protectionist chemical companies told us they had communicated with Congress through their trade associations. Michigan congressmen were also approached in the interest of protection by considerable numbers of chicory-growers and processors of maraschino cherries.

All in all, it would seem that the supporters of HR 1 in Detroit were more effective in expressing their views on a broad national level than they were in impressing these views on their own Congressional delegates. Perhaps the congressmen and senators from Michigan had come to take for granted the liberal-trade views and interests of the Detroit community. It is our distinct impression, however, from interviews with members of Congress and their staffs, that even convinced adherents of a liberal-trade policy were disturbed by the protectionist mail they were receiving. It is exceedingly difficult to make any clear statement as to the relative impact of protectionist and antiprotectionist influence on the final voting behavior of the Michigan senators and the representatives from the Detroit area. An analysis of votes in the House and Senate in the years 1953, 1954, and 1955 shows that representatives from the Detroit area and the Michigan senators voted fairly solidly against protectionism on some nine votes that came before them. There were exceptions, of course: Republicans voted against the Gore amendment in 1954, regarded by administration supporters as an attempt to embarrass the Republicans rather than as a legitimate effort to extend the Reciprocal Trade Act. Representative Kit Clardy (Rep.), defeated for office in 1954, was a solid protectionist. Another representative, Victor A. Knox (Rep.), was a protectionist, and, although he was from northern Michigan, his views were important to the Detroit community because of his important committee membership in the House.

Although the liberal-trade supporters might on the basis of this voting record claim credit for having influenced their own Congressional delegation, a closer look at what happened would put this claim in doubt. Detroit businessmen were Eisenhower Republicans and regarded the extension of the Reciprocal Trade Act as a Republican measure. Yet Michigan Republicans, whether in the House or the Senate, judged either by their voting records or by their statements of policy, were less consistently in favor of a liberal-trade policy than were their Democratic colleagues. Furthermore, no member of the Michigan Congressional delegation was an active spokesman for the Detroit point of view. During the House hearings, Rep. John Dingell (Dem.) complained that Canada was discriminating against the Detroit brewing industry by not permitting American beer across the border, and that was about the extent of it!

The Detroit business community's slight impact on its Congressional representatives could be explained simply by its lack of interest, but that would account for it only partly. A good portion of the efforts of men like Coleman was expended through national organizations. Various business firms also worked through their national trade associations. Their effect may have been stronger on congressmen and senators other than their own. There was some impediment to communication, because the majority of representatives from the Detroit area were Democrats, and its businessmen Republicans.

We happened to observe both sides of such an event of malcommunication. One member of the Michigan delegation, a Democrat with a long-standing affiliation with labor unions, was perturbed at the amount of protectionist mail he was receiving. He opposed protection on grounds of principle. He was looking for some course of action which would simultaneously alleviate the human problems connected with the plight of several businesses in his district and also permit him to support a liberal-trade policy without committing political suicide. Two businessmen from Detroit visited his office to persuade him to vote in favor of HR 1—an action on which he had long been decided. But in the interview, each party assumed the other to be on the other side of the fence, since they represented such disparate points of view on so many other issues. The businessmen interpreted the congressman's concern over his protectionist mail as opposition on the basic issues. The congressman, for his part, concluded that the businessmen were insensitive to the suffering of workers who were thrown out of their jobs. We knew from our interviews with both parties that these images were incorrect, that each saw the issues in substantially the same light, but the initial malperception' that they had of each other thwarted any opportunity they had to work together. One of them afterward grudgingly admitted that he had probably entered the discussion with a chip on his shoulder. Although the strong position of local organized labor, combined with the stand of the CIO, probably helped the liberal traders on the local scene, the same circumstance seems to have impeded communications between the business community and the labor-elected representatives in Congress.

Whatever reservations have to be made, Detroit was the city which came closest to being solidly organized behind the Eisenhower trade program. However, even there it was an item of relatively low priority. Yet, with a homogeneity of interests among the leading businesses of the community, a relatively few persons taking vigorous initiative were able to organize the community even—or perhaps especially—on an issue on which there was not a great deal of active involvement. Moreover, once the dominant firms in the community had expressed their views and these views were reflected in the policy statement of the Board of Commerce, it became difficult for protectionists to gain an effective audience locally.

The Detroit situation suggests the power which a few individuals may exercise if they take the initiative in a somewhat amorphous situation. The status of the automobile industry in Detroit created a situation in which sentiment for a liberal foreign-trade policy could be mobilized. The main initiative, however, did not come from leaders of the automobile industry, but from John Coleman and members of the staff of the Board of Commerce and others like them. Even within the automobile firms, it was the push of staff men which was largely responsible for the limited number of public statements made by leaders of the industry.

In these community studies, we have distinguished between local, or horizontal, communications and industrial, or vertical, ones. In Detroit, the domination of the local scene by the liberal traders forced protectionists to turn their efforts to the national scene, through their national trade organizations and in direct communications to Congress. For a variety of reasons, the largest firms in Detroit preferred not to communicate directly, or at least openly, with Congress on this issue. Locally, they supported the Board of Commerce and helped in efforts to get smaller businessmen interested. Nationally, they worked through trade organizations and pressure groups. But, in the channels to Congress, protectionist pleas had a much larger voice than an examination of Detroit community activity would have led one to expect.

Giant firms, such as the Big Three of the automobile industry, are in a complex situation so far as expressing their policy views is concerned. Their position is that of the adolescent of huge stature who cannot help but be conspicuous, who is both proud of his strength and afraid of it. A single speech by Ford attracted national attention. G.M. made no public statements, but its policy was known throughout the community. Even on an issue which was not of top priority for them, automobile manufacturers could scarcely hold an opinion, let alone express it, without this opinion being known and having a powerful effect on the attitudes and actions of others. The overwhelming importance of this industry for Detroit's economy made people in and about the city hyperresponsive to its orientation on foreign-trade policy.

Power is often illusory. In a democracy, those who have influence, wealth, and power may not be free to use it. The price of holding power may be self-denial. The penalty for using power may be to be stripped of it. The auto-makers in Detroit, the DuPont company in Delaware, the bankers in Wall Street—each illustrates the caution and incapacity which the desire to keep power imposes on those who possess it.

Chapter 16

Delaware:
Where the Elephant Takes Care
Not to Dance among the Chickens

DuPont was the principal reason we chose to study Delaware.[1] DuPont is a $2,000,000,000 corporation which has grown up in a state with only one Congressional district. And DuPont is traditionally protectionist. Some State Department employees with years of experience in commercial policy regarded DuPont as one of their most serious opponents, just as some protectionists so regarded the State Department.

It happened that, in 1953-1955, both senators from Delaware were on the Senate Finance Committee, which handles tariff matters; this is quite unusual.[2] Both leaned toward reciprocal trade, as did the Delaware congressman (when we started our study, Herbert Warburton (R.), who was succeeded in 1955 by Harris McDowell (D.)). In a knock-down, drag-

---

[1] On Delaware politics, see Paul Dolan's chapter on Delaware in P. David, R. Goldman, and M. Moos, eds., *Presidential Nominating Processes in 1952* (Baltimore: Johns Hopkins University Press, 1954), Vol. 2.

[2] Colorado also had two senators on Finance; the retirement of Senator Edwin C. Johnson (D.) in 1955 changed that. The remarkable thing about the Delaware senators both being on the committee is that they have no great seniority, whereas both Colorado senators enjoyed considerable seniority.

out fight on Reciprocal Trade Act extension, would not these legislators be under considerable pressure? Would not Delaware business and farming interests try to influence them? And would not DuPont, unquestionably the greatest of these interests, exert the most pressure?

The answer to all these questions, as it turned out, was "No." A business can be too big to be politically effective along some lines.

" 'Every man for himself,' said the elephant as he danced among the chickens," may well have described the attitude and outlook of big business in the days of Rockefeller and Carnegie and the railroad robber barons. But nowadays many really big corporations are not eager to dance among the chickens; the consequences are or may be too unpleasant.

□ The Corporate Setting

DuPont, because it is located in the very small state of Delaware, is more of an elephant among chickens than most of the other great corporations; Anaconda is the only similar situation that comes to mind. American Telephone and Telegraph, for instance, although great on a nationwide basis, is nowhere locally pre-eminent. General Electric is in the large state of New York. Ford and General Motors are cheek-by-jowl in Detroit. The Mellon interests are in Pennsylvania, but are there scattered among a number of different corporations. Standard Oil has been cut up into separate companies.

To the average outsider, DuPont is Delaware, Delaware DuPont. Thirty-odd years ago, *The Nation,* in a very serious though superficial evaluation, described the state as "the ward of a feudal family." The notion persists, and it persists in part because DuPont, willy-nilly, means so much more in Delaware than any other corporation.

There are probably more than 100 DuPont households scattered through greater Wilmington, the great majority of which draw their influence and their wealth from the company; together, they control an extraordinarily high proportion of the total personal wealth of the state, a much larger proportion than any other family in any other state. Not surprisingly, therefore, many of the charities of the state are DuPont-planned, DuPont-directed, DuPont-named.

It might follow from all this that Delaware senators and congressmen would fall into line with whatever stand DuPont takes. But DuPont has had many unpleasant experiences because of its size, its uniqueness, and its success. In 1912, it was required by court order in effect to set up two separate and competing companies—Atlas and Hercules. It has been under continuous surveillance and attack for alleged violation of the antitrust laws ever since. In 1961, it lost a major suit, being ordered to divest itself of its General Motors stock. Probably one reason why the central management of DuPont did not focus on such matters as the tariff during 1953-1955 was that it was under assault in antitrust suits.

Even more important in setting the company's public-relations policies was the great Nye Committee munitions investigation of the mid-1930's. DuPont, perhaps more than any other corporation, was pilloried as a satanic munitions-maker, gleefully piling up profits and creating wars. "I think," said one DuPont not close to the company's management, "that that investigation made [the company] feel they should be very cautious and lean over backwards."

And there is a certain local suspicion of the DuPonts. One of the most skillful Delaware political analysts said of Francis V. DuPont, for some years the leading Republican in the state[3] and not connected with the company, "There is only one reason he is not U.S. senator; his name is DuPont, and that would hurt him."[4]

It is not only that a senator dare not be for DuPont, but DuPont does not dare have a senator, and particularly a Delaware senator, in its pocket and would go a long way to avoid creating this impression.

Of course, DuPont is continually involved in relationships with the United States government, but, like most big corporations, it tends to deal directly with the relevant agency, rather than requesting Congressional aid. In the case of most corporations, this arises as much as anything out of the fact that business bureaucrats would rather deal with government bureaucrats, without being bothered by the temperamentally differing politician as an intermediary. In the case of DuPont, this tendency is probably reinforced by fear of appearing to pick on somebody not its own size. The executive arm of the government can stand up to it; there is more danger that a Delaware senator will look as though he cannot.

The cynical reader may believe that we have been taken in. Is it not possible that DuPont slurks or slithers or works with great quietness to get Delaware senators or congressmen to follow its lead? After all, until 1948 a Delaware senator was a DuPont in-law. But if DuPont influences them on such matters as the tariff, it is by subtle maneuver, not by any overt pressure. And we do not believe that it does. In any event, it was not successful on the protectionist issue if it did make any such effort in 1955. The Delaware senators and congressman supported reciprocal trade.

DuPont's position in some respects resembles that of the great overseas investors—Standard Oil, for example. Because many people suspect Standard Oil of being an agent of imperialism, because for this

---

[3] From 1953-1955 F. V. DuPont was U.S. commissioner of roads.

[4] However, Alexis DuPont Bayard, New Deal candidate for the Senate in 1952, uses his middle name, when he could be simply Alexis Bayard.

reason the United States government will be more reluctant to intervene on its behalf than on behalf of some small hat manufacturer, such a corporation in some ways, on political issues which are minor to it, has less power than smaller aggregations of wealth. And yet it will be held responsible for efforts that it cannot or does not take any part in. So also with DuPont in Delaware.

Very probably this reaction to the position of great power which DuPont and Standard Oil possess is not the only corporate reaction. Perhaps Anaconda in Montana or the tin companies in Bolivia have behaved very differently. But the point is that, within DuPont and Standard Oil and some other great companies, there has grown up a tradition of restraint based on a calculation of long-run welfare. This restraint may be compared with the doctrine of judicial restraint. Like judicial restraint, this corporate restraint breaks down from time to time, and the notion is differently interpreted by different officers and divisions; nevertheless, it makes a difference between DuPont and Standard Oil and, on the whole, Inland Steel on the one hand and some more politically aggressive firms like Westinghouse on the other.

What has just been said explains in part why DuPont was not more vocally protectionist. DuPont would have aligned itself considerably more actively than it did with such chemical companies as Dow and Monsanto (two of the four firms which have campaigned most energetically for protection) were it not for the general policy of corporate restraint.

DuPont, Standard Oil, and other large companies are far more likely to have on their staffs a number of people who have held significant governmental decision-making positions than are such groups as cherry-growers or woolen-worsted manufacturers. They will consequently be far more aware of the facts that legislation is effected through a series of administrative steps and that at each stage in the administrative process an interested party usually has the right to ask adaptation of the decision in such a way as to avoid injury to him. Big companies have the legal resources and administrative contacts to take advantage of such rights; small companies do not.[5] For large companies, this activity in the administrative sphere is far more attractive. It usually avoids the publicity which may spotlight the attempt to participate in the legislative process and is less likely to demand the time of top management. Government administrators would often prefer to deal with the specialist in the corporation who knows most about the topic, whereas senators or legislative committees are believed to be more accessible to prominent people.

However, too much influence may backfire at the administrative

---

[5] For this reason, the campaign against "five-per-centers" hurt small business more than it did big business.

level, too; and there are many people in government who lean over backward to avoid being pressured by the powerful. A company such as DuPont also has to pay the cost of lending top officials to government. Although some government agencies may see things a little more as DuPont does as a result of present or past service of DuPont officials in such agencies, many DuPont officials may see things somewhat more from the government agency's standpoint. In particular instances, even though he may disagree with the government standpoint, a corporate executive with a government-service background may be more hesitant to bring undue pressure on an official for whom he has some sympathy than will a manufacturer of toy marbles or a garlic-grower who has never had occasion to acquire such a fellow-feeling.

Officials of big corporations also come to realize that their relationships with government are continuous and that, if they press too hard for victory on one particular problem, even if they win, it may jeopardize their chances of success on some future and more important problem. The relations of corporate officials with government are in this respect like those of members of Congress with each other, as we note below. A businessman or a Congressional colleague who presses a congressman too hard on one issue may get the better of him, but the price may be a considerable loss of credit and potential support on future issues.

That DuPont will not push too hard too far was recognized in several of our Delaware interviews. Two examples will suffice.

1. A politician who believes DuPont to be protectionist for the excellent reason that a DuPont officer [6] waited on him to present arguments against the Reciprocal Trade Extension Act was later discussing with us the vast volume of mail sent to congressmen and senators against the act by Monsanto and Westinghouse. One of us inquired as to whether DuPont did anything of this sort. An expression of surprise crossed his face. "Oh, no; the company would not allow that sort of thing. Two or three letters, that would be the most." Other politicians expressed the same view.

2. Through a holding company, DuPont in effect owns the Wilmington papers. These papers, however, we were told by the editorial staff, have always supported reciprocal trade, and the company has never raised the issue, nor has it crossed the editors' minds that it would. To be sure, Fred Singer, a DuPont official whom we shall have further occasion to meet, has written the editors several times and, we believe, has discussed the issue with them; but the editors felt themselves under no more pres-

---

[6] Actually, from what we know, the DuPont officer undoubtedly identified himself as representing a trade association, but the politician had forgotten this.

sure from him than a college professor in one branch of a university would if a scholar in another branch criticized his views on some scientific theory.

Monolithic DuPont?

Both the DuPont family and the DuPont company have a wide variety of interests and orientations; there is no one point of view to which all adhere. Outside Delaware, the public picture of a DuPont is that of a rather conservative businessman. Actually, the founder of DuPont, E.I. DuPont, was a close friend of Jefferson, and, in every generation since, including the present, there have been several DuPonts whose views and attitudes have been definitely Jeffersonian and who have therefore tended to oppose the protectionist viewpoint which the interests of the company seemed to dictate. Aside from this, there have been family schisms, and some of the most prominent local DuPonts might not see eye-to-eye with the company.

Even among those DuPonts most directly responsible for building the company to its present eminence there seems to have been a difference of opinion on the tariff. Three brothers followed each other as president; it is generally reported that Pierre, the first of them to be president, in contrast to his brothers, opposed the protectionist viewpoint. Pierre, it may be noted, was more closely involved with General Motors, serving as its president at one time, than were the other two. At the time of our study, DuPont owned about one-fifth of all G.M. stock. This certainly was a consideration to offset DuPont's tendency as a chemical company to favor protection.

There is very real difficulty in discovering what DuPont's true interest is because the company has so many irons in the fire. A DuPont economist in Wilmington said: "Don't ever talk of DuPont as being in *an* industry; it is in a lot of industries." The same economist estimated that, for all DuPont products, exports constitute only about 6 per cent of sales; but he added: "It might well be that a man in one division would decide that he wanted to join the Henry Ford group [the Committee for a National Trade Policy]. The sales manager for finishes, selling a fair amount of paint abroad, might want to support all this reciprocal trade, whereas the rayon-yarn people, who are very alarmed about foreign imports, would be on the other side. This whole problem is pretty academic to the people in nylon; they just would not care. . . . There is no over-all company policy."

DuPont had ten separate operating divisions. For many purposes, they acted as separate companies. Each division had or could have its own tariff representative, an officer charged with analyzing the situation of the division. We discussed various major products with different officials and repeatedly heard the theme, "Each division has a different focus." One man, for instance, continued, "Explosives are primarily concerned with quick service, shipping, and timing; foreign competition would not matter. Film and cellophane—they don't get into export much and are not adversely affected by imports." Another official added: "On balance, I think our paint department would gain more than it would lose by a reduction of tariffs. But at the other extreme is the dyestuff business, which requires a combination of labor and technological skill, dependent on plodding, ordinary Ph.D.'s who in Germany get 25 per cent less salary than here, so that alone gives the Germans a very substantial advantage."

Repeatedly, we heard the argument that, since DuPont's bread and butter, synthetic organic chemicals, can and will be produced more cheaply abroad than in this country, DuPont needs protection. But there were a host of conflicting considerations. "Top management," we were told, "don't wish their position to be interpreted as extreme protectionist; they are trying for a middle-of-the-road position."

Who Speaks for DuPont?

Fred Singer was chairman of the Tariff Committee under the Executive Committee of DuPont; this is the tariff committee for the central corporate staff, as distinguished from the tariff representatives who work for the operating divisions, described above. A tariff representative said: "Oh, the tariff representatives of the different divisions may see each other occasionally, but they act quite independently; when they get together, it is usually just to hear Singer. But that central committee of his cannot tell any of the ten divisional managers anything; if the manager wants to do anything, he can; he is the kingpin."

But Singer could and did devote a good deal of time and effort to the cause of protection. He was a stalwart supporter of the American Tariff League. He also served on the policy committees of eight different trade associations; he was or had been chairman of several of them. In these capacities, he made statements and wrote reports. For example, he testified before the House Ways and Means Committee in 1955 in opposition to the proposed reciprocal-trade legislation as chairman of the International Trade and Tariff Committee of the Manufacturing Chemists Association. At no point in his testimony did he refer to DuPont in any way. However, since few people knew or recognized the trade association name and everybody had heard of DuPont, he was usually identified by readers and listeners as a spokesman for DuPont, rather than for whichever trade association he was at the moment representing.

The question whether he did in fact speak for DuPont's top management is an interesting one. On the one hand, the indirect approach through trade associations could be a tactic, designed to avoid controversy. On the other hand, Singer could be viewed in the same light as a university professor who testifies. When Seymour Harris, Harvard economist, testified for protection of the textile industry at the same hearings, no one supposed that he was speaking for Harvard, and everyone recognized his right to academic freedom. DuPont could have given Singer a similar freedom without endorsing his views. To choose either this or the more manipulative interpretation as the explanation is probably to impose more simplicity on reality than was there.

History of the Notion that DuPont Is Protectionist

The great development of the United States chemical industry took place during and immediately after World War I. It occurred because of the protection against German competition and the seizure of German patents resulting from the war. The chemical industry has therefore been regarded and has on the whole regarded itself as a beneficiary of protection.

In the interwar years, several DuPont economists—Edmund Lincoln, for instance—were particularly articulate spokesmen of protectionist views. It is generally believed that they played an influential part in the behind-the-scenes planning of the postwar tariff acts. These men were either dead or retired at the time of our study, but they were remembered in Wilmington and throughout the chemical industry.

This history has had its effect on the community. The Wilmington chapter of the American Association of University Women is naturally composed to a considerable degree of wives of DuPont men. A prominent member told us that the chapter "disagrees with the stand of national AAUW on several matters, such as the tariff."

□ Other Delaware Businesses

The two other big Delaware chemical companies, Atlas and Hercules, were separated from DuPont as a result of antitrust action in 1912. We were told in several interviews that the president of one of these companies had privately expressed considerable support for freer trade, and we got the impression that the other company did not care much about the issue but might lean toward reciprocal trade. But both were willing to let the trade associations to which they belonged—and there are several in the chemical industry—speak for them. None of the company officials most likely to know had great interest in or a clear impression of what the trade associations actually did say. Communications from the associations on foreign economy policy received little circulation within the companies.

It was not, of course, only DuPont's influence which kept such firms from supporting reciprocal trade. It was the cumulative weight of the numerous protectionist firms in the chemical industry. An official of one of these firms said in effect that the firm was neutral on reciprocal trade because "the whole chemical industry buys and sells from each other; [so] we have important customers who definitely are for protection, and these things make a difference. Personally, I think the customers are making a mountain out of a mole hill."

Two Wilmington firms in fields of industry which would place them in a protectionist milieu—although neither apparently themselves suffered from foreign competition—were owned and managed by old Quaker families. The managers had the attitude that good Quakers are supposed to have, and, hence, in principle both firms supported reciprocal trade.

In another industry, one firm intended to oppose reciprocal trade because its trade association had asked it to. Though its export manager had not been abroad for many years, exports ran to 7 per cent or so of gross. Yet, the export manager was delighted to oppose reciprocal trade because he was so irritated at foreign restrictions on trade.

Other Delaware firms on the whole showed even less interest than these. International Latex, which has since been sold, had done nothing and had been exposed to no pressures or requests on foreign economic policy.

Dover is the capital and second city of Delaware. An informed person there told us he had heard "no complaints about and no discussion of foreign trade or imports." The community was in 1954 occupied in tremendous expansion due to a newly established air base.

□ Rural Delaware

Outside Wilmington, Delaware's population is predominantly agriculture-based. The poultry business is large; broilers and other chickens are processed, as well as raised. The poultry processors or growers have many political problems in the state and area—stream pollution, general nuisances, and the like—and any political activity goes into these. How much of the poultry is ultimately exported was not known; records did not enable one to tell.

There is also a good deal of processing of sweet corn, lima beans, and other crops. There are apple-growers who, according to a state agricultural authority, sell abroad. Most of the wheat-growers are also in dairying as part of a diversification program, and dairying was generally protectionist. Thirty per cent of Delaware wheat went to foreign lands.

At the instigation of American Farm Bureau Federation officers, because "Secretary of Agriculture Benson said he wanted to know how farmers felt in regard to issues on foreign trade," a series of discussion meetings on the subject was held by farmers throughout the state. About 500 people took part. Raised-hand votes showed a considerable margin in favor of lower tariffs. The senators and congressman are supposed by the farm organizations to have heard about the results, but in fact Congressional representatives remembered them only vaguely or not at all.

We asked a farm leader if he knew how DuPont and other companies felt on tariffs: "No," he replied, "I have often wondered about these matters and would like to know whether industry feels it would gain or lose by a tariff. I just don't know how they feel."

□ What the Congressmen Heard and Did Not Hear

Substantially, the congressman and senators from Delaware in 1954-1955 appeared to have heard very little from the state about the Reciprocal Trade Extension Act. One of them said: "On the Randall Commission, I am sure I did get some letters or calls, but I cannot even recall them. No doubt somebody did [call]." Since all three Delaware legislators were alert, attentive men, this means that the calls were probably not very significant. One legislator said:

> No, I don't hear much at all on this issue. . . . There aren't any real problems of voting on reciprocal trade. I have always voted for it and I just don't hear much on that; so far as any particular complaint or gripes or so forth on that, there just haven't been very many.

Another said:

> I've talked directly with the chemical companies about problems of interest, and I have received no particular specifications as to their views . . . certainly they would be the most concerned; . . . therefore, we have no special reason to expect to hear much when any legislation is introduced.

The third thought that the chemical industry might have a predominant interest, had heard something from farmers, from machine-tool makers from outside the state, and "pretty heavily from the leather industry"—he was not sure whether in or out of the state. "The greatest interest," he remarked, "may well reflect the views of the Farm Bureau." "It is rare that we have a person of unlimited means make a demand on us," he said, commenting on the self-restraint of wealthy Delawareans.

None of them heard from Delaware labor on the issue in 1954 or 1955. Some apparently random letters were received from outside textile or electrical workers against HR 1 in 1955.

In 1955, the three received considerably more mail. The Delaware League of Women Voters was noticeable in support of reciprocal trade. Apparently all three legislators received more pro- than anti-reciprocal– trade mail from the state, although a good deal of anti mail from outside. But, as a staff member of the Finance Committee put it, "so many people have come in on all these things . . . , we just haven't been able to bear in mind which was which." Against the background of other business, the mail and visits on HR 1 were that unimpressive!

There was awareness in the Congressional delegation that different divisions of DuPont might have different views on HR 1. They knew DuPont employees personally. The Northern Newcastle Young Democrats Club, composed, according to the congressman, "largely of DuPont chemists, young businessmen, etc.," approached one congressman in favor of the Reciprocal Trade Act. This is one of the very few instances we encountered of a local political organization taking a definite stand with its congressman or senator for reciprocal trade; in Midland, Michigan, where Dow Chemical is located, the local Republican organization passed a resolution which it sent to the senators against the Reciprocal Trade Act; but, in general, party organizations everywhere stay out of policy issues of that sort.

□ Conclusion

In general, Delaware congressmen and senators appeared to be free to choose for themselves, without much pressure, on foreign economic-policy issues. No interest in the state vociferously opposed reciprocal trade; and, although DuPont may have leaned in that direction, senators and congressmen in a state as small as Delaware·knew the rifts and cross-pressures within DuPont and also knew that there were other issues on which DuPont felt much more strongly. Nor did any interest in the state vigorously support reciprocal trade. Such instances as there were of injury by foreign competition created no stir. Wilmington had approximately full employment. If he had been so minded and had chosen to dramatize it, a Delaware senator or congressman could probably have got some following and attention by speaking up for old-fashioned protectionism. The vulcanized-fiber plants, some of the textile plants, DuPont, and the traditional conservatism of several areas provided sources from which applause, votes, and some sympathy might have been given to a man who tried to defend American industry against "cheap foreign labor."

On the other hand, a Delaware senator or congressman who chose to dramatize the issue might also have crystallized the latent freer-trade concern in Atlas, Hercules, and International Latex and among some of the farmers. Either way, protectionist or reciprocal trade, he could have made an issue for himself which would have attracted some favorable attention and support, and at least as much from interests of moderate size and power as from the great.

As it was, none of the four men who occupied the three seats on Capitol Hill—Senators J. Allen Frear (D.) and John J. Williams (R.), Representatives Herbert Warburton (R.) and Harris McDowell, Jr. (D.)—focused on trade or the tariff, though the two senators were on the Finance Committee. There was no constituency reason why they should. So far as the record shows, all four supported the Reciprocal Trade Act as requested by the administration.[7]

---

[7] The only deviation was that in committee Senator Frear voted for a two-year instead of a three-year extension of the 1955 Reciprocal Trade Act.

Chapter 17

Wall Street:
The Sleeping Giant

Wall Street is, of course, not a community. "I have no idea who [the congressman] is," a Wall Street bank president told us. "I know the congressman in Westchester, where I live. I don't consider the congressman in this district as representing us; he represents the Turks and Chinese who live here." Yet it seemed worth studying those few square blocks in lower Manhattan as if they were a community. The world views them as such, and those who work there form an ingrown group linked in a net as closely knit as that of the business community in many a town.

□ The Myth of Wall Street

The accusations against Wall Street could be piled as high as a mountain. The defenses, too, would make at least a small hill. Some of these allegations played a part in the reciprocal-trade controversy.

Wall Street was widely seen, particularly by protectionists, as a center of the freer-trade drive. This view was less frequent than the notion that the promoters of freer trade were in mass-production industries, such

277

as auto. But, in the haze of ambiguity in which public argument takes place, such views easily merge. Marxism and populism led the public to identify heavy industry with the banking community which finances it.

Among economic sophisticates, a second and more telling argument established an image of the New York banking community as low-tariff advocates.[1] The foreign business of Wall Street banks is considerable. A relatively few of the largest banks, most of them in New York, and perhaps one or two others in each of the major port cities do the overwhelming bulk of foreign-trade financing, currency exchange, and the like. Even more important in the eyes of those who know the details is the fact that in recent years enormous dollars accounts have been established in these banks by foreign interests. No one claimed to know the size of the foreign deposits or, for that matter, the volume of foreign-trade financing which passes through the classic portals of these temples of finance. Yet the amounts were undeniably massive.[2]

The allegations about Wall Street's part in the reciprocal-trade debate are but special instances of the usual stereotypes about Wall Street: that it is a colossus of power and that it plays puppeteer to American life, pulling the strings and making things go the way it wishes.

□ The Organization Banker

It cannot be denied that there is a great power potential buried in the vaults of Wall Street. It is our thesis, however, that, in this controversy,

---

[1] We concentrated on Wall Street bankers and did not include the stockbrokers who are so much identified with the image of Wall Street. This latter group has little relevance to foreign-trade policy. We realize in retrospect that we failed to interview those smaller bankers and "five-dollar stock" underwriters who tend to finance the riskier and more adventurous enterprises, including much foreign investment. In reading what follows, account should be taken of this bias toward the top.

[2] No banker to whom we spoke was willing to make a quantitative estimate of his foreign deposits or of those of other banks. Reluctance here was backed up by genuine ignorance. The foreign deposits are not clearly identifiable; segregated statistics are not kept. It is also not feasible to estimate the importance of the foreign business as a whole to any bank, for the figure would be a composite of the importance of foreign deposits, foreign letters of credit, foreign exchange, foreign loans, foreign investments, etc. Annual reports seldom indicate any one of these figures, and, when they do, it is only in an occasional comment, not in a regular series. It used to be said as a rule of thumb that foreign business was perhaps 10 per cent of the domestic business for the large coastal banks, but this is a fairly meaningless statement, in view of the high concentration of such activities in the few largest of them. It was currently asserted in Wall Street circles that foreign funds in the United States were on the order of ten billion dollars. It is also generally asserted in Wall Street comments that the easiest way for a bank to make money is by financing foreign trade. Since the war, Wall Street has supplanted London as the world's financial center, partly because of the stability of the dollar, but even more because of the low interest rates in this country. American banks have been somewhat cautious in filling the new role into which they have been cast, yet that role has acquired considerable importance for them.

Wall Street played a small part because it was afraid to use the power that it had. The banking community was conspicuously silent. Judiciousness and balance became indistinguishable from apathy.

Throughout the rest of the United States, in our hundreds of interviews with businessmen, we seldom found ourselves recognizing the current stereotype of the corporate man: conformist, deindividualized, bureaucratized, and moderate to the point of vapidity. Wall Street was the exception. Even here the stereotype was oversimple and overgeneral, possessing only that kernel of truth that a stereotype can. Still, one could recognize the elements of reality around which the myth had taken shape.

Bankers view themselves as the servants of business, of *all* business. Hardly an interview passed without the cliché that bankers cannot take sides on issues because their clients are found on all sides.

The banker is a consultant. All types of firms tell him their troubles and their plans. He sees their books and their balances. Said one banker from a medium-sized industrial city, "I am in the export department. I would be crazy not to be for exports"; but also, "I sit on the credit committee of the bank, in addition to my work for this department, and there I can see how imports affect our businesses. I see accounts that would not be collectible if we dropped our protection."

At a big coastal bank with extensive foreign business, an officer told us how local businessmen raised the tariff issue with them. He reported an implied threat by a manufacturer who wrote complaining about the bank's presumed liberal-trade policy and pointed out that his firm maintained a very large deposit with the bank. Actually, the bank had avoided an official policy on trade. It had been invited to join the Coleman committee, but it did not do so. The committee to which the invitational telegram was referred was composed of men who were personally liberal traders, but they found grounds—"the telegram . . . did not really explain what the Coleman committee was going to do"—for turning down the request. The bank, our informant said, tried to take narrow and circumscribed specific stands for fear of alienating customers.

At another such bank, a respondent said, "Banks don't commit themselves. Of course the officers vary, but, when they speak up, they are always very careful to speak as individuals. I have never heard a banker who wasn't careful to say that he was not speaking for his bank. . . . Banks are very cautious and 'mealy-mouthed.' "

At the same institution, another man said: "It is very hard for banks to plead a case because they are not in business for themselves. They are not like manufacturers. They are doing a service for all kinds of business and cannot oppose their clients."

Our interview at one of the giants of the banking world deserves to be quoted at somewhat greater length, for it illustrates not only the caution of a banker arising from the diversity of his clients but also a conformity in way of life. The interviewer reported:

> I started by asking if there was much discussion of trade-tariff matters. . . . He said it goes on all the time. I asked where. . . . Such discussion takes place within the bank [not with outsiders] . . . the higher officers of the bank all ride down to work and home from work in a private railroad car that is owned by the bank. They live in some common area in Westchester or Connecticut.

> I asked the tenor of the discussion of the Randall Committee report in the car the day that it appeared. . . . The general feeling was that the Randall Commission had done as good a job as it could, and they hoped that Europeans wouldn't destroy the effectiveness of the committee report by belittling it as inadequate. . . . The bank digested the report and circulated it to all its relevant staff people.

> I asked about discussions outside the bank. He said that they do not conduct propaganda, that is not their function. They are a service industry and not like the manufacturer. They serve all kinds of people. Tariffs are a sensitive issue, and many of their customers are on the other side. They are not trying to run the country, so they will not engage in any propaganda on this subject. . . .

> I asked about pressures from customers. . . . He said that their clients send them their news letters and speeches, but he has never heard of anyone threatening to close an account. I asked what is done with these news letters and speeches, and he said they get circulated to the people handling those accounts.

> I asked if they . . . participate in the Coleman committee. He answered that they were not. . . . He said it is bank policy. A policy committee decides such things so all the officers will act in the same way.

> I then asked about communications between them and their correspondent banks outside New York. He said that issues such as the trade issue do not come up with their correspondent bankers. They all realize that there is an element of dynamite in the issue.

With only one of the giants was the situation different, and there because of the leadership of one top officer. Here is the picture as drawn by an officer of that bank:

> Z had always been willing to speak on trade policy. . . . That was a particularly courageous thing to do. . . . He did not fear to speak out his views, despite the threat of the loss of an account from a customer. . . . He knows of no case in which the bank actually did lose an account because of Z's expressed views on tariffs.

> I asked . . . whether Z's speeches were in a personal capacity or as chairman of the board. . . . He wouldn't admit the distinction. Z always spoke as chairman of the board and could not speak in any other way. . . .

Other banks [of a comparable kind], he said, are less willing to speak out . . . are concerned with their responsibility to their different clients.

I asked about the consequence of the difference of opinion he had mentioned between the foreign and domestic departments of [his] bank. I asked if the domestic people would feel hesitant to express an opinion contrary to that of the head of the bank. He said that they would, that, once the chairman of the board had expressed a view, others would not publicly take an opposed view, although they might try to persuade him within the bank. I asked in view of that fact whether there was not some discussion within the bank before the head of the bank took a position, whether there wasn't some across-the-table conferring. He said no, that was not the way it was done. Z would express his opinion in a speech, and then the others simply followed.

The caution we have been discussing permeates the environment. One respondent who has since broken out of Wall Street to make a great deal of money as an innovating entrepreneur in a cut-throat business described with dismay the blandness of his colleagues. Each week he went to a luncheon with a half-dozen heads of major banks and banking institutions, the top of the multibillion-dollar New York banking community, each bringing along a staff man. "At these luncheons," he said, "no one ever expresses a strong opinion. Someone will raise a matter by saying, 'What do you think about thus and so,' and each one will make a noncommittal comment. When the sense of the group is clear, then there may be stronger expressions, but on the whole they regard it as a sign of adolescence and immaturity to hold strong views." These big banks, opined our respondent, were built by men of different stripe, but, with time and bureaucratization, bland, "other-directed characters" were taking over.

We asked if our respondent had heard any discussions of HR 1 at his luncheon group or otherwise in recent months. He said that there were those in the group who were not interested in it and those who were for it; there were certainly no opponents in that group. The discussions consisted not of advocacy but of general comment on current developments.

Is this power? The answer is more a matter of semantics than of fact. Said a Wall Street financial consultant: "The bigger the banks are, the less influential they are. The only banks that have any influence are the pipsqueak banks in the small towns. Those are the bankers who know their congressmen."

No one can deny that potential power resides in the community where all major American business is financed. Nor could one deny that the grave and timid men who manage finance are skilled and sophisticated in the ways of the world and of politics. They may be short on fierce passion, or ideology, or crusading zeal, but they have a proven ability to work and prosper under a multitude of conditions. Perhaps these traits account for the fact that, in the Roosevelt and Truman administrations, Wall Street's representation in the higher posts of government was, if anything, more extensive than later under the Republicans, for whom, with few exceptions, they voted. When the New Deal needed a businessman for office, it found him among its moderate, not among its crusading, enemies. In many of our Wall Street interviews, we came upon a real concern with the recrudescence of the right wing in the Republican Party. Said one Wall Street respondent:

> Hauge [Eisenhower's economic aide] is liked by [their] type of progressive Eastern businessman . . . ; they regard him as their man. They consider the Eisenhower administration weak, but they like what it is doing and are impressed by its continuing to obtain public popularity. . . . One of the things they particularly like about the Eisenhower administration is that it seems to have smashed the right wing of the Republican Party, which these people regard as a menace to them.

But they were not happy with Eisenhower. "He is trying to do the right thing," but his good will did not seem to be enough. Said one respondent, who had just come to Wall Street after a Washington career:

> He was very much impressed by the hardheadedness and frankness of the men in the firm. They cannot afford not to speak the truth to each other, since it costs money, and they speak rather scathingly about the administration. . . . Even at the top, they do not think much of the competence of the administration.

The state of chronic frustration in politics that lasted twenty years under the Democrats had continued for Wall Street under the Republicans. What power they had did not get them what they wanted.

And yet it would be wrong to portray these as men without power. True, one may question whether unused power is power at all. But the power of Wall Street is not always unused. It is seldom used in matters of broad public policy, for experience of retribution is too common. But it is often used in much more detailed, petty, but still worthwhile matters closer to "legitimate" business problems than to broad politics.

> I asked V if his job was with political problems. He said it might turn out to be, but they had no political problems. He referred to the list of officers and said, "At least they have no political problems that they cannot solve." He said in a joking way, "You know what they say about Wall Street is right. All the communications do come in here." To draw him out, I argued, saying: "How many congressmen do they control, in contrast to a small-town banker?" He said, "Yes, but they have no trouble in speaking to any congressman they want to through a businessman in his own area." The bank acts as adviser to hundreds

of banks.[3] He described their procedure when there was a bankers' convention here. The firm holds three cocktail parties a year. . . . Each person in town is assigned to someone in the firm whose job it is to see that he has a good time. . . . There is no line handed down, . . . but in this way they know hundreds of people whom they can influence. . . . *W* is probably on twenty boards of directors and the officers among them had contact with hundreds of directors, who in turn had contact with hundreds of others. . . . I asked whether they take advantage of this situation to get on the telephone and speak to fifty people to get them to do something on a political issue such as the trade issue. *V* indicated that this wouldn't ordinarily be the case, but "if they get worked up enough that is exactly what they will do." Something like that had happened against the Bricker amendment, about which *W* and a lot of people in Wall Street got quite excited. I asked, does it occur to them in the normal course that a way . . . of making money is by getting some changes in rules or regulations. *V* answered that . . . this manipulative approach would tend to be limited to narrower questions, such as the particular phrasing of a Treasury regulation . . . potentially subject to change by their action.[4]

Thus, our Wall Street respondents had the means whereby they could have expressed their internationalist and freer-trade views. They were, however, actually silent. Few joined the Coleman committee, few spoke up, and none of the available channels of pressure were brought into use. In some banks, there was active internal discussion; in others, there was not even that; but in none of the major ones, with one exception, did any individual actively support the administration's trade-policy drive in the 1950's. These men were open to information which reached them in large quantities, but were not inclined to act on it. They were receivers, not sources, of vigorous communication. In 1962, it must be conceded, they were somewhat more active. They were more immediately alarmed by the gold outflow which had replaced the dollar gap. They shared the general alarm over exclusion from the Common Market. The most active bank had one officer devoting full time to organizing the banking community on behalf of the Kennedy trade bill. But, even in 1962, the most the banks achieved was subdued persuasion.

□ Channels to the Outside World

The banks were, however, sources of much detailed factual information about foreign economic developments. Many of the big banks which

---

[3] A part of the power of the big New York banks comes from their relations with correspondent banks throughout the country.

[4] He added that, "This sort of thing is more or less turned over to the lawyers. . . . They will ask for advice and information from their Washington lawyers."

specialize in foreign business—the First National City Bank, for instance—put out bulletins with wide circulation and respectful readership.[5] Most important of all, the banks that finance foreign trade are sources of individualized information for businessmen about foreign markets. Let us quote an interview on this matter.

> The foreign division has the task of stimulating interest in foreign trade. . . . It was frequently difficult to get people to go into export. We asked him what was the main resistance. His reply was that it was emotional. They tend to overestimate the technical difficulties of exporting. They were also overconcerned with getting payment. He said he told them that, if they exercised as much caution in getting credit ratings for foreign concerns as they did with domestic concerns, they could actually expect better rates of payment. . . . Finally, he said they are concerned that foreign businessmen would not exhibit the same high level of morality that American businessmen would. . . .
>
> A banker in Europe might correspond with him, saying that he had a textile manufacturer who wanted to find a market for a certain kind of fabric, and he might go to a wholesaler or distributor in the . . . area and ask him if he wanted to handle these. . . . He was a middleman for the exchange of information between companies engaged in foreign trade.

A number of export managers and other respondents included their banks among sources of information on foreign firms and markets.

Thus, a few individuals in the big banks are important gatekeepers of information about world affairs. Almost all the top bankers travel abroad. An annual report of the Irving Trust Company, one of the banks heavily engaged in international business, mentions:

> Among other highlights of the year was the increased frequency of field travel by Irving officers in their assigned territories abroad. During 1956 they traveled more than 200,000 miles in Asia, Europe, Africa, the Western Hemisphere, Australia, New Zealand. The purpose of these trips is to maintain close contact with our customers, to develop new business for the bank, and to obtain first-hand information on conditions in foreign countries.

Top officers of the biggest banks generally hear more from foreign clients than would top executives in other fields. For example, the respondent whom we quoted above about the handling of letters and speeches circulated by customers, when asked about information from foreign sources, said that their foreign clients send them approximately as much material as do their domestic ones. He also mentioned a recent visit to the United States of Lord Balfour, the head of Lloyd's, and the series of dinners and functions which ensued. Such contacts with visiting foreigners are numerous. But, aside from letters, travel, and contacts with European

---

[5] The First National City Bank *Bulletin* had a circulation of 220,000 at that time.

travelers here, the sources of foreign information of most of the banks' officers is that which we find for all intelligent big-businessmen—the mass business media. The respondent who talked of Lord Balfour and of letters from his foreign customers went on to say that in general he would not know anything except what he saw in the papers.

In each leading bank, however, there are a few people in lower echelons whose job it is to keep informed on foreign economic developments. We remind the reader of the previously quoted description given by the manager of the foreign division of a large East Coast bank of how one man on his staff read the *Neue Zürcher Zeitung* daily, whereas, for the rest, the foreign news meant *The New York Times*.

Nonetheless, these few individuals who specialize in knowing particular foreign situations, in addition to correspondence from a few dozen American employees overseas and perhaps from foreign employees who may number in four figures, provide the large international banks with some basis of specialized knowledge which is large compared to that in the hands of even exporting industries. Other businessmen rely on foreign departments of this type and on the few gatekeepers within them for specific foreign information.

The impact of this specific and detailed foreign-business information should not be underestimated, despite the fact that it does not concern matters of broad national policy. Its effect is to draw otherwise-reluctant businesses into the fields of foreign trade and investment. As noted, a sense of unfamiliarity, puzzlement, and lack of knowledge are primary obstacles to becoming involved in foreign ventures. Specific information helps to overcome these resistances. Once involved in foreign business, travel, and contacts with foreign clients, a greater awareness of foreign political issues may follow.

Among our interviews, there were some at a mammoth financial institution which in the past few years has become heavily involved in foreign investment in line with this pattern. At the time of our first interviews, the firm was intellectually convinced of the usual Wall Street position in favor of expanded foreign business, but emotionally, at top levels at least, was deeply opposed to their becoming themselves involved abroad. They had taken a table at a Coleman committee dinner, at a cost of perhaps $300. As one of those who went described it:

> They do this frequently for such affairs when an important client asks them. . . . S, being a fairly low man on the totem pole . . . gets pushed into these things. He suggested that we not regard attendance at the dinner as indicating actual support of the committee. There wasn't much discussion of the subject matter at the dinner across the table on an informal basis, but he did hear a few grumbling remarks . . . , the tenor being that such things as those Henry Ford was saying were all very well as a general matter. What about the pinch when it hurts?

The president of the same corporation told us that international trade was not part of his business. He paid attention to it only as any ordinary citizen would. He said that at one time they had been extensively engaged in overseas operations. Then, sometime between 1925 and 1930, they made a policy decision to leave that field and liquidated their overseas investments. He described the foreign operations as "a pain in the backside." Exchange difficulties were their first reason for not wanting to get into foreign operations. Second, they were too specialized and intricate. An overseas operation that might account for 1 per cent of their profits might take "half of his time." It did not pay for itself in man-hours. There had been pressure from a major client for them to get into the international field, but they had systematically avoided it. On the other hand, his general views, "for what they are worth," he said, were that "it is a vital necessity for us to stimulate more foreign trade for the United States . . . . If we don't import enough to permit the other countries to live and breathe, we cannot export to them. I am definitely in the low-tariff or no-tariff group." But, as one of his assistants put it, for becoming involved themselves, it was a you-first-my-dear-Alphonse matter.

Within three years, however, they had become deeply involved in foreign financing, and a number of their officers were traveling abroad to arrange it. The pressure that brought about this reversal consisted of a flow of information about opportunities too profitable to pass over. In 1953, the president of the company was still resisting: "If we put out a lightning rod, we would be struck dead in fifteen minutes," was how he described the flow of suggestions of foreign opportunities. Three years later, the firm had become a leading international investor.

□ Summary

Wall Street banks were very much involved in the practical business of foreign trade and international finance. They were a channel for technical international economic information. Although banks took little direct part in the reciprocal-trade controversy, they played a vital communication function in the transmission of the kind of information which has made American business concerned with world affairs.

Contrary to the myth that Wall Street runs America, we found the bankers there even more reluctant to exercise their power in foreign economic policy than DuPont and the Big Three of the automotive industry. Handicapped in part by high visibility and ill repute, the Wall Street bankers felt the additional inhibition of seeing themselves as the servants of business—that is, of all business. They were reluctant to fight openly for any policy which might antagonize any client.

Perhaps these inhibitions stemmed as much from personal psychology as from external pressures. By selection and training the Wall Street banker is a man of judiciousness, subtlety, and balance, rather than a crusader.

He is also a man with extensive contacts in the business world. These help him take effective action on political matters he considers crucial, and with a minimum of fuss and feathers. This raises the question of whether Wall Street bankers were not indeed active on behalf of the Reciprocal Trade Act, but so skilfully and inconspicuously that their activity could not be detected. We have dealt with the same problem in previous chapters in connection with other business giants. True, failure to find a needle in a haystack does not prove that it is not there. But we searched diligently. We had friends on the inside and on the other side. We talked not only to people in Wall Street but also to those whom they would have been influencing and those who tried to get them to exert influence. Covert maneuvering that we failed to detect was undoubtedly present, but, if so undetectable, it could not be a significant factor in the situation.

Chapter 18

New Anglia

New Anglia and its metropolitan area, with a population of three quarters of a million, had about 150,000 persons at work in industry. Forty-four per cent of employment was in manufacturing, as against a national average of 25 per cent. Textiles were the city's number-one industry and also its number-one headache. Before World War II, more than half of all manufacturing workers were in the textile plants. By 1954, textile workers accounted for less than one third. The textile industry was collapsing; other industries were growing or holding their own. From 1939 to 1952, textile employment dropped by 17,000, while metal and machine employment rose by exactly the same figure. Employment in accessories—such things as buttons, key rings, and the like—doubled. The city had grown since before the war, and employment was well up since then. But, in the few years just preceding the political events we were studying, the decline of the textile industry had brought a noticeable year-by-year shrinkage in total employment and with it some significant amount of suffering. Unemployment in one suburb ran to 32 per cent.

New Anglia is an old Yankee town. Yankee families still dominate the university and the old established firms in textiles and some other fields. The men who work in the mills, however, come from new waves of Americans. French Canadians, Italians, Irishmen, and Jews have long since left the Yankees in a minority. The Democrats have sewed up the area, with all five congressmen and the mayor.

New Anglia has a strong cultural tradition. One newspaper, *The Times,* was nationally noted as a well-edited, crusading, liberal Republican paper. An autographed photo of Wendell Willkie hung over the editor's desk. *The Times* carried a large amount of foreign news and took an internationalist editorial stand. In the past it had backed the reciprocal-trade program. There was in New Anglia an active League of Women Voters; a World Affairs Council, which tried in principle to reach all strata of the public; and a branch of the Council on Foreign Relations, a small, elite group of community leaders who met over dinner once a month to hear a speech and discuss foreign affairs. Perhaps the strongest stimulus for such discussions was the university, which took its community responsibilities with earnestness.

A town-gown educational program emphasized cooperation of the economics department with local businessmen. The discussion groups under that program included one on foreign trade.

New Anglia had a tradition of concern with tariffs and trade; it was a protectionist tradition. There was a time in American history when New Anglia was one of the two main centers of protectionist activity in the country. One of the major protectionist tariff bills of an earlier era carries the name of a New Anglia congressman. This tradition may have left its mark, particularly on the old textile industry, but in none of our interviews was it ever mentioned. Protectionism was no longer an article of ideological faith. It persisted strongly in New Anglia because of present interests, but not one respondent discussed it as a dogma sanctified by its past.

Protectionism was still the dominant view in New Anglia, though probably not that of the majority. It was the view of the textile industry, which expressed itself loudly through industry channels, and to a small extent it was the view of the accessory industry. It was not the view of the metal-products industry or of the town as a whole. In New Anglia, channels of communication about trade and tariffs were overwhelmingly vertical and represented industries, not the town. Communication between industries was negligible.

Perhaps the best illustration of the strictly vertical character of communications about tariffs in New Anglia is the story of Arthur White, a member of an old New Anglia family. He was the president of a top factory in the town, a man whom we would expect to be a leader of local opinion, and in fact he was. He was the man whom we were most often told to see when we asked who the business leaders were. He, or rather his family, were major stockholders in the newspaper. His company manufactured machinery.

In the fall of 1953, his industry was in somewhat of a slump. After the war, the demand for its product had been tremendous both at home and abroad, but by the fall of 1953 the pent-up demand was satisfied. The Korean War was over, and the European economy had not only been restored but was starting to be a source of supply. A number of respondents told us of European machines entering the country in competition with White's.

Our interviewer went to see White with the unquestioned expectation that he was about to interview a strong protectionist alarmed by the growth of foreign competition. He found himself at a lecture on Adam Smith. White described himself as in general a free trader. "We want to trade with the world, so the world must be free to trade with us." Less than 10 per cent of the X machines sold in this country are imported. "That 10 per cent is the fertilizer that will make the industry get up and go." Believing in free trade as a principle, he would have liked to see a long-range scheme with annual tariff reductions over a period of twenty-five to fifty years.

Our interviewer left confused. He was sure that in several conversations he had been told that White was a protectionist. At the newspaper, he had been told that the editorial policy was for low tariffs, but that the owners were on the other side. To check his impression of White's reputation in town, he went to a phone booth to ask three men who should know: an editor on the newspaper, a business journalist, and a Chamber of Commerce executive. One said that he frankly didn't know where White stood. The second said that White had never expressed himself, but thought that he was in general against reciprocal trade. The third said that at one time an elder White had been very much disturbed by foreign competition [an error too!] and that from the standpoint of self-preservation White would want barriers to imports, but that the interviewer had better make sure for himself. Clearly, the images of White and where he stood were based on surmise, but they nevertheless circulated through town and may have had some impact.

That finding became even more dramatic when our interviewer later discovered that White, far from being secretive about his views, was on the publicized list of members of the Committee for a National Trade Policy, the low-tariff pressure group. No one in New Anglia had told us that because no one knew it. Communications on tariffs were going through industry channels. General literature was not being read. White, because of the position of his firm and people's guesses as to where he must stand, had become a symbol of the need for tariff protection. He was important in the influence process as the symbolic leader of industry in New Anglia, but the communications from him which influenced people came mostly out of their own imaginations as to what reality must be.

White was not being silent. What limited the diffusion of his views was that they were expressed through industry, not community, channels. His firm had a long tradition of interest in exports. They have foreign-trade connections going back a century and still continuing. Exports were once, though no longer, a major portion of their business. For some time, they had been strong supporters of the International Chamber of Commerce. In their own trade association, they spoke up for a low-tariff policy and opposed those elements in the industry which favored protection. But all these actions were within the channels of their industry. White was explicit that he did not discuss these things with people in other businesses. Pressed on whether he ever discussed foreign economic policy with any of the textile people, he recalled one exceptional occasion when he had. He asked "one of the old bucks of the textile industry," who was having dinner at his home, what effect free trade would have on his business. "The man harumphed and grunted, but did not answer." "Ordinarily," White said, "I don't bother with them; they're not in my business." White also told us that he could recall only one time when he had received a telephone call on the tariff from a friend in the community. A textile man called to ask if he did not think it terrible that a British firm had got the Chief Joseph Dam contract, presumably assuming that that brought the issue home to White's machine firm. But for these two exceptions, the channels between White and the rest of New Anglia business were completely blocked for discussion of tariffs, however much communication flowed through trade associations.

The point can be exaggerated. We picked up a few clues of cross-industry communication. The head of the foreign department of a bank was a strong protectionist. His argument was based on the problems of local firms. The university discussion group on foreign trade brought together professors, newspaper people, exporters, and textile men—perhaps a dozen leading citizens. But here, also, controversial communication was cut out by defining the subject as a factual exploration of the volume of New Anglia exports. The League of Women Voters held some meetings. The newspaper ran a few stories and editorials, but made no major point of this issue in view of the conflicts of attitude about it within the community and within the newspaper itself. Some local businessmen concerned with export markets had formed a foreign-trade club which met once a month for dinner and a speech. Its 160 or so members included export managers and others from all the leading firms of the town, yet it had not made itself heard outside the fraternity of those middle-rank executiv ˜s whose job called for an interest in the foreign field. The editor of *The Times* had not heard of its existence.

Yet the foreign-trade issue was not a dead one. Within the textile industry it assumed the dimensions of a small crusade. At least three unions and two trade associations went to work and successfully swung the congressmen to protection, even though they were liberal Democrats. Two congressmen each reported 1,000 letters from one of the unions, and one reported four to five hunderd letters from a trade association. These were, of course, standard letters and therefore largely discounted, but, in the absence of other communication than that from the textile industry, the congressmen could not know what the community feeling was. One told us early in the year that he wished he knew where New Anglia people stood and that if we found out we should let him know. "When you hear something from the unions, it is hard to know whether it is just something that the national office told them to say." The businessmen were solidly Republican, so he did not have much contact with them.

Yet, the volume of communication from the textile interests to Congress was considerable. The main sources were two textile trade associations, with a single executive director, and two textile unions and their locals. The independent union worked closely with the trade association on tariff questions. They submitted a joint statement to the Randall Commission against lowering bars to imports. The CIO union wavered, but ultimately supported protection, pushed along by the trade associations. A woman CIO official was about to talk on a radio panel on foreign economic policy, giving the national CIO line. "But then Mr. Reiley came along." Reiley, the New England executive of the trade association, showed her how bad reciprocal trade was for their workers, and she pulled out of the panel. "As a practical matter," she said, "I don't see how we can do anything else" but oppose the reciprocal-trade program. The independent union was more vocal. Every local president wrote a personal letter to his congressman. The trade association, which was affiliated with the Strackbein committee, was even more active, its director being an old hand at lobbying. "During the last twenty-five years," he said, "I have appeared before every committee in Congress." Although this man's inspiration lay behind almost every letter from New Anglia to Congress, he made no effort to organize community support. He seemed to imply that he had never thought about the idea, since he said that he might some time in the future, although he had not in the past.

The textile people were the only group of which the New Anglia congressmen had a clear image. The accessories industry was divided and confused, and those who talked about it from outside had the general impression that it was protectionist, but for some reason did not express itself. The congressmen said that they did not hear from accessories people, but they noted Japanese competition and drew conclusions from it which in this case were partially correct. The over-all picture in New Anglia was that of a community in which foreign-trade discussions were solely along business lines, in which they were extensive only in one industry, and in which images of what was happening in other industries was largely the result of surmises or imaginary communications derived from small clues in past political attitudes or market information.

We should, however, note one recent occasion when an attempt at community organization was made. Although exceptional, it also illustrates how much of image-formation arises from surmises rather than from actual communication. It was an occasion on which New Anglia opposed the protectionist side. In 1953, New Anglia was regarded on Capitol Hill as the center of opposition to the second Simpson bill, which would have increased import quotas on residual fuel oil.

The story of the Simpson bill and of the lobbying activities for and against it is partly told elsewhere in this volume. Suffice it here to note that the bill was backed by the coal interests and domestic independent oil producers in the hope of recapturing some of that part of the coastal fuel-oil market which was then being supplied by tanker imports from Venezuela and elsewhere. Among the largest consumers of imported residual fuel oil are the industries of New England, and, among them, those of New Anglia. When the Simpson bill came before Congress, resolutions and letters began to flow in from such organizations as the New England Council and from unions and leading New England businessmen. Public opinion seemed aroused. On Capitol Hill, congressmen took notice, and the New England delegation led a successful fight to kill the bill. New Anglia was the center of the opposition, and the New Anglia congressmen its leading spokesmen. So it looked from Capitol Hill.

Actually, New Anglia feeling was not strong, and the image the congressmen received of their constituencies was just as partial as the image they later derived from the cry for protection of the textile industry. As one congressman said, at the time of the Simpson bill debate he thought everyone in the area was on the same side, and he acted accordingly, but since then he had heard differently. A protectionist trade association executive said: "Well, the attitude around here may have been correctly interpreted by the New England Council [which opposed the bill], but I doubt it." Despite these statements, however, there was no support for the Simpson bill in New Anglia. As one man put it: "Everybody is against crime." The significant point is that "no one was too excited about it."

On Capitol Hill, New Anglia symbolized the opposition to the Simpson bill. In New Anglia, the battle was viewed as an outside one, to which the city gave some mild support. "New Anglia was a little ruffled about the Simpson bill," we were told, "but not as much as other parts of New England. The Boston people said it would be tough if the Simpson bill passed. All we did was to agree." For most business leaders or their trade association executives, the issue was difficult to recall six months later. At the Chamber of Commerce, the name "Simpson bill" rang no bell, but "residual fuel oil" was recalled. Our respondent thought a moment and then said that the Chamber had taken a stand on that. Another trade association executive responded to neither symbol, but recalled the controversy when it was described at some length. He could say only that they had not been involved.

The responses of industrialists were similarly vague. Indeed, one big industrialist who uses residual fuel oil had never heard of the matter at all. Another, a strong protectionist, said after some hesitation: "The importers had a case there. There's no sense in too much protection of the oil industry. If it has enough money to invest abroad the way it does, it doesn't need much protection."

The last statement, in its convoluted reasoning, illustrates neatly our central point, that people restructure small bits of information to make imagined communications conform to their expectations, but often quite at variance with the facts. Just as Arthur White symbolized protectionism for New Anglia although he was a free trader and just as New Anglia symbolized opposition to the Simpson bill on Capitol Hill although few New Anglians cared, so for this protectionist the oil industry represented the Simpson bill. In point of fact, though he did not know it, the great oil companies were the chief victims and opponents of the Simpson bill. Its backers were coal-miners and small, independent oil producers of the Southwest. The great companies were the ones who were selling residual fuel oil to New England. But these fellow-opponents of the Simpson bill annoyed our xenophobic respondent by their great investments abroad. So he turned the information around in his mind to make more sense to him. He put the great internationalist oil companies on the opposite side from himself.

New Anglia did not know that it was thought of as the heart of the fight on the Simpson bill. It knew that it was merely giving mild cooperation to a push from outside, but it did not know whence this push came. The most informed response about the source of the movement came from a *Times* editor who had written against the bill. He could identify an attorney from Boston who had come to New Anglia to point out to local firms what oil quotas would cost them in their fuel bills. As a matter of fact, unknown to our respondent or at least unremembered, that attorney was sent by a Washington firm which represented Venezuelan manufacturers who were selling in the United States. The message which came to Congress from New Anglia had its source far from New Anglia. But it would be incorrect to conclude that New Anglia was thereby badly represented. The Simpson bill would have hurt New Anglia. It would have increased its fuel costs, and, even more important, that added item of cost might have been the last straw for some more of New Anglia's marginal textile mills. If some additional mills had closed and unemployment increased, then the Simpson bill might have been far more dreadful for the city than anyone there realized. New Anglia's interest was represented because an outsider cared enough to organize communications in and from New Anglia. The usual flow of foreign-trade discussion strictly within industry lines was supplemented in this one instance by editorials, by letters from dozens of leading citizens, and by resolutions from the leading civic organizations. But that alone would not have been enough to create in Washington an image of a really agitated community. Politicians are skeptical souls, ready to spot the public-relations man's put-up job. The communications from New Anglia carried conviction because they said the logical thing for New Anglia to say. They fitted the congressmen's image of reality. There was every reason why people in New Anglia should have felt strongly against the Simpson bill. It would have hurt them. So, when congressmen heard what seemed to be the voice of community feeling, they accepted it as such.

Chapter 19

Four Inactive Communities

In each community study thus far, we have asked why some community was not more active on the trade issue than it was. In Detroit, Wilmington, and Wall Street, powerful interests were inhibited by their very size and power. In New Anglia, community expression was blocked by the conviction that trade was a business matter, to be discussed through industry channels. Yet, muted as discussion may have been, in the communities reviewed so far foreign trade was a substantial issue. In the four communities at which we are still to look, various factors kept attention to trade matters minimal. In Midwest, community expression was discouraged by the futility of addressing Congressman Stubborn. Appalachian City was so depressed that only one issue interested it—its own development, which it did not see as related to tariffs. The Fifty-third Congressional District was too inchoate to act as a community, and those few industries within it which might have sought foreign markets found exporting too much bother. Textiletown, which had once been a protectionist center, lost interest in the issue to the extent that it began to prosper again. Thus, many factors could block citizen mobilization on a given public issue.

□ Midwest, Indiana

Midwest is a city of 50,000 persons located southeast of Chicago. It is a highly diversified manufacturing and business area. In 1953, it had over 200 industrial firms. Whereas New Anglia and Textiletown had passed the peak of their economic growth, Midwest was booming. Describing business conditions in 1953, the Chamber of Commerce announced proudly: "Midwest business was the best in history. . . . City building permits were up 37 per cent; retail sales showed a 20 per-cent increase in the first six months of the year. Employment was 60,000, more than 10 per cent higher than in 1952." As can be seen from comparing the population and the number of persons employed, many people came in from surrounding towns to work in Midwest. In late 1953, when we first visited Midwest, it was glowing with business optimism. The recession of 1954 affected this mood briefly, but by early 1955 business was again prosperous throughout the area.

Among the seven installations having over 1,000 employees, only one—the Acme Stationery Company—was locally owned, one was a state institution, and the other five were manufacturing subsidiaries of large national corporations. Midwest was once known as an important center for the manufacture of a household product which later was caught in a squeeze between the do-it-yourself movement and imports of higher quality. Most firms in that line had gone out of business by the fall of 1953; a few lingered on. The remaining industries, all thriving, ranged from metal processing, chemicals, building supplies, and dairy products to miscellaneous manufactures, processing, and distribution. Diversity was certainly the hallmark of Midwest business. But, even of the smaller companies, a large portion were owned by outside organizations, a matter which was something of a sore point in Midwest.

Midwest was chosen for study partly because of its small size and the diversity of its business and partly because it belonged to that area of the assertedly isolationist Great Plains on which Col. Robert R. McCormick of *The Chicago Tribune* had bestowed the name "Chicagoland." A crucial factor affecting our choice of this city was its Congressional representative, Rufus Stubborn. Congressman Stubborn was, and still is, a highly influential and highly conservative Republican congressman. He has been an implacable foe of every foreign-trade act of recent years. He proudly boasts that he has cast a vote for protection on every opportunity since entering Congress. One of his constituents described him as the only man who managed to remain consistently to the right of *The Chicago Tribune.* Another man referred to him critically as "a fossil. . . . He doesn't even believe in the typewriter." But nobody questioned his integrity. It was generally conceded in and out of his district that he voted as staunchly on principle as any member of Congress. In selecting Midwest for study, we assumed that we would find it to have little direct interest in foreign trade, which proved to be correct, and that its businessmen would reflect the isolationism so usually attributed to Chicagoland and stand firmly behind the protectionism of Representative Stubborn, which proved to be largely incorrect.

Midwest had little active interest in foreign trade. The secretary of the Chamber of Commerce was aware of no local discussion of foreign trade or foreign-trade policy. A few months previously, he had distributed to his membership the liberal-trade declaration of the Detroit Board of Commerce, but he had received no response. Like several other respondents in the community, he said: "If you find out anything about how people around here feel about it, would you come back and tell me?" The president of the largest bank in town gave us the same picture of Midwest business and was equally curious about the opinions of his fellow-businessmen.

The lack of concern of Midwest businessmen over foreign trade results largely from their preoccupation with the Midwestern market. Not only do they sell their products there, but often the distance from the coasts protects them from imports which must pay the additional cost of transportation to the Midwest. Said an executive of a company manufacturing industrial chemicals: "Well, we sell all our stuff here in the Midwest, and maybe some of these industrial chemicals are being imported and sold on the coast, but they never come in this far." Most of the business in Midwest had grown up in response to demand in the regional market. Most of the manufacturers in the city did not think beyond the Mississippi Valley when contemplating their prospects, and the needs which they were serving were often sufficiently specific to discourage competition from Eastern or foreign firms.

There were exceptions, of course, but these had surprisingly little effect on the community, and they produced almost no communications, either on the local or the national level. Many people in town expected that the head of the major remaining firm making the household product mentioned above would be concerned over foreign imports. They knew of his industry's plight, though they had not heard directly from him. When interviewed, he was indeed pessimistic about his business and did blame imports. But the imported product actually cost more than twice as much as his own. Recognizing that even a price advantage was not going to save him, he was reconciled to his fate. "People," he said, "seem to go for these fancy foreign designs nowadays and that word 'imported' fascinates them." In the past, his trade association had sought protection and failed; he felt that it was useless to try again. He had not approached his congressman: "I like Stubborn, and he is a good congressman, but he cannot do anything against the avalanche of free traders."

Two of the largest businesses in town, each having over 1,000 employees, were branches of national organizations which were very much involved in the fight over foreign-trade policy. Neither of the heads of the local branches had received instructions from the home office to take any action on the local level. As a matter of fact, they did not know that their national organizations had taken a stand on the issue. Fortunately for company policy, both men favored a liberal-trade policy, the same stand as their national organizations.

Locally, the only active interest in liberalizing trade policy came from the American Farm Bureau Federation and the farm-equipment manufacturers. The local leader of the Farm Bureau explained that he made a practice of indoctrinating the farmers in the policy of the national organization. "Actually, the farmers around here wouldn't be interested if we hadn't created the interest," he said.

The Midstate Barrow and Plow Company needed no outside stimulation. Their exports had dropped off, and their domestic sales were slumping because of the difficulties the local farmers were experiencing. The officials of Midstate had already been in touch with one of the state's senators, who was sympathetic to their position. But neither the farmers nor Midstate Barrow and Plow had spoken with Representative Stubborn on this subject. They knew his stand and felt that he could not be moved from his position. Stubborn, on his part, was not aware of Midstate's interest in 1953. When he was interviewed in the fall of that year, he reported that a representative of Midstate had risen to ask him a question about foreign trade at a public meeting on the preceding evening. Representative Stubborn interpreted this as an interest in protection. He commented: "They must be getting hurt by imports." But by 1955, when interviewed again, he had learned that the officials of Midstate were in favor of a liberal-trade policy. "But they haven't talked to me. They know where I stand."

The farmers' interest in the export market continued to increase during the period from 1953 to 1955. In the spring of 1955, we covered a meeting of the local Farm Bureau with Congressman Stubborn at which a whole series of issues was raised, yet the topic of foreign trade was still never mentioned. After the meeting, we asked the head of the Farm Bureau why he had not raised that issue. His answer was: "You know, we get along swell with Rufus on a whole bunch of issues and he helps us out. We know we cannot change his mind on foreign trade. He knows where we stand. So we just let him worry about it a little."

We had expected Midwestern isolationism to be reflected in the attitudes of Midwest's businessmen toward foreign-trade policy in much the same way as it was in Representative Stubborn's thinking, but we were wrong. Virtually nobody to whom we talked favored protection in principle. Almost everyone spontaneously referred to the region as the heartland of isolationism and speculated on what they regarded as the all-pervasive influence of *The Chicago Tribune*.[1] But, even though on most issues Colonel McCormick still stood firmly planted in the nineteenth century, the majority of businessmen of Midwest had moved into the second half of the twentieth. Even the head of the household-equipment firm said: "In the broad view, I understand that these countries have to get trade with us to exist, and I know that they need the trade to get funds to pay back their debts to us; but they can start erasing barriers somewhere else, just not in this industry." A local merchant, generally regarded as the most influential Republican in town, said:

> I'm a reprobate Republican. I've come to the position that, with the terrific interdependence of nations, what affects one must eventually affect all. We are the biggest and wealthiest nation in the West, and I think it is up to us to help out the poorer ones. . . . I say only two courses are open. . . . You invest money in ventures in their land, or you help Europeans trade in this country. . . . We must trade with them. We have no choice.

The secretary of the Midwest Merchants Association was several times identified as an extremely close personal friend of Rufus Stubborn and almost certain to reflect his point of view on foreign-trade policy. But, when interviewed, he gave us a classical lecture on the benefits of free trade. The most powerful union official in town took a point of view unusual for a representative of labor. After arguing for more liberal trade policies, he said: "Some industries would not like it, like watches and toys. . . . They have to suffer somewhat, but these are small industries, and we have to put up with this much suffering."

One could not say that Midwest was a hotbed of free-trade sentiment. Some men indicated that their support for lowering trade barriers was strongly influenced by their hope that this would make it possible for us to "stop pouring money into Europe," a semi-isolationist position which may well have derived from the editorial policy of *The Chicago Tribune*. Others, such as the president of the stationery manufacturing company, the largest locally owned business, approached the matter cautiously:

> I am in the middle of the road. I do not believe in the stone wall of the old days because we are too much of a world power. We cannot just sell and sell and never buy. But, on the other hand, . . . labor is going

---

[1] Actually, *The Chicago Tribune* favored the Reciprocal Trade Act because it promised to reduce the expenditure of public funds on foreign aid. An editorial writer with whom we talked was one of the few people we met who understood and accepted the literal meaning of the slogan, "trade, not aid."

to have to accept wage cuts before we get free trade, and they won't do that. After all, we cannot compete with expensive American labor against cheap European labor.

Although Midwest had little active interest in foreign trade, the majority of its leading citizens favored a liberal-trade policy. Congressman Stubborn was aware of both facts. "I think that 85 per cent of my voters are simply not interested, and of the remaining 15 per cent, I admit that probably the majority would want lowered trade barriers." He felt that they were mistaken. "This is true of the entire country and has been accomplished through government propaganda over the years. The average person has not thought the problem through, and, if he ever starts to, you will see a real change in thinking."

The only person interviewed who shared Representative Stubborn's principled belief in protection was the president of the Teamsters Union, the second most influential union leader in the area. "Lowering of tariffs," he said, "means that American workers will have to compete with lower wage brackets of foreign countries." He had not indicated to the congressman, however, what he felt on foreign-trade policy. Indeed, he took Stubborn to be a free trader! "He is against labor on everything else, so he must be opposed to us on this. . . . He never pays any attention to what we want, so why bother to talk to him?"

The most marked feature of the situation we observed in the city of Midwest was its lack of participation in the making of foreign-trade policy. To some extent, the behavior of businessmen in Midwest was like that of businessmen throughout the country. But their inactivity was compounded by the immovability of Representative Stubborn. As we have seen, people who were strongly opposed to Stubborn's protectionism did not bother to talk to him on the subject, even if they were on good terms with him. The head of the Farm Bureau deliberately avoided the topic of foreign trade while raising other issues. The head of Midstate, when asked if he believed it useful to approach legislators, replied: "Certainly. We contact them all the time. We really believe in the representation system, and we intend to let our position be known." The one leader in town who shared Stubborn's views on this issue had not approached him because on all other problems his union had found itself constantly opposed by Stubborn. People do not expend much energy on a hopeless cause once they perceive it as hopeless. Whatever effective communication took place was not addressed to Stubborn. Midstate contacted one of the senators. Two national corporations had not even informed their local representatives of their own stand, but their central headquarters were active on the national level. This phenomenon is not peculiar to Midwest. Large corporations seldom mobilize sentiment on the local level, where they have their branches. In any event, Representative Stubborn felt little pressure. When a congressman makes his position on an issue crystal-clear and makes it equally clear (as did Stubborn) that no amount of pressure will budge him from his position, the flow of communications from the opposing side dries up.

Another general point that Midwest illustrates is the effect of diversification and general economic health on attitudes toward an industry which seems to be suffering from foreign competition. The household-equipment industry had been one of the mainstays of Midwest's economy before World War II, yet its difficulties in the years 1953-1955 caused scarcely a flurry in the community. Any slack in employment in this industry was being taken up by others, and there was little disposition for the community as a whole to rally behind the household-equipment industry and demand protection for it.[2]

☐ Appalachian City

We chose to study Appalachian City because it was the kind of city in which opposition to imports flourishes. The heart and soul of the hostility to trade liberalization was to be found in the Eastern mountain regions. Coal, handblown glass, pottery, textiles, toy marbles, clothespins, and a number of other industries in these regions all suffered from foreign competition. The area as a whole had been plagued by unemployment. Its plants were old. It had benefited little from the war and postwar booms. Even during World War II it had a labor surplus. Of its working-force population, we would judge that well over 60 per cent have at some time since 1948 suffered a considerable period of idleness. Of those employed in 1953-1955, a sizable proportion worked in communities far from home, and others, especially in the mines, were engaged in marginal labor. There was the constant fear that the biggest plant in town would close down altogether, with as little notice as it had given in laying off about 10,000 workers seven years previously.

The region was Republican in heritage. Despite the New Deal, many of its unions were still Republican, because the mountains had historically been the strongholds of antagonism toward seacoast slave-holders and merchants.

---

[2] This was in marked contrast to the situation in Elgin, Illinois, approximately 100 miles away from Midwest. The Elgin Watch Company was the main industry in that town, and its troubles because of Swiss imports were known not only in Elgin but throughout Chicagoland. Even in Midwest, when an interviewer asked if anyone in the area were being injured by foreign imports, the answer was more likely to be "Elgin Watch" than "household equipment." Because the Elgin Watch protest had attracted community support, it came to symbolize the threat of foreign imports to the entire region, just as did that of the Waltham Watch Company in New England.

Congressmen as different as Wayne Hays (D., Ohio), Thomas Jenkins (R., Ohio), Cleveland Bailey (D., W.Va.), John P. Saylor (R., Pa.), and William C. Wampler (R., Va.)—all from the Appalachian Mountain region—had spoken strongly, urgently, and passionately for protectionism on the ground that they were representing the needs and desires of their people and their districts. Indeed, if it were not for these mountain men, the protectionist movement in Congress would have been a shadow of itself, not so much because it would have lost votes as because it would have lost men with convictions. The New Englanders or Southern textile congressmen who opposed the administration on reciprocal trade lacked altogether what these mountain men felt—the conviction of right-eousness.

We therefore expected to find some protectionist support in Appalachian City. It is coal country, and its coal industry was dying. The most aggressive of the local mine operators told us: "In 1947 two or three car-loads of coal a day would go down from here to Metropolis. Now, all twenty of us operators together are lucky if we send down a carload a month." Appalachian City was once a center for beautiful handblown glass. There were still 100 or so workers in the industry, mostly on a three-day week. The big cities now get their handblown glass from Middle Europe. The city had two small instrument plants. They were among the few growing industries in town, and their only serious competitors were Swiss and German. The Big Chemical Company believed itself threatened by Japanese and perhaps German competition. It had a plant at Southern City in another state, and there its management and workers waited on the congressman to express their opposition to the extension of the Reciprocal Trade Act. In Appalachian City, they did nothing. Coal-carrying railroads were one of the two or three largest industries in town; as the demand for coal had gone down, not only in the country but in the entire region, their workers suffered repeated layoffs, mostly due to dieselization, but partly also to Venezuelan oil imports.

Yet nobody made any complaint about foreign imports or asked for protection. With the exception of three or four dozen letters sent the congressman in 1955 (he received somewhat more in 1953 on the Simpson bill for fuel-oil quotas), nobody had done anything for protection. One organization did pass a resolution against the Reciprocal Trade Act, but three months later both of the officers had forgotten about it. (Their stenographer remembered.) The local newspapers thought the final adoption by Congress of the Senate amendments worth two brief paragraphs on the front page of the afternoon edition. The Pittsburgh papers, not far away, devoted about two and a half times as much space to the story. Not even the local United Mine Workers officials gave the impression of having paid any serious, systematic attention to the issue.

Appalachian City's Own Problem

There were many reasons for this lack of concern, but one stands out above all others: Appalachian City had its own very serious problem. Leading business and trade-union interests in the community were convinced that the city had to get a new industrial base. So intense was the focus on this that it shut out attention to such problems as that of the tariff.

The tariff issue may easily be crowded out by other matters unless there is a predisposition to pay attention to it. Channels of communication get overloaded. The typewriter and the mimeograph machine make it much more difficult for a national organization to focus the attention of its locals on a few clear purposes than was formerly the case. National, state, and regional headquarters can and in most instances do send out reams of communications to their local chapters. One important business interest organization sent its local chapters sixty-eight separate missives on different topics in one month. Consequently, much of the information that comes from national headquarters is simply disregarded or forgotten by local chapters. Sometimes it is not even read; the organizations in Appalachian City which had received communications from headquarters on the Randall report or the Neely amendment were simply unaware of these measures.[3]

Even when communications were read, action was seldom taken. For example, a protectionist union sent its large and powerful Appalachian City local a letter about its position on reciprocal trade. When one of us talked with the unusually competent and orderly business agent of this local a few months later, we asked him whether he had heard from anybody about the international trade-tariff issue.

"No. . . . Well, actually, you know, all I know about it is what I get from headquarters. Now where is the stuff?" A four-minute search failed to locate it. "I can find everything they have sent me but that; but they did send it to me and the Executive Board has never mentioned it." Later he said: "Now, we [the local] worked real hard on this minimum-wage matter; sent delegations to Washington three times on that. We've done a lot on that." Minimum wages were for this local one of the issues which crowded out the tariff. The same business agent explained why, in the community as a whole, nobody paid any attention to international trade or protection. "Of course it is not surprising we should not hear anything about it [tariff] around here," he said. "We have our own problems

---

[3] One of the reasons for the tremendous use of the long-distance telephone by many national organizations lies in this flood of communications. Since they ask for so much in writing, the easiest way to impress upon local branches which ones are to be stressed is by telephoning about them. Consequently, any association that wants to cut its long-distance telephone bill might well begin by cutting its postage bill.

in Appalachian City." The theme was repeated in interview after interview. "We have our own problem . . . we aren't much interested in this tariff business."

This theme was not only repeated, it was demonstrated. The people we interviewed and taxicab drivers and waiters all would start talking about the search for new industry. The latest rumors were reported with all the concern and involvement of a group of Asian students discussing colonialism. Anyone coming to Appalachian City, they felt, wanted to hear about industrial development. That was the urgent and pressing business. In fact, almost everyone in business and industry in Appalachian City either was or had been actually engaged in the formation of the redevelopment program; it was a community movement.

And "our problem" was not seen as related to protection. In New England areas, like New Anglia, where there was also unemployment, Congressman Second could and did say that unemployment was his first problem, the tariff his second, "but they are really the same."

Congressman First, from another New England area with an almost identical economic situation, regarded the tariff as tenth or fifteenth among his problems. Congressman First was more concerned with government contracts and equalization of labor legislation so that New England would not be at a disadvantage compared with other parts of the country. The difference in views as to the importance of the tariff between Mr. First and Mr. Second related to what they linked to the common problem of unemployment—did they see the tariff or something else as an effective attack on the problem?

The same factor explains Appalachian City's indifference to tariff matters. Since it had in the redevelopment program an alternative focus of attention for its economic worries, concentration on the threat of foreign imports served no psychological need. For much the same reason, protectionists were right in regarding the Kennedy retraining and reconversion provision in the Trade Expansion Act as dangerous to them. They promised to focus the concern of injured industries on matters other than tariffs and quotas.

The Potential for Protectionism

If, earlier in the period of adaptation to unemployment, foreign imports had been singled out by any leading local organ of opinion as an explanation of the difficulty, Appalachian City might have been quite amenable to the thesis. But the handblown-glass business had been declining gradually from year to year, without any sudden shock. The local mine operators were thoroughly agreed that their troubles were due to John L. Lewis and the depletion of the best coal. Before Venezuelan fuel oil began to come in, most of them had already cut their employment. If, when they laid off 10,000 workers seven years ago, the owners of the Big Chemical plant had said, "It is those foreign imports," people might have believed them. But, as it was, anyone who cared to inquire learned that this particular plant was the most expensive of the dozen or so the company owned. If some prominent local figure in 1948-1949 or even in 1954 had beaten the drums for protection, it might have made a difference. But no one did. And, as a result, conditions which ordinarily lead to protectionism led in Appalachian City to redevelopment. Redevelopment kept the citizens too busy to concern themselves with protection.

□ Textiletown, New Hampshire

Textiletown, like Appalachian City, was selected for study because it had earned the reputation of a "distress area," with much of the distress being attributed to foreign competition. This reputation had been generated a few years previously when Textiletown attracted national attention by its appeals for federal help. Textiletown was created and for a long time dominated by the woolen-worsted industry. The last of the textile booms was during World War II. In 1946, the industry employed 28,000 people in Textiletown, but, at the time of our interviews, late in 1953, most of the mills had moved South, and textile employment ran to only 6,000 or 7,000 persons. Furthermore, at least half this employment was threatened by the prospect of some of the remaining mills closing.

In Textiletown, too, the principal community goal was the creation of more jobs. It was claimed that eighty-one new companies had come to Textiletown, creating 8,000 jobs. The largest of these took over an old plant in a neighboring town, employed 1,000 persons, and broke ground for a plant in another adjacent town, which would employ 3,500. The smaller enterprises included paper, knitting, machinery, rubber goods, shoes, and plastics. Unemployment in the Textiletown area was still estimated in 1958 at 9,200 out of a total work force of about 54,000, or slightly less than 16 per cent.

This is a sizable figure, but, oddly enough, little hardship showed through. Bank deposits and the number of depositors were up. Retail merchants continued to show annual gains in volume of business. These facts were much discussed among more thoughtful business people in the town. Labor union officials said there had been more migration than the authorities either knew or acknowledged and that many workers were commuting longer distances to other jobs.

Interviews about the plight of the woolen-worsted industry in Textiletown were scarcely ever sentimental, loyal, or nostalgic. More often the remarks were vindictive, angry, or disgusted. The atmosphere was a little like that which attends the passing of a tyrant—some relief and sense of liberation, but also feelings of being cut adrift and of being ineffectual in the face of new responsibilities. There were few eulogies. The mills, one was told, never really interested themselves in the community. The local banker said that they never even banked in the city. When things got rough, said a local prominent citizen, the first thing they did was to cut down their contributions to such local causes as the Community Chest. Retail merchants were generally glad to have more than one kind of payroll around. Labor people said that one could still invite trouble by mentioning the name of a certain woolen-company executive in any local bistro. In general, the mill executives we spoke to returned these compliments in kind. Textiletown labor, they asserted, had cut its own throat, and Textiletown people could not understand the problem.

Businessmen's attitudes about the textile industry fell for the most part into three groups: (1) hope that the industry would survive in Textiletown as part of a more diversified economy; (2) no hope for survival, with some regrets; and (3) no hope for survival, with no regrets.

The tariff problem was a minor difficulty among Textiletown's current troubles. It rarely came up in discussions of local business affairs. In almost every case, inquiry brought the issue forward in the interviewees' minds for the first time in months or even years. The local newspaper's editorial writer could not recall when he had last written on the subject. It was a matter of interest to note that, a few days after our conversation, he came out with a full-column editorial reaffirming a strong protectionist position in tariff matters. This was, of course, the traditional Textiletown position on the tariff, which was reaffirmed in general whenever occasion arose.[4]

The traditional attitude arose from the historic position of the woolen-worsted industry. It was shared by other local interests in shoes, leather and rubber goods, and fisheries. In Textiletown itself, however, the intensity of feeling and readiness to act in the matter had been materially reduced by the decline of consumption and in the size and importance of the woolen-worsted industry. Thus, the local Chamber of Commerce, which up to five years before was largely dominated by the textile interests and which took relatively strong action on the matter when the Reciprocal Trade Act was up for renewal (a public advertisement campaign, letters to Congress), was now hardly interested in the question. It felt no strong pressure from its broadened constituency and was now generally inclined

---

[4] It was contradicted only when local interest required it, as in the spring of 1953, when local industry and business joined in strong representations on the matter of residual oil, taking, like the businessmen of New Anglia, an antiprotectionist stand on that one issue.

to pay much less attention to the interests of the woolen-worsted companies.[5] In fact, we were told, "the Chamber is now taking no stand on the tariff question. There are too many different interests . . . for us to be able to do this now." A Chamber official was frank in explaining the Chamber's new position:

> We have to all intents and purposes written off the woolen-worsted industry. It is going or gone and we don't really care any more. Hence this whole matter [tariffs] does not seriously concern us and will not, unless we discover that some of our new constituents have strong feelings on the subject.

The editor of the local newspaper, *The Times and News,* reflected a similar decline in interest and response to textile stimuli. News affecting the industry was culled from trade papers by a reporter whose regular assignment was City Hall and who did this as a side assignment. One such item, picked out of a Boston paper, reported a speech by the secretary of the National Association of Wool Manufacturers on the tariff issue. The item as published by the *News* ran only a few paragraphs. The next day, the local contact man for Atlantic Mills sent over the full text with a strong letter requesting that more space be given the remarks. The paper did not comply.

Although interest in the question was low at the time, there was no indication of a serious shift away from traditional attitudes, which remained protectionist. Of the persons interviewed, only three indicated free-trade or freer-trade views. All others expressed protectionist views of varying intensity, but none was planning any action in relation to them. Even the woolen-worsted spokesmen indicated that they did not expect much local action, but thought the national association would conduct the campaign adequately.

The latent attitude of the district was well represented by its congressman, who said he had always voted protectionist in deference to the needs of his constituents (textiles, shoes, tanneries, and fisheries). Although he felt that trade must be increased in the national interest, he said that his primary responsibility was to represent his constituency. He had opposed the imposition of quotas on residual fuel oil at the time of the Simpson bill. He could be relied on to go along with the interests of his district as he saw them and as the trade associations reported them to him.

The major lesson to be learned from Textiletown was that community support for protectionism was closely tied to the general economic health of the community. In its period of acute distress, when unemployment was high, the town was mainly dependent on the woolen-worsted

---

[5] In the last few years, the Chamber lost $5,000 in annual income through liquidation of textile mills.

industry. As unemployment decreased, through re-employment and migration, and as the town's business diversified, protectionism became a low-key issue in Textiletown. Despite the fact that it was still the predominant sentiment of the business community, it was doubtful that it would become active. There was no sting of urgency.

☐ The Fifty-third Congressional Distict

We began with the expectation that we would find people with economic interest in protection or reciprocal trade taking political action on the matter. We thought that this would be especially true in districts where the congressmen were undecided or were of great importance, owing to their committee assignments.

We therefore conducted interviews in Delaware, where both senators were on the Finance Committee, which handles tariff legislation, and where DuPont was allegedly protectionist. We thought that these senators would be under pressure.

We also conducted interviews in Textiletown, a woolen-worsted center, where the congressman in a public speech had expressed his doubts about what to do. We chose Midwest, where the dominant interests were presumably in the direction of reciprocal trade, but the congressman was a hard-shell protectionist of considerable influence. Then we chose Detroit, supposedly the center of reciprocal-trade sentiment, which had a member on Ways and Means. For similar reasons, we selected Appalachian City and New Anglia.

Then, we thought, we would study some towns where there was no particular reason to pay attention to the reciprocal-trade issue, where there were no dominant interests clearly related to it, where the congressman was not particularly influential and was on a committee which dealt with other matters, and where the senators' position was not likely to be affected by what they heard from the area.

We chose three market areas (Able and Baker counties and the city of New Zanzuel) in the Fifty-third, a long district extending down from the fruit-growing foothills of the Appalachians to the coastal plain, a district with no apparent reason for interest in foreign-trade legislation. Actually, our discoveries about the low visibility of and slight attention to the issue in such places as New Anglia, Detroit, and Midwest made our study here less important, since it simply confirmed our general findings. However, interviews in this district gave us clues as to why some manufacturers who might export are in fact not much interested in developing foreign trade.

The only people who ever think of the Fifty-third as a unit are the politicians. There is little exchange of information between different sections of the district. The communities differ widely and have little reason to consider each other.

Able County: A Suburb

Thirty years ago, Able County was predominantly a dairy and truck-garden area, dependent on the big city of New Paris, but with its own vitality. Increasingly over the years and rapidly since World War II, the hamlets have been blotted out as independent entities. By the time of our study, Able had become a middle-class suburb of New Paris. The predominance in New Paris of insurance companies, scientific research organizations, universities, and hospitals meant that Able's population was highly educated. But because they work in New Paris, the politics of the rest of the district meant less than nothing to them. A poll in Able indicated that many college graduates registered in one of the political parties did not know the name of the Congressional candidate for whom they voted.

Baker County: Dairying

North of Able is Baker, and Baker is above everything else dependent for its prosperity on the dairying industry. Milk market regulations and prices were of great importance, and a fair number of the people in the county apparently recognized the political issues involved in protecting New Paris milk markets against Indiana milk. However, none of those with dairying interests with whom we talked had heard anything about the great campaign of the national dairy associations for excluding foreign dairy products.

New Zanzuel: Could Reciprocal Trade Become as Vital as FEPC?

In the hills above Baker lies New Zanzuel, where one big union organized not only the tank plant but six other plants in town. The local union officials knew of and approved of the CIO stand in favor of reciprocal trade. But, so far as they knew, it did not matter one way or the other to the tank plant or the other industries in town.

The union officials also knew of the CIO stand on FEPC and the elimination of racial discrimination, and, although race relations were not a particularly sore or embarrassing subject in town, they pushed FEPC very strongly indeed. This seems to be a good example of personal choice on the part of a few people determining the focus of interest of a good many. Each union member contributed one cent a month to the union

FEPC committee, which thereby acquired an operating budget on which to build a program.

So far as we were able to find out, no industry in New Zanzuel had raised a finger recently for or against reciprocal trade.[6] A manufacturer of insecticides said: "Yes, sir, we are in constant touch with the State Department, the Pan-American Union, the World Health Organization. . . . No, we never heard any discussion of tariff matters." And it was indeed obvious that its able and alert officers had never heard of the Randall Commission or proposals for changing reciprocal-trade legislation. "We are very much interested in taxing cooperatives."

"It Is Just Too Much Bother to Try to Export"

One assumption sometimes heard in discussion of the politics of international trade is this: businessmen who could increase profits by increasing their export market will be eager to do so and will push for freer trade. This may sometimes be true, but apparently it is often just too much bother for many manufacturers to export, except to Canada.

The three manufacturers in Baker who were engaged in export reported their problems as: (1) dependable translators; (2) currency convertibility; and (3) finding out about rates of exchange, letters of credit, and the like. Tariffs were not among the reasons given by manufacturers who did not attempt to build an export trade. One reason given was the load of nonroutine work involved in exporting, which, since it is not routine, may fall on the higher levels of management as a personal responsibility. A medium-sized manufacturer of household goods told us: "It just would not be worth our while to export; cost of handling does not pay. We had a representative in Central America, but the terrific amount of detail did not pay."

To get dependable translators or advice on marketing abroad, letters of credit, and the like, they would have to send to New Paris. Indeed, even in such a large city as Kansas City, a manufacturer we knew was more irritated than pleased at a Venezuelan inquiry. He did not know anybody locally who could precisely translate the technical terms in the Venezuelan inquiry, and it took him a good many hours to locate such a translator.

Thus, although there were several firms in Baker and New Zanzuel which could export profitably, it was unlikely that any of them would do so. Since those which could profit most by exporting were doing well

---

[6] A physician had complained to one of the senators about the high duties imposed on surgical instruments, a nearly unique example, in our reading of Congressional mail, of a consumer or small-businessman objecting to tariffs.

enough without it, they were not very likely to bother. Ten per cent additional effort or ingenuity put into increasing their American market would probably yield as good or better results—with fewer headaches. So the congressman from this district was not likely to hear from potential exporters: "Let's do something about making foreign trade easier." And, indeed, he did not.

The Fifty-third District had little reason to become involved in the trade debate. Few of its industries were either threatened by imports or tempted by export markets. But, even if they had been, it is doubtful that the Fifty-third as a whole could have been organized for any common goal; it was too inchoate.

Chapter 20

Lessons of the Community Studies

It is always an open question what one learns from case studies. The communities we studied were not a representative sample of anything. Furthermore, our approaches to them were by no means standardized. From each community we tried to learn what it, distinctively, had to teach us. Basically, these community studies must be viewed as sources of ideas and insight which must be checked against other information and against one's own intuition and experience. A number of propositions which seem to have some generality emerge.

We have suggested two contrasting models of how communications on foreign-trade policy might occur, one "horizontal," the other "vertical." Horizontal communications were those organized on a community basis. Our impression is that such communications, cutting across industry and interest lines, are conspicuously rare.

Most communications bypassed the local community, either by being sent directly to Congress or by originating within industries and being channeled into the national scene by trade organizations. Neither the local community at large nor the local business community was structured to favor community-wide communications on foreign-trade policy.

Only in Detroit did horizontal communications appear to be significant. We would probably have found such horizontal communication in Textiletown, had we studied it a few years earlier, but not at the time of our interviews.

Having observed the reciprocal-trade controversy in areas other than the ones where we made our eight community studies, we are aware of a scattering of communities across the country which were successfully organized on this issue. They were generally organized, if at all, to favor protection. Pittsburgh Plate Glass, for example, succeeded in getting its neighbors to communicate with Congress on its behalf. But such actions are exceptional. The League of Women Voters stimulated a good deal of discussion within its ranks in many local areas, but, to the best of our knowledge, in no instance was the League successful in organizing the community over-all. Nor was the League accepted as the voice of the community.

If there is an agency which is regarded as the legitimate voice of the community on economic matters, it is probably the local Chamber of Commerce. But in very few of the areas with which we were acquainted did the Chamber become such a voice. Secretaries of Chambers of Commerce tended generally to favor the Reciprocal Trade Act, but such men virtually never take the initiative in stirring up and organizing local sentiment. They have too many other things to do. Besides, if they did so, the chances are that even a single industry with a protectionist position would be able to exercise an effective veto. On the other hand, where there has been an appreciable amount of local protectionist sentiment, local Chambers have often taken such a position.

Detroit looms as an obvious exception to what has been said. The Detroit Board of Commerce actually did take a good deal of initiative. And, as we have pointed out, protectionist voices on the Detroit scene were rather effectively quieted. Protectionists were forced to resort to vertical communications. Businessmen with protectionist positions either communicated directly to Congress or worked through their trade associations on the national level.

There is reason to doubt the efficacy of community organization on national policy issues. It is fair to say that the Detroit business community came as close to taking an official position as did any other. Yet, the volume of protectionist communications to Congress was at least as great as the volume of liberal-trade communications, and we have no way of knowing to what extent the congressmen and senators from Michigan were impressed by the fact that the Detroit community had to some extent gone on record as favoring a liberal-trade policy. When we looked at Detroit from the vantage point of Congress, it did not appear very different from any other city.

It is interesting to note, however, how often a community is perceived as organized and united when our studies showed that this was not so. New Anglia is perhaps the most striking example. Within a few years it was seen by its Congressional representatives as militantly organized against the protectionist Simpson bill and then as strongly protectionist. Yet, our investigation showed that only a few men were actively involved in the opposition to the Simpson bill and that some of them had entirely forgotten about the issue within a year. Similarly, of the variety of business interests in New Anglia, probably only the textile ones were in any significant way actively protectionist.

The congressman from Textiletown assumed that his district, as a whole, was in favor of and need of protection. He seemed to be right on the first point and wrong on the second. He overlooked the new industries which had moved into the district.

To the practitioner of politics it may be distressing and to the academic student of political affairs intriguing that such firm conclusions were based on such slim evidence. Throughout our study, we found men confusing the part with the whole. We shall develop this thesis at greater length in our discussion of Congress, but here it is sufficient to point out that a relatively few voices, well exercised, sometimes created the impression of unified community sentiment and that this happened on both sides of the issue. Public spokesmen, be they congressmen or others, have a sharp ear, attuned to complaints that foreshadow discontent. They react, not to actual opinion, but to their image of what opinion could become if not forestalled by action on their part. And often they are right. The very lack of concern for small grievances might well crystallize a genuinely hostile community sentiment. But, whether foresightedly or foolishly, the fact remains that men often feel the pressures of supposed public opinion when there are only a few stray voices.

Much "communication" was actually inference. We found many businessmen and congressmen who assumed that they knew what another person's stand on foreign-trade policy was because they knew a few objective facts about him—his party affiliation, the business he was in, his association in other matters, and the like. As an illustration, we may recall the protectionist union leader in Midwest who assumed that Rep. Rufus Stubborn must be in favor of a liberal-trade policy because on all other issues he was opposed to the union leader. Or there is Mr. White in New Anglia, who was thought to be a protectionist because competing foreign machines were being imported.

Much of the inference which takes place actually inhibits the flow of communications. Speculation occurs when communications are inadequate. We have cited a number of instances in which one man did not talk to another because he assumed that the other man disagreed with him.

Or, even if they did talk, as in the case of the Detroit businessman who visited a liberal Democratic member of the Michigan Congressional delegation, both parties misunderstood the situation because ambiguous behavior was interpreted in terms of prior expectations. Such failures of communication between the business community and Congress were common in large metropolitan areas where the congressman was likely to be a Democrat and assumed by businessmen to be *ipso facto* antibusiness.

In general, the community studies reinforced the conclusion suggested by our survey of businessmen and our study of Congress—that men tend to communicate with those they think not opposed to their position. Rather than concentrate on changing the opinions of antagonists, they try to convince the neutral or activate the already-convinced.

In the absence of better information, congressmen often had no choice but to assume that whatever significant communications were directed to them were indicative of the interests of their constituency as a whole. Congressmen may be skeptical of the mail they get, but act on it nevertheless. It is often the only clue they have as to what constituents think; and, even if the letters are recognized as not being representative of all the voters, they still represent the views of those who care enough to write. Only when congressmen received conflicting communications in substantial volume or impressive character did they feel constrained to explore seriously the nature of their constituency's interest; and then the questioning usually concentrated only on those groups which were already communicating with Congress. Seldom did the congressman ask how these interests fit in with the community as a whole.

In our studies both of the community and of Congress we were impressed with the latitude which congressmen have in representing their districts. A congressman must respond in what appears to be a serious and constructive way to the problems of his constituents, but he is free to be leader instead of led in deciding what response is appropriate to the problem. He must be attentive to the views of his petitioners, but attention is not agreement, and only a recurrent pattern of disagreement alienates them. A congressman like Rufus Stubborn could hold a position on foreign-trade policy which he accurately diagnosed as opposed to that of the small proportion of his constituency which had attitudes of any intensity. He could do this because there was not much opposition sentiment and because he was tied to his constituency on a variety of issues and pleased them on most. Furthermore, in other districts, such as the Fifty-third District, the congressman had opportunities to create an issue where none existed—a function of the congressman that is seldom recognized. He could have won support from an appreciable group of voters regardless of which side he took. The opponents would probably have remained uninterested and unorganized.

The practice of "corporate restraint" by large firms came as something of a surprise. To a great extent, we shared the common notion that bigness and potential power are unmixed blessings in controversy. But, even before we began our community studies, we ran into evidence that very large firms were reluctant to appear to be throwing their weight around too much. In the oil industry, for example, representatives of small oil interests told us that the giant companies went to great pains to appear not to be using their full power. Of course, the representatives of the small firms painted a picture of subtle *sub rosa* use of power by the large companies. But the appearance of virtue requires some part, at least, of the practice thereof. The representatives of large companies knew that there were severe limits to what they could do by way of maneuvering behind the scenes.

Just how much influence large companies exercise is impossible to state with precision. It is true that they lend personnel to the government. An economist from one of the larger oil companies did a major part of the drafting of the president's message in 1954. But, as we pointed out in the chapter on Delaware, this influence can work in both directions. The viewpoint of the government probably gets expressed in company councils by the men who have had a tour of duty in the government.

At this point, we should look at the community study data in the light of some of our survey findings. It will be remembered that, on our sample survey, the men from the larger firms were considerably more active in communicating with Congress. We do not think that the policy of corporate restraint extends so far that the heads of very large firms will not feel free to make their views known to congressmen. This is scarcely throwing one's weight around. Though it may be argued that a letter or telegram from the head of DuPont or General Motors constitutes more pressure than one from a small clothespin manufacturer, the right of petition is recognized for all citizens. Although the doctrine of corporate restraint does not prevent the head of a large firm from stating his case, it does inhibit him from using his full power against a congressman who does not agree with him. In addition, the small businessman is likely to evoke more sympathy from the congressman. His plight usually appears more acute. For example, we had close contact for several years with the legislative aide of a Western senator. Both wealthy oil interests and small sheep-growers in his state were petitioning him in opposition to a liberal-trade policy. He was at least as concerned with the plight of small sheep-growers, whom he perceived as the "real people," as he was with that of the wealthy oilmen, even though the latter furnished the backbone of his financial support in campaigning.

The curse of bigness is most significant where the company fears adverse public reaction, which may result in further governmental regulation or in prosecution. But this was not the primary factor which immobilized Wall Street banks. The banks were caught in cross-pressures from their clients. Similarly, Atlas and Hercules in Wilmington did not come out for a liberal-trade policy apparently partially because of pressures within the chemical industry. In our experience, these inhibitory cross-pressures almost always act to the benefit of the protectionists. Although contrary instances existed, most cases of the exercise of the veto we observed were ones in which a protectionist businessman complained because his banker or other business associate favored a liberal-trade policy. This is perhaps inherent in the nature of things, since in general it is more difficult for the man with a liberal-trade self-interest to demonstrate that he will suffer directly and immediately from a protectionist policy.

Our survey data already indicated that protectionists have a number of advantages in pushing their point of view. These advantages become clearer when we look at them in operation in the communities. Detroit and such port cities as San Francisco and New Orleans had been able to create the impression of being organized in favor of a more liberal trade policy. Granting this, we would nevertheless contend that it is easier to organize community sentiment for protection than against it.

Community discussions tend to center on injured industries. Among causes of injury, one of the most conspicuous and apparently remediable is foreign competition. True, it is often acknowledged that the difficulties have other causes also, but an easy therapy to prescribe is that of raising tariffs. However, in varying degrees Appalachian City, Textiletown, and New ,Anglia demonstrate that this is not the only way in which the problem can be viewed. Appalachian City, despite the fact that it was full of conditions which might have made it protectionist, did not see the problem as one of foreign competition, but rather of the need for general regional redevelopment. The men of Textiletown began by seeking protection. When they failed in those efforts and saw the textile industry substantially lost, they were forced to rephrase their problem as one of getting more and diversified new industries. New Anglia textile industries were also suffering from foreign competition, as well as from Southern competition and from obsolescence. One congressman from the area saw the problem as foreign competition, the other as a general need for economic development and aid. The problem of declining industries was not always viewed as one of foreign-trade policy.

Factors that decided whether an injured industry generated protectionist feelings in a community were the general economic health and diversification there. In Midwest, we found one industry that was injured virtually to the point of extinction, with imports being one of the identifiable causes. Yet, the economic life of the city as a whole was good, and there was virtually no chance for the surviving manufacturer in that industry to generate any public support for himself. This contrasted with the situation in Elgin, Illinois, not too many miles away, in which the Elgin Watch Company was the mainstay of employment. Actually, because the Elgin Watch Company had diversified, it was not doing badly in the 1950's despite Swiss competition. Yet, the mere possibility of damage to Elgin rallied the community to its support.

The timing and circumstance of injury can also considerably affect the community response. The coal and handblown-glass industries were strongly protectionist in general, but not in Appalachian City itself. The coal industry in the immediate vicinity of that city had already suffered its major setback before the importation of foreign fuel oil became sufficiently large for it to be regarded as the cause. And, in the case of handblown glass, the decline had been long and gradual, so that the impact of foreign imports was not sharp and dramatic. These conditions did not rule out the possibility of these industries turning to protectionism, but they made it less probable.

Finally, the community studies show that foreign-trade policy was only one among many issues with which American businessmen were concerned and that for most it was an item of relatively low priority. Our selection of communities was strongly biased toward those in which we expected to find active interest in the debate over the Reciprocal Trade Act. Our selection of men to interview was similarly motivated. Nevertheless, in every community that we studied, foreign-trade policy was less important than one or more other issues. For some individuals, it might have been vital, but it was never so for the community as a whole. This is, in part, why we found so little horizontal communication. The handful of men who were deeply concerned would have found it difficult to arouse a similar degree of interest among others. Accordingly, they turned directly to their congressman or senators and/or to their trade associations. On this final point, the Reciprocal Trade Act in 1953-1955 may have been a poor issue for which to expect community-wide activity. There are other issues on which local business, even if not the community as a whole, can feel common and urgent cause. The St. Lawrence Seaway and urban redevelopment are examples of such geographically defined matters. On such issues, we would expect to find a good deal of communication within the community; the business community might speak with a single voice, rather than in scattered voices heard more loudly in Washington than around the corner at home.

PART IV

The Pressure Groups

PART IV

Chapter 21

Dramatis Personae

□ Lobbying and Related Activities

Historically, the tariff has been a favorite concern of lobbies. Its story has more than once been written as a history of lobbying tricks, stratagems, and propaganda devices. The classic picture of a pack of wolves descending on Capitol Hill and buying, bullying, or cajoling congressmen is given in Schattschneider's excellent study.[1]

If one approached the history of the 1954-1955 debate with a naïve faith in classic democratic theory, expecting to find a group of statesmen on Capitol Hill who had been selected by their constituents for their superior wisdom and who were expected to deliberate seriously and freely about national interest, it would come as a shock to discover some of the things that occurred alongside such deliberations. It would be a shock to find a series of hired spokesmen for special interests enjoining congressmen to do favors for toy-marble-makers, bicycle manufacturers, cherry-growers, fishermen, importers, and others. It would come as an even

---

[1] E. E. Schattschneider, *Politics, Pressures, and the Tariff, op. cit.*

greater shock to discover that a significant number of congressmen might act on the basis of such representations. If our starting point were naïveté, we might describe this set of facts by saying that lobbies had a colossal influence.

But our starting point was not naïveté. We follow several generations of muckraking exposés and of the "group approach" to politics.[2] Our initial expectation was that, the facade once penetrated, we would find the decisive events in tariff legislation to be a series of deals worked out between subtle and richly financed interest groups and congressmen pressured by them. It thus came as a surprise to discover that the lobbies were on the whole poorly financed, ill-managed, out of contact with Congress, and at best only marginally effective in supporting tendencies and measures which already had behind them considerable Congressional impetus from other sources. We do not deny that there were large numbers of pressure groups. We are certain that, whatever the outcome, it would have been quite different if all the organized interest groups on one side had been silenced while all those on the other had remained vocal. However, it is in the nature of the democratic struggle that that does not happen. When we look at a typical lobby, we find that its opportunities for maneuver are sharply limited, its staff mediocre, and its major problem not the influencing of Congressional votes but the finding of clients and contributors to enable it to survive at all.

Lobbying also proved unimportant compared to other functions of pressure groups. Lobbying and pressure groups have become so identified with each other that it is often forgotten that pressure, or interest, groups also have other functions and programs.[3] In 1953-1955, their effect in buttonholing, cajoling, and persuading congressmen was far less than their effect in organizing and channeling communications. The predominant influence which a group like the Committee for a National Trade Policy had was as the recognized spokesman for the freer-trade point of view. Whether it functioned well or badly, aggressively or with restraint, it was the place to which a newsman would turn if he wished a statement from that side about a legislative event. It was the source to which a congressman would

---

[2] The academic proponents of the group approach to politics trace their origins to Arthur Bentley, *The Process of Government* (1908). Outstanding contemporary examples of this approach are David B. Truman, *The Governmental Process* (New York: Alfred Knopf, 1955), and Donald C. Blaisdell, *American Democracy under Pressure* (New York: Ronald Press, 1957). Also of interest is the monograph by Bernard C. Cohen, *The Influence of Non-governmental Groups on Foreign Policy-making* (Boston: World Peace Foundation, 1959). The conclusions of Blaisdell and Cohen correspond closely to many of our own.

[3] The federal Regulation of Lobbying Act of 1946 was unclear on the definition of lobbying. In 1954, the Supreme Court ruled that the act pertains only to direct efforts to influence legislation. Indirect efforts are not legally lobbying. For a discussion of this problem of definition, see Blaisdell, *op. cit.*, pp. 82 ff.

turn for facts he needed or to which his assistant would telephone to line up witnesses for a hearing. It was the place where a businessman would expect staff-type thinking to be done for him. The arguments it used would become the arguments all on that side would repeat. And, just as the CNTP in that way dominated and set the tone of much of the communications process for the side of freer trade, so the Nationwide Committee of Industry, Agriculture, and Labor on Import-Export Policy did for the side of protection, the National Coal Association for the coal industry, the Manufacturing Chemists Association for the chemical industry, and so on. These associations became nodes in the communications process. What they knew or failed to learn, what they heard or did not hear, what they said or failed to say, had a profound effect on what other people learned, heard, or said. These other people were not merely the general public, but, more importantly, their own members, the press, the administration, and congressmen.

Thus, although lobbying by any given pressure group was relatively limited in effectiveness, the presence of pressure associations astride the communications process was important indeed.

□ The Organizations

We shall not try to list all the interest groups that were active around the issue of Reciprocal Trade renewal [4] but merely to convey an impression of the types of organizations aligned on either side. They fall easily into four groups:

1. Special associations formed for the exclusive purpose of promoting or opposing protection.

2. Large, multipurpose associations, such as the Chamber of Commerce, National Association of Manufacturers, and League of Women Voters, all of which played some role in this, as in many other, legislative controversies.

3. Trade associations of manufacturers or dealers in particular products.

4. Law and public-relations firms which worked for any of the above types of groups or for individual firms.

In the 1950's, there were four important organizations designed especially to influence foreign-trade policy:

---

[4] The number of potential interest groups is very large. In 1949, the Department of Commerce estimated there were 4,000 trade, professional, civic, and other associations, to which could be added more than 200,000 local and branch chapters; cited by Truman, *op. cit.*, p. 58.

1. The American Tariff League,[5] founded in 1885 with headquarters in New York City. This venerable organization published attractive pamphlets and a newsletter, *Topics*. Its president for ten years was H. Wickliffe Rose, president of the Linen Thread Company. In 1956, he was succeeded by Carl H. Helfrich, vice-president of the Forstmann Woolen Company. The chairman of the League's executive committee was Fred G. Singer, a vice-president of DuPont. The full-time executive secretary of the League was Robert H. Anthony.

2. The Nation-wide Committee of Industry, Agriculture, and Labor on Import-Export Policy, with headquarters in Washington. This organization was formed in 1953 by O. R. Strackbein, who in 1950 had already formed the similar National Labor Management Council on Foreign Trade Policy. Strackbein was formerly an AFL organizer, then from 1924 to 1930 a trade commissioner with the Department of Commerce overseas. He also served as special expert on tariff matters for the U.S. Tariff Commission. The group he organized was supported by some labor unions, particularly the United Mine Workers, and such industries as wool, bicycles, glassware, and chemicals.

3. The Committee for a National Trade Policy, with headquarters in Washington, was organized in 1953 to mobilize support for renewal of the Reciprocal Trade Act and for a liberal-trade policy generally. The first chairman of the board was John S. Coleman, president of the Burroughs Corporation, Detroit. Other original officers were: William L. Batt, Sr., formerly of SKF, secretary, and Harry A. Bullis, chairman of the board, General Mills, vice-chairman. The full-time president was Charles Taft, brother of the late senator.

4. The Committee on Foreign Trade Education was formed in New York in 1954 by B. A. Rittersporn, Jr., a young public-relations man and the committee's executive director. This committee of young business and professional men and women, most of whom had originally been in the Young Republican clubs in 1952, operated in the publicity and public-education field on the low-tariff side. It alone, of the four organizations listed, had disappeared from the stage by 1962.

Of the large, multipurpose organizations which played a role in this debate, the most important were:

American Federation of Labor
Chamber of Commerce
Committee for Economic Development
Congress of Industrial Organizations
International Chamber of Commerce
League of Women Voters
National Association of Manufacturers

---

[5] In May, 1959, the American Tariff League changed its name to the Trade Relations Council.

In some general sense, all might be said to have favored a liberal-trade policy, but, as we shall see, the very nature of such organizations tended to make it difficult for them to take an effective stand.

The trade associations that interested themselves in this issue probably numbered in the hundreds. Among them by way of a sample we might list:

> American Dental Trades Association
> American Farm Bureau Federation
> American Glassware Association
> American Lace Manufacturers Association
> California Walnut Growers Association
> Cardboard Association
> Cordage Institute
> Hardwood Plywood Institute
> Hothouse Vegetable Growers
> Independent Petroleum Association of America
> International Brotherhood of Bookbinders
> Manufacturing Chemists Association
> Marble Industry of America [toy marbles]
> National Association of Button Manufacturers
> National Association of Cotton Manufacturers
> National Cheese Institute
> National Coal Association
> National Council of American Importers
> National Foreign Trade Council
> National Milk Producers Council
> Tuna Research Foundation
> Tungsten Institute
> United Mine Workers
> United Textile Workers of America
> Wyoming Wool Growers Association
> Etc.[6]

Some of these associations acted directly, as did some of the companies in them. But they also frequently hired a law firm or public-relations firm, often, but not always, in Washington. These agents, sometimes merely consultants and advisers, in other instances did most of the work. The law and public-relations firms engaged in Washington practice are many. By way of example, we might mention two that were important on each side in the 1950's.

> Pope, Ballard and Loos, a Washington law firm. Carl Loos since 1915 and later John B. Breckenridge, a member of the firm, represented such groups as the bicycle interests; the California Almond Growers Exchange; the Fig Institute; the National Creamery Associa-

---

[6] As an indication of what may occur under "Etc.," in the late spring of 1959 there was an appeal before the Tariff Commission filed by The Pacific Northwest Chewing and Creeping Red Fescue Association. The issue: imported grass seed.

tion; the American Butter Institute; the Dairy Industry Committee; stainless-steel flatware; the Pin, Clip, and Fastener Association; the American Fluorspar Producers; California Walnut Growers Association; North-West Nut Growers; and Sunkist Growers.

Selvage and Lee, a New York public-relations firm with Washington offices. Among its clients have been the Strackbein committee and some large manufacturers of a protectionist inclination.

Cleary, Gottlieb, Friendly, and Ball, a law firm. George Ball, who in the Kennedy administration became under secretary of state, was then its Washington partner. In line with Ball's personal convictions, the firm has had at various times a number of clients interested in freer trade. Among them have been the Venezuelan Chamber of Commerce, the Cuban sugar-planters, the Coal-Steel Community, the Common Market, the French government, and the French *patronat*.

Peabody and Associates, public-relations firm in New York City, representing major Philippine interests. One of the staff at the time of the study was Curtis J. Hoxter, formerly with the International Chamber of Commerce, who specialized in international trade relations. He was a volunteer aide to the White House staff on the foreign-trade issue.

This is a sample of the dramatis personae. Some were lobbying organizations; it is important to emphasize that not all were. It is important to remember this because the law has introduced a rather fine and perhaps unreal distinction between the lobbyist—the man or organization who attempts to influence legislation for a client—on the one hand and either the citizen petitioning in favor of his own views or the publicist who may work for a client via the media of public opinion, the press, and the like, on the other hand.

□ The Staff Men

Who were the men who conducted these institutions' work? The National Milk Producers Council, for example, campaigned for protection, but it was a professional staff man, not a parade of straw-hatted farmers, who appeared on Capitol Hill. Such a staff man was apt to be a lawyer or, as in this case, a journalist. Such a farm representative might be, and in this case actually was, from a farm background, but he was apt to be a man who had spent many years, in this case close to forty years, as a professional executive in Washington. There were not many such organizers of the battle. There are no reliable figures, but in all there were a few thousand key men working for the kinds of organizations listed above through whom the various interests spoke, a few score of whom concerned themselves principally with foreign-trade issues. Such men are gatekeepers in the communications process. From the businessmen whom they represent they learn, or at least think they learn, what those men want. But, having an ethos of their own, they perceive their clients' interests through their own spectacles. The wants of their members, thus translated, they in turn communicate to policy-makers, or at least they create circumstances for such communication by stimulating letters, promoting interviews, and the like. And, again, what they communicate is affected by their own needs and experiences.

In personality, the professional spokesmen represent the full range of American business and professional types. Examples can be found to contradict any generalization; yet patterns do emerge. We cannot do more than suggest the types of patterns, for we have not made a sample survey of Washington lobbyists. Dr. Lester Milbrath, while at the Brookings Institution, conducted just such a survey, with results confirming many of our own.[7] From our experience, we can suggest only what we learned in dealing with a very select group of lobbyists and public spokesmen—those who happened to be of major significance in the development of the particular controversy we were studying.

There were some differences between spokesmen on the opposing sides, differences which had at least some effect on what each side communicated. The stereotype of the egg-headed free trader and the hard-headed protectionist proved to have a germ of truth when we looked at the spokesmen. A list we drew up of the dozen key staff men on the side of freer trade consisted half of lawyers, as would anyone else's similar list. With few exceptions, they were from top law firms and from top schools. They were sophisticated men, with considerable intellectual stature. Charles Taft is an example. Scattered among the nonlawyers in anyone's list would be one or two economists, again of fairly considerable stature. There might also be a retired businessman or two. The remainder are apt to be people, usually young, who have made careers as political staff aides, for example, ex-Congressional assistants and organizers of public-information activities. Of these, the division between Republicans and Democrats turns out to be fairly even, but all must be rated as moderates in their own party. There are, it must be said, hardly any ex-professors eligible for such a list.

On the protectionist side, we also found lawyers, perhaps even in higher proportion at the top level. The rest are former newsmen, ex-congressmen, career publicists, public-relations men, and the like.

Though there is little major occupational distinction between the professionals on the two sides, there is a subtle difference that one cannot help but note. It stands out best, perhaps, when comparing the lawyers. The Ivy League is less prominent among the protectionists; so are the

---

[7] Lester W. Milbrath, *The Washington Lobbyists* (Chicago: Rand McNally & Co., 1963).

great and famous law firms. Most of the top freer-trade staff men come from metropolitan backgrounds; few of the protectionists do. On our own list of top staff men on each side, not one Southerner turns up on the low-tariff side, although the South is the home of free-trade feeling in America. Of the staff men on the protectionist side, nearly half are Southerners by origin. These and other facts suggest a difference in what might be vaguely called urbanity or cosmopolitanism, although it is certainly not a difference in intelligence. The top spokesmen of both sides are mostly able, intelligent men, but there is a subtle difference which, if we had the data, could presumably be indexed by a tabulation of the number of their acquaintances on the faculties of major private universities. For at least half of the top professionals on the low-tariff side, this type of contact would be a major item in their social life and career. The same is probably not true—except for one at most—of the top protectionist organizers. Given this difference in the social identifications of the key organizers on the two sides, the similarities are even more striking.

Tho role of trade-association executives is not highly regarded by American business. These staff aides share the reputation of men who have never met a payroll or who have tried and failed. A cliché is that, if they were any good, they would be in business for themselves instead of talking for business. Coupled with that sentiment is suspicion that the trade association has its own ax to grind, one which may be different from that of the business firm.

These attitudes are in part reciprocal. The association men have no undiluted admiration for the men they represent. Theirs is the attitude of the professional toward the amateur, the committed person toward the uncommitted. They complain of stupidity, lack of foresight, laziness, unwillingness to act, and lack of devotion to the cause. As one association executive told us,

> The people in the business frequently aren't worked up about this sort of issue. They regard things which we think of as very important as on the fringe. We'll start an activity—you have to beat 'em over the head to make 'em realize that they're supposed to do something about it—and yet you take a representative group of members and they'll all tell you, "Oh yes; it's very important, very vital"; and they'll vote to continue it.

Apathy is only one of the complaints that the association executive may have about his "bosses." The complaints run the full gamut of those made by anyone who works for others. One man, for instance, told us bitterly of an attempt to have him removed.

Perhaps most revealing was a discussion among trade-association executives at a conference of their own society, where the issues were:

> What would you do if:
>> a past president is running for political office and wants the trade-association secretary to distribute a speech of his?
>> a member comes into the trade-association office saying, "I didn't get the contract. Those God-damned bureaucrats," and wants to have his congressman make trouble for the bureaucrat with whom the trade-association executive has been working for years to build up a smooth relationship?
>> a prominent member comes to town, in effect trying to take over the headquarters for his own campaign for the Bricker amendment?

To all these problems, the practical answers of the assembled association executives were many. For example: distribute the political speech in plain envelopes; get the prominent member a good hotel room and an attractive public stenographer. The common thread in the answers was a prescription for how one should behave toward authorities with power over you, who, however, do not understand your business and whom you must manipulate if you are to do the job they demand of you.

This is the dilemma of the trade-association executive. He is convinced he knows his job better than do the men for whom he works. But, if he attempts to be a "statesman," as one executive of our acquaintance did, his efforts and his job are likely to be short-lived. His most successful role is not that of initiator of policy, but that of an arbitrator among conflicting forces in his organization and as a mouthpiece for the policies that result from this arbitration. He must also mediate between his organization or its members and his contacts, the men outside the organization on whom he relies when he wants to get something done. Though he may appear to the outsider to be a free-wheeling, high-pressure operator, his self-image is more often that of a man caught in a web of conflicting forces which keep him from doing a job nearly as effectively as he could—"if they would leave me alone."

Chapter 22

Quasiunanimity—
Premise of Action

In our study of Detroit, we noted that the liberal traders had captured the
Board of Commerce and had used it as an instrument for forwarding their
own policy despite the several articulate protectionists among its members.
This was a rather unusual situation. The usual pattern in American business and trade associations is one of unanimity, or, more accurately, quasiunanimity.[1]

Sometimes the minority preserves the façade of such unanimity if it
does not feel that it has too much at stake. It then keeps its peace and does
not obstruct. To quote one interview,

> His views are not the views of the association. . . . The association
> . . . has to be restrictive. . . . They have to look out for the interests of

---

[1] Truman, *op. cit.*, has an interesting discussion of the problem of group cohesion, pp.
156-187. Although both his and our discussion cover much of the same ground, unless
we read him incorrectly, he does not anticipate the second part of our argument, i.e.,
that unanimity (or cohesion) is maintained by the use of multiple group memberships
for purposes which might produce conflict within a single given group. Truman sees
multiple group memberships as a source of conflict, but does not emphasize that they
may also reduce conflict.

> all the different parts of the industry. . . . While he wasn't much con-
> cerned with tariffs and trade and can be detached, the association has
> to try to protect anyone they can get protection for.

Thus, there can be dissent when the minority is relatively indifferent. The
dissenters maintain the appearance of unanimity by self-restraint.

At other times, when the minority feels strongly on the issue, restraint is imposed on the majority. In this common situation, multipurpose
organizations duck the controversial issues. Here is a description by one
trade executive of conflicts of interests within his organization.

> It is necessary to distinguish different parts of the . . . industry.
> There are manufacturers of finished . . . products which are competi-
> tive with imports. There are manufacturers of finished . . . products
> which are noncompetitive with imports. There are manufacturers of
> unfinished parts which are competitive with imports, and there are
> manufacturers of unfinished parts which are noncompetitive with im-
> ports. The viewpoint of each would be different. . . .

That association took no stand at all on general tariff policy.

The problem becomes especially crucial in such catchall, multipurpose organizations as the Chamber of Commerce and the National Association of Manufacturers. Since such organizations are supposed to represent a wide range of interests in a wide range of businesses, special efforts
are taken to avoid generating any avoidable internal conflict. Cautious
procedures are employed for reaching a policy position, and spokesmen
are confined to stating that position without elaboration, for fear that even
the most cautious elaboration may produce dissension.

The pattern in the U.S. Chamber of Commerce is typical. The
Chamber has over 3,000 affiliated local chambers with more than 1,500,000
individual members. In most cases, policy statements are recommended by
one of the Chamber's specialized committees. They are reviewed by the
board of directors and then sent to a vote, either by referendum or at the
annual meeting. Each year the president of the Chamber for that year
appoints such committees as the Foreign Commerce Department Committee or the Committee on International Political and Social Problems. He
makes these appointments with the advice of the full-time managers of the
various departments of the Chamber, who thus exert a degree of influence
on the direction the committees may take. When a committee has formulated a policy statement, it is sent out for consideration at least six
weeks before the annual meeting. If consensus is reached at that meeting,
the policy statement is then published and ordinarily holds for three years,
although it can be changed at any time. The procedure is majority vote,
but there is a general understanding that no stand will be taken if opinion
is sharply divided.

Once a policy has been adopted, any person testifying for the Chamber is limited to it. One respondent told us that he would never testify for the Chamber of Commerce again because, once he said his piece as expressed in the official resolution, there was no more he could say. If asked other questions, he must simply reply, "The Chamber has no position on that." This leaves Chamber witnesses relatively impotent, but maintains the possibility of unity for an organization purporting to represent all American business.

In this weak form, the Chamber supported the administration's trade program both in the 1950's and 1962. In 1962, however, the Chamber faced the problem of what to do about an embattled minority. In January, the Chamber's Foreign Commerce Committee endorsed the Kennedy program by a large majority. In February, the board of directors did the same, on the grounds that they were interpreting the still-binding general resolutions of past conventions. Chamber representatives testified accordingly at the House hearings. Dispute arose, however, over the bill's readjustment provisions. The board resolution attached minor strings to its endorsement of such aids, but, when the fiftieth annual convention met in May, protectionist groups led a bitter attack on such federal subsidies to business and "back-door" federal control of state unemployment benefit systems. Even though the protectionist attack was not directly on the trade issue, it would have left the Chamber leadership in the position of having its testimony repudiated. An unusual two-hour floor battle ensued, in which the official resolution was first rejected; much later, when, the protectionists alleged, half the delegates had left, a motion to reconsider was passed and the directors upheld. Such things happen, but only rarely, and the tension generated makes clear why an association that wants to represent all business cannot often afford such controversial stands.

The NAM procedure is similarly based on committee work and board action. However, it seldom presents policy statements for a general vote by the members because it believes that only people with an active interest in a specific topic and who are informed on it should express an opinion. It, too, has an International Relations Committee. There are about 165 people on the committee, about half of them active, the rest joining to keep themselves informed on what is going on.

At the end of October, 1953, the NAM and its International Relations Committee went through a minor crisis. For some time, the NAM had been moving toward a more liberal trade policy. Strong influences were pushing it to adopt a statement supporting the President's program, as had the Chamber of Commerce and the Committee for Economic Development. NAM President Charles R. Sligh, Jr., had undergone a substantial conversion in views, attributed by his associates to his travels to Europe and contacts with European businessmen. During 1953, he had delivered speeches in which he had, for example, urged the United States to "work at a long-term tariff policy that will encourage the foreign producer to study his productivity problems, his merchandising and sales problems, and then compete intelligently in our markets over here." Some of the protectionist companies of the NAM had complained bitterly about these statements of personal views.

At the same time, the appropriate staff members of the NAM, almost to a man in favor of a liberal-trade policy, had been working hard with the members of the International Relations Committee, again overwhelmingly on the liberal-trade side, to draft a 400-page research report. This was the basis for a resolution drawn up by a steering group of the International Relations Committee and adopted by the committee in the middle of October. The board of directors was to decide on it on October 29. On the outside, the high powers of the Eisenhower administration were vigorously working on their business friends, for their strategy was in part to have all three major business associations—the Chamber, the CED, and the NAM—united behind the President's policy. A high administration source, for example, told us on October 20 to "watch for some surprising statements that will appear within the next month from some large business organizations." Arrangements were made to have Henning W. Prentiss, Jr., past president of the NAM and chairman of its International Relations Committee, testify before the Randall Commission on the afternoon of October 29, the very day of the board meeting, so that he could with full dramatic impact report the new policy. This was to be a major element in the strategy of winning a liberal report from the Randall Commission.

As the day of the board meeting approached, tension mounted and discussion increased. The NAM staff members who had guided this move could not predict the outcome. At the committee meeting, where they had expected a sharp fight, none developed. But in the board it was a different story. The majority was clearly for the resolution, but some individuals threatened to resign from the association if the resolution passed. The NAM remained without a policy.

Prentiss had to testify before the Randall Commission as follows:

> The board of directors of the National Association of Manufacturers met today in New York to discuss the tariff and related issues.
> For many years, the association has not endeavored to deal with the specific issue of the tariff.
> It was our feeling that the membership was so evenly divided that no majority opinion could be established sufficiently strong to carry influence with those concerned with the development and implementation of national policy. Something over a year ago, however, following discussions in the board and in the International Relations Committee, the conclusion was reached that the topic should be put under study.
> After several months of research and discussion and deliberation

on the part of the International Relations Committee and the board of
directors, the following resolution was adopted by the board early this
afternoon:

> . . . *Whereas, the National Association of Manufacturers has
> never adopted any position as to individual tariff rates and has
> no current policy as to other tariff matters, and*
>
> *Whereas, it is impracticable for the association to generalize
> in the national interest on a matter such as tariffs, which is so
> specific to the divergent points of view of its more than 20,000
> members and their employees,*
>
> *Therefore, be it resolved that:*
>
> *The National Association of Manufacturers does not pre-
> sume to speak in any way for its members as to tariff matters, and*
>
> *Be it further resolved, that:*
>
> *No existing positions or policies of the association on inter-
> national economic matters shall be construed to be a position on
> tariffs.*

The NAM and the Chamber of Commerce are constrained by the
fact that they must try to speak for the full range of American business.
They necessarily take positions only when business is relatively united.

But are specific industry associations more daring? Yes, but only
to a degree. Here, too, we generally find the controlling principle to be
quasiunanimity.

For example, the National Electrical Manufacturers Association
had on the surface been one of the most active of the trade associations on
the issue of protection; yet a close view reveals that it had taken no position. In July, 1953, the association decided to have a study of foreign-trade
policies made. The occasion was the one-year extension of the Reciprocal
Trade Act and creation of the Randall Commission. Accordingly, it had
Donovan, Leisure, Newton, and Irvine make an analysis of legislation,
treaties, and regulations affecting the ability of American manufacturers to
compete with foreign producers, and it commissioned the National Industrial Conference Board to make a study called "United States and its
Foreign Trade Position," which actually deals with electrical machinery.
The more controversial phase of this, "The United States Electrical Manufacturing Industry in its Relation to the Security, Health, Safety and
Welfare of the Country," was in turn subcontracted to Stone and Webster,
an engineering corporation. To quote the NEMA,

> All three organizations participating in the study were instructed
> to present factual conclusions only and to make no attempt at analysis,
> evaluation, or recommendation. In view of this objective and factual
> approach, O. Glenn Saxon, Professor of Economics at Yale University,
> was asked to make an analysis and evaluation of the three documents
> and to prepare his own conclusions and recommendations as to foreign
> economic policy.

Note that nowhere had the association taken a stand. In April, 1954, however, a group of manufacturers in their own name issued some "Recommendations of Electrical Manufacturers on Foreign Trade Policy." The signatories included manufacturers representing $3⅓ billion of annual sales and more than 235,000 employees. They included Westinghouse and eight departments of General Electric, but not General Electric as such. Sensitivity to conflicting interests reached down even below the corporate level. The chairman of the board of G.E. testified before the House committee, supporting the Trade Agreements Act "in broad effect."

Many trade associations and also many major companies adopted this permissive pattern, evading an official position while permitting action which smacked of one. A vice-president of a very large company, himself a strong, able, and vocal protectionist, said of his company:

> They really had no general stand except a very broad "goody-goody" policy. He said this was because of conflicting interests in the company. . . . "I am having a rough time in trying to persuade the company to come around." . . . "You know, you will find very few companies, except possibly one which has just a single main product, that has a clear stand on policy. . . . The trade associations . . . have 'to take a stand except, of course, if they represent businesses with conflicting interests. . . . If you have equal and conflicting interests in an organization, you get no action. . . ." Each department at [his company] has its own export division, and "I have a hell of a time with the export managers."

Although the company has what this vice-president considers virtually no policy, in the public eye it is a leading protectionist company, and that primarily because of this man's dynamism and effective public action.

Executives of trade associations expressed concern over the danger of prejudicing their organizations' strength by attempting to take stands on issues on which unanimity was absent.

> An organization of this kind has a wide diversity of interests, and it should not get embroiled in tariff fights. You don't get anywhere; you split your organization; you decrease its effectiveness; you end up with a weak-kneed position which doesn't express anything. I am speaking frankly now; the businessmen who are interested have their own trade associations who can go to bat on it. . . . There is a definite feeling that it is better to have a strong association . . . rather than to weaken and debilitate the association by inside rows. The main position is to keep the organization strong.

A variant way of avoiding internal friction is for a parent body to have a policy but not to enforce it on its members. The best example of this was the labor movement. As noted in our chapter on Detroit, the national CIO leadership strongly favored a more liberal trade policy, but many member unions and even the United Auto Workers locals associated with bicycle manufacturing favored protection for their industries. National officials of the CIO and UAW were extremely anxious to avoid putting any appreciable pressure on their locals. The only difference between the stance of the CIO leaders and that of typical trade-association executives is that the CIO leadership did view itself as a policy-forming unit, whereas trade-association executives typically view themselves as arbitrators between forces in the organization and as the members' mouthpiece. National labor leaders have more freedom in setting policies than do trade-association executives because AFL-CIO affiliates and locals are unlikely to secede if in disagreement with a national policy. But the labor leadership, too, felt impotent to prevent dissenting members from expressing their points of view.

Thus, throughout, there is a pattern of avoidance of issues, suppression of controversy, and at least the pretense of unanimity.

Sometimes issues cannot be avoided. What happens when there are sharp differences of opinion in American trade associations? Here, the pattern is one of multiplication of associations. Most business firms belong to several associations, and large firms belong to scores. An industry is apt to have many associations covering the variety of interests represented within it. In the textile industry, for example, a quick count reveals fifty-one associations, and these do not include those concerned with either raw fibers and thread or garments and finished products. For some purposes, such as research, the widest unity of the industry is feasible. Thus, there is a Textile Research Institute, an American Association of Textile Technology, and a Textile Economics Bureau. There is also a Textile Salesmen's Association, a Textile Export Association, and a Webb-Pomerene Act Association. For other purposes, since the interests of different fabrics are competitive, there is a National Association of Wool Manufacturers; a Burlap Council; a Corduroy Council of America; an American Lace Manufacturers Association; a National Federation of Textiles, for rayons and other man-made fabrics; and many others. There was no nation-wide cotton association, for the Northern and Southern cotton textile industries were too sharply antagonistic to each other. There was, at the time of the study, the National Association of Cotton Manufacturers, which was the association of the Northern firms, and the American Cotton Manufacturers Institute, that of the Southern firms. Since then, under the impact of the merger movement, firms increasingly find themselves manufacturing more than one textile, so the Northern group has organized the Northern Textile Association to permit representation of firms whose interests extend beyond cotton.

Partial coalition and partial conflict of interests is the pattern throughout. Woolen manufacturers share with wool-growers an interest in research and in the promotion of the use of wool, but they are at odds on whether these be American or British woolens. The manufacturers' and growers' interests converge in wanting protection against woolen fabric imports, but they find themselves in conflict regarding imports of raw wool. Cheap raw-wool imports help the American manufacturer compete with his British rivals, but hurt the American grower. In conflict with both the manufacturers and the growers, importers want free trade in general. Thus, a multiplicity of associations is called into being to reflect these varied interests. Alongside the National Association of Woolen Manufacturers, the American Wool Council unites the producers and the dealers with the manufacturers. For purposes of wool promotion, the Wool Bureau unites the entire American industry. It is represented in the American Wool Council with the British International Wool Secretariat. Separated from these associations to represent special interests are the American Trade Association for British Woolens and, for the fabric wholesalers, the Woolen Jobbers Association.

This pattern of multiplication and division permits each association to follow the rule of quasiunanimity within its range of issues and to permit those of its own members who have a different viewpoint to express it through another and more appropriate association. Often, these divergent bodies actually operate from the same headquarters and share personnel. There are some business firms in the field of association management which provide staff and offices for a large number of very small associations. For the larger associations, which have their own staffs and offices, it is also convenient to have several faces for different purposes. Thus, the National Coal Association has in its large and well-staffed Washington office the Coal Exporters Association. The former has been the voice of protection for the coal industry and has played down the prospect of the coal export market; the latter has the duty to maximize that prospect, whatever it may be.

Situations constantly arise which call for discretion on the part of officers and staff members of trade associations. We think, for instance, of the president of a trade organization who was also president of a company which had taken a strong protectionist position. But, we were told, "They dissociate themselves from the association in such matters since they . . . recognize that their interests are different from the rest of the association."

To summarize, it is difficult to get multipurpose business associations to take stands on controversial issues. The broader and more heterogeneous the organization, the greater the probability that some subgroups will dissent on a given issue. In a sense this means that, the more an organization represents the business community as a whole, the more unlikely it is to become committed on such an issue as foreign-trade policy. For the man who is seeking organizational support, there are ways out of this dilemma. There is a good chance that, in the multiplicity of business and trade organizations, one of those to which his firm belongs may be substantially united on the particular issue. Another possibility is to form a new organization to work on the specific problem. Thus, in 1953-1962 we found in the special-purpose organizations—the Strackbein group, the Committee for a National Trade Policy, and the like—firms grouped together which had nothing in common except support for or opposition to the Reciprocal Trade Act.

Chapter 23

Further Difficulties
of the Pressure Groups

The efforts of business and trade associations to avoid disintegration over controversial issues lead to a proliferation of organizations and particularly to the formation of specialized pressure groups designed to deal with specific issues. Even such single-minded groups had difficulties we did not anticipate. They suffered from shortages of money, skilled personnel, information, and time.

□ "All That Money Being Thrown Around"

The image of lobbyists wallowing in ill-gotten and ill-spent lucre is one of the great myths of our time. There are few very-well-paid lobbyists even at the peak of the profession. However, there have been legislative issues on which a great deal of money has been spent. A dramatic example of an attempt to "buy" legislation was the Natural Gas Bill of 1956, though the exposure of paper bags full of cash defeated that bill. We think such instances to be atypical, but we are interested now in how much money the foreign-trade pressure groups had for their range of activities.

The reciprocal-trade controversy, like that over the Natural Gas Bill, was one on the outcome of which many people stood to gain or lose large sums of money. Despite that, the men we observed were not over-fed lobbyists with lush bankrolls throwing swank cocktail parties, but rather hard-working organizers devoting an excessive portion of their time to raising enough money to keep their organizations going and constantly skimping on obvious things to do because the money was not available.

The lobbyists themselves are the source of part of the false public image of men with unbounded resources. Each side vastly overestimates the other. Each pictures the other as having an unlimited budget, an enormous staff, and all the operational possibilities which they themselves wish they had but feel frustrated because they have not. Each side sees itself as David against Goliath.

Let our respondents speak for themselves. Here are some comments by people on the low-tariff side describing the campaign of the protectionists:

> The coal people spent $1,000,000 in the first half of this year [1953] on the tariff fight.
> X said the interesting thing this year will be the . . . broad plastering of the Strackbein group. They have just hired a high-priced public-relations counsel to work for them who will spread the idea all over the country. I expect the Committee for a National Trade Policy, on the other hand, will spend most of its time at the telephone and do a hand-tooled job.

Here is what the protectionists say about those on the low-tariff side of the issue:

> "You know, we are just amateurs at this game." We replied, "Well, if you are amateurs, who are the professionals?" He said, "People like the Ford people. We just have a typewriter and a mimeograph machine, and they have all sorts of money and resources."

Some independent oil producers to whom we spoke,

> . . . indicated . . . admiration and . . . even envy of Standard Oil of New Jersey. They said, for example, it is probably the only organization that has the facts and figures of what is going on in the coal industry. We asked them how Standard Oil was able to influence policy, and they said it was largely through their resources. When the government runs into a problem, it goes to them, and Standard gives them the data and sometimes even lends them personnel to work on problems for the government for a long period of time. We asked them what kept them from doing the same, and they shrugged their shoulders and said, "Simply money."

Another protectionist said:

> Ike has lines out to all the mass-production industries. You know, he has people like Wilson of General Motors, and all through the campaign you could see him around with people like this. He thinks that these people are the important people in the country. And the Coleman committee speaks for this group.

An interviewer reported of a protectionist lobbyist:

> I asked him if he thought they had been getting a fair break from the press. He laughed and said that [the press has] a stand and that therefore they gave fuller reporting to the other side. . . . Newsprint, pulp, and pulpwood are all on the free list. Together, the imports of them are $800,000,000 a year. He said that this means more to them than the second-class rate, and they are organizing a big fight on that.

Another reported:

> I then asked what he thought would likely be the outcome of the trade debate in the light of this political situation. He said, off the record, that Eisenhower will get what he wants. I asked if that doesn't discourage his [trade association] members from doing anything. He said that they feel desperate, they don't think they'll win. "They feel like Custer's last stand." [Our] industry is a $50,000,000-a-year industry. In Washington that doesn't mean a thing. It is chicken-feed.

The contestants on both sides would be shocked to discover how impotent their rivals feel. For example, one public-relations firm was described to us on several occasions as the leading one on the protectionist side. Here was what our interviewer found when he called on the firm in Washington:

> The offices of U, V, Y, and Z, though at a good address, were surprisingly modest. Four small rooms led into the reception room. There were one or two secretaries around and one man besides X. . . . X was fiddling inexpertly with a pile of papers. . . . I asked him when his firm had become involved in the trade issue. He said that they had started on it last year when they represented A until July, when his money ran out. . . . In addition to representing A, they also worked for a group of big companies in the electrical and chemical fields . . . as more of an information service than public relations, since these companies were afraid to do anything. They lost that account, too. . . . X said that his firm will probably get out of this field. . . . Their present tariff accounts are the B industry and C industry. The big companies, in particular, won't stick their necks out. . . . He said that Strackbein got a little money from the big companies he had mentioned before, but not much.

On the low-tariff side, the story was much the same. The history of the Committee for a National Trade Policy can be written largely in terms of a struggle with finance. It started with a plan which called for the raising of $300,000. By the end of the first year, it had succeeded in raising about $200,000. The overhead amounted to $15,000 or $16,000 a month. Simple arithmetic shows how little money was left for campaign activities. None of the top staff people were particularly adept at or interested in fund-raising, so a professional fund-raiser was employed. He did not succeed and was dropped. Every mailing and advertisement had to be measured against the funds in the treasury.

A draft budget of October, 1953, though, like any other budget, not fully conforming to what actually happened, sheds some light on the operation. The budget was divided between operations and special activities. Operations included salaries, offices, and fund-raising. Salaries for fourteen employees, five or six of them clerical, were to come to about $11,000 a month. Rent and office costs were under $1,400 a month. Costs of fund-raising were estimated at $5,000 a month. Had these expenditures not been cut, and they are certainly not unreasonable for an organization intended to carry on a vigorous nation-wide campaign, the entire $200,000 would have disappeared there. The major budgeted special activity was preparing a mailing list of 100,000 names. That was expected to cost about $35,000. That would have been, for the most part, a one-time expense, but certainly an essential one for an effective organization. Lack of money prevented the completion of that job. After the first year, the financial position of the organization became even more stringent.

We have some less complete figures on other organizations. For example, the combined advertising and public-relations budget of the Swiss watch manufacturers in America reached $2,000,000 a year. Of this, most went for watch advertising which served both institutional and commercial purposes. (How can one distinguish the political effects of a Swiss watch advertisement from its sales purposes?) About $250,000 of the $2,000,000 went for public-relations activities in the campaign against tariff increases. Outside of that budget, there were some activities paid for by American assemblers using Swiss movements. There were also legal costs incurred in Tariff Commission hearings and activities of the Swiss Embassy which might well be chargeable in a complete accounting of what it cost to attempt to avoid a tariff increase.

One can argue that the sums expended on such a case are large or small, depending on the approach one takes. The total sums spent by all parties in a fight on a major national issue in which many millions of dollars are at stake may be very large indeed. In the instance of Swiss watches, the nonadvertising expenditures by one side may have substantially exceeded $500,000 a year. But that figure includes all the relevant activities of all the firms, all the trade associations, all the law cases, and also the relevant activities of the Swiss government. On the other hand, the sums available to any one lobbying or public-information organization or program are apt to be much too small to enable it to act in any decisive fashion or to acquire any megalomaniacal fantasies. The $120,000 to $150,000 a year that the major public-relations firm representing the watch assemblers received as its fee had first to cover its overhead and salaries. What was left for campaign purposes was hardly a stupendous figure.

We have no reason to believe that any one of the pressure groups on the trade issue wanted to buy votes. We know that Congressional votes were in general not available to be bought. But even if a group wished to turn from propaganda to corruption, no one of the organizations had the discretionary funds to undertake such an enterprise. Presumably, the funds of the natural-gas interests referred to above were more centrally channelled. However, as we have already indicated, the reciprocal-trade controversy was a more normal situation.

The failure to recognize the multiplicity and diversity of spending bodies, each with its individual goals, leads to a false image of pressure group processes. The total sums spent somehow leave the impression of plutocratic giants, able by their wealth to totally distort the public process. Clearly, if one takes the few instances concerning which we have reasonably reliable figures and projects those figures over the total number of organizations operating in this field and if one then adds to these organizational expenditures the amounts spent by business firms and individuals in their own contributed time and effort—for example, arranging meetings, making speeches, writing letters—one cannot escape the conclusion that the reciprocal-trade controversy cost the participants many millions of dollars a year. Yet, wherever one looked at the persons actually spending that money, one saw only harassed men with tight budgets and limited campaign funds, once their essential organizational overheads had been met.

□ Lack of Skilled Personnel

A profession needs an ideology to justify itself. Without a proud self-image, it will not attract its full potential in personnel. A man and his family are proud of the practice of law. Most mothers would say, "I didn't raise my boy to be a lobbyist." As long as that situation prevails, the best talent will not be found in pressure politics. One of our respondents described legislative work as a young man's game. A family man moves from it to more stable occupations. Many lobbyists were in fact older, but those were not generally the most gifted men. This is a difficult point to document. We have no evidence on intrinsic ability; yet it is our distinct impression that, except for a few highly capable men at the top of the heap, the best men leave the field.

□ Lack of Knowledge

The lack of money and personnel is compounded by such other problems as inadequate information. It takes able men and much money to do good research, and research is one thing every lobby needs. Facts are their stock in trade. Research is needed to write speeches, to put out pamphlets, to prepare testimony, to find the arguments which will convince doubters. It may not be research as the academician conceives it, but, such as it is, it takes much of the organizer's time.

At one level, if one asked what these association organizers did, we would answer in these terms: they produced publicity; they arranged meetings; they stimulated letters, articles, and speeches. In so doing, they raised the level of public discussion and awareness of public policy. We do not mean for a moment to suggest that they were educators in intent or that their products would meet the normal standards of scholarship. We suggest only that the net effect of all this discussion, counterdiscussion, statement, and correction is a certain degree of enlightenment.

The scholarly researcher may be both intrigued and disturbed as he observes the research activity conducted by interest groups and the standards of integrity in it. The prevailing attitude was least self-consciously expressed by one public-relations man from whose interview we quote:

> He said: "We did a survey recently which showed 300,000 unemployed as a result of foreign imports. That's probably about right, although no one can prove it one way or the other. . . ." I asked if some of the protectionists whom he dealt with who responded to particular injuries didn't have some trouble rationalizing their view in terms of the big picture. He said, "No, it doesn't bother them for long. They convince themselves that theirs is the national interest." He then cited himself as an example. He said: "Often I have doubts when I take a job, but after a while I find I am convinced. I like to tell myself that it is because I know more about the subject, but that is not really it. If that were it, why would I always find I am convinced of the side I am working on?" I suggested to him that there might be limits to this process. He said: "That's right. You don't get into a job in the first place if you don't like the looks of it. . . ." He said that he did a job on the oil cartel. "There are seven companies that divide up the world between them. We publicized that, and it is probably true."

In short, the job of an operator is to seek those facts which build his case. The operator here, as in psychological warfare, as in law cases, as in all fields except pure research, is balancing three standards. He wants the facts that will support his case, that will not kick back by exposing him as deceitful, and that are reliable because he himself objects in principle to lying. His assumption is that, since he is on the right side, there must be some facts that will help, not hurt. His job is to find them. He has no taboo against stating with great certitude something that is only probable or against stating broadly something that is only partially true; but he does not want to make his case out of whole cloth, nor does he believe that he can successfully do so. As one respondent put it:

> He said that they tried to get informational bulletins out, and then he said half-apologetically, "We call them informational bulletins, but some people don't think they are just information. . . . You know, we may slant the data a little bit our way, but it has to be sound; we see to it that it is sound because we cannot get caught off base."

Thus, a large part of the activity of the organizers consists of research, and one of the reasons for their relative ineffectiveness is the lack of good research on both sides. Congressmen frequently said that they would talk to anybody who would bring them really fresh information. Bored to death by hearing the same old stories, they often expressed a real craving for some solid facts that they could believe. One may wonder whether this was not to some extent a search for a *deus ex machina,* a wistful feeling on the part of congressmen that there must be some objective answer that would get them out of difficult decisions. Yet, receptive to facts they were, whatever the reason.

Thus, information is often power. A complex example is provided by the petroleum industry. For good and sufficient reasons, major oil companies are afraid to be overtly politically aggressive. They collided with the antitrust laws once, and they have been a symbol of big business in the public mind. They hesitate to lobby, and they would probably never dream of organizing their employees in a letter-writing campaign. Their time-perspective is a long one, and they recognize that self-restraint on a momentary issue will in the end pay off in public acceptance of the industry. It is therefore somewhat of a mystery how these few large firms succeeded in holding off oil-import quotas as long as they did against the much more vigorous demands of the American independent producers for protection. The answer lies in part in the fund of expertise and knowledge which they have accumulated. As noted in a quotation above, when the government needs expert personnel for staffing policy jobs in the administration of petroleum, it is likely to find them among men who have worked for the major oil companies. When one needs facts about the world petroleum situation, he is likely to find them in the excellent library organized by Standard Oil of New Jersey. Indeed, in their fight against Standard and the other major producers, the independents turned to Standard Oil to get the basic data with which to fight them. The sensitivity of the big companies to public relations, their unwillingness to be aggressive, and the power that knowledge gives them are all illustrated by the fact that, when the independents went to Standard to get the data with which to fight Standard, the latter helped them and asked no questions. Standard thus won the respect and the frustrated awe which, we have noted, was felt by those who opposed it, but on the basis of imperfect knowledge.

Though information can be power, it is a power usually untapped by the pressure groups we studied. The amount of factual information most of them had assembled was limited indeed. Neither side budgeted much for research. The Coleman committee initially had some rather large research plans, but these were the first casualties of budgetary stress. One highly placed respondent noted that:

> The figures which really substantiate a case of damage are never presented. Everyone claims damage, but when you ask them to prove it there just isn't any. The only statistics that are ever quoted are Picquet's.[1]

Another, who worked for a public-relations firm, also complained that Picquet's volume had become a bible for reciprocal-trade supporters and a target for protectionists, since it had almost a monopoly on the facts.

□ Lack of Time

The harassment we observed was not only financial. The life of a Washington pressure-group organizer is not a leisurely one. That is both its charm and its agony. In working for any legislative cause, whether as a lobbyist or as a congressman, there is just too much to do. An executive of a trade association has to concern himself, not only with national policies, but also with organization finances, membership, meetings, bulletins and magazines, correspondence, inquiries, staffing, and the like. He must follow legislative and administrative developments, not only on tariffs, but also on government contracts, taxes, and regulations of all sorts. He has to collect economic statistics, business news, and scientific and legislative reports. If he is in a single-issue organization, such as the CNTP or the Strackbein committee, he is concerned with changes in tariff rates and regulations for each of the products listed in the tariff rules. He is concerned, not only with the Reciprocal Trade Bill and all its ramifications, but also with customs simplification, GATT, OTC, Buy-American legislation, agricultural legislation, and such administrative proceedings as Tariff Commission escape-clause proceedings and State Department reciprocal-trade negotiations. In this day of big government, there is never enough time to do more than select from among its complexities what to cope with, or else to drift, pushed by events into a few

---

[1] Howard S. Picquet, *Aid, Trade and the Tariff* (New York: Thomas Y. Crowell, 1953).

of the many things one might do. Most pressure-group activity is emergency fire-fighting. There is seldom time to do much more. Long-range planning goes by default.

□ Summary

We have noted some difficulties which pressure groups face in attempting to do an effective job: lack of funds, adequate personnel, knowledge, and time. A close look at the pressure groups revealed them as something far short of the omnipotent, well-oiled machines that are portrayed in political literature. Most surprising to us was the lack of money. We have not contended that all pressure campaigns are similarly impoverished, but most are. The heart of the matter lies in the number of organizations among which the available funds are divided. The statement that "millions of dollars were spent on each side" proves to be meaningless until one has ascertained what proportion of these "vast sums" has gone into the overhead of the organizations. The balance available for external spending is what counts if the pressure groups are to have any appreciable effect.

Chapter 24

Pressure Group or
Service Bureau?

Our survey of business leaders as well as our community studies showed that men tend to make and maintain contact with those who agree with them. This tendency also characterized the staffs of the pressure groups. An impediment to the effectiveness of these organizations was a deep resistance to approaching unfriendly people. Perhaps the kind of person who becomes a public-relations man or a lobbyist is more than usually other-directed and anxious to be approved and to please. Perhaps the lobbyist is simply the victim of a calculation that he is unlikely to convert any enemies; his most effective use of time is thus not to debate with his opponents but to stimulate his friends to act. That calculation is certainly part of the operational code of the American lobbyist, whether it is the result of bitter experience or whether it is a rationalization of a distaste for being rebuffed. We know that very few lobbyists spend any substantial amount of time working on those who do not already agree with them, and it became clear to us as outside observers that the result was frequently the missing of opportunities. The events of 1962 again require us to qualify our generalizations. The liberal traders had learned some lessons

350

by then.[1] The strategy in 1962 was developed by men who already in 1953, in the Simpson bill controversy, had recognized the advantages of a direct approach to affected industries. In 1962, the liberal-trade high command successfully approached the textile industry and unsuccessfully approached the chemical industry. The basic 1962 strategy of splitting the protectionists by concessions to some of them necessitated negotiations with those foes. We shall have more to say about the textile case. The campaign by the administration on the chemical industry was carried as far as a private meeting between Howard C. Petersen, the President's special assistant on trade policy, and industry leaders in February at a session of the Manufacturing Chemists Association in New York. But, these exceptions notwithstanding, we observed no more common mistake than that of failing to push people who were movable because it was assumed that they were on the other side.

This became obvious to us as we watched the controversy from Capitol Hill. We note below how few were the congressmen who had heard anything from the major pressure groups and how many there were who were genuinely puzzled as to how they should vote and who would have appreciated clear indications of where their constituencies stood and what the issues were. They were the highly committed spokesmen of each side with whom in fact the pressure groups were in contact. There was a handful of protectionist spokesmen in Congress who were in constant communication with the major protectionist lobbies. There was also a handful of spokesmen for reciprocal trade who were in constant communication with the Coleman committee and with the Randall staff. For either set of lobbyists to have approached congressmen who were fully committed to the other side would have been indeed a foolish waste of effort and source of annoyance. It might in fact have been dangerous, for, as we have noted elsewhere, legitimate communications that do not annoy a congressman are not viewed as pressure, whereas those which threaten him are. A lobbyist approaching a real enemy is apt to invite a blast in *The Congressional Record* or elsewhere about selfish interests bringing pressures to bear.[2]

In short, it makes sense to avoid one's out-and-out opponents in Congress. But what of the moderates and mildly interested people in the middle? A lobbyist is a busy man. It is quite a chore to keep himself informed as to the views and desires of over 500 congressmen. Yet, to some

---

[1] We do not believe that one cause of the change was that a few of the proadministration organizers had read some chapters of this manuscript, but we owe it to the reader to note that this possible confounding of the evidence existed.

[2] An example of how "pressure" may backfire is the reaction in the fall of 1959 to the threatening letter that labor leader James Carey sent to congressmen who opposed his views on the labor reform bill.

extent each side tries to do just that. Late in 1953, Mrs. Rachel Bell, who had worked on the Hill on a series of international issues starting with the Committee to Defend America by Aiding the Allies, drafted for the Coleman committee a list of all the congressmen and where they might be expected to stand, based on past voting records modified by recent public statements. Our interviewer, familiar as he was with this issue, immediately spotted what he considered a number of wrong estimates. He asked, for example, about Congressman X, who was listed as undecided. After some discussion, it became clear that there was no knowledge at the CNTP that this congressman had issued a strongly protectionist statement approximately a year before. This is not a criticism, for, conversely, there were scores of congressmen on whom the committee had information where we would have pleaded ignorance. It is simply one more evidence of the enormity of the task. Eighteen months later, when a vote was taken, the list of the senators proved less than two-thirds correct, although thirteen had been listed as undecided. In the House, the prediction was three-quarters correct and one-quarter wrong, with a still larger proportion than in the Senate listed as undecided.

Thus, there was a great deal of uncertainty as to who stood where. In part, this was due to ignorance by the predictor; in part, it arose from the fact that many congressmen had not made up their minds.

This situation adds to the significance of the fact that lobbyists fear to enter where they may find a hostile reception. Since uncertainty is greatest precisely regarding those who are undecided, the lobbyist is apt to neglect contact with those very persons whom he might be able to influence. It is easy from an academic armchair to point this out and call it foolish, but if one puts oneself into the shoes or swivel chair of a harassed organizer, it is easy to see how it happens. The morning begins with a desk loaded with unfinished jobs and unanswered mail. There are hundreds of things which should be done, if only one could find the time for the effort required. Possibilities flash across the mind in the twinkle of an eye. One possibility may be to telephone a good friend, the assistant to a congressman, to ask that some article be read into *The Congressional Record*. Another may be to telephone the executive of another association with whom one works regularly to ask that it send a representative to a meeting. Another may be to line up a speaker in response to a request. Still another may be to arrange a luncheon with a possible source of funds. Finally, there may be the chronic awareness that he really ought to get in touch with any one of four or five congressmen about whose stand he is quite vague. Most of the first four possibilities simply involve picking up the telephone and having a pleasant conversation with a sympathetic and familiar colleague. Raising funds is painful, but the pressures to do it are never absent.

Approaching an unfamiliar congressman, however, immediately raises problems. To begin with, the fact that one views him as a question mark means that one's contact is limited. Our hypothetical organizer is puzzled. Perhaps he can write a letter to a businessman in the congressman's district and ask for information on likely reactions and on lines of approach. Until he gets an answer, he had better not walk brashly into what might prove a difficult situation and might do more harm than good. Some time later he gets an answer. Perhaps it doesn't tell him much, or perhaps it reinforces his notion that he ought to do something, but he may still need to find a way to make proper contact. Should he ask a mutual friend for an introduction? If so, he has put himself in debt to that friend, who may or may not be an advocate of his cause.

It is so much easier to carry on activities within the circle of those who agree and encourage you than it is to break out and find potential proselytes, that the day-to-day routine and pressure of business tend to shunt those more painful activities aside. The result is that *the lobbyist becomes in effect a service bureau for those congressmen already agreeing with him, rather than an agent of direct persuasion.*[3]

□ Breakfast at the Willard

This tendency to "work with our own people" was true on both sides of the controversy. One of the high points in the activities of the Strackbein committee was its cooperation with Congressman Simpson during the time that he served on the Randall Commission. The commission's deliberations were held entirely in executive session. Clarence Randall felt from the beginning that his only chance of getting a unanimous report was to avoid public controversy, for that would force members of the commission with special affiliations to make statements for the

---

[3] Other writers have made essentially the same point. Blaisdell, *op. cit.,* p. 12, says: ". . . few lobbyists are crude enough today to attempt to persuade a legislator against his better judgment or against what he believes to be the majority sentiment of the people he represents." Cohen, *op. cit.,* p. 14, comments: ". . . policy makers are not often persuaded to act (or not act) in favor of persons or groups with whom they are in basic ideological or political conflict. But more positively, there generally appears to be a close affinity between the policy makers and the individual or group whose position he is persuaded to support." Cohen goes on (p. 15) to cite an earlier study by John W. Masland ("Pressure Groups and American Foreign Policy preceding Pearl Harbor," *Public Opinion Quarterly,* Spring 1942, p. 121), in which Masland says: "The representatives of these various groups cultivated personal contact with members of Congress and of the Administration who were favorably inclined to their views. Fred Libby and Dorothy Detzer for many years worked closely with isolationists in Congress. General Wood moved into the office of Senator Wheeler for several days to assist in planning opposition strategy to revision of the Neutrality Act. Around the State Department, Clark Eichelberger found doors open at all times and consulted freely with officials, giving and receiving advice."

record which would be hard to reverse later. He himself adopted a policy of refusing to meet the press, and he urged his example on all commission members. Congressman Simpson, presumably in the minority on the commission, apparently felt that these rules of procedure were to his disadvantage. He maintained virtually daily contact with Oscar Strackbein in order to keep running pressure on the commission.

The commission, it will be recalled, permitted only two days of open hearings. Among those who testified was Strackbein. A few days later, his Nation-wide Committee of Industry, Agriculture, and Labor on Import-Export Policy held a meeting at the Willard Hotel, at which it adopted a resolution calling for the removal of Clarence Randall as commission chairman. The keynote speaker was Representative Simpson. Simpson himself avoided calling for Randall's removal, but his speech gave the meeting its newsworthiness. There seems little doubt that this meeting was arranged in response to Simpson's desire and to help him in his conflict with Randall. In this instance, the Strackbein committee was able to score because it could make itself an auxiliary of a person with power.

□ Helping Senator Gore

A similar high point of activity and effectiveness was reached by the Coleman committee in June, 1954, when it was able to put itself at the service of Sen. Albert Gore (D., Tenn.). To understand how a committee organized by Eisenhower supporters at the President's request ended up working for a Democratic senator, we need to know the background.

The administration had recognized the rising resistance to the Randall Commission proposals and had therefore agreed to a temporary, one-year extension of the Reciprocal Trade Act. To the ardent supporters of reciprocal trade, this was a defeat and in the eyes of some a sell-out. They anticipated continued uncertainty among foreign businessmen as to the prospects in the American market, and uncertainty is, as we have noted, at least as important as high tariffs in restricting trade development. They also foresaw the next renewal as coming in a less favorable juncture, although administration strategists believed, on the contrary, that time would work in their favor. In any case, the more ardent reciprocal-trade supporters saw themselves as betrayed. On the Senate floor, Senator Gore seized on this situation. He introduced an amendment giving the administration exactly the bill it had originally wished, with a three-year extension. This was obviously a political gesture designed to embarrass the President; the Democrats were offering him what he wanted after he had agreed to relinquish it. Randall and President Eisenhower resolved their dilemma by adhering to the agreement they had reached. They opposed the Gore amendment and urged their Republican supporters to vote against it.

The Committee for a National Trade Policy, however, made the opposite decision. It had long sought leadership from the White House which it did not feel it was getting. Now, for the first time, it suddenly found itself with strong leadership and a chance to be of service. True, nobody expected the Gore amendment to pass both houses of Congress. Still, rationally or irrationally, the staff of the CNTP saw in this unexpected event the chance to strike at least one blow for liberalized trade. It went into vigorous and forceful action. For that one and only time during the period of this study, it acted with some of the characteristics usually attributed to a pressure group.

Senator Gore recognized that one of his major problems was to persuade people, particularly Republicans, that his motion was not merely a slick political trick designed to embarrass the administration. To demonstrate that he was acting out of deep conviction and a sense of the importance of the issue, he decided to introduce the bill with a thoughtful four-hour speech. He instructed his assistants to prepare one.

For this they needed help, as they also did for the rounding-up of votes and support. First, they telephoned Clarence Randall and, quoting his own words to him, said they were getting him what he wanted and were sure that Randall would be glad to help. They wanted staff writers and a list of names of people whose supporting statements could be obtained. Randall was ambivalent but annoyed, feeling that the whole thing was political gunplay. As tactfully as he could, he declined and suggested that Gore's assistant approach the CNTP. When the CNTP picked up the Gore proposal, Randall was in fact perturbed, although of two minds. In retrospect, at least, he has said that it was perfectly proper for the CNTP as a bipartisan group committed on the issue to take the stand it did.

On Friday, June 18, one of Gore's assistants telephoned Meyer Rashish at the CNTP. That was the first time that they had had direct dealings. Between that Friday and the following Thursday, when the vote was taken, there were about four days available in which to prepare the speech. Working on it, besides Edward Robinson, William Allen, Senator Gore's assistants, and Rashish, was John Sharon, a general political aide of George Ball. Robinson also called upon Harold P. LaMarr, assistant to Howard Picquet in the Legislative Reference Service of the Library of Congress, whose job it was to prepare such material for congressmen.

One of the key decisions involved in writing the speech was to put the emphasis on lower American tariffs as a countermeasure to the

Soviet trade offensive. We had been wondering for some time during 1954 why the liberal traders did not make use of this argument. The decision to use the approach was made by Senator Gore himself. It grew in part out of a clipping file which LaMarr and Picquet maintained. During the previous months, they had been struck by the rapid accumulation of material on the Soviet trade offensive and the fact that it was not being discussed in the context of American trade policy. From Gore's point of view, the anti-Soviet argument had the distinct advantage of putting stress on American exports of agricultural products, a topic to which he also wished to devote a considerable portion of the speech.

The next problem was that of lining up votes. Gore himself lined up the Democrats. Charles Taft was assigned the job of trying to obtain a half-dozen Republican votes to offset the few Democratic defections that were inevitable. Taft spoke to Senators Irving Ives (N.Y.), James Duff (Pa.), Margaret Chase Smith (Maine), George Aiken (Vt.), Prescott Bush (Conn.), and Frank Carlson (Kan.). Ives and Smith left the impression that they would vote for the bill. Duff telephoned the White House to ask how he should vote; he voted nay. Margaret Chase Smith did not show up for the vote.

On the Democratic side, the leadership, specifically Lyndon Johnson, had been won over and asked the whip to line up votes. In the end, the Gore amendment lost only six Democrats, but, with no Republicans supporting it, it could not pass. The key to the Democratic side was thought to be Senator George. A few Democrats—such as Matthew Neely of West Virginia, Pat McCarran of Nevada, Johnson of Colorado, and Pastore of Rhode Island—had been written off from the beginning because of needs for protection in their constituencies. Gore spoke to George three times in the hope that he might support the bill. On June 15, however, after some persuasion by Millikin, with whom he had a close working relationship in the Finance Committee, George withdrew his support from the movement for a three-year extension because "the President has backed up on his own proposal." At that moment, it looked as though the Gore proposal were dead. The odds were so strong against it that, in the opinion of Gore's associates, the protectionists fell down on the job. "They felt so safe they weren't even buttonholing anybody." Yet, as the political advantages for the Democrats became clearer, the rest of the Democrats in the Senate lined up ever more solidly. Adlai Stevenson, who had adopted a policy against becoming involved in legislative controversy, stepped out of his usual role, despite some Democratic National Committee opposition. He issued a statement supporting the move. This helped to remove the impression that it was a one-man effort on the part of a junior senator. Immediately after the reading of the Stevenson statement, however, George rose to oppose the Gore amendment. Still, only six Democrats opposed the bill.

The story illustrates many points, but the one with which we are concerned here is the activity of a pressure group when it is functioning at full steam. Its role became that of an auxiliary service bureau for a senator with whom it was in complete agreement. Its staff provided him with information, they helped him in writing, they arranged for statements of support (notably Stevenson's), and they even assumed the task of approaching a half-dozen amenable Republicans.

□ Summary

All in all, the staff members of pressure groups, hard-working though they were, could scarcely be characterized as crusaders anxious to engage the enemy in open combat. Their major contacts, both in frequency and effectiveness, were with friends of their cause. We shall see in the next chapter how they served to activate and bolster groups and individuals who actually tried to influence the legislative outcome. Here we have seen that their best contribution was when they could become auxiliaries to a legislator, not propagandists to him. Their direction of influence was almost the reverse of what is usually assumed. They helped carry issues from the Congressional forum in which they were formulated to the larger community of interested citizens as much as they worked the other way around.

We are not saying that pressure groups never apply, or strive to apply, pressure or that lobbyists never lobby. We are not saying that pressure groups never approach persons opposed to their position or those who are on the fence and ripe for conversion; indeed, they did much more of it in 1962 than in the period we principally studied. We are saying that they do these things far less often than one might think and that the pressure groups are more likely to organize and stimulate other people to perform these activities. These other people are generally congressmen, businessmen, public figures, and the like whose application of pressure usually is regarded as more legitimate than is the same activity if carried out by a paid representative of some special interest.

Chapter 25

Organizing Communications—
Two Protectionist Examples

The objective of the national pressure groups was to influence Congress or, at times, the administration. Their approach was sometimes direct, sometimes indirect. Their methods were usually conventional. They got people to write letters. (Quite massive letter barrages did come from Westinghouse and/or people stimulated by Westinghouse, a few chemical companies—notably Dow and Monsanto—from Southern textile regions, and from people in a few such special situations as the cherry-growers of Michigan and Oregon and the makers of toy marbles of West Virginia.)

They arranged meetings. (The Southern textile people, for example, in 1955 held scores of regional business meetings at which amendment of HR 1 was advocated.)

They did research. They issued statements and press releases. They published bulletins and sent out mailings. The Coleman committee, for example, put out eleven mailings between September, 1953, and February, 1954. To some, the volume of their statements was the proof of their activity and, by implication, of their effectiveness.

Besides reacting to news events, they tried to create news. The

Coleman committee brought a delegation to Washington to be received by the President. The National Association of Cotton Manufacturers at its annual meeting gave a medal to the prominent Keynesian liberal economist, Seymour Harris. The *pièce de résistance* was a speech by him advocating protection of the New England textile industry. To get maximum press coverage for this man-bites-dog story of a liberal economist supporting protection, the other major speeches at the function were ones with no possible news value. One was an educational disquisition on atomic energy and another was a diet of solid humor.

In a similar vein, the Committee on Foreign Trade Education organized an annual Cordell Hull Award which it gave in 1954-1955 to Albert Gore and in 1955-1956 to Paul G. Hoffman at the Waldorf-Astoria Hotel.

Other groups, of which the outstanding was the League of Women Voters, organized discussion groups around the country. The League also ran surveys of local business opinion.

But all these events were no more than standard publicity routines. They had little direct effect on congressmen. What effect, if any, direct or indirect, did they have?

The answer seems to be that, although the pressure groups' propaganda activities did not persuade anyone by the direct impact of what was said, by engaging in such apparently futile activities those organizations arrogated to themselves the roles of authoritative spokesmen for particular sides or interests. By thus seizing a portion of the field of battle, they became effective organizers of the communications process. Two case histories will illustrate these points.

□ Organizing Southern Protectionism

Our first case is that of the American Cotton Manufacturers Institute, which represents the Southern section of the industry. There is no question but that their work was effective. Table 25-1 reveals how Congressional voting among traditionally free-trading Southern congressmen in textile areas shifted in favor of protection in 1955 and back again in 1962.

The methods used by the ACMI to produce the 1955 shift were classic and unoriginal. The institute had workers in members' firms write letters and had its members adopt resolutions, testify, and buttonhole. The question is why these methods worked better for them than they did for similar groups elsewhere. The answer lies partly in the peculiar politics of the American South. There one finds the politics of the closed corporation much more than in any other section of the country. The small-town

TABLE 25-1

RELATION OF HIGH TEXTILE EMPLOYMENT TO PROTECTIONIST VOTES BY SOUTHERN REPRESENTATIVES *

	Textile employment, 1950	Vote by representative														
		1922	1930	1934	1937	1940	1943	1945	1948	1949	1951	1953	1954	1955	1958	1962
Total number of protectionist votes cast from ten Southern states		8	16	3	5	7	8	6	3	2	19	12	1	10	22	17
Textile districts:																
Georgia, 4th District	22,830	L	L	L	L	L	L	L	L	L	L	P	O	P	P	L
Georgia, 7th District	24,000	L	L	L	L	L	L	L	L	L	L	L	L	P	P	L
N. Carolina, 9th District	61,700	L	L	L	L	L	L	L	L	L	L	L	L	P	P	P
N. Carolina, 10th District	41,800	L	L	L	L	L	L	L	L	L	L	L	L	P	P	P
N. Carolina, 11th District	39,170	L	L	L	L	L	L	L	L	L	L	P	L	P	P	P
S. Carolina, 3rd District	36,300	L	L	L	L	L	L	L	L	L	P	P	P	P	P	L
S. Carolina, 4th District	51,000	L	L	L	L	L	L	L	L	L	L	L	O	O	L	L

L = liberal-trade vote; P = protectionist vote; O = no vote.

* Votes 1922-1953 compiled by Mr. Jonathan Levin; textile data and votes compiled by Mr. William R. Leitch. The votes reported here are all final votes on the bill itself, not votes on the often-more-significant test roll calls along the way, such as that in 1955, on the motion to recommit. Thus, it is important to note that the sixteen Southern protectionist votes cast in 1930 were part of the lopsided majority by which the Smoot-Hawley Tariff Act was passed, whereas the one Southern protectionist vote in 1954 was one among the mere fifty-four die-hards who opposed the compromise one-year extension. The ten Southern protectionists in 1955 were among 110 die-hards who voted against the final bill in that year.

elite of Georgia or South Carolina brings together the local businessmen and politicians in more tightly knit personal relationships. In the past, this meant that the congressmen spoke as free traders for cotton and its world market. It also meant that the Southern representative was not deluged by letters or visits from pressure groups. The only representatives on Capitol Hill who did not have to work like slaves were some Southern representatives. Their crucial local relationships were well established, and each party to the relationship knew where the other stood and why. Communication was less often needed than in other constituencies.

The industrialization of the South with the spread of the textile industry has changed this in many ways. It has changed the economic interest of some constituencies. It has equally changed the political pattern. For many Southern congressmen, the battle on HR 1 in 1955 was the first time they had personally experienced a massive, stimulated letter-writing campaign, in which workers in factories were encouraged to write by the thousands. It was something new, and it therefore signaled important and different developments at home. Used a second time, it might not be as effective.

Although the protectionist campaign in the South was something new, in other ways its effectiveness arose from the persistence of the old South, or at least the forms of its persistence. Many of the Southern mills are not Southern at all, but parts of Northern combines. Yet their local managers, often the old owners, are still part of that relatively small, tightly knit, small-town elite with face-to-face relationships of which the congressman is a part. Thus, the ACMI's real effectiveness arose not so much from its own testifying, lobbying, or organizing as from the fact that it stimulated action by members who had the ear of their congressman to a far greater degree than do the members of most trade associations. They were geographically localized and politically influential. The ACMI's policy was not to speak for the industry but to have the local manufacturers speak for themselves. The ACMI held scores of industry regional meetings throughout the South to tell their members how endangered they were. From that point on, the operation worked to a large extent by itself. The combination of the newness of the demand for protection and the mass campaign methods shocked Southern congressmen into attention.

The ACMI was able to inject itself effectively into an established communication pattern. It did not need to convert by the force of its arguments. Southern congressmen were predisposed to respond to the changes which had been occurring in the economy of the South. By its activities, the ACMI determined that HR 1 became the issue which signaled these changes. If one looked only at its own activities and audience, they would seem very minor, but, by setting the processes of communication going at the right moment, it proved to be a very important catalyst indeed.

In 1962, it was equally important, but in the opposite direction. The Kennedy administration decided that, to get its bill through Congress, it had to break the opposition of the textile industry. As one of the most geographically dispersed and severely hurt industries, it could be a major source of opposition. It had been in 1955. It was also particularly vital for a Democratic president, who could not count on many Republican votes and needed to keep his Southern cadres in line. In February, a five-year, nineteen-nation agreement was signed, by which European countries which had quotas on Japanese textiles agreed to ease those quotas; the United States got the right to impose such quotas to protect home industry. A letter of thanks for help to the textile industry and its workers, signed by scores of congressmen, went to Kennedy. Then, in March, the President raised the tariff on carpets in an escape-clause action and banned eight varieties of cotton imports from Hong Kong. At the same time, many other such matters of administrative regulation were carefully left pending to give the textile industry a lively sense of possible favors still to come, depending on good behavior.

In the last days of March, the ACMI assembled for its annual meeting in Palm Beach. For three days, the directors debated and met with presidential aides. At the end, they unanimously recommended and the convention adopted a resolution expressing appreciation for the administration's "unprecedented degree of thoughtful consideration" and saying: "We believe that the authority to deal with foreign nations proposed by the President will be wisely exercised and should be granted by the Congress."

Within the first two weeks of this strange honeymoon, a number of Southern Democratic votes from textile areas switched to support of an administration-backed tax bill, and the administration pushed a textile-import bill through the House to implement the nineteen-nation agreement. In addition, the administration moved to give cotton-growers an 8.5-cent-per-pound subsidy and to balance this with a corresponding import tax on cotton textiles. It was thus that the heart of the protectionist coalition was smashed in 1962, and the only complaining voices were those of a strange combination of textile importers, Europeans who saw liberal-trade words being implemented by protective practices, and protectionists from other industries who saw their allies wooed away. Once again, the ACMI proved effective on behalf of its members, but again not by direct lobbying. Its effectiveness arose from its ability to speak for its members and determine their line; in this case, the line was to avoid lobbying.

☐ The Fight against Foreign Oil

Our second case takes us back to the Simpson bill of 1953 and the Neely amendment of 1955. The Simpson bill was principally designed to hold imports of petroleum products, particularly crude oil and residual fuel oil, to 10 per cent of domestic production. For reasons of strategy, the bill was framed in broader terms. It provided for a long list of products on which, if imports should reach certain levels, quotas would be imposed. The Simpson bill became the center of Congressional debate on foreign-trade matters in 1953. After a vigorous battle, it was finally defeated. It lost again in 1954. In 1955, substantially the same proposal was incorporated into an amendment to the Reciprocal Trade Act by Senator Neely. The Neely amendment was defeated, but the administration accepted a watered-down substitute which provided that the Office of Defense Mobilization might find that imports of a product were reaching levels where they endangered national defense. Under those circumstances, quotas could be imposed.

The impetus behind this drive for petroleum import restrictions came throughout from the coal-mining interests, and more specifically from the National Coal Association with the cooperation of the United Mine Workers. Also actively interested were those domestic oil producers without foreign wells. These small oil companies [1] were organized in the Independent Petroleum Association of America. A third industry which played a part in the campaign was that of the coal-carrying railroads. These three sets of interests combined to form a body called the Foreign Oil Policy Committee, but the specific interests of the various groups were by no means identical.

The bituminous coal miners were particularly concerned to reduce, if possible, the imports to the East Coast of residual fuel oil from Venezuela. Before 1953, residual-fuel-oil imports had been less than a quarter of total residual-fuel-oil consumption, but virtually all the imports were used in the Eastern states, where imports came to 45 per cent of residual oil consumed. Eastern coal miners in Pennsylvania, West Virginia, and other states felt themselves in a competitive situation. The petroleum importer might answer that the decline of coal was due largely to other factors. Between 1946 and 1952, coal used by railroads decreased by 64 per cent, owing to dieselization. This accounted for a 72,000,000-ton decline in the use of coal, whereas total residual-fuel-oil imports were the equivalent of only 31,000,000 tons of coal. There was another 33,000,000-ton decline in coal use for space heating and as a fuel in homes. Residual fuel

---

[1] Facetiously referred to as, "You know, men with only two Cadillacs."

oil is not very extensively used for these purposes. Here, coal's loss was largely to natural gas and fuel oil not of residual types. But coal-mining is a sick industry, and oil imports seemed to be the place where a defensive attack could be effectively launched. There seemed little hope of stopping dieselization or the shift to home-heating by oil. However, an attack on oil imports might be launched with some hope of success.

In part, it could be launched because the domestic oil producers shared an interest in this attack. The threat to the domestic oil producers came not from residual fuel oil but from the import of crude oil to be processed in American refineries into the full variety of petroleum products. Most of these products are not effectively competitive with coal, though they are completely competitive with the same products distilled from American crude oil.

The obvious basis for an alliance between the American independent oil producers and the coal-miners was for both to work for an over-all quota on imports of petroleum products, including both crude oil and residual.

Such a blanket quota would, however, have an ambivalent effect on the third party in the alliance, the coal-carrying railroads. For many of the railroads in the Middle Atlantic states, coal shipments have historically been the most important source of revenue. Coal, a heavy, bulk product used in enormous quantities and transported in almost no other way, has been the backbone of their prosperity. They therefore stood to benefit from restrictions on residual fuel oil. Ironically, however, these same railroads are rapidly dieselizing their own engines. They stand to benefit from low diesel-oil prices and thus from crude-oil imports. These same Middle Atlantic railroads are in many cases also major conveyors to and from the docks of America's leading ports. Furthermore, the railroads even carry some oil. Thus, railroad interests were complicated and varied from railroad to railroad. Although they would gain from restrictions on residual fuel oil—though by how much it would be hard to gauge—they stood to gain in all other ways from extensive foreign trade and cheap diesel fuel.

Despite all these divergencies of interest, coal, oil, and the railroads formed an alliance and waged a vigorous fight, first for the Simpson bill and later for the Neely amendment.

The public image projected was of an even wider alliance. The Strackbein committee took as its central program, not an increase of tariffs, but the establishment of a system of quotas as described in the Simpson bill. The issue became one, not merely of petroleum quotas, but also of textile, lead, zinc, copper, and brass quotas and many others. The public image created was that of a series of hard-pressed industries, actively united to achieve a common objective.

Yet, when one looked behind the façade, something quite different appeared. We saw the coal-mining industry, and more specifically the National Coal Association, with a strong assist from the United Mine Workers. We also saw, when we looked closely, a handful of men mobilizing a larger number of passive supporters in whose name they acted under a variety of hats.

Even the petroleum independents were to some extent passive allies of the coal association, though they did indeed do a certain amount of active organization and propagandizing on their own. They sent out a report to their members and others about every two weeks and much more often in crucial periods. Many of these reports dealt with natural-gas regulation and similar topics. On various occasions, they were about the trade issue. Number 704, for example, on March 3, 1955, reported the introduction of the Neely amendment. It stated: "This legislation is consistent with that endorsed by this association and the twenty other associations cooperating on the oil imports problem. It needs the enthusiastic support of every domestic producer." It appended the text of the Neely bill, a speech in Congress by Rep. Tom Steed (Dem.) of Oklahoma, a list of the seventeen cosponsors of the amendment, and the names of the members of the Senate Finance Committee.

Congressmen from oil-producing states received substantial communication on the subject of import quotas (and other issues) from the members of this group. Representatives of the association testified frequently, and its general counsel, Russell Brown, and assistant general counsel, A. Dan Jones, were active figures in Washington protectionist circles. Yet, by the standards of the National Coal Association, the petroleum independents were somewhat passive. On various occasions and from various sources we were told, with dark hints but never with substantial fact, of supposed pressures exercised by the Big Five of the oil industry on "small independents to prevent their taking a firm restrictionist stand." Those big companies which import from abroad are also the major customers for the Texas and Oklahoma producers who wanted to stop the foreign imports. There was at least a general consciousness that producers might be antagonizing their primary customers if they were too aggressive. It should be added that this was a mutual feeling. The oil giants were equally fearful of provoking their suppliers or of appearing to bring pressure to bear. The subject was highly charged and was discussed only by hints and implications.

Leaving aside all matters of pressure, oil independents actually shared only partially the interests of the coal people. We noted some reasons above. In addition, as their wealth increased and their investment grew, independents in increasing number began to find themselves with investments abroad. Indeed, at one point, advisers to Venezuelan interests had suggested that the Venezuelan government pick a handful of the key restrictionist independents and give them favorable opportunities for Venezuelan oil investment, a suggestion not taken up by the Venezuelans. Nevertheless, this process of shifts in investment was at work. In the eyes of the coal interests, "Some of the large independents and some of the very small independents have vacillated on this issue. . . . Some have backed away from their earlier protectionist stand." Conversely, to avoid saying that they were working together, a leader of the oil independents told us that in general they were "going in the same direction as the coal people." "The goals," he said, "are the same, but we have different ideas about how to get at them. . . . The coal people were too inflexible on the Simpson bill. They asked for too much."

The big oil companies recognized that coal producers, rather than the oil independents, were their major opponents. We were told by an executive of one of the Big Five,

> . . . that most of the largest [independents] have stayed quite quiet. Only two or three have spoken up mildly. He said possibly they did this out of consideration for the interests of the largest of the companies, acting on the implicit premise that "the big companies stick together." The people who support Russell Brown are quite few.

Abundant evidence as to who were the instigators of the oil-quota drive appeared in examining the Foreign Oil Policy Committee. Its address was 802 Southern Building, Washington, the address of the National Coal Association. Members included presidents of four coal companies; the vice-president of the United Mine Workers and another coal labor man; the executive secretary of the American Retail Coal Association; Tom Pickett, executive vice-president of the National Coal Association; the president of the Anthracite Institute; and the president of the American Coal Sales Association—in short, ten coal men out of eighteen members. In addition, there were two vice-presidents of railroads, two representatives of railroad labor, a vice-president of a lead and zinc company, the vice-president of the National Federation of Independent Business, and O. R. Strackbein. There was also one vice-president of an oil company, and he came from Pennsylvania, not Texas or Oklahoma. Clearly, coal was speaking for oil.

Now, what of the role of the third major party in the alliance, the railroads? At the hearings on the Simpson bill, testimony for the coal-carrying railroads was given by James M. Symes, then executive vice-president of the Pennsylvania Railroad. He also signed a statement submitted to the Randall Commission. In the course of our interviews with railroad executives, a number discussed the history of these statements. Said one:

> The House Ways and Means Committee held hearings on the measure introduced by this Pennsylvania congressman—what's his

name—to limit oil. The coal companies had a perfectly obvious interest. They came to us and asked us to testify. . . . Let me emphasize, the coal companies and two of the coal-carrying railroads . . . took the initiative in this matter on both occasions—before the Randall Commission and before the Ways and Means Committee. . . . There were two reasons why they wanted the Pennsylvania to testify. One: the Pennsylvania probably carries the greatest or about the greatest amount of coal. Two: Mr. Symes is an extremely good witness due to manner and experience.

We interviewed men at the two coal-carrying railroads named as instigators. They did not seem to remember the matter. "Very likely not," we were told by a man who had worked on the testimony and who was not surprised at this lapse of memory. But he did assure us that counsel from the two railroads,

did go over the testimony the first time. . . . On the second occasion, since the testimony before the Randall Commission was about the same . . . we checked with them by telephone. . . . An assistant vice-president in charge of traffic knew someone at the X and Y railroad and talked to him. I asked him to prepare me a list of the railroad people from these different roads.

Our interviewer asked about the list. The respondent could not remember how it had been compiled, but a secretary got it from the files. In each case, it was the vice-president in charge of traffic. The railroads were the New York Central; Baltimore and Ohio; Chesapeake and Ohio; Norfolk and Western; Virginian, Louisville and Nashville; Illinois Central; Western Maryland; and Nickel Plate. "All of them replied 'O.K.' except the X. They didn't reply. We got in touch with them by telephone and they said 'O.K.' " The replies in the file were strictly formal. "The V and W railroad concurs," "The X and Y concurs in the presentation by Mr. Symes."

The pattern that emerges is that one railroad agreed to make a statement as requested by the Coal Association and by two other railroads. The statement was prepared and sent to the vice-president in charge of traffic of each of the relevant railroads. A letter came back saying "O.K.," and the industry was on record. How far the industry had any deep or genuine feelings, how far its stand was known even to itself, remains to be seen.

Indeed, there is little evidence of much strong feeling. One informant told us:

The National Coal Association "asked us to do it and I shouldn't be surprised to find out that they were responsible for the [two initiating roads'] egging us on; although I don't know that, I strongly suspect it."

Here is what we found when we went to other railroads that had signed the Symes testimony. Said the president of one:

Well, we've got to keep our skirts pretty clean. We've got to be careful. A lot of our customers sell goods abroad. . . . We can't show partiality to different customers in making rates or in considering their interests. We have to play both ends against the middle, but X per cent of our tonnage . . . is from coal. The utilities use this foreign oil and . . . might resent our stand. We sit in and counsel with the coal companies. So far as I know, we don't give the coal companies any money for this fight. Maybe we do. I think maybe we did some time ago. . . . We did contribute John Doe's services to them. As far as I know, that was the extent.

He apparently did not recall the Symes testimony. He said:

We asked our officers to write to congressmen about this residual fuel business. We published it in the company magazine. We asked officers in the different divisions as well as at headquarters. . . . Bear in mind we must ride the fence on this. . . . I believe that, when Mr. X was vice-president in charge of traffic, he had a meeting of coal-carrying railroads to discuss this. The officers never went to congressmen as a group and talked to them about this, but they were encouraged to talk to their congressmen individually. No, we never took up the matter with unions. No, we never took up the matter with stockholders either. We have to be careful, we have to be pretty cagey. We have business relationships with customers who are big shippers and want more imports. We let the coal people carry the ball. We work with all phases of industry. Why, Standard Oil itself is one of our big shippers. . . . I was explaining to Senator X the other day that a congressman is in the same position as a railroad man. You have to be nice to everybody; he might be a customer. In the plumbing-supply business, you only have to be nice to plumbers, but here to everybody. . . . Yes, we almost have to be on both sides of everything, just like a politician. We have to be for tariff, against tariff; you want it done away with in order to keep it; either way, somebody's likely to say, "The hell with you, you're against me."

Another railroad that had signed the statement:

There is no question about the coal people being interested. We may do something about it, but so far we haven't done anything on it. Of course, we check articles in magazines. . . .

[Interviewer:] Have the coal people asked you to do anything about their problems?

[Respondent:] Well, that would be the business of the representatives in Washington . . . , it wouldn't be our business. . . . We have heard nothing here about any discussions on foreign economy policy. . . .

Another executive of the same railroad:

The National Coal Association is spearheading this drive, if you call it a drive. They are trying to enlist the railroad's cooperation—that's true—but we have a diversity of interests. [To interviewer:] What did you think of the Randall Commission's report? It sounds interesting. . . . Along with other railroads we have attended the meetings of this National Coal Association group—they call it the Oil Import Policy Committee or some such thing. . . . But definitely on this we've been noncommittal. . . . There is no question that doesn't have merit on both sides. It is just impossible to understand the merit of the State Department position and its ramifications for us here—mind, I am now speaking as a citizen; as a railroad official, I have no opinion. We might possibly be looking at this thing from a too-selfish angle. By "we," I mean people in coal, not railroad necessarily. You'd have to ask other railroads which attended these meetings if they have done anything, but to my knowledge none of them have. . . . I've attended two of these Foreign Oil Policy Committee meetings. No, we have not contributed to it in any way, just attended.

Another railroad:

We were invited by the Foreign Oil Policy Committee of the National Coal Association to take part in this; invited to serve on this committee. . . . The National Coal Association has or had meetings in various sections of the country, and we have had someone there to learn the feeling of the people. . . . These men are not selected to speak. . . . We just posted our people and told them the favorable and unfavorable parts of the situation as it affected us, but no consistent efforts were made to influence members of Congress. . . . This oil business, while it is important, is not so important that we have a fixed program for it. . . . We follow it . . . and do something, but we wouldn't take the lead; we would look to the coal people to take the lead on it.

A railway labor official:

The brotherhoods are, to be sure, working with these coal people, but we aren't. . . . I have told them that, if there is any industry in the U.S. that benefits from foreign trade, it is the railroad industry. We have been asked, yes, to help the coal people. . . . That ex-Texas congressman [Pickett of the NCA] asked me. I told him the small amount of loss involved was not worth fighting about.

What did the Pennsylvania Railroad do after Symes' testimony?

No, we did not release either of Mr. Symes' statements to the press, although I think, as part of the testimony before the committee, the first one did get some coverage. No, there was no reference to it in our house organ. No, we did not call it to the attention of the unions. No, we have made no statement on any other aspect of foreign economic policy. . . . There has not been any other representation on this coal matter and oil matter by anybody from the Pennsylvania Railroad. There have been no informal contacts with senators or congressmen, so far as I know, not even by our representative in Washington. I think the coal people felt the primary burden was theirs, and this was only a minor part of our concern. And we felt that, too.

Finally, one more revealing quote from a railroad man on the problem of conflict of interests. Our interviewer wrote:

Later on I asked about wheat, etc. What would the railroad feel about the argument that what it loses on coal it gains on wheat, etc.? And I asked whether the railroad had taken any general stand on the Randall Commission reports. "No, I think, quite frankly, the railroads don't quite know what their policy was. It is certainly true that what hurts us one place may help us another, and so forth, but we don't know how. There might be some criticism, justifiably, in my opinion, of the lack of definite policy. The railroad's policy is pretty much an *ad hoc* one. They take each issue as it comes along. I realize this approach might be stigmatized as short-term and even shortsighted. It is pretty hard for businessmen to make up their minds. . . . I think it is generally true that American businessmen form their views on economic issues on an *ad hoc* basis. . . . They don't know how to do it any other way. Every big company ought to have a staff of economists around. We don't. . . . We do employ witnesses, economists. . . . The Association of American Railroads does have an economist on its staff who is supposed to do this sort of thing, but one guy can't do much for the industry.

Clearly, the railroads were not firmly opposed to oil imports. In effect, they had done a favor for a customer. One wonders what would have happened if, before the National Coal Association took the initiative, an exporters' association had approached the same railroads to ask them to present testimony for expanded foreign trade. They might conceivably have testified on the opposite side and in doing so have been equally convinced that they were acting rationally for their self-interest. One wonders, also, what would have happened if both sides had approached them more or less simultaneously. Presumably, they would have done nothing. But what actually happened was that they were organized by the National Coal Association, and that fact determined the stand they took. On the record, the railroads were cited as unified in support of quotas on oil imports.

This takes us back once more to the National Coal Association. It was an unusually effective and ably led trade association. Its executive vice-president was Tom Pickett, first a practicing lawyer in Texas, then a prosecutor, and subsequently a member of Congress. The cost of being a congressman became too stiff, and in 1952 he decided not to run again. He was planning to go back to Texas when the coal job came along. Pickett is a breezy, open, large-boned man who is willing and able to talk and who treats one as an old friend from the first moment of meeting: "You'll find that I am the easiest man to get to know that there is." Cut out for a job of organization and persuasion, he is not a man to whom ideological liberals are likely to warm up any more than he is likely to warm up to them. As an anti-New Deal, anti-Fair Deal Democrat, he ran for re-election to Congress on the slogan, "The Man who Stopped FEPC." To him, the members of the State Department were striped-pants do-gooders, more interested in what happens on the other side of the border than in what happens here. Pickett was the dynamo of the oil-quota campaign, supported on the broader public front by Strackbein, a man of equal ability.

Even the coal industry, despite the vigor of Pickett's representations and the depth of John L. Lewis' convictions, is not solidly united on foreign-trade policy, although it is far more nearly so than most industries. As one coal man put it:

> They're all in favor of the reduction of imports by quantitative limitation. There is, however, a difference in the degree of interest of different firms in this. Some of them are very active; some don't care much. . . . The captive coal mines . . . section of the . . . industry is not affected by residual-fuel-oil competition because its market is directly to the steel companies. Since Big Steel has this source of supply, it doesn't give a damn about the coal industry as a whole. The steel industry has now been expanding production to the point where it has reached the saturation point of the domestic market, so . . . Big Steel is looking for foreign markets. . . .

A spokesman for a trade association of "captive" coal mines said:

> There is a bit of division of opinion . . . so I don't want to be pinned down myself. . . . Clarence Randall and Inland Steel belong to our organization, and I personally have taken no part in this lobby. . . . We are concerned with statistics, labor contracts, and safety, and legislation immediately related thereto; that's all. . . . The whole issue is sort of taboo in our shop. We don't discuss it.

Another source of divergence is coal exports. The volume of these has been extremely variable. At times, they have been a significant matter for the industry. The reciprocal-trade advocates blame the coal industry itself for failing to develop this potential market. The coal people are far less sanguine and feel that they cannot regularly and ordinarily compete in the overseas market. There is a Coal Exporters Association. However, it shares its offices and telephone number with the National Coal Association—a situation unlikely to permit it to develop a strongly independent view.

The conflicts of interest are sufficient to occasionally dampen the vigor of Tom Pickett's efforts. Those who know him have no doubt that Pickett would like to say things to and about his opponents, particularly the State Department, that he does not. There have been occasions when his statements brought repercussions from cautious members of his association. There is a feeling around the offices of the Coal Association that, despite the perpetual conflict over rates between coal shippers and railroads, any criticism of the railroads is taboo. Many coal people are heavy owners of railroad stock, and, equally important, they regard the railroads as consumers. The taboo, necessary or self-imposed, acted as a brake on the oil-quota campaign, since, as we have seen, the railroads were not fighting the battle all-out.

The complications, restrictions, and balancing of multiple interests pervade all aspects of the controversy. Within the National Coal Association, such conflicts of viewpoint are actually at a minimum. The association is relatively free to be aggressive and to fight as best it can for the policy it advocates. It also has able leadership. With these advantages, it has been able to build a nominal coalition in whose name it has carried on a campaign purporting to represent a wide segment of American industry. It achieved thereby a modicum of legislative success.

This story of partial success demonstrates the limitations and also the potential of lobbying. The major effect of the lobby is seldom that which gives it its name. It is seldom successful in buttonholing congressmen, in persuading, in working behind the scenes, and in buying or bullying votes. In the instances we cited, as indeed in most cases, the major effect achieved by small activist groups was in building a series of fronts through which they could speak. Since such fronts come to be regarded by the general public and Congress alike as the representatives of important interests, those who controlled what these groups said controlled thereby the accepted image of what the issues were and how the major interests felt about them.

□ Summary

Judged by the outcome, both the campaign of the American Cotton Manufacturers Institute and that of the Foreign Oil Policy Committee may be regarded as successful. A substantial group of Southern congressmen voted against the Reciprocal Trade Act in 1955, despite long-standing Southern tradition, and voluntary quotas on oil imports were put into effect in 1955.

Certainly, other factors were also at work. For example, the Georgia Congressional delegation may have been influenced by Gov. Herman Talmadge's adoption of a protectionist position in his senatorial campaign against Senator George. We agree with the statement of Blaisdell: "No simple, categorical statement can be made about the effect of pressure groups on American democracy. Only one thing is certain: the difficulty of determining the effect." [2] Yet, both campaigns were successful in their immediate objectives. The ACMI did get Southern businessmen to write to their congressmen, and the coal industry succeeded in forming a coalition of coal, oil, and Eastern railroads in what appeared to be united opposition to oil imports.

Other writers have referred to "catalytic groups" and to the important role of coalitions. Blaisdell talks of them in these terms:

---

[2] *Op. cit.,* p. 11.

> Groups of this type [catalytic groups] are sensitive to the subtle but important political difference between acceptance and support and between rejection and opposition. This is the difference between passive and active attitudes and is shrewdly exploited by catalytic groups. Rarely, if ever, strong enough in their own right to swing the balance of power . . . , such groups form coalitions with stronger groups. . . .[3]

But the notion of a coalition does not by itself express adequately the various aspects of the cases we have discussed.

The catalytic action of the ACMI and the National Coal Association accomplished more than the addition of numerical support to its position. It changed the qualitative nature of the campaign. It put itself in a position to determine what people thought were the issues and thus what they chose to discuss. It pre-empted this gatekeeper role among its followers as well as before outsiders. In place of hired lobbyists approaching Congress, Southern congressmen were approached by men, many of whom they knew personally and who were regarded as having a legitimate involvement in the issue. But these businessmen approached Congress only because the ACMI had informed them that an issue existed and that others were doing the same. We shall have occasion below to discuss the congressman's concern over distinguishing between spontaneous, legitimate petitions and stimulated pressure. As indicated, the ACMI campaign could have been seen by the Southern congressmen as stimulated if they had had more experience with protectionist appeals. But the ACMI did succeed in creating the appearance of a relatively broad, spontaneous appeal by affected businessmen, rather than that of an organized pressure campaign. It did so not by trickery but by virtue of the fact that a politically influential group of members was ready to take its word as to what the problem was and to act "spontaneously" accordingly.

The success of the National Coal Association underscored the latitude in possible definitions of self-interest. It is our impression that most discussions of the formation of pressure-group coalitions take the self-interest of the parties for granted. But it was by no means clear that the self-interest of the small oil companies and particularly of the railroads lay in combining with the coal industry in opposing oil imports. In fact, in both of the campaigns discussed, the pressure groups not only activated but defined the self-interest of the members of the coalitions. In the textile industry, there were many problems bothering Southern operators, not the least of which were competition with Northern mills and concern over unionization. But the ACMI managed to get them to focus on the issue of foreign imports. The National Coal Association perhaps performed a more adroit feat in getting oil and railroads to collaborate on a single issue on which all three could be united even though there were a number of

---

[3] *Ibid.,* pp. 8f.

actual and potential conflicts among the three. It is our best guess that the railroads could equally easily have been organized on the opposing side.

On the one hand, we are claiming that pressure groups are less omnipotent than popular literature and exposés would lead us to believe. On the other hand, we argue that the catalytic group has more leeway than has ordinarily been assumed. Because the self-interest of business is complicated, it is possible for a resourceful organizer to have a considerable amount of latitude in swinging quite diverse groups to his side. The power of the pressure organization seems to be that it is recognized as the voice of its supporters. Thus, what it says is endowed with a kind of canonical authority as the expression of their point of view. Its power lies in that slight aura of legitimacy, not in having any capability for persuasion or coercion.

Chapter 26

The CNTP—
Spokesman for Reciprocal Trade

A thesis of the preceding chapter was that the pressure groups we observed were most successful when they organized and stimulated activity by others. The two examples cited were on the protectionist side of the controversy. In this and the next chapter we shall depict three liberal-trade organizations and activities: the fight *against* oil-import restrictions, 1951-1953; the Committee for a National Trade Policy; and the League of Women Voters.

□ The Fight against Oil-Import Restrictions

The CNTP grew up in 1953 out of a number of antecedents. Perhaps the most important of these was the fight in 1951 and 1953 against oil-import restrictions, a fight finally lost in 1955. In 1953, the Washington law firm of Cleary, Gottlieb, Friendly, and Ball, representing the Venezuelan Chamber of Commerce, helped mobilize opposition to the Simpson bill and, earlier, in 1951, to another proposal to limit oil imports. In these campaigns, the firm developed an effective approach to such efforts, an approach whose influence may be noted in the 1962 campaign for the Kennedy trade program.

They operated on the principle that, to produce results, it was necessary to appeal not to a generalized public opinion but to an existing real interest that would both stimulate men to action and be recognized as legitimate by Congress. They believed also that many businessmen were not aware of their interests—specifically, that many did not export to Venezuela directly but sold to dealers and had no clear idea of how much the Venezuelan market might mean to them. As in the case of the National Coal Association and the coal-carrying railroads, their problem was to alert a group to the presence of an interest. They made studies of the exports of various American industries to Venezuela. They then sent letters based on this research to manufacturers in those fields showing each that his firm had sold X million or X thousand dollars worth of products on the Venezuelan market and that the stoppage of the flow of dollars to Venezuela would cut off that market. Would the manufacturer please write his congressman?

They followed up such letters on the telephone or with a personal call locally from one of their correspondent attorneys. In the 1951 and 1953 petroleum-import campaign, they established relationships with law firms in Chicago, Cincinnati, Baton Rouge, San Francisco, Los Angeles, Boston, Louisville, Cleveland, Pittsburgh, Portland, Philadelphia, and Baltimore.

There were at least two obvious reasons for their use of lawyers in this connection. As a law firm, their good contacts were with lawyers. Perhaps even more important, they recognized that businessmen are used to taking advice from lawyers, but resist taking advice from other independent professionals, such as public-relations men. This operation has been described by Charles Taft, who was one of the correspondent attorneys on the earlier case. Taft was on the stand for the Committee on a National Trade Policy, being grilled by Congressman Simpson. He was able to make his point only after parrying a number of Simpson's thrusts.

> Simpson: Whom do you represent lobbying besides this group?
> Taft: I do not represent anybody at the present time. . . .
> Simpson: You no longer represent Venezuela?
> Taft: I never represented Venezuela.
> Simpson: You or anyone in your firm?
> Taft: No, sir.
> Simpson: You deny it?
> Taft: Certainly I deny it. I never represented Venezuela at any time. I represented the Venezuelan Chamber of Commerce, which has more than half American members.
> Simpson: Let us not equivocate.
> Taft: That is not equivocation. I do not represent a foreign government and I never have.

> Simpson: You represent Venezuela in what?
>
> Taft: My job was to go to American producers in Cincinnati, Ohio, who are selling to Venezuela and tell them, if they let this quota go on residual oil, they would stop doing business with Venezuela.

Taft was soberly predicting, not threatening, when he conveyed that message. The moral which the law firm saw in the success of this operation was that the only effective approach was a coldly factual one. On that basis, they approached 500 firms in one campaign and got aid from 150 of them.[1] Occasionally, the correspondent attorneys tried to use their personal influence with businessmen they knew; this seemed invariably to fail.

The "coldly factual" approach was particularly effective in New England, where much of the imported residual fuel oil is consumed. Here, the approach was not only to businessmen who sold to Venezuela but also to industries and utilities which burned residual fuel oil. Cleary, Gottlieb, Friendly, and Ball prepared a four-page statement on the ways in which New England was vulnerable to fuel-oil quotas; 4,000 copies were sent to businessmen with whom they had contact. The New England Council was aroused. From such industries as traditionally protectionist textiles, protests flooded into Congress. All in all, an image was created in Washington of violent New England opposition to the bill, and the New England congressmen took the lead in opposing it, despite the protectionism of many of them on other matters.

Here, again, one might ask what would have happened if, for example, the Strackbein committee had approached them first with a plea to cooperate in trying to get textile quotas along with oil quotas. One also wonders what would have happened if there had been a simultaneous approach by both sides. In any case, an image of New England attitudes was created, the unreality of which we have spelled out in the chapter on New Anglia. Its unreality parallels almost precisely that of the image of the coal-oil-railroad bloc on the other side.

These early campaigns of Cleary, Gottlieb, Friendly, and Ball resembled the protectionist campaigns previously described in several respects. The basis of the appeal was not abstract principles, the national interest, the interests of the world at large, or personal friendship, but direct economic self-interest. But, since the self-interest of the men approached was by no means clear to these men themselves, an essential part of the

---

[1] One other significant contribution they made to the defeat of the Simpson bill was in getting an expression from President Eisenhower against it. They believed, rightly or wrongly, that he had made a deal to accept the bill in return for a compromise by the supporters of oil imports on another aspect of the trade program. To block this deal, they planted a question in one of the press conferences during the fight on the Simpson bill, and Eisenhower, in answering the question, came out against the bill, thus scuttling any implicit or explicit commitments that may have existed and putting him on record.

campaign was defining this self-interest and alerting businessmen to it. These early campaigns of C.G.F.&B. resembled in several respects the protectionist campaigns discussed previously. The result was the same in all the campaigns we have discussed; they produced an appearance of unanimity and involvement in the business community that far exceeded the reality of the situation. The role of the organizer was not one of lobbying or of direct approach to Congress, but rather that of organizing segments of the business community by giving them a voice and stimulating them to contact Congress on a common theme.

As already indicated, the two petroleum-import campaigns provided one image of how the CNTP should be organized: a factual approach based on self-interest, buttressed by research to define this self-interest.

□ Siring the CNTP

The oil-import campaigns just described form part of the prehistory of the CNTP, not only in the experience acquired, but also through the person of George Ball, then Washington partner of C.G.F.&B. America's ever-increasing participation through the last decades in a world economy owes a recognizable debt to the deep convictions of this rather retiring man. His beliefs in Western unity and the crucial role of freer trade in achieving it have since found public expression in the Kennedy trade policy, which Ball as under secretary of state was instrumental in developing. In 1953 and 1955, though not yet a name in the news, he was already a man with wide business and political contacts, a liberal Democrat often credited with having started the 1952 Stevenson boom.

Ball's efforts for a general antiprotectionist organization stem from not later than the middle of 1952. At that time, he discussed the possibility of such an organization with Paul Hoffman, William Clayton, Stanley Holm of General Electric, officers of the International House in New Orleans, and Ralph Straus. He had in mind an organization formed by exporters to promote imports. He felt that the costs of its activities would run on the order of $250,000 a year. He recognized that the task of doing the kind of analysis that had been done on exports to Venezuela for all export industries to all countries would be a formidable one, but he still argued for its importance, since the exporters themselves often do not know their own interests.

Another early lead in the formation of the Committee on a National Trade Policy stemmed from Ralph Straus, a businessman of the Macy department store family. His interests in trade liberalization stemmed from his overseas experience while working for the United States government. In 1949, he was approached by Paul Hoffman, head of the Economic Cooperation Administration, about going to Europe on a mission of four businessmen to prepare a report on ECA operations. Straus joined them. Among other things, the report recommended as one device for closing the dollar gap that the ECA appoint someone in each country or area whose job it would be to promote exports from that country to the United States. On December 1, 1949, Hoffman asked Straus to take over the job of organizing such a unit in Europe. Straus discussed it with Richard Bissell and William Foster, Hoffman's assistants. Straus told them that he would not take over such an assignment unless the men in charge in the field understood it and wanted it. Foster suggested that Straus go to Europe to talk to Averell Harriman and Milton Katz, then in charge of ECA in Europe, to get their reaction. He went. They liked the idea, and he took the job. By June, 1950, Straus had established his arrangements in all the countries of Western Europe. His agency worked with export associations and the relevant ministries in those countries. However, the agency did not last long. It was under constant attack, and, on June 30, 1951, it was abolished "for budgetary reasons." Straus was naturally disappointed, although some European governments continued the same activities on their own.

Straus came back to the United States convinced that the job that he had tried to do of promoting European exports was one that should be done permanently by the State, Commerce, or Treasury departments and one that needed the backing of an American citizens' organization. None of these ideas fructified immediately, but he continued to discuss them with such men as Paul Hoffman, William Clayton, Stanley Holm, and George Ball. At the end of October, 1952, he wrote William Draper about the need for a citizen effort for a liberal-trade policy. He said that to promote imports there was a need for a new association financed by exporters. He felt that the organization should be headed by a prominent businessman of the highest repute, exactly the pattern later followed by the Coleman committee. These efforts, however, did not lead directly to the Coleman committee. They seemed to reach a dead end late in 1952.

The next initiatives came from entirely different directions. One of these was Philadelphia, which had been the home of the so-called Batt committee, a group of prominent citizens which had played an important part in campaigning for Congressional support of the Marshall Plan. William Batt, Sr., president of SKF, was the chairman of the older organization. One of the spark plugs of the group was Mrs. Eleanor Woolf. Some of the same people saw the need for a new group on the foreign-trade issue.

But the initiative that finally led to the formation of the CNTP came when Harry Bullis, chairman of the board of General Mills, at the urging of persons close to the President, called together a group of business-men in New York. The assembled group included Joseph Spang, Jr., of Gillette, Gen. John J. McCloy of the Chase National Bank, Straus, Walter Louchheim, and Ball. They brought in Charles Taft, whose family repre-sented the respectability of Midwestern conservatism, as president of the new organization. Originally, Bullis had been pressed to take the chair-manship, but he declined under the burden of other activities. Bullis urged John Coleman, president of the Burroughs Manufacturing Company, to accept the chairmanship. Coleman had some hesitancy, but, upon a tele-phone call from Harold Stassen, then at the White House, he agreed to accept.

□ The CNTP in Action

Charles Taft, it will be recalled, had been one of the correspondents of George Ball on the earlier petroleum campaign, and a brilliantly suc-cessful one, in Ohio where he was dealing with people with whom he had had long contact. The new plan was essentially an adaptation and develop-ment of the methods used in the Venezuelan campaigns. Because of the broader character of the issues, it was recognized from the first that a cer-tain amount of general educational activity that was not essential, on such matters as petroleum quotas, would be called for. Our first interviews made it clear, however, that the conception at that stage was distinctly one of a hardheaded appeal to the self-interest of exporters and that the methods to be used were not dissimilar from those that had proved successful with the Simpson bill. The largest commitment in the budget proposed in October, 1953, was for the preparation of a list of names of 100,000 businessmen with a clear self-interest in export markets and freer trade. It was recognized from the start that locating such people by research on individual companies would be prohibitive, but there was much discussion of possible short cuts, ways to get industry and other summary data that would be meaningful and that would make it possible to go to a business-man and say, "You are selling about so-and-so many dollars' worth of goods to country Y." The plan thus called for significant preparatory research followed by the development of a highly focused mailing list, to be put on IBM cards.

So far, the operations seemed highly purposeful, professional, and action-oriented. From here on, the story of the committee is that of a change of role into a relatively diffuse, educational, statement-releasing operation.

The original plans quickly went down the drain. A mistake was committed almost on the day of birth of the committee. It set out, as we have noted, to raise $300,000. Its first act, before any publicity had been issued and before people knew the names of the committee members or its stand, was to send to a large selection of top business leaders lengthy telegrams appealing for membership and funds. Needless to say, the results of the fund drive were disappointing.[2]

An even more serious error, perhaps, was the fact that virtually no one was consulted outside the small group that met and decided to act. There had long existed certain small and perhaps only partly effective groups on the side of liberal trade. Among these, perhaps the most important was the United States Council of the International Chamber of Commerce, not to be confused with the United States Chamber of Commerce. For years, it had been carrying on a campaign on behalf of American international business and foreign trade. Representatives of that group had not been included in the initial consultations, and Lee Pierson, its chairman, was not put on the original Coleman committee board. In the months that followed, at least some of the people who had been associated with that organization, both at the level of leadership and of the staff, worked directly with Clarence Randall, Gabriel Hauge, and the White House staff, rather than with the CNTP. A list of affiliated organizations which the CNTP circulated did not include the U.S. Council.

Another group that felt aggrieved was the importers. For many years, the National Council of Importers had been waging a small-scale fight for freer trade. Importers are not particularly aggressive or vocal. They are on the whole small businesses and have small resources. To a considerable extent, they are immigrants, first-generation Americans, or foreigners and feel reticent in American politics. Furthermore, they feel, as apparently congressmen and others do, that theirs is a somewhat foreign interest.[3]

---

[2] One practice which increased the impression that the Coleman committee was only a fund-raising activity was that it dropped people from the mailing list unless they replied to the appeal for funds. Respondents were not obliged to send funds, but most people do not answer a letter asking for funds unless they are enclosing money. Thus, many interested people received nothing from the Coleman committee but the initial request for funds.

[3] In sitting in meetings of the study group of top importers and manufacturers, we constantly noted the reluctance of importers to present their case in a positive fashion. Their main contention seemed to be that they weren't really hurting American industry. Many features of foreign-trade legislation have changed since Schattschneider wrote his study of the passage of the Smoot-Hawley tariff, but the tactical plight of the importer seems to have remained about the same. One of the characteristics which he noted is that about nine-tenths of importers had their headquarters in New York City. This in itself limited, and still limits, their ability to enlist support on a broad geographical basis. Second, he points out, "In this organization of attitudes the importer is almost fatally handicapped. He is the agent of foreign interests that have no standing in court, and

Nevertheless, they have for many years been going through all the normal motions of an interest group. They foster research, prepare statements and documents, circularize their membership, and keep members informed on legislative developments and on whom to write. They had recently formed a council of trade associations concerned with importing. Although it had been planned that one member of the board of the Coleman committee, who was an ex-president of the council, would be given a chance to interest that group, a number of the individuals who had been prominent in importers' activities received telegrams asking for money before they had been approached or consulted.

Thus, off to an inauspicious start, the committee from the beginning used the mass, written message rather than the individual one. It was hamstrung by the need to cope with fund-raising, membership recruitment, and all the problems that we have already described. The funds were never adequate to conduct the research originally planned.

Furthermore, the CNTP soon gained the intellectual stamp of a debating society. It became an organization largely devoted to issuing statements and disseminating economic analyses. Although the CNTP did effectively occupy the position of spokesman for its side, the development of the action-oriented strategy originally contemplated became impossible in the 1950's.

In June, 1955, a pamphlet was issued over John Coleman's signature, part of which was devoted to reviewing the activities of the CNTP up to that point. Enumerated were:

> . . . Sought, and received, support for the trade program from almost every major civic, business, farm, and labor organization.
> . . . Policy recommendations . . . presented to the *President's Commission on Foreign Economic Policy* [the Randall Commission].
> . . . Studies and reports made by our committee on such questions as tariff levels and the effect of imports on domestic production and employment [have] already been given wide circulation.
> . . . Then, recognizing that to many people foreign commerce seems unrelated to their personal interests, we undertook to pinpoint the trade issue on the local level.
> . . . Through the efforts of our legislative committee, increasingly representative groups of businessmen participated in the numerous public hearings relating to the trade issue.

Of all the CNTP activities listed by Coleman, the fourth—"pinpoint the trade issue on the local level"—came closest to the organizers'

---

does business on sufferance . . ." (*op. cit.,* p. 161). To some extent, the importer of 1953-1955 was in a slightly better position, since foreign interests were at least nominally accepted as legitimate in the discussions of this latter period. The importers themselves, however, apparently were not sufficiently convinced to be willing to speak up with vigor and confidence.

original concepts of what the committee should have done. Between 1953 and 1955, several economic surveys were made to determine the self-interest of local communities in foreign-trade policy. The unit was sometimes a Congressional district and occasionally an entire state. So far as we know, only one survey was actually carried out by the CNTP, this being in the First Congressional District of Iowa. The U.S. Council of the International Chamber of Commerce covered the Eighteenth District of Pennsylvania, the district represented by Congressman Richard Simpson. The Legislative Reference Service of the Library of Congress also responded to the request of four congressmen with studies of their specific districts. Additional ones were carried out by the League of Women Voters. All such studies of which we are aware, with the partial exception of one in Rhode Island mentioned in the next chapter, came to the conclusion that the district in question would benefit from more trade.

These studies received a fair amount of publicity. The one on Representative Simpson's district was gleefully reported in *The Washington Post* on May 24, 1953. Simpson's private and public reaction was that the study was nonsense.

The study of the Eighth Indiana District requested by Congressman D. Bailey Merrill was reported in the February, 1954, issue of *Harper's.*

The CNTP distributed its own report, *Iowa and World Trade,* both in a detailed and in a summary form and publicized it and the other studies in a brochure entitled *Documenting the Evidence.*[4]

These studies of localities, one of which the CNTP carried out and the others of which it publicized, were as close as the CNTP came to its original intention of a pinpointed appeal on the basis of self-interest.

☐ Some Difficulties of the CNTP

As the committee had difficulties, complaints and disappointment increased. People started to look for a scapegoat. Our interviews abound

---

[4] Neither document is dated, but both were presumably issued late in 1954. In 1962, there was substantially more research of the same sort done. The Department of Commerce supported studies of how many workers in various localities and industries depended on exports for their jobs. Such an "Export Origin Study" was prepared for each state. A Washington research firm received a contract to draw lists of firms and their key executives (listed by Congressional districts) who would have an export interest. All these materials were issued by the CNTP. In short, the committee's original program was more nearly implemented nine years later.

Even in 1962, the CNTP's main function was general propaganda. The detailed bargaining with trade representatives was done by government officials. The de-emphasis on broad-sweep propaganda in 1962 is illustrated, however, by the fact that the CNTP budget was some 20 per cent lower in 1962 than in 1955 or 1958.

with criticisms. Cleary, Gottlieb, Friendly, and Ball dropped the committee as a client in order to be free to take other accounts where they felt they would be more effective.[5] There were those who found the committee's activities too academic and called it a study group.[6] We were told in the White House itself that the committee was inept, that there was no one there who understood organization, that Taft liked to go up to the Hill and talk to the boys, and that Coleman likewise did not provide organizational leadership. (In return, committee staffers complained about lack of leadership from the White House.)

A frequent criticism of Coleman seemed to be that, when he took the job, he had not realized what he was in for. He soon found himself in the midst of a controversial issue, with many of his close friends at the top level of business on the other side, accusing him of being a "one-worlder."

The main criticism of Taft was that he stressed propaganda activities more than organizing. One of the things of which he did a great deal and which had been explicitly excluded by the original plan was public speaking. Such generalized appeals as addressing Chambers of Commerce, Rotary Clubs, international-affairs groups, and the like had originally been dismissed as ineffective. "You have an itinerary, not a program," he was told by a critic.

There was another and still more serious problem for the Coleman committee. That was the question of who should take the lead. We described above one occasion, that of the Gore amendment, when the Coleman committee proved extremely effective in action. Then, Senator Gore took the lead. But the CNTP was organized to work with the White House, and most of the time there was a "dear-Alphonse" act going on between the White House staff and the Coleman committee staff. Clarence Randall is a man of the highest and strictest standards. When he accepted a government job, he recognized that he was bound by law not to lobby. Few public officials in recent years have interpreted this injunction as preventing them

---

[5] The Venezuelan activities had come to an end before taking on the CNTP, and the latter was dropped before taking on the planters of Cuban sugar. There was felt to be an incompatibility between representing the CNTP and representing a single special interest.

[6] In the first half-year of operation, the Coleman committee concentrated on sending out a number of mailings. These were: (1) the telegraphic appeal to join; (2) an invitation to the kick-off dinner in New York; (3) a copy of the speeches made there; (4) Coleman's statement to the Randall Commission; (5) the committee's proposal to the Randall Commission; (6) a letter from Taft to the members on the importance of working with other organizations in their communities; (7) Report Number One of the committee; (8) a report from Coleman on the activities of the committee in its fund-raising and a request for funds; (9) a letter on the Randall Commission report and a press release about it; (10) a copy of the Randall report; (11) a letter asking people to become active on the issue in their own trade associations.

from trying to mobilize public opinion behind themselves. Certainly Kennedy and his staff did not. Clarence Randall did; he stuck to the letter of the law. In his image of the situation, a prairie fire of public support could be set only by a private committee set up to do the job outside the government. He and his staff could do no more than follow where the Coleman committee led them, adding to the movement whatever aid White House blessing could render. The White House could receive delegations, communicate with Congressional leaders, and prepare presidential statements, but it could not take the lead in organizing a campaign for legislation.

The view of the Coleman committee staff was precisely the reverse. They viewed themselves as a service agency to help the White House staff when help was demanded. They felt that only the President had the stature and leadership to decide what the objectives and strategy should be. Once the President gave a lead, they recognized that their role was to mobilize public support for it.

Thus, each waited for the other. At one point, we interviewed one of the top officials of the Coleman committee and asked what they were doing at the moment.

> He said there wasn't anything much they could do now because there wasn't any bill before Congress or any action to be taken. . . . He said that they will stick close to the Randall Commission recommendations, but there isn't anything they can do for the moment. Any effort now would be waste effort until there is a specific bill to support.

An officer of the committee also attributed, not to himself, but to the board the view that they could do nothing.

> We have a number of people on our board and committee who are willing to support the President in whatever he wants, but they are not willing to go further than he wants. . . . Of course, a committee like ours can only be effective insofar as the administration lets it be and wants it to be. We can go around and do things which, for example, the secretary of labor cannot do because of his official position; but we are basically a kind of extra arm for the administration. And, when the administration is inert, as this one is, why, there is very little our committee or a committee of this type can do. . . . When it became clear to me around the first of March that the administration was not going to go very far, I felt it was best for us to play it quietly, do what we can, but there is not too much we can do.

On the other hand, a consultant for the White House staff gave the reverse picture. He indicated impatience with the difficulty he had in getting action out of the committee.

> Public relations is a kind of intelligence operation, he said. The day before the [President's] speech was delivered, he got hold of the release which Strackbein had written as his immediate answer to the President. . . . He took it over to [X, at the Coleman committee]. . . .

> If X were good for anything, he would have jumped . . . to prepare an immediate blast in reply, but X didn't.

Another White House man said:

> I'm in a terrible spot and I cannot do anything about it. I'm a civil servant, and I'm prohibited by law from engaging in any propaganda. I can't have anything to do with them [the Coleman committee].

Some critics around the CNTP felt that, although Randall wanted the Coleman committee to take the lead, he also wanted it to be a captive of the White House. Cited as the major instance was the episode of the Gore amendment, when Randall at first expressed annoyance at the committee's support of Gore. The relations between Randall and the committee, although close, were never smooth. Dissatisfied as he may have been, however, Randall always felt that there was nothing he could do. The Coleman committee was the public spokesman for freer-trade sentiment. He waited for it to start a movement to which he could respond. When it did not do so, he could only express frustration.

☐ The Effectiveness of the CNTP

To judge the net effectiveness of the CNTP in the 1950's is not simple. Certainly, the committee failed completely in its original objective to wage a cold-facts campaign based on self-interest, bolstered and defined by research. We have attributed this failure to shortages of funds and to the temperament of the people who eventually staffed the committee. Either factor would have been a sufficient cause.

Although early plans included a certain amount of general educational activities, it was not intended that these should become the major part of the CNTP's work. Yet Taft's speeches and the various general mailings turned out to be the committee's main business, as opposed to focused messages, directed at the individual's self-interest and designed to stimulate him to direct action.

The committee did succeed in making a certain amount of news and in stimulating communications in the mass media. For example, Taft's speeches were reported in the press. It also established itself as the spokesman for reciprocal trade. It is difficult to assess the practical value of such a symbol, but there is gain to a cause if its adherents feel even vaguely that it has leadership, that someone is fighting for it.

In establishing its symbolic leadership, the CNTP also established itself as a place to go to for information and help. Thus, as we have already pointed out, Senator Gore went to the committee for assistance in his fight to push reciprocal trade through the Senate in 1954.

Some of the committee's stronger supporters told us that it succeeded in swinging a number of Congressional votes in 1955. The number that could be directly attributed to the CNTP was apparently at most under half a dozen.

All that has been said may well undervalue the long-run effects of the CNTP. The original estimate of its founders that a cold-facts approach based on self-interest would be the most effective way of generating support for a particular reciprocal-trade bill may, indeed, have been correct. Such an approach would be the appropriate counter to the opposition claim that liberal traders were impractical. The appeal to self-interest would fit well with our own earlier observation, based on the survey data, that immediate and clearly perceived self-interest is the most effective stimulus to action. That was the approach to which the administration basically turned in 1962, and with much better short-term results than earlier. But it must be conceded, in any assessment of the effectiveness of the CNTP in 1954-1955, that the more general and diffuse appeals which it then used produced effects which are difficult to observe. But for the basic changes in business attitudes generated in the 1950's, the Trade Expansion Act would not have passed in 1962, no matter what deals were made in its favor. "Sleeper effects" and effects mediated through public opinion and various other filters may be substantial, but they manifest themselves only with the passage of years.[7] Perhaps, in the end, they are the most permanent effects, for devices which produce action without conviction may yield only one-time successes, whereas even defeats are only temporary for the truly converted.

---

[7] Cf. Bernard Berelson, Paul F. Lazarsfeld, and William McPhee, *Voting* (Chicago: University of Chicago Press, 1954), which supports the conclusion that few changes of basic atttitude occur during an election campaign. Such changes occur slowly during the intervening four years. The effect of campaign action in producing votes must be distinguished from its effect, if any, on the development of attitudes. Cf. also Carl Hovland, Arthur Lumsdaine, and Irving Janis, *Experiments in Mass Communication* (Princeton: Princeton University Press, 1949), on the "sleeper effect." Persuasion for opinion change showed effects often after a delay, during which new information was gradually worked over by the recipient.

Chapter 27

The Ladies of the League

One pressure group, the League of Women Voters,[1] violated almost all the generalizations we have made. During the period of our study and for some time previously and thereafter, the League of Women Voters was actively concerned with foreign trade and militantly in favor of liberalizing America's policy. Although it is a broad, multipurpose organization, it was not inhibited from action by minority dissent, if such dissent existed. In contrast to other pressure groups, the League had very good resources for doing research, and it gathered much information to bolster its position. League members knew the positions of their congressmen and senators, and they wrote to them by the thousands. The members of the League showed no timidity in approaching men or women whom they knew to be opposed to their position. Although the League certainly did not have unlimited financial resources, its large numbers of willing, intelligent, and trained volunteers made possible a prodigious output of activity.

---

[1] Since the term "pressure group" has been so closely linked with special interest, a general-interest group such as the League may object to the label. The fact remains that the League was very active in trying to influence a government decision.

In short, the League was free of many of the disabilities of other pressure groups. Yet, it had its own distinctive disadvantages.

When our study began, in the fall of 1953, the League of Women Voters had already been concerned for some time with foreign-trade policy. In February, 1952, the national board of the League issued an excellently prepared memo entitled "The Citizen and International Trade," a thirty-one–page pamphlet covering a wide range of issues from a liberal-trade point of view. The educational program for League members continued throughout 1953. *The National Voter* carried articles on foreign-trade policy. In March, 1953, a handbook [2] was issued, suggesting courses of action: calling a meeting of "representatives of such groups as business, labor, agriculture, chambers of commerce, etc."; setting up a speakers' bureau; getting local newspapers to print editorials, feature articles, and news stories; setting up window displays; getting librarians to put books and pamphlets on display; distributing leaflets in the community; informing the community of the status of legislation; arranging radio and television programs; and, finally, "conduct a mock Congressional hearing on international trade." By the beginning of 1954, the number-one item on the League's agenda was: "Support of U.S. trade policies that will help solve national and international economic problems."

During 1954, the League must have been by several orders of magnitude the most active group to be found on either side of the trade controversy. The intensity of involvement of the League members matched the extent of its activities. We heard numerous anecdotes of League-member wives of protectionist businessmen bringing "the gospel" into the home.

When one local opinion poll was conducted by League members, the women directing the poll found that they had to be very careful in instructing the interviewers that under no circumstance were they to tell the respondents the "right answers," at least not until they had answered the questionnaire!

Our estimate was that more than three-fourths of the Congressional mail supporting the Reciprocal Trade Act originated in the League. But the activities of the League were far from restricted to writing to representatives in Congress. It carried on a campaign of public education of the broadest sort. Mock Congressional hearings were held in such places as St. Louis and Louisville. League members did, or attempted to do, everything that was suggested in the handbook of March, 1953, and they did it throughout the country.

In February, 1954, a phonograph record was made available "suited

---

2 "A Workshop: International Trade and International Economic Development," Publication #210, March 1953.

to small home groups, large club audiences, or regular radio broadcasting." On one side, the president of the U.S. Chamber of Commerce and the president of the CNTP, on the other side, the assistant secretary of commerce and a prominent journalist preached the gospel of increased world trade.

One distinctive feature of League activities was the conduct of studies on the local level. The most frequent type of study was a survey among local businessmen on what they thought was their own self-interest in foreign-trade policy. Such surveys were sometimes supplemented by traditional economic studies based on published data and by opinion polls of the general public. It was estimated that 530 local Leagues in forty-one states conducted 11,229 interviews, with 3,500 League members doing the interviewing.[3] These studies were publicized in newspapers, on radio and television, and communicated to Congressional delegations.

The research quality of these studies varied, but was generally good. In some instances, the cooperation of professional research organizations was enlisted. The League itself had some competent personnel. We became quite accustomed to meeting charming housewives who turned out to be professionally trained economists! When they were not already trained, many of them learned quickly. We have in mind a voice teacher who with little prompting drew a competent sample of her city and kept plying her advisers with sharp and pertinent questions. However, when mailed questionnaires were used, the results looked disturbingly biased. The bias seemed to be against reciprocal trade, though still favorable on balance.

An example of a good local study is "Connecticut's Foreign Trade," by Mrs. Ragnar D. Naess,[4] then international trade director of the Connecticut League. Mrs. Naess' study begins with a review of the available data, historical and economic, on Connecticut's foreign trade and concludes with the results of personal interviews and mail questionnaires from Connecticut businessmen. The conclusion of the study is that Connecticut, despite certain industries which might be faced with difficult but not insurmountable problems, would benefit from a more liberal trade policy. Furthermore, Connecticut businessmen were generally in agreement with a liberal-trade policy.

The Connecticut study was typical of most in its conclusion that the interests of the area would be served by a liberal-trade policy. The single clear exception of which we are aware was the study made in Rhode Island, where 35 per cent of the businessmen who responded said that

---

[3] Cf. *Facts and Attitudes on World Trade* (Washington, D.C.: League of Women Voters, Publication #234, n.d. [1955?]), p. 1.

[4] League of Women Voters of Connecticut, 404 Farmington Avenue, Hartford 5, Connecticut, February 1954.

they would be hurt by a more liberal trade policy, 48 per cent felt that it would have no effect, and only 17 per cent viewed it with favor.[5] With this exception, the local studies invariably found that the community as a whole would benefit or thought it would benefit from a more liberal trade policy. That should hardly have been a surprise, since the cases of injury usually involve only a small proportion of the industries and workers within a community.

Whatever might be said for or against the League's local studies, they constituted a major source of new information in the controversy of 1953-1955.

The League's studies were used only partially as information for Congress. Perhaps more importantly, they were used to make news and stimulate communications in the mass media of the communities. The study of public opinion in the New York metropolitan area made in March, 1954, is a case in point.

Early in 1954, the New York City League decided to poll the opinions of the metropolitan area on foreign trade and related matters. They enlisted the assistance of Elmo Roper and Associates, the Bureau of Applied Social Research at Columbia University, and members of our own staff. (Our participation was made contingent on two circumstances: that we be permitted to remain neutral as to the subject matter of the issue and that we be permitted to analyze the data for our own purposes.) From the moment it was decided to undertake the survey, it was skillfully publicized. Stories appeared in the metropolitan papers in anticipation of the event, and it was signaled in such neighborhood papers as *The Riverdale Press.*

The plan for a survey was communicated to the senators from New York state and to a group of New York representatives. These gentlemen complimented the League on its sense of civic responsibility, and their testimonials were in turn converted into another press release.

After the survey was completed, one of us was asked to present an analysis of the findings to a meeting of League members, invited guests, and the general public. This meeting was announced in the New York press. The analysis was presented by us in a painfully nonpartisan fashion, which we felt the League accepted very graciously. The next morning, the local papers carried a story of the meeting. Finally, Rep. Franklin D. Roosevelt, Jr., introduced a report of the survey into *The Congressional Record* on March 25, 1954.

Although the New York City League of Women Voters had more resources on which to draw than did most local chapters, their mode of exploitation of the metropolitan survey was not atypical. The ladies of the League would not have used our terminology to describe what they were

---

[5] *Facts and Attitudes, op. cit.,* p. 14.

doing, but they were organizing and stimulating public communications to serve the cause of the Reciprocal Trade Act. The letters which League members wrote to Congress may have been of minor importance compared with their general stimulation of public discussion of the issue.

We have said that the League was unusual in being a broad, multi-purpose organization which succeeded in generating unified activity on the controversial issue of foreign-trade policy. The League is composed of women dedicated to the general interest of the country, against a back-ground of generally internationalist sentiment. The arguments used by League officials in presenting the cause of reciprocal trade to their mem-bers were couched strongly in terms of values that the members already shared. Indeed, there was little that could be said on the side of protec-tionism in this era, except the national-defense argument, that would shake the ladies of the League in their faith in reciprocal trade, so long as they held so tenaciously to their commitment to the general interest.

The fact that certain industries were having difficulties was granted. But, as in Mrs. Naess' study of Connecticut, it was pointed out that the sources of these difficulties were broader than foreign competition, that foreign competition had a gradual impact which permitted time for read-justment, that most workers could find other jobs in the community, and, finally, that these problems were minor compared with the benefits to the wider community. These arguments would be agreed to by virtually any professional economist, although they certainly would not placate a protectionist. What is relevant in this context, however, is that they were likely to be effective with a group sharing the League's values.

All in all, the League leadership had little trouble with its local branches. We heard that, in five cities, ranging from very small to very large, there was some disagreement with the League's support of a liberal-trade policy, but apparently not to the point of actual dissent. As one League officer said: "No League has ever differed with us on foreign economic policy. On the Bricker amendment, there were Leagues which did differ sharply." Each League, state or local, which did not take action on the national program was required to make a positive report as to why it differed from the policy or had not taken action. Up to that point (mid-1954), the only Leagues which had not taken action were new or very weak ones. However, Leagues in the coal area had not been overly active. Taking all these reservations into consideration, defections were minor, and the League must be credited with having done a remarkable job of producing united activity among a large number of dedicated and intel-ligent women.

How effective was all this activity? By its very nature, the League's activity is difficult to evaluate. Its efforts were broad and involved general public enlightenment, which might or might not have some influence at a later day in a roundabout fashion.

Certainly, the efforts of the League were highly successful in stimulating interest and activity among its members. There is also no doubt that this activity reverberated outside the organization. It is our impression that the League also succeeded in establishing itself in many quarters as the spokesman for the general interest in the reciprocal-trade controversy, in much the same way that other organizations established their claims to speak for various special interests.

However, the image of the League as a voice of a liberal-trade policy must have been of low salience. When we asked our sample of business executives what sorts of people generally favored low tariffs, more than half cited businessmen of some sort, 10 per cent cited college professors and economists, but less than 1 per cent cited "women's organizations." We had frankly expected the League, in particular, to be cited more often than that. We feel certain, on the basis of our many conversations in this period, that these same men, if asked whether the League favored high or low tariffs, would generally have guessed correctly. But it looks as though they did not think of the League as an important group in the controversy.

The League had two big advantages: its members are women, and they are strongly identified with the general interest. This meant that League members were assured of a courteous hearing from even the surliest of opponents. We have already noted that League members had the courage to approach the opposition. The League officer whom we have quoted reported spending a good deal of time attempting to soften up a protectionist spokesman. In another instance, a local League was advised to work on a congressman who voted for a protectionist measure. Compared to the members of other pressure groups, the ladies showed a considerable disposition to face up to people who disagreed with them.

Whether or not they had an effect on the people who disagreed with them is another matter. For example, we interviewed the congressman mentioned above on whom the local League was supposed to work, and, although he had sufficient opportunity and pretext for introducing the topic, he made no mention of the fact that the local League had been in contact with him. Without doubt, the activities of the League must have had some positive effect on persons in a state of indecision. But, in our judgment, the League was singularly ineffective with congressmen and senators of any protectionist inclination.

As pointed out below, virtually all congressmen and senators, a few very staunch protectionists excepted, agreed that the *general* interest would best be served by reciprocal trade. For most congressmen, a protectionist inclination meant only a realization that some local industry was having difficulties and that foreign imports were involved. Such moderate protectionists were looking for a conciliation between the particular interests of those constituents who were being injured and what they admitted to be the general national interest. For such men, the League's insistence of the general interest was only a source of irritation, since it accentuated rather than reduced their conflict. In this situation, the sex of the League's members and their devotion to the general interest stood them in poor stead, since it enabled the congressman in conflict to dismiss them as "lady do-gooders" urging an impractical source of action on a man who saw himself as compelled to be concerned with the welfare of a few dozen or hundred constituents who were having serious trouble.

Here are the statements of two protectionist congressmen:

> I don't get three—well, ten—letters a year urging the low-tariff side. Oh, some women's groups put on a postcard campaign, but they don't even know what a tariff is.

> Oh, the League of Women Voters sent in a lot about the free-trade position. I have a feeling it doesn't amount to much. The League isn't . . . a potent force, and all their letters are so . . . stilted, right out of a textbook.

The above quotations are undoubtedly harsh, but they are not atypical. Holt and Barlow, having studied the passage of the Reciprocal Trade Act in 1949, cite the following statement of a member of the staff of the Senate Finance Committee as typical:

> Women's organizations have no significant influence on Congressmen on RTA [the Reciprocal Trade Act]. Their representatives appear at the hearings claiming to represent hundreds of thousands of women, who are actually unaware of the significance of RTA. These representatives often are simply sold a bill of goods by the State Department and by import interests, who also support lecturers and literature, and are very eloquent and persuasive. These women appear before the committees talking "peace" and "more world trade," but the slightest questioning on economic issues can instantly embarrass them. Since the Congressmen are chivalrous, they don't press the lady, but let her go on her way.[6]

The quoted evaluation is not only harsh, but also unfair. The League's members were more deeply involved and its spokesmen better informed than this statement concedes. But all of the above statements are accurate in one thing; namely, they reflect the fact that there is a double

---

[6] J. Robert Barlow and Robert T. Holt, "The Reciprocal Trade Agreements Act of 1949: A Case Study" (unpublished manuscript, Princeton University, 1954), cited in Cohen, op. cit., p. 16.

standard in politics, whereby women, as "guardians of the hearth," are seen as noble but impractical partisans of the good.

The activities of the League undoubtedly produced some real results. However, the League was in a poor position to make an impact on convinced opponents. Its arguments were still general-interest arguments which dismissed the difficulties of injured interests in terms which congressmen and senators could consider as doing little to deal with the immediate, urgent situations of particular industries.

Obviously, it is difficult to balance the limited impact of the League as an organization operating in the short run to affect votes on a particular bill against its long-run educational achievements. Some of the assessments quoted above seem unduly harsh, since they take no account of the mediated effect of the League's activities as they were filtered through the general public, the mass media, and other intermediate agencies. Such effects, although they may or may not be great in the long run, cannot be assessed by looking at the immediate responses to League efforts by those to whom they were addressed.

Chapter 28

The Pressure Groups—
A Summary

It is apparent from the preceding chapters that our study of the reciprocal-trade controversy led us to reservations about the extent of influence that has characteristically been attributed to pressure groups. We heartily concur in an assessment by Cohen, based on a review of the literature on the role of pressure groups in the formation of foreign policy:

> . . . a "legend" of pressure group potency in foreign policy appears to be accepted and passed on without evidence to new generations of students and researchers. . . . [A great] substantive failing of the literature of pressure groups and foreign policy . . . is the repeated discussion of the interests, intentions, or actions of specific pressure groups in lieu of any specific discussion about or investigation into, their *actual* effects . . . the interest groups themselves seem generally willing to foster the belief that their opinions or actions have in fact had some important effect on policy. This apparent equation of interests and activity with influence is found frequently in basic texts in the field. . . .[1]

However, our argument should not be taken to imply that the groups we observed had no effects whatever. Strackbein and Simpson em-

---

[1] *Op. cit.*, p. 2.

barrassed the Randall Commission by their "breakfast mutiny." The ACMI swung some Southern Congressional votes. Cleary, Gottlieb, Friendly, and Ball organized a campaign which got some New England protectionist congressmen to vote against the Simpson bill in 1953. The CNTP helped Senator Gore come close to pulling off a genuine coup. The National Coal Association formed the Foreign Oil Policy Committee to speak for itself, railroads, and independent oil producers, in itself no mean feat, and may possibly be given credit for the eventual imposition of quotas on oil imports. The League of Women Voters, at the very least, generated a good deal of publicity for the liberal-trade point of view. Of course, in no instance were we able to trace a chain of causation as impressive as the poet's apocryphal kingdom which was lost for want of a horseshoe nail. History is seldom so conveniently organized. But we have tried to identify the reasons for the successes and failures of the various pressure groups, even though we hesitate to assess their over-all impact.

We may have created the impression that protectionist pressure groups were more effective than were the proponents of the liberal-trade cause. This may or may not be so, but there are several factors which produce this impression, even if it is not so. One factor was our more intimate acquaintance with the liberal pressure groups. For example, we knew in detail the early plans and aspirations of the CNTP and were therefore aware of the extent to which this committee did not succeed in achieving its own goals. If we had been taken into similar confidence by members of protectionist groups, we might have recorded more failures on the part of such groups. Second, and more important, it is in the nature of protectionist and antiprotectionist causes and campaigns that the efforts and effects of the protectionists are easier to identify. The antiprotectionist forces draw more support from persons identified with the general interest and in turn direct more of their efforts to public education. The effects of such efforts are more difficult to trace. In the American system, the protectionist tactic of mobilizing people and groups on the basis of direct self-interest is more effective over the short haul in producing political action than is a more diffuse approach attempting to reach larger groups on the basis of the general interest. That is manifest, not only from the apparent effectiveness of protectionist groups, but also from that of liberal traders when they adopted similar tactics as in the anti-Simpson-bill campaign and the Kennedy administration efforts of 1962. Protectionists almost always used such pinpointed mobilization of directly involved special interests. It must be emphasized that, whatever successes such tactics may have had in the short run, the long-run trend in the period we are studying was toward a gradual rise in liberal-trade sentiment. A new view of America's role in the world forced the protectionists onto the defensive and compelled them to retreat. An image of the general interest which was diffused through myriad channels of mass media and citizen discussion promised in the end to triumph over rear-guard actions by even the cleverest of pressure groups.

The stereotype notion of omnipotent pressure groups becomes completely untenable once there are groups aligned on both sides. The result of opposing equipotent forces is stalemate. But, even taken by themselves, the groups did not appear to have the raw material of great power. We noted shortages of money, men, information, and time. It was a particular surprise to us to find how dilute vast sums could become when divided among dozens of pressure groups.

We were further unprepared for the fact that most activities of pressure groups involved interaction with people on the same side. It resembled modern warfare, in which only a small proportion of the troops ever make contact with the enemy and the vast majority are involved in servicing front-line soldiers—in this case mainly the senators and representatives who were waging the battle within Congress. Direct lobbying was a very minor activity. The major efforts of the pressure groups went into persuading businessmen to write or talk to congressmen and to testify at hearings; into working with sympathetic members of Congress; and into general public relations and education, with a special emphasis on the business community.

But, on the other hand, there are certain areas of initiative that are not reflected in the usual treatises on pressure groups. These areas hinge on the complexity of the notion of self-interest. Scholars have assumed that interest groups had clear interests, of which they were aware. A number of the campaigns we have described show clearly that a pressure group's function is frequently to define the interest of its partisans. For example, neither the interest of New England textile manufacturers in supporting oil imports nor that of the Eastern railroads in opposing these imports were in any way self-evident. Offered the proper coalition, they both might well have been persuaded that their interest was in the opposite direction.

How typical was the reciprocal-trade fight of 1953-1955? Cohen's review of the literature suggests that it was quite typical of the way in which pressure groups function on foreign policy in general. In one way, however, it was not characteristic of all legislative struggles. Although it is true that vast sums were at stake, the immediate pay-off was not as evident as it is in many other instances. During the passage of the Smoot-Hawley tariff, when specific rates were being set, a businessman knew fairly precisely what he had to gain or lose if tariffs were set at a particular level. This is also true of the natural-gas legislation which has been before Congress at various times in recent years. Investment counselors made their estimate of certain stocks contingent on whether that particular legislation passed Congress and the president. But the Reciprocal Trade Act is primarily an authorization for the administration to act in a rather broad and unpredictable fashion. No one knows exactly what will happen and what it will mean to him. For a protectionist, even a liberalized escape clause or definition of injury only improves his chance of a favorable hearing from the Tariff Commission and a favorable presidential review. The benefits for the proponents of the act are even vaguer. For this reason, we believe that there was relatively little motivation for "rough stuff" in the pressure-group activities during the 1953-1955 controversy. For example, we heard only one rumor of bribery. Although our conclusions probably have fairly general application, it should be noted that, on some issues, the amount of energy expended on traditional lobbying practices would be higher. When one group has much to gain and no one has much to lose, the results achieved by a single pressure organization may approximate those magical ones often attributed to such groups.

It is tempting to speculate on the extent to which the pressure groups have themselves generated their traditional image. They have certainly aided in the growth of a myth. They are inclined to exaggerate their own effectiveness and at the same time to overrate the resources of the opposition. In full good faith, each side depicts the other as well-heeled professionals, whereas "we are amateurs operating on a shoestring." The public and the sound arguments are portrayed as "on our side," but the other side succeeds only because it is rich, unscrupulous, and conniving. It would be interesting to know how much of the generally held notions about pressure groups come actually from propaganda the pressure groups have put out about themselves and the opposition.

PART V

The Congressional Process

PART V

Chapter 29

The Job of the
Congressman

We have been converging on Congress by steps.[1] We began with a consideration of the broadest group which might conceivably be involved in the making of foreign-trade policy—the general voting public. From there we moved to the American business community—the broadest group which might be assumed to be especially involved in the issue. Then we looked at a number of communities—primary units in which interests may be organized and expressed. Finally, our attention was turned to the organized interest groups whose purpose was in whole or in part to influence Congress in its decision on the Reciprocal Trade Act.

[1] This part of the book is based on "Congressmen and the People They Listen To," by Lewis Anthony Dexter, submitted in partial fulfillment of the requirements for the Ph.D. to Columbia University, 1959, here drastically condensed. The data arose mostly from interviews conducted by Dexter and the other authors. Dexter's major assignment in 1954-1955 was to observe and to interview on Capitol Hill. In all, about fifty members of Congress were interviewed, some several times. An equal number of closely affiliated persons, such as administrative assistants, were interviewed, some on a continuing basis. These interviews were supplemented by information from other sources. No attempt was made to tabulate the interviews, since they followed the journalistic principle of asking each man about those matters on which he had something interesting to say, rather than the survey principle of asking each man the same thing.

It should be noted that the very organization of this book implies certain assumptions about the democratic process. assumptions which in this section we wish to bring under explicit scrutiny.

In the classical literature on democracy, notably in the writings of Burke, a lively debate concerned the question of whether the elected representative of the people should represent their interest as *he* sees it or as *they* see it. In either event, public opinion is regarded as pertinent, whether it be a constructive force guiding the representative's behavior or a corrupting force to which he makes concessions for the purpose of getting elected.

A neoclassical view of the democratic process, stemming from behavioristic political science, says in effect that it is naïve to think of legislators either as arriving independently at a decision in the general interest or as responding to the wishes of the general public. Organized special interests, according to this view, exercise the determining influence.[2] The general public, it asserts, lacks the capacity to make itself heard and, most especially, lacks the capacity to reward and punish legislators. The pressure groups which are articulate in presenting their views to Congress command attention because they, the pressure groups and not the general public, act to influence who will and will not be elected. In this view, organized pressure is the dynamo of politics.

One may well hold that all three models of the democratic process are correct in some instances and degrees. There are times when legislators out of their independent judgment arrive at decisions in the general interest. There are times when they respond to public opinion to the extent and in the sense they understand it, either because this corresponds to their ideal of democracy or because they wish to be re-elected. There are instances in which legislators succumb to the pressures of special-interest groups, as well as those in which they are under such pressures but resist them. A more sophisticated statement would hold that, in most legislative decisions, all three models apply to some extent. Often, the pressure of special-interest groups and of public opinion act as countervailing forces, offering the legislator independence in reaching a decision of his own choosing. Thus, what is involved is, not a single process, but a set of interacting processes.

This would, in any event, seem a sufficiently complicated way of looking at things, and it is approximately the model of the democratic process which was in our minds when we designed our study and gathered our data. Yet, even this eclectic model proved insufficient when it came to

---

[2] Cf. Schattschneider, *op. cit.*; E. P. Herring, *Group Representation Before Congress* (Baltimore: Johns Hopkins Press, 1929); and D. Truman, *Governmental Process* (New York: Knopf and Company, 1951).

understanding just what went on in Congress. It was an inadequate representation of the forces and processes at work there.

The flaw in that model of the legislative decision-process was that it postulates certain issues and certain alternative solutions to them as given. It assumes that these issues are somehow there in the legislative arena and that the legislator finding the issues before him must pay attention to them and reach decisions on them. It pictures the legislator as much like a student before a multiple-choice examination, in which he faces fixed alternatives and selects an answer among them. The model with which we started and, for that matter, most decision theory concerns that kind of situation of defined options. The question asked by such theory is what groups or interests or forces operate to determine a choice, the alternatives being pre-defined.

What we actually found, on the contrary, was that the most important part of the legislative decision-process was the decision about which decisions to consider. A congressman must decide what to make of his job. The decisions most constantly on his mind are not how to vote, but what to do with his time, how to allocate his resources, and where to put his energy. There are far more issues before Congress than he can possibly cope with. There are very few of them which he does not have the freedom to disregard or redefine. Instead of choosing among answers to fixed issues, he is apt to be seeking out those issues that will meet fixed answers. He can select those issues which do not raise for him the Burkean dilemma; that is, he can select those issues on which he feels no special tension between his own views and those of his constituents.

The issues or answers the congressman chooses to deal with are largely determined by the kind of job he as an individual wishes to do. The model of the legislative decision-process toward which we inevitably moved was one dealing with the congressman's choices about his career, his professional identity, his activities, rather than one dealing primarily with choices about his policies. It was also a model which took as the relevant criterion for choice the over-all needs of his position, rather than the views on specific policies held by special groups of the public. Any model is a simplification which accounts for only a part of the observations. What we are asserting is that looking at how a congressman defined his job helped us account for his behavior on reciprocal trade as much as did looking at the foreign-trade issue or at the involvements in it of his constituents and other groups.

We were thus forced to look at the Congressional process from a different perspective. What compelled us to do so was our own specific relationship to the problem under scrutiny. Frequently, social-science studies of public events proceed historically. The scholar begins with an event and seeks out antecedents that constitute a seemingly adequate explanation for the occurrence that is the focus of his interest. The actual nature of the consequent event serves him as a criterion of the relevance of prior events. He can ignore aspects which he might have thought relevant but for the wisdom of hindsight.

Our study was a historical one in the sense that we were interested in a single occurrence and its antecedent circumstances. But, since we were studying the event in the making, we could not use hindsight to know what would prove relevant to an event the ultimate shape of which we could not yet know. In the latter respect, our investigation was similar to an analytical-predictive one. In a strictly analytic study dealing with the interrelationship of a limited number of variables, the scholar's theoretical interests serve as a criterion of relevance. He is free to ignore factors which fall outside his theoretical scheme so long as this scheme yields a satisfactory pay-off. In an analytical-predictive study, statistical predictions are made on the basis of a limited analytic model. If a sufficient proportion of events in a given category are predicted correctly, one is satisfied.

Our study was also different from these in that we were trying to anticipate ("predict" would be too pretentious a word) what was going to be significant in a single instance, and we could not remain content with the general validity of our model. Thus, we could not study the single event, the controversy over the Reciprocal Trade Act, by itself. We had to look at it in the context of the other things which were going on in Congress at the same time. As we shall illustrate at length, this is not a simple statement of the truism that "everything is related to everything else."

Our frame of attention had to include more of what was going on in Congress while the Reciprocal Trade Act was being considered than it would if we had had knowledge of subsequent events to guide us. This section of the book is a systematization of certain features of the Congressional process that came to our attention while we were thus trying to anticipate and understand the events as they were taking place. It is an essay on some aspects of the Congressional process and not a history of the passage of the Reciprocal Trade Act in 1954 and 1955.[3]

□ Choosing a Job

It is a cliché that the main job of a congressman is to be re-elected. There is much truth to it, but there are various ways of getting re-elected. Somehow, the congressman must do things which will secure for him the esteem and/or support of significant elements of his constituency. This he can achieve in many ways. He can seek for himself a reputation as a national leader, which may sometimes impress his constituents. He can work

---

[3] For the history, see chaps. 3-5.

at press relations, creating and stimulating news stories and an image of activity. He can be a local civic leader, attending and speaking at community functions. He can make a reputation for himself in the field of legislation. In some states, he can be a party wheel horse and rely on the organization to back him. He can get people jobs and do social work and favors. He can become a promoter of certain local industries. He can conduct investigations and set himself up as a defender of public morals. He can take well-publicized trips to international hot spots. He can befriend moneyed interests to assure himself a well-financed campaign. He can befriend labor unions, veterans' organizations, or other groups with a numerous clientele and many votes. The one thing he cannot do is much of all these things. He must choose among them; he has to be a certain kind of congressman.

The reason he must choose is the scarcity of resources. Resources are various; they include time, money, energy, staff, information, and good will. All these have one common characteristic—there is never enough. They must all be budgeted and used with discretion. Opportunity is striking constantly or at least standing outside the door, but it is only occasionally that one has the wherewithal to capitalize on it. The skill of a congressman is to make the choices which, with the resources at hand, will get him the greatest results in doing the kind of Congressional job he has chosen to do.

Furthermore, his choices are not discrete. Choices on the use of scarce resources are never independent, for what is used for one purpose cannot be used for another. The choices are linked in other ways, too, for Congress is both a social system and part of a larger social system. The individuals with whom a legislator interacts in one transaction may be the same ones involved in another. The choice to spend time and effort in winning a particular friend can hardly be independent of another choice which would make of that person an enemy.

For these reasons, a rational congressman who has decided what kind of congressman he wants to be would then use his resources according to strategies consisting of whole packages of related acts. His stand on a particular issue would be far less dependent on what was specifically involved in that issue than on its role in a general policy or strategy on which he was working. Congressmen are no more rational political men than the businessmen whom we previously examined are rational economic men. Yet, to the extent that they are partially that and that a "maximizing" [4] model helps us understand their behavior, the model must be one relating continuing strategies, all aimed at achieving a certain kind of job success,

---

[4] Actually, as already indicated, we believe Herbert Simon's concept of "satisficing" is more appropriate, though less familiar.

not one dealing with strategies to maximize success on discrete issues. The skillful congressman—and, in this respect, most congressmen are skillful —makes his choices in terms of ways of living in a continuing political system. He constantly weighs his future relations with his colleagues.

A skillful congressman also takes account of the strategies of the other players in the Capitol arena and the rules of the game there. He is part of a multiperson game in which the goals of the different players vary and in which each defines them for himself; in which the pieces are the scarce resources which can be allocated; and in which the optimal strategies depend on the coalitions which can be formed, the procedural rules of the house in which the game is being played, and the power and the goals of the other players. Voting strategies depend on many things besides the pros and cons of issues. A senior senator, for example, can seek for himself the mantle of statesman with some chance of success, thanks to unlimited debate and his ability to balance special interests in one part of the state against those in another. A representative has far less chance of playing that particular kind of game. Again, a congressman can afford to vote the popular position in his constituency although he believes it wrong when he knows that there will be enough Congressional votes to defeat him anyway. He may have to vote his principles with courage when he thinks his vote is going to count. But, even then, he may, if skilled at parliamentary procedure, satisfy his constituents by dramatic votes and gestures at moments when they cannot succeed.

How a congressman defines his job, the importance of choice in the use of his time and resources, the continuing character of Congress as a social system, and the constraints of procedure and interaction form the substance of this section. The congressman is typically thrust unprepared into a specialized milieu and confronted with a massive volume of highly technical legislation, with most of which he can deal only superficially. Counting on the assistance of a modest staff, he must work within the framework of a committee structure and is burdened with the additional task of servicing myriad personal requests from his constituents. These pressures combine to make time one of the congressman's most critical resources and the study of its allocation and husbanding a key to the legislative process.

□ Allocating Time

The scholar tends to approach his problem as though it had equal salience in the minds of men dealing with it on a practical basis. But we have already observed, in our study of the business community, that foreign-trade policy was only one of many issues crying for the American businessman's attention and not one of the most pressing. What has been said of the businessman must be said doubly of the congressman. There are infinite demands on him, which he must meet with finite means. Both the scholar and the newsman often miss this point in their assumption that congressmen can pay attention to all issues of national policy. We began our study with two major interests: legislation and communication. We wanted to know what congressmen did about tariff legislation, and we wanted to know what and who influenced them in what they did. We tended to assume that the issues of public policy which were crucial to us were as crucial to the men with whom we were talking. Yet, few congressmen viewed tariff legislation as their primary concern, and the way in which many of them noticed what they read and heard about reciprocal trade was in large part a consequence of the fact that tariff legislation was simply one of several competing interests for them.

The low priority assigned tariff matters and the effect of that on what congressmen heard and did may be examined by considering their allocation of time. We could equally proceed by looking at the allocation of any other resource, particularly good will, for that is one of the most essential commodities in which a politician deals—there are limits to the frequency with which he can draw on his available fund of it. But let us look here at the consequences of the shortage of time in the congressman's life. A congressman is a member of what sociologists call a free profession, in that he makes his working schedule for himself. His job is undefined and free, not only in schedule, but also in content and in standards of achievement. As a result, he lives under a heavy burden of multiple choices, and, what is more, the choices he has to make are far more fateful than those most citizens make. The citizen may conceive of the congressman tackling his highly responsible choices with the same care and awe with which the citizen imagines himself tackling the few really responsible choices which he makes. But, by the very nature of their busy lives, congressmen cannot do this.

Let us consider the ways in which a congressman may occupy his time. He may concentrate on any of the following aspects of his job:

1. Legislative planning—the working out of legislation in committee.
2. Legislative criticism—an unpopular role in the House, but one common in the Senate.
3. Parliamentary procedure—specializing in rules and regulations for the conduct of Congressional business.
4. Legislative tactics—like Lyndon Johnson when he was majority leader, or James Byrnes in an even earlier period.
5. Investigation.
6. Public education—rallying support for causes through forums, speeches, articles.
7. Personal advertisement and campaigning—birthday and condolence

letters to constituents, congratulations to graduating high school seniors, news letters, press releases, trips back home.

8. Seeing visitors and shaking hands.

9. Personal service—rectification of bureaucratic injustices; facilitating immigration of relatives of constituents; arranging military leaves, transfers, and hardship releases; helping confused constituents to route their inquiries to the right administrative offices; providing information on social security rights, etc.

10. Representation of local or state interests—Sen. Wiley (R., Wis.), ranking Republican on the Foreign Relations Committee, reported: "In 1939 on the occasion of the 75th anniversary of the Wisconsin cheese industry, it was my pleasure to preside over an appropriate celebration in Washington. It featured the world's largest cheese. . . . The cheese was eventually cut up and distributed . . . to Senators, Representatives, Congressional employees, newspapermen and others. . . . I am satisfied that advancing the interests of one of the foremost food industries of my state . . . is one of the jobs for which I was sent to Washington. . . ." [5]

11. Participating in national political organization or campaigning— for example, Sen. A. S. Mike Monroney (D., Okla.) has been chairman of the Speakers Division of the Democratic National Committee.

12. Development of local political organization and leadership—many senators are state political bosses, for example, the late Sen. Pat McCarran in Nevada.

A congressman might decide that his chief responsibility is, after all, legislation. Even so, there is far too much legislation for any particular legislator to attend to all of it. During the Eighty-third Congress, 1953-1955, which we were studying, the following legislative issues were among those considered:

1. Reciprocal Trade Extension acts of 1953 and 1954
2. Customs simplifications bills
3. Cargo Preference Act of 1954
4. Excise tax
5. Complete overhauling of federal tax system
6. Social security revision
7. Unemployment compensation measures
8. Appropriations measures
9. Amendment to the Constitution [6]
10. Civil service pay raises
11. The lease-purchase bill
12. Revision of health-welfare-grant formulas

---

[5] A. Wiley, *Laughing with Congress* (New York: Crown Publishers, 1947), pp. 136-141. This book probably has the best treatment of the Congressional work load. It is one of the indispensable books about Congress for anybody trying to find out what Congress does. Especially valuable is Chapter VI, "The Office Inferno," particularly pp. 90-96.

[6] A resolution providing for the replacement of House members killed in a national emergency.

13. Flexible price supports
14. Reduction of wheat acreage
15. Reduction of the Air Force
16. Establishment of an Air Academy
17. Building of twenty merchant ships
18. Upper Colorado development
19. Niagara Falls development
20. Highway aid
21. Commercial use of atomic-energy patents
22. Range improvements by private interests on public lands
23. Alaskan statehood
24. Hawaiian statehood
25. End of price controls
26. Revision of the Taft-Hartley Act
27. New health insurance law
28. Windfall profits
29. The Bricker amendment
30. Wiretap bills
31. Suffrage for eighteen-year-olds
32. Raising the federal debt ceiling
33. Tidelands oil
34. Sale of government rubber plants
35. Abolition of the Reconstruction Finance Corporation
36. The St. Lawrence Seaway
37. Special Refugee Immigration Law
38. Interest rate rise for Federal Housing Administration
39. Excess profits tax
40. Bill for twenty-six new judgeships
41. Witness immunity measures
42. Ten plans for government reorganization
43. Rise in postal rates.

In addition, during the Eighty-third Congress members of the Senate were confronted with a number of other time-consuming issues which were not properly legislative but were more important than many laws in terms of policy. Prominent among these were the censuring of Sen. Joseph McCarthy (R., Wis.), the proposal to unseat Sen. Dennis Chavez (D., N.M.), and the confirmation of appointments to major commissions, cabinet and diplomatic posts, and judgeships. Some appointments were highly controversial. The appointment and confirmation of ex-Representative Joseph Talbot (R., Conn.) to the Tariff Commission seems to have been regarded in many quarters as as great a protectionist victory as passage of the Fuel Oil Quota (Simpson) Bill would have been.

In the same session, the Senate and House conducted at least sixty-five investigations, some of which had specific legislative purposes. Finally, it should be considered that interested members of the House and Senate may and do devote long hours of work to legislative proposals that never reach the floor or achieve serious consideration in committee.

Only painstaking and continuous study can give a legislator command of the often complex details of any one of the many proposed pieces of legislation. Few congressmen can or do master more than a handful of them. A congressman with years of service may in time develop expertness in a particular field of legislation, but the best-informed of our lawmakers are fully acquainted with only a fraction of the bills that come before each session.

Furthermore, even if some particular legislation is the major focus of interest of a given congressman, usually, if he is to be re-elected, he cannot completely ignore other aspects of his job.[7] Said one administrative assistant:

> You know this business; it is like trying to deal with a great immovable beast or cleanse the Augean stables . . . you just cannot do much. . . . The Senator is now a member of fourteen important subcommittees, and he just cannot split up his time. . . . Now there is the [particular] subcommittee— . . . and all those questions are tremendous and vital questions. . . . Yet, you try to get these senators [members of the subcommittee] even to agree to meet at any one time and you cannot even do that . . . they are so independent and rushed and all doing things their own way.[8]

Not only is the congressman himself overcommitted, but he is surrounded by similarly busy men. A salient fact about the congressman's job is that what he does is invariably accomplished through other people, most of whom are as busy as himself. He becomes involved in a complex web of interdependence with colleagues and constituents as a result of the fact that each must work through the other to get what he wants, whether it be re-election, the passage of a piece of legislation, or service from a congress-

---

[7] For a variety of reasons, House members, if they are so minded, are freer to "take it easy" than members of the upper body. They represent a smaller constituency. Crucial decisions in the House are usually made by the leadership. Also, each member of the larger House is on fewer committees.

[8] A senatorial assistant rejected the idea of having an intern from the American Political Science Association in his office because "the intern has lots of ideas—mostly good—but every single one of them means more work." We should note that among the duties of a congressman is running his own office and staff. By 1959, House members received approximately $40,000 a year for the maintenance of staffs. They were permitted to employ as many as eight persons. In addition, members were allowed $1,200 per session for stationery, 2,700 minutes of telephone service, 12,000 words of telegraph service, $600 a year for official office expenses in the district, and $200 a year for air-mail and special-delivery stamps. Very few members employ as many as eight persons or spend quite the maximum. Few congressmen receive office space adequate for that number, and the use of a staff that large is likely to involve the personal financing of some office expenses.

The amount available to senators for staff purposes varies from state to state. The average expense appeared to be more than $50,000 a year. This usually permits the senator to employ two or three professional persons as legislative and administrative assistants and two or three clerks.

man. To anticipate a point which we shall develop later, it is highly naïve to think of a congressman as being under pressure from one direction or even as being under cross-pressure from two opposing directions. More typically, he is under simultaneous influence and demands from many directions, a large number of which are relevant to the issue with which the scholar or interest group is concerned only in that they compete with that issue for the congressman's time and energies.

However, our purpose is not to argue that congressmen are busy people but to show specifically that their busyness affected their reaction to the reciprocal-trade extension.

Busyness blocked effective communication of constituents' views to their congressmen. A congressman can seldom readily inform himself as to how his constituents feel about any issue. A sense of acting in the dark about public opinion plagued many of the legislators we interviewed. On the simplest level, communications with respect to foreign-trade policy had to compete with, and frequently were lost in, the welter of other communications. This is particularly true of conversations which congressmen and their assistants had with other people. In 1955, a senator's assistant commented:

> You know, so many people have come into the office in the last two weeks on all these things—rubber disposal, stock market, reciprocal-trade extensions, and taxes—I just haven't been able to keep in mind which was which; and I think it is pretty difficult for the Senator to keep track, too.

One representative who was very much concerned with the Reciprocal Trade Act complained about his impossible work load. He had recently been back to his district; he could remember vaguely that a number of people had talked to him about tariff and foreign-trade policy, but he could not recall who had wanted what.

Both these men belonged to the committees which handled reciprocal-trade extension. Yet, even for them, it was but one issue among many. They had no time to give more than a hurried glance to communications about it. As a result, they, too, had only the haziest notion of what public opinion in their constituency really was. The communications they received were poorly remembered and ill-understood. Most messages left only the impression that something had been said, not a clear recollection of what was said. We find that the net effect of communication was to heighten attention to an issue, rather than to convey specific content about it.

Chapter 30

Some Areas of Initiative

Congressmen feel much freer than most outsiders think. They need not be unduly constrained by demands from constituents, interest groups, or party. Their freedom is secured by a number of conditions. For one thing, constituents and pressure groups are often satisfied with a fair hearing, not insisting on a specific conclusion. For another thing, American political parties seldom impose discipline in regard to issues.

Among all the conditions that make congressmen free, there is one that deserves special attention; that is the fact that a congressman's own decisions largely determine what pressures will be communicated to him. Paradoxical as it may seem, their "freedom" comes from the excessive demands made on them. The complexity of their environment which seems to congressmen to rob them of initiative thrusts initiative back on them, for, when the demands on a man's resources clearly exceed his capacity to respond, he *must* select the problems and pressures to which to respond.

□ A Congressman Determines What He Will Hear

There are additional ways in which a congressman largely determines for himself what he hears from the public. Several mechanisms converge to place a congressman in a closed communication circuit. For one thing, like anyone else, a congressman indulges in selective perception and recall of what he hears. Most messages received by a congressman change saliency more than they change his attitudes on the subject with which they deal. They raise its saliency so that he thinks about it more and becomes more prone to express whatever predispositions he has regarding it. Beset by competing stimuli, he perceives the original message hurriedly, seeing in it what he expects is there. The effect of the stimulus is thus that he reacts more, but reacts in terms of his own accumulated predispositions, not in terms of the content of the communication. Messages serve more as triggers than as persuaders.[1]

Second, a congressman must select those persons within his constituency on whom he is going to build his following; he cannot react to all equally. Third, a congressman must discount as phony much of the material he receives, and the discounting process can lead to a variation of readings. Last, and perhaps most significant, the attitudes of a congressman in large measure control what messages will be sent to him, because they determine, often overdetermine, the image people have of him.

Of course, congressmen do get mail of all kinds, including some with which they are bound to disagree. Although the large bulk of issue mail is supportive, there are exceptions, and sometimes there may be large sacks of mail demanding that a congressman take a difficult or unpalatable stand. When that happens, the congressman wants to know how seriously to take those demands on him. Do they represent his constituents' deep feelings or are they the product of a slick promotion? He wants to know something of the degree of spontaneity, sincerity, and urgency of these communications. The congressman's experience with other communications on the same and other issues is his touchstone for assessing the degree to which his mail is stimulated or spontaneous. Thus, a Senate mail clerk commented on one set of letters: "This mail is surprisingly unstereotyped; . . . although the stationery may have been given out, the message was not. It is quite different from other heavy pressure mail."

Lack of experience with protectionist mail probably accounted in part for the responsiveness of Southern congressmen to it in 1955.[2] North-

---

[1] See Raymond A. Bauer, "The Communicator and the Audience," *Journal of Conflict Resolution,* II (March 1958), No. 1, 67-77.

[2] See Chap. 25.

ern congressmen, more experienced with protectionist arguments, frequently commented, "There is nothing new here."

In general, experienced congressmen and their staffs are quite tough-minded and skilled at assessing their mail. They are unlikely to feel pressure from the mere existence of numerous demands on them. That being the case, the demands that seem compelling to congressmen are apt to be those which fit their own psychic needs and their images of the world. Things interior to the congressman's mind largely determine what events he will perceive as external pressure on him. He unconsciously chooses which pressures to recognize.

One way or another, the congressman must simplify the complex world. We interviewed two congressmen from the vicinity of New Anglia. It will be remembered that there was considerable unemployment in the textile industry around New Anglia. Northern textile unemployment may be interpreted in a variety of ways—as a result of technological obsolescence, foreign competition, Southern competition, and so on. Congressman Second, in virtually these words, said: "Unemployment and the need for protection are the same issue." He saw textile unemployment as the result of foreign competition. But Congressman First, when asked about foreign-trade policy, began immediately to talk about Southern competition and about the failure of the administration to grant defense contracts to the distressed New Anglia area. Rather than seeking relief via tariffs, he was trying to get from the Office of Defense Mobilization a "certificate of necessity" for a steel mill in New Anglia. He commented: "By and large, on . . . the tariff . . . New Anglia businesses feel it is New Anglia against the South, and New Anglia is getting a raw deal every time."

We had the opportunity of observing both congressmen at a breakfast meeting organized by New Anglia textile interests. One speaker talked about foreign competition; another stressed Southern textile competition. Both Congressmen First and Second questioned the speakers. From their questioning, it might seem that Congressman First had heard one speech and Congressman Second another.

Another congressman occupied himself with doing personal favors for his constituents. The district from which the congressman came was very similar to that served by another congressman who reported a heavy influx of protectionist mail. We knew the industries in the first's district to be generally very active in favor of protectionism. But that congressman, although he frequently returned home, reported hearing little or nothing on tariff problems. Either his concentration on problems of personal service discouraged communications on tariff problems or he was so absorbed that he did not notice them.

In the Senate Office Building, the mail rooms were in the basement, a long walk from the senators' offices. That fact, added to the volume of mail a senator receives, made it far less likely for him to be aware of what was in his mail than was a representative, whose mail clerk was right in his office. In one senatorial office, the senator's administrative assistant was under the impression that they had received no mail on foreign-trade policy. One of us took a walk over to the senator's mail room. The mail clerk said that the mail on foreign-trade policy was first or second in volume of mail on any issue. However, the senator and his assistants were heavily involved in several other issues, and the mail clerk had not forwarded the reciprocal-trade mail, since, in her judgment, there was nothing that the senator could do about the issue at the moment.

In that instance, the filter against pressure was not strictly psychic. The barrier was selective communication, which, however, stemmed directly from the clerk's awareness of the senator's selective attention. We shall meet this mechanism again below. But, whatever the mechanism, the result was that effective pressure was limited to topics on which the congressman chose to recognize it.

We add another point that reinforces the notion that congressmen interpret the pressures on them. Many communications to congressmen leave the recipient in the dark as to precisely what is wanted of him. Communications to Congress are frequently ambiguous, and it is not surprising if the ambiguities are resolved in consonance with the congressman's other interests and activities. A letter reporting industrial distress might be seen as a plea for tariff protection by Congressman Second and as a plea for selective allocation of defense contracts by Congressman First. Yet, both would regard themselves as truly and effectively expressing the plea of the constituent.

The work load of the congressman and his staff reduces the precision with which congressmen interpret that high proportion of mail which is only partially on target. For example, a large volume of protectionist mail was received from employees of the Westinghouse Corporation in protest against U. S. government purchase of foreign electrical installations. Although the mail was ostensibly directed against the extension of the Reciprocal Trade Act, it is probable that the issue confronting Westinghouse—government purchasing of foreign electrical equipment—should have called for mail asking an administrative tightening-up of the Buy-American Act, not for tariff legislation. But few congressmen had the time or staff resources to investigate this problem. Our impression was that many congressmen were not clear as to what was wanted of them by the Westinghouse Corporation. The mail might have had some effect on trade-legislation votes, but the effect, if any, may have been quite unrelated to the specific situation affecting Westinghouse.

The fact that a large part of the mail, and other communications, too, are only partly on target is one which cannot be too strongly emphasized. Sometimes it makes action to meet the request impossible, for many writers ask for something that is procedurally or otherwise impracticable. They may ask a congressman to support a bill which is still in a committee of which he is not a member and where he has little influence with any member. For him to comply in any way other than by a polite reply to the correspondent would require a major investment of effort and good will. He would have to go out of his way to testify or to approach some of his better-placed colleagues.

On the other hand, the fact that petitioners are vague about what they want also helps make political action possible. Political action requires the formation of coalitions. Coalitions are held together by the glue of ambiguity which enables persons to perceive diverse goals as somehow akin. There are not enough people with an interest in the Buy-American regulations, for example, to produce Congressional action. Nor are there enough who care about oil quotas to get such action. Nor are there enough who care about specific tariff rates as such. The only way any of them could achieve legislative effectiveness was to mobilize all of them as a coalition around some issue which might serve at least as a wedge for those whom it did not serve directly. Such a bloc was organized each time against the trade acts. Had it ever succeeded, its success might have led ultimately to administrative yielding on the interpretation of Buy-American legislation too. The administration would most likely have yielded to what it would have seen as a general protectionist direction in the political atmosphere.

Indeed, it happens more often than not in public-policy debates that the issues around which mass opinion is mobilized are not the crucial ones in the minds of those who frame legislative policy. This happens often enough so that congressmen are well attuned to grievances as an index to the sources of public alarm, rather than as specific guidance on legislative drafting. A congressman is concerned to allay the discontent of those who appeal to him. The complaint is a signal to him to do something, not a command as to what to do. Like a doctor, having made a diagnosis, he often has a range of choices of treatment open to him.

We consider now another range of alternatives among which a congressman must choose. Almost every district is composed of a complex of interests, and congressmen are faced with the task of deciding just whom they represent. They cannot give attention and energy equally to all. They must select some for whom they can become valued allies and from whom they can command more than passive support. They must find groups which have money, votes, media of communication, influence, and political desires which a congressman can further. A congressman must seek to make himself an important figure to some such groups within his constituency. These may change over time. A congressman elected by labor votes may throw off this harness by turning to business support. But, at any one moment, a congressman must relate to some key groups within his constituency, for a constituency is a social structure, not an amorphous mass. Thus, Rep. Henderson Lanham (D., Ga.) came from a district with both farming and business interests. He had associated himself with the business group. Their protectionist interests, rather than the farmers' stake in international trade, were communicated to him, for people write and talk more to a congressman whom they know, and he listens more to them.

Although a congressman's established relationship to a particular group may increase the probability of its members communicating with him, this established relationship does not necessarily make him more compliant to their interests on a specific issue. This is a point so important and so overlooked in the pressure-group model of the democratic process that it deserves emphasis.

In the first place, the direction of influence is as apt to be from the congressman to his closer constituents as the other way around. Citizens value a relation to a congressman and are apt to be guided by him.

Second, established favorable relationships between congressmen and groups in the constituency are invariably based on a range of issues. It is rare that any one of these is of such paramount importance that a group would renounce its allegiance to a congressman who had pleased them on many other issues. We had an illustration of this in Midwest. It will be remembered that the farmers talked to Congressman Stubborn on a range of issues on which they expected a favorable reaction from him. However, they were so certain of his opposition to trade liberalization that they did not even raise that subject. A congressman wins the allegiance of multipurpose interest groups through both legislation and services. This allegiance, then, can buy him freedom from pressure on almost any individual issue on which he has firm personal convictions.

We may thus enunciate the general principle that whether a group will communicate with a congressman and whether the congressman will respond to the interests of that group are functions of the relationship between the group and the congressman on a *range* of issues. We offer as an example our impression that some groups interested in both the St. Lawrence Seaway bill and the Reciprocal Trade Act gave priority to the former and did not communicate on the latter for fear of exhausting a finite supply of Congressional good will.

Our basic conclusion, we repeat, is that a congressman determines —consciously or unconsciously—what he hears. He hears most, for instance, from interest groups with which he is congenial; but he can cut off communication on single issues on which he is at odds with them. It is not surprising, therefore, that our old friend, Congressman Second, who interpreted textile unemployment as a foreign-trade problem, reported receiving more foreign-trade mail than did Congressman First, who saw it as a problem of Southern competition. Congressman Second reported it first or second in importance; Congressman First's assistant placed it in tenth or fifteenth position.

It is, we judge, usually truthful when two congressmen on opposite sides of an issue each say that "80 per cent of my mail supports me," for people write less to congressmen with whom they disagree.

The busyness of Congressmen First and Second forced each to specialize. Each chose a specialty congenial to himself from among the many of potential appeal to his constituents. Their specialties in turn determined what pressures were placed on them, for among the demands to which a congressman is most likely to respond are those which he has stimulated himself.

Belief that a congressman is busy with other matters will dry up the flow of communication to him on a given subject. The late Sen. Joseph McCarthy had twice succeeded in getting the Reciprocal Trade Act amended to place a quota on the importation of foreign furs. But this was before he became involved in the investigation of Communism. In 1954, an informed source commented: "None of the Wisconsin dairy or fur people would go see Joe. He's too busy and out of that world. They'd go see Wiley or Thye or Humphrey's assistant, but not Joe—he doesn't follow that sort of thing any more." The image of Senator McCarthy had become that of investigator of Communism rather than that of representative of local and state interests.

Thus, an anticipatory feedback discourages messages that may not be favorably received from even getting sent.[3] A congressman very largely gets back what he puts out. In his limited time, he associates more with some kinds of people than with others, listens to some kinds of messages more than to others, and as a result hears from some kinds of people more than from others. He controls what he hears both by his attention and by his attitudes. He makes the world to which he thinks he is responding. Congressmen, indeed, do respond to pressures, but they generate the pressures they feel.

In making that assertion, we take leave of the traditional theory of pressure politics as expounded both by the politician and the political scientist. The political scientist observing Congress gives too much credence to the way the congressman himself describes the situation. The congressman often sees himself as buffeted by a torrent of inexorable demands on his time and effort. Like any busy executive, he sees himself responding to stimuli that come to him from without. What he does not realize is that

---

[3] Relevant experimental evidence on this point is to be found in Claire Zimmerman and Raymond A. Bauer, "The Effect of an Audience on What is Remembered," *Public Opinion Quarterly*, XX (1956), 1, 238-248.

the nature of these forces on him are largely self-made. His own sensitivities determine which demands he feels to be important and which he forgets and sloughs off. One congressman with an eye on issues will listen with concern to arguments put forward by constituents, whereas another congressman with an eye on local social groups will feel no pressure from pompous statements about issues as he tries to keep track of births, marriages, and deaths. The representative who is known to have arranged for the nonquota entrance of relatives of members of a given ethnic group will receive similar requests from other such persons. The congressman who establishes his home office in a working-class section, where his secretary gives advice on social-security cases, will get such cases, which perhaps take more time than any other service. The congressman who has interested himself in taxes will hear about taxes, and the one who has cultivated groups interested in foreign trade will hear about tariffs. The congressman's activities determine which of his constituents know him and the contexts in which they know him, and their past experience tells them to what their congressman will respond. If he has come to church suppers before, he will be invited again. If he has given speeches on foreign policy, that is what he will be invited to do. The job is largely what the congressman makes it.

□ A Congressman Is Relatively Free

One implication of the fact that the congressman makes his own job and hears what he chooses to hear is that he can be a relatively free man, not the unwilling captive of interest groups or parties. There may seem to be a conflict between the two pictures we paint of the congressman harassed by many demands and of the congressman relatively free. But, as suggested above, it is precisely because the demands on him are excessive that he must be selective, and therein lies his relative freedom.

Early in our study we talked with a veteran congressman who said:

> You know, I am sure you will find out a congressman can do pretty much what he decides to do, and he doesn't have to bother too much about criticism. I've been up here where a guy will hold one economic or political position and get along all right; and then he'll die or resign, and a guy comes in (from the same district) who holds quite a different economic or political position, and he gets along all right, too. That's the fact of the matter.

The reasons for this are many. In American political practice, neither the party nor the executive branch exercises more than slight control over a member of Congress. The reader will probably note how seldom in this and the historical chapters we refer to the mechanism of party or to direct executive intervention. The weight we give them is the weight they seem to deserve. In 1953-1955, each (the Executive more than the party) played a role in forcing a few key votes at a few crucial moments, but, for the rest, theirs was a reserve power kept out of the picture. Rayburn stepped in at a breakfast described in an earlier chapter to pressure a few Democratic votes in the House in 1955. The White House did give leadership to Republican senators about how to vote on the Gore amendment, and it did have a representative meet with Senators Byrd and Millikin during the 1955 Senate committee deliberations to decide which proposed amendments would be incorporated in the bill. These were all highly important moments, but in no one of these three isolated but vital cases did the guidance affect more than a score of congressmen. Over the two years which we studied most intensively, the overwhelming majority of congressmen would have felt no more pressure toward conformity to party or administration views than that which they generated within themselves from reading the newspapers and knowing what the President and party leaders were saying.

In 1962, the White House intrusion into the life of Congress was much more direct, aggressive, and insistent. Presidential aides talked repeatedly to a large number of key congressmen and often did so in an overt bargaining manner. Yet these direct appeals did not switch the most votes. It was the indirect effect of the administration's approach to and conversion of the textile lobby and to numerous other businessmen that indirectly affected Congress. Congressmen recognized the hand of the administration in the extraordinary change whereby most of the special-interest lobbying in 1962 was for trade liberalization, not protection. But congressmen responded to this change in atmosphere because of what it showed about the shifting balance of forces in the country, not because the President asked them to go along. On the contrary, many congressmen, including Democrats, so resented the unusual intrusiveness of the Kennedy administration's tactics that they would have preferred to vote the President down. If party and administration had much direct weight at all in the House in 1962, it was precisely because congressmen had not listened to them much on a variety of issues. Congress had rebuffed the President on a whole series of proposals: long-term foreign aid, a Department of Urban Affairs, tax reform, aid to education, and the like. Both the President and numerous Democrats in Congress wished to pass some legislation that would create a party record of success for the approaching elections. To the administration, the Trade Expansion Act had the charm of something that might actually succeed in passing, so it was given a higher priority. Conversely, the selection of this bill as a Democratic show piece may have led some Democratic representatives to go along. But such mutual recognition of a chance for agreement cannot be called a result of administration pressure.

The sanction that counts much more than party or executive leadership in the Congressional picture is that of re-election by the voters of one's district. But in that regard, too, the congressman is quite free. There are limits on what is morally or sociologically conceivable. Few, if any, congressmen could announce adherence to Communism and be re-elected. But the latitude is wide and of course wider on any one given issue than on all issues put together. A congressman creates an image on the full range of issues which affects his chances of re-election, although even over the full range his freedom is much more substantial than is often realized.

☐ Summary

A congressman is free, as we have already noted, because each district is ordinarily a complex and he can choose the elements out of which he wishes to build his coalition. As Congressman Stubborn said about his district: "It is a good district, because, if the farmers are mad at you, the cities won't be; and, if the cities are, the farmers won't be; so you can be free."

He is freed from a slavish dependence on the elements in his coalition, not only because he can change it, but, even more, because, once he has built a coalition, he tends to lead it. His closest supporters, who may originally have rallied around him because they wanted him to take certain stands, come to be his men. Within very broad limits, when he shifts, they shift. They gain prestige by being close to a congressman, and they fear to break a relationship which may some day be useful for important purposes. Once the leader has committed himself, his supporters are inclined to go along.

He is free also because the voters seldom know just what they want. Mostly they want evidence that he is concerned with their problem and is addressing himself effectively to it. Often he is viewed as the doctor who should recommend the appropriate cure. The larger number of constituents, and the ones the congressman likes, are the ones who come in to say, "Congressman, this is my problem." Those, such as the League of Women Voters, who come in with a list of recommended votes are, fortunately for the comfort of the congressman, fewer.

Indeed, even where the constituent frames his appeal to his congressman as a highly specific demand, the congressman is quite free to disregard it. Few constituents deny their vote to a congressman who generally listens to them just because he differs on any one issue. Furthermore, for every demand on one side, there is a demand on the other. The congressman who saw his job in no more imaginative light than doing what his constituents or large groups of them wanted would not only face impossible problems of doing that job, but would also soon find himself offending enough other constituents to undermine his chances of remaining in office.[4] He must view the demands with a more creative eye, seeking to invent formulas that will catch the imagination of constituents rather than taking all requests at face value.

Finally, a congressman is free also because, as we shall see in the sections to come, the procedure of Congress is so complex that it is easy for him to obfuscate where he stands on any issue and what he has done about it.

---

[4] Cf. Anthony Downs, *An Economic Theory of Democracy* (New York: Harper & Bros., 1957), for a demonstration of the proposition that, by following the majority on each issue, a legislator is likely to court defeat by a coalition of passionate minorities.

Chapter 31

Congress as a
Social System

We have confined our attention to the way in which the context of other activities affects incoming information and the way in which the congressman perceives and interprets it. The action which he takes on the basis of such information must also be placed in the context of his other activities. Though it is easy enough for the scholar to abstract one vote on one issue, congressmen act on a complex of issues, rather than on a single one. The typical congressman acts, not as if some bill were the only one to be decided, but as if it must be disposed of in such a way as simultaneously to facilitate desired actions on other issues, too.

In the first place, any one bill compounds many issues. Thus, one congressman who indicated general support for the Reciprocal Trade Act voted against it in the House. In his district, there was considerable unemployment related to foreign imports. He was disgruntled that the Ways and Means Committee had not given him something he could represent as a token of his concern for the problems of business in his district. Then he added: ". . . and then there is another thing, that damn Eisenhower. I just cannot see why we should give him more power, can you? He . . .

425

is so incapable." Where some people might see one issue, he saw three: national interest in a liberal-trade policy, his district's interest in protection from foreign imports (which he wanted to acknowledge on a token basis), and the delegation of powers to the president.

In the second place, action on any one bill affects action on other bills, too. The single enduring issue that complicates the consideration of all individual issues is the necessity for the congressman to maintain effective working relationships with other congressmen. In the words of Speaker Sam Rayburn, you have to "go along" to "get along." Some congressmen voted on the Reciprocal Trade Act primarily out of friendship for other congressmen. One intended to vote against the party leadership's wishes because of local problems. A second congressman, from a neighboring district, voted with the first so that the other man would not be the only one from the state to stand against the party leadership.

Few issues present themselves as a clear legislative black and white, and there are few uncompromising fighters on any issue. In an interview with Stewart Alsop, then Vice-President Nixon stated forcefully the requirement for compromise in politics: "You know, you come to Washington, you have great ideas and there you are in the committees or on the floor of the House, and you have an inability to implement your ideas. . . . You've got to learn how to play the game." [1]

The complication of other issues, role conflict, and the realization that there are infinite demands on Congress' finite time result in congressmen usually being interested in a viable, rather than in a definitive, solution to the problems with which they are faced. The Reciprocal Trade Act, though extended in 1955, was sufficiently amended so that both sides could claim victory. Indeed, as we have had occasion to note, it was difficult to tell which side won the contest without knowing how the act was to be interpreted administratively.

The same was true of the Trade Expansion Act of 1962. So many protective practices were introduced on behalf of textiles and other industries to get a bill passed that no one could tell whether the long-run potential for trade liberalization under the general provisions of the act would in the end offset them. At no point in the period we studied did a trade bill pass which closed any major issue with a clear decision for one policy or the other. We do not regard this circumstance as unusual.

A legislative enactment is seldom a clean decision of important issues. It is normally a verbal formula which the majority of congressmen find adequate as a basis for their continuing a policy struggle. It sets up new ground rules within which the issue may be fought out. The ground rules will reflect the balance of forces, but the minority is seldom so weak

---

[1] "Nixon on Nixon," *Saturday Evening Post*, July 12, 1958, p. 26.

on a major issue that it has to accept a once-and-for-all decision. The formula must usually offer them the chance of later reversal, keeping the big issue alive. The trade bills were just such formulas. They only authorized executive consideration of trade policy, leaving it open to further politics and propaganda to influence what administrative action would actually be and whether it would be liberal or protectionist. They allowed the congressmen and their followers on both sides to continue their efforts on behalf of the policies about which they cared. The large majority of congressmen of all tendencies agreed that some bill had to be passed. The old bill was about to expire, and having no bill at all would have created the worst possible situation in the eyes of all but a handful of protectionist extremists. Some bill was required, if only for the sake of having a functioning escape clause. Failure to pass some act would also have harmed the Congressional system in ways having nothing to do with foreign trade. It would have damaged the public image of Congress, as similar failures to act have hurt in such countries as France. It would have brought the Congressional leadership into bitter conflict with the White House. It would have injured American prestige abroad and thus have had severe consequences for foreign policy and defense spending. It would have tied up other bills in a legislative log jam. There was agreement on the need for action, but none on what action to take. Thus, the framers of the bill had to get some bill out so that the system could continue to function, but a bill that would force Congress as little as possible to make determinations on the issues which divided it the most. Once such a bill had been hammered out, it was helped through by members on both sides of the main issue, for example, Sen. Eugene Millikin (R., Colo.) and Rep. Robert Kean (R., N.J.). Each had other business to get on with, to which he could proceed on the basis of the text adopted.[2] Not the least of these goals was achievement of an effective, smooth-running Congressional system, a goal far more important than almost any one bill and one to which we now turn our attention.

Congress is not a temporary convocation. It is an ongoing social system which must preserve itself intact and which deals with problems on a long-run, rather than a one-shot, basis.

Because Congress is a social system, what comes out in the form of legislation often, and probably usually, differs from what one would

---

[2] In the interviews, a recurrent theme by partisans of each side was that their struggle, though unsuccessful, was justified by the effect it would have at the next renewal. The protectionist theme in 1955 was: this is the last time "they" will be able to get through a tariff-cutting bill; the corner has been turned. The administration theme was: this is the last gasp of protectionism; "we have laid the basis for a liberal-trade policy." Judging by the ease of the 1958 renewal, the administration may have been right in 1955. Failure to resolve issues in 1954 and 1955 may have bought the time needed for public opinion to mature.

predict from an enumeration of the opinions of individual congressmen.

Suppose that, in the elections of 1954, a voter wished to cast a ballot to facilitate protectionist legislation by Congress. Suppose that, in his district, he faced the choice between a protectionist Democrat and a free-trading Republican, either of whom would be a freshman.[3] He would probably have been ill-advised to vote for the protectionist Democrat. The Democrat might have added one protectionist vote in the House. We say *might* have because, being a freshman, he might also have given in to the persuasive efforts of Sam Rayburn *et al.* and gone along with a liberal-trade policy in the hope of digging himself in with the Democratic leadership. But, in the House in particular, legislation is written mainly in the committees, and our freshman, a protectionist Democrat, would certainly have not got on the cherished Ways and Means Committee, where tariff legislation is written. The free-trading Republican, however, might have contributed to a Republican majority in the House. Had a Republican majority organized the House, the Ways and Means Committee would have been chaired by a Republican and dominated by a majority of Republicans ranging from mildly to militantly protectionist. Considering the composition of that committee in that period and the protectionist inclinations of Republican Congressmen James Utt (Calif.) and Victor Knox (Mich.), who were in fact displaced from their committee positions by the Democratic victory in 1954, the chances of a protectionist bill being fashioned by the Ways and Means Committee would have been greater with a Republican House. Thus, our hypothetical voter might have been well-advised to vote for a free-trade Republican if he wanted a protectionist law to come out of the House.

Of course, there is no logical reason why tariff legislation should at present be considered by the Ways and Means Committee of the House. Historically, it made sense, since the tariff was an important source of revenue. In the present, tariff legislation could just as reasonably, and perhaps more reasonably, be considered by the Foreign Affairs Committee, which, incidentally, is burdened with far less work. However, to make this shift would raise very delicate questions. If some members of the Ways and Means Committee who are more interested in foreign-trade policy than in taxation wanted to shift to the Foreign Affairs Committee, problems of seniority would arise. All in all, such a shift could cause considerable disequilibrium in the social organization of the House of Representatives, and it is not likely.

---

[3] We present this as a hypothetical case. It has, however, some similarities to the 1954 New Jersey election of Clifford Case (R.) to the Senate. The public-relations firm which organized the right-wing campaign against Case on the grounds of his affiliation with the Fund for the Republic also represented some protectionist business groups. Had they won their fight against the Republican liberal trader, Case, they might have hurt the interests of their protectionist clients.

But it made a good deal of difference that tariff legislation was considered, not by the Foreign Affairs Committee, but by the Ways and Means Committee, if only because of its heavy work load, let alone the difference in committee memberships on the Republican side. The deferment of a decision in 1954 was to a large part due to the fact that the Ways and Means Committee was occupied with tax reform and other legislation dear to the heart of Chairman Daniel Reed (R., N.Y.) and did not have sufficient time for hearings. In 1955, additional legislation was introduced which might have taken much of the steam out of protectionist arguments. But, because of the work load, Ways and Means never got around to considering this legislation.

The fact that Congress is an organized body with its own institutions and procedures was far from a self-evident proposition to the people who were trying to influence Congress on foreign-trade policy in 1953-1955.

We have commented on the importance of committees for the passage of legislation. In the House, this is especially true, since bills are often reported out of committee under the closed rule, which makes it impossible to amend the bill on the floor. A member can vote either for or against the bill as presented. There are two principles which can be deduced from this simple circumstance. First, committee members on Ways and Means are much more important on foreign-trade measures than are other representatives. However, so far as we could ascertain, Ways and Means members received but little extra mail on the issue by virtue of their committee membership. The picture is slightly complicated,[4] but there was by no means the concentration of mail one would expect, were this simple principle grasped. Second, there was little or no point in writing the average congressman advocating amendments to the Reciprocal Trade Act for specific products. (In 1955, there was a brief possibility that the bill would be opened to amendments from the floor, but this was an unusual circumstance.) Nevertheless, congressmen from Michigan, for example, were confronted with mail which asked them to vote for the Reciprocal Trade Act, but to except cherries by giving them a protective tariff. Many other congressmen were petitioned for protection for specific products and industries. Given the way in which legislation is passed in the House, these instructions constituted something less than a clear-cut mandate to the congressmen. They could not vote for reciprocal trade and for protection for the cherry industry or any other interest. They had to vote for or against HR 1 as reported out of committee.

---

[4] It looks as though committee members received a disproportionate number of press releases and other canned communications. This suggests that some interest groups were thinking at least in part of the importance of the committee. However, such canned communications are precisely the type of communication that is least effective with most congressmen. (Cf. the discussion of stimulated communications below.)

Congressmen specialize according to their committee assignments far more than most laymen realize. Most legislative work is done in committee. A congressman can therefore ordinarily be effective in drafting and pushing legislation only in a field covered by his committee. Over the years, members of committees become experts in their subjects. Other congressmen follow the lead of committee members in whose general point of view they have confidence. Thus, a generally protectionist representative who was not on Ways and Means might not do anything about tariff legislation, except that when it got on the floor he would vote for those amendments supported by Dan Reed. Most creative work in framing amendments and strategy and Congressional in-fighting would have been done by committee members.

That the pressure groups were not fully alert to exactly how Congress functions may also be demonstrated by their inattention to the conference committee. The Senate and House versions of HR 1 were referred to a joint conference committee, as happens when the bills passed by the two houses do not agree. That committee had a good deal of leeway. For example, it could have settled on substantially the original House bill and dropped most or all of the senatorial amendments. Would this, then, not have resulted in a bill which the Senate would reject? Not necessarily. In the interests of keeping the system moving, there is a strong Congressional bias against rejecting a conference committee report. Amendments which a large majority of either house has inserted as an absolute condition for passing a bill may be quietly dropped if the conference committee has not accepted them. Congressmen, knowing that, will often propose and/or vote for some measure with the intent of demonstrating that they are alert to their constituents' needs, tacitly understanding that it will be amended in conference. Oregon's Sen. Wayne Morse (D.) inserted into the Senate bill such an amendment to protect the cherry- and nut-growers.

The opportunity for modifying the bill in conference existed not only in the abstract. It was known that Jere Cooper (D., Tenn.) and Wilbur Mills (D., Ark.), the major House conferees, were dissatisfied with the Senate version and were apparently ready to fight for a substantial revision. This was an attractive opportunity for pressure groups to converge on a small group of men, the Senate-House conferees. But nothing of the sort happened. Perhaps the pro-reciprocal-trade groups were simply tired and had in effect disbanded their effort when the amended bill passed the Senate. Perhaps they were guilty of neglect or a political blunder, although they certainly knew the basic facts. In any event, they seem to have been inadequately sensitive to established institutions and procedures of Congress.

There are many other examples of how communications with Congress fail because the public has too simple a notion of what goes on there. Congressman Amiable, commenting on his wide experience in a state legislature and in Congress, complained, "You always hear from business too late." Businessmen and their representatives respond to the news. They write to protest a bill when their newspaper or magazine reports it, and that is when it is reported out of committee for general debate. But, by that time, especially in the House, it is difficult to amend. If a communication arrives while the committee is still meeting, a member may feel free to work for the adoption of an amendment. But, once he has voted, he is under obligation to go along with other members of the committee. He can scarcely afford to sacrifice his long-term working arrangements with the other congressmen for this one issue. The very petitioners from his district have many interests. If he wants to serve his district, not only at the moment, but over the years, he must preserve his colleagues' respect.

Sometimes an alert trade-association secretary warns his members to write soon enough. In practice, we found relatively few who did so. However, what such a trade association gains in superior tactics it may lose in the appearance of being organized in its efforts.

When mail does come in time to influence the decision on a bill, subsequent amendments to the original bill may make it irrelevant. A communication which was initially clear in its intentions may become unclear in its implications as the Congressional process wends its way. A note which said simply, "Vote for free trade," was presumably in favor of HR 1 as originally reported out, a reasonably liberal trade measure. But what about HR 1 as amended by the Senate? At least one representative voted against it as a protectionist measure! Would our hypothetical congressman make his free-trade correspondent happy by voting for or against the amended version?

There is one more relevant point which bears directly on the workings of Congress. Its established procedures are sufficiently complicated to make it often hard to tell exactly what stand a congressman did take on a particular issue. In many instances, a congressman will cast a record vote for a proposal only when he is sure it will be defeated, or against it when he is sure it will pass. The reason for this may be twofold. The leadership may release him if his vote does not matter, recognizing his need to impress his constituents. He may in fact be opposed to the measure, but want to get a vote in favor of it on his record. If he has guessed wrongly on how the votes divide, he can usually change his vote when the count is toted up. On the crucial votes in the House in 1955, the leadership in fact won by one vote, according to *The Congressional Record*. But at one time, members report, it had lost by seven votes. The leadership usually has enough of a reservoir of political credit to have a few votes switched if it would otherwise lose by a narrow margin.

A particular measure may involve a complex of issues. For example, the open-rule proposal was defended on grounds that the House should not be gagged. Certainly, whether in good conscience or not, a congressman could have voted for debate under an open rule and claimed that he was nonetheless for HR 1. Such things happen, and they happen regularly. We cannot help but remember the bemused comment of a trade-association representative who said, "I don't know what the hell happened with 'em," referring to several senators who promised to vote "his way" but apparently did not. Aware of the complexities of the Congressional process, he knew that he could not take their apparent reneging on a promise as deception on their part, for they may have been hoping to serve him later.

If pressure is to be effective, there must be some clear criterion of yielding to the pressure. In view of the complexity of the Congressional process, we suspect that an adroit congressman could confuse the issue in a majority of instances. A look at the voting pattern of HR 1 suggests that a considerable number of congressmen were doing just that. That is one reason why, after the open rule and the protectionist Reed amendment were beaten by the narrowest of squeaks, HR 1 went through with a considerable margin. How can one account for the representatives who first voted to kill the bill and then to pass it? Among other things, they were putting themselves on record on both sides of the issue. To protectionists, they could say that they voted to have the bill changed, but when they were beaten they had no choice but to vote for it, rather than have no bill at all. To freer traders they could say that they voted for the bill. If challenged on their earlier votes, they could defend these in terms of desiring freer debate and improvements in the law.

The complexity of the organization and procedures of Congress reduces the effect of external voices on it. Its social organization exerts constraints on what any single congressman can do. It also enables him to confuse the issue as to what he has in fact done and why he did it. Clearly, influencing Congress is more than a matter of pressuring individual congressmen. The job is to approach the right congressman at the right time and in the right way.

Chapter 32

Communications—
Pressure, Influence, or Education?

We started with the notion that public officials would see themselves as under almost constant pressure from those who have a stake in the decisions they make. That seems to be the conventional belief about pressure politics put forth in textbooks and journalistic accounts. It may in fact be an accurate description of what happens in some cases, such as post-office pay raises, patronage matters, in getting contracts for highway jobs, and similar issues on which the interests of the parties are clear, immediate, unequivocal, vital, and relatively uncomplicated by other relationships with the congressman which must be considered under the heading of long-run good will. But, for most general legislation, the picture is much like what we found in the foreign-trade area.

The first lesson we learned is that vigorous pushing of an interest is not necessarily regarded as pressure. One of our early talks was with an administrative official who had prepared a report minimizing the defense aspect of foreign economic policy. During the committee hearing, he had said with some exasperation to a questioner, "I suppose next you will tell me the toothbrush-makers need protection for national defense reasons." (We have changed the product.) Angry letters instigated by a lobbyist came to him from all over the country protesting his offense against that minor industry. But when our interviewer asked him, "Did other people put pressure on you in a similar way?" the official "looked . . . incredulous and said, 'Why he [the lobbyist] didn't put any pressure on me.' " Our interviewer insisted, but the respondent said vehemently: "No, I didn't have any pressure on me at all; if you are reasonable with these people, they are reasonable with you."

"Reasonable," "legitimate," and "threat" turned out to be key words.

We continued for a while to use the word "pressure" in our interviews, but steadily ran into the response: "What do you mean, 'pressure'? I wasn't under any pressure. It was all perfectly legitimate."

Or, as Congressman Second from New Anglia told us: although "the tariff was number two or perhaps number one" in what he heard from his district, "nobody's tried to pressure me. Yes, there have been a lot of letters about the damage they are suffering, but there has been no pressure—by that I mean no threats."

Vigorous representation of a partisan interest turns out to be per se legitimate, providing it is "reasonable," that is, devoid of threat.[1] Said one assistant, speaking of organized labor, "It's true the senator opposed repeal of Taft-Hartley publicly, and they criticized him for it. But that was all in the game. Some of them may have thought he was sore about the way they took after him, but he expected it. He wasn't sore."

Most congressmen, and we believe to a lesser extent personnel in administrative agencies, believe strongly in the right of petition. Furthermore, they often regard the communications which come into their offices as helpful and instructive. True, persistent pleading of a cause to which the congressman is firmly opposed may eventually have an abrasive effect on his nerves. But, to our surprise, we found many congressmen looking to mail and personal contacts as sources of information on vital issues. This was more true of representatives than of senators, who are blessed with more adequate staffs.

We think it fair to say that, on general legislative problems, communications from constituents are seldom pressure—in the congressman's eye. The congressman perceives in them little or no element of external threat, which is what distinguishes petition from pressure. We have already seen that the constituents from whom the congressman hears are generally friendly and hesitate to alienate him on any single issue. Recall the farm delegation which approached a group of Southern congressmen

---

[1] Cf. our fuller report on this point: Frank Bonilla, "When is Petition 'Pressure'?" *Public Opinion Quarterly*, XX (Spring 1956), No. 1, 39-48.

arid said: "The national told us to pass the word along; we're in favor of reciprocal trade, but we shan't get mad if you vote against it." We repeatedly ran across the theme: "So-and-so has gone along with us on so many issues that we wouldn't think of opposing him because he disagrees with us on this."

The word "pressure" does exist in Congressional parlance. It is used, for example, to explain the opposition's behavior, sometimes described as "opportunistic yielding to pressure." "Opportunism" and "pressure" are handy terms to explain why someone disagrees with you.

There is also reference to pressure on oneself. Sometimes the term "pressure mail" was applied to mail on the Reciprocal Trade Act. But "pressure" (if on oneself) most frequently referred to influence exerted by other congressmen or by the administration. An example of such pressure was Rayburn's injunction to freshman congressmen on the morning of the key foreign-trade votes that to "get along" they had better "go along." What made it pressure was the implied threat of disapproval by the powerful party leadership on which fate in Congress depends.[2] Similarly, the administration can apply pressure by threats to withhold patronage. Individual congressmen can also apply pressure by implying that they will not cooperate on other issues with the person being pressured. One congressman said that Rep. Cleveland Bailey (D., W. Va.) was "real rough" in attempting to get him to go along on a protectionist measure.

But does not the expression of a constituent's view and/or interest incorporate an implied threat to vote against a congressman who disagrees with him? It may. There have unquestionably been individual instances of congressmen being defeated because of their unpopular stand on a single issue. However, what is important is the fact that congressmen, though they definitely respond to mail and other communications, do not usually perceive in them any cause for alarm. One senator, out of curiosity, had his staff check on the writers of 100 letters he received advocating support of a higher minimum wage. It was found that seventy-five writers were eligible to register, but, of these, only thirty-three actually were registered. Furthermore, the letters advocated his support of a measure on which he had been particularly active, and the content of the mail showed no realization of the stand he had so publicly taken. The senator could scarcely get excited about these letter-writers, as sources of either opposition or support, on the basis of that issue. He might, however, respond to their petition as a legitimate request and an opportunity to make some voters among them familiar with him as a person.

Approximately the same result might generally be expected from

---

[2] We do not consider this a contradiction of our earlier statement that, in Congress, party discipline is much less important a factor than in most legislatures.

an analysis of the mail. The reader will remember that most of the businessmen in our sample who had communicated with Congress were not aware of the position taken by the man to whom they had written. The probability is that they also did not follow up to see how he voted. Congressman Simpson received a number of letters and postcards in 1953 urging him to vote against the Simpson bill! We found that even some of the people active in the major interest groups were not aware of how key members of Congress had voted on the Reciprocal Trade Act.

In view of such circumstances, it is little wonder that congressmen do not regard partisan communications to them as a source of pressure in the sense of an implied threat. However, to say that incoming communications are not perceived as pressure is by no means to say that congressmen are not responsive to them, particularly to mail from constituents.

Indeed, the mail is the congressman's main source of information on foreign-trade policy. Whenever we asked a congressman if he had heard anything about foreign-trade policy, he almost inevitably answered in terms of mail. We cannot say whether this is true of other issues, but it is our distinct impression that congressmen are far more conscious of what the mail says about foreign-trade legislation than they are about any other exposition of foreign-trade matters.[3]

Visitors and telephone-callers have an impact similar in character to that of mail. They are listened to as indicators of feeling back home. They too, however, seldom use pressure, nor do the professional lobbyists.

> You know all these guys who come in here never talk about issues at all. I've seen lots of them supposedly lobbying. . . . We go out to lunch, but they don't necessarily talk about anything. [We] just know a good guy may be going out of business because he doesn't get more trade or so. It's the spirit that influences.

"The spirit" may be imperfect as a communication medium, but small talk does serve the congressman as a protection against having to reply with a face-to-face "No." Furthermore, congressmen frequently ask questions of visitors in ways which channel their comments in the direction desired. One congressman asked a delegation whether any of them really favored reciprocal trade. They did, but, on receiving this cue, they talked about other things. The typical business visitor to a Congressional office comes with not one problem, but several, and in general congressmen are much more experienced and expert at diverting visitors than visitors are in forcing congressmen on a point.

One source of word-of-mouth information is fellow-congressmen and other members of the Capitol Hill work force. The structure of Con-

---

[3] This is, of course, not true of members of the relevant committees, who spend a great deal of time in hearings.

gress is such that every member has to specialize. As we have noted, the congressman cannot do all the things his job calls for. He can operate effectively only on that special part of the legislation which comes before the committees on which he sits. A given representative or senator sits on one or two committees, and one will be of particular importance to him. Over a period of years, a capable congressman becomes an expert on the subject matter of his committee assignments. One man becomes a specialist on immigration and another on conservation, one on foreign policy and another on taxes. Among the specialists on any topic, there will be men of different character and viewpoint. Thus, congressmen develop an implicit roster of fellow-congressmen whose judgment they respect, whose viewpoint they normally share, and to whom they can turn for guidance on particular topics of the colleague's competence. Each congressman tends to follow the lead, not of any one person, but of a roster of specific colleagues sorted by topics.

Members of the House on the whole associate with other congressmen and assistants whose views are like their own. Much of the social life of Congress is passed with other members of the same party and their wives. It is especially from among these friendly associates that a congressman picks out as a mentor on a particular topic a man who is on the appropriate committee and who is a specialist on that topic. Communication with such a person may often be no more than an exchange of two sentences: "How should I vote on such-and-such bill?" and an answer.[4] Or it may be a validation of the authenticity of a partisan claim, for example, "Are oil imports really hurting your people?" Occasionally it will be fuller conversation, but even in the usual brief form it may be very effective.

Another source of Congressional information is the published word. With regard to reciprocal trade, except for newspapers, this played very little part in the legislative information system. With few exceptions, there was among our Congressional interviewees little indication of familiarity with the economic literature on international trade. On the other hand, perhaps a dozen congressmen referred to some item in the press, and several had evidently obtained ideas from newspaper columns. No respondent mentioned specialized, for example, business, newspapers. A few did refer to recently issued reports prepared by government agencies or interest groups, but these had been skimmed, rather than read. Congressmen seemed to have read somewhat less than had executive department officials whom we interviewed. It must, however, be remembered that there is little available in print which copes with the problem the congressman faces on tariff policy. What he essentially needs is material which

---

[4] A member of a state legislature told us that she could walk onto the floor during a roll call and count even on members of the opposition to tell her reliably what would be the "right" vote *for her,* considering her allegiances and interests.

reconciles the claims and desires of his individual constituents with over-all national economic problems. What he finds in print are for the most part theoretical and high-level discussions of national interest and economic policy, on the one hand, and discussions of the plight of some one industry, on the other, not material balancing the two.

We might also mention that we can recall nothing to indicate that nation-wide opinion-poll data had any appreciable impact on Congress. Members of the administration were anxious that our survey of business should be published [5] so that they could use the results. (We do not know whether they were ever used.) Some representatives did informal public-opinion polls in their own districts. But, on the whole, in the reciprocal-trade controversy, members of Congress paid little attention to general public opinion as it could have been ascertained by formal polling techniques.

Despite the fact that, on issue after issue, the mail has been shown to be not representative—in 1954-1955 it was about ten-to-one protectionist—and despite the fact that there is no reason to suspect that letter-writing on any given issue has any relationship to voting or political influence, the mail is nevertheless seen as the voice of the district or state. As is to be expected, many congressmen and senators run counter to the mail in obedience to dictates of conscience, party, or committee; but, when they do so, many of them appear to think that they are defying something very significant.

Why is the mail taken so seriously? First of all, members of Congress and their staff have no alternative but to spend an enormous amount of time reading and answering mail, and a busy man would be less than human if he were to believe he was wasting so much time. Second, congressmen often operate in a near-vacuum, uninformed about what their ultimate employers, the voters in their district or state, really want. The mail gives a sense, perhaps a spurious one, of receiving instructions on some issues. Such instructions give the man a sense of being in contact with his constituents and some notion, again perhaps spurious, as to what is likely to please his constituents and result in his re-election. Third, many junior members of the House, having no important role on major committees, appear to be frustrated at their inability to take any demonstrably effective action on major issues. Answering constituents' mail is one thing they can do which gives them the feeling of acting effectively. Fourth, writing to one's congressman is an expression of the citizen's right of petition—treasured by most congressmen—from perceived inequities

---

[5] This was done in Raymond A. Bauer, Suzanne Keller, and Ithiel de Sola Pool, "The Shift in Business Opinion on the Tariff," *Fortune*, April 1955.

of legislation or administrative action. Finally, some congressmen, whether realistically or not, appear to regard their correspondence as rational academic discussion of issues of national importance. Much Congressional correspondence serves no visible political or legislative purpose.

But mail must be "genuine." It must not be junk—that is, press releases or other broadcast mailings—nor must it be stimulated. Stimulated mail is not entirely easy to define. In its pure form, it consists of virtually identical postcard messages written at the instigation of a single company, union, or interest group. (One company even mailed the postcards for its workers, fearing that they would not know who their congressman was.) Congressmen look for signs of stimulation—similarity of phrasing ("They all used the same argument") or even stationery ("They handed out the paper") and time of mailing ("You could tell the hour or minute someone pushed the button"). Indeed, it is hard to fool a congressman as to when mail is stimulated. Some organizations urge their members to write in their own words, on their own stationery, and as personally as possible. Congressional assistants tell us that perhaps one in fifty persons who write such a letter will enclose the original printed notice from the organization urging an individualized, apparently spontaneous letter. But some mail which would have to be regarded as stimulated in the literal sense does not necessarily have the impact of stimulated mail. Pittsburgh Plate Glass, for example, succeeded in getting people in the community—doctors, lawyers, mechanics, school teachers—to write to their congressmen, and these letters appeared to reflect genuine involvement in the effect on Pittsburgh Plate of foreign competition.[6]

Most of the mail sent on the Reciprocal Trade Act was in some sense stimulated. It is our guess that, among the Eastern and Southern congressmen on whom we concentrated our attention, Westinghouse, Dow, Monsanto, and Pittsburgh Plate Glass may have stimulated 40 per cent or more of all the mail received on the issue in 1954. In addition, there were the coal, small oil, watch, bicycle, and textile interests, as well as such small groups as the nut- and cherry-growers. All of this mail was protectionist and outnumbered pro-reciprocal-trade mail about ten to one. Mail in favor of reciprocal trade was equally stimulated, and perhaps by even fewer prime movers. Our impression is that three-fourths of all antiprotectionist mail was stimulated directly or indirectly by the League of Women Voters.

Stimulated mail and junk is discounted (some congressmen do

---

[6] But note that even this well-worked-out and individualized effort was not enough to disguise the fact of stimulation. The congressman who showed us the material and the present authors were fully aware of the campaign, or we would not be discussing it in this passage. We doubt that there is much stimulated mail which passes undetected.

not even regard it as mail) because it does not convey the impression that the writer is genuinely involved in the issue.

> Congressman to Secretary: Jane, am I right that we haven't received mail from more than five people on this tariff business?

> Secretary to Congressman: Yes, except, of course, for the pressure groups.

Stimulated or interest-group mail is the type of communication most likely to be regarded as pressure because it comes close to being an implied threat to mobilize votes against the congressman. Even though, as indicated above, there is every reason for him to discount this threat, it cannot be completely discounted. One lobbyist told us a story from an earlier phase in his career when Speaker William Bankhead said to him, "Look, I've got 400 letters on this bill." "But, Speaker," the lobbyist replied, "you know those are stimulated." "Of course they're stimulated," said Bankhead, "but they're there." The person who has been stimulated to write may be stimulated to vote. Though we are convinced that the likelihood is not great, a shred of suspicion remains. Although the term "pressure" is not often employed about mail, it is almost exclusively applied to such stimulated mail.

The conventional description of congressmen as under pressure carries with it the implication that the communications addressed to them are an undesired burden. But, more often than not, the congressman welcomes communication. One congressman who was having difficulty making up his mind complained that no one came to his office to see him. The only time he saw a lobbyist was when he sought one out! Still others indicated that, on the Reciprocal Trade Act and on other issues, they wanted more communication.

Said one newly appointed assistant: "You know, I was very much surprised at how few representatives of organizations come around to make themselves known." Said another: "I used to be a lobbyist myself. . . . It is a peculiar thing and rather incredible to me—the scarcity of contact with Washington trade-association or labor-union representatives." The assistant of another who was a key figure in the reciprocal-trade fight said: "I absolutely had to beat them over the head at our lobbying organization to find out what I wanted to find out; I had to push and push them on this to get the information." And one congressman, when asked what he had heard from the lobby groups on his side and whether they had pushed him, said: "Hell no, it's just the other way around; it's me calling them up and trying to shaft them to get off their fat rears and get out and do something." To many congressmen, the interest organization is a source of information about the attitudes of significant groups in his public, a source of research data and speech material, and an unofficial propaganda ally to help him put his own case forward. This one speaks of "our lobby."

The reader will recall that, in the chapter on lobbies, we noted that they became effective when they served as private auxiliaries to congressmen or other persons in a public-policy-forming position. Frequently, the lobby is a service agency for a movement led by or even initiated by a congressman.[7] The congressman who told us that he had to telephone "his" lobby to get them going was not telling us a man-bites-dog story. He was describing a usual state of affairs. For his own career reasons, a congressman wants to be a leader of movements with public appeal. He may define as his profession the mobilization of opinion and the propagation of viewpoints on public issues. Success in that profession, as in any other, depends on creating a product that the public wants and becoming a leading purveyor of it. But, as is also true in business or education, the supplier does not wait passively for wants to appear. He helps create the want. Businessmen spend billions to create wants for their products. Educators educate; they do not wait to be told what the students want to learn. Congressmen promote movements for legislation. Men like Richard Simpson and Cleveland Bailey, not to mention their precursors, gave form and vitality to protectionism as a program for coping with ills. It was in the United States Congress, not somewhere in the hinterland, that the ideological initiative for protection has been historically centered. And the men who made themselves national figures by taking this initiative led, rather than were led by, hired staff men working in private association offices.

Thus, we note once more that the congressman is not entirely a passive instrument with respect to the communications coming to him. To a large extent, he determines whether he is communicated with, in what manner, and on which side of the issue. We have already seen that businessmen and interest-group representatives tend not to communicate with persons who disagree with them. We recall the case of Congressman Stubborn whose obduracy stopped liberal-trade communications from coming to him; no registered voter, he said, wrote him favoring reciprocal trade. That represents but one side of the coin, however.

The other side is that of congressmen who, by their manner and conduct, communicate their desire for communication. In contrast to Congressman Stubborn, we may consider Congressman Serious Consideration, an indecisive man who called a meeting in his district of people interested in the Reciprocal Trade Act. By publicizing his own indecision, he stimulated his constituents to speak up. The circumstances under which

---

[7] Cf. Stephen K. Bailey, *Congress Makes a Law* (New York: Columbia University Press, 1950). The Full Employment Act, the adoption of which Bailey describes, was conceived in Congress. The liberal congressmen who got it written then pressed the unions and liberal organizations into reluctant support of the measure.

he called the meeting virtually ensured its being dominated by persons with protectionist interests.[8] He voted against HR 1.

Several members of Congress told us: "I tell my people that I want such-and-such a type of letter; otherwise, I won't pay any attention to it." In this way, they produce the letters they want.

Congressman Special, in three months, had, he claimed, received 2,000 letters supporting his position and not one letter opposing it. The reason was that he had spoken up and down the country and his own district on the evils of a low-tariff policy, calling the Reciprocal Trade Act an evil product of intrigue, advocated by Karl Marx and worked out by Harry Dexter White.

It is true, as we have seen in preceding chapters, that a large proportion of businessmen and a surprising proportion of representatives of interest groups communicate perfunctorily with congressmen without first ascertaining their views on the issue in question. But it is also true that, when a congressman's stand becomes known, that fact determines to a large extent what communications get sent to him.

In closing this chapter, we should repeat a previously noted fact which partly explains why pressure groups do not appear to exercise so much pressure with regard to general legislation when viewed from Congress as they appear to when viewed by outside observers. We have pointed out that, during the reciprocal-trade controversy in 1953-1955, lobbyists tended to establish liaison only with the congressmen and senators on their own side. They acted for them as outside men stimulating general public interest in the issue, testifying before committees, or providing staff services for the congressmen and senators. The tactical basis of pressure-group activities seemed to be to assist men already on their side to do the job of persuading fellow legislators. Direct persuasion of uncommitted or opposed congressmen and senators was a minor activity of the lobbies.[9]

---

[8] He asked in effect how the bill would affect his district and heard from industrial interests in his district. He did not ask how it would affect America's world interests. He did not invite foreign spokesmen or foreign-affairs specialists.

[9] Was the reciprocal-trade situation unique or typical in regard to lobbying? It is instructive to note the full range of items on pressures on Congress which appeared in the press during a sample period (July, 1959). Boston industrialist Bernard Goldfine, who had gone out of his way to "maintain good relations" with friends in the national government, was convicted of perjury in refusing to disclose to a Congressional committee all of his activities. The Teamsters Union had been lobbying against labor legislation before Congress. When the lobbyist tried to apply pressure in the classical sense, saying, in effect, "We'll get you," it backfired on him, and he apparently ended up with less support than he had at the beginning (cf. *Time*, July 27, 1959, pp. 12-13). In these same few weeks, Robert Kennedy, then counsel for the Senate Rackets Committee, appeared on several television shows and called for a flood of mail to Congress. His appeal was answered, and thousands of letters poured in. But at the very same time a comparable volume of mail was received in protest against the mistreatment of wild horses!

One of the results of the Kennedy appeal reported from Chicago was that so many people were calling to find out who their congressman was that a special telephone service had to be installed. In the meantime, Jack Paar, master of ceremonies of one of the television programs on which Kennedy appeared, shamefacedly reported to his audience that he had telegraphed Senator Javits only to find out that Javits had long been working fervently for the very legislation that Paar urged him to support. During the same period, there was a considerable furor over the pressure tactics of missile manufacturers to obtain contracts. Several weeks of investigation seemed to confirm the fact that little pressure, if any, had been applied, or at least that the people to whom it was applied did not regard it as pressure (cf. "Gates Approves Ex-Officers' Jobs," *New York Times,* July 8, 1959).

All in all, the picture was what we would have expected. Actual pressure is likely to backfire and is a dangerous activity. In the case of the missile program, even a moderate amount of self-serving promotion appeared to generate disproportionate counteractivity. Both Goldfine and the Teamsters Union ended up worse off than they were at the beginning. Kennedy and "Wild-Horse Annie" showed that it was possible to stir up a considerable amount of activity in the form of writing to Congress. But both campaigns of letter-writing seemed to have more head than beer.

Chapter 33

Conflict of Roles

Congressmen suffer from many role conflicts. The trade-act debates drew attention to the disparity between the national interest and that of the district, with its local business and industry. There seems little doubt that a comfortable majority of the members of both the House and the Senate saw increased international trade as in the national interest. But they could not divorce themselves from concern for local businesses which might be relieved of some of their difficulties by increased protection from foreign competition. Certainly, Senators Wayne Morse (D., Ore.), Paul Douglas (D., Ill.), and the late Senator Alben Barkley (D., Ky.) were men who generally thought in national, rather than local, terms. Yet, during the Senate debate in 1953-1955, each of them spoke out for the protection of local products—Oregon cherries and nuts, Illinois and Kentucky fluorspar. The strengthening of the escape clause in the 1955 and 1958 extensions of the act may be regarded as a device for reducing this role conflict. It permitted the congressman to reconcile two competing roles—general public service and special service to his constituents.

The role conflict between national and constituent interest on the tariff issue is widely recognized. Most histories of recent tariff politics have, indeed, centered on the story of the conflict between national interest, as expressed in the principles of free trade, and "selfish local interests" seeking protective legislative advantage. Role conflict over general public service versus constituent service occasionally operates in the opposite direction, too. In 1953, we found some New Englanders who appeared to favor protection in principle speaking out against quotas on fuel-oil imports which would discriminate against them.

The general issue of what a congressman should be, a defender of broad principles or a defender of his constituency, is far from simple. Considerable argument could be mustered for the view of Congressman District who said:

> I'm here to represent my district. . . . This is . . . my . . . belief as to the function of a congressman . . . what is good for the majority of districts is good for the country. What snarls up the system is these so-called statesmen-congressmen who vote for what they think is the country's interest. Let the senators do that. They are paid to be statesmen; we aren't.

The U.S. House of Representatives is above all a communication node which serves to unify a large and heterogeneous land by bringing into confrontation a group of men representing its various parts. The House is an instrument for bringing 435 pairs of critical eyes to bear on proposals drafted by persons who cannot possibly think of the particular implications of their general principles for every town, profession, or interest group in the country. The House is also the agency that forcefully brings special considerations of equity to bear on bureaucratic decision-makers operating in the framework of abstract and general policies. In short, the concern of the House with what may be the particular consequences of policies to minor local individuals and industries is one of its great functions and values. It could not perform that function without receiving much communication of petitioner complaints and paying faithful attention to them. The congressman who thinks of his job in terms of favors to constituents can make a good case for so thinking. And, because there is a case to be made for serving both constituent and national interests, he feels role conflict.

A number of factors operate to bring into the House men of a temperament oriented toward a concern with their constituents' special interests. The newly elected representative's expertness has usually been in human relations and community activities. He knows many people, relates to them easily, listens well, and talks well. Clearly, he has proved himself good at getting elected in his own district, and for purposes of getting elected it helps to have a deep and genuine concern for what the district wants. Such a man is not necessarily prepared by his previous career for specialized technical work in the areas of public policy in which he must legislate, nor does he normally have a wide background on issues of major public policy or foreign affairs. We noted above that congressmen are busy men; we might have added that they are typically not good managers of their time. The man who gets elected is more likely to be the one who enjoys sitting at the cracker barrel or at a lengthy meeting, who will talk to his friends and neighbors patiently, who will listen to complaints at length. He is not often an efficient organizer for whom objectives take precedence over persons. Congressmen, on the whole, by selection and usually by temperament, think of the particular man thrown out of work, the particular firm driven out of business, and the particular misfortune which may befall.

Indeed, we formed a hypothesis, and it is no more than that, that much of the conflict between Congress and the administration, particularly the State Department, and most of the protectionist bias of the House arise from a difference between two personality types: one oriented to particular relations with persons and another which abstracts from persons to principles. Representatives seemed most often to be of the former kind, administration spokesmen of the latter. No sharper clashes on tariffs occurred than when officers of the State Department, or for that matter of the CNTP, testified in hearings. These liberal traders preached from broad principles. They would not consider questions about injury to local industries, asserting instead that American national interest required trade concessions. Members of Congress often pointed out what that would do to some handful of miners or factory workers somewhere, whereas State Department spokesmen, not denying the problem, tended to answer that, regrettably, the interest of a handful must give way to national interests. A favorite phrase of a State Department man who worked on Congressional relations was, "You've got to think in the over-all." The result was fuming anger on both sides. The State Department men saw the congressmen who grilled them as narrow-minded defenders of selfish, as against national, interests. The congressman, unsatisfied in his search for usable answers, saw the diplomat as cold, unwilling to do anything for a suffering human being who faced unemployment and whom the congressman knew, or at least thought of, as a man of flesh and blood.

The events of 1962 again require partial qualification of these generalizations. The Kennedy approach to politics was more prone to solution of particular problems, less ideological than that of his predecessors. Also, the readjustment provisions gave the liberal traders something to say about injured industries other than that they must yield to the general good. Furthermore, in 1962 primary responsibility for dealing with Congress was transferred to a small group of highly political individuals, much more like congressmen in their approach than like administrators. George Ball, the key administration figure on foreign trade, had always understood the advantages of hard-headed individualized arguments. He also understood the incapacity of the State Department in Congress. In 1961, he submitted to the President a series of decision-questions including, "Who would take the lead if an important bill were to be proposed?" The answer was that the State Department could not and that only the White House could. That part of the White House staff —Meyer Feldman and others—which actually piloted the bill through innumerable bargains and negotiations to final passage, were political men to the core, contrasting sharply to the industrial administrators Eisenhower had used. In 1962, the career administrators and professional men in both the State Department and White House, the men who had created the bill, still found themselves in the sort of conflict with politicians which we have been describing, but not with congressmen directly. Their problem was with their own political emissaries to Congress. Perhaps a couple of times a week, they wrote or spoke to Feldman or other Congressional liaison agents appealing to them not to buy passage of the bill by concessions of principle.

It is not clear to us whether the American political system would be better or worse off with a Congressional pattern that put more emphasis on matters of ideology and principle instead of on the particular needs of living constituents. Suffice it to note that there is role conflict and, in the House at least, a heavy loading in favor of looking after one's district.

Mail from the district or state is most important for alerting the congressman to the perceived self-interest of constituents. By and large, most protectionist mail took the line, "Save my job. Don't let HR 1 throw me out of work." There was a good deal of reference to low foreign wages.

Where such mundane appeals could be bolstered with appeals to the national interest, this was also done. Almost invariably, it involved some aspect of national defense: preservation of skills (watchmakers, glass-workers), development of natural resources (oil, fluorspar, zinc, copper), avoiding becoming dependent on foreign sources of supply (for turbines and the like).

The impression we got from our talk with congressmen and their assistants was that the direct interest of their constituents in potential losses in jobs and in business motivated them more strongly than did protectionist considerations of national interest. This circumstance must be looked at closely. If their constituents had had no interest to the contrary, the majority of congressmen would have favored the Reciprocal Trade Act as being in the country's interest. However, as we have estimated, about 90 per cent of the communications were protectionist in tone. With most congressmen being oriented toward a more liberal trade policy as favoring the national interest and with most communications favoring protection, it was statistically probable that the net impact of mail was to move congressmen toward protection. This added to the sense of conflict between representation of the district or state and more general service to the nation. To the extent that protectionist communications included an argument of national interest (chiefly national defense), such considerations helped to reconcile this role conflict. But it is our guess that the national-defense argument would have persuaded very few congressmen if it had not been linked with the interests of their constituents. The reverse is by no means equally true.

It should be restated that the assertion of special interests by constituents was not considered as pressure or improper, but rather as legitimate expression of interests which it was the congressman's job to represent. We quote from one congressman who said that there was no pressure on him:

> I discussed this issue in the campaign. . . , I . . . said then I was in favor of free trade, that it was a Democratic policy and principle. Besides, I am personally fond of Cordell Hull. . . . Between election and the vote I, to some extent, changed my mind. Partly, I saw unemployment, so much of it, during the campaign. The long line of people out of work. The reason was foreign imports. . . . I talked with the laboring people on this, and their representatives in Washington. . . . A representative of the union and of the producers came in to see me, and the representative of one of the synthetic plants, a big one. . . . I heard from the League of Women Voters and several individuals who were well learned in favor of the program. Actually, I wasn't going to vote against the program at all. . . . You know I was very eager to see reciprocal trade extended. I have a lot of crops in my district which export. I heard nothing from them or any of their organizations. They didn't wait on me at all.

The congressman's complaint that he had not heard from people with a direct interest in a liberal-trade policy as contrasted with "learned" people concerned with the general interest may be interpreted as a desire on his part to build up a counterpressure to offset protectionist pressure, so that he could feel justified in persisting in the liberal stand he preferred. The major pressure on this and other congressmen came from within, in the form of a desire both to serve the national interest and to represent his district. What he was seeking was an articulation of the antiprotectionist interest in his district so that he could feel that he would also be representing his district if he supported the Reciprocal Trade Act.

Spokesmen for reciprocal trade did not help him, however. Until 1962, instead of arguing low-level district advantage, they couched their argument in lofty terms. The League of Women Voters seemed especially inclined that way. Partisans of general-interest pressure groups will find little encouragement in the response which League mail received from most congressmen. It was regarded as general, uninformed "do-goodism." As a matter of fact, we had the impression that some, perhaps many, congressmen were irritated to be asked to act in the national interest or, still worse, in international interests against those of their constituents. Such an appeal could only engender guilt in the man responding to pressure and bring into focus his role conflict. It also made him angry at those ladies who forced him to feel guilty for doing the humane and kind thing for friends and neighbors who had elected him.

We should note here that the role conflict of which congressmen are most aware focuses on only two of many possible roles. The two categories of identification, district and national, are not the only ones possible, although they are the only ones American legislators think much about. None talked about representing class or party or humanity. These were not choices which were ever thought of as proper roles and so caused no role conflict.

When interviewed, the majority of congressmen spontaneously discussed their conception of their role. Although asked about tariff views, they answered in terms of how they saw their job, of their obligations to their constituents and to the nation. The majority had explicit theories on those points which they found it easy to express and which they felt to be pertinent to the tariff issue.

The same was not true of their views of party. In our free-flowing, unstructured interviews they seldom spontaneously introduced party program, party obligations, or party-building as considerations relevant to their tariff stand. Some Republicans referred to their early days, when people did identify Republicanism with high tariffs and Democracy with low, but that was recognized by all as a bygone era. Some Democrats referred to Rayburn's attempts at discipline, but with resentment. Although, where possible, they would have preferred to act in ways helpful to the party, no one expressed a feeling that the criterion for a right tariff stand for himself as a congressman was party interest. American parties do not command the kind of loyalty that makes their organizational progress a criterion for public policy.

Class was hardly mentioned at all. Its absence is worth noting, for there are places in the world where a representative would feel a duty to judge legislation by class interest. In our interviews, the closest thing to such an attitude was expressed by a handful of men who identified with small against big business and defended tariffs in those terms. The plight of American workers was often referred to, but not in opposition to American business.

Finally, specific foreign interests were hardly mentioned at all. This is important to us because of our central interest in international communication. We started out to learn how and how much foreign considerations were brought to bear in American discussion of foreign-trade matters. In fifty formal interviews with congressmen, not one spontaneously mentioned anything implying any obligation to take into account the interests or concerns of specific allies. Some talked about strengthening the system of alliances or strengthening the American position abroad, but none alluded to the needs or desires of foreigners, except as instrumental to American needs. In interviews in the State Department, the executive branch, and also with a good many businessmen, there were specific references to the economic needs of certain foreign countries, without accompanying reference as to how it served America to take account of these needs. In those interviews, there was at least some direct identification with things foreign. Nothing of the sort happened in Congress. Role conflict was universally defined as that between local and national interests.

Chapter 34

The Congressional Process—
A Summary

The Reciprocal Trade Act was a good test case for some established notions of the Congressional process. The issue was one on which communication from constituents and interest groups to Congress was extensive—which is not always the case, even for issues of considerable legislative consequence. We found that congressmen who had received a good deal of mail on the Reciprocal Trade Act had not received a single letter or postcard on some other major issues before Congress. There are issues which may outdraw foreign-trade policy, but it was sufficiently close to the top to provide a test for some of the established propositions about the relationship of the congressman to the public.

The classic problem of representative government is that of whether the representative should take instructions from his constituents or serve their interests in the manner which his own judgment indicates to be best. Some congressmen fell near each end of the continuum. Some saw themselves as leaders who knew better than did their constituents what was good for them. Our old friend Congressman Stubborn was obviously such a person. On the other hand, there was Congressman District, who complained: "It's those so-called statesmen who snarl up the system." Congressman District saw his job as one of finding out what his constituents wanted and then giving it to them in their own terms. Those of his colleagues who thought in terms of national interest or the long range merely "snarled things up."

The reader may note that we are once again discussing a topic that has been central throughout the book: how self-interest affects the formulation of public-policy views. We find with congressmen, as we did with businessmen and lobbyists, that its effects are subtle and indeterminate. For congressmen, businessmen, and lobbyists alike, a good description of the form of their goal-oriented behavior is to say that they are serving some interest. But for each there is an infinity of ways in which that interest can be seen. Along with the pious norm of national interest, American congressmen recognize a genuine duty to their districts. Fortunately for their peace of mind, these conflicting norms are indeterminate until the congressman's own operational code and the communications he receives give them some content. Congressmen Stubborn and District go about the job of serving their constituents differently.

Let us look for a moment at the type of congressman who sees his job as that of obeying his constituents' instructions. Political philosophers and commentators down to Walter Lippmann in our day have regarded this man critically. But, in our opinion, the criticisms have been on the wrong grounds. They have been based on an assumption which our own experience denies, namely, that it is possible for a politician to simply do what his constituents want. In fact, that option is an illusion. No congressman would long be re-elected who showed no more imagination in interpreting his constituents' needs than to vote at each point in time as his followers felt at that time. At the minimum, a political leader must guess where his followers are going and get there first.[1] The voters do not know that next year or a few years later they may have turned against their present views. They may have abandoned isolation or become alarmed at unemployment or have realized the excesses of McCarthy. The congressman who too faithfully bespoke their earlier concerns may thereby lose.

Furthermore, it is in fact impossible for a politician to ascertain his constituents' views on any large issue with sufficient precision to obtain for himself a clear set of instructions. In the chapter on the foreign-trade opinions of the general public, the major thing that opinion-poll data showed is that there was no informed, crystallized opinion on the issue.

---

[1] Stephen K. Bailey's *Congress Makes a Law, op. cit.,* provides a classic description of Congress trying to make a record of concern for the unemployed at a moment when there were still few of them, but when Congress expected that a few months later there would be many.

The questions the pollers used to cull out uninformed voters were exceedingly lenient, yet even such mild screening devices rejected from one-fourth to one-half of adult voters. Among those who earn the accolade "informed," a full half really had no crystallized opinion. And, of those with crystallized opinions, most based those opinions, not on information, but on deductions from more generalized attitudes.

Could a congressman rely on such generalized attitudes as his guide? He would have found that more people said they favored lower tariffs than said they favored higher tariffs. But, in voting on foreign-trade policy, the congressman is not dealing with abstract principles. Congress in 1954 and 1955, 1958 and 1962, did not vote on tariffs, but on the details of the administrative devices for handling tariff negotiations, details which admittedly had some predictable relation to what might in the future happen to tariff rates, but details also related to general notions of fairness, executive power, and so on. Key votes occurred on such matters as the openness of debate in the House, the finality of rulings by the Tariff Commission and the president, and the payment of readjustment subsidies. Opinion-poll data show that any slight restating of the conditions and rewording of the question can produce enormous apparent changes of opinion. To what is the congressman to look in this situation? In terms of the specific issues with which congressmen were faced, there was nothing like a clear mandate from the people.

Moreover, we have glossed over another important consideration. The would-be agent of his own constituency is not interested in what the general public wants, but in what his own constituency wants, and there were few local polls, and those few were largely amateur jobs.

Polls of their districts which congressmen conducted invariably involved questions which virtually predetermined the distribution of responses. A press release of May 20, 1954, by the Committee for a National Trade Policy summarizes a number of such polls, all of which quite naturally favored a freer-trade position. Congressman George Bender of Ohio asked: "Do you approve of the Reciprocal Trade Program?", a question which we saw in an earlier chapter was bound to get an affirmative response. Similarly, Rep. Joel Broyhill (R., Va.) asked: "Are you in sympathy with the Reciprocal Trade Program?", and Rep. William Widnall (R., N.J.) asked: "Do you believe that the Reciprocal Trade Law should be continued to assist in our foreign trade?"

It is probably just as well that Congress paid no more attention than it did to the opinions of the general public as measured by polls. But the sources of information which they did use were, if anything, even less revealing of the state of opinion. Communications to Congress from business represented neither the opinions nor the interests of the business community at large. That was equally true in individual states and Congressional districts. Even less can these communications be considered representative of the interests and opinions of the general public or of such special groups as labor, nor even of those segments of the public which really cared about the issue.

The expression of opinion at a given time represents the opinions of those who, under a given set of circumstances, have been persuaded to momentarily focus their attention on an issue. The factors which determine who will express his opinion are largely accidental to the issue. Thus, in 1954-1955, there was no mass writing by purchasing agents in protest against the tariffs on goods which they bought for their companies. This was partly due to the fact that they bought through brokers and were unaware of the tariffs on foreign goods which they did or did not buy. It was almost certainly also due to the fact that they saw their function as the limited one of "purchasing" in an existing market rather than as influencing the nature of that market. A few purchasing agents were persuaded to write in 1962.

One of the factors, accidental to the issue, which affects expression of opinion is, of course, the congressman himself. No matter how faithfully he wants to represent the wishes of his constituency, he must make choices as to what issues to concentrate on, what means (legislative or service) to use, and which groups in his constituency to represent. In choosing between competing groups to represent, he is in a high proportion of instances responding to the part as though it were the whole. Even the least statesmanlike of congressmen willy-nilly does much to determine what he is told to do. Thus, the fact that a particular congressman sees it as his job to follow the instructions of his constituents is not predictive of his behavior until one observes him as he goes about the virtually impossible tasks of trying to find out what those instructions are.

Thus, neither the basic dichotomy between the image of the representative as agent and as leader nor the related dichotomy between district and national interest is by itself predictive of what a man will do. Virtually any policy can be rationalized in terms of either national or local interest. The choice affects the congressman's rationalizations more than his action.

The pressure-group model of the Congressional process was not invalidated by our investigation, though it fitted neatly only a small part of the behavior we observed. We noticed much activity that has ordinarily been fitted to the pressure-group model. Interest groups were organized, spent money, and got in touch with Congress. Substantial segments of the public wrote their congressmen. But this single word, "pressure," whether in the congressman's or the scientist's sense, is still a poor description of the Congressional facts. We do not deny that there are individual instances of what the congressman called "pressure," that is, when a congressman is coerced into doing what he does not want to do. But we do not see this as the modal relationship between congressmen and the public. Nor do we find a linear causal relationship analogous to fluid mechanics—"the pressure is applied here and the results come out there"—as an accurate description of the influence of the public on Congressional decisions. We have spelled out the mitigating factors at great length: the congressman's support of the right to petition, the discounting of pressure mail, the multiplicity of ties which relate the congressman to stable interest groups, the congressman's own desire for information and education from his constituents, the intervention of Congressional procedures in the linear equation, the pressure from other congressmen and the administration, the congressman's ability intentionally or unintentionally to obscure the question of whether he has in fact conformed to pressure, and the tendency of interest-group representatives to approach those who are already on their side. We are not saying that the intention of interest groups and/or of the general public is not to exert pressure. We are saying only that the congressman usually does not respond to these efforts as pressure and that the application of pressure is conspicuously less effective than might be assumed if one did not take an exceedingly close look at what actually happens.

Again, we must stress the transactional nature of the relationship between the congressman and the constituent. Each acts upon the other, and much that appears from a simplistic view to be pressure on the congressman is actually a result of the congressman's actions on the constituency —the communication of his own stand, his identification with particular interest groups, his activities in general.

The matters which we have reported appear to be more than minor aberrations, more than noise in an otherwise-orderly pressure-group model. The pressure-group view of Congressional proceedings evolved in large part out of the study of tariff legislation prior to the passage of the Reciprocal Trade Act. It is highly probable that the pressure-group model was more appropriate when Congress itself was setting tariff rates. The change in procedures for the handling of tariff-making may account in great part for the difference in the picture painted by us and that painted by so competent a scholar as Schattschneider. The picture has certainly changed since 1931. Indeed, one point on which the large majority of congressmen were agreed (one must except a few of the most ardent protectionists) was that they did not wish to return to a system whereby Congress itself set individual tariff rates. That system generated too much pressure on individual congressmen by industries seeking favors. Congress has found it far more comfortable to decide matters of general tariff policy and the procedure for seeking favors, but to leave individual decisions in the hands of administrators. This means that the individual business interest appeals to Congress only for an intermediate goal, namely, that general rules be framed in ways likely to result in favorable action on later petitions. That fact reduces the frequency and urgency of appeals to the congressman. By thus passing the buck, Congress has reduced its own power. A congressman's power is in large part the favors he can perform. If patronage is eliminated, if nominations to West Point or Annapolis are removed from his hands, if tariff-rate-setting is turned over to the executive, the legislator is deprived of ways to win the support of constituents. But each of these powers is a two-edged sword. If there are more appeals for help than he can handle and if the intensity of them is such that they generate threats and anger against him, then he may be glad to yield a part of his power, letting someone else take the blame for decisions and reserving to himself only the role of critic and issuer of statements. That is what Congress has done in the Reciprocal Trade Act, and most congressmen are happy they have no more power on this score than they now have.

But, if pressure politics no longer satisfies as an explanation of what happened regarding reciprocal trade, this is not just because of a change in the times. We are probably also reflecting a characteristic stage in the development of a discipline. The pressure-group model was a sophisticated refinement of previously naïve views of the Congressional process. It may now be time for a still more complicated view of the process of influence on and in Congress.

A case can always be made for the elaboration of explanatory models, since one can always dream up some additional variable which exerts or could exert influence on the phenomena studied. But such elaborate models complicate the investigator's life, and the simpler ones usually have greater generality. Therefore, the plea for elaboration should be made cautiously and responsibly. We make it because we feel that the simpler model did not do the job for us.

Abstracting a single issue for study may produce quite an erroneous impression of what is going on. That is not merely to say that everything is related to everything else. Many things which happened with respect to foreign-trade policy in 1953-1955 are understandable *only* in the light of the other activities which engaged the business community, Congress, and the administration. These other activities were major determinants of what happened to the Reciprocal Trade Act.

The characteristic organizational structure and procedures of Congress must be kept in mind to understand the success or failure of attempts to influence legislation.

Moreover, the appropriate general model is not one of linear causality, but a transactional one, which views all the actors in the situation as exerting continuous influence on each other. All the actors are to some extent in a situation of mutual influence and interdependence; A's influence on B is to some extent a result of B's prior influence on A.

Finally, we may repeat what we learned about the impact of communications on the specific outcome of the Reciprocal Trade renewal. It has become clear in retrospect that few direct messages had any significant effect on the outcome. We can easily list some exceptions. The most striking one is the letter from one Southern textile manufacturer to Congressman Lanham. This letter from a respected source against a background of similar letters led Representative Lanham to make direct inquiries of the writer, which, in turn, led him to change his views, and that, in turn, influenced perhaps a dozen or more nearly crucial Southern votes.[2] Other exceptions were a few messages from the White House. Word from the White House certainly beat the Gore amendment, although at some point it would have been beaten anyway. Word from the White House also led to the acceptance of certain other amendments, such as the Millikin one. Barring such few exceptions, no message to Congress in the two years of debate can be shown to have had a direct, determinate effect on the outcome. For the rest, the communications process set a crucial backdrop against which the drama was played out.

That does not minimize the role of the communications process. Without it, knowledge, attitudes, action would all have been impossible. What we are asserting is that any specific prediction or causal statement about Congress and the Reciprocal Trade Bill would have to link communication as a process with such other variables as Congressional procedure, congressmen's images of their roles, the pressure of time, and so on. An example may make the point clear. Communication certainly made many congressmen aware of the underbidding of American turbine-manufacturers by Swiss and British bidders and also of the rejection of some of the low foreign bids by the U.S. government. Congressmen read about that in the press and about American and foreign protests. Occasionally, they also learned about them from lobby literature. They knew, too, about the mail from Westinghouse asking for protection. But that issue was not before Congress. Those communications constituted an indirect influence on the atmosphere of the discussion and most particularly on the atmosphere in which amendments to the Reciprocal Trade Act were considered;

---

[2] There is an unpredictable element of chance in the response to particular communications. "I've seen it a dozen times," said the senatorial assistant. "One time, some letter or call will come in . . . and nobody will pay any attention to it. It might say, for instance, the miners are all worried about this foreign fuel oil. Another time, a call will come in in the same words almost, and everybody will get worried about it; it might be that the state chairman was in the day before and says we're not doing so well in such-and-such a county, so we all jump to the conclusion that it's fuel oil that's hurting us there. Or it may be just accident; one time, the senator is preoccupied . . . another time, he listens eagerly."

but the amendments were of greater relevance to cherries, textiles, or petroleum than to turbines. The structures that controlled attention and the capacity for action, determined, as much as the communications received, the interests of which Congress could become conscious and to which it could respond.

Appendix to Part V

The Study and
The Literature on Congress

In reporting on any social institution and its operations through the analysis of a particular case or situation, it may be helpful to indicate the degree to which the case or situation limits the validity of the generalizations and how the approach to it may differ from that followed in other studies in the same general field. This is, after all, a case study and, as such, different from such valuable works as Bertram Gross' *Legislative Struggle*,[1] Robert Dahl's *Congress and Foreign Policy*,[2] and James Robinson's *Congress and Foreign Policy Making*.[3]

It appears to us that the most significant factor differentiating our study from other analyses of pressure groups, of campaigns to influence legislators, and of Congress is this: we tried to follow up several aspects of the problem almost simultaneously. We differ from Schattschneider [4] in giving a lower rating to the influence of lobbyists, in part because their influence and that of trade associations may have been greater in the Hoover administration than it now is and in part because of our effort to trace back the diverse influences to which congress-

---

[1] New York: McGraw-Hill Book Company, 1953.
[2] New York: Harcourt Brace & Co., 1950.
[3] Homewood, Ill.: The Dorsey Press, 1962.
[4] *Politics, Pressures, and the Tariff, op. cit.*

men are exposed. We are much impressed by the work of White,[5] Matthews,[6] Fenno,[7] Carroll,[8] and others on how Congress and its committees operate as a social institution or a work group. But our continuing attention to the constituencies of several members, to sociological role and status, to the mail, and to lobbyists made us, we believe, expand the focus and framework. We find that Huitt's [9] approach to Congressional role-taking is in accord with what we observed and inferred; to oversimplify, it states that there are many differing roles which the individual can assume in quite highly structured groups.

Of course, no book is ever entirely different from its predecessors, but there may be some distinctive differences between our effort and that of some of the closer predecessors, such as Bailey's study of the Full Employment Act [10] or Riggs' study of Chinese exclusion.[11] *Inter alia,* the transactional analysis here employed makes the concept of "power" and "pressure" in the ordinary political-science sense of the terms somewhat more difficult to employ; Arthur F. Bentley himself pointed out to one of us in 1936 that he had long since abandoned these notions as not useful for systematic analysis. There are probably a few cases where popular interest is greater or procedure is simpler than in the instance of foreign-trade legislation, and there are certainly many where popular interest is less, where there is little expression of group interest, and where legislators make decisions on their own. There are certainly in some appropriations matters (river-and-harbor measures, for example, and probably the National Defense Highway Program) cases where direct, naked financial interests is much greater and more influential on some members. There are presumably also instances where a constituency or an interest is strongly unified in favor of one point of view, although such instances are far more difficult to locate than seems to be the case at first blush. But, even so, a good many influential people in such instances probably have several issues with much higher priorities. Very small industries—for instance, toy-marble manufacturing—may be genuinely unified and emphatic on their interest, but, within any large industry, conflicts of emphasis, if not of actual preference, are numerous. So, on the whole, our case seems to us typical of any issue having economic implications for a number of industries and where, through a historical process, institutional alignments and expectations have been

---

[5] William S. White, *Citadel,* "The Story of the U.S. Senate" (New York: Harper & Bros., 1957).

[6] Donald Matthews, *U.S. Senators and Their World* (Chapel Hill: University of North Carolina Press, 1960).

[7] Richard Fenno, "The House Appropriations Committee as a Political System: The Problem of Integration" (mimeographed; available from author, University of Rochester). Paper read before the American Political Science Association, 1961.

[8] Holbert Carroll, *The House of Representatives and Foreign Affairs* (Pittsburgh: University of Pittsburgh Press, 1958). This work and ours are close in many ways. An unpublished study by Dwaine Marvick of the House Appropriations Committee and the members' constituencies (Ph.D., Columbia, Public Law, 1952) is also similar.

[9] Ralph Huitt, "The Outsider in the Senate, an Alternative Role," *American Political Science Review,* 55 (September 1961), No. 3, 566-575.

[10] *Congress Makes a Law, op. cit.*

[11] Fred W. Riggs, *Pressures on Congress,* "A Study of the Repeal of Chinese Exclusion" (New York: Columbia University, Kings Crown Press, 1950).

established. What would be characteristic of some really new and unexpected issue—as some of the New Deal legislation was—is difficult to deduce from our study, because in this instance there had been an enormous amount of previous learning of relevant roles by many participants.

One similarity, however, applies to all legislative bodies except those in very small states and provinces. The great majority of members of such bodies are brokers of interests, forced to engage in a series of calculations about priorities, procedures, and the like, whether explicitly or implicitly, and therefore do not represent (with such rare exceptions as Sen. George Malone of Nevada) one special interest or doctrine. T. V. Smith, in *The Promise of American Politics,*[12] paints the legislator as the broker of ideals. From the standpoint of a man whose training was as a specialist in ethics, this seems comprehensible, but ideals from the standpoint of many politicians are simply one kind of interest, a point which is hard for the educated nonpolitical professional to realize without falling into the opposite error of glorifying power or becoming cynical.

However, the ways in which interests and ideals are influential, the manner in which roles are chosen, the method in which legislation is analyzed, the degree to which long-term considerations can be taken into account, the extent to which party is a dominant variable—all these are quite different in different legislative bodies. The Massachusetts legislature, for example, does not seem particularly similar to the U.S. Congress, nor is the British Parliament. But we need more comparative transactional analyses of legislative behavior before much can be said on this point. At present, it is difficult to generalize about the relevance of studies of the U.S. Congress to other legislative bodies.

---

[12] Chicago: University of Chicago Press, 1936.

PART VI

Conclusions

Chapter 35

Conclusions

☐ Historical Significance of Recent Trade Legislation

We have been studying events that marked the end of some of the most stable historical features of American politics. No longer could it be said, after 1953, that the Republican Party stood for protection and the Democratic Party for lower tariffs. Furthermore, though this period did not by any means mark the end of protectionism in American politics, by the time Congress acted on President Kennedy's Trade Expansion Act of 1962, protectionism in principle seemed to be at an end. Protectionism had become a doctrine of exceptions.

With recognition of America's role in the world, the slogans of the new internationalism became the accepted clichés from the time of the 1954-1955 debate. The ideological consensus proclaimed that foreign trade was a good thing, that high tariffs were to be avoided, that we should be helping or drawing closer to our Free World allies, and that we could not sell abroad without also buying abroad. Protectionists, on the defensive, rarely denied these principles. They had to fall back on pleas of special circumstances. Historic Republican principles ceased to give them support

465

and comfort. The reversal of what constituted Republican orthodoxy symbolized the transformation of America from a nation seeking its destiny by
cutting its ties with the Old World to one seeking its destiny allied with
that world.

The renewal of the Reciprocal Trade Act in 1954-1955 was a sign,
not only of the end of isolation and an end to one historic definition of
Republicanism, but also a sign of the end of the New Deal era, in the sense
that New Deal policies had lost their distinctiveness and had been incorporated into the common American heritage. A Republican administration felt free to adopt as the most cherished item of its legislative program
a Roosevelt measure which transferred tariff-making from the legislative
to the executive branch. In 1962, protectionism was a rear-guard action to
limit a transfer of still-greater powers to the president, but the issue of
principle had long since been settled in favor of executive tariff-making.

The tariff bills of 1955 and 1962 were events that a historian of our
times might note for serious discussion. But it was not the importance of
these events in their own right that drew our attention to them. We were
interested in the Reciprocal Trade renewal because it provided a case study
of a national policy decision into the making of which there entered
simultaneously information about both foreign and domestic matters. It
was the domestic impact of knowledge about the outside world that we
set out to study.

Most of this study has been devoted to establishing the facts on the
information and attitudes that were present and how they were distributed
among the population. We have examined who believed and who said
what. The sources from which they acquired such information have often
been a matter in which we have relied on inference, the effects of it almost always so. As we now sum up our conclusions, it is to these infer-
ences that we turn. We wish in the closing pages not so much to review
the facts as to take note of patterns in the effects of communications and
most particularly of those patterns which probably apply wherever men are
reaching national decisions under the impact of persuasive messages from
a multitude of global sources.

□ A New Look at Communication

Perhaps the most important thing we learned is that individual communications act on people more as triggers than as forces. Students of communication working in psychological laboratories have experimented with
the interrelation of several variables, for example, the contents of a communication, the characteristics of the experimental subjects who hear it,
and the response of these subjects to the message in it. That kind of analysis

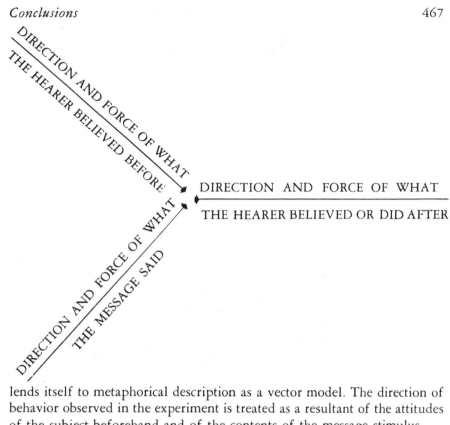

DIRECTION AND FORCE OF WHAT
_____
THE HEARER BELIEVED OR DID AFTER

lends itself to metaphorical description as a vector model. The direction of behavior observed in the experiment is treated as a resultant of the attitudes of the subject beforehand and of the contents of the message stimulus.

That vector model is not necessarily naïve. It does not treat propaganda as all-powerful, as do some popular writers on persuasion these days. The model allows appropriate weight to inertia against change rooted in the hearer's prejudices and made effective by mechanisms of psychological defense.

Our data add one more to the large number of case studies in which the mechanisms of selective exposure and perception have been documented. As others have before us,[1] we, too, found that persons read and heard expositions of the views they already believed. Protectionists attended to protectionists, liberal traders to liberal traders.[2] That finding can be fitted into the vector model; it characterizes the vectors which impinge upon one another.

The vector model also encompasses findings as subtle as the "sleeper

---

[1] For a handy review, see Carl I. Hovland, "Effects of the Mass Media of Communication," in Lindzey, ed., *Handbook of Social Psychology* (Cambridge, Mass.: Addison-Wesley, 1954), Vol. II, pp. 1062-1103.

[2] In qualification, we note that this proposition may not fully apply to those who have really serious responsibilities to attend to different views, e.g., members of the Ways and Means Committee or of the staffs of the CNTP or Strackbein committee.

effect," in which the fact that messages come from disapproved sources is gradually forgotten, while their contents come to be accepted. The vector pattern which expresses that finding shifts through time, so that vectors which were earlier opposed to each other come to be seen as having the same direction.

What phenomena do not fit this vector model of communication effects? Let us take a situation we noted early in the volume. There, we found that, among the general population, liberalism on foreign trade was highly correlated with education and social status. The lower in the social spectrum one looked, the more latent protectionists one found and also the more people unaware of the foreign-trade issue. Under such conditions, any propaganda campaign which increased popular attention to the issue would probably thereby increase manifest protectionist sentiment by bringing otherwise apathetic persons, who tended to have a disproportionate number of latent protectionists among them, into the area of discourse. That would be true whether the campaign which alerted the public was conducted on behalf of protection or conducted, as by the League of Women Voters, on behalf of freer trade. The direction of the stimulus in such a situation matters little. What matters more is that the reservoir of uninformed protectionism at the bottom of the cultural ladder is apt to be tapped by any campaign sufficiently vigorous to catch the attention of the whole public. Any sort of popular propaganda on foreign-trade matters could trigger the protectionist potential.

We have cited another example of a situation where the metaphor of a trigger releasing a fixed potential (in determining the character of which the trigger plays no part) seems more relevant than the metaphor of vectors. Repub'ican electoral compaigning in 1954, whether the contents were free-trade or protectionist, served to strengthen protectionist efforts, for a Republican majority in Congress would have served to bring some of the most powerful and protectionist congressmen into leading positions on the appropriate committees. In a local constituency contest between a protectionist Democrat and a free-trade Republican, protectionists would have been well-advised to vote for the free trader, and free traders for the protectionist, not only with an eye to close committee votes, but also to the power which the leadership of a Congressional committee may have on the molding of public opinion.

In both these examples, the reversal of the stimulus content in the response content is the result of a social mechanism. In neither case is the vector model of individual behavior denied. In the first example, League of Women Voters propaganda, for instance, might make each individual more liberal than he was before, but have the effect of activating a larger number of slightly modified protectionists than of slightly accentuated free traders. A similar thing may also happen within the psyche of a single individual if that psyche contains several discrete and not fully consonant attitudes.

Take, for example, the New Anglia businessman who believed in protection in principle but for whom the immediate problem is that he was using imported residual fuel oil at the time of the Simpson bill discussion. Protectionist literature from the National Coal Association on the cost difference between coal and imported residual fuel oil designed to show why coal needs protection could well mobilize his awareness of his interests in cheap imported fuel oil. He might well be stimulated by the propaganda to express general protectionism in the occasional context of civic discussions, but in his office he is organized to act on the concrete business problem. The office mechanisms are geared so that a stimulus supporting his general views would, as its primary effect, mobilize action on matters of specific business importance. If these happen to require that he go contrary to his own generalized attitudes and those of the stimulus communication, no matter. Furthermore, since the action of advocating one side of an issue generally tends to shift the actor toward belief in the views on behalf of which he acts, the net effect of propaganda on its recipient's attitudes may be indeterminate in those instances where it causes him to act contrary to the persuasive message of the stimulus material.

Specific action by a businessman or politician contrary to his overall views was a common phenomenon. It is not clear to us whether a majority of letters to Congress from our generally antiprotectionist survey-respondents were anti- or proprotectionist. Since they were more apt to write on specific business problems than on their more general views, the net weight of their correspondence may have been to undercut their general views.

What we have been saying does not deny the vector image of communication. It merely adds some important complications. First, there lies latent in individuals a great collection of traces of previous communications. Any new communication may serve to change this massive structure only imperceptibly, but it may at the same time set it into action in directions determined by the structure itself more than by the trigger stimulus.

Second, the event triggered within the system may itself have more effect on the system than does the original stimulus. Arguing for one's own views in reply to a challenge may have more effect on one than does the challenge.

Third, within an individual many latent attitudes may be simultaneously present. The structure of social controls and social relations may make some of them easier to express than others. Thus, even stimuli which have a persuasive effect on a man's thought may trigger quite opposite expressions.

Fourth, where a stimulus is addressed to a population of individuals, structural determinants may result in its mobilizing different proportions of those who agree and those who disagree with it. If it mobilizes more of those who disagree, the stimulus may boomerang.

The image of the communications process with which we emerged from this and other studies is that the communication is one input into a complex sociopsychological system. The effect of the communication on that system is, to a greater degree than is usually acknowledged, a function of the structure of that system. The impact of a given communication is of itself essentially indeterminate. Effects can be predicted only if one has quite detailed knowledge of the state of the system into which the communication is being fed.

Thus, the study of communications in real-life situations is a study of complex structural facets of society. It is not enough to examine a message flow between the black boxes. One needs to know the transforming characteristics of the black boxes.

We looked inside five sets of black boxes which constituted the system of foreign-trade discussion: (1) the individual businessman as reader, traveler, communicator; (2) the business firm, small, medium, and large; (3) the communities in which the businessman lives; (4) trade associations and lobbies; and (5) Congress. What have we learned about the behavior of each of those as it finds itself in complex transactions involving its own purposes and the environment of the outside world—global, national, and local?

To the individual businessman, knowledge of the outside world came in a number of ways. It came in part through the printed word, but what came that way was surprisingly general and unfocused. Our respondents read *Time, Business Week, The Wall Street Journal, The New York Times,* and other such journals. They read a great deal. They also read trade papers. But, in making specific business decisions, they did not do research in published sources. They read what the editors chose to provide. Even men with wide foreign business did not read publications from the places where they carried on that business. Knowledge of foreign economic affairs came either from the most general news sources or, more vividly, from correspondence and personal experience.

In the interpersonal communication network on which businessmen rely for making specific decisions, knowing a man who knows is more important than knowing of a source that has the information. The mails, the telegraph, and the telephone bring knowledgeable men from anywhere in the world into an effective businessman's immediate contact net. By translating the percentages of men exposed to various communications into a rough time-series measure, we can get a picture of what volume of communications on the specifics of foreign trade comes to the average business leader. Such a translation of percentages into frequencies is, we must emphasize, only a presentational device, for it is subject to statistical fallacies. We make this rough translation in order to arrive at a partially postulated ideal type. Every few days, an American businessman will spot some item on foreign-trade policy as he skims in a cursory way through his newspaper or news magazine. Ninety per cent of the big-businessmen and 46 per cent of the small had heard of the Randall Commission report; 74 per cent of the big-businessmen and 59 per cent of the small had heard of President Eisenhower's message on foreign economic policy, both of these being recent events. But it is only about half a dozen times a year that a big-business executive will read an article or listen to a speech specifically on that topic, and the head of a firm with only 100 to 1,000 employees will seriously inform himself in that way perhaps twice a year. Once a year, the typical big-business executive will also attend a meeting at which the topic is foreign business. The smaller businessman may do that only once every three years. About as often again, each of these men will find himself at another meeting at which this topic is part of the business. In addition, about twice a year, the business executive of either size of firm finds himself in a discussion of this topic with some acquaintance who is not a business associate. Four times a year, the big-businessman will have a similar conversation with a business associate outside his firm, the small-businessman maybe twice a year. About four times a year, the big-businessman will also discuss these matters with his foreign-trade manager; this is a less typical event for a small-businessman. Every few months, the big-businessman also has a discussion of such matters with some other official of his firm, something which the typical smaller businessman does about twice a year. All in all, purposive communication activities going beyond a review of the day's news and dealing with foreign trade and related matters are engaged in by an ideal-type head of a major American business firm about once every two weeks. A similar head of a smaller firm may engage in such communication less than once a month. About two-thirds of these communication events are conversations.

Of all channels of information about the world abroad, one of the most significant was travel. The heads of firms whom we studied are a highly traveled group of men. They go abroad an average of once every two years. And, what is more important, those who frequently travel abroad behave quite differently from those whose horizons have not risen above their provincial environment.

Those who do not travel much behave to a certain extent as some critics of our study told us all businessmen would. "Tell me what a man makes and I will tell you where he stands on foreign trade," is what we were told. For those businessmen who have not traveled abroad, one can do that fairly well. They answer questions on national policy in the role of a spokesman for a particular firm. But not so the men who had traveled.

For them, prediction from product to viewpoint was less feasible. In the course of their experience, they had changed their frame of reference. It was not that they had acquired the foreign views with which they came into contact. On the contrary, travel placed them in the role of spokesmen for America in a foreign environment. In that broadened role, they learned to speak for a self-interest that went beyond their particular industry. They became more internationalist in the sense that they took more foreign facts into account in their calculations, but, in another sense, they became more nationalist. They came to answer questions in the light of what seemed to them the interests. of America in the world, not the interests of one firm in America.

□ The Concept of Self-Interest

One way to describe this book is as an attempt to relate the study of communication to the study of economic man.

The world of social science has been divided between users of two different models of man. In most of psychology and sociology, including the study of communication, men are seen as subject to influence. They are the objects of action by causal forces. Conditioning stimuli, punishments and rewards, persuasive devices produce predictable attitudes and behavior in them. Economics had proceeded by a different model. Men are seen as rational, maximizing animals, and the scientist attempts to deduce what a maximizer ought to do to live up to the maximizing postulates. Sometimes maximizing theories assume that what he ought to do is what he will do.

In this study, we have tried to make the empirical-influence model and the teleological-maximizing model meet. The student of communications will describe the formation of attitudes in a businessman as the result of propaganda stimuli to which he is subjected. The student of the economic man will see his actions as determined by his economic goals. Which way is it? Are the economic views of businessmen myths which their culture has instilled in them or are they rational calculations?

The answer is that these two alternatives are not opposed. In fairly complex ways, they are interrelated. The influence model and the maximizing model are simultaneously true for the behavior of businessmen.

Businessmen do, indeed, follow their own self-interest. They do it consciously and continuously. It is a rare businessman who says, "My business would be helped by protection, but the national interest calls for freer trade. I yield before higher considerations than my pocketbook." That happened few times in our sample of observations. More often, rationalization justified the pursuit of self-interest. By that statement, however, we do not mean that each man started with a fixed self-interest and that such other considerations as his views of the national interest yielded to it. On the contrary, it is our conviction that a man's self-interest is as vague a concept as is that of national interest. Self-interest, too, can be redefined. Rationalization means viewing what is self-serving and what is good as identical. That satisfying state is sometimes achieved by changing the image of the good to conform to perceived self-interests. But the identity can as well be established by changing one's beliefs as to what is self-serving.

To say that a man's goal is promotion of his self-interest is a purely formal and tautological assertion. A man's interest lies in the achievement of whatever it is he desires. Interest, in that respect, is like the Aristotelian concept of the good as an end or the economic concept of utility. That which is sought is the good; that which is desired has utility. The statement that men seek their self-interest asserts a truth about behavior, but the truth is only that men seek that which they seek. The truth asserted is that behavior is purposeful. What can be conceived of as self-interest is as varied as are men.

In the calculations of self-interest that occurred continuously among our subjects, the aspects of the conception that varied included *whose* self-interest, in the light of *which facts*, and *over what time periods*.

Consider, first, whose self-interest is maximized. Certainly, it is seldom the interest of the physically individual human animal. The executives we interviewed viewed themselves merely as agents of groups. Corporation presidents like to comment that they are only hired hands. Their proper goal is not personal enrichment from the treasury of the company, but the advancing of a collectivity which is designated as "the firm."

But "the firm" is a vague concept. Is it the stockholders only, or is it also employees, management, and customers? We recall the case of the protectionist firm which stood to benefit from a reversal of American liberal-trade policies if its balance sheet were taken as the criterion of self-interest. But the firm in question happened to be controlled by British investors. Where did the self-interest of the firm lie? Was it in an improved balance sheet at the expense of an American economic policy which would have adverse economic consequences for British business, or was it in the acceptance of a poorer return on this one investment under an economic policy of clear advantage to the alien majority but not to all of the stockholders? For the sake of the historical record, we may mention that it never even occurred to the American management of the firm to take account of the fact that the major stockholders were British. The immediate balance sheet of the American firm was the sole criterion they used. That is a fact of communications and ideology which helped define what "the firm" meant and what its self-interest meant in this instance.

Consider, also, the cases where a man's self-identification was as a manufacturer and not as a merchant, or where his feeling for his employees prescribed his conception of self-interest. A lace-manufacturer had all the merchandising outlets required to do well in selling either his own lace or lace bought abroad. But the very suggestion that he close his plant and be an importer brought fury. It would be at the cost of the jobs of his men. And, besides, he said with pride, "We are manufacturers, not merchants." He too was protecting the self-interest of a firm, but a firm conceived as a certain body of men or even as a certain physical plant, not as an undifferentiated sum of financial capital which could be used in whatever way would make the most money. The balance sheet did not define the firm for him.

Perhaps one might also say that our lace-manufacturer was serving a self-interest that was measured in pride and respect and that went beyond money. The point is too obvious to labor. Not only must we ask whose self-interest is to be maximized, but, also, what are the social values in terms of which it is measured?

Then there is the matter of time discounts. Is it a short- or long-run goal that the maximizer seeks? What is the trade-off between a relatively likely small short-run loss and a possibly large long-run gain? There are at least two time discounts operating: one for waiting and one for the uncertainty that the future introduces. What these discount rates are for any individual is something not for maximizing-theory but for a theory of personal psychology to explain.

The time discounts which we found operating, particularly in smaller firms, were remarkably large. One of the great weaknesses of the liberal-trade side was that a clearly predictable short-run loss to foreign competition was far more productive of vigorous business action than a possible much larger ultimate gain in foreign business from a liberal policy. The long-run prospect of gain was too indirect, too "iffy," to be a basis of action for men with an American business psychology.

In very large firms, that was less true. A giant firm might aim, not at maximizing immediate profit, a policy which might only call antitrust action down on its head, but rather at securing a stable 6-to-8 per-cent return. Plans in such firms are often made on a twenty-year basis.

We have so far considered three aspects of the formal concept of self-interest which help make concrete this otherwise highly abstract concept. They are: who is the self, what value does he maximize, and over what time period? The answers given by any person to these questions are obviously subject to the operation of influences. By changing businessmen's notions about these matters, communications change policies without in the least modifying the formal feature—that action remains the pursuit of business interest.

All this is even more clearly true of a fourth concretizing aspect of purposive behavior—information. To have knowledge about a market for a product may justify entering it. A man without such information would be following his business interest by refraining from investment. Indeed, one of the greatest weaknesses of the liberal-trade side was the prevailing ignorance among American businessmen about foreign markets and the cost to them of acquiring such information. Over and over we were told that "the American market is our primary one." Foreign opportunities might exist, but they were not worth the trouble of learning about them. There is a wide dissatisfaction in the American business community with the available means of acquiring information about foreign markets and foreign opportunities for investment. U.S. commercial attachés are widely dismissed by businessmen as "incompetents who never met a payroll." Published sources are, as we have noted, not well used. Specialized consulting services are only now beginning to function widely. The best information source, in the eyes of most businessmen, is to go abroad and to talk there to trusted business colleagues.

Under such conditions, foreign investments and promotions occur partly by chance. The presence within the management of a firm of a man with experience in a particular country is the most important factor in leading the firm into that country. In the absence of such contacts, an aura of uncertainty blocks action. It is not only uncertainty about the facts, but also uncertainty about whether it is worth the effort to get the facts. The calculation of self-interest depends both on the stock of knowledge already at hand and on a guess about which unknown facts might be worth acquiring. These are clearly social facts about the existing system of communications.

If the picture is, indeed, as we have just described it, then we can disregard as irrelevant and naïve most arguments about the relative role of ideology and economics in influencing public-policy decisions. The formal acts of economic calculation acquire their concrete content only through acts of communication and social influence. Conversely, economic calculation is one of the processes which occur inside the black boxes into which communications are fed. Neither a simple study of influence processes nor a simple study of economic interests without their interactions could have yielded much understanding of the behavior of our business respondents.

☐ Structural Factors in Communication and Decision-Making

We have looked thus far at the businessman as an individual and how structural facts about his life and role interact with the messages he receives to determine the decisions he makes.

But the businessman acts within the framework of the business firm. That framework is not uniform. In almost all our survey results, the most dramatic statistical differences were not those which interested us originally. They were differences between the large, medium, and small firms. These represent differing ways of life for their chief officers.

The head of a small firm, especially one with under 400 employees, is essentially a manager of operations. His look is inward, to problems of production, or, if outward, it is toward problems of marketing. He has few men in specialized staffs around him. In contrast, the head of a giant corporation deals most of the time with such staffs. Production has long since slipped from his immediate attention. He works with people, statistics, and memoranda, and not with things. The heads of large and small firms differ, too, in sociological characteristics: ethnic background, rural-urban origins, education, and the like. Thanks to their competence but even more to their staffs, the big-businessmen read more, know more, and do more, particularly with respect to the external environment.

On foreign economic matters, the heads of big firms are far better informed and more apt to be interested. On the other hand, they are likely to have conflicting interests in the various sectors of their companies. The heads of small firms are more often not at all interested in foreign economic issues. However, in the rare cases where foreign trade affects them, it can be a life-or-death matter.

The administrative structure of American corporations has some significant effect on their export-mindedness, and often unfavorably to liberal-trade policies. In the first place, Canadian sales are generally under the sales manager, not under the export manager, and are not included in foreign-trade calculations. Top management, when it quotes export figures, generally quotes export-department figures, disregarding Canada, the largest foreign customer. Second, the export manager, even in large firms where he heads a department, is not usually a vice-president. He is apt to report to the president through the vice-president for sales, the very man who is most concerned with foreign competition. Furthermore, since the United States levies import duties and not export duties, the effects of American tariffs on the problems of the export department are only indirect. Congressional action never threatens to tax export sales directly. At worst, tariff increases create a situation in which world markets might deteriorate, foreign countries might retaliate, or domestic costs might increase. But, since all these effects are still only possibilities, the export manager worries about them indecisively. Finally, the purchasing department, which might have an interest in tariff reduction, seldom even knows how much tariffs have contributed to the prices it pays. It usually has no competitive concern with duties. If a tariff results in higher price for a raw material or component part, it raises it for all domestic industrial consumers alike, and this increase can be passed on in increased prices. Unless the firm's product faces competition from foreign manufacturers or from functionally equivalent but not identically made products, a uniform price increase in the domestic market does it little harm. In that respect, there is no symmetry between the injury done the sales department by a cheap foreign import and that done the purchasing department by an expensive one.

All these structural facts deeply affect what American business leaders hear from within their firms and in turn what they say to the world. What they say is in large part said for them by others. Our study therefore moved from the businessmen to the lobbies and associations which talk for them.

Here, once more, we found important structural facts influencing the message flow. The associations must maintain a quasiunanimity within themselves. Multipurpose organizations are hampered by fear of saying things which would offend some of their members. The focus of such organizations becomes internal morale-building activities instead of external representation.

The single-purpose organization does not suffer this limitation; it may become an aggressive lobby. But none of the lobbies we observed were the powerful monsters they are reputed to be. Underfinanced, they had to spend much of their time recruiting members and raising funds. Poorly staffed and overworked, they generally became effective, not as lobbies persuading public officeholders, but as service bureaus auxiliary to the efforts of those public servants.

Indeed, in many instances, and the most important ones, the relation between officeholder and lobby is exactly the reverse of what the public thinks. The protectionist leadership in the United States clearly lay inside the United States Congress. Congressmen Richard Simpson and Cleveland Bailey and Senators Malone and Eugene Millikin were far more important defenders of a waning ideology than were the more-or-less inert American Tariff League or the clamorous but relatively unsophisticated Strackbein committee. The business interests that sought protection were, of course, an essential ingredient in the picture, since congressmen for whom protection was a major platform plank greeted every business request as one more piece of evidence of the need for protection and one more opportunity to gain political supporters. It was the congressman, however, who opened the path to business pleas, and it was he who stimulated and guided the protectionist lobbies in their every effective move. The lobby became the congressman's publicity bureau. Indeed, without a congressman working with it, a lobby found it difficult to do anything the press would consider newsworthy.

On the liberal-trade side, it was only slightly different. There, the lobby spoke largely for the White House. It was organized at the White

House's request. It tried to act as the White House's private arm. Without White House support, it would have been a mere shell, were it to have existed at all. Indeed, its frustration and relative failure in 1953-1955 was very largely because the White House and Clarence Randall, the President's special aide, adhered to the letter and spirit of the law against executive lobbying. Randall had scruples against covert manipulation of a private lobby. He waited frustrated for the private lobby to start a tidal wave of public opinion which would push upon him.

It rarely happens that way. It never happened in the events we studied. The time the Coleman committee became effective in the 1953-1955 period was when Senator Gore launched a legislative drive and called on the committee to provide staff, publicity, and contacts. Then, with a public figure to lead them, their staff and technical skills became meaningful.

What we have said about lobbies already indicates our view of the role of Congress. Congressmen have a great deal more freedom than is ordinarily attributed to them. The complexities of procedure, the chances of obfuscation, the limited attention constituents pay to any one issue, and the presence of countervailing forces all leave the congressman relatively free on most issues. He may feel unfree because of the great demands on his time, but, consciously or unconsciously, by his own decisions as to what he chooses to make of his job he generates the pressures which impinge upon him. He hears from voters about those things in which he himself chooses to become involved.

The great decisions a congressman must make are not so much those determining the position to take on individual bills, but rather decisions as to what kind of a congressman to be, what sorts of things to specialize in, how to allocate time, and how to project himself into a role of leadership.

A congressman needs issues in the public eye. He needs people who want favors from him. His stock in trade is his power to take action on things citizens care about. If there were no clamorous demands giving him the opportunity to show his worth, he would have to create them. And that, indeed, is what he habitually does.

Congress is not a passive body, registering already-existent public views forced on its attention by public pressures. Congress, second only to the president, is, rather, the major institution for initiating and creating political issues and projecting them into a national civic debate. Congressmen are often the leaders in that debate.

To say, as we are doing, that congressmen create public opinion is not to deny that they must also attend to it closely. But the attention a congressman pays to what his constituents think is a complex matter.

Constituents seldom come to clear conclusions on technically feasible steps within the congressman's competence early enough to urge action that could affect legislation. Public opinion is more often a reaction when the decision process is all over; it likes or dislikes the result. The intelligent congressman looks to his constituents, not for instructions, but for clues as to what their reactions might be in future, hypothetical circumstances. The congressman listens, not only to actual constituents conveying injunctions to him, but also to constituents whom his imagination anticipates and to their reactions to future events which he can foresee better than they can.

There is, then, no straight-line process in which businessmen receive messages about foreign economic affairs, respond by messages to their trade associations, which in their turn respond by messages to congressmen, who to some measure respond by action. The low saliency of foreign-trade matters and the competition of other matters for time means that at every level there is only a limited amount of actual communication and a great deal of speculative imagination of what each relevant group must be thinking and feeling. The flow of information is going both ways. For example, the messages about foreign economic affairs often start with the congressman or the trade association and are spread via domestic media. Except by means of foreign travel, little substantial foreign information comes directly to the businessman. The people who most actively frame the issues to be discussed and debated are the symbolic leaders in Congress and the Executive. They generate the public concerns which come back as pressures on them.

☐ Decision-Making as a Social Process

One way or another, decision-making is much talked about by academicians and by practical men of affairs, much observed, and sometimes even achieved. The predominant tendency is to regard it as an intellectual process which usually proceeds according to a certain formal order, such as definition of the problem, consideration of alternate courses of action, data-gathering, and selection of the most appropriate course of action. This is far from what happens. Not only do these intellectual steps fail to exhaust the factors which determine decision, but they falsify even what takes place on the strictly intellectual level. But consideration of the intellectual aspects of problem-solving is a digression. What most impressed us was the extent to which decision-making is a social process and imbedded in a stream of social processes.

In one respect, the assertion that decision-making is a social process is more or less self-evident. In business organizations or in Congress, certain social units—committees or officers—are formally designated to deal with such a matter as tariff legislation. The composition of such groups, their formal mandate in the larger organization, and the type and volume of other business such a group has assigned to it all affect the outcome of any single issue. We have already discussed at some length how structural features of American business firms, of the business community, and of Congress affected the outcome of the events we studied.

In addition, we learned that we could not isolate foreign-trade policy as an issue with anything like the ease that we expected. What a man said about foreign-trade policy was very much a function of his involvement in other issues. General Motors and DuPont could well have been more active than they were, had it not been for the antitrust suit in which they figured. The delegation of farmers in Midwest did not raise the issue of foreign-trade policy with Representative Stubborn because they chose to expend their finite resources of good will on issues on which they had a chance of influencing him.

In 1954, the Ways and Means Committee of the House failed to hold hearings on the Reciprocal Trade Act for a variety of reasons which bore mainly on other issues: the committee, and especially its chairman, Congressman Reed, were tired from the long tax hearings, and the White House was reluctant to put pressure on Reed, in part because of its desire to maintain good relations with the conservative wing of the Republican Party.

Any given issue must compete with other issues for those scarce resources which determine the outcome: time, energy, attention, money, man power, and good will. Where a given issue stands in priority affects not only the fight for resources but also the whole manner of its handling. If a matter has very low priority, it gets no attention, and nature is left to take its course. This was true of certain members of the general public (about 50 per cent) who did not know that a fight over trade legislation existed. Or an issue such as the Reciprocal Trade Act may be accorded a status of second priority. This not only affects who handles the problem— second-rank officers rather than the top business brass—but also which courses of action may be attempted. In a fight of second priority, one must be careful not to take actions which would jeopardize higher-priority objectives.

An issue not merely consumes resources, but is often also an opportunity for creating them. Some congressmen went along with the leadership on foreign trade solely to generate good will which they could expend on objectives of higher priority to them. The skillful operator is alert to these opportunities to obtain resources. He may, for example, place a supplicant in his debt by pretending to be coerced into doing what he wanted to do in the first place.[3]

In general, an issue of relatively low priority is likely to be used to generate resources for use on issues of higher priority. But, since priority is itself a relative matter, we cannot assess the priority given any one issue except by reference to all issues which compete or might compete for position.

We have already spoken of good will as one of the resources that affect the outcome of issues. Good will is but an aspect of the large problem of maintaining effective social relationships. Since virtually every decision involves working with or through other people, whether in business, in the public arena, or within Congress, it is necessary for each actor to zealously guard his relations to these others. What he will guard depends somewhat on his own style. He may prefer to use fear rather than good will in order to influence others to go his way. But, whatever mode of relationship he prefers, he must apply himself to keeping it in working order. This means that only on very occasional issues of highest priority can he act as a truly free agent. In all other instances, he must take care to keep his supply of good will, respect, fear, and the like, at an adequate level and, furthermore, to act in a sufficiently patterned manner so that others will know what to expect of him and that they can count on him. This does not mean that he will always do what is predictable, but that he will do so in such situations and to such an extent that others will continue to respond as he wishes them to. Thus, he cannot often violate agreements, or others will stop making agreements with him; nor can he fail to carry through on threats, or others will lose fear of his threats.

In such respects, the social aspects of decision-making constrain a man's freedom of action. But, for the knowledgeable man, the social aspect of decision-making also offers opportunities. We have mentioned how a congressman may make it virtually impossible for his constituents to know how he stood on a given issue. The business administrator can and does do the same thing. How did DuPont stand on protection? It seems impossible to be certain. An important officer, Frederick G. Singer, was active in the American Tariff League in 1953-1955, but the company per se took no stand. It could be maintained, and quite possibly correctly, that Singer was acting as a private citizen, even though many knowledgeable people thought of him as acting for the company.

---

[3] Strategies more complex than simple advocacy of whatever one wants can be found increasingly discussed in the literature on nonzero sum games and games with communication. Cf. Thomas Schelling, *The Strategy of Conflict* (Cambridge, Mass.: Harvard University Press, 1960), and Duncan Luce and Howard Raiffa, *Games and Decisions* (New York: John Wiley & Sons, 1958).

It often seemed to us that the term "decision-making" was a misnomer. What we saw did not often warrant so intellectual-sounding a label. At some point, it was possible to say that an issue existed, though how it arose was not always clear. For example, in tracing the history of the Committee for a National Trade Policy, we identified several streams of influence. Several people were trying to organize several different things. It might be possible to specify when and under what circumstances the question was first posed: "Should we form just such a committee?" But people were working on the matter long before that idea came to exist as one alternative about which to decide.

Not only may the formulation of a problem not have taken place deliberately, but the decision, also, may not have been deliberate. Under the pressure of circumstances, a man does something that seems small, and suddenly he finds himself committed to something much larger than he envisioned. He may give a small speech and suddenly find himself a spokesman. Or the actions of subordinates may create conditions which determine his line of action. His decision is to recognize the inevitable.

We have pointed out that in 1954-1955 the CNTP became more of an educational society than the hard-bitten lobbying group it had set out to be. Was this the result of a decision? Decisions were made about fund-raising which failed to produce the funds thought necessary for the original plan of action. Decisions were made to hire certain personnel. At a later date, as a result of those decisions, the CNTP existed as an organization with personnel and funds of types which determined what it did. Was there a decision about debating versus lobbying?

In any study such as ours, the question of whether a decision has been made at all should be regarded as a moot point. It is an issue that should be settled on empirical grounds in each instance. The label "decision-making" probably cannot be abandoned entirely, but it is necessary to call attention to how far this phrase fails to describe what happens in a social group between the time that an issue is recognized and the time that one or more persons are committed to a course of action.

Sometimes, the length of time between these steps may itself be so compressed that a person may first realize that he is confronted with an issue when he finds himself already committed to a course of action. A congressman may make a routine commitment to support a given piece of legislation and find only afterward that one or more of his constituents are adversely affected by it. In such instances, the retrievability of a decision becomes a crucial issue in its own right.

One of the ways in which the usual model of decision-making differs from the model which emerged from this study is its assumption of much more clear-cut outcomes than apparently occur in many situations. The passage of the Reciprocal Trade Act in 1955 proved not to be the culmination of a fight. It turned out to be but one phase of an ongoing controversy and an ongoing process of Congressional activities. While we in designing our study were looking forward only to the final vote on the act, the members of Congress were setting their sights on other legislation coming up in that session of Congress and also on the next time when the Reciprocal Trade Act and other foreign-trade legislation would be considered. In the end, both sides claimed victory, and even outside observers were not in agreement as to which side had won. It would be difficult to prove that any decision was actually made on trade liberalization in 1955. The passage of the bill was a decision only about procedures to be followed in the further conduct of the controversy. The same thing could be said of the 1962 law, the operation of which was bound to depend heavily on the policies of the Common Market. The 80 per-cent provision, allowing some tariffs to be cut to zero, will affect a significant number of commodities only if Great Britain joins the EEC. That was still an imponderable at the time of the bill's passage. The Reciprocal Trade Act and the Trade Expansion Act are sets of directives and licenses to the executive branch. The directives were unclear, the licenses varied. There was no way of knowing for certain just how the Tariff Commission, the president, and other parts of the executive branch would interpret the provisions of this legislation. Such indeterminacy is not equally present in all legislation, but it is widespread.

We said previously that it should be regarded as a moot point whether a decision has in any meaningful sense been made. Even when, as in the case we studied, some decision has been made in a meaningful sense, it still does not mean that the decision should be regarded as the terminal phase of a sequence of events. The decision may be a workable formula designed to keep the decision-making apparatus operating on this and related issues. It may be something between a resolution of conflict and a tabling of issues, with perhaps a little bit of passing the buck involved.

□ Social Science and the Political Process

Any study of political matters, and especially a study of the relationship of business to politics, is likely to be interpreted as in itself a political document. Ideas are weapons, and, even where the analyst or scholar protests his neutrality and loyalty to the facts, other people are likely to handle his ideas and reports and findings as weapons—weapons which they can use, weapons directed against themselves, or weapons helpful in parlor games for the entertainment of themselves and friends. "Scientific inquiry," in other words, "has latent as well as realized functions, inadvertent as well as intended results. This dual and uncontrollable quality of scientific inquiry . . ." [4] is sometimes, perhaps usually, influential in determining how a report is written and what its authors emphasize. We have found ourselves in preliminary versions of this book accused of forging weapons for purposes which we did not have in mind.

Ideas are weapons, not only for or against relatively specific legislative proposals, but, regardless of the intentions of the scientist or scholar, for supporting or upsetting habitual ways of looking at the segment of reality which is under discussion. A report which suggests that reality operates in a manner differing from the reader's expectations engenders more or less discomfort. And, depending on his previous expectations, a reader is likely to interpret the report, if it deals with political matters, as having a conservative or a liberal orientation.

Our experience is that readers tend to feel that our orientation is conservative. We have found objection not so much to our findings as to the fact that the findings might be correct. There are those who would prefer that the facts we report not be so.

We have reflected on the unhappy reaction from some of our professional colleagues. As a matter of fact and intention, our work is not, so far as we can see, conservative in any traditional sense of the term, nor is it liberal. But, for the case which we have studied, it tends to cast doubt on the stereotype of pressure politics, of special interests effectively expressing themselves and forcing politicians either to bow to their dictates or to fight back vigorously. Our presentation of the congressman as one who is part of a transactional process, who can himself signal what communications he wants, and who has a good deal of latitude in those which he heeds is not precisely in accord with the stereotyped picture. Nor do we portray the lobbyist and the business interest conventionally when we show them faced by many priorities, often deliberately restrained in exerting pressure or woefully ignorant of where pressure could be profitably exerted.

What we believe we are doing is extending and qualifying certain insights recently ably restated by V. O. Key in his *Public Opinion and American Democracy* [5] and earlier by Bernard Berelson in *Voting* [6] and still earlier by Walter Lippmann in *Public Opinion* [7] and *The Phantom Public*. [8]

Those authors compared a popular version of the theory of democracy with the facts of democratic politics.

What Mr. Lippmann did was to destroy a straw man. He did it thoroughly. He refuted the more extravagant beliefs about the role of

---

[4] C. Vincent, *Unmarried Mothers* (New York: The Free Press of Glencoe, 1961), p. 263.
[5] New York: Alfred A. Knopf, 1961.
[6] Chicago: University of Chicago Press, 1954.
[7] New York: Macmillan and Company, 1922.
[8] New York: Macmillan and Company, 1929.

the average man in selfgovernance . . . , demolished whatever illusion existed that "the public" could be . . . equipped to decide the affairs of state. The average man . . . exhausted his energies earning a livelihood . . . , looked at the comics rather than attempting to inform himself. . . . Even if he were willing to devote his spare time to the study of public issues, the information available to him was both inadequate and unenlightening.[9]

Public-opinion pollsters, by showing how many issues do not in fact get much public attention, and political behavior specialists, by showing how many issues are decided by a relatively small in-group, have confirmed this picture many times over.

But it was only with Berelson's concluding chapter in *Voting* that due recognition was given to positive functions that are served when voters behave as human beings, not as stereotypes of good citizenship. A society where no one was apathetic about any issue, Berelson showed, would be chaos, indeed. The citizens of a democracy may not behave as some theorists wish they would, but it is thanks to the ways that they do behave that democracy functions.

If Lippmann, Berelson, Key, and others have shown that, for good or ill, the ordinary man does not conform to Rousseauian prescriptions of citizenship, what we have done here is to say a similar thing about his political betters. They, too, fulfill their roles while uninformed, preoccupied, and motivated by adventitious private goals. If such facts disqualify men for a role in affairs of state, it is difficult to say who would be qualified. We believe we have shown that, the rush of events being what it is and the limitations of time and energy being what they are, no leading politician could meet the test. A political theory which expects a statesman to act with that degree of deliberation on all issues which he might at best achieve for one issue at a time is clearly unrealistic.

We have often asked ourselves why it is that most existing literature portrays the policy decision-process in what we came to feel was an overly intellectualized way. Certainly it is not because previous writers were less aware than we of the complexity of reality or because they failed to note how often policy-makers depart from norms of orderly action. Rather than a failure of knowledge, we feel that it is an urge by writers to make their descriptions of events neat and satisfying which accounts for the way decision-processes have been described.

Most political behavior studies have, for example, tended to concentrate on the cases where someone made a purposeful decision or was thought to have done so, not the cases where there was nothing to say or report because of inaction, indifference, or ignorance. And, in general, students of political science ask questions in such a way that people are

---

[9] Key, *op. cit.*, p. 5.

encouraged to report something happening, rather than inattention, indifference, unconcern, ignorance. American social science has tended to show business as an active, aggressive agent, always taking part in politics for its own purposes. Such studies as A. Eugene Staley's *War and the Private Investor*,[10] which present a different picture, have attracted too little attention and been almost forgotten.

Now, our methods of interviewing focused on communication, and we were as much interested in noncommunication as in communication, in what did not happen as in what did. Accordingly, we found that, in a number of instances where something could have happened, where a special interest could have been effective, where a politician might have been under pressure, inaction or ignorance seemed to prevail. We found businesses leaning over backward not to exert pressure; we found politicians discounting or utterly unaware of pressure campaigns directed against them; we found politicians inviting, rather than resisting, pressures. In other words, we think we differ from most previous reporters of pressure-group behavior in that we asked what did not happen, as well as what did.

Another consideration that shaped the earlier literature is the appeal of melodrama. We have suggested that pressure is sometimes a phantom or at least weak and ineffective. That is not what political scientists generally observe nor what lobbyists, journalists, and congressmen themselves report. Why? A journalist can make a much more interesting and credible story about heavy pressure than about the tepid sort of relationship presented in our chapters. A congressman, eager either to build himself up or denigrate his opponents, can castigate the special interests and wicked lobbyists on the other side. A good many lobbyists have obvious enough self-serving reasons for building themselves up and, what is not generally realized, much stronger reasons for building up the forces of evil on the other side. We have sacrificed drama by stressing complexities and qualifications.

In a carefully restricted and precisely defined sense, the introduction of complexities and qualifications into a simple picture may be regarded as conservative. But, of course, this is not the major basis for the objections which we have experienced. Social scientists do not generally object to complexities!

A more important source of discomfort is that we are questioning cherished notions in the conventional criticism of society.

We have said that pressure groups which we observed were more inept than we had anticipated. This will presumably be interpreted as a defense of such groups, since it implies that pressure groups taken in-

---

[10] Chicago: University of Illinois Press, 1935.

dividually are not as dangerous as they have been made out to be. It could, however, be taken as a criticism of the people who run these groups; and we expect that some of them will be irritated with us for our judgment of them.

We have minimized the role of such factors as evil intentions, crookedness, and cynicism. We have conveyed the impression that most of the men with whom we were in contact were convinced of the rectitude of their positions. This may also be taken as a defense of them, for it denies the easy assumption that the men on the other side are cynical opportunists. But almost every issue is sufficiently complicated for arguments to be made on both sides.

We have also suggested that the picture of congressmen as influenced by pressure groups is not always valid. The people supposed to make decisions, officeholders, often really do make decisions. Congress as a body can to a great extent be its own boss. This means that the notion that the special interests decide, a qualification some adopted to the notion that the people decide, in its turn needs qualification.

Furthermore, we have made statements which will be taken as a defense of big business as against small business. We find that the notion that big business interferes rudely and violently with the democratic process needs qualification. This notion is based on a long historical stream of writings, but, so far as our reporting goes, it was not true on the tariff in the period since 1953.

We also picture the heads of large firms as active in public affairs, well-informed, with a broad perspective. (For most American readers of books like this one, these are positively valued statements and will be taken as praise.) In general, it may be said that, the larger a firm is, the more concern its chief officers must have for the interaction of their own behavior and that of the economic, social, and political environment in which they operate. For one thing, their own actions may have predictable second-order consequences back on themselves via the economy as a whole. Also, once a business reaches a certain size, it acquires a good deal of social visibility. Because it can have an effect on the economy or on the society as a whole, public agencies keep an eye on it. This does not necessarily mean that every head of a large organization develops a social conscience. But he must at least acquire a sensitivity to the reactions of those people who do have social consciences and to the reactions of politicians who may capitalize on the social consciousness of others.

The head of a big business firm has great potential for influencing public policy in the direction which he prefers. But, particularly in the past few decades, he has seen a growth of forces acting to constrain him from doing so and impelling him to be subtle in his political behavior. We know of no evidence that would enable either us or anyone else to answer the question of how these two opposing tendencies relate to each other summatively. But it is our suspicion that the relative power of big business in American politics has declined in the past fifty years and that the manner in which power is exercised has become more responsible. We believe it to be beyond controversy that the new situation of big business in American society demands qualities of mind on the part of the leaders of these big firms that make them generally closer in attitude and thinking to the intellectual community than are the heads of smaller firms. In general, the larger the firm, the more the head of the firm is forced by his role to think in broad economic, political, and social terms. This does not mean that he becomes a theorist, a term which many of them despise, but that he must attend to the same set of variables as do academic theorists.

There are certain trends in American social science—naturalism, functionalism, and transactionism—which are at present making themselves felt in the analysis of political phenomena. Each of them serves as a source of irritation to the reformer and the moralist, since they appear to be defenses of the *status quo*. Naturalism is simply a disposition to study phenomena in a nonnormative fashion. It is no more than the application of the scientific precept that one understands prior to evaluating. Functionalism [11] is a mode of social analysis that takes as its point of departure the notion that various social phenomena may be useful in the larger social context in ways that would not immediately strike the eye. Transactionism, among other things, obscures the direction of causality by stressing the interdependence of events that were once viewed more simply. An example would be our proposition that the congressman determines the sort of letters that come to him just as certainly as the sort of letters that come to him determine the behavior of the congressman.

These trends in social analysis could lead toward conservatism. For instance, our contention that pressure groups are not as effective as sometimes alleged could lead to complacency. The notion that congressmen lead pressure groups as much as pressure groups influence congressmen could have a similar effect. The discovery of latent functions for a given phenomenon may be taken as a justification of that phenomenon. Thus, our proposition that many legislators find pressure groups to be useful sources of information might be interpreted as a justification of them. There is no more necessity for this conclusion than there is for interpreting the law of gravity as a reason for letting little old ladies fall into manholes. If things tend to fall to the earth at a given speed under given conditions, this knowledge is an excellent resource in our attempts to keep from falling those things that we wish not to fall. Similarly, our

---

[11] For a discussion of the complications of functional analysis, see Kingsley Davis, "The Myth of Functional Analysis," *American Sociological Review,* 24 (December 1959), No. 6, 757-772.

naturalistic knowledge of political and social phenomena can serve a normative purpose.

Another reason why our report may be interpreted as conservative is that we appear to approve, and certainly make no objection to, the political processes which we describe.

There are, indeed, values associated with the stability of any existing and tolerably benign political process. It can be argued that political processes are more important than specific political decisions. This notion is best exemplified in the Anglo-American legal tradition that the courts should operate according to due process of law, regardless of any extrinsic factors which lead judges and juries to feel subjectively certain of guilt, innocence, worthiness, or wickedness. There are points at which any of us would admit that results are more important than processes. Many Frenchmen felt that the problem of Algeria was more important for France to solve than it was for France to preserve normal parliamentary processes. Perhaps the issue of thermonuclear arms control is more vital than any institutional process of politics. But such issues must necessarily be few if a political system is to long survive.

The underlying proposition here is that political societies operate best when the political institutions are accepted by the consensus of the society and when they permit compromise, adjudication, bargaining, and deals. They operate best when sharp breaks in the customary way of doing things are rare and are introduced gradually. As Sir Walter Scott said, "All . . . good has its rateable proportion of evil. Even an admitted nuisance of ancient standing should not be abated without some caution." [12]

As individuals we have both enthusiasms and objections to various items in the several pieces of legislation passed between 1953 and 1962. But in this we are, so far as we can guess, simply in accord with every member of Congress who voted for the bills.

In particular, it seems to us that the escape clause as it operates cannot restore things to the *status quo ante* and merely adds an additional measure of uncertainty and instability and that "hope which deferred maketh the heart sick." We would prefer that before trade regulations or negotiations are set, those who are likely to be injured be given a stronger initial opportunity to seek relief, but, once a decision has been in effect for a year or more, action to reverse what is then the prevailing situation should be made more difficult or impossible. The prospect of unpredictable change via the escape clause has a most discouraging effect on business investment in trade expansion.

We have been particularly concerned with the problems of how American leaders learn about the outside world, how they integrate that

---

[12] *Guy Mannering*, Chapter VI.

which they learn with their own immediate concerns, and, finally, what leads them to action. We saw, and this fact makes some people unhappy, that the intelligent and influential men we studied seldom acted on the basis of ideology or conviction alone. In 1954-1955, the liberal-trade plea that national interest had to be put ahead of self-interest received passive acquiescence from most American businessmen. The majority of them had accepted the doctrine of internationalism. That acceptance was the prerequisite for the long-run success of liberal-trade views and for the ultimate decay of protectionism. Immediate action required, however, more than general conviction. Action, to occur, had to be appropriate to a man's specific role. It also usually took place in response to a danger which it was the actor's job to combat. The protectionists understood this principle all through the decade and hardheadedly appealed to people in their business roles on the grounds of competitive threats. The Kennedy leadership in 1962, having also learned this lesson, reversed the liberal strategy. While doing less, perhaps, than the previous administration to build ideological capital for the future through dissemination of liberal-trade doctrine, it did more of what counted in the short run, namely, pinpointed organization of those relatively few individuals whose role in life was such that it made sense for them to invest time, effort, and good will in the issue. For ordinary citizens, as for congressmen, there are many good things to believe in. What determines action is not the merits of an issue per se but its relation to the actor's chosen pattern of life. To understand a citizen's action, just as much as a congressman's action, one must look primarily at the man and his whole round of life, not at the issues taken in isolation. In 1962, as contrasted to 1955, the liberal-trade leadership understood this principle and mobilized specific and appropriate business interests to respond to the new threat and challenge of the Common Market. Only when the liberal-trade organizers learned thus to alert robust motives of perceived interests among people whose job it was to care did they translate vague internationalism into effective expression.

That may not be the way we would like to have seen it, but that is the way it was. The study of politics by American intellectuals has been too much confused by the indiscriminate mixing up of what should be with what is. A more realistic understanding of American politics may help those communicators who are striving for important social goals to work toward them effectively, not futilely. It may, we hope, enable readers who are seeking to improve American political processes to distinguish real dragons from false windmills.

Index

Activity on trade issue; *see* Political activity on trade issue

Adjustment subsidies, 12, 43, 48, 74, 76, 78, 305, 362

Agriculture and agricultural products, 13, 16, 28, 72, 74, 236, 273-274, 299, 309-310, 323, 328, 356, 358, 378, 429-430, 439, 444, 458

Aiken, George, 356

Allen, William, 355

Alsop, Stewart, 426

American Association of University Women, 272

American Bankers' Association, 25

American bottoms, shipping in, 7, 12, 19, 48, 112

American Cotton Manufacturers Institute, 79, 359, 361-362, 372-373, 397

American Farm Bureau Federation, 274, 299, 301, 327

American Federation of Labor, 41, 326, 338; *see also* Congress of Industrial Organizations

American Foreign Trade Council, 163-164

American Institute of Public Opinion (Gallup poll), 7, 81-86, 91, 100-101

American Tariff League (Trade Relations Council), *xiii,* 271, 326, 477, 481

Anthony, Robert H., 326

Aron, Raymond, 5

Association of American Railroads, 370

Australia, 62, 164, 284

Automobile industry, 129, 249, 251-260, 263, 278, 286

Bailey, Cleveland, 61, 64, 303, 435, 441, 477

Bailey, Stephen K., 35, 441, 452, 460

Ball, George, 40, 74, 167, 328, 355, 375, 377-380, 384, 397, 447

Bankhead, William, 440

Barkley, Alben, 68-69, 444

Barlow, J. Robert, 394

Batt, William L., Jr., 42-43, 326